The new Emily Post's
⋙ETIQUETTE⋘

◆§ *Published by Funk & Wagnalls*
for the EMILY POST INSTITUTE, INC.

The Emily Post Book of Etiquette for Young People
Children Are People
Emily Post Wedding Etiquette
The New Emily Post's Etiquette

The new Emily Post's

ETIQUETTE

by Elizabeth L. Post

FUNK & WAGNALLS • NEW YORK ॐ

Designed by Carol Basen

Manufactured in the United States of America

Library of Congress Cataloging in Publication Data

Post, Emily Price, 1873–1960.
  The new Emily Post's Etiquette.

  Published in 1922 under title: Etiquette in society, in business, in politics and at home; in 1928: Etiquette, the blue book of social usage; in 1968: Etiquette.
  1. Etiquette.   I. Post, Elizabeth L.   II. Title.
BJ1853.P6 1975   395   74-14667
ISBN 0-308-10167-7
ISBN 0-308-10168-5 (thumb indexed)

  2 3 4 5 6 7 8 9 10

Preface ⪦

It is not uncommon today to hear someone ask, "Are manners still important? Isn't etiquette outdated, or hypocritical?" Or even, "Do manners and etiquette, as we used to recognize them, exist at all?"

Of course they do! And they are just as important to us now as they were to previous generations. But they are different manners, new manners, and this is as it should be, because our life-style is new. Yesterday, privacy, self-discipline, and formality were the rule. Today, openness, freedom, and informality are the qualities that we live with. The formalities that our parents worked hard to learn are outdated, and the informalities that we practice seem right for *now* —so natural to us that we are scarcely conscious of the difference. Manners evolve of their own accord, influenced by current life-style, and the best survive until that style changes again, and they become obsolete.

To be able to answer the question "Is etiquette important?" one must have an understanding of the true meaning of the word. There is no simple definition or synonym, but to me "consideration" comes the closest. All good manners are based on thoughtfulness for others, and if everyone lived by the Golden Rule—"Do unto others as you would have others do unto you"—there would be no bad manners in the world. There have been many attempts to define "etiquette" over the years, but my own particular favorite was found in an old grammar book. It is,

> *"Politeness is to do and say*
> *The kindest thing in the kindest way."*

The type of person for whom books on etiquette hold an interest has changed almost as much as manners themselves. Until the first edition of *Etiquette* was printed in 1922, the idea prevailed that manners held little interest for anyone other than the rich, or members of so-called "society." An etiquette book printed in Chicago in

1882, for example, stated that the rich needed good manners "to give finish and éclat to their homes and their wealth"; the middle class needed manners "to gain admittance to the homes of the rich"; and the poor needed manners "to help find solace for the 'sting of poverty.' " Today, fortunately, our attitude toward manners is far more sensible. As Peg Bracken writes, "Once a proof of your breeding, manners are now an indication of your warm heart and good intentions as well."

A knowledge of etiquette—and good manners—carries many advantages. It imparts a comfortable feeling of security, self-confidence, and self-respect. Unquestionably, we enjoy every experience more if we feel that we need not worry about how to face it—if we know that instinctively we are doing the right thing.

There is a deep basic need in all of us to conform and to be liked. Acting according to accepted standards helps us to avoid criticism and to become popular members of society. Of course, it is most important that certain standards be maintained. Just because "everyone does it" does not make an action correct or even acceptable. Each standard that is lowered or forgotten must be replaced by another—one that is more suitable to life today. The fact that we live less formally does not mean that we need live less agreeably. But it does mean that we must have a knowledge of what is considered right, or wrong, for our times. It was true many years ago, and it is still true today—we are open to criticism if we flaunt convention too defiantly.

Finally, good manners simply make one more attractive, and who does not, "deep down," want to be as attractive as possible? Manners—those that are described in this book, and, perhaps, some that are not—have survived or become accepted because they have proved over many years to be the pleasantest, most practical, most considerate, or least offensive way of doing something. They are not, as some people think, "rules," but rather "guideposts on the road to good taste."

This new book, then, is designed to *help* you. In no way is it intended to complicate your life, to make it more difficult or less fun. Rather, it should make life easier and smoother. Nor is every reader expected to follow all the suggestions to the letter. Each person must read it, consider what advice is applicable to his circumstances, and then adopt those parts of the book that will be of most help to him.

In a comparison of Emily Post's original *Etiquette* with this edition, certain facts emerge. First, and most obvious, *manners* have changed tremendously in fifty years. The clothes we wear, the way we talk, the parties we give, our ideas on how to bring up our children are as different as night from day. (Running throughout this book are some short excerpts from the original edition which will show just how different). The second, and more important, is that *etiquette* has not changed. It is a code of behavior, based on consideration and kindness, and manners are the outward evidence that we live by that code. The conclusion, then, is that, while manners and each individual "manner" must be constantly redefined and revised, Emily Post's definition of etiquette is as valid today as it was in 1922. She wrote: "Beneath its myriad rules, the fundamental purpose of etiquette is to make the world a pleasanter place to live in, and you a more pleasant person to live with." There is no need to redefine that. The way of life of those who accept the code has not changed over many centuries—and, I hope, never will.

Contents ❧

CONTENTS &

PART FOUR • AS OTHERS SEE YOU

PART FIVE • ADVICE FOR TRAVELERS

PART SIX • PARTIES, PARTIES, PARTIES

PART SEVEN • SUCCESSFUL ENTERTAINING

PART EIGHT • SPECIAL OCCASIONS

PART NINE • WEDDINGS

PART TEN • GOOD MANNERS FOR EVERY DAY

CONTENTS ❧

PART ELEVEN • ON HOW TO DRESS

PART TWELVE • HOME LIFE

PART THIRTEEN • YOU AND YOUR FAMILY

The new Emily Post's ETIQUETTE

Part One

THE ART OF CONVERSATION

❧ **1** ❧ *Introductions, Greetings, and Farewells*

The words we say when we meet someone, whether or not we ever expect to see him again, create a first impression that may have far-reaching consequences. As a result, the forms used on such occasions are very important. An automatic and easy familiarity with these forms will leave you free to turn your mind to the more complicated art of making the newly introduced acquaintance feel at ease.

It also helps you to avoid that dreadful moment—which all of us have experienced—when suddenly you can't recall your best friend's name! You are so busy trying to remember the proper order of the introduction that the truly important factor—the identification—is driven right out of your mind.

If you are one of the many who panic at the mere thought of having to make an introduction, spend a little time studying the basic rules. There are only three, and once they are ingrained on your consciousness you will find there is really nothing to fear.

1

THE BASIC RULES OF INTRODUCTION

Rules for introductions have actually become much less rigid in recent years, and there is considerable variation in the phrases used, yet certain forms must still be followed.

To begin with, one person is always introduced *to* another. This is achieved in two ways. First, by actual use of the word *to:* "Mr. Johnson, I'd like to introduce you *to* Mrs. Borden." Second (and most generally used), by saying the name of the person *to whom* the other is being introduced first without using the preposition *to*.

"Mrs. Borden, may I introduce Mr. Johnson."

Now here are the three basic rules:

1. A man is always introduced *to* a woman.

"Mrs. Harper, I'd like you to meet Mr. Woodward."

"Sally, this is my roommate, Hank Jones. Hank, this is Sally Farthingham."

"Mr. Pitt, may I introduce you *to* my mother, Mrs. Black?"

2. A young person is always introduced *to* an older person.

"Professor Higby, I'd like you to meet my niece, Ginny King."

"Aunt Sally, this is my roommate, Linda Carroll."

3. A less important person is always introduced *to* a more important person. This is the only complicated rule, as it is sometimes difficult to decide who *is* more important. There are several guidelines that will help you. Except for members of your family no woman is ever presented *to* a man unless he is: the President of the United States, the head of another country, a member of a royal family, a church official, or an older man in a high position such as a governor. Members of your family, even though they may be the more prominent, are introduced *to* the other person as a matter of courtesy.

"Bishop Frost, may I present Miss Hinman?"

"Professor Boggs, I'd like you to meet my stepfather, Dr. Simons."

"Governor Heard, my niece, Miss Weinberg."

The latter form—simply saying two names—is, of course, the simplest, and it is perfectly correct. However, it seems to me to be rather formal and "disinterested," and when introducing people under ordinary circumstances, it is much friendlier to say, "I'd like you to meet . . ." or "I'd like to introduce . . . ," and so on. Other acceptable phrases are: "Mrs. Smith, have you met our new neighbor, Sarah Cross?" "Jennie, may I introduce Frank Hood, my brother-in-law?" "Jane, do you know my cousin, Jack Campbell? Jack, this is Jane Smithers, my roommate."

When said with enthusiasm, "This is . . ." is the warmest introduction of all. When a youngster introduces his favorite teacher by
saying, "*This* is Mrs. Street, Mom," or a father proudly says to his boss,
"Mr. Ford, *this* is our son, Jamie," the pride and affection are there
for everyone to see.

OTHER HELPFUL HINTS

There would be very few problems if we could all make ourselves look forward to meeting new people. As Jennie Grossinger
wrote, "To me there are no strangers, only friends I haven't met
before."

One should always use the name that the newly introduced pair
will use in talking to each other. Even though you may call your
stepfather by his first name, your roommate should not, so you would
introduce the former not as "my stepfather, Jack," but as "my stepfather, Mr. Hill."

It is always helpful to include an identifying phrase. "My new
neighbor, Joan Simms," "This is Jack Woods, our family doctor," or
the family relationship, "my sister Jean," "my cousin, Sue Brody,"
etc., all help new acquaintances immediately. Such phrases also automatically provide a conversational opening for two strangers who
might otherwise hesitate to start out with, in effect, "Who are you?"

Not many years ago anyone introducing two couples to each
other would have said, "Mr. and Mrs. Smith, Mr. and Mrs. Brown."
Today when the couples are contemporaries the first names are
always included. This is natural, since most people—especially
younger ones—call people of their own age by their first names as
soon as they are introduced. Should one couple be older, however,
their titles would be used, since the younger couple would call them
"Mr. and Mrs." after being introduced.

Although in all of these cases the name of the woman, the older
person, or the more prominent person *should* be said first, if you
inadvertently say the wrong name first, you have a "safety valve."
All you need do to correct your slip is to say, "Mr. Carruthers, I'd
like to introduce you *to* my aunt, Mrs. Franklin."

INTRODUCING FAMILY MEMBERS

Remember, when introducing members of your family the other
person is always courteously given precedence. This is not only polite, but makes it easier to explain your family relationship. "Mary,
my sister," or "my cousin, Frank Seward," can only come at the *end*

of the introduction. For example, a mother introducing a man and her grown daughter would say, "Mr. Schley, I'd like you to meet my daughter, Mary." If Mary is married, her last name may be added: "My daughter, Mary Corbin."

On formal occasions a man introduces his wife: "Mr. Brown, may I introduce my wife?"

To a younger man or a business acquaintance, a husband would say, "Jim, I want you to meet my wife" (never "the wife"!). Then he adds, "Mary, Jim Buyer." If they are all the same age he probably just says, "Mary, this is Bob Ace," indicating that he expects his friend to call his wife "Mary."

A wife introduces her husband to friends as "John" and to acquaintances as "my husband." You may always use the forms "my husband" and "my wife," because they are proper no matter to whom you are talking. "Mr. Jones" or "Mrs. Jones" are only used when introducing an employee to one's husband or wife.

A woman formally introduces her son's wife to acquaintances as "my daughter-in-law," but to friends she simply says, "Mary, Dick's wife." A son-in-law is introduced in the same way. The more formal "my daughter-in-law" or "son-in-law" depends for its warmth on the tone of voice in which it is spoken. And this is, of course, an extremely important point in all introductions: By tone, the same words can convey every shade of feeling, from cool indifference to affection.

The introduction of a parent-in-law as "Father" or "Mother" is well meant, but can be confusing. It is better to say, "This is my mother-in-law," or if you prefer, "This is Bill's mother." When introducing other relatives-in-law, say, "my brother John's wife," or "John's wife." These identifications are clearer than "my sister-in-law."

INTRODUCING STEPPARENTS

When a child has always lived with his stepparents and has been given their name, he almost invariably calls them "Mother" and "Father" (or derivatives of those names) and introduces them in that way. When he has come to live with one stepparent, or two, later in life, the situation is different, because he may well retain his own name. Since this can be extremely confusing when introductions are necessary, the relationship should be made clear at once. There is nothing objectionable or derogatory in the terms "stepmother" or "stepfather," and the simplest form of introduction, said in the warmest tone to indicate an affectionate relationship, is, "Mrs. Jones,

I'd like you to meet my stepfather, Mr. Casey," or "Mrs. Jones, do you know my stepmother?" In the latter case it is not necessary, although perfectly proper, to say the stepmother's name, as it would be the same as their father's and their own.

The same rule holds true when the parents are the introducers. A man would correctly introduce his wife's son by a former marriage, "Jack, I'd like you to meet my stepson, Jimmy Winters."

INTRODUCING EX-FAMILY MEMBERS

Many divorced persons retain a close relationship with their ex-husband's or ex-wife's family, even though they remarry. Frequently there are children involved, who love and are loved by their grandparents. The same is often true when a son or daughter dies and the husband or wife remarries. Questions inevitably come up on how these "ex" members of the family should be introduced, or should introduce their former parents-in-law.

If the introduction is *very* casual and there is little chance that any of the people involved will see each other again, there is no need to make any explanation at all. But if that is not so and the new acquaintanceship is likely to continue, it is important to explain the relationship as clearly as possible. The former mother-in-law would say, "I'd like you to meet Mary Dunbar. She is John's [or, "my son's"] widow and is now married to Joe Dunbar." Had she been divorced from your son, you would say, "She was John's wife and is now married to. . . ." Her introduction of you would be, "This is Mrs. Judson, Johnny's grandmother," or, "my first husband's mother."

FORMS TO AVOID

Although the worst sin of all is to make *no* introduction, there are certain phrases that should be avoided.

Never phrase your introduction as a command. "Mr. Jones, shake hands with Mr. Hoagland," or "Dr. Jennings, meet my cousin Joe," are neither friendly nor courteous. Don't call one of the people you are introducing "my friend," unless it is very obvious that he or she is very close to you, in which case you might say "very dear friend." You may say "my aunt" or "my sister" or "my cousin," but to pick out one person as "my friend" when neither is particularly close implies that the other person is not.

Do not repeat "Mrs. Jones—Mrs. Smith. Mrs. Smith—Mrs. Jones." To say each name once is enough, except when one is foreign or difficult to pronounce, in which case repeating the name a second time, and slowly, is helpful.

When you see someone you would like to meet at a party, and there is no one about to introduce you, don't walk up and say, "What is your name?" which is abrupt and unflattering. Start by giving your own name, and if that doesn't elicit the information, you can almost always find a third person later and ask, "Who was the attractive woman in the green dress?" The next time you see her you will be able to say, "I'm Joan Barnes, Mrs. Goldberg. I understand you are visiting Sue King," or whatever is appropriate.

FORMAL AND CEREMONIAL FORMS OF INTRODUCTION

The most ceremonious introduction possible is: "Mrs. Cartwright, may I present Mr. Thompson?" *Present* is more formal than *introduce,* but "may I introduce" is equally proper.

TO THE PRESIDENT OF THE UNITED STATES

The correct introduction of a man or a woman is: "Mr. President, I have the honor to present Mrs. [or Mr.] Williams," or "Mrs. Williams of Chicago," if further identification is really necessary.

Both men and women respond in the same way. That is, Mrs. Williams (as well as Mr. Williams) bows. If the President offers his hand, Mrs. Williams gives him hers. She does not offer hers if he fails to make this gesture of courtesy—as is most unlikely.

TO CHURCH DIGNITARIES

To a cardinal one says, "Your Eminence [or in England, "Your Grace"], may I present Mrs. Williams?"

A non-Catholic bows or curtsies but a Roman Catholic drops on the right knee, places the right hand, palm down, under the cardinal's extended hand, and kisses his ring.

A woman is always presented *to* church dignitaries. Mrs. Williams would reply to these introductions by saying to an archbishop, "How do you do, Your Excellency?" or to a monsignor, "How do you do, Monsignor Ryan?" She would speak to a priest as "Father Kelly" or simply "Father."

TO OTHER DISTINGUISHED PERSONS

The following persons are all presented *to* women by their proper titles. A foreign ambassador is presented, "Your Excellency, may I present you to Mrs. Williams?" A senator is introduced, "Mrs. Williams, may I present Senator Davies?" A senator is always "Senator Davies," even when he is no longer in office. But the President of the United States, once out of office, becomes "Mr.," although he is referred to as "The Honorable."

Former governors or ambassadors are also properly "The Honorable." On ceremonial occasions you would present "The Honorable John Jones, former governor of the State of Blank." Among friends, of course, "The Honorable John Jones" may be introduced simply as "Mr. Jones," or "John Jones."

Doctors and judges are always introduced and addressed by their titles. Protestant clergymen are "Mr.," unless they hold the title of doctor, dean, or canon, in which case the surname is added to the proper title. A Catholic priest is "Father," whatever his other titles may be. Rabbis are called "Rabbi," with or without surname, or "Dr." if they hold a doctorate.

If you are introduced to a prominent person and the one making the introduction has not spoken clearly or has not used a title (as he should have), the safest thing for you to say is, "How do you do?" If the conversation continues and the person's title is still not mentioned, you may address any gentleman as "Sir." In fact to avoid repetition of long titles like "Your Royal Highness" or "Mr. President," it is preferable to say "Ma'am" or "Sir" occasionally.

For a chart of titles to be used in addressing and introducing important persons, see Chapter 7.

WHEN TO INTRODUCE

Introductions are always required when a guest of honor is presented to other guests. If you arrive after the receiving line has dispersed, you must introduce yourself because it is considered very rude to go to an entertainment given in honor of someone and fail to say "How do you do?" to him or her.

RECEIVING LINES

If the reception or party is a very big one for a stranger, the hostess receives, standing with the special guest. As each guest approaches, the hostess says, "Mrs. Famous, this is my neighbor, Mrs. Johnson"; "Mr. Prominent, our headmaster, Mr. Riley"; or simply, "Mrs. Notable, Mrs. Stokes." The guest of honor offers his or her hand, and the other guest says, "How do you do?" or "I'm so glad to meet you," and moves on.

When an invited guest has brought guests of her own to the reception she precedes them in the line and introduces them to the hostess, who in turn introduces her and her guests to the guest of honor.

On formal occasions when (as a guest) you do not know any of the people in the line, nor could they be expected to know you, you introduce yourself formally: "I am Charles Smith," or a woman would say, "I am Mrs. Charles Smith," and turning to her husband behind her, "and this is my husband."

At a smaller, friendlier party given for someone known to most of the people present, the guest of honor does not receive with the hostess, but sits or stands in a convenient place so that everyone can go up and talk to him or her. Whether there is a receiving line or not, a lady introduces herself not as "Mrs. Charles Smith" but as "Janet Smith" and her husband as "my husband, Bob."

Even at large balls and receptions the receiving line should be limited to four whenever possible. It is a necessary formality which is generally endured rather than enjoyed, and the shorter it is, the better.

WHEN A GUEST IS UNKNOWN TO THE HOSTESS

When you are taking a houseguest who is not known to your friends to a party, remember to introduce him or her to everyone you possibly can: This does not mean that you should make a grand tour of the room—but it is unfair to your hostess to expect her to look after *your* guest and to have a stranger's name at the tip of her tongue in order to introduce him to her other guests.

FORMAL DINNERS

At a formal dinner the host should try to see that every gentleman either knows or is introduced to the lady he is to take in to dinner, but this is not always practical at a very large dinner. The man who does not know Mrs. James Jones, whose name is in his "dinner envelope," should try to find out who she is and ask to be introduced to her. If even this is difficult, it is entirely correct for him to go up to her and say, "Mrs. Jones? I'm Henry Longfellow and I believe that I'm to have the pleasure of taking you in to dinner."

Strangers sitting next to each other at the table should introduce themselves. A gentleman says, "I'm Arthur Robinson," and an older lady replies, "I'm Mrs. Hunter Jones." A younger woman says, "I'm Mary Perkins," and perhaps adds, "Bob Perkins' wife." Your neighbor's place card is a handy reminder if you do not quite catch, or do not remember, the name he or she gives you.

When a woman finds herself next to an unknown man at a dinner party she may start talking to him without telling him her name. But if he introduces himself to her she immediately says, "I'm Fanny Bogart."

Whether they exchange names or not, people who find themselves seated together at any table must accept the obligation of talking. To sit side by side without speaking is a great discourtesy to your hostess, as well as the person next to whom you are sitting.

ONE PERSON TO A GROUP

On formal occasions when a great many people are present, a stranger is not introduced to every person there. He should be introduced to several people and then he may talk with those near him with or without exchanging names.

Let us suppose you are the hostess at a small, formal luncheon. While guests are arriving you stand near the door. Mrs. King and Mrs. Lawrence are sitting quite close to you. Your new neighbor, Mrs. Jones, comes in. You go and shake hands with her, and if she apparently knows no one, you say, "Mrs. King, this is Mrs. Jones, my new neighbor." If Mrs. King is young she will rise, shake hands with Mrs. Jones, and sit down. Since Mrs. King is about the same age as Mrs. Jones she merely extends her hand and does not rise. Having said "Mrs. Jones" once, you do not repeat it immediately, but turning to the other lady sitting nearby, you say, "And this is Mrs. Lawrence." You can also look across the room and continue, "Mrs. Robinson, Miss Frost, Mrs. Jones." The two nod but do not rise.

At a less formal party, or one made up of young people, first names would be used instead of "Miss" and "Mrs."

It is much more effective to name those already present before naming the new arrival. Mrs. Jones is paying attention, of course, but one who is chatting with someone else may need to hear her own name before her attention is called to the name of the new arrival.

The well-meant practice of leading a guest on a tour around the room to make sure that he—or more especially she—is introduced to everyone is totally unnecessary and invariably a failure. The poor stranger is hopelessly confused by too many names, and the hostess is often interrupted by the arrival of other guests.

The best procedure is to leave a stranger with a nearby group, introducing her or him to them. Even if the hostess does not complete these introductions the stranger will not be marooned, because in a friend's house people should *always* talk with those near them. The good hostess, however, will make every effort to see that all her guests are introduced during the course of any party of moderate size.

OTHER OCCASIONS

Introductions are required on many, many occasions; in fact on any occasion when two strangers meet in the company of a mutual friend. This may be when two friends are walking down the street or riding on a bus and a third, known to one of the two, approaches. It may be in a business office when an employee is talking to his boss and a client known to one of them only, comes in. It could happen in the hall at school, at a wedding reception, on an airplane, or anyplace you can name. *Whenever* this situation occurs an introduction is in order. Whether you forget a name, put them in the wrong order, or make any other mistake, some form of introduction is better than none at all. It is inexcusably rude of the one who knows the other two to chat with one and leave the other—unacknowledged and left out—standing by like the invisible man.

INTRODUCING ONESELF

Under a friend's roof, at any sort of social function, guests are free to talk with whomever they wish. When the hostess or a mutual friend is not nearby to introduce two strangers they should take it upon themselves to make the introduction. It is very simple—one simply says one's own name with some identifying remark: "I'm Frank Peters. My wife and I live two houses down the street." The other replies, "I'm Jim Stout—I'm visiting Cindy and Bob Jones for the weekend."

Women who are contemporaries introduce themselves to each other (or to a man) as "Mary Reeves." However, an older woman introducing herself to a much younger woman would say, "I am Mrs. Sardo," as that is the name by which the younger one would call her.

Otherwise, a woman does not identify herself as "Miss" or "Mrs." The use of the first name serves as extra identification, and the other person can easily determine her marital status. If it does not come out in the course of the conversation, if interested, he or she may ask a third person.

At a very large party (a dance or a wedding reception, for example) it is not necessary to speak to people you do not know, unless you and another guest find yourselves apart from the others. In such a case you simply make casual conversation, and if the other seems happy to talk, you should introduce yourself with an identifying remark: "I'm Sally's cousin," or "I live next door to Bill."

There are many occasions when you have a good reason for wanting to meet someone, and then it is quite proper to introduce yourself. For instance, you would say, "Mrs. Simms, aren't you a friend of my mother's? I'm Jane, Mrs. Pinkham's daughter." Mrs. Simms says, "Yes, I am. How nice to see you."

WHEN INCORRECTLY INTRODUCED

We have all, at one time or another, been incorrectly introduced. One's title may be wrongly given, the name can be confused or mispronounced, or the identification may be erroneous. It is only sensible and kind that the person being introduced correct the error immediately. If, for example, a hostess introduces a man to a group as "a surgeon who has just moved to Greenwich" when he is really a general practitioner, he should explain this to the new acquaintances—and the hostess, if she remains there—at once. He should also make a correction should she refer to him as "Mr." instead of "Dr.," or call him "Dr. Donald" instead of "Dr. McDonald."

When someone is introducing a stranger to a number of people and consistently says the name wrong, the person being introduced should correct the host as soon as he realizes it is not just a slip of the tongue. He should do so not with annoyance, but if possible, by making light of it. All he need say is, "I know it's confusing, but my name is "Light," not "Bright," or "Just so you can find me in the phone book, I'm Bob Lord, not Jim Lord."

WHEN NOT TO INTRODUCE

You must never introduce people to each other in public places unless you are certain beyond a doubt that the introduction will be agreeable to both.—Emily Post, 1922

At a small party it is quite all right for the hostess to introduce as many people as she can, but at a large one such as a wedding reception, repeating never-to-be-remembered names is a mistake—unless there is some good reason for doing so. For instance, a friend might be chagrined if he were not introduced to a celebrity or a person in whom he had a special interest.

11

An arriving visitor is never introduced to someone who is taking leave. If two people are engaged in conversation, a third should not approach expecting them to interrupt their talk for introductions.

THE "NONINTRODUCTION"

Sometimes it happens that in talking to one person, you want to include another in your conversation without making an introduction. Suppose you are talking in your yard to a gardener, and a friend joins you. You greet her and then casually include her by saying, "Mr. Smith is suggesting that I dig up these daisies and put in delphiniums." Whether or not your friend makes any comment she has been made part of your conversation.

There are other occasions when a halfway introduction seems most appropriate. Suppose, for example, you wish to make a maid's name known to a guest. "Olga, would you please take Mrs. Jones's coat for her?" Or you might say to your guest, "Mary, this is Olga. She'll be glad to take your coat for you."

In many homes one person is employed who helps in so many ways that she becomes more than a housekeeper and is often known as a "mother's helper." These people frequently are almost members of the family and are treated as such. They are always introduced to guests, especially to houseguests. The hostess might say, "Mary, this is Sally Jones, whom we couldn't manage without. Sally, this is my friend, Mrs. Charles." If Sally is on hand to take wraps from dinner guests she is introduced in the same way. An older woman, especially one whose employers are a young couple, may be called and introduced as "Mrs. Jones."

WHAT TO DO WHEN INTRODUCED

WHAT TO SAY

"How do you do?" followed by the name of the person you have just met is a traditional and acceptable response to a formal introduction. However, if you think about it, the phrase "How do you do?" has little meaning. Therefore, except on very formal occasions when tradition is important and desirable, I prefer the less formal responses: "Hello," or "I'm very glad to meet you" (not "Pleased ta meecha"). In the case of an older or prominent person the addition of the name adds a note of respect, and repeating the name is a great help, too, in committing it to memory.

If you have not heard the new name clearly, you may ask to have it repeated. "How do you do?" or "Hello" may be said gladly or casually, and they may be varied in emphasis, depending on the degree of warmth you wish to convey. In any event, when Mrs. Fox has been introduced to Mr. Struthers and replies, "How do you do, Mr. Struthers?" he nods and need not say anything more, or he may say, "I'm very glad to meet you."

When you meet someone whom you have heard a great deal about and have wanted to meet, you may of course say, "Oh, I am so *glad* to meet you," and then go on to say, "John Brown speaks of you all the time," or whatever may be the reason for your special interest.

WHEN TO SHAKE HANDS

As already said, it is unforgivably rude to refuse a proffered hand, but it is rarely necessary to offer your hand if you prefer not to.—Emily Post, 1922

Men usually shake hands when they are introduced to each other, even if they have to cross a room to do so. Ladies may do as they wish. Boys and girls both shake hands when introduced to adults.

When a man is introduced to a woman she generally smiles and says, "How do you do?" or "Hello." Strictly speaking, it is her place to offer her hand or not, as she chooses; but if he should extend his hand she must give him hers. Nothing could be ruder than to ignore spontaneous friendliness. Technically, it is the place of a man to whom another is being introduced to offer his hand first, but the gesture is usually simultaneous.

Many Europeans shake hands each time they meet, even if they have seen each other several times previously the same day. Americans traveling abroad should be prepared for this and ready to shake enthusiastically, especially in Latin countries.

There is no fixed rule about shaking hands on parting. Nearly all rules of etiquette are elastic, but there is a wide distance between rudeness and reserve. With the same gesture you can be courteously polite and reserved with someone who does not appeal to you, or you can be welcoming and friendly to another whom you like on sight.

THE PERSONALITY OF A HANDSHAKE

A handshake can create a feeling of friendliness or of irritation between two strangers. No one likes a "boneless" hand that feels like a jellyfish, and what woman does not wince at the viselike grasp that cuts her rings into her flesh and temporarily paralyzes every finger?

The proper handshake is brief, but there should be strength and warmth in the clasp, and one should at the same time look at the person whose hand he takes. In giving her hand to a foreigner, a woman should relax her arm and fingers, for it is customary in many countries for him to lift her hand to his lips. A hand should have life even though it is passive—a relaxed hand does not mean a wet rag.

AMPUTEES AND INVALIDS

When you meet someone whose right arm is missing extend your right hand even though he cannot shake hands in the normal way. He will take it with his left hand and will feel less self-conscious because you have made no unnatural gesture to accommodate his disability.

If for some reason—due to an injury, arthritis, or any other disability—it is painful for you to shake hands, you certainly should not feel that you must do so. When someone offers you his hand simply say, "I'm so glad to meet you but forgive me if I don't shake hands. I have arthritis [gout, a sprained finger]," or whatever the trouble may be.

WHEN TO RISE

Hosts and hostesses always rise to greet each arriving guest. Members of the host's family, including young people, also rise as a guest enters the room, although they do not all necessarily shake hands. With this exception: A youngster who is sitting and chatting with an adult need not rise as each new guest comes in. He should stand up instantly, however, if the guest is brought over to be introduced.

A woman does not stand when being introduced to someone at a distance. Nor does she rise when shaking hands with anyone, unless that person is much older, or very prominent, is someone she has wanted to meet for some time, or is someone with whom she wants to go on talking. In the first case think before you leap. Some women would hardly feel complimented if a woman only a few years younger were to jump up for them.

A man always rises when a woman comes into a room for the first time, and remains standing until she is seated or leaves his vicinity. He does not jump up every time a hostess, or another guest, or a member of his family goes in and out. A husband rises for his wife when she comes in after they have been apart for a time, just as she rises to greet him when he comes home from the office. This is not a matter of manners but simply of saying, "I'm glad to see you."

In public places, a man does not rise for every strange woman who happens to approach, but if a woman stops to talk to him he stands as he answers her.

When a woman client goes to a man's office on business he should stand up to receive her, offer her a chair, and should not sit down until after she is seated. When she rises to leave he gets up, stands for as long as she remains, and then goes with her as far as the door, which he holds open for her. He does not rise for his secretary or for coworkers in his office.

In a restaurant when a woman greets a man in passing, he merely makes the gesture of rising slightly from his chair and nodding.

For additional details see Chapter 16, "In Restaurants."

NAME "BLACKOUTS"

When you are talking with someone whose name you are struggling to remember and a friend joins you and looks inquiringly from you to the nameless person, there is nothing you can do but introduce your friend to the stranger by saying to the latter, "Oh, don't you know Mrs. Neighbor?"

Hopefully, the stranger will be tactful and understanding enough to announce his own name. If he says nothing, however, and Mrs. Neighbor makes matters worse by saying, "You didn't tell me your friend's name," the situation reaches the height of embarrassment. The only solution then is to be completely frank, admit you do not remember the name, and ask them to complete the introduction themselves.

If you didn't learn another thing from this book I would consider it a success if I could persuade you, when meeting someone who obviously does not remember your name (or even someone who *might* not remember it), to offer it at once. *Never* say, "You don't remember me, do you?" and then stop. Start right out with: "Hello, I'm Kitty Blair, I met you at the Kennys' last Easter." I promise you, you will have made a fast friend! If everyone would do this automatically when he met anyone but his closest friends, the world would be a happier place.

INFORMAL GREETINGS AND FAREWELLS

"Hello" is the universal form of greeting in America, and it is acceptable in any situation except after a very formal introduction. Even comparative strangers say "Hello" in passing, and it is the friendly response to a first-name introduction: "Sally, I'd like you to meet Joan," and Sally says, "Hello, Joan, I'm glad to meet you." First-name introductions like this are frequently used by teenagers and young unmarrieds. Last names should be included, however, when a young person is being introduced to an adult, to provide a better identification.

Even more informal is the widely used "Hi." A friendly greeting for people who already know each other, it should never be said in answer to a formal introduction, but it is universally used, and accepted, by the young.

In the business world "Good morning" is the usual greeting before the lunch hour; after lunch "Good afternoon" is proper. But because the latter sounds somewhat stilted it has largely been replaced by "Hello."

"Good afternoon" is used, however, as a phrase of dismissal, indicating that an interview is ended, a class is over, etc. Acquaintances and business associates say "Good-bye" or "Good night" on parting. Closer friends usually say "So long," "See you later," or whatever they like.

GREETINGS IN PUBLIC

For one person to look directly at another and not acknowledge the other's bow is such a breach of civility that only an unforgivable misdemeanor can warrant the rebuke.

A "cut" is very different. It is a direct stare of blank refusal, and is not only insulting to its victim but embarrassing to every witness. Happily it is practically unknown in polite society.—Emily Post, 1922

A nod or tipping of the hat on the man's part and a nod and smile on the woman's are all that is necessary when casual acquaintances pass by accident. In theaters, restaurants, shops, or any public place, people stop to speak to acquaintances as long as the greeting does not create a situation that may disturb others around them, as it would in a narrow aisle. If they are too far apart to speak without shouting they simply smile and wave.

It is safer to nod to someone whose face is familiar than to run the risk of ignoring an acquaintance. It is often difficult to recognize people whom one has met when they are wearing a different type of clothing—a bathing suit rather than street dress, for instance.

The habit that is most often interpreted as rudeness is absent-mindedness. Absorbed in their own thoughts, people do not hear the voice or see the motions made by someone trying to speak to them.

They may walk right by a friend without noticing him. Although it is annoying to be passed by an "unseeing" acquaintance, one should be careful not to confuse absentmindedness with intentional slight.

Except at a wedding people greet each other in church with a nod and a smile. At weddings people do speak softly to friends sitting near them, but one does not expect to enter a church and hear an undignified and unceremonious babel of voices. If you go to a church other than your own and are seated next to a member of the congregation you recognize, you should, of course, quietly say, "How do you do?" But you do not greet anyone aloud until you are out in the vestibule or on the church steps, when you naturally speak to your friends as you meet.

THE ANSWER TO "HOW ARE YOU?"

Tact produces good manners. To a chronic invalid or someone in great sorrow or anxiety a gay "Hello, Mrs. Jones! How *are* you? You look fine!" is really tactless, however well intended, since a truthful answer would make the situation emotional. In such a case Mrs. Jones can only reply, "All right, thank you." She may be feeling that everything is all wrong, but to let go and tell the truth would open the floodgates disastrously.

"Fine, thank you," or "Very well, thank you," is normally the correct and conventional answer to "How are you?" unless there is reason to believe that the person asking *really* wants to know the state of one's health.

TAKING LEAVE

When someone making a formal call is ready to leave he or she stands up at a pause in the conversation. To those with whom he has been talking he says, "Good-bye. I hope I'll see you again soon," or simply, "I'm glad to have met you." The others answer that they were delighted to meet him too.

In taking leave of a group of strangers—whether you have been introduced or not—you nod and smile a good-bye to those who happen to be looking at you, but you do not attempt to attract the attention of others who are unaware that you are leaving.

If you must leave a large party early you find your hostess and say good-bye without calling more attention than necessary to your going. It might suggest leaving to others and so lead to the premature breaking up of the party.

⚛2⚛ Names and Titles

THE USE OF FIRST NAMES

Only a century ago it was not unusual for a wife to refer to her husband as "Mr. Jones" and to call him "Mr. Jones" when she was speaking to him, even in private. The use of first names was restricted to children, brothers and sisters, close cousins, a very few lifelong friends (of the same sex, of course), and perhaps a girl and her fiancé. Ridiculous as these customs now sound, the pendulum sometimes seems to have swung a bit too far in the other direction. Titles of respect, and family titles such as "Aunt," "Granny," "Cousin," etc., are becoming the exception rather than the rule.

Strangers who have just been introduced immediately start to call each other "Jack" and "Sue," and at a party in the home of friends people always use first names after being introduced. If you don't you will surely be thought stiff and unfriendly. Certainly if two people find each other attractive and discover common interests even though there is a considerable difference in their ages it is perfectly correct for one to say to the other, "Please call me Barbara."

However, this trend is not popular with everyone, and a certain amount of discretion must be used. As George Stevens wrote, "I propose that anyone who calls me George the first time we meet should be prepared to recognize me the next time."

Here are some occasions on which first names may not be used *except by specific request:*

To a superior in one's business, unless it is obviously the office custom.

To a business client or customer until requested to do so.

To a person of higher rank (a diplomat, a governor, a professor, for example).

To professional people offering you their services (doctors, lawyers, etc.), who are not personal friends.

18

To an older person.

We all know people of middle age and older who seem to think that being called "Sally" or "Jack" by Tilly Teenager and Freddy Freshman will take them back to the same age level. "Sally" or "Jack" may suggest a camaraderie that "Mrs. Collins" or "Mr. Sears" does not. But one wonders how Mrs. Collins would feel if she could hear those same youngsters calling her "Old Sal" behind her back.

When an older person calls a younger person by his first name the younger is not to take it as an invitation to respond in the same way. But if Mrs. Collins and Mr. Sears prefer to be "Sally" and "Jack," and specifically ask the young person to call them by those names, no one else has a right to object.

When trying to decide if you should be on a first-name basis with someone you have just met, whether or not you are of the same generation is a good general guideline. Suppose you are around thirty. A new neighbor, Mrs. Newcomb—ten or fifteen years older than you—moves in next door. You like each other and are soon calling each other "Janet" and "Rose." But she has a fifteen-year-old daughter, while your children are four and six. Do the youngsters call you and Mrs. Newcomb by your first names? They do not. Even though Ginnie Newcomb is as close to your age as her mother is, you are of different generations. To help foster the respect that has been so lacking in recent years it is most important to maintain the titles that are a sign of that respect.

Sometimes parents who have always been known to their children's friends as "Mr. and Mrs." begin to feel awkward about retaining those titles as the age gap lessens. To those who have brought up this question I can only say, Do whatever seems most natural. If you think that you *and* the youngsters would feel comfortable about it you can suggest that they start calling you "Harriet" and "Jim." But if it would make you feel awkward it would undoubtedly make them more so. So, in most cases, even though emotionally you are closer than you were when they were children, I would recommend going on with the titles that have always been natural and right—in their eyes—for you and Mr. Jones.

PARENTS

It is a flagrant violation of good manners for children to call their natural parents by their first names, and furthermore, it undermines the respect that every child should have for his mother and father. It is all very well to want to be "pals" with your child, but you are *not* the same age and you do not have the same abilities and interests.

There is little to be gained by pretending that you do. An attitude that accepts and takes advantage of the age difference is far more satisfactory. One simple mark of recognition of this difference is the use of your proper title. If you deny your position by rejecting the use of "Mother," "Father," or their derivatives you are undermining the natural parent-child relationship. You are trying, instead, to be a brother or sister. Not only do the terms show your child's respect for you, but they give him the security he needs with real parents who accept the relationship and are proud of it.

AUNTS, UNCLES, AND GRANDPARENTS

Aunts and uncles are often called by those names, but not necessarily. Those who are younger than the parents often prefer to be called by their first names only, and this is perfectly permissible. For example, my children call my brother, who is considerably older than I am, "Uncle." But his children, who are closer to my age than to his, call my husband and me by our first names. However, in introducing an aunt or uncle the term should always be used, both to show respect and to explain the relationship: "My aunt, Mrs. Singer."

With the possible exception of a young stepgrandmother grandparents are always called "Grandmother," "Grandfather," or a derivative thereof.

DEFINING SOME OTHER RELATIONSHIPS

Your brother-in-law is either your sister's husband or your husband or wife's brother. The same holds true in reverse for your sister-in-law. Their spouses are *not* in-laws but are courteously *referred to* as "sister-in-law" or "brother-in-law" when there is a friendly relationship. They are not defined as in-laws legally.

The children of siblings are first cousins. The children of first cousins are second cousins. Your cousin once removed is your first cousin's child. In other words a cousin once removed is separated by one generation. Second cousins are of the same generation.

STEPPARENTS

The question of what children should call their stepparents is difficult because the circumstances are so variable, and the answer must depend on what seems best in each case.

A child should *never* be forced to call a stepparent "Mother" or "Father" or any nickname having that meaning, especially if his own parent is living. If the child *chooses* to do so, it is a compliment to the stepparent and should be encouraged.

If a child does not, and probably will not, know his own parent, then he would regard a stepparent who has brought him up as a natural parent and say "Mother" or "Father." This is especially true if he has stepbrothers or stepsisters whom he hears using those names. But if the child is older when one parent remarries, the situation is quite different. If he has known the stepparent for some time he may call him or her by a nickname or first name. Actually, a nickname seems to be the best solution, if one can be found that is appropriate and not a derivative of "Mother" or "Father."

NAMES FOR PARENTS-IN-LAW

The question of what a bride is to call her parents-in-law has no definite answer either, and the choice of names is purely personal. Only in unusually formal families does one hear "Mr." and "Mrs.," which to most of us sound very cold. Even "Mr. and Mrs. B." seems warmer and more intimate than "Mr. and Mrs. Brown." More often parents-in-law are called by names that mean "Mother" and "Father," but are not the names that the bride uses for her own parents. Or perhaps they are called "Mr." and "Mrs." until a grandchild's nicknames—"Mimi" and "Poppy," for example—gradually become theirs. When a son or daughter has a special nickname for a parent the new husband or wife usually uses that same name. And this is one case, especially if the parents are young, when a younger person may call the older by a first name.

Whatever name is decided upon, there is often a difficult period, and sometimes hurt feelings, before the solution is found. The new daughter-in-law is too shy and embarrassed to bring up the subject, and her husband's parents, in turn, don't want to "push" her into too much intimacy.

The parents, simply because they are older and have more self-confidence than the bride, should make the move. Rather than sitting back and wondering why Cindy still calls them "Mr. and Mrs. Pool" when they are so fond of her, they should *suggest* that she call them by the name their son uses, or if that is what she calls her parents, another form of "Mother" and "Father." Or they may prefer that she use their first names. All that need be said is, "Now that you and Dick have been married awhile and we know each other so well, we'd love to have you call us Mom and Dad, or would you prefer Kate and George?" In any case it is up to the parents to make the move, and the daughter- (or son-) in-law should, of course, comply.

If the shoe is on the other foot and you are the devoted daughter-in-law whose parents-in-law have given you no hint at all, you are free, if you wish, to break the ice. But don't just start right out with

"Kate" and "George"—ask them what they would like you to call them, since you feel "Mr. and Mrs." is much too formal.

When a mother writes to a son and daughter-in-law who call her "Mom" and "Jean" respectively, she signs her letter "Mom." She has been "Mom" to her son for longer than she has been "Jean" to her daughter-in-law, and "Mom" seems less strange to the latter than would "Jean" to the son.

The less intimate relationships of aunts, uncles, and even grand-parents need not pose a question, because the bride calls all her husband's relatives exactly what he does, and he in turn does the same.

YOUR CHILDREN'S IN-LAWS

Unfortunately English, unlike several foreign languages, has no single word to describe your son's or daughter's parents-in-law. In Hebrew the word is *machatoonom,* and in Spanish, *consuegros.* Sue Shymer in her book *Keep Your Mouth Shut and Your Pocketbook Open* suggests that we coin a neuter version of *machatoonom* and call our co-in-laws *mockitoons.* But until Mr. Webster accepts the word we must simply refer to them as "my daughter's in-laws" or "John's" or "my son-in-law's parents."

OTHER ADULTS

The custom of calling family friends "Aunt," "Uncle," or "Cousin" when no such relationship exists has generally gone out of style. When really intimate friends are devoted to the children and feel that "Mr. [or "Mrs."] Surname" does not express the affectionate relationship, they may suggest nicknames for themselves or even specifically request that the youngsters call them by their first names. The children should comply, but the parent should make it clear that this is a special case, and he is only to use the first name because it is requested. Otherwise a child addresses all friends of his parents as "Mr. [or "Mrs."] Surname."

REFERRING TO HER HUSBAND OR HIS WIFE

Usually—and correctly—a lady says "my husband" when speak-ing of him to an acquaintance. But to a friend or to the friend of a friend, she speaks of him as "John." This does not necessarily give the other person the privilege of calling him "John" when they meet.

In the same way, Mr. Comstock speaks of his wife as "Edith" to friends whether they themselves call her "Edith" or "Mrs. Comstock." But to a man or woman who is a stranger, he speaks of her as "my wife." Thus when the Duke of Edinburgh, accompanying Queen Elizabeth II, was hailed by a former shipmate in the British Navy, he correctly introduced him to "my wife."

NAMES OF SAFETY

The so-called names of safety—properly used by every man, woman, or child when speaking to a stranger about any member of the family—are "my wife," "my husband," "my daughter," "my mother," or as necessary, "my sister, Alice," "my son, George." These forms are correct for every occasion; whereas, should Mrs. Jansen, whom you have met before, speak of her husband as "Mr. Jansen," she would be very rude.

WHEN NOT TO REFER BY THE FIRST NAME

In speaking *about* other people "Mr.," "Mrs.," or "Miss" are generally used if the person with whom you are talking does not know the one to whom you refer. You only speak of absent friends by their first names when you have referred to them often enough so that the person to whom you are talking realizes who they are. For example, to a close friend to whom you had often spoken about your college roommate you might say, "I'm so pleased—Jane is coming East to visit me next month." But in speaking of someone you have mentioned only once or twice, a word of identification is necessary. "Yesterday I ran into that nice Mrs. Brown who was on the cruise with us last year."

ANNOUNCING ONESELF

ARRIVING AT THE DOOR

When an adult member of the family comes to the door in answer to your ring, you never call yourself "Mr." or "Mrs." or "Miss." If he does not know you identify yourself by a sentence or two: "I'm John Grant, a friend of Jim's at the office. Is he home?" or "Susan and I met at the Barrys' cocktail party. I told her I'd drop by."

If a child answers the door you say, "I'm Mr. Grant," or "Mrs. Smythe," and "Would you please call your mother for me, if she is at home?"

If the door is answered by a maid who does not know you and

if you are not expected, you say, "I'm Mr. John Grant. Is Mrs. Jones in?" If you are expected, you merely say, "I'm Mr. Grant," and you may add, "Mrs. Jones is expecting me." A woman uses "Mrs. Grant" in both cases.

THE BUSINESSMAN ANNOUNCES HIMSELF

When you enter an unfamiliar office, say to the receptionist, "Good morning. My name is Roger Short. I have a ten-o'clock appointment with Mr. Byre." If you have one, offer your business card. It helps the receptionist give your name correctly to the person you wish to see or to his secretary. And some firms keep the card as a record of each visitor.

If you do not have a specific appointment it is helpful to give a little information about your business. "Good afternoon, I'm Roger Short of the Schmid Corporation. I'd like to see Mr. Byre about our line of lubricants."

ON THE TELEPHONE

Introducing oneself on the telephone is described in Chapter 58.

THE USE OF "DR."

When the title "Dr." indicates a degree required for the practice of a profession, as in medicine, dentistry, or veterinary medicine, it is used instead of "Mr." at all times. Protestant clergymen who are doctors of divinity also use the title.

An *earned* title indicating that a man or woman has received a doctorate in history, philosophy, literature, etc., is generally used professionally, although it varies according to the feelings of the owner of the degree and the customs of his particular institution or academic field. In private life he may, if he prefers, continue to call himself "Mr." But in any formal situation where other people are introduced as "Mr.," "Mrs.," or "Miss," rather than by first names, it is a mark of recognition and respect to use the title "Dr." The distinction, in that case, is in the social setting rather than in the type of degree. In general, it is better to "Dr." a man who would rather be "Mr." than to "Mr." a man who would rather be "Dr."

He also may have "Ph.D.," or whatever the appropriate letters may be, printed following his name on his business stationery and cards. Although he might, under the circumstances mentioned above, use "Dr." on his social cards he would not use the letters of his degree.

THE USE OF JR., 2ND, AND 3RD

A man with the same name as his father uses "Jr." after his name as long as his father is alive. He may drop the "Jr." after his father's death, or if he prefers, he may retain it in order not to be confused with his late father. This also helps to differentiate between his wife and his mother if the latter is still living and does not wish to be known as "Mrs. Jones, Sr."

When a man is named after his father who is a "Jr.," he is called "3rd." A man named after his grandfather, uncle, or cousin is called "2nd."

The following diagram may help to clarify these relationships:

John Silas Acres

John Silas Acres, Jr.   *Robert Smith Acres*

John Silas Acres, 3rd   *John Silas Acres, 2nd*

The wife of each of these men uses the same suffix after her name as her husband does, i.e., "Mrs. John Silas Acres, 3rd."

Some family names are carried on through three or four generations. There is John (Sr.), John Jr., and Johns III, IV, and V. This presents a real problem when John (Sr.) dies. Do they all retain the title they have always been known by or do they all "move up"? There is no rule. Moving up creates a problem of identification, and there is bound to be confusion among acquaintances who used to know John Jr. as John III, or there can be a problem with bank and charge accounts, etc. But moving up does avoid more generations of the same name and thus more confusion. Many people feel the complications outnumber the advantages and prefer to retain their same titles, and I am inclined to agree. However, I feel that too many men having the same name is confusing at best, and after number III the next son should be given a different middle name so that he does not use any numeral at all.

THE USE OF "SIR"

"Sir" is a title of respect, but it implies an inferior position, in some way, on the part of the speaker. Therefore it is never used between people of equal age and status. No matter how charming a gentleman may be, a woman of the same age does not address him as "Sir." On rare occasions an older man may say "Sir" to a contemporary, especially if he doesn't know the other's name. It is also used as a means of addressing distinguished people and may be used instead of too many repetitions of a formal name and title.

In the South many youngsters are taught to address their elders as "Ma'am" and "Sir." This is considered correct since it is the local custom, but they should be taught the distinction between using the term for a family friend and using it for a waiter or employee. I have heard young people calling a waiter "Sir" in an effort to be polite, and this is incorrect—they, like adults, should simply say "Waiter."

It is perfectly correct for a salesperson to call a customer "Sir," or for a pupil to so address his teacher—in short when there is an age difference, or when one is in the position of serving the other.

SPECIAL USAGE OF WOMEN'S NAMES

A DIVORCÉE'S NAME

Until recently, unless a divorcée took back her maiden name and used the title "Miss," her only possible form of address was her maiden name combined with her ex-husband's last name. Mary Jones who married John Smith, after divorcing him became Mrs. Jones Smith. This is still absolutely correct, but today many find it stiff or confusing. Divorce was uncommon years ago; and when it occurred the divorcée, who was apt to remain in the same town or city where she was well known, seldom remarried. Therefore her maiden name was known to all of the people around her, and its use identified her and also declared her divorced state. But today many divorcées move; they look for a new life in a community where their maiden names mean nothing and are a source of considerable confusion to people they meet. They are naturally introduced as "Mary Smith," and new acquaintances have no way of making a connection with someone they hear of as "Mrs. Jones Smith." An acceptable alternative now is "Mrs. Mary Smith." With this title she establishes both her identity and her divorced status.

A divorcée may also prefer to use her given name as opposed to her maiden name when the combination of the two last names is ludicrous or unmanageable. "Mrs. Mary Lipwitz" is certainly easier for both Mary and her friends than "Mrs. Hobenzollen Lipwitz." "Mrs. White Black" could not fail to cause considerable amusement, if not confusion.

It is quite true that the title "Mrs." should technically be used only in conjunction with one's husband's name, but in the interest of simplifying an awkward custom an allowance may be made for those who prefer this form of address.

When a woman divorces two or three husbands, she drops the previous husband's name each time and retains either her maiden name or her first name with the name of her last husband. Della Smith married Bob White, then Frank Green, and is now divorced from him. She forgets the White entirely and calls herself "Mrs. Smith Green" or "Mrs. Della Green," whichever she prefers.

Many young divorcées who have no children take back their maiden names. When they do this they should use the title "Miss," as they should not call themselves "Mrs." Maiden-name. If there are children involved she should keep her husband's name, which is the same as theirs, and call herself "Mrs."

UNMARRIED MOTHERS

When a girl is unmarried but has a child she is referred to as "Miss," or if she wishes, "Ms." Getting married changes a woman's title to "Mrs.," having a child does not.

A MARRIED WOMAN'S LEGAL NAME

A woman's legal name consists of her given name, her maiden name, and her husband's name. Except in a few instances—for example, on income tax forms—the middle name is shortened to an initial. The title "Mrs." is never used with the legal signature with the possible exception of a professional woman who wishes it to be known that she is married, but does not wish her husband's name to appear. In that case she may put "Mrs." in parentheses before her signature.

She uses her legal name as her signature on all business correspondence, on bank accounts, and all legal documents.

Many women are christened with two names and are called by both. Mary-Louise, Elizabeth-Ann, Mary-Beth, are inseparable in some cases. When these girls marry, the requirement that their maiden name be used as their middle name makes the whole thing entirely too long. So the maiden name, in this one case, may be dropped; Mary-Louise Harper, who married Bob Morgan, may call herself Mary-Louise Morgan. But Betsy Hancock Smith, who married James Layton, becomes Betsy Smith Layton—not Betsy Hancock Layton. Susan Jean Franklin, who has always been known as Jean and has never used the "Susan" at all, may, when she marries, drop the Susan and become Jean Franklin Jones.

A WIDOW'S NAME

A widow, until she remarries, keeps her husband's name. She is known, not as Mrs. Mary Scott, but as Mrs. James Scott.

When she remarries she has the option of using her first husband's name as a middle name, or of dropping his name and using her maiden name. If she was married for a long time, and if she has children, she will undoubtedly prefer to keep the name of a man with whom she spent many years, and which identifies her with her children.

PROFESSIONAL WOMEN

IN SOCIAL SITUATIONS

A woman who is a medical doctor, a dentist, etc., is addressed by, and introduced with, her title, socially as well as professionally. She may or may not prefer to be known as "Dr." on an envelope addressed to her and her husband *(see Chapter 6)*, but in speaking, the "Dr." is always used.

The rules for women who have earned a law degree, Ph.D., or any other degree, are exactly the same as those described on p. 24 for men holding the same degrees.

MISS, MRS., OR MS.?

Traditionally, when there is no way of knowing a businesswoman's marital status, she has been addressed as "Miss." This is still perfectly correct, but many professional women today prefer the more impersonal "Ms." It does on occasion avoid what is sometimes an embarrassing error, and therefore I believe it serves a useful purpose in the business world, or in circumstances where a woman, for professional reasons, does not wish her marital situation to be revealed.

I do not, however, think it is necessary or appropriate socially. Most women are perfectly happy with and unashamed of their state —whether it is married or single—and have no reason to hide it. Furthermore, contrary to the business situation, in social surroundings it is usually very helpful to use "Miss" or "Mrs." when making introductions or referring to someone, because many people are embarrassed to ask right out: "Are you married?"

"Ms." has no meaning (other than "manuscript"), and "Miz" or "Em Ess," the only possible pronunciations, are either unattractive or unwieldy. Therefore I think it should be avoided socially, unless, of course, someone has made it clear that that is the title by which she wishes to be addressed.

NAMES LEGALLY CHANGED

Whatever the reason for changing the name by which one has been known, social and business associates should be notified of the change if embarrassing situations are to be avoided. The quickest and simplest way of telling them is to send out formal announcements:

Mr. and Mrs. John Milsokovich
Announce that by Permission of the Court
They and Their Children
Have Taken the Family Name of
Miller

⤙3⤚ Words and How We Use Them

Nothing reveals our background, training, self-discipline, and education as quickly as the words we choose and how we pronounce them. Well-educated people, for example, invariably use certain expressions and appear to avoid others instinctively.

To speak English properly is not difficult, but it requires study. The dictionary is meticulous in its definitions, and rules of grammar determine each word's use. These matters can be learned by anyone who cares enough to try. The shades of meaning, however, may vary from one place to another, and there are, of course, local or regional dialects and accents. Usually, to speak as the best-educated people in one's hometown speak is sufficient for all social and domestic purposes. Be sure, though, not to confuse the educated with the caricature—the "lady" with the comic-strip "society" manner who says "pahdon me" and "chahmed" and talks of the elegant affairs she attends.

Of course there are certain exceptional people who overcome the handicap of lack of education. Their language is simple, and they may be guilty of committing certain grammatical errors, but this is far better than the extreme of pretentiousness. A genuine, sincere man or woman can go anywhere and be welcomed by everyone, provided that he or she is a person of naturalness, wit, and warmth.

PRONUNCIATION

REGIONAL AND FOREIGN ACCENTS

Traits of speech typical of certain sections of the country or accents acquired from foreign-born parents are not to be confused with pronunciations whose origins are in carelessness, laziness, or deliberate misuse.

30

An Irishman may have a brogue as rich as Irish stew, while another person may speak in a soft Southern drawl, a flat New England tone, or a rolling Western style. The very crisp Boston accent is considered by some the best English spoken in America. In the South there is a softness, with "I" turned to "Ah" and a tendency toward a drawl. People from Chicago say "Chicawgo," eat "chawk-lut," and drink "waaatuh." Philadelphia's "haow" and "caow" for "how" and "cow" are as typical as the twang of the Midwest. All the variations merely indicate the part of the country we are from. "Bot" and "thot" may sound ugly to those who say "bought" and "thought," but it is very possible that "bought" and "thought" sound equally ugly to the others. Yet regional variations are in no way unacceptable. To some the speech of others may sound too flat, too soft, too harsh, too clipped, or too drawling, but it should not sound uncultivated. Only to those involved in making public speeches to the entire nation—perhaps a candidate for federal office—could a markedly local accent be a handicap, because it might suggest to the listeners a mind limited to that particular locality and uninformed about the broader issues.

As a general rule, therefore, when you look up the pronunciation of a word in your dictionary, you need not be concerned because you say the "ou" in "out" or the "a" in "add" in a way quite unlike the recommended. As long as the sound you produce is natural to you and consistent with your general speech pattern and your region's, you are quite correct—for *you.*

CARELESS AND IGNORANT PRONUNCIATIONS

Anyone can pronounce common English words properly with the help of a good dictionary and the willingness to use it. Too many errors are the result of nothing more nor less than laziness. Differences such as those between "wash" and "wawsh" or "cahn't" and "can't" are unimportant, but an educated person doesn't commit errors such as "cherce" for "choice" and "erl" for "oil."

THE USE AND MEANING OF WORDS

REGIONAL EXPRESSIONS

The meanings of words as well as their pronunciations vary from one section of the United States to another. In one town the local grocer will put your purchases in a "bag" while in another he provides a "sack." An expression common in Dallas might as well be

Greek when the Texan uses it in Vermont. No one can be expected to know each and every one of these regional words and phrases. But we ought to be aware that such differences exist, especially when we find ourselves in another part of the country or talking with a visitor from another city. To use obscure colloquialisms with no concern for the listener's understanding—and hence his feelings—is hardly polite. If you are the listener don't hesitate to ask the meaning of a word or phrase you do not understand. Otherwise the conversation may slip into misunderstanding and confusion for no good reason.

SLANG

Funk and Wagnall's *Standard College Dictionary* defines *slang* as follows: "Language, words, or phrases of a vigorous, colorful, facetious, or taboo nature, invented for specific occasions or uses, or derived from the unconventional use of the standard vocabulary." A slang expression, although often short-lived, may achieve wide use, and in the evolution of language many words originally slang have been adopted by good writers and speakers and have ultimately taken their place as accepted English.

The fact that slang is apt and forceful makes its use irresistible. Coarse or profane words are unnecessary, but so many other entertaining or descriptive expressions are in common use that their exclusion from everyday conversation would be absurd.

To be an asset to your conversation, slang must be fresh and applicable or it is as unappetizing as cold gravy. Moreover, using slang is like underscoring written words; to be effective it must be sparingly done. It is all too easy to fall into the habit of using too much, or of depending on it, to express ideas that it cannot adequately convey.

"BAD" LANGUAGE

The question of four-letter words or sex terms has become far more complicated in recent years. A generation ago they were simply taboo, and to use them demonstrated a complete lack of education and manners. Today many of these formerly unmentionable words are casually used by people of refinement, in almost all the plays on Broadway, and in every best-selling novel. It makes no sense to tell a child or young person that he can't use these words when he hears them on all sides and when his contemporaries are using them without a second thought.

However widely four-letter words may be used, however, they are offensive to many people and should *not* be used indiscriminately. I firmly believe the pendulum will swing—is already swinging, in fact—away from pornography, perversion, and absorption with nudity and sex, and toward a more moral and modest attitude. As it does, the use of "bad" language will fade away. The overemphasis on sex is bound to wear itself out, and with it the overprevalent use of "sexy" words.

In the meantime young people should be taught the meaning of the words they pick up, and when and how to use them. They should consider whether or not the word is offensive to their listeners. To their contemporaries, it probably is not—to their grandparents, it is. As one father I know said to his son, "Look, Joey, that word doesn't bother me particularly but I know Mom doesn't like it, so let's not use it around the house, OK?" This put the emphasis on the right spot—the word itself isn't so important, but the fact that it may offend is.

FOREIGN WORDS

Sprinkling foreign words indiscriminately through your speech is not a sign of great education—in fact it sounds pretentious—but an occasional word, used in its proper sense, adds color and spice to English speech and writing. There are many foreign words that have become an accepted part of our language, and we should be familiar with their meaning and pronunciation.

We cross paths so often with the many foreigners living in the United States that it is easy to increase one's knowledge of their languages. We have Italian grocers, German bakers, French and Spanish waiters—to name only a few—all of whom are delighted if you show an interest in their language, how it sounds, and what it means. In fact, if you ask the waiter how to pronounce "parmigiana," he very well may tell you not only how to say it, but how to cook it. Everyone loves to be an expert, and foreigners as well as Americans like to have you express interest in their language and their customs.

A visit to a foreign country is no excuse for using the native pronunciation of its cities when you are back home talking to fellow Americans. If you come back from France speaking of Paris as "Paree" to all your friends, you will not only sound pretentious, but you will be a laughingstock. If you happen to run into a Frenchman, you may say the name of his country or cities as he does, but to other Americans, use the accepted English pronunciation.

The French and other foreign terms used on restaurant menus are too numerous to learn all at once. Many good cookbooks contain glossaries of these terms and provide an excellent source of reference. In any case the waiter or headwaiter is always available to explain the dish to you if there is no translation, and you may make a note of the words for future use.

WORDS AND PHRASES TO AVOID

There are certain words and phrases that should be avoided at all times, either because they sound pretentious, make you seem uneducated, or the meaning you give them is simply incorrect. For example no one who speaks easily and well "arises," or "retires," or "resides" in a "residence." He gets up, goes to bed, and lives in a house. In other words everything that is simple and direct is better form than the cumbersome and pretentious.

Other expressions are provincial; and if you want your speech to be pure, avoid them unless they are indigenous to you. They are often words whose correct meaning has been corrupted by incorrect usage, and they include such terms as:

reckon or *figure,* when you mean *think*
visiting with, when you mean *talking with*
allowed as how when you mean *said*
drapes, when you mean *draperies* or *curtains*
folks, when you mean *family*
leave me, when you mean *let me*
Pardon me when you mean *Excuse me* or *I beg your pardon*
party when you mean *person*

WORDS OFTEN CONFUSED

The born gentleman avoids the mention of names exactly as he avoids the mention of what things cost; both are an abomination to his soul.
    A gentleman never takes advantage of another's helplessness or ignorance, and assumes that no gentleman will take advantage of him.
—Emily Post, 1922

I'm sure there are a number of words whose meanings are often confused, but three sets come to mind that are closely connected with etiquette.

Lady and Gentleman. These meaningful words have become so discredited by misuse that those to whom they most accurately apply rarely use them. Instead they have substituted for them the less precise words *man* and *woman.*

However, an understanding of the true meanings of *lady* and *gentleman* is helpful to an understanding of the true meaning of good manners. To say that no man cheats at cards or to say that no woman makes a public spectacle of herself would be false. Each of these statements is true of a gentleman and a lady but not necessarily of a man or a woman.

The fact that someone does a service for you is no reason to assume that she is not a lady. A lady is no longer "a woman of superior position in society." I refer to the female who cleans my house for me as a lady, because she is one.

There are many occasions when our conversation would be more precise and more flavorful if we did not avoid the use of these two words. And there are many definitions of them to help you decide when they should be used. Oliver Wendell Holmes wrote that a "gentleman was a man who, though not trying to be a gentleman, filled all the qualifications by instinct." Ralph Waldo Emerson said that the word *gentleman* "denotes good-nature or benevolence: manhood first and then gentleness." Holmes also thought it took three years to "polish" a gentleman, and he might well have agreed with the anonymous writer who said, "To be born a gentleman is an accident: to die one is an achievement."

And a lady, as Peg Bracken says, is simply "a woman in whose presence a man is a gentleman."

Home versus House. In its true meaning *home* conveys the spirit, the personality, and the hospitality of your house. *Home* is not a synonym for *house.* A house is a solid structure built of wood or brick or stone. You can love your home, be at home, do whatever you please at home, and you can eat home cooking. But if you are sensitive to nuances, you never put a piece of furniture in "the home" unless you mean a charitable institution. You would say, "Our home was an old Georgian house," but not "We had a Georgian home."

Formal and Informal. Formal is a synonym for *ceremonial.* A formal party is conducted according to rules of established forms of ceremony.

In some houses—Mrs. Worldly's, for instance—formality is inevitable no matter how informal the invitation may be.

On the other hand, the Kindharts can invite a hundred guests and achieve a party that is strictly informal. Ordinary pleasant social intercourse between friends and neighbors could never be characterized as formal.

While the word *formal* used to mean the extreme degree of correctness it is currently used to mean somewhat less.

An elderly gentleman and his grandson were sitting together at a beach club when young George called out to a passing friend, "Hey, Jim, are we going formal tonight?"

Jim answered, "I think so."

Grandfather looked at George's shorts, bare feet, and T-shirt. "Tell me," he said, "what do you mean by 'going formal'?"

The boy shrugged and replied, "I don't know, exactly. I guess it means we've got to put on ties."

CULTIVATING AGREEABLE SPEECH

INCREASING VOCABULARY

Irritating speech is like a badly tuned car engine—each knock and thump disconcerts the listener. He hears the "er-er-and-er," shares the frantic search for a word or the effort with which each word is pronounced, and never hears the thoughts the speaker is trying so desperately to convey.

One of the best ways to cultivate taste in words is by reading good books. It must be remembered that there can be a vast difference between excellence and popularity and that many books on the best-seller lists have no literary merit.

Although we have many fine American authors the works of two English writers, Rebecca West and Winston Churchill, are outstanding as sources of flawless English. And it is true that Winston Churchill's war memoirs have a value of "matter" as well as "manner" of writing English that sets a high standard. Rebecca West's writing is invaluable to those who are interested in finding an example of English at its *best*.

The best way to cultivate both vocabulary and a perfect pronunciation, apart from associating with cultivated people, is to get a small pronouncing dictionary and read it word by word, marking and studying any that you have used and mispronounced or those you wish to learn. Or choose a book and read it aloud to yourself, looking up words you come across that are not familiar to you and learning the meaning as well as the correct pronunciation.

There are excellent books available containing vocabulary-building instructions, with exercises to help you increase your knowledge of words and test your achievement. The consciousness of these exercises may initially make you sound a bit stilted, but by using your new vocabulary constantly, you will soon overcome this tendency.

A postscript of encouragement is that plain speech is much more pleasing and friend-making than the self-conscious use of a broad vocabulary that is not really natural to the speaker.

A PLEASING VOICE

The expression "You know she is a lady as soon as she opens her mouth" is not an exaggeration. A pleasing voice is the first requirement for charm of speech. A low voice—low in pitch, not in range—is always more appealing than one that comes out in a high squeak. On the other hand, a voice uttered with so little strength that it threatens to be extinguished is even more trying. Socially *and* in a business office it is annoying to have to ask a "mumbler" to repeat what he has said. Making yourself heard is chiefly a matter of enunciation; if you breathe properly and pronounce distinctly, a low voice carries well and delights the listener's ear.

Shouting is not only earsplitting but is also extremely bad form, since it attracts the attention of everyone within hearing. As a nation we do not talk too fast so much as too loudly. Some of us twang and slur and shout; others drawl, and still others race ahead at full speed, but the speed of our speech does not matter so much. It is pitch that is important, along with pronunciation and enunciation, both of which are essential to the listener's comfort.

$\cdot$4$\cdot$ The Good Conversationalist

The cynics say that those who take part in social conversation are bound to be either the bores or the bored; and that which you choose to be, is a mere matter of selection. The cleverest woman is she who, in talking to a man, makes him *seem clever.* —Emily Post, 1922

Ideal conversation is an exchange of thought and not necessarily an eloquent exhibition of wit or oratory. Fortunately for most of us, it is not essential to have a special gift of cleverness to be someone with whom others are delighted to talk. An ability to express our thoughts and feelings clearly and simply is sufficient for ordinary conversation among friends.

Conversation should be a matter of equal give-and-take, but unhappily it is frequently all "take." The voluble talker monopolizes the conversation without giving anyone else a chance to do anything other than wait for the turn that never comes. Only on rare occasions does one meet a brilliant person whose continuous talk is a delight.

There is a simple rule by which one who is inclined to "run on" can at least refrain from being a pest or a bore: Stop and think.

DON'T PANIC, THERE'S NOTHING TO FEAR

If you dread meeting strangers because you are afraid you won't be able to think of anything to say, remember that most conversational errors are committed not by those who talk too little but by those who talk too much.

Many people for some reason are terrified of silence, and they generally have great difficulty in carrying on a conversation. This terror is something like the terror felt by those who are learning to swim. It is not just the first stroke that overwhelms them, but the thought of all the strokes that must follow. The frightened talker

38

doesn't hear a word that is said to him because he is trying so desperately to think of what to say next. So the practical rule for continuing a conversation is the same as that for swimming: Don't panic. Just take it one stroke (or word) at a time.

The old sign at railroad crossings—STOP, LOOK, LISTEN—is excellent advice in many circumstances other than when you are waiting to cross the tracks. In conversation *stop* means not to rush ahead without thinking; *look* means to pay attention to the expression of the person with whom you are talking; and *listen*—meaning exactly that—is the best advice possible, because everyone loves to sit next to a sympathetic listener. Remember, though, that a sympathetic listener *really* listens. A fixed expression of sympathy while your mind wanders far away won't fool anyone but the most self-centered conversationalist.

THINK BEFORE YOU SPEAK

Nearly all the faults or mistakes commonly made in conversation are caused by not thinking, that is, by lack of consideration. Many people who really should know better and who are perfectly capable of intelligent understanding let their brains remain asleep—they are too lazy to be considerate. They go out night after night to parties, day after day to business, and absentmindedly chatter away without ever taking the trouble to think about what they are saying and to whom they are saying it!

For example, would a young mother dwell on her baby's cute tricks to a bachelor sitting next to her at dinner if she *thought?* No, she would understand that only her closest friend (and a female friend, at that) would care for more than the briefest mention of her children. An older mother can be even worse, because she not only bores her hearers but prejudices everyone against her children. I remember the advice I once received from an older and wiser friend: "My dear, there is no point in discussing your children with new acquaintances—they either have some of their own, or they don't." In the case of the doting wife or mother, someone should point out to her that her lavish praise is not merely boring to her friends but actually handicapping those whose image she wants to enhance.

Many of us do not have anyone to instruct or remind us about our thoughtless and inconsiderate talk. Only by careful listening to our own words and strict attention to the reactions of our listeners can we discover our personal inadequacies. The burden of thinking before speaking is our own. Dorothy Sarnoff wrote: " 'I' is the smallest letter in the alphabet. Don't make it the largest word in your vocabulary. Say, with Socrates, not 'I think,' but 'What do you think?' "

PLEASANT TALK

HUMOR: THE RAREST OF GIFTS

If you know anyone who is both interesting and amusing, you will, if you are wise, do everything you can to lure him to your house frequently, for he can "make" your party. His subject is unimportant; it is the twist he gives to it, the personality he puts into it, that delights his hearers.

There are those who can tell a group of people that their train broke down, or that they had a flat tire, and make everyone burst into laughter. But the storyteller who constantly *tries* to be funny is generally a bore, and the majority of us, if we wish to be considered attractive, are safer if we rely on sincerity, clarity, and an intelligent choice of subject.

FISHING FOR TOPICS

> *Notwithstanding the advertisements in the most dignified magazines, a discussion of underwear and toilet articles and their merit or their use, is unpleasant in polite conversation.*—Emily Post, 1922

In talking to a person you have just met and about whom you are in complete ignorance, the best approach is to try one topic after another just as a fisherman searches for the right fly. You "try for nibbles" by asking a few questions. When one subject runs down, you try another. Or perhaps you take your turn and describe something you have been doing or thinking about—planting a garden, planning a trip, or an interesting article you have read. Don't snatch at a period of silence. Let it go for a little while. Conversation is not a race that must be continued at breakneck pace to the finish line.

When you find yourself seated next to a stranger at a party introduce yourself before starting your "fishing." Then there are all manner of openings, and if you are shy, have some of them fixed in your mind before you go to the party: If your hostess has told you something about your dinner partner, you might say, "I understand you're the man who went out on the Roberts' boat last week. That must have been fun." If you know nothing about him at all, you could ask, "Do you live in Homeville, or are you just visiting?" From his answer, hopefully, you can carry on a conversation. He will probably ask where you live and what your husband does. It's simple enough, but be sure to give him the opportunity to talk.

Another helpful gambit—and one that wins instant popularity —is to ask advice. "We are planning to drive through the South. Do you know any particularly good places to stop on the way?" or "I'm thinking of buying a television set. Which brand do you think is best?" In fact it is safe to ask his or her opinion on almost anything: politics, sports, the stock market, the current fad—anything.

COMPLIMENTS

We all love to receive compliments and tend to love those who offer them. Therefore I often wonder why so few people give them. I suspect it is sometimes because most people have an inborn aversion toward being too personal, and some are shy or embarrassed. Still others are simply thoughtless and don't stop to think how a complimentary word can brighten someone's day. But if you are one who finds it hard to give a firsthand compliment, you need not hesitate to give a "compliment once removed." "I saw Margie May yesterday, and she told me what delicious cookies you made for the PTA meeting." This gets you double credit—once with the person you're talking to, and again when it gets back to Margie.

So let me urge you to speak up. The next time you have a nice thought about someone, tell him. If we all did it more frequently the world would be a happier place.

Be sure however, a compliment is sincere. Archbishop Fulton Sheen once remarked that "a compliment is baloney sliced so thin that it is delectable. Flattery is baloney sliced so thick that it is indigestible."

If you are the one being complimented you will want to show your appreciation and pleasure. Don't simper and don't belittle whatever the compliment referred to. For instance if someone says, "What a lovely dress," don't say, "Oh, well, it was very inexpensive, and I don't think it fits very well." The appropriate way to respond to any compliment is to say, "Thank you," or "I'm so glad you like it," or "Aren't you nice to say so."

FORBIDDEN GROUNDS

HANDLING "SORE SUBJECTS" WITH CARE

The tactful person keeps his prejudices to himself and when involved in a discussion says, "It *seems* to me" thus and so. He does not say, "That's not so!" which is tantamount to calling the other a liar. If he finds another's opinion totally unacceptable he tries to change the subject as soon as possible.

If you care too intensely about a subject, it is dangerous to allow yourself to say anything. That is, if you can only expound your own fixed point of view, then you should never mention the subject except as a platform speaker. But if, on the other hand, you are able to listen with an open mind, you may safely speak on any topic. After all, any mutually interesting topic may lead to one about which you don't agree. Then take care! Much better to withdraw unless you can argue without bitterness or bigotry. Argument between coolheaded, skillful opponents may be an amusing game, but it can be very, very dangerous for those who become hotheaded and ill-tempered.

THE TACTLESS BLUNDER

It is like rubbing salt into an open wound to make such remarks as "Bobby's complexion has gotten so much worse since he went away to school!" or "I suppose you feel lonely since the death of your daughter," or "Are you and Hank really getting a divorce?" These examples may sound exaggerated, yet these and similar remarks are constantly being made by people who have not the slightest excuse for making them and who should know better.

Other examples of tactlessness include such remarks as "Twenty years ago you were the prettiest girl in Philadelphia," or, to a woman whose son has just married, "Why is it, do you suppose, that young wives always dislike their mothers-in-law?"

If you want to be popular don't talk about the unattractiveness of old age to the elderly, about the joys of dancing and skating to the lame, or about the pleasure of a garden to one who must live in an apartment.

It is needlessly unkind to ridicule or criticize others, especially for what they can't help. It is also a habit that may turn the tables on you. A young girl who hoped to make an impression said to the boy sitting next to her, "How *can* you go out with that drip?" "Because," he answered, "she's my sister."

UNPLEASANT TYPES

THE BORE

One definition of a bore is "one who talks about himself when you want to talk about yourself." This is superficially true, but a bore might more accurately be described as one who insists on telling you at length something that you don't want to hear about at all. He insists that you hear him out to the bitter end in spite of your obvious boredom.

THE WAILER

One of the fundamental and commonsense rules of all conversation is that you talk about things that will be interesting and agreeable to the listener. It seems unbelievable, therefore, that so many people can talk about nothing but misfortunes, sickness, and other unpleasantness. Don't dwell on your own problems. Your audience has them, too, and won't be entertained by yours. Only your nearest and dearest care how many times you have been in the operating room.

THE SENTENCE-FINISHER

Some people are quicker to find a word or phrase than others. They have an irresistible urge to supply that word or to finish a sentence for one who is slow in finding the exact expression he wants. If you are inclined to do this use all your strength to resist the temptation. It makes the other speaker feel inadequate, you may change his meaning by supplying a word he did not intend to use, and finally, you put yourself in the position of appearing to try to steal the limelight from him.

THE CONTRADICTER

There was a popular song some years ago that went, "It ain't what you say but the way that you say it," and that is true of contradictions, too. Everyone has a right to express his viewpoint as long as he doesn't say didactically, "You're wrong and I'm right." If you wish to express an opposing view, or "contradict," say, "I *think* it is this way or that way," and give your reasons for thinking so. And then listen carefully to the other person's side.

THE SHIFTY EYE

Nothing is more disconcerting than talking with someone who does not look directly at you. His eyes may wander here and there as though he is looking for any escape route, or he may stare fixedly at something behind you, as though it is far more interesting than you. Some people do this while they are talking themselves; others only while listening. Both are lacking in that primary obligation of a good conversationalist—being a good listener. When you are talking to *anyone,* look at him, not in a fixed stare but constantly enough so that he feels he has your undivided attention.

THE STORY-SNATCHER

We all know people who can't let anyone else tell a story to the end. They must jump in and correct the details and then finish the story. This is particularly common between husband and wife, and also between parent and child. It is a habit that is particularly annoying if it happens frequently, and it has been the cause of many a marital battle. Avoid it yourself, and if you are the victim of a story-snatcher don't suffer in silence. Many people don't even realize they are doing it and even less do they realize how annoying it is to everyone who is listening. If, after a gentle hint from you, the offender continues to steal your stories, break in, each time he does it, with, "all right, *you* tell it." This will stop all but the thickest-skinned story-snatcher.

THE SECRET-TELLER

Another social pariah is the one who, when part of a group, is constantly whispering or talking in low asides to one person alone. The others cannot fail to feel that either he is talking about them or they are missing some especially juicy tidbit. This also applies to speaking a foreign language that most of the group does not know. It is exactly like telling a secret and is equally rude.

ONE WHO MAKES PERSONAL REMARKS

As mentioned above, compliments and other favorable personal remarks are not only permissible but desirable. But unpleasant remarks, or remarks that make another person uncomfortable, are definitely in bad taste. The old adage "If you can't say something nice, don't say anything at all" is very good advice.

There are occasions, however, when one wonders whether or not he should make what might be construed as a critical remark. This occurs perhaps when you don't know whether you should tell your friend that her slip is showing, or that she has a run in her panty hose. The answer depends on whether she can correct the situation or not. If there is a place where she can go to shorten her slip straps, or a store nearby where she can buy a new pair of panty hose, by all means tell her. If not, calling attention to her problem will only make her self-conscious and aware of a fault of which she might otherwise have been uaware, or at least have thought was unnoticed.

Women frequently ask whether they should call an unzipped fly to the wearer's attention. Unless you are total strangers, do. The slight embarrassment to you and the man at the time is nothing compared to the mortification he will feel when he discovers the condition and wonders how long it existed. If, however, you have just been introduced, leave it to someone who knows him better.

Another good resolve to make and stick to, if you want to keep your friends, is never to speak of anyone without, in imagination, having him or her overhear what you say. You have heard the exclamation, "I'd say it to her face!" Be sure, if you say it, that you mean it, and then—nine times out of ten—think better of it and don't say it anyway. Preaching is all very well in a schoolroom or pulpit, but it has no place in social conversation. That is supposed to be a happy pastime; telling people disagreeable things to their faces or talking behind their backs will not endear you to your friends.

FOR THOSE WHO TALK TOO MUCH

There are seldom regrets for what you have left unsaid. "Better to keep your mouth closed and be thought a fool than open it and remove all doubt."

Don't pretend to know more than you do. To say that you have read a book and then reveal that you have understood nothing of what you have read makes you look like an idiot. No person of real intelligence hesitates to say, "I don't know."

People who talk too easily are likely to talk too much and at times imprudently. Those who have vivid imaginations are often unreliable in their statements. On the other hand, the "man of silence" who rarely speaks tends to wear well among his intimates, but he is not likely to add much to the gaiety of a party. In conversation, as in most things, the "middle road" is best. Know when to listen to others, but know also when it is your turn to carry the conversation.

Try not to repeat yourself, either by telling the same story again and again or by going back over details of your narrative that seemed to interest or amuse your hearer. Many things are interesting when told briefly and for the first time; few bear repeating.

ANSWERS TO PERPLEXING REMARKS

SNOOPERS

How do you answer personal questions about the cost of a gift, a furnishing, or a piece of clothing?

You are under no obligation to give out this sort of information if you do not wish to. You can simply resort to "I don't know [or "remember"] what it cost." Or if you wish to play up the value of the article, say, "More than I probably should have paid," and if you wish to play it down, "Not as much as you'd think."

Inquiries about your rent or mortgage, your children's allowance, or the amount you pay your maid fall into the same category. They are in poor taste and should be given short shrift. You cannot quite say, "None of your business," but you can say, "I'd rather not talk about that, if you don't mind. With the cost of living what it is, the whole subject is too depressing. . . ." and change the subject.

ANSWERING "HOW OLD ARE YOU?"

Most women and many men over thirty do not like to be asked their age, and it is a very thoughtless question. However, it *is* frequently asked, and there are a number of ways of parrying the question. You might say, "Old enough to know better," you can be as indefinite as "Over twenty-one," or you can use my particular favorite, "Thirty-nine [or forty-nine, or whatever] and holding."

ETHNIC AND OTHER INSULTS

What can you say when someone makes derogatory remarks about a group, a person, or a nationality, in your presence?

There is no excuse for remarks of that nature, and you should make that clear. Tell the speaker quite frankly that you find their remarks objectionable and do not wish to listen to them, and then walk away. If you do not feel *that* strongly, just say, "Let's get off that subject," and introduce another.

CORRECTIONS

When a person pronounces a word incorrectly, or makes a grammatical error, should you correct him or should you repeat his error to avoid making him uncomfortable?

Two wrongs don't make a right. Don't correct him, but when the opportunity arises use the same word or phrase correctly and hope that he will recognize his mistake.

REPEATERS

Is it permissible to remind someone that he has told you the same story before, or must you just grin and bear it?

Good manners can often be combined with a bit of frankness. It is not only to your advantage, but to the speaker's, to stop him from frequent repetition, or he will soon be considered a bore. Making your tone as appreciative as possible, break in at a pause with, "Oh, yes, you told me about that trip—it sounded like such fun."

✌5✌ *Public Speaking*

Many excellent books have been published on the subject of parliamentary procedure (*Robert's Rules of Order* is one of the best), and in most high schools students are required to take courses in the subject and in public speaking as well. This chapter is intended not for experienced speakers or for those who have to run formal meetings frequently, but for the thousands of private citizens who may be called upon to speak at a club meeting, a PTA meeting, or a testimonial dinner. To the novice, public speaking can be a terrifying experience, but there are many simple rules that can be a great help in making the occasion a success.

INTRODUCING A SPEAKER

Today women as well as men are called on frequently to serve as masters of ceremonies or chairmen at dinners and are expected to introduce the speakers. When the appointed time comes, if he (or she) is on a stage or platform he rises, steps forward, and taps firmly on the speaker's podium or table to attract attention. If he is at a dinner table he simply rises, and the people near him immediately stop talking, which should be enough to bring quiet to the rest of the hall. If it is not, one or two people tap their glasses gently to call attention to the speaker.

An introductory speech should be extremely brief in order not to divert time or attention from the main speaker. A few sentences to identify him are all that is necessary. If he is very well known, you might open your introduction by saying, "Our speaker tonight is Mr. Jim Jones. I know that it is not necessary for me to tell you about him as we have all read of his exploits in Africa. We are most fortunate in having persuaded him to fit this evening with us into his busy schedule, and it gives me great pleasure to introduce—Mr. Jones."

If the speaker is less famous a few more remarks might be added to explain his background and the reason for his speaking to your organization. But avoid overdoing it and confine your talk to two or three minutes at the most.

Having made the introduction, sit down quietly until the speech is over. Then you should rise, shake hands, and thank the speaker for his time, his effort, and his excellent speech. *See also Chapter 16, "Conducting Meetings."*

PREPARING YOUR SPEECH

The greatest asset to a successful speech is having it well prepared and rehearsed in advance. It may be long or short, serious or humorous, but the confidence gained from the knowledge that your material is good and your presentation smooth is worth hours of preparation and practice. This does not mean that your speech should be rattled off like a memory exercise, and it should certainly never sound as if it were being read.

After you have written the speech, notes should be made (if it is long enough to warrant them) in large clear print on index cards or a small pad. These notes should be only an outline of the speech—a reminder in case you lose the train of thought. The speech should be rehearsed several times, first in front of a mirror and then, if possible, before family members or friends so that you will feel less strange when you stand before a larger audience. It is a good idea to try to express a thought in several different ways while you practice, for this tends to make your speech sound less "rehearsed" and more as if you were thinking about what you are saying.

Unless it is absolutely necessary don't write your speech out in full and then read it. No matter how familiar you are with the material, reading it makes it sound sterile, and you will rapidly lose your audience's interest. It is possible to use a written speech and refer to it only as you would to notes, but the amount of material on the page makes it difficult to keep your place. If you must write your speech out fully, either because of the amount of detail necessary or because of your lack of confidence, practice it even more assiduously so that you almost know it by heart and can look up frequently to keep your listeners' attention.

OPENING WORDS

There is a set formula for opening a speech that is helpful to an inexperienced speaker because he hears the sound of his voice for a second or two while repeating exact phrases that he has committed to memory. He must turn to the chairman first, and calling him by name, thank him for his introduction; he greets any distinguished persons present and then the audience: "Mr. Chairman, Senator Brown, and fellow members of Delta Psi, good evening," or "Mr. President, Distinguished Guests, Ladies and Gentlemen."

Some speakers begin by giving the audience a suggestion of the points to be covered in the speech, others with an amusing story or a pertinent quotation to introduce the subject. It is wise not to make too important a point in the opening paragraphs because the audience may take a few minutes to settle down to listen. Also, most speakers "warm" to their subject and will make their salient points more forcefully after they have overcome any initial nervousness.

USE HUMOR AND PROPS

Everyone enjoys listening to a speaker who tells an amusing story well, but it must have some connection with his subject. There is nothing worse than a poor attempt at humor that fails either in the choice of the story itself or in its presentation. This distracts the audience and leaves them searching for the point rather than listening to the speaker. Jokes, anecdotes, and quotations are all useful means of giving a talk variety and interest. But remember that the audience wants to hear what *you* have to say, not just a collection of other people's thoughts and actions.

If your subject permits the use of illustrations or slides, by all means take advantage of this. Not only does it make your preparation easier (although you still must rehearse, using the slides and perfecting the timing and mechanical details), but the attention of an audience is held more firmly when it is seeing as well as hearing.

THE IMPORTANCE OF YOUR VOICE

Closely rivaling your material and preparation in importance is the quality of your voice. A low-pitched voice is vastly more attractive than a high one, but it must be loud enough so that the audience need not strain to hear. Speak slowly rather than fast (between 90 and 130 words, or half a double-spaced, typed page, a minute), but vary the tempo or you will sound monotonous. A certain amount of variation in pitch is desirable, especially in telling a joke or story, and some words should be stressed for emphasis. All this is a matter of practice, and you should think of these points, as well as the content of your speech, while rehearsing.

If you are to use a microphone try to arrive early enough to test it with your own voice. If this is not possible make certain that someone has proved it to be working properly and try to watch the chairman while he is introducing you to see how close he stands, how loudly he speaks, and how he adjusts the height. Most people have a tendency to speak much too loudly into a microphone and to hold onto the stand, causing interference. If you have advance notice that a microphone is to be used try to practice with one beforehand.

THE DANGER OF RAMBLING

The inexperienced speaker's most serious fault is a tendency to talk too long. Almost invariably, at meetings where a number of people are allotted five or ten minutes to speak, the speakers must be cut off long before they have made their points. When you have been told, or have decided for yourself, the length of the speech, you must plan your remarks to fit that time limit and stick to your plan. In fact it is the obligation of the chairman (or committee) who invited you to speak to give you a time limit, and if he does not you should be sure to ask him about it. Notes will help you stay with the subject, but the extemporaneous speaker is in real danger of rambling too long on each thought as it occurs to him.

The most successful speakers say what they have to say concisely, simply, and without pretentious language or repetition. When your point is made go on to the next one—it is not necessary to explain the preceding one in other ways. Your listeners will go away thinking you a wonderful speaker if you end your speech before they become restless and while they are still hoping that you have more to say.

IN CLOSING

When your time is up or you have said all that you have to say, a brief summary prepares the audience for the ending. Sometimes an entertaining story in conclusion will leave them with a pleasant memory, and some speakers like to close by thanking the audience for their attention. You might also close with the thought you wish to leave in your audience's mind or by referring to what is next on the program: "I want to thank you all for giving me your attention, and now I know you are anxious for the fashion show to start." However you choose to end your talk do not let yourself fade away. Memorize your closing remarks carefully so that you will make them firmly and without apology.

WHEN CALLED ON UNEXPECTEDLY

If you happen to be called on unexpectedly to "say a few words" it is in very poor taste to contradict, out of embarrassment, the speech of the chairman who has graciously introduced you. To say

"I'm afraid the chairman has greatly exaggerated my abilities" is an impulse of modesty, but besides being discourteous to the chairman it all too seldom rings true.

If your knees begin to shake and you feel incapable of uttering a sensible word you must acknowledge the chairman's introduction at least briefly by some such words as "I'm sorry, I'm not a speaker but I do wish to thank you all for attending [supporting our cause]," and sit down. But if you are able to speak you should smile and think (whether or not you actually say it), "How nice of you to say that," and make at least a few remarks. Try to think of what you are saying rather than of the impression you are making. Remember, the speech that charms is the one that ends to its listeners' regret.

THE PROBLEM OF YOUR HANDS

One of the greatest problems for a public speaker is what to do with his hands. At a podium you may grasp the side edges with your hands and keep them there, moving them only to turn the pages of your notes or to make an occasional gesture. At a dinner table you may press your hands against the table, but only if it is high enough so that you need not bend over. Avoid the temptation to pick up a piece of silver or to finger your napkin or glass. And wherever you are speaking, if you are a man, be sure that you do not have loose change or keys in your pockets. It is a perfectly natural gesture for a man to put his hand in his pocket, but if it results in rattling or jingling, it is most distracting to the audience.

If you are using slides be sure that a pointer is available. Not only is it practical for indicating details in the pictures, but it also serves as a prop for you to grasp during the rest of your speech.

If there is no support of any kind available you must do your best to keep your hands reasonably still, clasping them before you or behind your back or simply letting them hang at your sides. Gestures are important to add emphasis to your speech, but avoid repeating the same movement again and again. Do not throw your arms about or move around so much that your listeners' attention is diverted from what you are saying.

Finally, do not, in desperation, grab the microphone. It *might* support you, but it will also create the most distracting and irritating crackle through the loudspeakers.

OTHER MINOR PROBLEMS

If you feel an urge to sneeze, or a need to cough overcomes you, don't worry about it—just do it. If it is a prolonged fit of coughing you should apologize to your audience; if not don't mention it at all. You should always have a handkerchief or tissue available. In the case of these "emergencies" simply pull it out, cover your mouth, turn your face away from the microphone, and get rid of the "tickle." It is in your own interest to see that there is a glass of water on the podium. It is perfectly permissible to take a sip at any time, and the slight pause can even be used to heighten suspense or emphasize a point.

Occasionally one sees a speaker smoking during his talk. Don't do it. It is distracting to the audience and a sign of insecurity in the one who is talking. Smoking, per se, is objectionable to many people, and the speaker is certain to lose the favor of a substantial proportion of his audience simply by doing so.

DRESSING FOR YOUR APPEARANCE

Men, unless the occasion is a formal one, wear business suits when they give a speech. If the men at the speakers' table at a dinner are wearing black tie, the speaker does too, and of course the same is true of a "white-tie" dinner. The only other exception to the rule of the business suit is a meeting of a golf or yacht club, where a blazer and slacks would be more appropriate.

The keynote of a woman's costume for speaking in public is simplicity. If the occasion is an afternoon meeting wear a suit or a simple wool dress in winter; choose a short-sleeved or sleeveless cotton or silk dress in summer. A good-looking pants suit is acceptable if the meeting is not too formal, and it is becoming to the wearer. Jewelry in the daytime should be confined to simple earrings, a pin, a necklace, and a bracelet, which must not jangle. Hats are optional. At an evening meeting, a slightly more elaborate dress or a cocktail suit is appropriate.

For a dinner speaking engagement the woman speaker should find out what the other women will wear and dress accordingly. The variety of costume might range from a very plain cocktail dress to a long dinner skirt or an evening dress, depending on the formality of the occasion. In all cases, however, the dress should not have a very low neckline and should not be too elaborate in design. Jewelry for evening naturally may be more elaborate than that worn in the daytime, but it should not be so brilliant or worn in such quantity as to be distracting.

Shoes should go with the rest of your costume, but be sure that they are very comfortable, especially if the speech is to be long.

TOASTS

The custom of toasting goes back almost as far as history itself. Ancient warriors drank to their pagan gods, more civilized Greeks and Romans drank to gods too, and early Norsemen drank to each other. Almost every culture practiced toasting in some form, and the custom gradually evolved into today's toasts to love, friendship, health, wealth, and happiness.

One story has it that the term itself originated in England in the seventeenth century, when it was customary to float a bit of toast on a drink. A well-known belle of the day was in the public baths (in Bath where then, as now, the waters were considered "salubrious"). Her lover scooped up a little of the bath water, added the customary toast, and having drunk to her health, offered the glass to a friend. The friend commented that he didn't really want the water but he'd enjoy the toast.

THE MECHANICS OF MAKING A TOAST

Men, frequently, and women, occasionally, are called on to make a toast, and it can be a perplexing experience for those who are not accustomed to it. Unless one knows he will be called on and can plan in advance, his mind is apt to go completely blank.

The best solution is simply to say exactly what you feel. Toasts never need be long, and if you do panic when called on unexpectedly, you can get away with something as brief as "To Joe, God bless him," or "To Jack—a wonderful friend and a great boss."

But if you wish to appear more poised and more eloquent you must add a few remarks—a reminiscence, praise, or a relevant story or joke. The toast should, however, always be in keeping with the occasion. A touch of humor is rarely out of place, but toasts at a wedding should be on the sentimental side, those in honor of a retiring employee nostalgic, and so on.

On ceremonial occasions there is generally a toastmaster, and if not, the chairman of the committee or the president of the organization proposes the necessary toasts at the end of the meal, and before any speeches. At less formal dinners anyone may propose a toast as soon as wine or champagne is served. The toasters need not drain their glasses. A small sip each time allows one to drink numerous toasts from the serving.

Many people do not touch alcohol, including wine, at all, even for toasts. These teetotalers should not turn their glasses upside down. They may, of course, refuse the wine when it is passed and merely rise empty-handed or raise the empty glass when the toast is drunk. However, I feel it is less conspicuous (and implies less criticism of the drinkers) if they say to the waiter, "Just a little, please," and then raise the partly filled glass to their lips without drinking. Or if it seems expedient they may ask the waiter quietly to bring them a soft drink. Years ago one was not supposed to toast except with an alcoholic beverage, but today one may participate in the toast with whatever liquid is available. In any case, one must rise and join in the spirit at least—it would be extremely discourteous to remain seated.

REPLYING TO A TOAST

The person being toasted does not rise or drink the toast. Instead a man rises and drinks to his toasters in return, either saying, "Thank you," or proposing his own toast to them. While a woman is perfectly free to make toasts if she wishes to, her reply to a toast is simply a smile and a nod in the direction of the speaker. She may also raise her glass toward him in a gesture of "Thanks, and here's to you, too."

SOME SAMPLE TOASTS

The following toasts are intended only to give you some ideas for various occasions. They must be changed to fit the particular circumstances, of course, and a word or two of your own feelings will always add a personal touch.

A FATHER'S TOAST AT HIS DAUGHTER'S ENGAGEMENT PARTY

1. Now you know that the reason for this party is to announce Mary's engagement to John. I would like to propose a toast to them both, wishing them many, many years of happiness.

2. Mary's mother and I have always looked forward to meeting the man Mary would choose to marry. She lived up to all our expectations when she picked John. We want you all to know how pleased we are to announce their engagement tonight. Please join me in wishing them a long and happy marriage.

A BEST MAN'S TOAST AT THE REHEARSAL DINNER

1. For some time I have been worried about Mary and John's apparent incompatibility, but looking at them tonight I see how wrong I have been. So please join me in a toast to John's income and Mary's patibility.

2. John and I have been friends for a long time now, and I have always known what a lucky guy he is. Tonight all of you can see what

I mean when you look at Mary. Please join me in a toast to both of them. May this kind of luck continue throughout their lives together.

A BEST MAN'S TOAST TO THE BRIDAL COUPLE AT THE WEDDING RECEPTION

1. To Mary and John—a beautiful girl, a wonderful man—and the happiest couple I ever hope to see!

2. To Mary and John—may they always be as happy as they look today.

A BRIDEGROOM'S TOAST TO HIS BRIDE AT THE WEDDING RECEPTION

1. I'd like you all to join me in a toast to the girl who's just made me the happiest man in the world.

2. All my life I've wonder what the girl I'd marry would be like. In my wildest dreams I never imagined she would be as wonderful as Mary, so please join me in drinking this first toast to my bride.

A BRIDEGROOM'S FATHER'S TOAST AT THE REHEARSAL DINNER

1. I would like to ask you to join me in drinking a toast to two wonderful people without whom this wedding could never have been possible: Mary's mother and father, Mr. and Mrs. Brown.

2. I don't need to tell you what a wonderful girl Mary is, but I do want to tell you how happy John's mother and I are to welcome her as our new daughter-in-law. To Mary and John.

TOAST TO A RETIRING EMPLOYEE OR A MEMBER OF THE FIRM

1. It is often said that nobody is indispensable, and that may sometime be true, but for all of us there will never be anyone who can replace Joe. Although we will miss him greatly, we know how much he is looking forward to his retirement and we wish him all the happiness he so richly deserves in the years to come.

2. I know that every one of us here tonight thinks of Bob (Mr. Smith) not as an employee (employer) but as a friend. When he leaves we will suffer a very real loss both in our organization and in our hearts. At the same time we rejoice that he will now be able to enjoy the things he wants to do, so let us rise and drink a toast to one of the finest friends we have known.

ANNIVERSARY TOASTS

1. Many of us who are here tonight can well remember that day twenty-five years ago when we drank a toast to the future happiness of Mary and Bob. It is more than obvious that our good wishes at that time have served them well, and therefore I would like to ask that all of you—old friends and new—rise and drink with me to another

twenty-five years of the same love and happiness that Mary and Bob have already shared together.

2. John, I'd like to propose a toast to you on your fiftieth birthday. It has been a wonderful party tonight, and all of us wish you health, wealth, and the years to enjoy them.

TOAST TO A SECOND MARRIAGE

For this I am indebted to Samuel Johnson: "Here's to a second marriage—the triumph of hope over experience!"

TOAST TO A GUEST OF HONOR AT A
TESTIMONIAL DINNER

1. We are gathered here tonight to honor a man who has given unselfishly of his time and effort to make this campaign so successful. Without the enthusiasm and leadership that Bob Jones has shown all through these past months we could never have reached our goal. Please join me in drinking a toast to the man who more than anyone else is responsible for making it possible to see our dream of a new hospital wing finally come true.

2. Ladies and gentlemen, you have already heard of the magnificent work our guest of honor has accomplished during his past two years in Washington. Right now we would like to tell him that no matter how proud we are of his success in his chosen career we are even more pleased to have him home with us again. It's great to have you back, Jim!

FOREIGN TOASTS

Since the custom of toasting originated in Europe, and is still more widely practiced there than here, well-traveled Americans are bringing home toasts from abroad. A knowledge of the most common of these can be very useful, but if you are not sure of the pronunciation use the equivalent English toast instead. The following examples all mean, translated, "To your health."

French—*A votre santé.*

Spanish—*Salud.*

German—*Prosit.*

Swedish—*Sköal.* (This is often taken to mean that the toasters must empty their glasses, but that is not necessarily so in the U.S.)

Yiddish—*L'Chayim.*

Part Two

CORRESPONDENCE

❧6❧ *The Appearance and Style of Your Letters*

The letter you write, whether you realize it or not, is a mirror that reflects your appearance, taste, and character. A sloppy letter—the writing running up and down, badly worded, badly spelled, reveals the sort of person who probably is messy and disorganized in other ways. Conversely, a neat, clean, attractively written note portrays a person who has those happy characteristics. Therefore, while it is not quite true that a person's future can be read in his handwriting, his character may well be revealed. Furthermore, a messy letter implies a lack of interest and care on the part of the writer.

HANDWRITING VERSUS TYPEWRITING

The mechanical nature of the typewriter itself simplifies such matters as the evenness of margins and the regular spacing of lines. But it also cannot help but destroy some of the intimacy or personal feeling of the letter. Writing letters by hand is more difficult, but it is possible to learn to make graceful letters, to space words evenly, and to put them on a page so that their appearance is pleasing. No matter how badly formed each individual letter may be, the page as a whole will look fairly neat if the writing is consistent and the lines level.

You can make yourself write neatly and legibly and you can—with the help of a dictionary if need be—spell correctly. If it is difficult for you to write in a straight line make a lined guide and practice with it. If you find it impossible to keep an even margin, draw a very light perpendicular line that can be erased at the left of the page so that you can start each new line of writing on it.

Avoid such passing fads as dotting your *i*'s with a circle or using no capitals at all. Your letters may look very "in" at the time, but if these practices become a habit they look rather foolish in an older person's correspondence.

All these calligraphic complications can, of course, be avoided by using a typewriter. So many girls have taken typing at some time during their education that they write much faster as well as more neatly by machine. There is no longer any rule against using a typewriter for most personal letters, and if you prefer it, by all means do so, especially if your handwriting is illegible. However, there are three types of letters that should always be handwritten unless you are actually disabled. They are:

Notes of condolence

Formal invitations and replies

Thank-you notes

In the case of the last mentioned, if your thanks are simply part of a longer personal letter, the rule could be waived, and you could, if you customarily do so, use your typewriter.

PERSONAL STATIONERY

Suitability should be a factor in choosing your stationery, just as it is in choosing your wardrobe. For a handwriting that is habitually large pick a paper of a larger size than you would choose for writing that is small. The shape of paper should also depend somewhat upon the writer's usual spacing of the lines and on whether a wide or narrow margin is used. For example, low, spread-out writing looks better on a square sheet of paper; tall, pointed writing looks better on paper that is high and narrow.

The texture of the paper—whether it is rough or smooth—is a matter of personal choice. However, everyone should have one box of good-quality paper in a conservative color and shape to be used for condolence notes, answers to invitations, etc. This "good" paper need not be personalized if that seems extravagant, but all leading writing-paper companies sell high-quality solid-color or bordered paper in excellent taste.

If the paper is thin (airmail paper, for instance), envelopes with colored linings should be used so that the writing cannot be read through the envelope, or you may fold a blank sheet outside the pages. The monogram or address may be stamped on the paper in a color to match the lining.

A MAN'S PERSONAL PAPER

A man's writing paper should always be conservative. White or cream, gray- or granite-colored paper, is the best choice. The color of the engraving (or printing) should be black, gray, dark green, brown, or dark blue, and his ink should match, or complement it.

The most practical man's paper is a single sheet seven or seven and one-fourth inches by ten or ten and one-half inches marked in plain block or Roman letters at the top center. His name (without title), his address, including zip code, all appear. His telephone number is optional. This paper can be used for typewriting or handwriting and for all types of correspondence. It is folded in threes to fit into a seven-and-one-fourth- or seven-and-one-half-by-four-inch envelope. For purely social correspondence he may also have a family crest—if he has one—engraved in the top center or the upper-left-hand corner. If it is engraved in the corner his address and telephone number may appear at the right. In the United States, however, this is apt to appear ostentatious on a young man's stationery.

A MARRIED WOMAN'S PAPER

White, cream, light blue, gray, or light green are the proper colors for the "conservative" paper mentioned above for formal correspondence, and also for business letters. For personal letters there are no longer many restrictions, and a woman may choose any pattern or combination of colors that pleases her. Blue paper with a green border, pink with purple, orange with brown are good examples of attractive combinations. It may be stamped with a monogram, initials, or her name and address—in the center or upper-left corner —in a contrasting shade, or a color to match a border. Ink should match the printing or engraving, or should be chosen to complement the color of the paper.

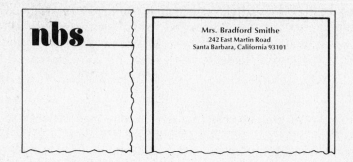

The paper is smaller than a man's, approximately five and one-half by six and one-half inches, and it may be single or double. If you type most of your letters you should get single sheets, which may be used for both typewritten and handwritten letters.

A married woman's social paper is engraved "Mrs. William Frost," rather than "Mrs. Mary Frost." A professional woman may use her professional name without title—"Jane Author" rather than "Mrs. Robert Author"—on paper used for business correspondence.

PAPER FOR EVERYONE IN THE FAMILY

Paper suitable for use by all the members of a family has the address engraved or printed in plain letters at the top. Frequently the telephone number is put in small letters under the address or in the upper-left-hand corner with the address in the center. This paper is especially practical if you have a country or vacation home, as it can also be used by your guests. Some people have a small map printed in the corner of their vacation-home paper to assist weekend visitors.

350 Chestnut Street
Philadelphia, Pennsylvania 19106

TELEPHONE 674-7572

18 Walnut Road
Peoria, Illinois 61602

AN UNMARRIED WOMAN'S PAPER

An unmarried woman's paper is the same as a married woman's in color and style. Her name at the top of the paper, however, is written without title. The envelope address does, of course, include the "Miss." The envelopes of stationery she uses for business purposes may be printed "Ms." if she prefers that title.

NOTEPAPER

For short notes, for acceptances or regrets, and for invitations, a supply of fold-over notepaper, half the size of a single sheet of woman's writing paper, is invaluable. It may be of any color or combination of colors you wish and engraved or printed with initials or with your name and address and telephone number. If not marked with initials or a name, it is useful for every female member of the family.

FOR THE YOUNG CORRESPONDENT

Many stationers sell paper for very young children. It is ruled, usually has an illustration of animals, toys, or something from a familiar story or nursery rhyme, and may come in a variety of shapes. It is designed to amuse the young child and make him consider letter-writing a pleasure rather than a chore.

A girl's first name—either Elizabeth in full or Betty—is popular for a young girl's personal correspondence, but it should not be used by an older woman. If her first name is not distinctive the younger girl may wish to use her surname also. Available, too, are attractive papers with designs in the upper-left-hand corners or along the left or in borders; usually flowers, birds, or perhaps a kitten or puppy. A name or monogram is not used, and the style of the picture varies with the age of the girl. The paper illustrated below would be suitable for a young teenager.

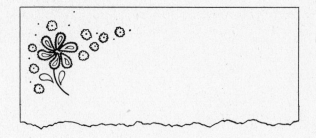

BUSINESS STATIONERY

A firm's business stationery should be carefully chosen, as the impression it makes may be widespread. It should be conservative, attractive, and of good quality, to indicate that the firm itself has those characteristics.

The most appropriate business-company stationery is a single sheet, white or off-white, measuring approximately eight by ten inches. This fits into the standard file, and folded in thirds, into a regular business envelope.

When it is to be used by various people in a company it carries the name of the firm and the address and telephone number in block or Roman letters at the top.

Many large companies have paper printed (or engraved) *for* their executives. In this case the firm's name and address are at the top center, and the executive's name and position are found in the upper-left-hand corner. The secretary does not type the executive's position after the signature.

Both men and women executives often have their personal office stationery in addition to the above. The man's paper is engraved with his name and the firm's address, without title unless he is a doctor, commander, etc. If necessary his secretary may include his position in the firm when she types his name below his signature. A woman's title does not appear on the paper but does on the envelope—"Miss," "Mrs.," or "Ms."

On business envelopes the return address should always be on the face of the envelope.

OFFICIAL WRITING PAPER

An ambassador or minister has his country's coat of arms—usually in gold—stamped at the top of writing paper and on cards of invitation for official or formal use. For his personal use and for the use of all who live at the embassy or the legation, notepaper is engraved merely

AMERICAN EMBASSY
LONDON

A governor's letter paper is stamped

EXECUTIVE MANSION
COLUMBUS
OHIO

and is usually surmounted by the state coat of arms. EXECUTIVE OFFICE is also correct as the heading for official letters. Paper engraved with EXECUTIVE MANSION, but without the coat of arms, may be used by the governor's family if the address is also that of their home. Otherwise their paper is engraved with the personal address.

A senator's wife has no right to use stationery headed THE SENATE, nor should the wife of a representative write on paper engraved HOUSE OF REPRESENTATIVES.

RETURN ADDRESSES

Although the U.S. Postal Service prefers that the return address appear in the upper-left-hand corner of the envelope, that is not particularly attractive on personal stationery and is impossible if the lettering is engraved. Therefore addresses are almost invariably stamped on the back flap. If, however, your paper is not personalized you will find printed address stickers very useful. These can be stuck in the preferred place on the front of unmarked envelopes and may even be used when the address is on the back, for business letters or others where it is important that the address be noticed.

PRINTING OR ENGRAVING?

Years ago writing paper was engraved or it was not marked at all. Today the cost of engraving and the amount of correspondence carried on by busy women has changed that entirely. If one can afford it a supply of paper with an engraved initial, monogram, or crest, to be used for special or formal correspondence, is practical and beautiful. For ordinary purposes, however, and for those who find the cost of engraving prohibitive, printed stationery serves very well.

All of the fine stationery companies also use a process called thermography, even, in some cases, to the exclusion of real engraving. The type is raised, and to the unpracticed eye, is indistinguishable from engraving. It is far less expensive than engraving, although more than plain printing, and is an excellent choice for those who wish their paper be handsome and of good quality.

CRESTS

Heraldry, with its medieval origins, is not an American institution, so the use of a coat of arms is as much a foreign custom as the speaking of an alien tongue. But when a family has used its family arms (or crest) continuously since the days when they brought the device from Europe—and their right to it is certified by the colleges of heraldry—its use is proper, if somewhat conspicuous.

It must be remembered, however, that the crest is the exclusive property of male members of a family, although it may be used jointly by husband and wife on some occasions. Its appearance on the paper of a widow or a spinster is as absurd as it would be to put "Esq." at the end of her name. Surprisingly few Americans, however, seem to be aware of this heraldic rule. A widow has no right to use her husband's crest on her letter paper. She may properly use the device on the shield of his coat of arms, transferred to a diamond-shaped device called a lozenge. She may also, if she chooses, divide the lozenge perpendicularly into two parts and crowd the device from her husband's shield into the left half and the device from her father's shield into the right half. A spinster uses her paternal arms on a lozenge without crest or motto.

SEALS

We are all familiar with a variety of seals—Christmas seals, Easter seals, Boys' Town seals, etc.—all of which help to raise money for the organizations that distribute them. They provide a painless way of supporting a worthy cause and at the same time make our correspondence gayer and more attractive.

Seals should not be used on notes of condolence, or on formal invitations and replies. Otherwise, they may be used on all personal letters and on business letters, too. Their appearance on your correspondence calls attention to the organization that sponsors the seal and gives proof of your support—thus encouraging others to contribute, too.

THE MECHANICS OF THE LETTER ITSELF

SEQUENCE OF PAGES

> *In certain cities—Boston, for instance—the last word on a page is repeated at the top of the next. It is undoubtedly a good idea, but makes a stuttering impression upon one not accustomed to it.*—Emily Post, 1922

Folded stationery sometimes causes problems about the proper order in which to use the pages. If a letter is probably going to be longer than one page but shorter than three it is customary to use the first and third pages, as this leaves the fourth (or outside) page blank and prevents the writing from showing through the envelope. For longer letters one may write first, second, third, fourth, in regular order; or first and fourth, then, opening the sheet and turning it sideways, write across the two inside pages as one. The sequence is not important, and there is no fixed rule.

One may write on both sides of single-sheet stationery, but not if it is airmail weight, as that shows through and makes the letter difficult to read.

On fold-over or informal notepaper, when the address is at the top and there is nothing in the center, the letter or note begins on the first page and follows into the center pages. The paper is opened flat and written on vertically as if it were a single page. If there is an initial, or design, or name in the center of the front page, the note begins at the top of the opened center pages if it is long enough to cover more than half, and on the lower half if it is to be only a few words.

YOUR HOME ADDRESS AND THE DATE

If your stationery is not marked with your address, it is only courteous and practical to provide it for your correspondent's convenience in replying. The upper-right-hand corner of the first page of your letter is the usual place for an address, but sometimes, especially on a short note, it may be included in the lower-left-hand part of the page, just below the level of your signature. In either case the date goes below the address.

Sincerely,
Mary Swenson
(Mrs. John Swenson)

45 Barton Street
Racine, Wisconsin
May 19, 19--

This placement is more appropriate for business letters than for social correspondence.

When your address is already engraved or printed on the stationery the date only is placed in the same place—in the upper-right-hand corner of the first page or at the end and to the far left of the signature. The form May 9, 1975, is preferable to 5–9–75.

On a friendly note "Thursday" is sufficient unless the note is an invitation for more than a week ahead, in which case you write "Thursday, January 9." The year is not essential except in business letters.

RECIPIENT'S ADDRESS

The correct form for business letters demands that the receiver's address be put at the left, below the level of the date and two lines above the salutation, exactly as it appears on the envelope.

June 7, 19--

Mr. James Johnson
Smith, Johnson & Co.
20 Broadway
New York, New York 10027

Dear Mr. Johnson:

Personal letters and notes, however, never have the address of the receiver anywhere except on the envelope itself.

THE SALUTATION

For business letters, unless you are writing to a person whose name you know, the salutation may be "Dear Sir," "Dear Sirs," or

"Gentlemen." When writing to a firm or organization composed of women, the salutation is "Dear Madam" or "Dear Madams." You should not use "Mesdames," any more than you would "Messieurs" instead of "Sirs." If you are writing to a specific member of the company—the secretary, treasurer, sales manager, etc.—but do not know the recipient's name, you use the singular "Dear Sir" or "Dear Madam." When the letter is to a firm in general, or a department of a firm, such as an order to a department store, you use the plural forms. When you are not sure whether or not the receiver is a woman "Dear Sir" is a better choice than "Dear Madam." Finally, if you know the name of the woman who will receive the letter, but do not know her marital status, you write to "Dear Miss Jones," or if you prefer, "Dear Ms. Jones."

The salutation on a business letter is followed by a colon, whereas a comma follows the name on a personal letter.

A form letter, or a very businesslike communication, when the writer and recipient do not know each other personally, starts in this way:

Mrs. Richard Worldly
4892 Third Avenue
New York, New York 10017

Dear Madam:

A more personal business letter, meaning a letter from a business or professional man to a customer or client (or vice versa) he knows personally, begins:

Mrs. Richard Worldly
4892 Third Avenue
New York, New York 10017

Dear Mrs. Worldly [or, if they are friends, *Dear Anne*]:

When you receive a letter addressed to "Dear Anne" it would be very unfriendly of you to start your reply with "Dear Mr. Brown."

The most formal beginning of a social letter is "My dear Mrs. Smith." "Dear Mrs. Smith" and "Dear Sally" are increasingly intimate. In this area your own feeling must be your guide, although it is perhaps better to err on the side of formality when you are not absolutely certain of your recipient's reaction.

In ordinary correspondence a man is always addressed "Dear Bob" when something less formal than "Dear Mr. Smith" is suitable.

Forms used in addressing distinguished persons or those in special categories are discussed elsewhere. *See Chapter 7.*

THE CLOSING

> *The phrases that a man might devise to close a letter to his betrothed or his wife are bound only by the limit of his imagination and do not belong in this, or any, book.*—Emily Post, 1922

It is too bad that, for personal letters and notes, the English language does not permit the charming closing of letters in the French manner, those little flowers of compliment that leave such a pleasant glow. But ever since the eighteenth century, English-speaking people have been busy pruning away all ornamental expressions; even the last remaining graces—"Kindest regards," "With kindest remembrances"—are fast disappearing, leaving us little but an abrupt "Sincerely yours."

The best ending to a formal social note is "Sincerely," "Sincerely yours," "Very sincerely," or "Very sincerely yours."

"I have the honor to remain . . ." is used only in correspondence to very prominent people in the government, diplomatic corps, or church.

The close of a business letter should be "Yours truly" or "Very truly yours." "Sincerely" is also correct. "Respectfully" is used only by a tradesman to a customer or by an employee to an employer. No lady should ever sign a letter "Respectfully," except as part of the long, formal "I have the honor to remain . . ." close of a letter to the President of the United States or to a bishop or a mother superior.

"Faithfully" or "Faithfully yours" are rarely used but are appropriate for a man on very formal social correspondence, such as a letter to the President of the United States, a member of the Cabinet, an ambassador, a clergyman, etc.

"As always" or "as ever" is useful to someone with whom you may not be on intimate terms, especially when you have not seen the person for some time.

"Yours" is often used on informal office correspondence.

"Sincerely" in formal notes and "Affectionately" or "Fondly" or "Love" in friendly notes are the most frequently used closings at present. Between the first and last two there is a blank; in English we have no adequate expression to fit sentiment more friendly than the first and less intimate than the others. "Cordially" was brought into use no doubt to fill this need, but it is infrequently used on purely social correspondence.

"Yours in haste" and "Hastily yours" are not so much bad form as rather carelessly rude unless for some reason your communication indicates real and necessary haste.

"Gratefully" is used only when a benefit has been received, as to a lawyer who has skillfully handed a case or to a friend who has gone to unusual trouble to do you a favor.

In an ordinary letter of thanks the signature is "Sincerely," "Affectionately," "Fondly," "Much love"—whatever your usual close may be.

Forms used in letters to distinguished persons or those in special categories are discussed elsewhere. *See Chapter 7.*

SIGNATURES ON LETTERS

On business correspondence, John Hunter Titherington Smith, finding his name too much of a penful for letters and documents, may choose "J. H. T. Smith" instead, or perhaps "John H. T. Smith." Of course, if he is writing a business associate with whom he is personally acquainted he signs simply "John" or "Jack" over the typed "J. H. T. Smith." Mail is addressed to him in the typed form (or the printed form, if the letterhead carries his full name).

A married woman always signs a letter to a stranger, or a business letter, with her legal name. If her stationery is marked with her full married name and address, "Mrs. Henry Mathews," her signature—"Mary Jones Mathews" or "Mary J. Mathews—needs no further explanation. But if it is not, she should give her married name (to which the reply will be sent) in one of the several ways. When she writes by hand she adds her married name below her signature, in parentheses.

> *Very truly yours,*
> *Mary Jones Mathews*
> *(Mrs. John Mathews)*

When the letter is typed, her married name is typed beneath the space left for her signature, where it need not be enclosed in parentheses.

> Very truly yours,
> *Mary Jones Mathews*
> Mrs. John Mathews

An unmarried woman may use the same form in a typed letter:

Sincerely,
Mary Mathews
Miss Mary Mathews

Or a single woman or a divorcée, when writing by hand, may use this style

Sincerely,
(Miss) Mary Mathews
[or] *(Mrs.) Mary Mathews*

If for some reason a woman does not want her marital status known she may use "Ms." in the parentheses, but only on business correspondence.

And a final warning about the signature: Avoid a flourishing unrecognizable one. While the reader may be able to decipher a word in a sentence because of its context, he cannot possibly make sense of an illegible signature if he does not already know who wrote the letter.

A PROFESSIONAL WOMAN'S SIGNATURE

When an unmarried woman starts her career using her maiden name she generally continues to do so throughout her professional life. She uses "Miss" in combination with that name even after she marries.

But many women start their careers after their marriage or marry after they are established and wish to have it known that they are married. Professionally called Mary T. Forsyth or Helen Horton Hughes, they use business stationery with their names printed that way. This can be most confusing to a correspondent. In order to make it clear what title he should use in addressing a reply, Mary or Helen may precede her signature with (Mrs.). This should *never* be done except on business correspondence—in all other cases their husbands' names are used below the handwritten signature when it is necessary.

SIGNATURES ON PERSONAL LETTERS

On ordinary friendly letters you sign the name by which your correspondent thinks of you. If he has a special nickname for you use that as a signature rather than what you generally call yourself.

If your name is a common one and you are writing to someone who might not recognize you by your handwriting or by the contents of your letter you must use your last name as well as your first. You may, if it seems friendlier, put the last name in parentheses.

When you are writing a letter for you *and* your husband (or sister, or whoever it may be) sign your own name only. It is not a sin to sign "Flo and Jack," but Jack is *not* writing the letter, and it is preferable to include him by referring to him in the text. "Jack and I had such a terrific time last weekend, and he especially asked me to tell you again how much he liked the golf course," "Jack joins me in sending thanks and love to everyone," etc. On Christmas cards and other greeting cards joint signatures are permissible.

OTHER SIGNATURES

The only times a woman actually uses "Mrs." in her signature are in a hotel register, on a business telegram, or on a charge account, and then it must be "Mrs. John Smith." A note to a household employee is signed "Mrs. Smith."

A married woman is listed as a member of a club or organization as "Mrs. William Franklin," not as "Nancy Franklin." Only if the organization is a professional one does she use her professional name and signature, whatever that may be. In all other cases—checks, legal documents of any sort, and as her signature on letters, she uses "Nancy Maiden-name Franklin," which is her legal signature.

Husbands and wives sign most registers as "Mr. and Mrs. William Franklin." However, when the owner of a boat you are sailing on or a home you are visiting asks you to sign his guest book, you always sign "Jean and Bill Franklin," using the last name so that future guests can see who else has enjoyed his hospitality.

A man registers at a hotel as "Robert Huff," without title, unless he is accompanied by his wife, when, naturally, he signs "Mr. and Mrs. Robert Huff." If their children are with them he may sign the register "Robert Huff and family."

On social lists, such as patrons or sponsors of a fund-raising party, a man's name is listed with his title. On professional or business listings he is simply "James Regent," and that is also the correct signature if he is signing reports, diplomas, etc.

FOLDING A LETTER

It is not very important which edge of a letter is inserted first into the envelope, but for those who wish to be strictly proper—insert the open, or unfolded edge, first. It should be placed so that when the recipient withdraws and opens it the writing will be right side up. The paper should be folded neatly—once for the envelope that is as deep as half the length of the paper, and twice for the envelope that is a third as deep. The paper that must be folded into thirds is used only as personal stationery for men or for business purposes. Women's personal letter paper should fold only once and fit into its envelope. Notepaper is the same size as the envelope and goes into it flat with only the original fold.

THE OUTSIDE ADDRESSES

Write the name and address on the envelope as precisely and as legibly as you can. If your writing is poor, print.

When you are writing to someone who lives in an American city be sure to use the zip code as it is an essential part of the address. Zone numbers are used in many foreign cities and are also an integral part of the address.

The address may be written with each line indented a few spaces:

> *Mr. Harvey S. Simpson*
> *4 Hillside Lane*
> *Clinton*
> *Ohio 20567*

or with a straight margin on the left:

> *Mr. Harvey S. Simpson*
> *4 Hillside Lane*
> *Clinton, Ohio 20567*

Either form is correct.

CORRECT USE OF "ESQUIRE"

The use of "Esquire" has virtually gone out of general use in the United States—except among a few conservative members of the older generation and among lawyers and justices of the peace. When "Esq." or "Esquire" follows the name, "Mr." *never* precedes it. "Esq." is frequently used in business correspondence from one lawyer to another. It may also be used by anyone else writing to a lawyer, unless the letter is to the lawyer and his wife, when "Mr. and Mrs. Hathaway" is correct. The salutation of a letter to him, regardless of the form on the envelope, is "Dear Mr. Hathaway."

TO A MARRIED WOMAN

No note or social letter should ever be addressed to a married woman—even if she is a widow—as "Mrs. Mary Town." Correctly and properly a widow keeps her husband's name, always. The correct form is "Mrs. Robert Town." The only exception is if you do not know the husband's name. In that case it is better to write to "Mrs. Mary Town" than to "Mrs. Town," which, unless she is the only "Mrs. Town" in the area, may never reach her at all.

UNMARRIED COUPLES OR "LIBERATED" WIVES

Men and women living together without benefit of matrimony are addressed as "Miss [or "Ms.] Jane Stuckey and Mr. Hugh Sidney." The same holds true when a married woman does not wish to assume her husband's name.

WHEN A MARRIED WOMEN IS A DOCTOR

Even though a married woman may be known both professionally and socially in conversation as Dr. Mary Flint (her husband's last name), there is some confusion when it comes to addressing social correspondence to her and her husband together. If her husband is a doctor, too, it is simple—they are addressed as "The Drs. Flint," or "Drs. Mary and Simon Flint." If, however, he is not a doctor she must decide whether or not she wishes to retain the title socially, which means that letters must be addressed to "Dr. Mary and Mr. Simon Flint"—an awkward and lengthy address. "Mr. and Dr. Simon Flint" is misleading, so for the sake of convenience many married women doctors do prefer to be addressed as "Mrs." on social correspondence.

YOUNG PEOPLE

Young girls are addressed as "Miss" from the very day they are born. Both the first and last names are used on envelopes—the only time a girl is addressed as "Miss Taylor" is on the inner envelope of a wedding invitation.

Boys may be addressed as "Master" until they are six or seven. After that they are addressed without title until they graduate from high school at approximately eighteen. At that time they take the adult title of "Mr."

"Messrs." may not be used to address a father and son. It is correct only in writing to unmarried brothers, or to two or more business partners, or members of a firm.

"PERSONAL" AND "PLEASE FORWARD" AND "OPENED BY MISTAKE"

In writing to someone at his home address you properly assume that no one else will open the letter. Therefore it is rude to write

"Personal" on it. But if you are writing a social note to a friend's business address, it is entirely correct.

"Please Forward" is correct if you know only a former address but not the current one.

It is not uncommon to open a letter addressed to someone else by mistake. It can easily happen if you live in an apartment house where letters are often put in the wrong box, or if your name is a common one. When this happens write"Opened by Mistake" and your initials on the face of the envelope, seal it with a piece of tape, and put it in the mail.

≈§7ε≈ Addressing Important People

At one time or another nearly every one of us either meets or has to write a letter to someone officially, a senator or a judge, or perhaps a clergyman or a professor, and we certainly do not want to appear ignorant because we address him or her improperly. Neither can we remember all the proper forms of address for all the personages we might ever need to speak to or write to. The chart in this chapter has been prepared to cover as many as possible of the situations likely to occur in the ordinary course of events—and some not so ordinary.

The chapter is devoted to official and formal occasions, for naturally a governor's friends continue to call him by his first name, and their wives continue to arrange their dinner and luncheon engagements with the governor's wife. Only when wedding or other formal invitations are sent to both husband and wife is it necessary to use the special forms included below under "Social Correspondence."

"THE HONORABLE"

"The Honorable" is an expression that causes considerable confusion. Federal custom in the United States bestows the title "Honorable," first officially and then by courtesy for life, on the President and Vice-President, United States senators and congressmen, Cabinet members, all federal judges, ministers plenipotentiary, ambassadors, and governors. State senators and mayors are also referred to as "The Honorable" while they are in office. The title is not used by the person himself on his visiting card, letterhead, or in his signature, nor does he say it when introducing himself.

PERSONAGE	BUSINESS CORRESPONDENCE	SOCIAL CORRESPONDENCE	BEGINNING OF PERSONAL LETTERS
THE PRESIDENT	The President The White House Washington, D.C. 20500	The President and Mrs. Washington The White House Washington, D.C. 20500	Dear Mr. President:
THE VICE-PRESIDENT	The Vice-President United States Senate Washington, D.C. 20510	The Vice-President and Mrs. Hope Home Address	Dear Mr. Vice-President:
THE CHIEF JUSTICE, SUPREME COURT	The Chief Justice The Supreme Court Washington, D.C. 20543	The Chief Justice and Mrs. Page Home Address	Dear Mr. Chief Justice:
ASSOCIATE JUSTICE, SUPREME COURT	Mr. Justice Katsaros The Supreme Court Washington, D.C. 20543	Mr. Justice and Mrs. Katsaros Home Address	Dear Mr. Justice Katsaros:

CABINET MEMBERS	The Honorable
	Gary George Gussin
	The Secretary of the Treasury
	  (or if a woman)
	The Honorable Joan Kidd
	Washington, D.C. 20220
		The Honorable (optional)
		The Secretary of the Treasury
		  and Mrs. Gussin
		  (or Mr., if the secretary
		  is a woman)
		Home Address
			Dear Mr. Secretary:
			or
			Madam Secretary:

ATTORNEY GENERAL	The Honorable Joseph Compton Attorney General Washington, D.C. 20503	The Attorney General and Mrs. Joseph Compton Home Address	Dear Mr. Attorney General:
FORMER PRESIDENT	The Honorable Alfred Edward Work Office Address	The Honorable and Mrs. Alfred Edward Work *	Dear Mr. Work:

UNITED STATES SENATOR	The Honorable
	John Wandzilak
	United States Senate
	Washington, D.C. 20510
		The Honorable and Mrs.
		  John Wandzilak
		  (or, if a woman senator)
		Mr. John Doe and
		  The Honorable Jean Doe
		Home Address
			Dear Senator Wandzilak:
			or
			Dear Senator Doe:

THE SPEAKER OF THE HOUSE OF REPRESENTATIVES	The Honorable
	Walter James Grevesmuhl
	The Speaker of the House of
	  Representatives
	Washington, D.C. 20515
		The Speaker
		  and Mrs. Grevesmuhl
		Home Address
			Dear Mr. Speaker:

MEMBER OF THE UNITED STATES HOUSE OF REPRESENTATIVES	The Honorable
	Henry Cobb Wellcome
	United States House of
	  Representatives
	Washington, D.C. 20515
		The Honorable and Mrs.
		  Henry Cobb Wellcome
		  (or for a woman member)
		Mr. John Jones and
		  The Honorable Helen Jones
		Home Address
			Dear Mr. Wellcome:
			or
			Dear Mrs., Miss., or
			  Ms. Jones:

AMBASSADOR OF THE UNITED STATES	The Honorable
	John Wilson Smith
	The Ambassador of the
	  United States
	American Embassy
	London, England
		The Honorable and Mrs.
		  John Wilson Smith
		  (or for a woman ambassador)
		Mr. John Fordyce and
		  The Honorable Martha Fordyce
		Home Address
			Dear Mr. Ambassador:
			or
			Dear Madam Ambassador:

* Formerly, letters were addressed, "The Honorable Alfred Edward Work and Mrs. Work." Today the more common usage is "The Honorable and Mrs. Alfred Edward Work." Both forms are equally correct.

BEGINNING OF BUSINESS LETTERS	CLOSE OF PERSONAL LETTERS	CLOSE OF BUSINESS LETTERS	SOCIAL INTRODUCTIONS AND IN CONVERSATION	INTRODUCING AS A SPEAKER	PLACE CARDS FOR FORMAL OCCASIONS
Sir:	Respectfully yours, *or* Sincerely yours,	I have the honor to remain, Most respectfully yours,	Mr. President *or* Sir (prolonged conversation)	The President *or* The President of the United States	The President (Mrs. Washington)
Sir:	Sincerely yours,	Very truly yours, *or* Respectfully yours,	Mr. Vice-President *or* Sir (prolonged conversation)	The Vice-President *or* The Vice-President of the United States	The Vice-President (Mrs. Hope)
Sir:	Sincerely yours,	Very truly yours, *or* Respectfully yours,	Mr. Chief Justice *or* Sir †	The Chief Justice	The Chief Justice
Sir:	Sincerely yours,	Very truly yours,	Mr. Justice *or* Mr. Justice Katsaros *or* Sir †	Mr. Justice Katsaros	Mr. Justice Katsaros
Sir: *or* Madam:	Sincerely yours,	Very truly yours,	Mr. Secretary *or* Mr. Gussin *or* Madam Secretary *or* Mrs. *or* Miss Kidd	The Secretary of the Treasury *or* Mr. Gussin *or* Mrs. Kidd	The Secretary of the Treasury *(or if the only one present)* The Secretary
Sir:	Sincerely yours,	Very truly yours,	Mr. Attorney General *or* Mr. Compton	The Attorney General *or* Mr. Compton	The Attorney General
Sir:	Sincerely yours,	Very truly yours,	Mr. Work *or* Sir	The Honorable Alfred Edward Work	Mr. Work
Sir: *or* Madam:	Sincerely yours,	Very truly yours,	Senator *or* Senator Wandzilak	Senator Wandzilak of Alaska	Senator Wandzilak
Sir:	Sincerely yours,	Very truly yours,	Mr. Speaker *or* Mr. Grevesmuhl	The Speaker of the House of Representatives *or* The Speaker, Mr. Grevesmuhl	The Speaker
Sir: *or* Madam:	Sincerely yours,	Very truly yours,	Mr. Wellcome *or* Mrs., Miss., *or* Ms. Jones	Representative Wellcome of Nebraska	Mr. Wellcome *or* Mrs., Miss., *or* Ms. Jones
Sir: *or* Madam:	Sincerely yours,	Very truly yours,	Mr. Ambassador *or* Mr. Smith *or* Madam Ambassador *or* Mrs. Fordyce *or* Sir *or* Madam	The American Ambassador *or* Our Ambassador to England, Mr. Smith	The Ambassador of the United States *(or if more than one present)* the Ambassador of the United States to *(name of country)*

† A woman does not use "Sir" in speaking to a man. Where indicated a man may use "Sir" in place of the title or name in any prolonged conversation.

PERSONAGE	BUSINESS CORRESPONDENCE	SOCIAL CORRESPONDENCE	BEGINNING OF PERSONAL LETTERS
MINISTER PLENIPOTENTIARY OF THE UNITED STATES	The Honorable James Lee Row The Minister of the United States American Legation Oslo, Norway	The Honorable and Mrs. James Lee Row (or for a woman minister) Mr. Arthur Johnson and The Honorable Susan Johnson Home Address	Dear Mr. Minister: or Dear Madam Minister:
CONSUL OF THE UNITED STATES	Mr. John Smith American Consul Rue de Quelque Chose Paris, France	Mr. and Mrs. John Smith Home Address	Dear Mr. Smith:
AMBASSADOR OF A FOREIGN COUNTRY	His Excellency Juan Luis Ortega The Ambassador of Mexico Washington, D.C. [Zip]	His Excellency The Ambassador of Mexico and Señora Ortega Home Address	Dear Mr. Ambassador:
MINISTER OF A FOREIGN COUNTRY	The Honorable Carluh Matti The Minister of Kezeah Washington, D.C. [Zip]	The Honorable and Mrs. Carluh Matti Home Address	Dear Mr. Minister:
GOVERNOR OF A STATE	The Honorable Joseph L. Marvin Governor of Idaho Office Address	The Honorable and Mrs. Joseph L. Marvin Home Address	Dear Governor Marvin:

State senators and representatives are addressed like United States senators and representatives, with appropriate addresses.

PERSONAGE	BUSINESS CORRESPONDENCE	SOCIAL CORRESPONDENCE	BEGINNING OF PERSONAL LETTERS
MAYOR	The Honorable Carson Lake City Hall	The Honorable and Mrs. Carson Lake (or for a woman mayor) Mr. and Mrs. Lawrence T. Wayne Home Address	Dear Mayor Lake:
FEDERAL JUDGE	The Honorable Robert Little Justice, Appellate Division Supreme Court of the State of New York Office Address	The Honorable and Mrs. Robert Little Home Address	Dear Judge Little:
LAWYER	John W. Fordyce, Esq. Office Address	Mr. and Mrs. John W. Fordyce Home Address	Dear Mr. Fordyce:
BISHOP, PROTESTANT EPISCOPAL	The Right Reverend John S. Bowman D.D., LL.D. Bishop of Rhode Island Office Address	The Right Reverend and Mrs. John S. Bowman Home Address	Dear Bishop Bowman:
CLERGYMAN, PROTESTANT (without degree)	The Reverend David Dekker Address of His Church	The Reverend and Mrs. David Dekker Home Address	Dear Mr. Dekker:
CLERGYMAN, PROTESTANT (with degree)	The Reverend David Dekker, D.D., (LL.D., if held) Address of His Church	The Reverend Dr. and Mrs. David Dekker Home Address	Dear Dr. Dekker:
CLERGYMAN, LUTHERAN	The Reverend Huey Brown Address of His Church	The Reverend and Mrs. Huey Brown Home Address	Dear Pastor Brown:
RABBI	Rabbi Paul Aaron Fine (or if he holds a degree) Rabbi Paul Aaron Fine, D.D. Address of His Synagogue	Rabbi (or Dr.) and Mrs. Paul Aaron Fine Home Address	Dear Rabbi (or Dr.) Fine:

BEGINNING OF BUSINESS LETTERS	CLOSE OF PERSONAL LETTERS	CLOSE OF BUSINESS LETTERS	SOCIAL INTRODUCTIONS AND IN CONVERSATION	INTRODUCING AS A SPEAKER	PLACE CARDS FOR FORMAL OCCASIONS
Sir: *or* Madam:	Sincerely yours,	Very truly yours,	Mr. Minister *or* Mr. Row *or* Mrs. Johnson	Mr. Row, the American Minister *or* Mrs. Johnson, the American Minister to Denmark	The Minister of the United States to *(name of country)*
Sir: *or* Dear Sir:	Sincerely yours,	Very truly yours,	Mr. Smith	Mr. Smith	Mr. Smith
Excellency:	Sincerely yours,	Very truly yours,	Mr. Ambassador *or* Excellency *or* Sir †	The Ambassador of Mexico	The Ambassador of Mexico
Sir:	Sincerely yours,	Very truly yours,	Mr. Minister *or* Mr. Matti	The Minister of Kezeah	The Minister of Kezeah
Sir:	Sincerely yours,	Very truly yours,	Governor Marvin	The Governor *(or if necessary)* The Governor of Idaho *or* Governor Marvin	The Governor of Idaho
Sir: *or* Madam:	Sincerely yours,	Very truly yours,	Mr. Mayor *or* Mayor Lake *or* Madam Mayor *or* Mayor Wayne	Mayor Lake *or* His *(or Her)* Honor, the Mayor	The Mayor of Easton
Sir:	Sincerely yours,	Very truly yours,	Mr. Justice *or* Judge Little	The Honorable Robert Little Judge of the Appellate Division of the Supreme Court	The Honorable Robert Little
Dear Sir:	Sincerely yours,	Very truly yours,	Mr. Fordyce	Mr. John Fordyce	Mr. Fordyce
Right Reverend Sir:	Sincerely yours,	Respectfully yours,	Bishop Bowman	Bishop Bowman	Bishop Bowman
Dear Sir:	Sincerely yours,	Very truly yours,	Mr. Dekker	Mr. Dekker *or* The Reverend David Dekker	Mr. Dekker
Dear Sir:	Sincerely yours,	Very truly yours,	Dr. Dekker	Dr. Dekker *or* The Reverend Dr. David Dekker	Dr. Dekker
Dear Sir:	Sincerely yours,	Very truly yours,	Pastor *or* Pastor Brown	Pastor Brown	Pastor Brown
Dear Sir:	Sincerely yours,	Very truly yours,	Rabbi (*or* Dr.) Fine	Rabbi (*or* Dr.) Fine	Rabbi Fine *(or if he holds a degree)* Dr. Fine

PERSONAGE	BUSINESS CORRESPONDENCE	SOCIAL CORRESPONDENCE	BEGINNING OF PERSONAL LETTERS
THE POPE	His Holiness Pope Paul VI *or* His Holiness the Pope Vatican City	Same as Business	Your Holiness: *or* Most Holy Father:
CARDINAL	His Eminence Alberto Cardinal Vezzetti Archbishop of Baltimore Office Address	Same as Business	Dear Cardinal Vezzetti:
ARCHBISHOP, ROMAN CATHOLIC	The Most Reverend Preston Lowen, D.D. Archbishop of San Francisco Office Address	Same as Business	Dear Archbishop Lowen:
BISHOP, ROMAN CATHOLIC	The Most Reverend Matthew S. Borden, D.D. Address of His Church	Same as Business	Dear Bishop Borden:
ABBOT	The Right Reverend James Kirk Address of His Church	Same as Business	Dear Father Abbot:
MONSIGNOR	The Right Reverend Monsignor Ryan Address of His Church	Same as Business	Dear Monsignor Ryan:
PRIEST	The Reverend John Matthews *(and the initials of his order)* Address of His Church	Same as Business	Dear Father Matthews:
MEMBER OF RELIGIOUS ORDER	Sister Angelica *(and the initials of her order)* *or* Brother James *(and the initials of his order)* Address	Same as Business	Dear Sister Angelica: *or* Dear Brother James:
UNIVERSITY PROFESSOR	Professor Robert Knowles *or* Mr. Robert Knowles *(or if he holds a degree)* Dr. Robert Knowles Office Address	Professor *(or Mr. or Dr.)* and Mrs. Robert Knowles Home Address	Dear Professor *(or Mr. or Dr.)* Knowles:
PHYSICIAN	William L. Barnes, M.D. Office Address	Dr. and Mrs. William L. Barnes Home Address	Dear Dr. Barnes:
DENTIST	John Sanford, D.D.S. Office Address	Dr. and Mrs. John Sanford Home Address	Dear Dr. Sanford:

BEGINNING OF BUSINESS LETTERS	CLOSE OF PERSONAL LETTERS	CLOSE OF BUSINESS LETTERS	SOCIAL INTRODUCATIONS AND IN CONVERSATION	INTRODUCING AS A SPEAKER	PLACE CARDS FOR FORMAL OCCASIONS
Your Holiness:	Your most humble servant,	Your Holiness' most humble servant,	Your Holiness *or* Most Holy Father	His Holiness, The Pope	His Holiness, The Pope
Your Eminence:	Your humble servant,	I have the honor to remain, Your Eminence's humble servant,	Your Eminence *or* Cardinal Vezzetti	His Eminence, Cardinal Vezzetti	His Eminence, Cardinal Vezzetti
Your Excellency: *or* Most Reverend Sir:	Your obedient servant,	I have the honor to remain, Your obedient servant,	Your Excellency *or* Archbishop Lowen	The Archbishop of San Francisco	The Archbishop of San Francisco *or* Archbishop Lowen
Most Reverend Sir:	Respectfully yours, *or* Faithfully yours,	I have the honor to remain, Your obedient servant,	Bishop Borden	Bishop Borden	Bishop Borden
Right Reverend Abbot:	Respectfully yours, *or* Faithfully yours,	I have the honor to remain, Your obedient servant,	Abbot Kirk	Abbot Kirk *or* The Right Reverend James Kirk	Father Kirk *or* Abbot Kirk
Right Reverend Monsignor:	Respectfully yours, *or* Faithfully yours,	I remain, Right Reverend Monsignor, Yours faithfully,	Monsignor *or* Monsignor Ryan	Monsignor Ryan	The Right Reverend Monsignor Ryan *or* Monsignor Ryan
Reverend Father:	Faithfully yours,	I remain, Reverend Father, Yours faithfully,	Father Matthews *or* Father	Father Matthews	Father Matthews
Dear Sister: *or* Dear Brother:	Faithfully yours,	Respectfully yours,	Sister Angelica *or* Sister *or* Brother James *or* Brother	Sister Angelica *or* Brother James	Sister Angelica *or* Brother James
Dear Sir:	Sincerely yours, *or* Sincerely,	Very truly yours,	Professor (*or* Dr.) Knowles (*within the university*) Mr. Knowles (*elsewhere, unless always known as* Dr.)	Professor (*or* Dr.) Knowles	Dr. Knowles *or* Professor Knowles
Dear Sir:	Sincerely yours, *or* Sincerely,	Very truly yours,	Dr. Barnes	Dr. Barnes	Dr. Barnes
Dear Sir:	Sincerely yours, *or* Sincerely,	Very truly yours,	Dr. Sanford	Dr. Sanford	Dr. Sanford

WITH OTHER NATIONS

We refer to our country briefly and casually as "America," but when we address anyone elsewhere in the Western Hemisphere we should remember that we have no monopoly on the name. Thus, although it is customary in both Europe and Asia to speak of or write to the American Embassy or the American Legation, it should not be done in Latin America or Canada. The address on a letter to one of our government representatives there always specifies "the United States of America."

Representatives of other countries who are living in the United States present no particular problems, since the ways of addressing them are firmly fixed by governmental protocol. But whether their wives are addressed as "Mrs. Shultz," "Madame Deauville," "Doña Maria," or some other title depends upon the usage of their particular nations. Women of Spanish descent retain their maiden names after marriage and add "of" and their husband's names. Helena Padilla who marries Jorge Ortega becomes Helena Padilla de Ortega, and is often referred to by old friends as Helena Padilla. In many instances a wife is addressed as she would be in her own country (that is, the wife of the Mexican Ambassador is addressed on envelopes as Señora Doña, and a line below, Helena de Ortega), but sometimes, especially when hers is a difficult or little-known language, she uses "Mrs." or "Madame."

In this age of international travel we may well find ourselves in need of information about the important personages of countries other than our own. Customs vary, of course, and no general rules can be made for the more than one hundred nations in the world. However, should you find yourself about to leave for Ghana or Japan or Finland there are many sources of help. Try the consulate nearest you or the embassy in Washington or the mission to the United Nations in New York. Information officers from all over the world are ready to help you and eager to facilitate your communication with their homelands.

FORMAL INTRODUCTIONS

When introducing any of the people listed in the chart formally—at a banquet as a speaker, or to another person of note—his full title is always mentioned. "Ladies and Gentlemen, the Honorable Gary Gussin, Secretary of the Treasury," or "I am honored to present the Most Reverend Preston Lowen, Archbishop of San Francisco."

In personal introductions the person of lesser rank is introduced to the more important person, insofar as possible. Since in this case the introducer is speaking directly to the people being introduced, he uses the forms listed under "In Conversation." "Mr. Ambassador, may I present Professor Carson?" "Mr. Chief Justice, I would like you to meet Senator Lake of Ohio."

Note that the President's and Vice-President's names are never used except when the speaker is not in their presence. They are introduced, "Ladies and Gentlemen, the President [Vice-President] of the United States," and spoken to personally as "Mr. President" or "Mr. Vice-President." In a prolonged conversation it is always correct to use "Sir" in place of the longer forms.

Governors are always addressed with title *and* name although they may be *referred* to as "The Governor."

MILITARY TITLES

Commissioned Army officers of all grades are addressed by their title (rank). The officer's name is generally added although it is not wrong to say simply "Captain" or "Lieutenant" when there is no chance of confusion. Noncommissioned officers are addressed officially by their titles although they may use "Mr." socially.

The Air Force follows the same customs as the Army.

Chaplains in all the services are called "Chaplain," regardless of their rank. Catholic chaplains are usually spoken *to* as "Father."

Doctors in the service are generally called by their rank although they may be called "Dr." socially when they are junior officers. Officially, they are addressed by their Army or Navy titles for as long as they remain in the service.

Warrant officers are called "Mr.," both officially and socially.

Naval officers from the rank of lieutenant commander (called "Commander" in conversation) up, are called by their titles. Officers below that rank are called "Mr." in conversation but are introduced and referred to by their titles.

Students at the United States Military Academy at West Point are "Mr." socially, but "Cadet" officially. Those at the Naval Academy in Annapolis are "Mr." socially and "Midshipman" officially.

In speaking to a first or second lieutenant in the Army, or a lieutenant junior grade in the Navy, you say simply "Lieutenant." His rank is made clear by his insignia, but it would be awkward to use the full title in conversation. In the same way, the various grades of colonels, generals, and admirals are spoken to simply as "Colonel," "General," or "Admiral," with their names.

Members of the regular armed services retain their titles after retiring. However, it is not in good taste for reserve officers who served for only a short time, or those who held temporary commissions during a war to continue calling themselves "Captain," "Major," or "Colonel." They do, of course, use the titles if they resume an active status in a reserve unit or in the National Guard. When this happens the initials of their service always follow their name. When the rank is used they write "Colonel Harold Gordon, U.S.A.R." (or N.G. or U.S.N.R. or U.S.M.C.R.).

Reserve officers who remain in the service and retire with pay after twenty or more years are, like a member of the regular service, entitled to use their military titles.

In contrast to the abbreviations of "Mr." and "Mrs.," which are *never* written in full, it is both correct and courteous to write out all military and naval titles when addressing a formal social note. However, informal communications may be sent to "2nd Lieut. John Smith," "Lieut. Johnson," "Lt. Cdr. Harris," or "Lt. Col. Graham," because the full titles are so long. Other ranks are more properly written in full.

When introducing or addressing a letter to someone who has both a military and an inherited title, military rank is put first: "Colonel, Lord London."

OTHER PEOPLE WITH TITLES

Every day we run into people who, officially, have a title. The police officer at the desk is Sergeant Biggs; the head of your fire department is Chief Ellsworth; the pilot on your plane is Captain Howe; etc. These people are always addressed by their title when they are on their job or when the matter is related to their work. Generally they do not use the title socially, although a man who has been a pilot for many years might well be so universally known as "Captain" that the title sticks, and he is referred to in that way at all times.

❧8❧ The Contents of Business Letters

Letters from business offices depend so thoroughly on the nature of the concern that little need be said except that they be clear, concise, and to the point. If you know exactly what you want to say and give considerable thought to the initial statement of your most important point you cannot go far astray. And when you have said what you intended to say, stop. A meandering last paragraph can destroy the entire effect of the letter.

"Personal" business letters written by a customer or client should also be as brief and explicit as possible. For example:

May 17, 1975

H. J. Paint Co.
22 Branch Street
New York, New York 10010

Dear Mr. Henry:
    Your estimate of $300.00 for painting my dining room and living room is satisfactory, and I hope you will start as soon as possible.

Very truly yours,
Ida Town
(Mrs. James Town)

AN ORDER TO A DEPARTMENT STORE

Whenever possible it is best to use the form found in the store catalog to place your order. If, however, you do not have the form, or are ordering from another source, your letter should include:

1. Name or description of article.
2. Quantity, size, color.
3. Price.
4. How paid for (C.O.D., check enclosed, or charge account).
5. How to be sent.
6. Address and date.

March 3, 1975
604 Lowell Drive
Dedham, Massachusetts 02026

Brown, Green, and Company
15 Beacon Street
Boston, Massachusetts

Dear Sirs:
    Please send by United Parcel the following merchandise:
    1 upholstered chair, No. 4337 in your January, 1975, catalog, in green, or second choice, yellow. $76.95
    1 wool bathrobe, catalog No. 264, size 12, in blue, or 2nd choice, white. $27.50
    My check for $104.45 is enclosed [Or, Please charge to my account.]

Sincerely,
Susan Smythe
(Mrs. Grant Smythe)

If you do not want to make a second choice, say so, rather than accept an item you really don't want.

Always make, and put away carefully, a copy of your orders. If your letter is lost, or the wrong merchandise sent, this is the only way you can possibly know (and prove) exactly what you have requested. If you have the facilities available for making a photocopy, that is the best way, but even a handwritten copy will serve the purpose.

TO REQUEST INFORMATION

Mrs. John Newhouse
Meade Place
Richmond, Virginia 23200

April 2, 1975

Manager
Loon Lake Lodge
Shiretown, Maine 12267

Dear Sir:
    Would you be kind enough to send me your information folder and your schedule of rates for Loon Lake Lodge? Your hotel was recommended to me by Mrs. Arthur Simpson.
    Would you also let me know what accommodations you have open for the month of August? We would require two double rooms with baths for my two daughters, my husband, and myself.

Very truly yours [or, *Sincerely*],
Mary Newhouse
(Mrs. John Newhouse)

TO MAKE A RESERVATION

The relationship of persons requesting rooms should be made clear.

MRS. WILLIAM FROST
6 LAKEWOOD AVENUE
JAMESTOWN, VIRGINIA 23081

June 3, 1975

Holiday Hotel
Framingham, Massachusetts 01710

Dear Sirs:
    Will you please reserve a double room and bath for my husband and me for the first weekend of August. We will arrive Friday evening the first, before six, and will leave Sunday afternoon the third.
    If a room is not available for that weekend please let me know at once so that we may make other plans. Otherwise, please confirm the reservation.

Sincerely,
Jane Frost

A LETTER FOR A MEMBERSHIP CANDIDATE

A letter of recommendation for membership in a club is addressed to the secretary and should follow this general form:

To the Secretary of the Town Club.

Dear Mrs. Brown,
Mrs. Walter Smith, who has been proposed for membership, is a very old friend of mind.
She is a charming and intelligent person. She has had a great deal of experience with fund-raising, and her knowledge should be of great value to our activities. I feel that she will be a tremendous addition to the club, and when you meet her I am sure that you will agree.

Very sincerely,
Ina Jackson

For other letters pertaining to clubs, see Chapter 60.

LETTERS OF RESIGNATION

A letter of resignation should be concise, but always polite. It should touch briefly on the reason for the resignation, but whatever that may be, it should never in any way give any indication of rancor or ill-feeling on the part of either the firm or the individual. Since resignations are almost always discussed in person and rarely come as a surprise, there is no need to do more than write a letter that will serve as a permanent record.

Mr. Henry Farthing
Associated Household Wares
14 Kent Place
Cincinnati, Ohio 45216

Dear Mr. Farthing,
It is with regret that I find I must resign from the firm. My health has been very poor in recent weeks, and my doctor has told me that I must retire from business if I wish to recover completely.
Our long association has been a very happy one for me, and I leave you all with sincere gratitude and best wishes for the continued success of the firm.

Sincerely,
Foster Hayes

In the case of an unpleasant parting, the letter should not reveal any signs of vituperation and should attempt to alleviate bitterness.

Dear Mr. Farthing,

I regret that I feel I must resign from the firm. An opportunity has been offered me by another company that will allow me more time with my family, and I feel that I should accept it.

I am sure a younger man will be better able to fill my position with your company. I leave Associated with the highest regard for you and other members of the firm.

Sincerely,
Robert Pugh

For letters of resignation from a club, see Chapter 60.

REFERENCE FOR DOMESTIC EMPLOYEES

The written recommendation that is given to a departing employee carries very little weight compared to the slip used by some employment agencies on which either "Yes" or "No" has to be answered to a list of specific and important questions. Nevertheless, one is put in a difficult position when reporting on an unsatisfactory servant.

Either a poor reference must be given—possibly preventing the employee from earning his or her living—or you must write what is not true. Consequently it is best to list truthfully any good qualifications and to omit the qualifications that are lacking except when the employee was disrespectful, neglectful, or dishonest.

This evasion helps solve the poor-recommendation problem, but as a result the good servant suffers unless one is very careful. In writing for a satisfactory employee, therefore, it is most important to put in every good point that you can think of, remembering that omission implies a failing in those characteristics not mentioned. All good references should include honesty, sobriety, capability, and a reason, other than unsatisfactoriness, for the employee's departure.

It is not necessary to begin a recommendation with "To whom it may concern" or "This is to certify." The form can be very simple. For example:

TWO HUNDRED MAPLE STREET

Selma Johnson has been in my employ as cook for two and a half years.

I really don't know how we will get along without her. She is a wonderful person—honest, sober, industrious, neat in her person as well as her work, has an excellent disposition, and is a very good cook.

She is leaving us—to my great regret—because I am moving away.

I shall be very glad to answer personally any inquiries about her.

Josephine Smith
(Mrs. Walter Smith)

February 17, 1975

LETTERS OF COMPLAINT

When it is necessary to write a letter of complaint you will generally get more satisfaction with a reasonable approach than with exaggerated accusations and anger. In any case, the person who receives your letter will not be the one who made the error, and he will be more disposed to make an adjustment if your letter does not irritate him and insult his company.

Merchandise does arrive broken, orders are confused, or goods are not of the quality advertised, and there are many other legitimate reasons for complaint. Intelligent letters from customers pointing out these errors keep a company on its toes, and for the firm's own good, should be given prompt attention.

Here is a sample of a sensible letter of complaint, containing all the necessary information.

September 15, 1975

Dear Sirs,

On July 21 of this year I bought a Roller Tricycle for my son, from your Jefferson Branch. The first time he rode it the right pedal came off. I took it to a local bicycle store, and they said they could not get the necessary part, so I took it back to the store where I bought it. They said to leave the tricycle, as they had to order a new bar for the pedal, and we did so. The tricycle is still there. I have called repeatedly and been told the part has not come in. In view of the fact that this was a brand-new tricycle that broke the first time it was used, I feel that we should be given a replacement, or the pedal should be replaced in some other way. My son will have outgrown the machine before it is fixed at this rate.

Thanking you for your immediate attention to this matter, I am

Sincerely,
William Dodge

Naturally, if a letter such as this does not get results it is sometimes necessary to write again in more forceful tones. Always keep
a copy of this type of letter in case the follow-up is necessary.

LETTERS OF COMMENDATION

It is sad but true that people in general are quick to complain
and slow to commend. Letters of complaint flow freely by the thousands; letters of praise trickle in by twos and threes. And yet, such
letters would undoubtedly do more to improve service in many areas
than those that tend to irritate or put a company (or individual) on
the defensive.

I can only urge you, when you are the happy recipient of extra
attention or fine service, to call it to the attention of the individual's
superiors, where it can do the most good. The employee will profit,
and so will the company whose reputation may depend on promot-
ing service.

When you are prompted to write a letter of commendation, first
do your best to get the name of the person or persons who rendered
the service and the name or title of the person to whom you should
write. Then describe the act or attitude that pleased you, and the
date on which it occurred. A letter containing these specifics is of
far more value than a more "general" commendation. However,
when you have not gotten or cannot remember all the details, the
less specific letter will still be appreciated, and is far better than
none.

The following letter is an example of a good letter of commendation:

BRANDT TOOLS, INC.
4500 MAIN STREET
MILWAUKEE, WISCONSIN 53200

Mr. S. N. Jones, Manager
Flight Service
American Air Lines
Love Field
Dallas, Texas 75235

Dear Mr. Jones:
The normal conduct of my business takes me over a good part
of the world via air travel, and from time to time there is an oppor-
tunity to write a complimentary letter about services that have been
rendered.

CORRESPONDENCE 🐦

Such a happy circumstance presented itself on January 26 on Flight 425 from Dallas to Phoenix, Arizona. The plane was full, and the three girls in the tourist section really did a job for you. They were not only efficient, but pleasant and cheerful to the point that it was really a pleasure to be on the flight.

The particular stewardesses involved were Sally Keene, based in Dallas, Juanita Velez of Dallas, and Gay Brooks, based in Chicago. Will you please see that my thanks are transmitted in some manner to these three girls.

Yours sincerely,
Henry Dorfuss

H. Dorfuss
President

⇜9⇝ *Personal Letters*

If you have a mind that is entirely bromidic, if you are lacking in humor, all power of observation, and facility for expression, you had best join the ever-growing class of people who frankly confess, "I can't write letters to save my life!" and confine your literary efforts to picture post-cards with the engaging captions "X is my room," or "Beautiful weather, wish you were here."—Emily Post, 1922

Letter-writing *is* becoming a lost art—in fact the practice of writing personal letters is diminishing to such an extent today that they threaten to become extinct. Since daily events are communicated by newspapers, radio, and television with great accuracy and dispatch, the circulation of general news—which formed the chief reason for letters in the stagecoach and sailing-vessel days—has no part in the hurried correspondence of the twentieth century. Yet people *do* write letters, and there are still some who possess a gift for the fresh turn of phrase that we see in old letters. It may be, though, that in the past the average writing was no better than the average of today, for naturally, the unusually gifted letters are the ones that have been preserved for us over the years.

THE LETTER EVERYONE LOVES TO RECEIVE

A perfect letter has always the effect of being a light dipping off of the top of a spring. A poor letter suggests digging into the dried ink at the bottom of an ink-well.—Emily Post, 1922

The letter we all love to receive is the one that carries so much of the writer's personality that he or she seems to be sitting beside us and chatting with us. To achieve this happy feeling of *talking* through a letter, one must employ certain devices in order to detract from the stilted quality of the written word. Here are a few specific suggestions that may help to make your letters reflect your personality.

It is absolutely correct to type a personal letter, as long as the writer is a proficient enough typist so that the number of errors does not distract the reader. It does however, destroy some of the personal touch.

Punctuation can add interest and variety to your letters, much as the change in tone of a speaker's voice adds zest and color to his story. Underlining a word or using an exclamation point after a phrase or sentence gives emphasis where you want it. A dash is effective instead of a longer, possibly more grammatical, phrase. "We went to a dance last night—what a party!" is more colorful than "We went to a dance last night, and it was a great party." Don't, however, overdo the exclamation points and dashes. A few add zest—too many become boring.

In a personal letter phrases typical of your speech should be used and not artificially replaced by more formal language. A young person who commonly uses the expression "a real doll" would sound most unnatural and self-conscious when writing, "She is a lovely girl."

Occasionally inserting the name of the person to whom you are writing gives your letter an added touch of familiarity and affection. "And, Helen, guess what we are going to do this summer!" makes Helen feel as though it will be of special interest to *her*.

The use of contractions is another means of making your writing natural. Since you would probably never say "I do not know" for "I don't know," or "I am so glad" for "I'm so glad," why write it that way?

Don't stop too long to think of *how* to say it. Decide what you want to say and then write it as quickly as possible; that way, it will seem as if you are truly talking to your friend.

And finally, brevity is infinitely more interesting than lengthy rambling. As Pascal wrote, "This letter wouldn't have been so long, but I haven't the time to make it shorter."

TO AND FROM FAMILY MEMBERS

Formerly, the "lady of the house," who had far more leisure than her hardworking husband, took care of all the social correspondence. This is still true in families where the man works and his wife is at home. This includes letters to the husband's parents, which should contain all the family news and specific messages from him. It is a good idea for a wife to leave space at the end of the letter for her husband to add a brief personal note to assure his family that he is interested and wants to keep in touch.

When a woman is working and has no more time at home for personal correspondence than does her husband, they should divide the letter-writing chores in whatever way seems most satisfactory, and should each try to include the other in the texts.

Parents of married children may either address their letters to the one who has been corresponding with them or write their letters to "Mr. and Mrs. Henry Fuller, Jr." If the father is writing to the son about a business matter, or the mother to her daughter-in-law about a pattern for a dress, naturally those letters are addressed to the one concerned.

When people other than husbands and wives are living together—a brother and sister, or an unmarried couple, for example—letters to both are addressed to "Miss Jane Moore and Mr. Samuel Moore," or "Miss Francis Poole and Mr. Robert Smithers," and the salutation is to both.

LETTERS THAT SHOULDN'T BE WRITTEN

LETTERS OF GLOOMY APPREHENSION

No useful purpose is ever served by writing *needlessly* of misfortune or unhappiness—even to members of one's family. Our distress at hearing about illness or unhappiness among those we love is intensified by the number of miles that separate us from them. For instance:

"My little Betty ["my little" seems so much more pathetic than merely "Betty"] has been feeling miserable for several days. I'm worried to death about her, for there are so many cases of mononucleosis around. The doctor says the symptoms are not alarming, but doctors see so much of illness that they don't seem to appreciate what anxiety means to a mother," etc., etc.

Or: "The times seem to be getting worse and worse. I always said we would have to go through a long night before any chance of daylight. You can mark my words, the night is hardly more than begun."

Neither of these letters serves any useful purpose, and can only worry or irritate the recipients, or depress them.

THE DANGEROUS LETTER

> *Letters between young girls and young men flourish to-day like unpulled weeds in a garden where weeds were formerly never allowed to grow.*—Emily Post, 1922

CORRESPONDENCE ॐ

Every day the mails carry letters whose fallout would be spectacular if they fell into the wrong hands. Letters that should never have been written are continually introduced as evidence in courtrooms, and many of them cannot, in any way, be excused. Silly women and foolish men often write things that sound to a jury, for example, quite different from what was innocently intended.

The safest rule is: Never write a letter to *anyone* that would embarrass you, were you to see it in a newspaper above your signature. Thousands upon thousands of people, inspired by every known emotion, have poured words on paper, and few of these made public have been a credit to the writer.

However, people *will* continue to declare their feelings in writing to absent loved ones, so if you are a young person—or even not-so-young—and are determined to write a love letter to someone of the opposite sex, then at least put it away overnight in order to reread it and make sure that you have said nothing that may sound different from what you intended to say.

Remember: Written words have permanency, and thoughts carelessly put on paper can exist for hundreds of years.

A FEW MORE WARNINGS

The light, jesting tone that saves a quip from offense cannot be expressed in writing, and spoken remarks that would amuse can become sharp and insulting when written.

Anger in a letter carries with it the effect of solidified fury. Bitter spoken words fade away once the cause is forgiven; written words are fixed on the page forever. Admonitions from parents to their children may very properly be put on paper—they are meant to endure and be remembered—but momentary annoyance should never be more than briefly expressed. A parent who gets into the habit of writing in an irritable or faultfinding tone to his children soon finds that his letters are seldom read.

One point cannot be overstressed: Letters written under strong emotion should be held for twenty-four hours and reread before being sent—or probably torn into small pieces and not sent at all.

THE DIFFICULTY IN BEGINNING

Most people who wonder how they will ever fill a blank sheet of paper find that the difficult part of a letter is the beginning. The instruction of a professor of English—"Begin at the beginning of what you have to say, go on until you have finished, and then stop"

—is just about as much help as was the instruction of the artist who proclaimed, "You simply take a little of the right color paint and put it on the right spot." Perhaps the following suggestions will be more helpful.

Even someone who loves the very sight of your handwriting could hardly be expected to enjoy a letter beginning, "I know I ought to have written sooner, but I haven't had anything to write about." Or one saying, "I suppose you think I've been very neglectful, but you know how I hate to write letters." Yet such sentences are written time and again by people who are utterly unaware that they are really expressing an unfriendly thought.

Suppose you merely change the wording of the above sentences, so that instead of slamming the door in your friend's face, you hold it open. "Do you think I have forgotten you entirely? You don't know, Ann, how many letters I planned to write you." Or "Time and time again I've wanted to write you, but every time I sat down to start I was interrupted by—*something.*"

It is unfortunate when the answer to a letter has been so long delayed that it must begin with an apology—at best an unhappy beginning. The examples above, however, show that even an opening apology may be attractive rather than repellent. After all, if you take the trouble to write a letter you have remembered someone in a friendly way; otherwise you would not be writing at all.

It is easy enough to begin a letter in answer to one that has just been received. You have fresh news to comment on, and the impulse to reply needs no prodding. Nothing can be simpler than to say, "We were all so pleased to get your letter on Tuesday," or "Your letter was the most welcome thing the postman has brought for ages." Then you take up the various subjects in Ann's letter, which should certainly launch you upon topics of your own.

Remember to answer all of her specific questions. It is not only unflattering to be given the impression that you read them hurriedly, but often very upsetting if long-awaited information is not forthcoming.

ON ENDING A LETTER

Just as the beginning of a letter should give the reader an impression of greeting, so should its ending express friendly or affectionate leave-taking. Nothing can be worse than to flounder for an idea that will effect your escape. "Well, I guess you've read enough of this," and "You're probably bored by now, so I'd better close" are obvious phrases of desperation. "The mountains were beautiful at sunset" is also a bad closing sentence because it means nothing personal to either of you. But if you add, "They reminded me of when we were all in Colorado together," you have established a connection, and you can go on to finish, "How I wish we were together again now."

When you leave a good friend's house you don't have to invent a special sentence in order to say good-bye. Leave-taking in a letter is the same. In personal letters to friends or family it is not necessary to use the standard forms of closing. One of the following is fine.

> *Will write again in a day or two.*
> > > *Martin*
> *Only have twenty minutes to get to work! So good-bye for now.*
> > > *Nancy*
> *Counting the hours till next weekend!*
> > > *Betsy*

NOTES OF APOLOGY

A note of apology should offer a valid excuse for breaking an engagement. Although you may have telephoned or sent a telegram a written explanation should follow.

> *BROADLAWNS*

> > > *Tuesday*

Dear Helen,

> *I do apologize for having to send you the telegram about Monday night.*

> *When I accepted your invitation I stupidly forgot entirely that Monday was a holiday and that our own guests were not leaving until Tuesday morning; Arthur and I could not very well go off and leave them!*

> *We were disappointed and hope that you know how sorry we were not to be with you.*

> > > *Affectionately,*
> > > *Ethel*

Occasionally an unfortunate accident occurs, which, although it may have been entirely beyond our control, requires that we send another type of note of apology.

Dear Mrs. Johnson,
Your little boy has just told me that our dog got into your flower beds and did a great deal of damage.
My husband will build the fence around his pen higher tonight, and he will not be able to escape again. I shall send you some plants to replace those that were ruined, although I'm afraid that new ones cannot compensate for those you lost. I can only ask you to accept my apologies.

Sincerely yours,
Katherine Pennybacker

THANK-YOU LETTERS

The most important qualifications of a thank-you letter are that it sound sincere and that it be written promptly. You use the expressions most natural to you and write as enthusiastically as though you were talking.

The following chart tells you when thank-you notes are obligatory, optional, or unnecessary.

Occasion	Obligatory	Optional or Unnecessary
Dinner parties	Only if you are a guest of honor.	Otherwise, always appreciated but not necessary if you have thanked your hostess when leaving.
Overnight visits	Always, except in the case of close friends or relatives whom you see frequently. Then, a telephone call would serve the purpose.	
For birthday, anniversary, Christmas, and other gifts	Always, when you have not thanked the donor in person. Here again, a phone call to a very close friend or relative is sufficient.	*It is never wrong* to send a note in addition to your verbal thanks.
Shower gifts	If the donor was not at the shower or you did not extend verbal thanks.	Many girls like to add a written note to their verbal thanks, but it is not necessary.
Gifts to a sick person	Notes to out-of-towners and calls or notes to close friends are obligatory as soon as the patient feels well enough.	

Occasion	*Obligatory*	*Optional or Unnecessary*
For notes of condolence	Thank-yous should be sent for all notes of condolence except for printed cards with no personal message.	
For congratulatory cards or gifts	All personal messages must be acknowledged.	Form letters from firms need not be acknowledged.
Wedding gifts	*Obligatory*—even though verbal thanks have been given. All wedding gifts must be acknowledged within three months, but preferably as the gifts arrive.	
When a hostess receives a gift after visitors have left	Even though the gift is a thank-you itself, the hostess must thank her visitors, especially if the gift has arrived by mail, so that the visitor will know it has been received.	
When a client is entertained by a salesman		Even though the entertainment is charged to the salesman's company it would not be remiss to send a note. It is not necessary, but might help to ensure a good relationship.

SAMPLE THANK-YOUS

LETTERS OF THANKS FOR WEDDING PRESENTS

Insofar as possible, thank-you notes for wedding presents should be written as soon as the gift is received. This is not always possible, but if they are not sent before the wedding, they must be written as soon as the bride returns from her honeymoon. Even for a very large wedding, when the gifts are innumerable, all thank-you notes should be mailed within three months.

The notes sent before the wedding are properly written on plain white notepaper, or paper engraved with the bride's maiden initials. Those mailed after the marriage may be written on full-size paper or notepaper, plain or marked with her married initials.

Wedding presents are sent to the bride, and she writes all the thank-you notes. But she should word her letters to include the bridegroom, especially if the gifts have been sent by friends of his. Some girls prefer to sign the notes with both their names. This is not incorrect, but the first way is more proper. She might write something like this:

Saturday

Dear Mrs. Beck,

How did you ever find those wonderful glasses? They are perfect, and Jim and I want to thank you a thousand times!

The presents will be shown on the day of the wedding, but do come over Tuesday morning if you can for a cup of coffee and an earlier view.

Thanking you again, and with love from us both,

Joan

More formally, the bride-to-be might write:

Dear Mrs. King,

It was so thoughtful of you and Mr. King to send us such a lovely clock. I have never been noted for my punctuality, and your gift will surely help me to improve. Thank you very, very much.

Looking forward to seeing you on the tenth,

Very sincerely,
Joan McCord

The salutation is usually addressed to Mrs. King only, but thanks to her husband is often expressed in the text. Otherwise, however, "you" is understood to mean "you both."

For a present received after the wedding the bride might write:

Dear Mrs. Chatterton,

The mirror you sent us is going over our living-room mantel just as soon as we can hang it up! It is exactly what we most needed, and we both thank you ever so much.

Please come in soon to see how beautiful it looks in the room.

Affectionately,
Mary Franklin

THANKS FOR GIFTS OF MONEY

When a gift is a sum of money the recipient should indicate how it will be used: "I'm so thrilled that with your $60.00 I'll be able to get the rotobroiler I've been longing for." "Your check for $50.00 is going into our 'sofa fund,' and we can't tell you how pleased we were to receive it."

If you have no such specific use to mention, you can simply say that it will be such a help in furnishing your apartment, building up your savings, or whatever. You should mention the amount just as you would mention the specific item in a thank-you note for a chair or an ashtray.

THANKS FOR CHRISTMAS AND OTHER PRESENTS

Thank-you notes for Christmas—and all other—presents should be written within two or three days of the time the gift is received. In the case of Christmas gifts they should be sent before New Year's Day, and certainly before young people return to school or college.

Dearest Aunt Lucy,

We just love our armchair! Jack says I'll never get a chance to sit in it if he gets there first. We both thank you so much and are looking forward to seeing you at Easter.

With much love,
Sally

Dear Kate,

I am just delighted with my jewel box—it is so unusual. You are really clever at finding what no one else can, and what everyone wants. I don't know how you do it!
Again, thanks so much.

With love,
Edie

THANKS FOR A BABY PRESENT

Dear Mrs. Foster,

No one else in the world can knit like you! The sweater you made for the baby is perfectly adorable on her. Thank you so much, from both of us.

Affectionately,
Robin

Dear Mrs. Cooper,

Thank you ever so much for the blanket you sent the baby. It is by far the prettiest one he has, and so soft and warm that I wish I had one just like it!

Do come in and see him, won't you? We love visitors—just let us know when you can come.

Affectionately,
Helen

BREAD-AND-BUTTER LETTERS

When you have stayed overnight, or longer, at someone's house, it is absolutely necessary that you write a letter of thanks to your hostess within a few days after the visit. Unless, of course, your host and hostess are your closest friends with whom you are on "family" terms, or relatives with whom you frequently visit back and forth. Even in those cases a note is in order if you will not see your hosts for some time. If you are all returning to the same town, perhaps after a weekend at their summer home, you should call them on the phone a day or so later, or before seeing them again, to repeat what a good time you had.

Don't be afraid that your thank-you note is too informal. If your hosts are older people they are always pleased with friendly and spontaneous expressions from the young. Never think, because you cannot write a letter easily, that it is better not to write at all. The most awkward note imaginable is better than none. To write none is the height of rudeness, whereas the awkward note at least fulfills the duty.

AFTER A HOUSE-PARTY WEEKEND

Dear Franny,

You and Jim are such wonderful hosts! Once again I can only tell you that there is no other house where I have such a good time and hate to leave so much.

Your party over this last weekend was the best yet, and thank you very, very much for including me.

> *With much love to you all,*
> *Betty*

Dear Mrs. Farthingham,

Last weekend was the high spot of the summer. Everything you planned was wonderful, but the best of all was the trip to the country fair on Sunday. I wish I could have brought every one of those vegetables home with me!

I truly enjoyed every minute with your family, and I thank you more than I can say for inviting me.

> *Very sincerely,*
> *Elliot*

TO A STRANGER WHO HAS ENTERTAINED YOU

When someone has shown you special hospitality in a city you visited:

Dear Mrs. Duluth,

It was so good of you to give my husband and me so much of your time. We enjoyed and appreciated all your kindness to us more than we can say.

We hope that you and Mr. Duluth may be coming East before long and that we may have the pleasure of seeing you then at Cottswold.

In the meanwhile, thank you for your generous hospitality, and my husband joins me in sending kindest regards to you both.

> *Very sincerely yours,*
> *Katherine Starkweather*

FROM A BRIDE TO HER NEW RELATIVES-IN-LAW

The following letter, written by a bride after paying a first visit to her husband's aunt and uncle, won her the approval of the whole family:

Dear Aunt Anne,

Now that we are home again I have a confession to make! Do you know that when Dick drove me up to your front door and I saw you and Uncle Bob standing on the top step—I was simply paralyzed with fright!

"Suppose they don't like me," was all that I could think. Of course, I know you love Dick, but that only made it worse! The reason I stumbled coming up the steps was that my knees were actually knocking together! And then you were both so sweet to me and made me feel as though I had always been your niece—and not just the wife of your nephew.

I loved every minute of our being with you, just as much as Dick did, and we hope you are going to let us come again soon.

With best love from us both,

> *Your niece,*
> *Nancy*

FOR THOSE WHO RECEIVE NO THANK-YOUS

I receive innumerable letters every week asking what should be done when no acknowledgment for a gift sent weeks or months before has been received. This is no time to stand on ceremony. After three months, at the outside, you must write and ask whether or not the gift was received. If the bride (or any other recipient) is embarrassed, that is fine—she should be, and perhaps will be more appreciative in the future. If her letter was lost she will tell you that she has written, and your mind will be at rest.

It is *inexcusable* not to thank the donor for *any* gift, and people have been driven to desperate measures to ensure some acknowledgment. One suggestion is to send all gifts insured. You then have a good reason to write and say, "Since I haven't heard from you I assume the gift I sent was lost. If this is so I would like to put in a claim for the insurance, so would you let me know as soon as possible whether you received it or not." One lady has become so annoyed with this frequent carelessness that when she sends a gift from a department store and has received no "thanks" in a reasonable length of time, she sends a postcard to the bride with two lines on the back:

I did receive the package from Altman's.
I did not receive the package from Altman's.

She claims she always gets results immediately, and I believe it. However, such measures may seem a bit strong—even rude, to some—and I would not suggest using them unless you *know* that your gift was received and that others, as well as you, have received no acknowledgments of their gifts. In that case, it is obviously not an error, and the bride deserves no consideration.

When the gift in question is a check, you might write, "I am quite concerned about the check I sent you for your birthday. It has been cashed and returned to me, but since I have received no word from you I am worried that it fell into the wrong hands and it was not you who cashed it. Would you let me know?"

PRINTED THANK-YOU CARDS

Cards with "thank you" printed on them, plain or with a floral design or pattern, have gained great popularity. When they are not too ornate or "cute" they are perfectly acceptable *as long as a personal message is written on them by hand*. It need only be a line or two, but it must express your own feelings—not those of the stationer —and it must mention the gift or the occasion. The following suggestions turn an impersonal thank-you card into a warm, personal note:

"How did you know that blue is my favorite color—the scarf you sent goes perfectly with my coat!"

"The fabulous book on mountain-climbing—with all those unbelievably beautiful pictures—has a place of honor on my desk. Affectionately . . ."

"The weekend was superb. I only hope we can give you half as good a time when you visit us next summer."

AN ENGRAVED CARD OF THANKS

An engraved card of thanks is proper only when sent by a public official to acknowledge the overwhelming number of congratulatory messages inevitably received from strangers when he has won an election or been otherwise honored by his state or country.

Executive Mansion is the established name of the house in which a governor lives; but if he prefers, all official letters may be sent from the Executive Office. For example:

EXECUTIVE MANSION [OR OFFICE]

My dear [*name inserted by hand*]:

I warmly appreciate your kind message of congratulation, which has given me a great deal of pleasure, and sincerely wish that it were possible for me to acknowledge it in a less formal manner.

Faithfully,
[*Signed by hand*]

TO WHOM ARE THANKS ADDRESSED?

When a gift is sent by more than one person—to your daughter Susie from "the Joneses" for example—to whom does she write? It would be awkward to name all of the Joneses in the salutation, so she addresses the envelope and the salutation to "Mr. and Mrs. Jones" and includes their children in the text: "Please thank Billy and Janet and Fred for me, and tell them how much I like the perfume."

A bride usually writes her thank-yous to "Mrs. Jones," on the assumption that Mrs. Jones actually made the purchase, but it is equally correct for her to write to "Mr. and Mrs. Jones" if both of their names are on the card.

A dinner-party thank-you (optional) is sent to the hostess, but thanks for an overnight visit are either sent to both husband and wife, or the husband is included in the text.

DIFFICULT THANK-YOUS

The most difficult thank-you letter to write is the one you owe for a gift that you can't bear. It is all very well to say, "It's the thought that counts," but we sometimes receive gifts that are so dreadful or so inappropriate that it is impossible to believe the donor thought at all!

However, we still don't want to hurt someone's feelings—it is always possible that he or she really did like the monstrosity you received—so you must write something. You need not lie. It is quite possible to find a phrase that can be taken to mean anything the recipient wishes. Consider the following examples:

"You do have the most original ideas—whoever else would have found such an unusual gurgling pitcher?"

"The silver and gold bowl is unique—it has become a real conversation piece in our house."

"The upside-down clock is simply fascinating—I've never seen anything quite like it."

None of the statements is untrue, and yet they indicate approval, if they don't actually give it.

LETTERS OF CONGRATULATION

All letters of congratulation except printed or "form" letters require an acknowledgment.

ON AN ENGAGEMENT

Dear Stella,
While we are not altogether surprised, we are both delighted to hear the good news of your engagement. Ted's family and ours are very close, as you know, and we have always been especially devoted to him. He is one of the finest—and now luckiest—of young men, and we send you both every good wish for all possible happiness.

> *Affectionately,*
> *Nancy Jackson*

Dear Ted,
Just a line to tell you how glad we all are to hear of your wonderful news. Stella is lovely, and of course, from our point of view, we don't think she's exactly unfortunate either! This brings our very best wishes to you from

> *Aunt Sue and Uncle George*

LETTER FROM A MOTHER TO A SON'S FIANCÉE

When it is impossible for a mother to go to meet her son's new fiancée, a letter should be written to her. The general outline is:

Dear Mary,
John has just told us of his great happiness, which, of course, makes us very happy, too. Our one regret is that we are so far away [or whatever else] that we cannot immediately meet you in person.
We do, however, send you our love and hope that we shall see you very soon, here if not there. Perhaps John can arrange to bring you here for a visit in the near future.

> *Sincerely and affectionately,*
> *Martha Jones*

CORRESPONDENCE ❧

ON THE BIRTH OF A BABY

Dear Sue,

We were so delighted to hear the news of Jonathan Junior's birth. Congratulations to all three of you!

May I come to see you and the baby the first time that I'm in town? I'll call and let you know when that will be.

Much love,
Helen

FOR A SPECIAL ACHIEVEMENT

Dear Mrs. Steele,

We are so glad to hear the good news of David's success; it was a very splendid accomplishment, and we are all so proud of him and happy for you. When you see him or write to him please give him our love and congratulations.

Sincerely,
Mildred Bowen

Dear Michael,

We were all so happy to hear of the confirmation of your appointment. The state needs men like you—if we had more men of your caliber the ordinary citizen would have less to worry about. Our warmest congratulations!

Jim

LETTERS OF INTRODUCTION

A business letter of introduction is somewhat different from a social one, although it carries the same implicit approval of the subject. It also implies the writer's request that the receiver pay due attention to the one being introduced. It should not be written casually nor for a person who does not merit the introduction.

A business letter of this type does not necessarily oblige the receiver to entertain the subject socially. If he wishes to, he certainly may, but generally his attention to the bearer's business is sufficient.

The social introduction is far more of a responsibility. Therefore, it is better to avoid writing a note of introduction in the beginning than to commit the error of inconveniencing a friend or acquaintance.

When you know someone who is going to a city where you have

other friends and when you sincerely believe that it will be a mutual pleasure for them to meet, a letter of introduction is proper and easy to write. But to send one to a casual acquaintance—no matter how attractive or distinguished the person to be introduced—is a gross presumption.

THE DIRECT NOTE OF INTRODUCTION

This note is carried by the one being introduced.

Dear Mrs. Miller:

Julian Gibbs is going to Buffalo on January tenth to deliver a lecture on his polar expedition, and I am giving him this note of introduction to you. He is a very great friend of ours, and I think that perhaps you and Mr. Miller will enjoy meeting him as much as I know he would enjoy knowing you.

With kindest regards, in which Arthur joins,

Very sincerely,
Ethel Norman

If Mr. Norman were introducing one man to another for business reasons, he would give his card to the visitor, inscribed as follows:

Introducing Julian Gibbs

Mr. Arthur Lees Norman

Mr. Norman would also send a private letter by mail, telling his friend that Mr. Gibbs is coming.

A LESS FORMAL LETTER OF INTRODUCTION

Dear Ruth,

I am giving this letter to George Perrin, a good friend of ours, who is going to be in Chicago the week of January seventh.

I want very much to have him get together with you and hope that this will find you in town.

Affectionately,
Louise Hill

109

At the same time a second and private letter of information is written and sent by mail.

Dear Ruth,
I have sent you a letter introducing George Perrin. He is in his thirties, very good company, and an altogether nice person.
He is very interested in modern art, and knowing that you know a number of artists, we thought you might be able to arrange some introductions for him.
I know it would be a pleasure for everyone concerned and hope you will be able to get together.

Affectionately,
Louise

All of the letters above impose a strict obligation on the people to whom they are delivered or sent to meet and to do whatever they can for the person being introduced.

PROCEDURE ON ARRIVAL

A letter of introduction is always handed to the bearer unsealed.

If you are a man and your introduction is written to a woman, either married or single, you go to her home, introduce yourself when you arrive, and give her your letter of introduction. She should, if it's possible, immediately invite you to cocktails or dinner. If you feel presumptuous in going directly to her home you may telephone and explain who you are and by whom you are introduced. She should, and undoubtedly will, set a time for you to meet, and when you arrive you give her your letter of introduction.

A letter to a man is mailed to his house, unless the letter is a business one. In the latter case, if there has not been time to mail the introduction ahead, you go to his office and send in your business card and the letter. You wait in the reception room until he has read the letter and calls you into his office. If at all possible it is much better to write or call him first, letting him know your business and when you will arrive. This will ensure his having time to see you, as well as prepare him to discuss whatever your business may be.

A woman carrying a social introduction mails her letter to the addressee and does nothing further until she receives an acknowledgment. She does not go directly to the recipient's home. But the obligation of a written introduction is so strong that there is little chance that the recipient will not contact her shortly.

When a man receives a letter introducing another man for business purposes, he calls the stranger on the telephone and asks what he may do for him. If he does not invite the newcomer to his house he may arrange a meeting or ask him to lunch or dinner at a restaurant, as the circumstances seem to warrant. But it is absolutely necessary that he show the stranger what courtesy he can.

THE INDIRECT LETTER OF INTRODUCTION

When the Franklins move to Strangetown an indirect letter of introduction is better than a direct one. An indirect letter is one written by Mrs. O'Connor to a friend of hers in Strangetown. As already explained, a letter of introduction *presented* by Mrs. Franklin puts its recipient in a position where she must do something for the Franklins, no matter how inconvenient or distasteful it may be.

If, on the other hand, Mrs. O'Connor merely writes to Mrs. Hartwell, "My friends, the Franklins, are going to live in your neighborhood," the latter is free to make advances only insofar as she feels inclined.

Mrs. Franklin, knowing nothing about this letter and expecting nothing in the way of hospitality, is far more likely to be pleased when Mrs. Hartwell calls on her than when she is invited to Mrs. Hartwell's house because the invitation is obligatory. A letter of introduction, as you can see, is usually an inconvenience and on occasions a very real burden.

THE LETTER OF CONDOLENCE

Intimate letters of condolence are too personal to follow a set form. One rule, and one only, should guide you in writing such letters. Say what you truly feel. Say that and nothing else. Sit down at your desk as soon as you hear of the death and let your thoughts be with the person you are writing to.

Don't dwell on the details of illness or the manner of death; don't, especially to a mother who has lost a child, try to convince her that her loss is a "blessing in disguise." Remember that a person with an aching heart will not wish to wade through interminable sorrowful thoughts. The more nearly a note can express your sympathy, and a genuine love or appreciation for the one who has gone, the greater comfort it brings.

Forget, if you can, that you are using written words. Think merely how you feel—then put your feelings on paper.

Suppose it is the death of a man who has left a place in the whole community that will be difficult, if not impossible, to fill. You remember all he stood for that was fine and helpful to others and how much he will be missed. All you can think of is "Steve—what a wonderful man he was! I don't think anything will ever be the same again without him." Say just that! Ask if there is anything you can do at any time to be of service. There is nothing more to be said. A line into which you have put a little of the genuine feeling that you had for Steve is worth pages of eloquence. A letter of condolence may be badly constructed, ungrammatical—never mind. Flowery language counts for nothing; sincerity alone is of value.

Occasionally a letter from one who has suffered an undeniably equal loss, who through experience can write words of encouragment and assurance that in time the pain will grow less, is of genuine help. But that sort of letter must never be written by anyone whose own suffering has not been equally devastating.

The few examples below are intended merely as suggested guides for those at a loss to construct a short but appropriate message.

Dear Mrs. Sutphen,

We are so very shocked to hear of the sorrow that has come to you.

If there is anything that either my husband or I can do, I earnestly hope that you will call upon us.

Alice Blake

Dear Mr. and Mrs. Conrad,

I know how little words written on a page can possibly mean to you at such a time. But I must at least tell you that you are in our thoughts and in our hearts, and if there is anything that we can do for you, please send us a message—whatever it may be.

With deepest sympathy,
Mary Newling

Or, one my husband received when Emily Post died: *"We have so much sympathy for you. It must have been wonderful to have had her as your grandmother."*

LETTER WHERE DEATH WAS A RELEASE

It is difficult to write a letter to one whose loss is for the best in that you want to express sympathy but cannot feel sad that one who has suffered so long has found release. The expression of sympathy in this case should not be for the present death, but for the illness that started long ago. The grief for a paralyzed mother is for the stroke that cut her down many years before, and your sympathy is really for that. You might write: "Your sorrow during all these years —and now—is in my heart; and all my thoughts and sympathy are with you."

TO WHOM ARE LETTERS OF CONDOLENCE WRITTEN?

Letters of condolence may be addressed in various ways. If you knew the deceased well but do not know his or her family, the note is addressed to the closest relative—usually the widow, the widower, or the oldest child. Some like to add "and family" on the envelope, and this is permissible when you feel that you are sending your sympathy to all rather than to one special person.

When you did not know the person who died but do know one of his relatives, you write to that person rather than to someone who might have been closer to him. In writing to a married person who has lost a parent you may write to the one whose parent it was, or if the other partner was close to his or her in-law the letter may be addressed to both.

Letters to children who have lost a parent may be addressed to Miss Lucy Field (the daughter), with Mr. John Field (the son) underneath. The salutation would read, "Dear Lucy and John."

I am sometimes asked if one should write to the surviving member of a divorced couple when the other dies. If they have maintained a friendly relationship, and you know that the survivor is truly upset by his or her ex-mate's death, naturally you should write. In most cases, however, the divorce indicates that they no longer wish to share each other's lives, so there is little need to send sympathy. The children of the divorced couple, even though they live with the surviving member, should receive notes if they have continued to see the deceased.

ACKNOWLEDGMENT

Notes of condolence should always be acknowledged—by the recipient if possible. If he or she cannot do it—for whatever reason —other members of the family should write the notes. The only exceptions to this obligation are when the expression of condolence is simply a printed form with no personal message, or when the writer asks that his note not be acknowledged. This is a thoughtful thing to do when writing a close friend, or someone you know will receive a great number of condolences.

CHANGE-OF-ADDRESS CARDS

Although this paragraph is concerned with printed cards rather than letters, it surely falls under the heading of personal correspondence.

When you are planning to move to a new address you will save yourself countless hours of writing, and your friends and business contacts hours of distress, if you have change-of-address cards printed. They are generally three- by five-inch cards that say simply:

> *After March first* [*or, On March first*]
> *Mr. and Mrs. Howard Trumbull*
> *will be living at* [*will change their address to*]
> *Short Pine Farm*
> *Craftsbury, Vermont 06572*

If you send cards *after* you move:

> *Mr. and Mrs. Howard Trumbull*
> *have changed their address to*
> *Short Pine Farm*
> *Craftsbury, Vermont 06572*

UNSEALED LETTERS

Properly, any letter given to a person (other than a commercial messenger) for delivery by hand is unsealed. Customarily, the person who will carry it seals it immediately in the presence of the writer, but this is not obligatory.

Exceptions may be made, of course, should there be a heavy or particularly valuable enclosure that might slip out after the time of writing. In this case, it is polite to explain why the envelope has been sealed.

TAPE CASSETTES AS LETTERS

Although nothing can replace the printed word as tangible evidence of love and remembrance, I would like to mention a form of "letter" that fills a great need for many people. That is the tape cassette. It does something that no letter can do—it brings the sound of your voice into the listener's home, and that in turn brings a closeness and an image that the written word cannot produce.

Tape recorders are not inexpensive and many people cannot afford to use them as a means of communication. But if you can, and your parents—or your children—are far away, I highly recommend this form of correspondence. It is a special treat for older people who are often lonely and feel forgotten and neglected. To receive a tape carrying the voices of children and grandchildren, and to be able to play and replay it when the loneliness creeps in, is a gift of immeasurable value. The tapes can also be erased and reused, and questions can be answered, stories told, and news reported far more fully than can be done in a letter. We have used tapes to communicate with my father-in-law, who lives in Italy, and with our son and daughter-in-law when they were in the Peace Corps in Africa. I can only say it has been a most satisfying form of communication in both cases.

One reminder, however: Make some notes of the contents of the tapes you receive, because once those tapes are erased and reused you will have no other way of remembering what was on them. This also eliminates the necessity of having to replay the whole tape when you are taping your reply.

ᵇ10ᵇ Greeting Cards

Birthday and anniversary cards, get-well cards, and all other messages of friendship are welcome evidences of good wishes from family and friends. The wide variety of cards now available makes the choosing and sending of them a pleasure rather than a chore.

But a word of warning is in order. The very fact that they are attractive and easy to find may on occasion lead to their abuse. Elderly Aunt Margaret will enjoy her birthday card only if you take the trouble to add a little note in your own handwriting expressing something of your own feelings about the day or giving her a bit of family news. A printed message, however delightful, cannot possibly make up for lack of personal attention.

I would like to quote from a letter I received recently:

While ill for some weeks I received a vast number of get-well cards. I was touched that so many friends thought of me, but I can't help my feeling of disappointment that so few contained a personal note, even one line. If one could realize how much even the shortest personal note enhances the card in the eyes of the receiver, more people would take the extra time and trouble to write something beneath the printed message.

Need I say more?

BIRTHDAYS, ANNIVERSARIES, ETC.

Only the most remarkable people can remember all the special dates that they should. The rest of us need "props," and I would like to make a suggestion or two to help you remember Aunt Hattie's birthday and Cousin Sarah's anniversary.

You can very easily keep track by making a month-by-month calendar showing only dates, and not the day of the week. My daughter-in-law made one as a Christmas present for me, and it hangs on

January	February	March
April	May	June
July	August	September
October	November	December

my kitchen wall—a constant reminder of our children's and friends' birthdays, anniversaries, etc. It is simply an illustrated chart of twelve boxes with the name of a month at the top of each, and lines to be filled in with the name of the person whose birthday or anniversary it is, and exact date.

A friend has another system. She keeps a book of all important dates on her desk. At the beginning of each month she gets out her book, writes a message, signs and addresses cards for each person listed, and keeps them in a pile to be mailed on the appropriate day.

The method doesn't matter. The important thing is that you keep a record of some sort and remember to use it. We can't always give presents and we can't always visit our friends to celebrate those special occasions, but we can show that we are thinking of them by sending a card.

Cards should be sent, insofar as possible, so that they will *arrive* on the date of the birthday, anniversary, or whatever.

CHRISTMAS CARDS

There is virtually no limit to the list of those to whom one may send Christmas cards, beginning with closest friends and ending with mere acquaintances. However, the custom that has become prevalent of sending a card to everyone with whom you have a nodding acquaintance is ridiculous and contrary to the spirit of Christmas. In many areas it has become a contest to see who can receive the most cards—each person who sent a card the previous year must be sent one, plus all the new acquaintances made during the intervening months. The tradespeople in most towns now send cards to their customers. This practice, unless there is a personal relationship involved, can be for no other reason than to bolster business. Surely the idea of a heartfelt greeting and sincere wish for a happy holiday cannot go with each and every one of these messages!

Christmas cards should be sent to people you really wish to greet but who are not quite close enough to you to exchange gifts, to good friends whom you may not have seen for some time, and most of all to those who do not live near you and with whom your Christmas card may be your only communication. In this last case a picture of your children or a new house is always appreciated. It need not be elaborate—a snapshot pasted on red paper, with "Merry Christmas" in green ink, is sufficient, although film stores and stationers make these cards up to order in attractive folders, with or without a printed message.

CARDS TO BUSINESS ACQUAINTANCES

When it is company policy to send a Christmas card to a client, it is sent to the man at his business address, in the name of the company—"The Hollister Hardware Company wishes you a Merry Christmas and a Happy New Year"—rather than sending a card to his home in the name of the president or other officer. But if the client is known to the executive socially as well as through business it may be addressed to husband and wife and sent to their home, even though he may not know her personally.

All personal Christmas cards should be addressed by hand, and even secretaries who are sending a great number out for their firm, or as the "personal business" cards of an employer, should make every effort to do so. Nor should they use a postage meter. It takes no longer to write the address by hand than to insert the envelope in the typewriter, type the address, and remove the envelope; and stamps can be affixed quickly and painlessly by using a wet sponge. A typed, metered envelope can easily be mistaken for an advertisement, and tossed, unopened, into the wastebasket. As one lady wrote, "A card with a typewritten address literally shouts, 'Business only!' " So I repeat, unless the number is overwhelming, or the secretary is physically incapable of writing, even the boss's cards should be addressed by hand.

ENGRAVED CARDS

Very few people send engraved cards today unless they are prominent in public life or hold an official position. These cards are very simple—they may contain the message and nothing more, or they may have a little decoration, perhaps a straight gold border or a simple design of holly leaves around the edge. The message usually reads, "Mr. and Mrs. Christopher Holly send you their best wishes for a Merry Christmas and a Happy New Year," or "Governor and Mrs. Herbert Black wish you a Happy Holiday and a Joyous New Year."

The engraving of names on Christmas cards (as opposed to printing) follows the rules for the engraving of names on visiting cards. A woman's name should never be engraved without the title of "Mrs." or "Miss," and a man's card includes "Mr.," "Doctor," or "Dr."

SIGNATURES ON CHRISTMAS, AND OTHER, CARDS

When cards are sent by husband and wife, the one who writes the names, courteously writes his or her own name last. To close friends, the last name need not be written; to others, it should be included. When signatures are printed, there is no rule about whether the husband's or the wife's name should be first, but the last name is always used. "Mary and John Godfrey" may seem more polite to Mary, but "John and Mary Godfrey" does, of course, follow the conventional "Mr. and Mrs." form. When children's names are included the father's name comes first—always. For example: "John and Mary Godfrey and John Jr." Cards sent by a family having several children might be from "The John Smiths—All Five"; or from "The

Smiths—John, Mary, Johnny, Marie, and Tim." There is, of course, no rule about anything as informal as this.

A title—"Mr.," "Mrs.," etc.—is never used on any other than engraved cards.

When printed cards are sent by a widow and her grown son together, or a widower and his grown daughter, the name of the parent goes on one line and that of the son or daughter on the line below. If written by hand, the parent's name would come first: "Henry Brown and Mary," or to those who call the parent and the daughter (or son) by their first names, "Henry and Mary."

Engaged couples may send cards together, with their first names either written by hand or printed to match the rest of the printing on an informal card.

Even though a married couple is separated (by distance) when Christmas, birthday, or any other cards are sent, the wife signs her husband's name with her own. The idea is, of course, to indicate that his thoughts are with the recipient too, even though circumstances prevent him from actually sending the card with his wife.

Older couples sending cards to younger friends sign their names "Helen and Fred Smith," rather than "Mr. and Mrs. Smith"—just as they would sign a letter. To sign "Mr. and Mrs." would sound very formal or would imply an inferiority on the part of the receiver.

When a husband and wife have each been married before and have children from both previous marriages the signatures can become very complicated if they try to include all the names. It is not incorrect to write "Pat, Jean, and Billy Smith," and "Bobby, Rich, Frank, and Carol Brown" under the parents' names, but it seems more practical if the parents sign "Bob and Sue" and add "and all the family" or "and children" after the signature.

CHRISTMAS CARDS AS NEWSLETTERS

Christmas cards are often used as carriers of news—and rightly so. They may announce a birth in the family by the signature— "Mary, Joe, and Joe Jr., born August seventh in Williamstown." They may carry unhappy news, too—"John and I were divorced in September, so please write me at my new address. . . ." Or a death is announced simply by the fact that a card comes from "Mary Cross" when always before it had come from "Bill and Mary." And of course, we all write brief news notes or special thoughts to people whom we have not seen, or do not see often. But there is another type of "newsletter" I would like to mention. That is the mimeographed history of the past year, which has no handwritten note added, and which often runs to four or five pages. The people who send these form letters mean well—they are trying to get all the news into this once-a-year communication, and they go to great trouble to do it. But the truth is that, outside of their closest friends, most people don't really care if the baby has six teeth, or that Johnny had his tonsils out. A handwritten note on a pretty card, possibly telling of the high points—a marriage, a birth, etc., would be much more appreciated. So if you want to have one of these letters printed up, fine, but I urge you to send out cards to the majority of your acquaintances and enclose the newsletter only to those who you are sure will be interested.

MERRY CHRISTMAS OR SEASON'S GREETINGS?

Many, many Christians send greeting cards to Jews at Christmastime and vice versa. This is a lovely thing to do, since it is a holiday time, and since both the Christian Christmas and the Jewish Chanukah fall in the same season. But care should be taken in choosing the cards. A Santa Claus card, a holiday or country scene, or elves, gnomes, animals, etc., with a "Happy Holiday" or "Season's Greetings," are ideal choices. A Christian should *not* send a religious card, especially one depicting the birth of Christ or other biblical scenes, nor one featuring "Christmas" which is not a significant day for the Jews, to a Jew. Nor should a Jew send a "Happy Chanukah" card to his Christian friends. Either, however, could, if he wished, send a card appropriate to the other's faith. In short, it is a matter of thoughtfulness. Greetings and wishes for happiness are always welcomed—but they should be expressed in the way that they will mean the most, and above all will not offend the recipient.

A CARD TO A WHOLE FAMILY

When you intend a card for the whole family but dislike the ambiguousness of "Mr. and Mrs. Meadows and Family," address the envelope to "Mr. and Mrs. Meadows" and then on the card itself write in ink, "Love to the children [or Jimmy and Ned], too," below the printed message. If the message reads "A Merry Christmas and a Happy New Year" or "Holiday Greetings," you may simply add "to all of you" or "to all the Meadowses" below.

A CHRISTMAS CARD TO SOMEONE IN MOURNING

A card to someone who is in mourning will be gratefully received if in some way it illustrates the promise of peace or comfort or if its message is one of love or friendship. But please do not send a gay or humorous card shouting "Merry Christmas and Happy New Year" to one who probably feels that he will never laugh or be happy again. Whether or not those who are themselves in mourning send cards depends entirely upon their own feelings. Naturally they would not send cards to mere acquaintances, but certainly there is no impropriety in wishing their friends happiness, if they can forget their own unhappiness enough to do so. On the other hand, no one could possibly want them to do anything that could add to their difficulties or emotional burdens.

ENVELOPES FOR CHRISTMAS CARDS

Christmas envelopes, their linings, the ink, can be as vividly colorful as you please. You should paste return-address stickers or write your address on envelopes. This not only complies with the U.S. Postal Service's request but is a help to those receiving the cards in keeping their lists in order. The Christmas seals sold to help support various worthy causes look gay on the back of the envelope. They should be applied to the tip of the flap or to the center of a square flap.

DISPLAYING CARDS

Christmas cards are joyfully displayed in any way the imagination can devise. They are hung from stair rails, mantels, in special containers, and even on streamers from the ceiling! They add greatly to the other decorations and express the warmth and love of the season. Anyone who comes to your house should feel free to examine and admire the display. So if you receive any cards with private personal messages it is best not to display them.

After the holidays they may be given to hospitals or other organizations, which find many uses for them, or they may be kept to decorate your Christmas packages the following year. The pages with messages and names are, of course, removed before using the cards again for decorating packages. It is not necessary to remove names from those given to hospitals, however, unless there is also a personal message on the page.

CUTTING DOWN YOUR LIST

For many people it is a sad and difficult thing to cut down a Christmas-card list, since many of the cards are the only communication they have with the people the cards are sent to. But older people often simply do not have the strength to keep up their long lists, or cannot afford to. Others simply get tired of it and wish to cut their lists down or stop entirely.

The bright spot to remember is this: Thousands of people don't —and never have—sent cards, and are not one bit less well liked because of it.

You may do it gradually by cutting your list down in this order: Eliminate first those from whom you have not received a card for a year or two. Then cut out all those in your own town to whom sending a card is just a habit—you don't really care whether you hear from them or not. Next leave off the people to whom you give gifts, and finally other good friends you see every day. Since they are *good* friends you can tell them what you are doing and why. If you cut down in that order, over one or two years, the remainder of your list should be only those far-away friends who really look forward to your Christmas cards—and you to theirs. Hopefully you will never have to eliminate them, too, but if you must, at least write a note on a card this year and explain that it will be the last.

~§11&~ Visiting Cards, Informals, and Business Cards

USING A VISITING (OR "CALLING") CARD

FOR A FORMAL CALL

Today the formal call is a thing of the past except in military and diplomatic circles. The calling cards that used to be left in great quantities at the homes of friends and acquaintances are now used almost entirely as enclosures with gifts and flowers, or for invitations and replies. Even for those last uses, the card has been largely replaced by an informal, and many women do not feel it necessary to have visiting cards at all, or they order only "Mr. and Mrs." cards for use as gift enclosures. Therefore, although the following information may seem outdated and unnecessary, if you are unexpectedly faced with the occasion to make a formal call, it is wise to be familiar with the correct procedure.

When the visitor rings the doorbell the butler or maid offers a card tray on which the visitor lays her card, and it is taken to the person being called on. As she leaves, the visitor leaves cards for the other members of the household on the tray, which is now on a convenient table in the hallway. The number of cards to leave is very simple. A woman leaves her own cards for ladies only, because she is not supposed to call on a gentleman. But her husband leaves a card for every man as well as for every woman.

That is all there is to it. But three is the greatest number ever left of any *one* card. In calling on Mrs. Town, who has three grown daughters and her mother living in the house and a Mrs. Stranger staying with her, a card for each would mean a packet of six. Instead, the visitor should leave three—one for Mrs. Town, one for all the other ladies of the house (not one for each), and one for Mrs. Stranger.

AS AN INVITATION

Although informals are more frequently used, calling cards make very practical invitations for all sorts of semiformal parties. You simply write the essential information in small neat letters in a lower corner, or perhaps above *and* below the engraved name.

Cocktails

Mr. and Mrs. Harvey Cole

Long Hill Farm
6 o'clock
Saturday, February 26

Saturday, April 7, at 4 o'clock

Mr. Anthony Dauber

Exhibition of paintings by
Henry Smith   Park Studio

```
┌─────────────────────────────────────┐
│                                     │
│    MR. AND MRS. HARVEY COLE          │
│                                     │
│    Dinner, 7:00 P.M.                 │
│    Tuesday, January 7th              │
│    9 Lakeshore Drive                 │
│                                     │
│    R.S.V.P.          687-4478        │
│                                     │
└─────────────────────────────────────┘
```

Replies may also be sent on visiting cards. Above or below the name, you would write "Accept with pleasure, the 7th," or "We'd love to come on the 7th," or "We're so sorry, will be out of town on the 7th," etc. *See Chapter 39, page 447.*

ENVELOPES

When visiting cards are frequently used as invitations, it is necessary to order a supply of matching envelopes meeting postal regulations. The mailing envelopes are somewhat larger than the cards themselves, but the color and quality of the paper prevent any appearance of a mismatch and the larger size ensures their safe delivery. The minimum envelope size accepted by the U.S. Postal Service is three by four and a half inches.

OTHER MESSAGES

Occasionally a calling card is enclosed with flowers sent as an expression of sympathy or congratulations, especially when it is a "formality" rather than extended to someone to whom you wish to send a more personal message. All that is required is to write "Congratulations on your new job" or "With deepest sympathy" above your engraved name. A card may also be sent as a thank-you for a dinner party—"Many thanks for a wonderful evening."

AS A BABY ANNOUNCEMENT

A miniature visiting card with your baby's name on it, attached by a ribbon to your card, makes the nicest birth announcement possible.

AS A GIFT ENCLOSURE

When sending a gift or flowers to anyone, it definitely adds a "touch" if you enclose your own card, rather than one picked out from the selection on the counter. Although you need not write any message at all, most people, if they know the recipient personally, like to write a word or two at the top of the card. To a bride you might write "Best wishes for your happiness" or "Love and best wishes to you both." On a card sent with flowers to a bereaved person or family the words might be "You are in our thoughts and prayers" or "We share your sorrow," but no message is written when the flowers are sent to "the funeral of John Smith" at the church.

When you are enclosing a card with a gift being sent to someone you know well, you may feel that your "Mrs. Franklin Carey" or "Mr. and Mrs. Franklin Carey" card is too formal. It is perfectly permissible to scratch out the entire name and write "Mary and Frank" above it. Or if it is to someone who might not think of you quite that informally (a young bride, for instance), you may scratch out all but the last name and write in "Mary and Frank." However, leaving the engraved name as it is, and writing whatever you wish above it, is correct in all circumstances.

Your card is put in an envelope that is either put inside the gift box or stapled to the paper around the flowers. If the message on the card is very personal it may be sealed; otherwise it is not. The name (without address) of the recipient is written on the envelope when the gift is being sent from a store, but if you are mailing the package yourself that is not necessary.

THE STYLE OF YOUR CARD

SIZE AND ENGRAVING

Of necessity, the width of visiting cards varies according to the length of the name, but a married woman's card is usually from three to three and one-half inches wide and from two and one-fourth to two and one-half inches high. (Very young girls customarily use a smaller card.) A man's card is narrower, from three to three and one-fourth inches long and from one and one-fourth to one and five-eighths inches high. The cards are made of white or cream-white glazed or unglazed bristol board of medium thickness, and they are not plate-marked (with raised border).

The most popular engraving, perhaps, is shaded Roman, but script is always handsome too. Various other letterings brought out by engravers from time to time are attractive, but all overly large or ornate lettering should be avoided.

Business cards may be of much thinner paper, so that more of them can be comfortably carried in a wallet or card case.

Mrs. John Foster Hughes

Mr. John Foster Hughes, Jr.

ADDRESSES

It is not incorrect, but it is unusual, to have an address on a social card. If you wish to do so, the address should be written out in full, with no abbreviations. Numerals may be used. The address is engraved in the lower-right-hand corner. More often, the address is simply written on the card by hand when it is requested or necessary.

NAMES AND INITIALS

To be impeccably correct, one should not use initials on a visiting card. A gentleman's card theoretically should read "Mr. John Hunter Titherington Smith"; but when the name is awkwardly long, he may have his card engraved "Mr. John H. T. Smith" or "Mr. J. H. Titherington Smith," if he prefers. His wife's card should be the exact duplicate of his, and not read "Mrs. J. Hunter Smith" when his reads "Mr. John H. Smith." She uses "Jr." if he does, and drops it, if he does, when his father dies.

WOMEN'S SOCIAL CARDS

A MARRIED WOMAN'S CARD

As stated above, a married woman uses her husband's name in exactly the same form that he does, and her card is approximately three and one-fourth inches by two and one-fourth inches.

A WIDOW'S CARD

A man gives his name to his wife for life—or until she remarries. A widow, therefore, should always continue to use her husband's Christian names. She is Mrs. John Foster Hughes—never Mrs. Sarah Hughes.

If a widow's son has the name of his father, the widow may have "Sr." added to her name when her son marries. This use of "Sr." is necessary if they live at the same address—or in the country, where no street numbers are used. If they live in different cities, both mother and daughter-in-law can be Mrs. John Foster Hughes.

If the widow lives in the same city but at a different address from her son and his wife, she can have her address engraved in small letters at the lower-right-hand corner and so identify herself.

A DIVORCÉE'S CARD

For many years a divorcée was known by her ex-husband's name, preceded by her maiden name. This is still perfectly correct, but can be very confusing and very awkward. Most divorcées today prefer to use their first names, and it seems sensible that they do so. Janice Forsythe, who is divorced from Robert Jones, has a choice, therefore, of having her cards engraved "Mrs. Forsythe Jones," or "Mrs. Janice Jones." If she legally takes back her maiden name, her card should be engraved "Miss Janice Forsythe"—not "Mrs. Janice Forsythe." If she has children she should retain her husband's name, which is the same as theirs, and be known as "Mrs." *For a further discussion of the divorcée's name, see Chapter 2, pages 26–27.*

A SINGLE WOMAN'S CARD

A single woman's name is written out in full (no initials) and from age ten or twelve on is preceded by "Miss." She should use her real name rather than a nickname unless the "real" name is *never* used or is objectionable to her.

A PROFESSIONAL WOMAN'S CARD

Single women who are medical doctors, dentists, veterinarians, etc., use the title on their social as well as their business cards. The social card would be "Doctor [written out if space permits] Jean Hamilton," and the professional card would be "Jean Hamilton, M.D." A married woman doctor would use the same forms on her own cards, but she has more of a problem if she and her husband want to have "joint" cards. They cannot be "Mr. and Dr. William Perry," since she is *not* Dr. William Perry. So she must make a choice between forgoing the "Dr." on their joint card, and letting it be "Mr. and Mrs. William Perry," or if he is a doctor too, "Dr. and Mrs. William Perry," or having their card printed, "Mr. William and Dr. Susan Perry," or "Drs. William and Susan Perry."

A woman who has an earned degree, but is not ordinarily called "Dr." in the pursuit of her profession, does not use "Dr." on her cards, but uses "Miss" or "Mrs." as indicated.

A registered nurse uses "Miss" or "Mrs." on her social cards, but uses her first and last names followed by "R.N." on her professional cards. She drops her title in this case and is "Sandra Smith, R.N."

MEN'S SOCIAL CARDS

A MARRIED OR SINGLE MAN'S CARD

A man's card is engraved with his title, "Doctor" or "Mr.," even though he may have "junior" after his name. "Mr." is never written "Mister," but "Doctor" is preferable to "Dr."

A bachelor whose job requires that he move about frequently may wish to have the address of a club where he can receive messages and mail, and perhaps stay when he is at his home office, printed on his card. The name of the club, and the address if he wishes, appears in the lower-left-hand corner.

THE USE OF "JR." AND "2ND" ON CARDS

The fact that a man's name has "Jr." added at the end in no way takes the place of "Mr." His card should be engraved "Mr. John Foster Hughes, Jr.," and his wife's, "Mrs. John Foster Hughes, Jr." "Junior" may be engraved in full; when it is, it is not spelled with a capital *j.* John, second, or John, third, may have "2nd" or "3rd" after their names, but II or III in Roman numerals gives a very handsome appearance.

MEN'S TITLES ON THEIR SOCIAL CARDS

Doctors, clergymen, military officers, and holders of title-bestowing offices all have their cards engraved with their titles: "Doctor Henry Gordon" (an M.D.), "The Reverend William Goode,"

"Colonel Thomas Doyle," "Judge Horace Rush," "Senator James Widelands."

Holders of earned degrees who have attained a high or prominent position in their field, or are universally known as "Doctor," may have that title on their cards. Other, less established professors or holders of degrees use "Mr." socially. The letters of the degree, no matter how high, do not follow the name. When necessary, the title may be abbreviated. "Lieutenant Colonel Sylvester Howe Heatherton," which could hardly fit on a three-quarter-inch card, may be written "Lt. Col. Sylvester H. Heatherton." Holders of *honorary* degrees do not use the title or the letters on their cards.

"Joint" cards read "The Reverend and Mrs. William Goode," "Judge and Mrs. Horace Rush," etc.

The correct card for a governor is:

The Governor of Nevada

on a card that is slightly larger or more nearly square than an ordinary man's card. Less correct, but not inadmissible, is his ordinary card with "Governor of Nevada" added in small letters under his name. Occasionally an overmodest incumbent objects to the correct form because he thinks it looks too self-important. But he must remember that the card is representative of the highest office of his state and not the card of a private citizen.

The card of a mayor may read:

The Mayor of Chicago

or if he prefers:

Mr. John Lake
Mayor of Chicago

A diplomat uses his title and "United States of America," rather than "America" or "American."

Finally, it may be well to add that titles of courtesy have no place either in a signature or on a visiting card. For example, the American title of courtesy, "The Honorable," unlike this title given to sons of British earls, viscounts, and barons, is never correct on a card.

The professional card of a doctor or surgeon is "James Smith, M.D.," even though his social card is "Doctor James Smith."

HUSBAND-AND-WIFE CARDS

"MR. AND MRS." CARDS

"Mr. and Mrs." cards are more useful to most of us than individual cards. They are used for invitations, as enclosures with presents, or for any communication that comes from both husband and wife. They are approximately three and one-half inches by two and one-half inches in size.

"Joint" cards often have the couple's address on them, as they are used for more practical purposes than the individual calling card. Titles such as "Doctor" and "The Reverend" must be abbreviated because of space. "Mr. and Mrs." cards are almost always enclosed with wedding gifts, and all presents that are given by both husband and wife. They are also used with flowers going to a funeral or to a bereaved family, and for invitations to dinners or cocktail parties given by the couple. An invitation to a tea, on the other hand, would be written on the wife's card.

Husband-and-wife cards are never left by the woman when she makes a call by herself. Nor can the husband use one if he makes a call alone. On official calls, their separate cards are left, even when they go together, but on a less formal occasion they might leave their "Mr. and Mrs." card.

Retired military officers and their wives often do not have a "joint" card, because "retired" is usually printed in the lower-right-hand corner, and would, if her name were on the card, refer to the wife too. However, they may, if they wish, have a card engraved with "General Paul Seaburn, retired," on one line and "Mrs. Seaburn" written below.

See pages 129–130 for husband-and-wife cards when the woman has a professional title.

CARDS FOR CHILDREN

Children's cards may seem extravagant and unnecessary today, but occasionally a parent or grandparent orders cards to be enclosed with gifts from the child. These cards are smaller than regulation size and are engraved without title.

THE PPC CARD

The PPC card is almost unheard of nowadays. But for those readers who might unexpectedly receive a card with those initials, I include this explanation. It is merely a visiting card on which the initials PPC (*pour prendre congé*—"to take leave") are written in ink in the lower left corner. This is sent by mail to acquaintances when

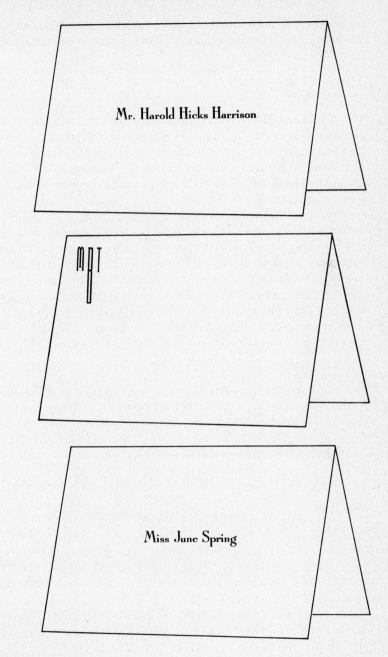

Informals (see page 134)

one is leaving and means nothing except "I've gone away—good-bye." It is in no sense a message of thanks or farewell, and no acknowledgment need be made.

INFORMALS

The small fold-over cards known as informals are convenient when you want, for example, to write a very brief note, but one that requires more space than is afforded by a visiting card.

Plain white informals of good quality are available at all stationers and are perfectly acceptable. If you wish, however, you may have them engraved, thermographed, or printed. This should be done exactly as you would have your visiting cards engraved. Or you may simply have your monogram in the upper left corner *(see page 133).*

Because informals are somewhat larger than visiting cards, the envelopes present fewer problems when it comes to mailing them.

Informals are correct and practical for invitations *(see Chapter 39),* but they cannot be substituted for visiting cards when you make a formal call. They may be enclosed with a gift *only* if you wish to write a personal message on the inner page.

BUSINESS AND PROFESSIONAL CARDS

Although business cards are never used for social purposes and must not be confused with visiting cards, their principal use is very like the original and now uncommon function of the visiting card: When an employee or an executive of a company makes a business call on another company or on a client or a prospective client, he sends in his card or leaves it as a record of his visit. They are also given to people the owner meets and with whom he wishes to keep in contact.

The card of a salesman, or anyone not in an executive position, has the name and address of the company printed in the center of the card with the employee's name in the lower left corner and the telephone number in the lower right corner. For sales purposes the ink may be colored and there may be an emblem or drawing on the card.

An executive has his or her name in the center with his or her position in the company in smaller letters under the name. The name and address of the company are then put in the lower left corner. It is helpful and convenient to have the telephone number in the lower right corner.

Business cards are approximately three and one-half inches by two inches in most cases. They do not require the use of full names to the extent that is usual with visiting cards. If a man is known simply as "Foster Smith" in his business life, for example, his card is engraved in that form. No title is used unless the name could belong to someone of either sex—"Francis" or "Gene," for example.

The writing on an executive's card is engraved or thermographed on good-quality paper, but it may be lighter and less expensive than that of a social card.

EXECUTIVE

Roger Holliday
Sales Manager

High Tide Corporation
Bowling Green Road
Columbus, Ohio 43200 614–921–7400

or

Stephen Sutphen

Vice-President
Rollins Engineering
Waynetown, Indiana 47899 317–873–1100

SALESMAN

Hardway Container Corp.
16 Centre Street
Ames, Iowa 50010

George Davis
Sales Representative 515–624–3888

Women's business cards are exactly like those of men except that they include "Miss," "Mrs.," or if the owner prefers, "Ms."

Part Three

OFFICIAL PROTOCOL

⋅§ 12 ᵇ⋅ *Precedence and Titles*

It is imperative that each new arrival in Washington—whether an official or a private citizen who expects to take part in the social life of the capital—learn first of all the proper titles by which each diplomat, government official, and military officer is addressed and the order of his rank. When a man has been promoted to high position the respect due his office should not be overlooked. And placing a foreign representative below his proper seat at a dinner table may actually influence diplomatic feelings between nations.

Precedence is the bane of the Washington hostess. It is easy enough to know that a general outranks a lieutenant, or a member of the President's Cabinet, a state assemblyman. The difficulty begins in determining, for instance, whether a general of the army should outrank the governor of a state, or whether a rear admiral or a justice of a state court should be seated "higher" at the table, or where to seat the archbishop of X and the duke of Y.

In Washington, even though the dinner is given for a guest of medium rank, those present of highest rank have the honor places on either side of the host or hostess. The person for whom the dinner is actually given is merely "among those present," unless those of higher rank agree to waive precedence. When Mrs. Frances Perkins was Secretary of Labor, during Franklin Roosevelt's administration, she waived her rank and said always to seat her wherever was most convenient.

The hostess who plans to entertain several government officials, military officers, or foreign diplomats must naturally try to arrange her seating without slighting any of her guests.

In an American house, the ranking foreigner should insofar as possible be given precedence.

In a foreign embassy in Washington, the ranking American is given precedence. The President of the United States takes precedence over the representative of the country that is receiving him. In the President's absence the Vice-President, the Chief Justice, or the Secretary of State—whoever represents the United States—outranks all foreign ambassadors. In the diplomatic service, the highest-ranking ambassador is the one who has been longest in residence in Washington—not longest in the service of his country.

Wives of officials, whether their husbands are present or not, assume their husband's rank. Widows are merely given a courtesy position. Exceptions are wives and widows of former Presidents, who do have a definite ranking in precedence.

As the protocol staff of the Department of State explains,

"The White House and the Department of State prescribe the protocol to be used only for ceremonies of state. The protocol differs somewhat for each ceremony and the rules used are not considered as binding at private functions. For this reason it is the policy of the White House not to make the rules public or to give out the order of precedence of Government officials."

Therefore the following list must be understood to be an *unofficial* order of rank among those in government service.

The President of the United States
The Vice-President of the United States
The Speaker of the House of Representatives
The Chief Justice of the United States
Former Presidents of the United States
The Secretary of State
Ambassadors of Foreign Powers
Widows of Former Presidents of the United States
The Secretary-General of the United Nations
United States Representative to the United Nations
Ministers of Foreign Powers (chiefs of diplomatic missions)

Associate Justices of the Supreme Court of the United States and Retired Associate Justices
The Secretary of the Treasury
The Secretary of Defense
The Attorney General
The Secretary of the Interior
The Secretary of Agriculture
The Secretary of Commerce
The Secretary of Labor
The Secretary of Health, Education, and Welfare
The Secretary of Housing and Urban Development
The Secretary of Transportation
Senators
Governors of States
Acting Heads of Executive Departments (in the absence of the Cabinet member)
Former Vice-Presidents of the United States
Members of the House of Representatives
Under Secretaries of State
Administrator, Agency for International Development
Director, United States Arms Control and Disarmament Agency
Chargé d'Affaires of Foreign Powers
Secretaries of the Army, the Navy, and the Air Force (ranked according to date of appointment)
Director, Bureau of the Budget
Chairman, Council of Economic Advisers
Chairman, Board of Governors, Federal Reserve
Under Secretaries of the Executive Department and Deputy Secretaries
Chairman, Joint Chiefs of Staff
Chiefs of Staff of the Army, the Navy, and the Air Force (ranked according to date of appointment)
Commandant of the Marine Corps
Five-Star Generals of the Army and Fleet Admirals
The Secretary-General, Organization of American States
Representatives to the Organization of American States
Director, Central Intelligence Agency
Administrator, General Services Administration
Director, United States Information Agency
Administrator, National Aeronautics and Space Administration
Chairman, the Atomic Energy Commission
Director, Defense Research and Engineering

Director, Office of Emergency Planning
Administrator, Federal Aviation Agency
Chairman, Civil Service Commission
Director, the Peace Corps
Special Assistants to the President
Deputy Under Secretaries of the Executive Departments
Assistant Secretaries of the Executive Departments
United States Chief of Protocol
Members of the Council of Economic Advisers
Active or Designate United States Ambassadors and Ministers
(career rank, when in the United States)
Under Secretaries of the Army, the Navy, and the Air Force
(ranked according to date of appointment)
Four-Star Generals and Admirals
Assistant Secretaries of the Army, the Navy, and the Air Force
(ranked according to date of appointment)
Lieutenant Generals and Vice Admirals (Three-Star)
Ministers of Foreign Powers (serving in embassies, not accredited)
Deputy Assistant Secretaries of the Executive Departments
Counselors of Embassies or Legations of Foreign Powers
*Major Generals and Rear Admirals (Two-Star)
Brigadier Generals (One-Star)
Assistant Chiefs of Protocol
The Secretary of the Senate

OFFICIAL TITLES

Just as there is a certain order of precedence in official circles, so are there specific forms of address that must be used. The following rules apply whenever the official is spoken to "in public."

Members of the Cabinet are usually addressed as "Mr. Secretary," but if several are present, they are addressed as "Mr. Secretary of State," "Mr. Secretary of Commerce." Ambassadors are called "Mr. Ambassador" officially rather than "Ambassador Kellogg." The Chief Justice is "Mr. Chief Justice"; another member of the Supreme Court is "Mr. Justice Lawton."

---

* The rank of rear admiral is divided into two categories: the "upper half" and the "lower half." Those of the upper half are equivalent to two-star major generals. Those of the lower half are equivalent to one-star brigadier generals, and may even be, depending on date of rank, outranked by a brigadier general.

The Chief Executive and Vice-President are always spoken to without the surname: "I appreciate the honor, Mr. President," or "Thank you, Mr. Vice-President." However, if the conversation is prolonged, they, and all the other officials mentioned, may be addressed as "Sir."

It is improper to call a governor "Mr." He is, in public, "The Governor" or, to his face, "Governor Jones," and less formally he may be addressed as "Governor," without the surname.

Captains, commanders, and all those of higher military rank are usually addressed by title and surname: "Colonel Johnson," "Admiral Boggs," etc. However, it is not objectionable to use the title only —especially when the occasion is not particularly formal.

TITLES ON PLACE CARDS

Place cards present another problem, for at official functions some carry only the title whereas others have title and surname. The following appear without names on all formal occasions:

The President
The Vice-President
The Archbishop of . . .
The Ambassador of . . .
The Minister of . . .
The Chief Justice
The Speaker
The Secretary of . . . or The Attorney General

So, too, at public dinners place cards are inscribed "His Excellency, the Archbishop of New York," "His Honor, the Mayor of Chicago," etc. "The Assistant Secretary of the Navy" is never used alone, however, because there is more than one assistant secretary in all executive departments. The same is true in the case of the following and similar titles:

Mr. Justice Fox
Senator Essex
Governor Lansing
Rev. Father Stole
Dr. Sanford

At a private dinner, when the title alone sounds overly stiff and formal, the hostess may modify the official form (except in the cases of the President and Vice-President) by adding the surname: "Ambassador Santorino," "Chief Justice Howard," "Secretary Knowles." For other notables she uses the names by which she would address

141

them in speaking: "Governor Street, will you sit here?" "Father Gaines, I'd like you to meet. . . ." Everyone else appears as "Mr.," "Mrs.," or "Miss." Remember that the object of a place card is two-fold: to show the owner of the name (or title) where he is to sit and to give his neighbors at the table a clue about how to address him.

·13· *An Invitation to the White House*

An invitation to lunch or dinner at the White House is somewhat of a command and automatically cancels almost any other engagement that is not of the utmost importance. The reply must be written by hand within a day of the invitation's arrival. If the recipient is not near Washington, his reply should be telegraphed or sent special delivery. There are very few acceptable excuses for refusing an invitation to the White House, and the reason must be stated in the note of regret. Unavoidable absence from Washington, the recent death of a close relative, or actual illness used to be the only possible excuses. Today "a wedding in the family" or "a vacation trip" reflects a less rigid attitude.

The correct forms for replies are:

Mr. and Mrs. Richard Worldly
accept with pleasure
the kind invitation of
The President and Mrs. Washington
for dinner on Thursday, the eighth of May
at eight o'clock

Mr. and Mrs. Robert Franklin
regret extremely
that owing to Mr. Franklin's illness
they will be unable to accept
the kind invitation of
The President and Mrs. Washington
for dinner on Friday, the first of May

The note to a hostess whose invitation they must refuse reads:

Mr. and Mrs. Richard Worldly
regret extremely
that an invitation to the White House
prevents their keeping
their engagement for dinner
Tuesday, the first of December

INFORMAL INVITATIONS

Informal invitations to dinner or luncheon at the White House are now used more frequently than formerly. They may be sent by letter or telegram, or may be extended by telephone by the President's secretary or his wife's secretary. The replies should be sent in the same form to whoever issued the invitations. Written acceptances (or regrets, when the reasons are valid) are sent on personal stationery, either engraved or plain.

A typical invitation might be worded something like this:

Dear Mrs. Heathcote,
Mrs. Washington has asked me to invite you to have lunch with her at the White House on Thursday, the sixteenth of May. Luncheon will be at one o'clock.

> *Yours truly,*
> *Eleanor Smithers*
> *Secretary to Mrs. Washington*

The reply might read:

Dear Miss Smithers,
Will you please thank Mrs. Washington for her kind invitation and tell her that I shall be delighted to lunch with her at the White House on Thursday, the sixteenth of May. Thank you very much.

> *Sincerely,*
> *Frances Heathcote*

DRESS FOR A LUNCHEON

To the luncheon Mrs. Heathcote wears a dress that she might wear to any similar gathering. Hats and gloves are not required for a luncheon or afternoon reception, although many women do wear either one or both.

DINNER AT THE WHITE HOUSE

An engraved invitation to the White House means black tie unless white tie is specified on the invitation. Women wear evening dresses, not pants, and if it is a white-tie dinner they wear long gloves.

All the names of guests expected at the White House are posted with the guards at the gate. You announce your name and wait a few seconds until you are recognized.

After the guests arrive, the President and his wife enter and speak to each guest and shake hands. Guests, of course, remain standing.

At a formal dinner the President goes into the dining room first with the highest-ranking woman guest. His wife follows with the highest-ranking man.

DETAILS OF WHITE HOUSE ETIQUETTE

Although customs vary somewhat during different administrations, the following details represent the conventional pattern from which each administration adapts its own procedure.

When you are invited to the White House you must arrive several minutes, at least, before the hour specified. It is an unpardonable breach of etiquette not to be standing in the drawing room when the President makes his entry.

The President, followed by his wife, enters at the hour set, and if the group is not too large, makes a tour of the room, shaking hands with each guest. If the occasion is a big reception the President and his wife stand in one place and the guests form a line and pass by to be greeted. In this case an aide serves as announcer. Gentlemen of rank precede their wives, and they are greeted first by the President and then by his wife. If a woman is wearing gloves she *removes* the right one before shaking hands with the President. If the President talks to you, you address him as "Mr. President." In a long conversation it is proper to vary "Mr. President" with "Sir" occasionally. You call the wife of the President "Mrs. Washington" and treat her as you would any formal hostess. You do not sit down so long as either the President or his wife remains standing. No guest, of course, ever leaves until after the President has withdrawn from the room, but the guests then bid each other good night and leave promptly.

Requests to see the President on a business matter should be made through one of the presidential aides—the one whose area of responsibility includes the subject you wish to discuss—or through your congressman. Your reason should be a valid one, you should be sure that no one else can solve your problem, and your letter should be stated in such a way that, if possible, the matter can be settled without a personal interview.

If you have a business appointment with the President, it is most important, again, that you arrive a few minutes ahead of the appointed time. No doubt you will be told how much time you are allowed. Make your call brief and, if possible, take less time than that allotted.

If a buzzer should ring when you are in a corridor of the White House, an attendant will ask you to step behind a closed door. The buzzer means that the President or members of his family are leaving or entering. This precaution is for their safety and their privacy.

Don't smoke unless you are invited to.

Gentlemen always remove their hats as they reach the White House portico.

GIFTS TO THE PRESIDENT

Not only should you avoid taking a present to the President unless it has been cleared with an aide, but you should not *send* anything to the White House without receiving permission from his secretary or one of his aides. You may have had a successful hunting trip and wish to send the President a brace of pheasants. The gift must be cleared with the proper authority; otherwise he will never see or taste it.

Furthermore, the President cannot accept personal gifts worth more than twenty-five dollars, and there is a strict rule against the gift of an animal. The only exception is a gift from a foreign country or ruler—for example, the pandas sent to Washington from China, following President Richard Nixon's visit there in 1972.

‹§14›‹ The Flag and the National Anthem

There are certain rules and customs connected with our flag that all of us should know and follow to show our respect for our country and our patriotism.

It is proper to fly the flag every day in the year between sunrise and sunset, although customarily it is not flown in inclement weather unless there is a particular occasion that requires its display. It may also be displayed at night as part of a patriotic display.

On Memorial Day, May 30 (or whatever day it is legally observed), the flag is displayed at half staff until noon and at full staff thereafter until sunset. Flag Day is June 14—the day when we especially celebrate this emblem by displaying the flag. Many of us display the flag on other national holidays too.

There are certain clear-cut situations in which the flag should never be used—for example, as decoration on a portion of a costume or athletic uniform, as embroidery on cushions, scarves, handkerchiefs, or applied to paper napkins or boxes. Of course it should never be used as a covering for articles on a speaker's table, or so placed that objects may be put on or over it. When a statue or monument is unveiled, the flag should never be used as a covering for the object to be displayed. It is unlawful to use the flag in a registered trademark that comprises "the flag, coat of arms, or other insignia of the United States or any simulation thereof." Some of these rules have been relaxed, and if you are in doubt you may write to the United States Flag Foundation, 115 East Eighty-sixth Street, New York, New York 10028. It goes without saying that the national emblem is never displayed in connection with advertising of any kind. When festoons, rosettes, or other draperies are desired, bunting of blue (uppermost), white, and red should be used, but never the flag itself.

DISPLAYING THE FLAG

When displayed over the middle of a street, the flag should be suspended vertically with the union (the blue field) to the north in an east-west street, or to the east in a north-south street.

When displayed with another flag from crossed staffs, the flag of the United States should be on the right (the flag's own right), and its staff should be in front of the staff of the other flag.

The flag should be raised briskly and lowered slowly and solemnly.

When flown at half-mast, the flag should be hoisted to the peak for a moment and then lowered to the half-mast position. And the flag should again be raised to the peak before being lowered for the day.

When flags of states or cities or pennants of societies are flown on the same halyard with the flag of the United States, the latter should always be at the peak. When flown from adjacent staffs, the national flag should be hoisted first and lowered last.

When the flag is suspended over a sidewalk from a rope extending from house to pole at the edge of the sidewalk, the flag should be hoisted union first.

When the flag is displayed from a staff projecting horizontally or at an angle from a window sill, balcony, or the front of a building, the union of the flag should go all the way to the peak of the staff (except when at half-mast).

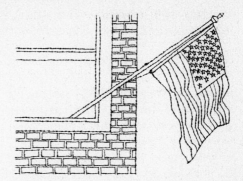

On a power boat the flag is flown from 8:00 A.M. until sunset. It flies from a staff at the stern when the boat is anchored, or if the boat has a gaff, may be flown from the gaff when under way.

The flag is flown from the stern of a sailboat in the harbor or under power, but is taken down while the boat is under sail.

When used to cover a casket the flag should be placed so that the union is at the head and over the left shoulder. The flag should not be lowered into the grave or allowed to touch the ground.

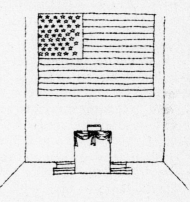

When the flag is displayed in a manner other than flown from a staff, it should be flat, not tucked or draped, whether indoors or out. When displayed vertically against a wall, the union should be uppermost and to the observer's left. When displayed in a window it should be displayed in the same way, with the union to the left of the observer in the street.

When carried in a procession with another flag or flags, either the American flag should be on the marching right, or when there is a line of other flags, it may be in front of the center of that line.

When a number of flags of states or cities are grouped and displayed from staffs, our national flag should be at the center or at the highest point of the group. If the flags of two or more nations are displayed, they should be flown from separate staffs of the same height, and the flags should be of approximately equal size. International usage forbids the display of the flag of one nation above that of another nation in time of peace.

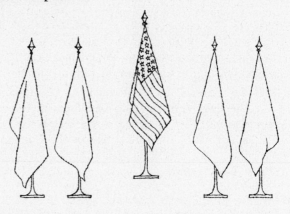

When the flag is used in a church—on the chancel or on a platform—it should be placed on a staff on the clergyman's right; other flags are on his left. When displayed in the body of the church, the flag should be on the congregation's right as it faces the chancel.

As an identifying symbol on an automobile the flag is flown on a small staff affixed to the end of the front bumper, on the right looking forward and within the line of the fender. When used this way, the staff should be tall enough so that the flag clears the car hood. Alternately, a small flag may be flown from the radiator cap. If the flag has become soiled or torn, it should be promptly removed and replaced.

The flag should *never* be hung upside down except as a signal of distress.

CARE OF THE FLAG

The flag of our country should be carefully protected in storage and in use so that it will not be damaged. Every precaution should be taken to prevent it from becoming soiled or torn. It should not be permitted to touch the ground, or water, or a floor. In handling the flag do not let it brush against other objects.

If it should get wet it should be hung smoothly until dry—never rolled or folded while still damp.

Flags should be dry-cleaned, not washed.

SALUTING THE FLAG

Whenever the flag passes by, as in a parade, men and women pay it their respects. Women stand quietly with hands at their sides, or they may place their right hands over their hearts if they wish. Men remove their hats and hold them, in their right hands, over their hearts. Men and women in the armed forces give the military salute as the flag passes.

When the salute to the flag is spoken at a public dinner or in church, men and women both stand quietly at attention while they repeat it or listen to the person giving the salute.

THE NATIONAL ANTHEM

Everyone, even very young children, should rise and remain standing during the playing of the "Star-Spangled Banner." It is not easy to sing, and you need not do so if you do not have the necessary range or "ear," but you must stand quietly until you hear "O'er the land of the free, and the home of the brave."

If you are on the way to your seat at a sports event, or in any public place, when the strain, "Oh say, can you see, by the dawn's early light," sounds, stop where you are and stand at attention until the end. Don't talk, chew gum loudly, eat, or smoke during the rendition.

At home, in private, when it is played on television or radio, it is *not* necessary to rise. But if at a large private party the orchestra plays the anthem at the start of the dancing, the guests *do* rise and show their respect.

The anthem is never played as dance music, nor are improvisations permissible.

When the anthem of a foreign country is played officially—as, for instance, in honor of a visiting team of athletes—everyone rises and stands at attention, and men remove their hats but they do not salute.

RULES FOR ALIENS

When the "Star-Spangled Banner" is played, aliens as well as American citizens stand. It is up to them whether they sing or not.

When the pledge of allegiance to the flag is said, aliens stand, but they do not repeat the words.

Aliens may display the flag of their own country on its national holidays. Out of courtesy, they may display the American flag also.

On *our* national holidays an alien should display the American flag or none—not his own.

When an alien attends a parade or other patriotic event he stands respectfully while the flag passes by, but he need not salute in any way.

Part Four

AS OTHERS
SEE YOU

~§ 15 ?~ *The Social Amenities*

Would you know the secret of popularity? It is unconsciousness of self, altruistic interest, and inward kindliness, outwardly expressed in good manners.

Good manners socially are not unlike swimming—not the "crawl" or "overhand," but smooth, tranquil swimming. (Quite probably where the expression "in the swim" came from anyway!)—Emily Post, 1922

The cardinal principle of etiquette is thoughtfulness. This implies a concern for the effect of your actions on those around you. Attracting attention to yourself, because it is usually objectionable to others, is contrary to that basic principle.

Many of the specific suggestions that appear in this and the following chapters are simply applications of this all-important rule. Just by keeping this one injunction in mind, you can save yourself and others embarrassment in many situations.

Young girls (and some boys), especially those with the figure for it, love to wear the wildest, most eye-catching clothes they can find. And on them the latest fashion in the fashion magazines generally looks sensational—and appropriate. But the vast majority of women, either because of their age or because of their shape, look far better in more conservative costumes. So unless you are under twenty-five and have a gorgeous figure don't wear conspicuous clothes.

Don't stare at people or bump into them deliberately or point at them. Whether on the street or in a building, don't talk at the top of your lungs. Avoid making personal remarks that may attract attention. And finally, never broadcast your private affairs, feelings, or innermost thoughts in public.

WALKING ON THE STREET

Years ago it was considered necessary for a man walking with a lady to stay between her and the street to protect her from runaway or obstreperous horses. The most dangerous thing he might protect her from today would be the splash of a passing automobile going through a mud puddle. In fact, my daughter, when she was living in New York, said that most of her dates felt they should walk on the inside to protect her from muggers or purse-snatchers who lurked in the doorways. This is an excellent example of *why* rules of etiquette change, although it is, at the same time, a sad commentary. While the old rule is no longer a necessity most women feel more feminine and "cared for" when their escorts follow the established pattern. A man need not hop back and forth each time they cross the street, but when they are continuing in the same relative position for some time, he should walk on the outside. Otherwise, if he prefers to ignore the curbside rule entirely, he should always walk on the lady's left.

A man should not sandwich himself between two ladies when walking or sitting with them. From one side he can look in the direction of both while talking with either one; whereas when he is between them he must turn away from one when he talks to the other. In addition, if the women happen to be intimate friends they may have a tendency to talk "across" him, forcing him to turn back and forth as if he were at a tennis match.

There is, however, an exception to this rule. When a bachelor is walking with two single girls it might cause considerable consternation if he chose to walk beside one, leaving the other on the far side. Therefore, in this situation, in spite of the disadvantages, it would be better if he walked between the girls.

Today a man rarely offers his arm to a woman in the daytime unless she is old and infirm. At night when going down steps or a slope, she is wise to accept his arm, not only because it is a courtesy, but because flimsy shoes can be difficult to manage when it is too dark for a woman to see clearly where she is walking.

A gentleman also offers his arm to a lady when he takes her in at a formal dinner or when he is an usher at a wedding. Otherwise couples walk side by side rather than hand on arm.

A gentleman does not grab a lady by the arm or the elbow and shove her along. It is only when he is helping her into a car, a taxi, or a bus, or up steep stairs that he should put his hand under her elbow. A man may also take a woman's hand and precede her through a crowd to make way for her.

AS FOR THE MANNERS OF PEDESTRIANS . . .

When anyone is run over by an automobile the driver's guilt is *invariably* taken for granted. Often the blame belongs to him, but often it does not. In other words good "pedestrian" manners are every bit as important to people who want to escape being injured as to people who want to avoid injuring them. When you are a pedestrian:

Don't cross before the light turns green or the signal reads WALK. Don't cross streets in the middle of a block. Don't dart forward after hiding behind a parked car and imagine that an oncoming driver, whom you yourself could not see, could know by means of clairvoyance that you were there. Don't, when the lights change while you are in the middle of the street, turn and run back to the side you started from. If you keep on going exactly as you were, drivers will automatically wait and give you time to pass in front of their cars. But those you have already passed cannot possibly be prepared to have you about-face and suddenly dash back again in front of the wheels.

One of the serious causes of pedestrian accidents is the practically universal (and very natural) habit of walking on the right side of a road that has no sidewalk. A pedestrian on the right side cannot see a car overtaking him. If another car is coming from the other direction, the pedestrian cannot even hear the car coming from behind him. Pedestrians should walk on the left-hand side of the road—always.

LADIES—OR GENTLEMEN—FIRST

In all ordinary circumstances, indoors or out, when a couple walks together, the woman precedes the man. But over rough ground he goes first and offers his hand if she needs assistance. He steps ahead of her to open a car door for her when she enters it, and he gets out first and holds the door for her when they arrive, unless she doesn't want to wait. He precedes her down a steep or slippery stairway. However, he follows her up *or* down an escalator, unless she asks him to go first to help her on or off. Although the idea of protecting her is quite out of key with, and in some cases, repugnant to, the capable woman of today, he should make the gesture of stepping into a boat first or off the bus first, for example, to be ready to help her. Femininity is still more attractive in a woman than masculine capability and in no way denies the fact that her helplessness is a thing of the past.

ON GOING THROUGH DOORS

A man should always stand aside and allow a woman to pass through an open door ahead of him. When approaching a closed, heavy door, however, it is far more practical and simpler if he pushes the door open, goes through, and holds the door while she follows. If the door opens toward them he pulls it open and allows her to go through first.

A woman steps into a revolving door ahead of a man if it is already moving, or if there is a partition in such a position that he can push it to start the door turning. Otherwise he steps in first and gets the door moving slowly so that she may step in the section behind him.

Any courteous person—man or woman—holds a door open for the person following him, unless that person is some distance behind. It is extremely rude (but unfortunately very common) to let a door slam shut in someone's face.

LADIES ON THE RIGHT

Years ago there was a rule of great importance: A lady was never seated on a gentleman's left, because according to the etiquette of the day a woman "on the left" was *not* a "lady." But today in America all that remains of this rule is that, when equally practical, it is always more polite that a gentleman seat a lady on his right. (The few surviving rules about placing a lady on the gentleman's right include the seating of a guest of honor on the right of the host or hostess or chairman, the rule that the bride walk up the aisle on her father's right and that she be seated on the bridegroom's right at all wedding festivities, and the military rule that the senior officer walk as well as sit on his junior's right.)

SEATING ON PUBLIC CONVEYANCES

Today, with women demanding equal rights in every field, men cannot be expected to treat them as the delicate petals they were supposed to be many years ago. A man who has worked all day is just as tired as the women next to him on the bus. If he has been fortunate enough to find a seat and the woman standing in front of him does not appear to be elderly, infirm, pregnant, or burdened with a baby or a heavy armful of any sort, he need not offer her his place. Of course he may do so if he wishes, and she may accept his offer or not as she wishes.

Young people, however, should be taught to offer their seats to older people, both men and women. Youngsters are stronger, they have not generally worked as hard, and furthermore, it is a gesture of courtesy and respect. A youngster traveling with his or her mother or father should offer his parent the empty seat, and it is up to the latter to accept if he wants to, or perhaps they may take turns.

A mother traveling with a very young child should keep him on her lap—not taking up a space he does not really need. Most cities do not charge fares to children under a certain age, and a good slogan, used for some time in New York buses, was:

> *Little enough to ride for free,*
> *Little enough to ride your knee.*

ELEVATOR ETIQUETTE

In a crowded elevator, such as those in department stores or office buildings, a man does not remove his hat, whether there are women passengers or not. It would take up far more room in his hand than on his head, and the hat could also be squashed if the crowd were particularly dense.

If the passengers nearest the door are men they get off immediately when the elevator stops. They do not try to step to the side to let women off. If one of the women is with a man but is standing further back, he gets off and waits for her outside the elevator.

In apartment houses, or private homes, a man does remove his hat when a woman gets on the elevator, and he lets her go out the door first, just as he would in any room in a house.

UMBRELLAS

When a man and woman are walking together, he generally holds the umbrella, if they have only one, since he is presumably taller. If there is a great difference in their heights the woman should carry an umbrella of her own, because one held far above her head will not keep her dry. Both men and women should be very careful not to poke other pedestrians with the umbrella point. Never walk with an umbrella held so that you cannot see ahead. The new plastic umbrellas and bubbles for women are excellent for this reason. When the umbrella is closed it should be held over the arm by the crook or strap so that it hangs close to one's side, rather than crosswise or with the point protruding in any way.

CHEWING GUM

It is hard to understand why so many otherwise attractive people totally destroy their appearance by chewing gum like a cow chewing a cud. There are people who chew it for therapeutic reasons as well as because they like the taste, and others just chew because it's a habit. Chewing gum, in itself, if it is done quietly and unobtrusively, is not unattractive. But when one does it with grimaces, open mouth, smacks, crackles, and pops, and worst of all with bubbles, it is in the worst of taste.

It should be unnecessary to remind people not to dispose of gum where anyone can possibly sit on it, step on it, or touch it. But is there anyone who has not been a victim of this thoughtlessness? When you are through with your gum, wrap it in any scrap of paper and throw it in a trash can. If no trash basket is available keep the gum, wrapped, in your pocket or handbag, until you find an appropriate receptacle.

POSTURE

There is no doubt that a person—man or woman—who stands and sits erect shows himself off to his best advantage. A round-shouldered slouch, with head thrust forward and stomach sticking out, certainly does little to make one appealing. Victorian parents used to insist that children sit up straight, and even the youngsters who hated that admonition grew up to appreciate it. Today it is common to see youngsters sprawling, slouching, and in all manner of contortions, with no one saying a word about it. But it *is* worth fussing about, and your children will eventually thank you if you encourage them to "Stand up!"

Men have less problem in sitting properly than women, because wearing trousers allows more latitude. As long as they do not slump way down in their seats, wrap their legs into pretzels, or thump or jerk nervously, they may sit pretty much as they please, with both feet on the floor, or one leg crossed over the other above the knee.

A woman has more trouble. If she is wearing a short skirt she is hard put to cross her legs without sacrificing her modesty. Crossing one knee over the other also tends to make the calf bulge unattractively. Years ago when chairs were firmer and more upright she could sit up straight easily enough using the back for support, but today overstuffed chairs are so deep and modern chairs so low-slung that most women cannot sit in, or get in or out of them, gracefully. Unless a woman is unusually tall her legs are not long enough to reach the floor comfortably, and she must tuck them up under her—at best an awkward maneuver. When a woman is seated in a chair of reasonably upright design, such as a dining-room chair, she should sit with her knees together, crossing the feet at the ankles if she wishes. When she has no choice but to sit in a deep easy chair, she should sit down somewhat sideways with a hand on the arm, rather than dropping into it like a rock. Then she may cross her legs or not, as she wishes, only remembering to pull her skirt down and keep her knees together if she wishes to retain her modesty.

Getting into a car—especially a taxi—is also awkward in a short skirt. The most graceful approach, rather than leaning over and half-crawling in, is to put one foot in, slide in sideways and sit down, then pull the other foot in. To get out, put both feet out and then edge forward and stand up.

DISPLAYING AFFECTION IN PUBLIC

Lovemaking is a personal matter and should take place in private. Public displays of physical attraction are embarrassing to the observer and are therefore in poor taste. Ardent embraces, passionate kisses, etc. (in spite of the current race to portray sex in all forms in movies, theaters, and literature), can only be as meaningful as they should when they do not become public property.

This, however, has little to do with the casual, affectionate kiss or hug with which we greet an old friend, or with a couple strolling companionably hand in hand. Men and women, married or unmarried, who are no more than good friends frequently greet each other with a brief kiss—not on the lips—and it is in no way offensive. Women, too, greet each other with a token kiss, or more likely a mere touch of the cheeks, but this seems to me rather forced, unless they are truly close friends or relatives who have not seen each other for some time. These gestures (which would have horrified the dignified ladies of the Victorian days), as long as they are brief and do not become in any way "sexy," are perfectly acceptable, and indicative of the informal and friendly relationships of today.

The best way to foil someone you know is a compulsive kisser is to hold out your hand quickly when you meet and use the hand-clasp to hold her (or him) off. She may try to pull you toward her, but hold your ground, because if you are overpowered, there is no remedy but to turn a "cold cheek."

THE QUESTION OF PAYING

It is much less customary than it used to be for a man to offer to pay a woman's way, especially if they happen to meet by chance. For example, if a woman and a man find themselves taking the same train and she stops at the newsstand to buy magazines, the man may start to pay for them. If she knows him very well and the total is small she perhaps lets him. But if he is someone she knows slightly or if she has bought several of the higher-priced ones, she says, "Don't bother. I have it!" and puts the money on the counter. It would be awkward for him to protest and bad taste to press the point. In this case, too, she buys her own ticket. On the other hand, if she has gone anyplace *on his invitation* he of course pays for everything.

A group of people going on an excursion or dining together in a restaurant should agree beforehand on the handling of the finances. "Going Dutch" (each couple or individual paying his own way) is more often done than not. To avoid the confusion of dividing and then paying the bill, it is far better for one man (or woman, but only when it is a women's group) to pay the entire bill and the others to pay him their shares later. *See Chapter 16.*

LIFE IN CROWDED CITIES

Consideration of others is essential for dwellers in city apart-ments so closely packed that every sound made by one family can be heard by several others. In fact sound seems sometimes to be intensified by the walls between. Children's play may not seem over-loud when you are in the same room with them, nor does the radio or television set when we are engrossed in the program. But to the family living on the floor below, the patter of little feet sounds like a stableful of Percherons. The disk jockey crashes through each sepa-rate convolution of a tired neighbor's brain. As for a musician's practicing—what manager of an apartment house has not been at his wits' end to solve this cause of complaint?

There are certain annoyances that can't be helped: Babies must sometimes cry, children scream, dogs bark, or someone get a hacking cough. The best that considerate people can do is try to soften such sounds as much as possible by shutting a window temporarily and by trying to train both children and dogs.

In nearly all apartment buildings there are always those who seem to have no feelings for others because their own sensitivity is on another wavelength. We must keep in mind that there can be sounds that greatly annoy some people—the unceasing sound of a television set, for example, or a record player—but that do not disturb others at all, whereas some of the things that we don't mind can quite possibly be unbearable to our neighbors. Only by being aware of this, and doing our best to minimize these irritations, can we make apartment living bearable.

PUBLIC CLEANLINESS

The subject is not a pleasant one, but no one can be unaware of the increasing messiness (at times actual filthiness) of the lounges and powder and dressing rooms of hotels, theaters, and movie houses. As for such places as waiting rooms in railroad terminals and rest rooms in overcrowded department stores or sports stadiums, the problem is becoming overwhelming!

Discarders of food containers and newspapers have always been conspicuous offenders, and the gum-scatterers have ranked with the graffiti artists in doing permanent damage. But in former years their destructiveness was held in check by employees whose present scarcity makes the orderliness of these places the responsibility of the public—in other words, each one of us.

In writing this, there are certain persons to whom I want to make a special appeal. At one extreme there are those who are really untidy. We all know people who throw ashes no matter where, set wet tumblers down on no matter what, drop wet raincoats on the nearest upholstered chair, and burn table edges with forgotten cigarettes. Women shake face powder on whatever is near them and leave hairs in the sink. Their behavior suggests that in their own homes they would not object if their beds were never made! In other words those who live in disorder can hardly be keenly aware of the disorder they make others endure.

In the second group are those who are careless because they take it for granted that someone will come along after them with dustpan and brush. These people, if made to realize there is no one other than themselves to tidy up, would ordinarily be more careful.

If only all of us who care about our surroundings would become sufficiently conscious of our obligation to act as deputy wardens the situation would be improved. In short, instead of refraining from showing criticism of others, it is sometimes our obligation to do what we have been trained not to do—frankly to correct them. For example, when a woman tosses a used paper towel at a receptacle and leaves it lying on the floor when it misses its mark, suggest that she make more effort by picking it up yourself, saying, "Didn't you notice that you missed the basket?" It would help, perhaps, if the signs seen in many rest rooms saying: PLEASE LEAVE THIS REST ROOM AS YOU FOUND IT, read, instead: PLEASE LEAVE THIS REST ROOM CLEANER THAN YOU FOUND IT. But signs seem to do little good. Having an attendant on duty seems to be the greatest help—people apparently take a little more care if they feel they are being watched. This is a sad commentary, but in the case of rest rooms—true!

Familiar and troublesome to all who have the care of public places is the discarding of chewing gum. I was told by a railroad official that the chewing gum ground into the marble floor of a crowded terminal meant hours of scraping that cost the building maintenance department a small fortune.

Perhaps the most flagrant examples of sheer thoughtlessness are the people who carelessly throw all manner of trash into toilets. In washrooms that have no attendants conditions are sometimes so bad that there is no answer other than a locked door. The owner of a department store was forced to hang a large sign on the door to the customers rest room that read: THIS WASHROOM CAN REMAIN OPEN FOR YOUR CONVENIENCE ONLY FOR SO LONG AS YOU COOPERATE IN HELPING TO KEEP IT IN ORDER.

Every city has the same problem in keeping its streets clean. All the campaigns, the special "Keep Our City Clean" weeks, the signs, the trash cans on corners, and the fines imposed for littering fail to solve the problem completely. As in the public washroom it is the duty of each and every one of us to take pride in keeping our cities and towns places of cleanliness and beauty and to impress others with the importance of the problem.

CONSIDERATION FOR THOSE WHO SERVE YOU

Don't forget that a little praise is not only merest justice but is beyond the purse of no one.—Emily Post, 1922

Only the lowest type of boor is rude to or inconsiderate of the people who serve him in restaurants, stores, or any public places. It can safely be said that this sort of discourtesy is a sure sign of insecurity. Those who have self-confidence do not need to act in that way in an effort to prove themselves superior. Good manners and thoughtfulness are so much a part of their nature that they treat everyone they come in contact with, with the same courtesy, whether there is anything to be gained by doing so or not.

ᵉ§16ᵉ~ *In Restaurants*

RESERVATIONS

Reservations are made in a man's name only, even though his wife may be accompanying him. A businessman's secretary, when calling a restaurant for a reservation, says, "I'd like to make a reservation for four for luncheon at twelve thirty—for Mr. William Frost." A wife, or the man himself, makes the reservation in the same way. However, when a single woman is hostess at a luncheon or dinner, even though there are men in the party, she makes the reservation in her own name.

ARRIVING AT A RESTAURANT

CHECKING HATS AND COATS

On entering a restaurant a man leaves his hat, coat, umbrella, and packages in the checkroom near the entrance. A woman may check her coat too, although some checkrooms are so small that the attendants will not accept a woman's coat, and in others they do not want to be responsible for a valuable fur. Generally she wears it until she is seated, then throws the shoulders back over her chair, with her escort's help if necessary. If she is wearing a hat she keeps it on.

BEING SEATED

After the coats have been checked the couple or the group wait at the entrance to the dining room until the headwaiter or hostess comes forward to ask about the number in the group and possibly about preference as to the location of the table. The spokesman for the group greets him by name if he knows him, and otherwise says, "Good afternoon" or "Good evening." If the group has no host (or hostess) one member should assume the responsibility for a host's duties. If many people are involved, an informal kind of decision may be made beforehand: "John, why don't you handle things this noon?"

This avoids the confusion that can arise when several people are addressing the waiter at once, leaving him in doubt about whom to listen to first—a state that never improves the service nor adds to the enjoyment of the meal. The person playing the host's role is only a spokesman, however, and is not expected to shoulder financial or other burdens that are not properly his.

Women generally walk behind the headwaiter, and the men follow them. But if a man is giving a dinner for six or more, the women would have to wait at the table until told by their host where to sit. In this case it causes less confusion if he goes in ahead of his guests. When a husband and wife are hosts the wife seats the guests, usually going first with the most important lady, and the host follows last.

When your group reaches the table the headwaiter pulls out the choice seat first (choice because it faces the room or the view or is out of the stream of traffic). If you are a woman with a man you take it at once, unless for some reason you prefer another seat. In this case you stand beside the other chair saying, "I'd rather sit here if I may." A woman who has another lady as her guest offers her the best seat, but if the hostess is a much older person the young guest should refuse, saying, "Oh no, Mrs. Cole, won't you sit on the banquette?"

If you do not like the table that has been offered to you, you may always say, "We would prefer a table with a banquette if there is one free," or "Could we sit a little farther from the door, please?" Any good headwaiter will try to accommodate you, but if he says, "I'm sorry, all the other tables are reserved," don't argue. Just say, "All right then, this will be fine," if you wish to stay, or "Thanks, but I think we'll try another restaurant that isn't so crowded," if you don't. In any case, if you really feel that you have been shabbily treated, don't return to that particular restaurant.

Where there is no waiter at hand to seat people the man seats his women guests. If he is with two women he helps first one and then at least make the gesture of helping the second. He should always help a guest before his wife, who by that time should have seated herself.

If there are four in the party and none is married, the ladies seat themselves facing each other. When one married couple takes another to dinner the host and his wife sit opposite each other exactly as they do at home. If, however, neither couple is giving the party they may sit in any fashion they prefer, usually with the women sitting opposite each other. At larger parties the guest of honor (if there is one) is seated at the host's or hostess's right, and the others alternate, men and women, around the table. Ordinarily men do not sit next to their wives.

When two men and a woman dine together she is seated between them, as is one man dining with two women. If a married couple is accompanied by a single woman she is seated on the man's right.

In a restaurant that has continuous sofa seats or banquettes along its walls the seating is necessarily somewhat different. When the room is spacious two people dining together are seated side by side against the wall, and the table, which is two places wide, is pushed in front of them. If there are two couples the women are seated on the banquette and the men face them across the table.

In a more crowded restaurant two diners who might otherwise be given wall seats side by side are seated opposite each other at a narrower table. The women is seated on the banquette with the man facing her. This inevitably makes if difficult for him to see their waiter, so in this case the woman can help out, either by telling him when she sees the waiter approaching, or by actually signaling to the waiter herself.

In a restaurant with booths the women go in first and sit against the far wall, facing each other across the table. The men then sit next to them on the outside. If a woman and two men are lunching or dining, the woman takes her place first against the wall. If one of the men is related to her, he sits across from her, and the one not related sits beside her. If this grouping is reversed, the two ladies sit next to the wall, and the man who is the husband of one sits beside the other.

WAITING FOR PEOPLE AT A RESTAURANT

Absolutely no lady (unless middle-aged—and even then she would be defying convention) can go to dinner or supper in a restaurant alone with a gentleman.

A very young girl may motor around the country alone with a man, with her father's consent, or sit with him on the rocks by the sea or on a log in the woods; but she must not sit with him in a restaurant. All of which is about as upside down as it can very well be.—Emily Post, 1922

When a group of women arrive separately to have lunch at a restaurant, the first arrival should wait for the second rather than go in and sit by herself. When two have arrived, unless they are early, they should ask to be seated, explaining to the headwaiter that others are joining them and asking him to see they are promptly directed to the table. This avoids overcrowding the entry and sometimes is the only way of holding a reservation.

When a girl is meeting a man at a restaurant and arrives first, she may do one of several things. If she knows he has made a reservation she may say to the headwaiter, "I believe Mr. Rodgers made a reservation for us. Please show me to the table and tell him I'm here when he arrives." If no reservation has been made, however, it is better for her to wait in the entry for him rather than assume the responsibility of choosing the table. Finally, if it is a nice day, she may prefer to walk down the street, window-shopping for a few moments, and return when she is sure he has arrived. This, however, is really a question of tactics rather than of etiquette.

Ideally a man waits for a woman in the entry, after first making sure she has not been seated. However, many city restaurants have tiny halls or entryways, and if all the people waiting for others stood there, no one could possibly get through. So if the area is crowded, or if there is danger of losing his reservation, a man may ask to be seated—especially if his companion (male or female) is late. He should keep his eye on the door, ready to wave and rise as the other approaches, and he should tell the headwaiter that he is expecting a lady—or a man—and to please be sure that his guest is brought in at once. A woman who does not see her escort when she arrives should go up to the headwaiter and say, "I believe Mr. Scranton has a reservation for two—has he arrived?" She will then be seated or not, as she wishes. The one who is waiting at the table, or at a bar in the entry, may order a cocktail before the other arrives, and may even order for his companion if he knows what he (or she) will want, and that he will arrive very shortly.

COCKTAILS AND WINE

When the diners are all seated, the waiter may ask if anyone would like a cocktail. The host asks the others what, if anything, they would like and gives the order to the waiter, or if there is no host each diner may give his own order.

No one should be urged to drink cocktails once he has refused, but neither should any guest feel uncomfortable because he would like one when his host does not. In fact if the host, or one member of a couple dining together, does not drink, he should say to the other(s), "I don't think I'll have a cocktail, but please do—I'll have a tomato juice while you're having your martini." If there are some guests who say "No" to liquor, the host should suggest that they have a soft drink while the others are having cocktails. It is impolite to order more than one or two cocktails when others are left with nothing in front of them and only the hope of a meal to sustain them.

If desired, wine should be ordered after the choices for the meal have been made, from the wine steward if there is one, or from the waiter, if there is not. The host, or whichever man may be best qualified, should choose a wine that goes well with the greatest number of choices of food. For instance, if more people have ordered chicken or fish, choose a white wine; but if more are having a steak dinner, pick a red. Or a bottle of each may be ordered. There are many people who enjoy a vin rosé, or pink wine, and it is often a happy compromise, as it goes well with almost any menu. Many restaurants also offer wine by the glass, and that is an ideal solution when two people dining together want different wines or they do not want as much as a bottle contains.

If you have a definite preference for red or white wine it is not incorrect to order either with any food. The choices stated above are simply those which, for the majority, result in the most pleasing combination of flavors.

You may choose expensive imported wines if you wish, but there are many excellent domestic wines at a fraction of the cost. Some of the imported wines at lower prices are delicious too, and one should not feel it necessary to spend a great deal to enjoy a good wine with dinner. If you do not recognize the names on the wine list, by all means ask your headwaiter's advice, giving him an idea of the type you prefer, and whether domestic or imported.

ORDERING THE MEAL

WHO GIVES THE ORDER?

For many years the rule was that the woman told the man what she would like and he gave the order—she never so much as spoke to the waiter herself. Presumably, the man was supposed to be the protector of his "shrinking violet," and besides, no woman ever spoke to any strange man. Today this is obviously ridiculous. When one couple is dining in a restaurant it is correct and practical to follow the old rule, but when there are more than two people and the waiter asks each one for his choice, there is every reason for the ladies to give him their orders directly. It is certainly less confusing, and there will be fewer mistakes made, especially if the group is large.

When the waiter looks straight at a woman and asks, "What kind of dressing would you like on your salad?" it is insulting if she turns away and relays her message through her escort. Many waiters ask the woman for her order first in an effort to be polite, and there is no reason why she should not answer directly.

When the man knows the restaurant and its specialties well, and sometimes when foreign food is served with which the woman is not acquainted, he should suggest some choices to her. If they are both unfamiliar with the type of food served he should ask the waiter to recommend one of the specialties of the restaurant.

Unless a woman knows that her host is very well off, she should show some consideration for his pocketbook and avoid ordering the most expensive items on the menu. Neither should she order the cheapest item, implying that she thinks he can't afford more. She should ask for a table d'hôte dinner if one is offered, or choose only a main course, a salad, and a dessert, if it is not. The man may always add more, with her approval, but she should give him the opportunity of economizing. A host who wishes to indicate that he doesn't need to spare expenses may say, "The filet mignon is excellent here—wouldn't you like to try it?"

THE DIFFERENCE BETWEEN TABLE D'HÔTE AND A LA CARTE

Table d'hôte means a set price for a complete meal, irrespective of how many courses are ordered. "Club" breakfasts and lunches, "blue-plate" dinners, or any meals at fixed prices are table d'hôte.

A la carte means that you order from a list of dishes and you pay the price listed beside each dish—even your salad and coffee.

Usually it is very easy to know which is which, because a price follows each item on an a la carte menu. No prices are listed on some table d'hôte bills of fare except at the top where the price for the complete dinner may be printed.

Another type of table d'hôte menu is the one that has a price beside each entrée. This price includes the choice of an hors d'oeuvre or a soup, a salad, and a dessert, and choice of coffee, tea, or milk. If any other items on the menu are followed by a price, there is an additional charge for them.

Very often a separate card or a box inset on the a la carte menu reads, "Special dinner $5.00," or whatever the price may be, and informs you that you can order whatever you choose on this special for five dollars, but that any item taken from the regular bill of fare will be charged for as an extra.

SALADS

Whether salad is ordered specially or comes with the meal it is generally—to my consternation—served before the entrée. I believe that this custom has taken hold because restaurants wished to keep the customer happy while his entrée was being prepared, and people simply became accustomed to it. In private homes salad generally was—and is—served with or after the main course, and as far as I am concerned that is where it belongs.

If you do not wish to eat your salad before your entrée don't ask the waiter to take it back, because this will upset him and you may never see it again. Simply put it to one side, and if you have the willpower, leave it alone. But keep an eagle eye on it! Many a diner has looked away for a moment and looked back to find his salad stolen—by the waiter who thought he didn't want it at all. To forestall this you may say to the waiter, when he brings it, "Please leave my salad here on the side—I'll eat it later."

RESTAURANT TABLE MANNERS

Although table manners are much the same whether you are eating at home or in a restaurant, there are a few special problems that do arise when dining out.

THE APPETIZER KNIFE

Restaurants offering appetizers requiring the use of a knife, such as a crock of cheese, often fail to supply an extra one for this purpose. Use the knife that has been provided for the entrée, leave it on your appetizer plate, and ask for a fresh one when the waiter brings the next course. Do not try to clean your first knife and then lay it on the table between courses.

INDIVIDUAL SIDE DISHES

Many restaurants serve vegetables and potatoes in small individual side dishes, which the waiter places strategically around your dinner plate. You may eat these vegetables directly from the small dishes, or you may (as I prefer to do) put them on your dinner plate by using a serving spoon or sliding them directly out of the small dish. You then ask the waiter to remove the empty dishes, thus avoiding an overcrowded table.

COCKTAIL TRIMMINGS

Olives, cherries, or onions served in cocktails may be eaten. If they are served on a toothpick or cocktail pick, simply remove them from the drink with it and enjoy them. If there is no pick, drink enough of the cocktail so that you will not wet your fingers, and then you can lift out the olive or onion and eat it in your fingers. Slices of oranges in old-fashioneds are not usually eaten as it is too messy to chew the pulp off the rind.

CUTTING BREAD AND POURING COFFEE

When an uncut loaf of bread is placed on the table the host slices or breaks off two or three individual portions and offers them with the rest of the loaf in the breadbasket or on the plate to the people beside him. This is then passed around the table, and each man should cut or break off a portion for himself and the lady next to him.

If coffee or tea is placed on the table without first having been poured by the waiter, the person nearest the pot should offer to pour, filling his own cup last.

ICED-TEA AND ICED-COFFEE SPOONS

If iced tea or coffee has been served in a glass with a saucer under it, the spoon used to stir the drink is placed in this saucer. But when there is no saucer the problem arises as to what to do with the spoon. If paper napkins are available put one on the table next to your glass and then put the spoon on the napkin. If no paper napkins are available the spoon should be placed with the bowl upside down on the edge of your butter plate, or dinner plate if necessary. A used piece of silver should not be put on the table, especially when there is a tablecloth. Some people like to leave the spoon in the glass and hold it back with a finger when they drink but I find this awkward and unattractive.

PAPER CONTAINERS

Many accompaniments to meals in restaurants are served with paper wrappers or in cardboard containers. The question of what to do with, for instance, paper sugar packets, comes up frequently. They should be crumpled up tightly and either tucked under the rim of your place or placed on the edge of the saucer or butter plate. This is preferable to putting them in the ashtray where a lighted cigarette may easily set them on fire.

When jelly or marmalade is served in a paper container it should be taken out with the butter knife (or dinner knife if there is no butter knife) and put on the butter plate. The top is put back in the empty container, which is left on the table beside the butter plate.

171

SUMMONING A WAITER

There is no hard or fixed rule for the best way to summon a waiter. In fact ways that are considered proper in some countries are downright insulting in others. For example a waiter who is hissed, whistled, or clapped at in the United States would probably run in the other direction, and yet those gestures are perfectly correct in certain other nations. The usual way here is to catch his eye and then raise your hand, finger pointing up, as if to say "Attention" or "Listen." If he refuses to look in your direction you may call "Waiter" (or "Waitress") quietly, or if he is too far away to hear you, ask any other waiter nearby, "Please call our waiter." "Miss" is also a correct term for a waitress, but "Sir" is *not* correct for a waiter, whether used by a woman, man, or youngster. Writing this paragraph reminds me of one of my favorite stories—that of the waiter whose tombstone was marked: GOD FINALLY CAUGHT HIS EYE.

PAYING THE CHECK

When everyone has finished his meal the host or spokesman catches the eye of the waiter or headwaiter and says, "The check, please." The check is brought facedown on a small plate and presented to the man who ordered the dinner. He looks at it, checks it quickly for mistakes, and returns it to the plate with the necessary money. When his change is returned to him he leaves the correct amount for the tip on the tray. If he has found an error he beckons the waiter and points it out quietly; the waiter makes the adjustment, either himself or with the help of the headwaiter or cashier. In no circumstances should a "scene" be made.

Many restaurants ask their customers to pay a cashier on the way out. This practice is especially common in large city restaurants and in those which are used mostly at the lunch hour. It is a great timesaver, as very often a waiter, when he has finished serving a table, gives his attention to other customers, and those waiting for their checks find it difficult to attract his attention. When you read at the bottom of your check "Please pay cashier," put the tip on the table, collect your belongings, and leave, with the host following the group, who wait in the entry while he pays the bill. A woman dining with a man accompanies him to the cashier and stands next to him in line, or if it is crowded, waits to one side. If he needs change in order to have the right amount for a tip, he pays the check and quickly returns to the table so that the waiter knows he has not been forgotten.

When a group is small the men wait for the ladies to precede them on leaving the restaurant. With more than six or eight people, however, this becomes unwieldy and each couple goes out together.

CREDIT CARDS

A popular and practical method of paying for restaurant dinners and entertainments is to use a credit card. This is a great convenience for those who dine out or entertain frequently but do not wish to carry large amounts of cash. The card is used as identification at any restaurant or establishment that is a member of the credit organization. All the customer has to do at the time is give the signed check and his card to the waiter for processing, after which he will be asked to sign a special voucher when his card is returned to him. The restaurant sends the voucher in to the credit-card company, which in turn bills the customer at the end of the month. The customer adds the tip to the voucher himself, after making sure that the bill is correct.

"GOING DUTCH"

"Going Dutch" (each person—or couple—paying his own way) is the universally accepted way of paying for a meal enjoyed with friends, except when one couple has actually invited the other to dine, or when a man has invited a girl on a date. Even the latter is often "Dutch treat" if they go out together regularly and have a prior agreement about who pays for what. Were it not for the practice of "going Dutch," most of us would rarely enjoy an evening out with friends.

The very best way of doing this is to ask for separate checks. When you order with two, three, or four couples this causes very little problem. However, in a larger group, separate checks are a nuisance for the waiter, and can become terribly confused. Then, when the man who has acted as host or spokesman (getting the table, ordering, etc.) gets the bill, he asks the other men for a sum large enough to cover their own share of the meal and the tip. If everyone has chosen items that cost more or less the same amount, it is best to ask each for the same amount of money. But if some have only had a soup or a salad, while others dined on steak and lobster, the spokesman should make appropriate allowances.

Men and women who go out together regularly very often share the cost of meals, especially when she is a wage earner and makes as much or more than he does. This is sensible and practical, but a man taking a girl out for the first time, or the first few times, pays

173

the bill. When the girls feels that it is time to suggest that they share and share alike, she should bring it up *before* they get to the restaurant. She should *not,* when the check arrives, say, "Oh, let me pay half." The man asks for the check and pays the full amount. She gives him her share at the time if he needs it, or later if he does not. When a man and woman who customarily share expenses join a group, she should ask him how he wants to handle it. Some men who are willing to accept a girl's assistance when they are alone would hesitate to do so in front of their friends.

WHEN A WOMAN INVITES A MAN

This is rarely a problem among young people who are accustomed to the new relationship between men and women, but it is a matter of concern to men who were brought up to feel that paying a woman's expenses was not only an obligation but a pleasure and privilege.

When a woman invites a man to dine with her for personal rather than business reasons and it is understood that she is paying the bill, there may be some embarrassment at the time the check is presented. The best solution is for the woman to have a credit card, or possibly a charge account at the restaurant. If the man is sensitive about it at all, the act of signing a slip of paper does not somehow seem so objectionable as having the woman check over the bill and count out the money while he sits helplessly by. In fact this situation can be so awkward that many women without charge privileges prefer to give their guest a sum of cash large enough to cover the bill before they enter the restaurant, thus relieving the man of any embarrassment before the waiter. Incidentally this solution also serves for the husband who has left his wallet behind or has insufficient money with him. Rather than have him embarrassed in front of the waiters or his guests, his wife may pass him the necessary sum without calling attention to his situation.

When a woman entertains a customer for her company she signs the check as her firm's representative. If they have not made arrangements for her to sign the check she pays cash, and if her guest protests and tries to pay himself, she explains that he is her company's guest and that the amount of this check is going on her expense account. Or again, if she has a credit card she may use it and present the bill to her employer. When a woman must entertain male clients frequently, she should request—and be given—a company credit card to be used for her business expenses.

WHEN A WOMAN INVITES A MARRIED COUPLE

A woman may invite a married couple to have dinner with her, but when she does she should make it clear that it's her party. She does this by saying when she invites them, "I'd like to *take* you to dinner." If the man offers to pay, as he probably will, she should be firm, saying, "No, this was *my* invitation, and I really want it to be *my* party." She should follow the same procedures described above for the mechanics of paying the bill.

WHEN WOMEN DINE TOGETHER

When several women are dining out together the problem of the check can cause concern to and confusion among the waiters, the nearby diners, and the women themselves. Women who are unaccustomed to paying checks have so much difficulty dividing them fairly that the cartoon of feminine heads clustered around the waiter's tab, captioned, "Now let's see, Ethel, you had the Tomato Surprise," is more truth than fiction. As described above under "Going Dutch," one way to avoid such a scene is to get separate checks. Or one woman may pay the entire check, and the settling up can be done later. If each one's debt must be figured at the table, make sure at least that the best computer in the group gets the chore so that it is done as quietly and simply as possible.

COURTESIES AND DISCOURTESIES

WOMEN APPLYING COSMETICS AT TABLE

At the end of a meal a woman may quickly powder her nose and put on a little lipstick, but to look in a mirror and daub at the face for any length of time is in bad taste.

The one never-to-be-broken rule is: Never use a comb at a restaurant table—or in any public place. Never rearrange or put your hands to your hair in any place where food is served. These rules apply to both men and women.

TASTING ANOTHER'S FOOD

Occasionally a couple—especially a man and wife—will order different dishes, and each wishes to try a taste of the other's. This is permissible if done unobtrusively. Let's suppose Mary wants to try Jim's moussaka. She hands her fork to Jim, who picks up a bit of the moussaka and hands it back to her carefully. She should not reach over and spear it herself, nor should he use his fork to give her the taste, unless he does so before he has used it himself. He could, however, before starting to eat, put a small portion of the moussaka on the edge of her plate.

VISITING AND TABLE-HOPPING

When a group enters a restaurant and sees people whom some know and others do not, they continue directly to their table, nodding "Hello" as they pass. A public restaurant is scarcely the place for mass introductions.

On the other hand, there are occasions when one or two introductions are suitable. All men at a small table rise when a woman is being introduced, as they do whenever a woman stops to talk. When the group is large only those closest to the visitor rise. If a woman stopping at a table is introduced to other women seated there, the latter never rise—even though they be young and the visitor quite old.

All the men at the table do not rise when another man stops on his way by. When someone comes up to speak to one of the diners, that man only should stand to shake hands. The visitor should then ask him please to be seated while he finishes what he has come to say. If he intends to say more than a few words of greeting he might ask a waiter for a chair (although table-hopping of this sort is not in good taste), or better yet, quickly arrange to meet later.

When a man is seated on a banquette and someone—man *or* woman—stops by to say "Hello," he merely nods and extends his hand. He need not rise. If he did he would either get cramps from the crouched position or he would upset the table trying to straighten up!

One husband solved this problem quite effectively. Gustav Gourmet, just about to eat a perfect soufflé, was forced to stand for a friend of his wife who stopped at their table. "Oh *please* sit down! You mustn't let your soufflé fall!" said she. Reluctant to sit down, he solved the problem by lifting the plate and eating—standing.

Let us hope that long-talking standees will take this anecdote to heart and pass the tables of their friends without pausing for too long a time.

TOO MUCH FOOD!

One of the most frequent complaints one hears these days when so many people are weight-conscious is, "Oh but they gave us such huge portions!" Many people are not only offended, but actually made ill, by the sight of an overloaded plate.

Children's eyes are almost invariably bigger than their stomachs, so the wise parent will select his youngster's dinner from the children's menu even though young Johnny insists that he can eat a whole portion of rib roast. Often even the children's portion is too much for a small child. An understanding waiter or waitress will not object to your requesting a separate plate and giving a toddler a small portion of your meat and vegetable. There is no harm in asking, and if the request is greeted with less than enthusiasm, don't insist, but choose the smallest and least expensive item on the menu for a "picky" eater.

Most men *do* eat more than their female companions, and while a man taking a girl out for the first time would not suggest this, a husband might well say to his wife, "Are you going to eat your other chop? If not, may I take it?" He lifts her plate close to his and takes the chop (or any untouched *unit* of food) onto his own, carefully. Although he could exchange the plates after she has finished eating, it is not attractive or sanitary to eat off someone else's plate, and furthermore he would be in the position of keeping his companion waiting while he went on eating.

This brings us to the subject of "doggy bags." Frequently so much food is served that no one can possibly eat it all. Many restaurants recognize this, but feel they must offer enough for the largest, rather than the smallest, appetite. So they offer the customer a plastic bag called a doggy bag to take home the remainder of the steak or chicken or whatever. Originally the idea was that these "scraps" would be given to the dog, but today the scraps are often so delicious and so expensive that they are fit for human—not canine—consumption.

For some years I resisted the temptation to approve these doggy bags—on the theory that while it was all right to ask to take home a bone for the dog, it did seem rather degrading to ask to take home a "bone" for the family. Until suddenly I realized that I had quite happily done just what I had advised others not to do. I was in Alaska where "men are men" and the portions are, to say the least, man-sized. I was served a steak that *three* New Yorkers could never consume at one sitting. Neither I—nor my companions—even thought of saying "No" when the waiter arrived and said, "Here's a bag to take home the meat for tomorrow's sandwiches."

TIPPING *(see also Chapter 67)*

It is difficult to give definite rules for tipping, because it depends upon where you go and the service that is given you. That is, if you

177

patronize luxurious restaurants, or if you have special requirements or are difficult to please, greater "compensation" is expected than if you choose simpler restaurants and receive less service.

WAITERS AND WAITRESSES

Fifteen percent is standard in any restaurant, or possibly 20 percent if you have been very demanding or the service has been unusually good. Ten percent is too little almost anywhere, except perhaps at a lunch counter or self-service restaurant, and never less than fifteen cents should be left anytime at any place.

Patrons who make a practice of tipping waitresses less than waiters are being unfair, because the service rendered is the same.

If you are having a party of ten, twelve, or more, 15 percent would be quite adequate divided among the waiters who serve you, and five dollars would be enough for the headwaiter if he has taken pains to give you extra service. On the other hand, no matter what the number in the party, if he has done nothing beyond seating you and handing you a menu, you give him nothing.

The waiter's tip is always left for him on the tray on which he brings the check. The headwaiter's tip is handed to him as you leave the restaurant.

WINE STEWARD AND BARTENDER

If a wine steward has served you he should receive 12 to 15 percent of the wine bill. He will make himself available to receive it when he sees you getting ready to leave. The bartender receives 15 percent of the bar bill if you have drinks at the bar. It is given to him when he gives you the check, or before you leave the bar.

CHECKROOM AND DRESSING ROOM

The fee to the checkroom attendant who takes care of a man's hat and coat in most restaurants is twenty-five cents—fifty cents in very exclusive ones.

The maid in a ladies' room never receives less than twenty-five cents in any restaurant or hotel and sometimes fifty cents in an expensive one. There is almost always a small plate with a few coins on it in a conspicuous place. If the attendant hands you a towel or performs some other service for you, you are expected to leave a coin of the same denomination as those on the plate—usually a quarter—but if she does nothing but sit and look at you, you need not leave a tip.

APPRECIATION AND COMPLAINTS

For some reason people voice their complaints much more often —and more loudly—than they voice their appreciation. One *should* complain in a restaurant—when the service is bad, when a waiter is rude or careless, or when the food comes in badly prepared or not as ordered. These are legitimate reasons for speaking up, and it is to the restaurant's advantage that you do so. Its livelihood depends on customers' approval, and if its faults are not called to the management's attention they cannot be corrected.

Complaints should be made quietly, without making a fuss or attracting the attention of other diners. They should be made first to the waiter (or person who commits the error), and if he makes no effort to correct the situation, the headwaiter or whoever is in charge of the dining room should be notified. Food that is cold should be taken back to be heated; meat that is not done as you requested should be replaced. Rudeness and laziness should be reported, but laziness should not be confused with pure inability to serve too many people. Often a waiter or waitress, because the tables are poorly allotted, or because another waiter is absent, works as hard and fast as he can, but still cannot keep up with the requests of the patrons. Diners should recognize this and make allowances. They may complain to the manager, so that more help can be sent to their area, but they should be careful not to put the blame on the waiter, who is no happier about the situation than they are.

If, after making a legitimate complaint, you receive no satisfaction from anyone, you may reduce the tip or leave none at all, and avoid that restaurant in the future.

On the other side of the coin, appreciative comments, as well as appreciation shown by a generous tip, are more than welcome. The tip is expected, but the extra "Thank you," "The food was really outstanding," or "The service was especially good," mean a great deal to someone who is trying to do his best. They also mean a great deal to the management, whose reputation is greatly enhanced by the customer who is satisfied and doesn't hesitate to say so.

HOSTING A RESTAURANT DINNER

The first thing a host must consider is the choice of restaurant. Do his guests like exotic food or good plain cooking? If they are from out of town do they have the proper clothes with them for an elaborate restaurant? Do they wish to see a place with a worldwide reputation? If a man is taking a woman to dinner would she like a small, intimate spot, or would she prefer to dance to a good orchestra?

Having reached a decision, the host must make every effort to see that the restaurant chosen meets the expectations of his guests. If he has picked a well-known restaurant he must reserve a table ahead of time; and even in an ordinary restaurant it is always safer to make a reservation in advance.

If he has ordered the dinner ahead of time he must try to check the dishes as they are served to make sure that everything is as he requested. If there are any omissions he quietly calls them to the attention of the waiter and makes sure that the missing items are supplied.

If dinner has not been ordered beforehand, it is the host's duty to take his guests' orders and give them to the waiter, or if the party is large, to make sure that the waiter gets the order correctly from each person. Again, if there are mistakes he must tactfully and politely see that they are corrected, without embarrassing his guests.

When he pays the check he does not display the total but puts the money (or the signed form if he pays by credit card) quietly on the plate and nods to the waiter that he may remove it. If he does not have the exact amount, including the tip, he waits for the waiter to bring his change, but if the sum includes both bill and tip, the host thanks the waiter and indicates that he is ready to leave by rising or by making some such remark as, "Well, let's move along or we'll never make the first act."

If the headwaiter has been especially helpful the host unobtrusively slips a tip (from two to five dollars, depending on the size of the group) into his hand and thanks him as he is leaving the restaurant.

SPECIAL TYPES OF RESTAURANTS

SMORGASBORD

The smorgasbord, an import from Sweden originally, has gained tremendous popularity in the United States. Actually it is a buffet, but a buffet of such variety and interest that it is more than worth the effort of serving yourself.

When a man invites a woman to dine at a smorgasbord restaurant he may go to the buffet alone and select her food for her. But I don't recommend that because it eliminates much of the fun of dining in such a restaurant. Aside from the fact that she would be left sitting alone at the table, a woman would hardly want to miss the opportunity of seeing the delectable displays of food and choosing a little of everything that appeals to her.

At this type of meal the individual tables are set as usual. The smorgasbord, which literally translated means "sandwich table," has one or more stacks of small plates to be filled with reasonable amounts of food. Since you are expected to make as many trips as you wish from your seat to the smorgasbord and back, you should never overload your plate and you should only choose foods that go well together each time you serve yourself. Leave your used plate and silver at your table for the waiter to remove while you are helping yourself to your next selection. You are intended to take your time. Start with fish, which should whet your appetite, then cold cuts and salad, followed if you wish by cheeses and a bit of fresh fruit or jello. You then choose your hot food, and end with dessert and coffee if your appetite is still there.

ORIENTAL RESTAURANTS

Japanese and Chinese restaurants offer interesting variations in service and food. Some Japanese restaurants have sections where the guests may remove their shoes, if they choose to, and sit on cushions on the floor at low tables, Japanese style. If you have very long legs, like my husband, or if you are taking older or crippled people to such a restaurant, you would not sit in that section, but you would request a regular table, which is always available for those who prefer it. Chinese restaurants have regular seating arrangements, but in most of them you may eat with chopsticks if you wish. Some restaurants suggest that the people at the table order different dishes, which are placed in the center of the table so that the diners may serve themselves from any or all of them. This is a delightful way to experiment with various dishes—and one that may be helpful in ordering the next time you go to a similar restaurant.

CAFETERIAS

There are few rules for eating as informally as one does in a cafeteria—other than ordinary good table manners—but there are certain niceties that should be observed. If there are racks available, men should remove their hats before getting their food. If there are no racks or hooks they should remove their hats when they sit down, putting them on an empty chair, or in their laps if necessary. When the restaurant is crowded and there are no empty tables it is perfectly all right to take an empty chair at a table already occupied, but one should say, "Is this seat taken?" or "Do you mind if I sit here?" When there are busboys who carry the trays to the tables they are generally given a tip of fifteen cents or a quarter, depending on the particular cafeteria and the amount of food on the tray. Diners who join a stranger are under no obligation to talk, but it is all right to open a casual conversation if the other person seems to be receptive. If he does not respond after an opening gambit don't bother him with further remarks.

LUNCH COUNTERS

When a couple goes to a lunch counter that is so crowded that there are not two seats together, it is permissible to ask a person sitting between two empty stools if he would mind moving down one place. Conversely, a person in this position should offer to move before he is asked.

Assuming that there is a place to put it, a man removes his hat before eating at a counter, as he would in any other restaurant.

Unless there is a sign saying: NO TIPPING, tips are expected. The minimum—for a cup of coffee only—is fifteen cents. When food is served the tip should not be less than a quarter.

~§17~ The Theater, the Opera, and Other Indoor Entertainments

The basic principles of conduct at any public entertainment are the same: Do not draw attention to yourself by noisy or conspicuous behavior. Do remember that others in the audience (as well as the performers) are entitled to your consideration.

THE THEATER

DINNER AND A PLAY

> *In New York, for instance, no young girl of social standing may, without being criticized, go alone with a man to the theater.*—Emily Post, 1922

In any audience there is almost certain to be a mixture of married couples who are enjoying an evening away from home, serious devotees or students of the drama, and theater parties of various sizes. One of the more delightful ways of entertaining people is to ask them to have dinner and go to a play.

When an unattached man invites friends to go to the theater he usually takes them to dinner in a restaurant, but if a host and hostess have a house or apartment in the city they are likely to have dinner at home. Among others, when this form of entertainment involves dining out, the evening is Dutch treat. If one member of the group wishes to, he (or she) may ask the others to meet at his home for cocktails, but the cost of dinner and the tickets is divided among the group.

It is absolutely essential that a host arrange for theater tickets well in advance. In New York, for instance, if you buy your tickets at the box office you must plan weeks ahead in order to get the seats that you wish for the most popular plays. If you plan your party on the spur of the moment, at best you will have to settle for a less popular play or one that has been running for some time, or else you must buy the tickets from a ticket agency, which charges more than the box-office price.

ARRIVING AT THE THEATER

On arriving at the theater the host (or hostess) holds the tickets in his hand so that the ticket-taker may see them, but he allows his guests to pass in ahead of him. If the usher is at the head of the aisle the host gives her the stubs and steps back, and the women precede him down the aisle. If, however, the usher is already partway down the aisle, the host may lead the way until he reaches her. If the party is large the hostess should tell her guests ahead of time in what order they are going to sit, so that they may arrive at their row in more or less that order, avoiding a great deal of shuffling about and confusion in the aisle.

The only fixed rule about seating in the theater is that a man should sit on the aisle. When there are two couples a woman should not go into the row first because it leaves her at the end of the line in a more difficult position for joining the conversation before the play starts and between the acts. Therefore, one man should go in first, followed by the two women, and finally the other man. Each woman generally sits next to the man who is not her husband.

When the party is larger a woman does lead the way into the row, and the others alternate, men and women, leaving the host, or one of the men if there is no host, on the aisle.

In the case of a man and a woman alone, she, of course, goes in first, and he follows, sitting on or nearest to the aisle.

WHEN THE PLAY IS OVER

The first man to leave the row naturally stands in the aisle for a moment, so that the lady who follows can walk with him, or if the crowd makes two abreast impossible, precede him. In nearly all situations a lady goes first. Only when the crowd is really dense does a man go first to make a wedge for her. In a theater party of six or more the first man should let the woman who sat next to him go ahead of him, but he does not wait to follow the others.

DRESSING FOR THE THEATER

It is perfectly correct for both men and women to wear daytime clothes to the theater. During the week the audience is likely to be made up of a large proportion of couples from the suburbs, and the man who has been at his office all day and has had no opportunity to change his clothes would hardly wish to see his wife arrive to meet him for dinner dressed in an elaborate cocktail or dinner dress. So if Mrs. Franklin has decided to combine her trip to the theater with an afternoon's shopping she need feel no embarrassment at appearing at the theater in a wool or cotton dress, or even a suit, or pants suit, although it should not be too sporty. Many women carry an extra piece or two of jewelry in their purses with which to dress up their "basic" black dresses for the evening.

On the rare occasions when a hostess plans a large theater party, perhaps to celebrate an anniversary, she may wish to make the evening more gala by requesting that the men wear "black tie." The only other time that more formal dress is required is on the opening night of an evening performance, when one attends by special invitation. Then the women wear cocktail or dinner dresses and the gentlemen wear tuxedos.

COURTESY AT THE THEATER

You must not be late! It is terribly unfair to others in your party to make them miss the beginning of a performance because of your tardiness. Other theatergoers dislike being climbed over after the performance has started. If your taxi breaks down or a flat tire causes a truly unavoidable delay, wait at the back of the theater until the first scene is over; then the usher can show you to your seat. If the first act is not divided into scenes you should wait until the chorus is singing a number, or the audience is applauding, or at least until there is a pause in the action, and then slip into your seat as quickly and noiselessly as possible.

Hats off! Even if a woman believes her hat too small to obstruct anyone's view she should be agreeable about removing it if asked to do so. Thoughtful women whose hats are likely to interfere with the view of those behind them take them off without having to be asked. Women or men who have huge Afro hairdos or wear tall turbans that cannot be removed should try to request seats toward the back of the theater. Nothing is more distressing than to pay for a good seat and then to see nothing of the performance because of someone else's thoughtlessness.

"Excuse me, please," is the natural thing to say when having to disturb anyone in order to get to or leave your seat in a theater, and if someone is obliged to get up to let you pass, you add "Thank you," or "I'm sorry." Should you by any chance have to pass someone a second time, you say, "I'm sorry to disturb you again," and "Thank you," as they let you go by.

In passing strangers, men as well as women face the stage and press closely to the backs of the seats they are facing, remembering, however, not to drag anything across the heads of those sitting in the row in front of them. Some women are very careless about their handbags, which, if swinging from a strap handle, bump into people beside or below them.

When you are seated you must give others enough room to pass. If the seats are far enough apart so that you can do this by merely turning your knees sideways, so much the better, especially if the play has started. But if there is so little space that the passersby have to step over your knees, you must stand and sit down again—quickly! Remember that during every second you stand, you are cutting off the view of all who are seated behind you.

There are certain ill-mannered men and women who practically refuse to allow anyone to pass once they are seated. It is quite true that having to gather up hat, program, and bag, and stand while each person on a long aisle leaves and comes back between each act can be far from pleasurable. But if you haven't sufficient self-control to be amiable about these annoyances you should forgo the discomforts of the theater and take your entertainment in front of your television set at home. If, for example, you do not wish to leave your seat between acts, why not try to get seats away from an aisle instead of on it?

Quiet, please! Most theater audiences are made up of mature people genuinely interested in the performance, but even they may irritate their neighbors through sheer thoughtlessness. Especially annoying are those who cannot seem to settle down when the curtain first goes up, who must finish that one important story or find a misplaced glove that could perfectly well wait until the intermission. Not much better are those who feel they must explain all the jokes to their companions; rarely is anyone enlightened, and all too often those nearby miss the next punch line. If you want to discuss the plot or the performance, wait until the act is over.

SMOKING BETWEEN THE ACTS

A woman usually goes out to the lobby with her escort if he wishes to smoke between the acts. But if a man is with a woman who does not smoke and prefers to remain seated, he may leave her briefly during one intermission, or if she has no objections, during both.

THE OPERA

The general rules are the same as those for the theater.

SEATING IN A BOX AT THE OPERA

Generally people dine together before the opera, and they all arrive at the same time. The gentlemen help the ladies to take off their coats, and one of them draws back the curtain dividing the anteroom from the box. The hostess places her more distinguished or older female guest in the corner of the front row nearest the stage. The seat farthest from the stage in the front row is always her own. The guest of honor takes her seat first, the hostess takes her place, and then the third lady goes forward and is seated between the other two. If there are eight, the fourth lady sits in the second row with two of the gentlemen beside her. The host and the other men sit in the back row.

One of the duties of the men is to see that the curtains at the back of the box remain tightly closed, so that the light from the anteroom does not shine into the faces of others in the audience.

Three or four couples often subscribe to a box at the opera together, sharing the cost and enjoying each other's company during the season. So that each member of the group may enjoy the better seats and no two men be always relegated to the back row (especially if it is an off-center box that does not offer a full view of the stage from all of its seats), these friends may agree to switch their seating arrangments around, even though it violates the old rule of "no gentlemen in the front row."

BETWEEN THE ACTS

> *In walking about in the foyer of the opera house, a gentleman leaves his coat in the box—or in his orchestra chair—but he always wears his high hat.*—Emily Post, 1922

Both women and men may visit friends in other boxes between the acts, but the women should have escorts if possible. They may go out to enjoy the refreshments that most opera houses provide or simply to "people-watch." No lady should ever be left alone in the box, however, and no gentleman may stay in a box other than his own after the lowering of the lights. In fact everyone should return as soon as the signal is given for the raising of the curtain, for it is very annoying to have people coming in after the performance has resumed, not only to the audience but to the performers as well.

THE AUDIENCE'S CONDUCT

It should not be necessary to point out that there must be no conversation during the overture or the performance. An enthusiastic audience may applaud at the end of an aria, and of course, after each curtain, but not for the entrances or exits of a performer.

DRESSING FOR MONDAY NIGHT

In New York and some other large cities there are still people who wear very formal dress for Monday night at the opera. In the boxes some of the men wear white tie and tails, and their companions wear long evening dresses and their best jewelry. This formality is not required, however. Dinner jackets for men and evening, dinner, or cocktail dresses for ladies are acceptable.

In the orchestra either a dinner jacket or a business suit is correct, and you will feel comfortable in whichever you choose. A lady may wear a long skirt or short dinner dress, or if her escort is in a business suit, a silk dress or a cocktail suit.

In the balconies daytime clothes are worn by both men and women.

DRESSING FOR OTHER EVENINGS

On evenings other than Monday, clothing is very much the same as that worn to the theater, but one may occasionally see tuxedos and dinner dresses. One never sees tails on other than an opening night, but men who have the opportunity to change from business clothes sometimes put on a dinner jacket, especially those sitting in the boxes.

CONCERTS

Many cities have weekly matinee concert performances during the winter season. These are attended almost entirely by women, many of whom have season tickets. The dress at these matinees ranges from tweed suits to afternoon dresses to pants suits, but less casual slacks should not be worn. The few men who attend wear business suits.

At evening concerts business suits and cocktail dresses or long skirts are worn by the older people and by everyone in the better seats. Businesswomen may wear their everyday clothes if they have no opportunity to change. In the balcony and the least expensive seats it makes little difference what you wear, as you will be surrounded by everything from blue jeans to hot pants.

APPLAUSE

The conductor and guest soloists are always applauded when they walk out onto the stage. Clapping stops as soon as the conductor steps onto the podium and raises his baton. Applause for the music is held until the end of each selection, when the conductor turns toward the audience and bows.

THE MOVIES

An evening at the movies is about as informal as anything can be, but consideration for others should still be observed. Unless you are attending a premiere or an elaborate benefit performance of some kind, when you would dress as you would for the opening night of a play, casual clothes are proper. "Casual," however, must be determined by the location of the theater and the other activities of the evening. For example, jeans might be quite proper in the country, but they would be quite out of place in the city, especially if you were going to a good restaurant first or a nightclub later.

FINDING SEATS AT THE MOVIES

The order in which a couple goes down the aisle in a movie theater is unimportant. When there are no ushers a man and woman go down the aisle together. Either one might say, "There are two— shall we take those?" The other agrees or suggests two farther down.

If you come in after the movie has started wait at the rear until your eyes have become adjusted to the darkness. By doing this you may avoid stumbling into the center of a row only to find that there are not the necessary vacant seats, having to back out, and tripping over unsympathetic spectators.

AUDIENCE PESTS

Talking, coughing, jingling bangles—not to speak of rattling cellophane when opening candy boxes—are annoying and disturbing to everyone in the audience. Very young people who go to the movies in droves often ruin the evening for others who happen to sit near them. If Julie and Johnny and Susie and Tommy want to talk and giggle they should arrange chairs in rows in a game room, turn on the radio or television, and sit there and chatter.

If those behind you insist on talking, it will do you no good to turn around and glare. If you are young they pay no attention, and if you are older you may discover that most young people think an angry older person the funniest sight on earth. The small boy throws a snowball at an elderly gentleman for no other reason! The only thing you can do is say amiably, "I'm sorry, but I can't hear anything while you talk." If they persist you can ask an usher to call the manager. However, perhaps the simplest thing to do, if there are other seats available, is to move.

The romantically inclined should realize that every word said above a whisper is easily heard by those sitting near them, and that two heads together are harder to see around than one.

But comparatively few people are anything but well-behaved. Most people take their seats as quietly and quickly as they possibly can and are quite as interested, and therefore as attentive and quiet, as you are, or they would not have come.

CIRCUSES, ICE SHOWS, AND RODEOS

It is almost worthy of a study in air currents to discover why with plenty of space all around, a tiny column of [cigar] smoke will make straight for the nostrils of the very one most nauseated by it!—Emily Post, 1922

As long as members of the audience obey the basic principles of thoughtfulness, behavior at such events as circuses, rodeos, or ice shows is unrestricted by rules. Clothing depends entirely on the weather, and as long as it is decent and appropriate for you, anything you choose is acceptable.

At any show where it is not necessary to hear the performers the audience may talk and shout as much as they please. In fact at such competitive events as rodeos part of the fun is cheering your favorite on.

But in spite of all this informality there are a few things to avoid.

As at the theater, don't be late. Even here it disturbs others who have arrived on time. Don't blow your cigarette smoke into your neighbor's face and don't let your enthusiasm get so out of hand that your voice may burst his eardrums. This is one time when it is perfectly all right to discard peanut shells, paper cups, wrappers, etc., on the floor, but be *sure* you don't discard them all over your neighbors' feet or shoulders.

18 Outdoor Events

Football, baseball, soccer, ice hockey, and basketball are integral parts of American life. Few parents of young boys have not had to wait their turn for the sports page of the Sunday newspaper. Beginning in the earliest grades, children learn teamwork and loyalty through participating in team sports. It is natural, therefore, that Americans grow up with an avid interest in one or many sports, an interest that sometimes becomes almost fanatical. In fact most professional games are so well attended that if you wish to get choice seats you must have season tickets or at least order them well in advance.

AT A PROFESSIONAL MATCH

At a sports event you need follow few rules other than those of ordinary courtesy. Arrive on time so that you do not disturb others in reaching your seat. You are expected to cheer for your team or your favorite player, but don't shout insults at the opposing team, as you may very well find yourself in a fight with your neighbor, and you will gain little by being escorted to the nearest exit by an usher or a policeman. Try to refrain from jumping up in moments of crisis; the people behind you are interested in seeing too, and you will be deluged with shouts of "Down in front!" Since smoke going directly into someone's face can be most irritating, hold your cigarette or cigar in such a way that it does not offend. If possible leave very young children at home. They lose interest very quickly at a long game, and the spectators around you will not appreciate repeated requests for candy, ice cream, sodas, or trips to the bathroom. In fact adults, too, who are seated in the middle of a row should try to restrict their comings and goings, and their purchases, to between periods or innings. If you do buy a beer or an ice cream have your money ready (the exact amount, if possible) and conclude the transaction as quickly as you can.

And last but not least, don't shove! If you have an appointment following the game, slip out quietly a minute or two before the end. If you leave when the game is over, walk slowly *with* the crowd, not *through* it, to the exit.

Clothing is as variable as the weather. At football or soccer or ice hockey games warmth is the first consideration. Above all, don't forget boots—a concrete floor is one of the coldest footrests known to man. At indoor arenas people in the boxes generally dress more formally than those in the balconies, where any costume seems to be acceptable. For the better seats at evening games, pants suits or wool dresses for women and sports jackets with ties or business suits for men are usually worn. Baseball, although it is our National Sport, is perhaps the least formal of all, and even in the boxes (unless you are the guest of an official) open sports shirts for men, flat-heeled shoes for women—in short, the most comfortable clothes possible—are the rule.

To sum up, if you do not act or dress in a conspicuous manner, and if you observe the basic rules of consideration for others, you will be able to get the most enjoyment out of any sporting event, as well as add to the pleasure of neighboring spectators.

AT COLLEGE AND SCHOOL MATCHES

One should never call out a name in public, unless it is absolutely unavoidable. A young girl who was separated from her friends in a baseball crowd had the presence of mind to put her hat on her parasol and lift it above the people surrounding her so that her friends might find her.—Emily Post, 1922

The rules of behavior are the same at any school or college match as they are at professional sports events. There are, however, a few suggestions for girls that may add to their enjoyment and to that of their escorts. In choosing your clothes remember to consider where your date may be taking you after the game. If there will be a cocktail party or a tea dance before you'll have a chance to change, carry a handbag that will hold a pair of suitable shoes to replace your boots, and wear a scarf if you have a hairdo that will be ruined in the wind. Many a girl has made a big hit by tucking a thermos of hot coffee or soup into a carryall, and even a "snack" if she has room.

If you are unfamiliar with the sport you are going to see, try to get some information about it in advance. Read the newspaper and find out the names of the outstanding players (especially on your date's team) and the standing of the clubs. Get a paperback about the game and be sure you know what to watch for, the basic rules and the penalties. You'll be way ahead of the girl who spends the afternoon asking stupid questions—"Why do they do that? What's the score? Which team is ahead?" Even more important, don't show your boredom or ignorance by talking "girl talk" with your escort's roommate's date!

Whether you feel any enthusiasm for your date's team or not, let him think you do. Disinterest or lack of loyalty to his school is as bad as or worse than lack of knowledge of the sport.

AT A PUBLIC BEACH

At a public beach the first rule is to avoid crowding—try not to choose a spot right on top of someone who is already there. Those who have children should choose places as near as possible to the spot where the youngsters are going to wade in and out of the water and dig canals and build sand castles. Not only is it dangerous to have little children paddling in the water far away, but it is natural for a child to fill his pail and run back and forth from his family to the water, kicking sand and spilling water over those who may be sitting in his path. Even though the children may be adorable their charm is not apparent to a sleeping sunbather on whom they have just splashed icy water!

It is also important not to let a child thrust his attentions upon strangers. Most people are inclined to like children, but remember, there are those who do not. Therefore, before letting Johnny make himself one of a group of strangers sitting nearby be sure to notice whether the strangers are showing particular interest in Johnny or whether Johnny alone is showing interest in them! If the latter seems to be the case call him back immediately.

Dogs are forbidden on most crowded beaches, but on more remote ones they are usually allowed and can give a lot of pleasure if they are properly controlled. In an area where there are other people a dog must be kept on his leash so as not to alarm small children or adults who are distrustful of animals. If your dog is to be free to run and swim you must find a deserted part of the beach, being sure to leash him again if a stranger approaches.

Children and dog owners are not the only offenders on the beach. Young people throwing a ball over, around, and between the sunbathers can be very annoying. An obvious display of affection is out of place, too. Couples who give languid back rubs, lie entwined like pretzels, to say nothing of kissing and caressing, make their neighbors thoroughly uncomfortable.

Although brief bathing suits, including bikinis, and trunks are now accepted wherever there is sun, it is not necessary to throw good taste to the winds.

Bikinis can look superb on a young girl with a beautiful figure. On an older woman, however, or one who even tends toward overweight, they are a disaster. Far from adding to her charms by a display of seminudity they draw attention to and exaggerate the imperfections in her figure.

PARKS AND PLAYGROUNDS

Behavior at a public park is virtually the same as at the beach. Again, don't crowd others if you can help it. Don't spread your picnic baskets and personal belongings over two or three tables when your share is one. Although picnic-table manners are less demanding than those at a table at home, they do not grant the children the privilege of eating like little savages and offending neighbors who cannot help seeing them.

Public parks and picnic grounds are excellent training schools in that they teach a child to take his turn and be satisfied with his own share of time with the slides, swings, seesaws, and all the other play equipment.

Most important of all, always leave public grounds as clean or cleaner than you find them. Papers, cans, trash, and broken bottles, so frequently strewn over picnic grounds and beaches, completely destroy the loveliest landscape. If each of us did his share by picking up his own mess, and *one item more*, our countryside would soon regain the beauty it has, in many places, lost.

~§ 19 ~ *Appearing on Television and Radio*

Except for the special requirements of makeup and clothes for a television appearance the rules are the same for a radio broadcast as for television. Since a radio program is always witnessed by members of the station's staff and sometimes by a studio audience as well, you should dress tastefully and appropriately; but because you are not appearing before a camera the style of your dress, your makeup, and your jewelry is entirely up to you.

DRESSING FOR TELEVISION

You can always get help in choosing the clothing for your television appearance by calling and asking the advice of the producer. A more satisfactory way is to watch the program two or three times and decide which costumes you think are the most suitable or would be most becoming to you. Pastel or even dark colors televise better than white or black—men's shirts as well as women's dresses. Choose clothes that are "slimming," because the television camera tends to make everyone look fatter than he or she is. Almost all networks have makeup artists on hand for their regular performers, and they occasionally see that a guest is properly made up before appearing. Be sure, however, that they know what your role on the program is to be.

You may wear jewelry if it is necessary to your costume, but remember that brilliant stones will be sprayed with wax to dull the glitter, and the wax may be difficult to remove. Otherwise, choose clothing that is most flattering to your face and figure and appropriate to the time of day and the type of program. A sports suit would seem out of place on an evening variety show, as would a low-necked cocktail dress on a morning quiz program.

YOUR VOICE AND MANNER

The most important thing to remember when you are appearing on either radio or television is that you are really a guest in the home of the listener or viewer. Your manners, therefore, should be the same as if you were in their houses in person. You should speak in a well-modulated voice, just as if you were in the same room with your audience. Remember, too, that a pocketful of jingling coins and a rattle of notes will sound far louder through the microphone than they would across a room, so check before the program begins to make certain you have eliminated all distracting and unnecessary noisemakers.

Once on the air, act natural and try not to show off. If other people on the program become noisy or the discussion becomes heated, don't compete. By waiting until the moderator calms them down or changes the subject you retain your dignity.

If you are appearing on behalf of a charitable cause or on an intellectual program, be sure that the interviewer knows exactly what your subject is and also let him know of any particular story or incident that you want him to ask you about. Otherwise you may have difficulty in bringing out the points you wish to stress. If you are a participant in a discussion group or on a panel show, listen to the views of the other members and don't concentrate on pushing only your own opinions. But prepare yourself thoroughly and be sure you have enough to say. Nothing is more disconcerting to a moderator or interviewer than to have a guest who can say no more than "Yes," "No," or "Maybe."

Don't talk down to or patronize your audience. You are a guest in the homes of people from every walk of life and you cannot possibly know more than each and every one of them. In other words don't *under*estimate the intelligence of your listeners. On the other hand, simply because they have chosen to listen to you, don't *over*-estimate their knowledge of your subject.

~§20§~ Conducting Meetings

Meetings may consist of three or four mothers who want to work out suitable arrangements for transporting their children to school, or they may involve hundreds of stockholders of the country's largest corporation. Almost all of us attend several kinds of meetings each year, and many of us find ourselves from time to time in the position of having to take charge. Situations vary, of course, but some rather generalized suggestions may be useful.

MEETINGS OF LARGE ORGANIZATIONS

The president or chairman of any large organization must run its meetings in strict accordance with the rules of parliamentary procedure. The standard reference book on the subject is *Robert's Rules of Order,* which is available in any library or bookstore. In addition to learning these rules and following them scrupulously the person in charge must control the meeting politely but firmly, so that it does not get out of hand through unnecessary arguments or unpleasant wrangling, and he should prevent discussion from wandering from the business of the day.

Furthermore he must be neatly dressed in the proper clothes for the time of day and the type of meeting. *See Chapter 5, "Public Speaking."*

BOARD MEETINGS

If you are elected chairman of the board of any organization, you will be called upon to hold meetings, probably once a month and possibly oftener. If the organization is of considerable size or importance (a hospital or a community-fund drive, for example) the meeting must be run with some degree of formality.

Before the members arrive, it is up to you and the secretary to

rarely enter a church without at least a scarf over their heads. In any case it is *always* correct to wear a hat to church, and if you like to wear them and feel that they are becoming to you, by all means do so. Don't let the fact that you are in the minority make you uncomfortable.

Men *never* wear hats in Christian churches—they *always* do in synagogues.

Gloves are worn less often than they used to be and generally only when the weather is cold. However, even in summer, light cotton or nylon gloves "dress up" your costume, and they are always correct. In the past gloves were kept on all during the church service—today they are removed. It is far easier to turn the pages of the hymnal or prayer book without gloves on, and in those faiths where the communion wafer is placed on the palm, gloves *must* be removed before going to the altar.

SEATING

When there are ushers at a service, all members of the congregation are escorted to a pew, although the women do not take the usher's arm as they do at a wedding. The usher leads the way to a vacant seat and stands aside while the arrival—whether single or a couple—steps in. Women precede their husbands into the pew, going in far enough to allow room for him—and for children or others who may be with them. Early arrivals at a wedding or first communion may keep the choice seats on the aisle so that they can see the proceedings, but at weekly services, those who are already in the pews should move over to make room for later arrivals, rather than force the newcomers to climb over them.

When a couple leaves their pew to go to the altar for communion, they need not "switch." The husband steps out and walks to the communion rail; his wife follows him. They return in whichever order is most practical, although, again, the man lets the woman go into the pew first.

THE OFFERING

Although there is no fixed rule about it a husband generally puts the offering into the plate for both himself and his wife. When a man takes a girl friend to his church he contributes for both of them, but when a woman asks a man to go to a service with her they generally each make a contribution.

BEHAVIOR IN CHURCH OR SYNAGOGUE

Reverence is the quality that guides one's behavior at all religious services, and while it is expressed in various ways, in most faiths quiet, attentiveness, and dignity are the ingredients.

It is perfectly correct to nod, smile, wave at acquaintances before a service starts, and if a friend sits down next to you or in front of you, you may certainly lean over and whisper "Hello." You should not, however, carry on a prolonged conversation, giggle, gossip, or otherwise make yourself objectionable to others around you. Introductions, too, should wait until after the service.

Occasionally a group of young people sitting together will forget themselves—and their neighbors. If their whispering and laughing becomes distracting and annoying, you have a right—in fact an obligation—to remind them of where they are. If they refuse to listen or pay attention to you, you should, after the service, report their behavior to the clergyman.

The roof of the church, in somewhat the same way as does a hostess's roof at her home, provides an excuse for strangers to become friends. Although you are not expected to speak to people you do not know at each service, those who attend regularly and recognize each other should feel free to chat casually after services. Also, in small congregations it is both proper and friendly to greet a visitor who you know is not a regular member of the congregation.

CHANGING YOUR PLACE OF WORSHIP

When you are changing from one parish to another or from a church of one faith to another, it is only courteous to inform the clergyman of your old church, or at least the parish secretary. In some denominations each parish is assessed according to the number of registered members, and therefore its financial condition can be harmed if a member who moves away is still enrolled but not contributing.

If your desire to make a change is due to the fact that you are not getting what you think you should from your particular faith, or perhaps your views are not compatible with those of the clergyman, your problem is more difficult. You owe him an explanation of your reasons for changing parishes, either by letter or in person. Although it may be difficult try to be very honest and clear, because while he may be hurt or upset at the time, your criticisms and comments may help him to see some of his failings and to serve his congregation better.

ATTENDING A SERVICE OF ANOTHER FAITH

When you have an opportunity to visit a church of another faith, or a synagogue if you are a Christian, do so. It is a broadening and enriching experience, and you will come away with more understanding of people whose beliefs are different from yours. If you are secure and sincere in your own beliefs, attending another service with an open mind will strengthen, rather than weaken, them.

Unless some part of the service is opposed to your religious convictions you should attempt to follow the lead of the congregation. Stand when they stand, sing when they sing, pray when they pray. If there is a part in which you do not wish to participate, simply sit quietly until that portion of the service is over.

A Protestant need not cross himself nor genuflect when he enters his pew in a Catholic church. No one must kneel if his custom is to pray seated in the pew. All he need do is bend forward and bow his head. But insofar as the proceedings are not objectionable to you, you will get more from the strange service, and perhaps be more comfortable, if you do as the others are doing.

Christian men keep their hats on in synagogues—there are yarmulkas available for visitors who come without a hat.

If you are taking communion in a church that is strange to you, watch what the congregation does and follow their lead. You will derive the same comfort and strength from the Host whether you receive it at the altar rail as do Catholics and Episcopalians and certain other communicants, or it is passed to you in the pew as in Presbyterian and some other Protestant churches.

When you attend church while you are away from home, you should make a contribution when the offering plate is passed. Even though you have contributed your full share to your home parish your donation is a way of saying "Thank you" to the church you are visiting. Also, while the larger part of your offering may go to that particular church a percentage goes to the church as a whole and helps in its support.

Part Five

ADVICE FOR TRAVELERS

❧22❧ *Planning Your Trip*

> *Certain sounds, perfumes, places, always bring associated pictures to mind: Restaurant suppers; Paris! Distinguished-looking audiences; London! The essence of charm in society; Rome! Beguiling and informal joyousness; San Francisco! Recklessness; Colorado Springs! The afternoon visit; Washington! Hectic and splendid gaiety; New York! Beautiful balls; Boston!*—Emily Post, 1922

There are some people who find it so pleasant to make plans for a trip that they truly consider the preliminaries "half the fun." But to the joys of poring over maps and collecting suggestions from your friends must be added certain practical preparations without which travel can be a nightmare instead of an exciting adventure. Dream of castles in Spain if you will, but don't forget that you may well be footsore and weary by the time you have actually toured your first one. Comfortable shoes, a good dinner, and a decent bed may make all the difference in your enthusiasm for the next day's expedition.

RESERVATIONS

ADVANTAGES OF A TRAVEL AGENCY

By far the easiest way to plan your trip is to go to a travel agency. If there isn't one in your own town write to one that has been recommended to you by a friend. Tell the agency just where you want to go and when and how—in fact give all the details you can and let them work out the best possible plan for you. This is their business, and they can do it better and more economically than you can. There is no extra cost to you, as they get their commission from the transportation company, the resort, or the hotel. A competent travel agency can of course arrange the most elaborate accommodations—from the best rooms in deluxe hotels to automobiles with chauffeurs. With equal interest the same travel agency will provide the equivalent degree of quality to those traveling on a limited budget.

MAKING YOUR OWN RESERVATIONS

If you are an independent type and do not wish to use a travel agency start well in advance to make your reservations. If you are refused at the first hotels or resorts you write to, you may have to wait days or even weeks before you have word from your alternate choice. It is not unreasonable to make the arrangements for a trip to a popular area six months or more ahead of time. In this case the reservations *must* be reconfirmed a week or two before your departure. It is also absolutely essential to request a receipt or acknowledgment (and don't forget to carry it with you) to be shown on your arrival. It is all too easy for a careless innkeeper or hotel manager to fill up the rooms with earlier arrivals and tell you cheerfully when you arrive, hot and exhausted, "But we have no record of your letter!"

Your travel reservations should be made at the same time as those for hotel rooms, and don't neglect your homebound ticket. Many people have found themselves in Europe at the end of the tourist season with days of waiting for a plane seat still ahead of them. With a little forethought you can plan your return date as definitely as that of your departure and thus prevent a last-minute case of jitters and impatience that could ruin your whole trip.

A tip to parents: When your son or daughter sets off for a summer of traveling, possibly with a knapsack on his back and no planned stopping places other than a list of youth hostels (inexpensive lodgings for bicyclists and motorcyclists found in every European country) be sure that he or she has a return reservation, either with him or held at the airline or steamship office for him. It is all too easy for a youngster to cable home: UNABLE TO GET SPACE UNTIL SEPTEMBER 15—three weeks longer than you had expected to finance him!

USING A GUIDEBOOK

If you are young enough so that you don't care where you spend the night—at an inn or in a field—or if you are fortunate enough to be able to travel during the "off" season when most of the tourists are at home, you may not need reservations. Nothing is more delightful than being able to drive at random, following whatever highway or byway catches your fancy and stopping for the night wherever you happen to be. And what a joy to have plans so flexible that you can leave a town that has little to offer the day after you arrive, or stay for ten in a city that has all the charm you have dreamed of!

To travel in this way is ideal, but there is one requirement—a good guidebook. By using its listings of available lodgings and eating places, you may avoid, first, hours of searching for a respectable hotel, and second, the danger of falling upon dirty accommodations or dishonest proprietors. Since the staffs of all good guidebooks regularly visit the places they recommend, their information is as accurate and current as can be found.

GETTING THE MOST OUT OF TRAVELING

If you want to get the most out of your travels, read as much as you possibly can, in advance, about the places you plan to visit. Ask friends who have been there to give you tips—about what to see, names of guides, places to stay, or clothes to wear. Borrow their books about the places on your itinerary and buy others that are recommended to you. Novels as well as more scholarly books give you a "feel" for a place even before you see it and often arouse your curiosity and interest about the less publicized features of the area.

Carry travel books and stories with you, too. A diary written by someone who has taken the same trip is invaluable. On a recent boat trip through the Canal du Midi in southern France, we had a book that provided us with so much practical information, so many hints about what to see, and so many interesting stories about the places we were passing that we called it our "Bible."

TRAVELING COMPANIONS

Some couples feel that they can never travel with anyone else—that companions would necessarily curtail their freedom to do what they please or that there would be too many different interests to have all of them satisfied.

Personally, my husband and I find that traveling with another couple, at least occasionally, is stimulating. You do more things than you probably would by yourselves, you get a more varied viewpoint about the places you visit, and even the most devoted husbands and wives get a little tired of nobody's company but their own from time to time.

You *must*, however, choose your companions carefully. If you like to be up and out on the sightseeing bus by 8:00 A.M., don't travel with people who sleep until noon. If you prefer picnics in the country and simple country inns, don't go with a couple whose idea of heaven is a nightclub in Paris. Be sure that your interests and your life-styles are reasonably similar. In the case of very close friends these differences might be overlooked, but only if each is prepared to compromise, or to go their own way and meet only at specified times.

When you are traveling with another couple, there is invariably a problem with expenses. Hotel bills and travel fares can be paid individually of course, but restaurant and bar bills and food bills—if you are doing your own cooking—are more complicated. The ideal solution is a "kitty." Each couple puts in the same amount of money at the beginning of the trip and replenishes the kitty with equal amounts whenever it is necessary. All food and liquor bills (or whatever has been agreed upon) are paid for from the kitty, and whatever is left over is divided evenly at the end of the trip.

LEAVING YOUR HOME IN ORDER

WHEN THE CHILDREN STAY AT HOME

If you wish to enjoy your trip to the full with a minimum of worries, there are several precautions that you must take to ensure the safety and well-being of the people and things you have left behind.

The first and most obvious responsibility is that of parents who must leave children at home. If you already have a reliable housekeeper who is capable of taking charge while you are away, there is no problem. She simply takes over the house with a few extra instructions and possibly extra pay if her duties will be substantially increased during your absence. Otherwise, if you do not have relatives who can come and stay at your house or invite your children to stay at theirs, it is absolutely essential to find a trustworthy person to care for them. Occasionally a couple, or a man if the children are boys, can be found, but generally the position of sitter or temporary mother is filled by a woman. She should be recommended either by a friend whose judgment is sound or by a reputable agency. If you do not know her personally, she should arrive two or three days in advance so that the children may get to know her while you are there to help them over any rough spots and so that she may become acquainted with your house and routine.

There should be definite rules laid down—especially if the children are teenagers—about what hours they are to keep, what they are allowed or forbidden to do, and with whom they may go out. Otherwise the sitter has no way of knowing what your basic standards are, and the young people will soon find out that they can have many more liberties than they are ordinarily allowed.

Your household should have a complete list of addresses at which you may be reached and also a list of relatives or friends who may be counted on to help in an emergency. An additional list of the names and numbers of the following people and/or services should be posted next to your telephone:

1. Doctors—pediatrician, general practitioner
2. Dentist
3. Plumber
4. Electrician
5. Gas company (if necessary)
6. Laundry and cleaners
7. Drugstore
8. Food stores
9. School
10. Husband's office number

If your absence is to be lengthy the person in charge should be shown the location of the main water valves, all gas pilots, the furnace reset button (if your furnace has one), the electric fuse boxes or circuit breakers, and fire extinguishers.

If you take care of these matters conscientiously before you leave, you will have little reason to be concerned about your family while you are gone.

WHEN NO ONE IS LEFT IN THE HOME

When you are leaving an empty house or apartment, there is a different set of precautions to consider. A house whose owners are obviously away is an open invitation to a burglar. Therefore, in order to make it appear occupied, the following suggestions should be followed. Don't forget to:

Cancel milk delivery.

Cancel newspaper delivery.

Request that the post office either hold or forward your mail. Nothing could better advertise your absence than mail and newspapers piling up at your door.

Have all laundry and cleaning delivered before you leave so that it is not left hanging outside for days or weeks.

Put all jewelry and small valuables in a safe or safe-deposit box.

Leave a light or two burning, or better yet, install an automatic light that goes on at dusk.

Check all locks on windows and doors and be sure that you take a key with you! Not a few people have been horrified to find on arriving home late at night that they had so thoroughly closed up their house with the key inside that they must either break a window to get in or spend the remainder of the night in a motel.

Leave a spare key with a friendly neighbor and ask him to check the house occasionally.

Put potted plants outside or make arrangements to have them watered by a friend. A neighbor's child is often happy to take over this chore for, possibly, fifty cents a week.

Take pets to the veterinarian's or wherever they are to be left.

Notify the police of your absence and ask them to keep watch over your house. Also, if you have a cleaning woman or anyone coming into the house legitimately, give the officer her name so that she will not be accused of unlawful entry.

Never give your travel plans or dates to your local newspaper in advance. There are people who watch the papers every day in order to take advantage of just such information.

There is no way that you can make your house 100-percent burglarproof, but the above suggestions will help to discourage any but the most professional thief. If you travel frequently and wish to go away feeling confident that all will be in order on your return, make a list of the above suggestions that apply to your house and check it off carefully before every trip.

TRAVEL DOCUMENTS

Several weeks before your departure you should apply for your passport, visas if they are required, and health certificates. If you already have them, make sure that they are still valid and in good order. These matters have to be attended to in person, although after you have filled out the forms and paid the fee at the passport office, your passport will be sent to you by mail. Your doctor will tell you where to get official health forms if he does not have them. You must go in person to the consulate of the country from which you wish to get a visitor's permit or visa. Everything else can be done for you; and if you are obliged to go on a suddenly planned trip a great deal of valuable time can be saved by having an experienced agent make your reservations and deliver your tickets to you.

It is advisable to get some foreign money in small bills and change to have in your hand when you land. There are restrictions as to the amount you are permitted to take in or out of some countries, and these should be checked before you leave. It is also very important to take the bulk of your money in traveler's checks, which can be replaced if lost and are accepted everywhere as readily as cash. Even though you have a letter of credit—a good idea if you want to have something to depend on for extra and unexpected expenses—there are many occasions when it is inconvenient or even impossible to go to a bank. *See also Chapter 26, "Currency and Language."*

A PRETRIP SCHEDULE

When you have spent months or even years planning the trip of your life you certainly don't want anything to go wrong. If you make your plans far enough ahead and implement them on a specific schedule, you will not forget anything and your day of departure will find you "calm, cool, and collected." Here is a suggested schedule leading up to a trip abroad.

ONE MONTH AHEAD

Make your travel reservations or go to a travel agency and enlist their services.

Apply for your passport if you do not have one. You can get the application blanks at government passport offices in large cities or at county courthouses in more rural areas. It generally takes ten days to two weeks after your application is sent in for the passport to arrive. At peak vacation seasons it may take longer.

If you are going to a country where a visa is required, you must apply at that country's consulate as soon as you have your passport. It is not necessary—legally—to get shots for some European countries, but many people take the precaution regardless. It is good insurance to be sure that your tetanus shot is up-to-date, and small-pox vaccinations and yellow-fever shots are required before returning to the United States from many areas. Hepatitis shots are a good idea, but since they do not last long the shot should be given just before leaving.

THREE WEEKS AHEAD

Make sure that your insurance is up-to-date and take out trip insurance if you wish to.

Get your wardrobe together and be sure that all your clothing is clean, no buttons are missing, etc.

Get your camera equipment ready. You can buy film all over the world, but sometimes they are out of the type you want, so take a supply with you.

Apply to the AAA for an international driver's license if you plan to rent a car in Europe. It is not required in all countries—your American license is accepted—but it is a good thing to have in case your plans change and you go someplace where the American license is not accepted.

Be sure that you have the luggage that you will need and that it is in reasonably good shape. If you intend to bring back a number of gifts or other purchases, you may want to take an empty canvas bag that can be folded into one of your own suitcases.

TWO WEEKS AHEAD

Get your "medical kit" together. Be sure you have a supply of the headache pills, laxatives, special prescriptions, and "travelers' tummy remedies" that work best for you. Put your pills and liquids in plastic, rather than glass, containers.

Have your eyeglasses checked and be sure to take an extra pair. Get a good pair of sunglasses if you don't have one.

Make up an itinerary of your trip to be left with your parents, your children, or anyone who might want to be able to reach you.

If you have a strong preference for certain brands of soap, cosmetics, shaving blades or lotions, etc., stock up on them now and put them with your luggage.

ONE WEEK AHEAD

Cancel all deliveries and put your valuables in a safe-deposit box or other safe place. Be sure some responsible person knows what steps you have taken.

Arrange for a cab, a driver, a friend, or whatever means you will use to get to the airport. Remember to make plans for getting *back* from the airport, too. Your travel agency will know about bus or limousine service in your area.

Pack your bags—heavier articles on the bottom and lighter on top. Put breakables between layers of clothing in the center.

Get your traveler's checks and some cash in the currency of the country where you will land. Ten dollars should be more than enough to take care of any immediate expenses—taxis, tips, etc.

◆§23◆ Motels and Hotels

MOTELS

All over America, and recently in foreign countries as well, motels have sprung up like mushrooms. They are becoming more and more luxurious as the competition increases, with some of them actually serving as resort hotels. The larger ones, and those belonging to national chains, are equipped with every facility for the traveler's comfort and pleasure, including swimming pools, shuffleboard courts, sunbathing areas, color television sets, and individual coffeemakers in each room. I know of one motel where there is a drive-in movie directly behind so that you may sit comfortably in bed and see a movie through your window before going to sleep, with the sound piped into each unit through a private speaker!

Motels can claim many advantages over hotels for the automobile traveler. Because the majority are on the outskirts of towns or between cities, you need not drive into heavy urban traffic to reach them. There is no parking problem, as your car is left directly in front of your room or unit. You may unload only what you need for the night—the rest can be locked up in the car. Especially important to a woman is the fact that, unless she is traveling alone, she need not be seen at all in her wrinkled travel clothes. Her husband simply goes to the office of the motel, registers, receives the key, and drives to the room allotted to them. There Mrs. Tired Traveler in her rumpled dress may slip in with scarcely a chance of being seen by anyone. If one does not expect to have breakfast in the motel dining room, to make any phone calls, or to incur any other charges, he may pay for the night on arrival and leave the next morning with no need to go to the office again.

Because of the immense popularity of motels as stopping places, it is wise, especially for a woman alone, to make reservations in advance. If you choose to stay in a chain motel the manager will be delighted to call ahead to the member motel in or nearest your next destination to reserve a room for the following night. Since you usually pay for this reservation at the time it is made and receive a written receipt you need not fear that your room will not be held for you, no matter how late your arrival. The larger chains will also help you plan your trip, providing road maps and lists of restaurants, entertainments, and points of interest, as well as the location of their own or associated motels.

One of the attractions of a motel is the fact that there is no need to tip. This is certainly true for the average traveler or businessman who stays one night—or at the most two—as a "transient." The only tip necessary in that case is at the bar or in the dining room, where the standard 15 percent is expected. Naturally, if anyone offers a special service he should receive an appropriate tip. If, however, you are making a motel (or "motor lodge" as the more complete chain motels are generally called) your headquarters for a prolonged stay you must reward the people who wait on you constantly. The chambermaid, bellhop, room-service waiter, and valet all offer their services in the large resort motels, and they should be tipped just as they would be in a hotel. *(See below, under "Hotels.")*

Dress is more casual in motels than hotels. Since the majority of patrons are spending only one night, they are not expected to unpack their luggage, and travel clothes are acceptable. Only in very luxurious motels are jackets and ties expected at dinner, and there are no restrictions on women's clothes. However, even the most exhausted traveler will enjoy dinner more and make the atmosphere pleasanter for the other diners if he freshens up and changes into a clean shirt (or fresh dress or blouse) before appearing in the dining room. Some motels provide the best dining rooms in town, and residents go there as they would to any other restaurant. It would add little to their "night out" if the transients all came in straight from a long day in the car—dirty, wrinkled, and bedraggled.

Otherwise there are few restrictions on behavior other than ordinary rules of courtesy. Don't play the radio or television too loudly or entertain until late in your room (most motel guests go to bed early to prepare for an early start or a day full of business meetings). Don't take the ashtrays or towels as souvenirs. Lock the door and turn out the lights when you leave, and keep your children from running around the halls and disturbing other travelers. Speaking of leaving, be especially careful if you are making an early departure. Don't call back and forth, don't slam the room door or the car doors, and don't race your engine or leave it warming up for a long time.

Motel traveling is a new way of life and a good one. With a little thoughtfulness and courtesy we can make it even better.

HOTELS

Because of their central locations in most cities and the services that they offer, hotels will never be completely replaced by motels. The business traveler arriving by plane or train naturally chooses a hotel in the center of town, near the offices of the companies he must visit. Tourists, other than those driving their own cars, usually wish to be in a central location where they can easily find transportation to museums, monuments, parks, historical sites, and other points of interest. Finally, many people, and certainly those making their homes in such accommodations, will never forsake the convenience and excellence of the services offered in first-class hotels.

TO ASSURE ACCOMMODATIONS IN HOTELS

You should always telephone, write, or telegraph in advance for accommodations in a good hotel. A typical telegram reads:

PLEASE RESERVE SINGLE ROOM WITH BATH AFTERNOON DECEMBER THIRD TO FIFTH.
REQUEST CONFIRMATION.
JOHN HAWKINS, 608 FALL STREET, GOSHEN, NEW YORK

A letter is a little more explicit:

Manager of the Lake Hotel
Chicago, Illinois

Dear Sir:
Please reserve two single rooms with baths or with a bath between for my daughter and me from December sixth through December twelfth. We will be arriving in the late afternoon, so please hold the accommodations.

Kindly confirm reservation to
Mrs. George K. Smith
Holly Lane
Brightmeadows, Illinois

Very truly yours,
Sarah L. Smith

Both letter and telegram should state clearly the hour of your arrival, the number and relationship of persons, the accommodations you wish, and the approximate length of your stay.

If you telephone be sure to request a written confirmation.

THE ARRIVAL AT A HOTEL

When you arrive at a big city hotel a doorman opens the door of your car or taxi and deposits your luggage on the sidewalk. If the hotel is crowded he will probably ask, "Have you a reservation?" If you say "Yes" all is well; but if you say "No" the reply may be, "Very sorry, but we are full." So don't take a chance. Wire or write ahead and ask for a confirmation. Hotels accommodate so many participants in conventions, expositions, etc., that it is wise to make your reservations as far ahead as possible as soon as your plans are definite.

If you have your room reservation a bellboy comes out, takes your bags, carries them into the lobby, and deposits them not far from the desk. In a typical hotel there is a counter with one or two men behind it. In city hotels desks are divided into areas labeled "Rooms," "Cashier," "Information," etc.

In any case you go to the section marked "Registration" and say, "I am Mrs. George K. Smith. I believe you have a reservation for me and my daughter."

If the desk clerk does not find a record of your reservation at once, you give him your confirmation. He is then obliged to give you a room, or if there has been such an error made that the hotel is completely full he will call until he finds you a room in a hotel of equal quality.

Generally, however, your reservation is in order, and he gives you a form to fill in and sign. He will ask how long you intend to stay, and you should reply with as accurate an estimate as possible. It is wise to specify the maximum number of nights you might stay, as it is far easier to give up the room than to extend the reservation.

A man registers as "John Smith, New York." He does not use "Mr." if he is alone, but with his wife he adds the title to their joint names: "Mr. and Mrs. John Smith, New York." If he is accompanied by his entire family "John Smith and Family" is acceptable. Nurses, employees, or those with a different name should be listed separately so that they may receive mail or messages.

If for any reason children are registered individually, "Miss" precedes the names of all little girls. Boys are registered with no title—just "John" or "Henry" or whoever—until they are eighteen or over.

One exceptional occasion when a lady signs her name "Miss" or "Mrs." is in a hotel register. "Miss Jean McLean" is correct, or "Mrs. George K. Smith"—never "Sarah Smith." A divorcée registers as "Mrs. Helen McCloud" or "Mrs. Smith McCloud."

If Mrs. Smith arrives first, she fills in the blank for both herself and her husband. When Mr. Smith arrives he says to the room clerk, "I think Mrs. Smith has already arrived and registered. What is the number of our room, please?"

As soon as you have registered, the clerk hands the key not to you but to the bellboy, who gathers up your bags and goes to the elevators. You follow. In your room the bellboy puts down your bags, turns on the lights, and opens the window or tests the air-conditioning unit. He receives a tip, usually twenty-five cents for each large bag, more if there are other packages, and an extra twenty-five cents for opening up the room.

SERVICE IN A GOOD HOTEL

Any service that you require is requested by telephone. You tell the operator if you wish to be called at a certain time or ask for the desk if you want to inquire about mail or give the name of a visitor you are expecting. You call the porter's desk if you have any inquiries about luggage or trains or reservations. You call room service when you want food or drinks sent up to you, and valet or maid service if you need a dress or suit cleaned or pressed.

If you want breakfast in your room you call room service and order it—this may be done the evening before, or you can call when you awaken. Most hotels have breakfast menus in each room, and you may choose from them. Presently the waiter brings in a tray with your order. In a first-class hotel he rolls in a long, narrow table that fits between twin beds or stands beside a single one. It is completely set: damask cloth, china, glass, silverware, thermos pitchers, and possibly chafing dishes to keep the food hot. In less pretentious hotels the waiter carries the breakfast in on a tray, which he simply sets down on any convenient table in the room.

It is entirely proper to open the door for the waiter, dressed in a bathrobe. He is used to carrying breakfast trays into the presence of all varieties of pajamas and negligees, and it is not necessary for even the most old-fashioned lady to be completely dressed to receive him.

After the waiter has arranged the breakfast and removed the covers from the dishes you sign the check and give it to him with a tip amounting to approximately 15 percent of the total. Most hotels will include an additional amount as a room-service charge, but this does not take the place of the normal tip to the waiter. If you wish, you may wheel the serving table (or place the tray) outside your door when you have finished in order to give yourself more space in a small room and to avoid being disturbed when the waiter returns for it.

You telephone maid service to have your clothes washed unless, as is often the case, there is a bag or receptacle marked for laundry in the bathroom. Pressing is done by the regular valet or maid, but in a small hotel a woman's dress as well as a man's suit may be sent to a cleaner. If there is no regular valet service, you ask a chambermaid, "Where can I have my dress [or suit] pressed?" She answers, "I will do it for you," or tells you who will.

PILFERAGE

An inexplicable urge seems to come over many otherwise decent, honest citizens when they are guests in a hotel. This is the urge to pilfer—to help themselves to articles that can be hidden away in luggage—exactly as if such things were put out as gifts to the guests from the management! Bath towels with the hotel's name on them, ashtrays, writing paper, soap, dining-room silver, and even bed linen disappear in such quantities as to be a major expense in every large hotel. These pilferers, when accused of stealing, say, "Not at all—the management expects these things to disappear!" How any normal law-abiding person can thus excuse what is technically petty theft I cannot understand. All I can suggest is that the next time you, or anyone traveling with you, is tempted to take home such a souvenir, say to yourself or to them, "That ashtray is hotel property; if I take it home with me it will have to be replaced, and I am no better than a common thief."

HOTEL MANNERS

Years ago a woman who entertained a man in her hotel bedroom was practically a "fallen woman." But today so many hotel rooms are designed as bed-sitting rooms that it would be foolish not to use them in that way. A woman traveling alone may ask anyone she pleases to have a drink with her in such a room, or simply visit, as long as she breaks none of the ordinary conventions of behavior. Noisy par-

221

ties, men visitors at unconventionally late hours, or anything that suggests questionable behavior is not permitted in a first-class hotel, whose success depends partly on its good reputation.

The woman staying alone in a hotel is also free to ask anyone she wants to the bar or dining room. There is not the slightest reason why a woman—of any age—may not stay in a hotel by herself and have men come to see her and be invited by her to lunch or dinner. It is not so much a question of suitable age as of suitable behavior.

A hotel guest—whether a woman or a man—going down to the dining room alone usually takes along a book or newspaper to avoid sitting eating bread and butter and looking at the tablecloth, which is scarcely diverting, or staring at other people, which is impolite, while waiting for one's order.

When visiting people who are staying at a hotel you ask the desk clerk to telephone them in their rooms or you call them yourself on the house telephone. If they are expecting you to come up, they tell you the number of the room, and you join them there. The room numbers are usually clearly indicated by arrows or signs.

If the friends you are visiting answer that they are coming right down, you wait for them in the lobby or the lounge, in view of the elevators.

WHEN YOU LEAVE THE HOTEL

When a long-term guest is ready to leave he goes to the cashier —or telephones from his room—to request that his bill be prepared. When he has finished packing he telephones for a bellboy to carry down his luggage. Having tipped the boy, he goes to the desk marked "Cashier," pays his bill, leaves his key, gives a forwarding address if he wishes any mail sent after him, and departs.

The one-night transient with little luggage carries his own bag and goes directly to the cashier when he is ready to check out.

TIPS

The following schedule of tips applies to transient visitors staying in the hotel (or the motel with services) for not more than a week. Permanent or long-term residents tip on a monthly or even twice-yearly basis rather than having to produce a perpetual stream of small change for every service. The amount, of course, would vary according to the quantity and quality of the service. Hotel residents must arrive at their own conclusions, possibly with the help of other permanent guests and even the hotel management.

The usual tip for a dining-room waiter in a first-class hotel restaurant is 15 percent of the bill, but never less than twenty-five cents in a restaurant with tablecloth on table. If you are staying in an American-plan hotel, at the end of each week you estimate about 15 percent of the week's total lodging and divide that amount among those who have served you, proportionate to the amount of service. Your waiter usually receives at least half of the 15 percent, and sometimes more. When you leave you give a tip to the headwaiter in proportion to the service rendered. You give him one or two dollars a week if he has done little, and five dollars a week if you are a family to whom he has been especially attentive. For a one-night stay you need not tip him at all.

The room waiter receives 15 percent of the bill for each meal. This is *in addition to* a set sum charged by the hotel for each meal taken to a room.

The chambermaid in a first-class hotel is given about two dollars a week per person, or one dollar a week in a small, inexpensive hotel. Most people do not tip at all after one night in a commercial hotel, but after a longer stay in a luxury hotel or resort the tip is expected. Give the maid her tip in person if she can be found. If not, leave it on the bureau in an envelope marked "chambermaid," or if you want to be sure she gets it, give the envelope to the desk clerk and ask him to see that she receives it.

Nothing is given to the doorman for putting a bag on the sidewalk, but twenty-five cents if he helps take the luggage into the hotel. He gets a quarter if he calls a taxi, but rather than tip each time when your stay is prolonged, tip a dollar or two at the end of each week.

For other standard tips to hotel personnel, see Chapter 67.

One piece of advice: While you need not tip lavishly you will not get good service unless you tip generously.

Tipping is undoubtedly an undesirable and undignified system, but since it happens to be in force, travelers who like the way made smooth and comfortable have to pay their share of it.

EUROPEAN HOTELS

Large, first-class hotels in Europe—those most frequented by tourists—are essentially the same as our best hotels in the United States. Before venturing into less well-traveled areas, however, be prepared for certain differences in facilities and service.

In European hotels all services other than your actual accommodations and meals are provided by the concierge. He corresponds to our head porter but has a much wider range of responsibility and is as important as the hotel management. He presents a separate bill, or his bill appears as a separate item on the hotel bill. The concierge and his staff handle luggage and mail, including the sale of stamps. They will make all your travel reservations for you or will arrange for car rentals. They will recommend restaurants and places of interest and make the necessary reservations or arrangements. They are happy to shop for you and will have packages delivered to you. In general, they are your "general factotum" and as indispensable to the average traveler as the hotel management itself.

Many foreign hotels do not have a telephone in each room. Instead they have a push-button device with charming little pictures of waiters, maids, or valets beside each button to indicate which one you must push. This system certainly overcomes the language barrier —at least until the maid arrives!

Many small hotels do not have bathrooms with every room. Most rooms do have washbasins, although in very small towns there may just be a pitcher of water and a bowl. In these hotels you use the public bathrooms on each floor, which are marked "WC"—a universally known abbreviation for "water closet" or "toilet." There may be two, marked for men or women in the language of the country, or there may be just one to be used by all guests. You must reserve a time for your bath with the maid on the floor. She will run the bath and give you the key and a towel. In many places an extra charge for each bath will be added to your bill.

Although the hotels in small towns may not be luxurious the desire to please and the friendliness of the help more than make up for the lack of elegance. The chef who proudly invites you to see his spotless kitchen, the chambermaid who smilingly brings you a cup of coffee when she awakens you in the morning, and the concierge who takes great pains to ensure that you miss nothing in this, the most beautiful town in Europe, all leave you feeling that it is the spirit of the place and not the physical comforts that enchant so many Americans who travel abroad.

▶24◀ On Plane, Train, or Ship

AIRPLANE TRAVEL

FIRST CLASS VERSUS ECONOMY

There are two main classes of air travel—first class and economy. Many airlines that run "commuter" operations or fly twin-engine jets or four-engine propeller planes do not offer any choice of accommodations; all seats are the same price, and all passengers receive the same services. On most scheduled flights, however, you must choose between the two classes. The economy-class seats occupy three-quarters or more of the space toward the rear of the plane and are more closely spaced, often with three on each side of the aisle. Meals and snacks are included in the economy fare, but if you wish alcoholic drinks (cocktails are served before meals on overseas flights and on most domestic flights) you must pay for them. Service is somewhat slower in the economy section, as two or three stewardesses or stewards must take care of an enormous number of people on a full plane. Because the difference in cost between economy and first class on an overseas flight is quite astronomical a vast majority of people, even the well-to-do, put up with the discomfort of more crowded conditions on a flight that rarely lasts more than a few hours on a fast modern jet.

For older people who may have difficulty in getting in and out of crowded seats or cannot stand long in line for washroom facilities, for disabled persons, or simply for those who prefer, and can afford, a bit of luxury when they travel, the first-class section has far more appeal. The seats are roomy, and there are tables between them so that passengers may play cards or comfortably spread out their business papers. Cocktails are free, meals are more elaborate, and champagne is served if you wish it. The steward or stewardess often has

225

only ten or fifteen passengers to attend, and therefore every request is taken care of at once.

LUGGAGE

Insofar as possible, airplane luggage should be light. There are strict weight limitations on overseas flights, where economy-class passengers are allowed approximately forty-four pounds, and first class, sixty-six. You may carry more, but you pay for the excess at a specified rate per pound. At this writing, there is no weight limit on domestic flights if you carry no more than two pieces of luggage.

The ideal luggage is made of a lightweight metal, such as aluminum, or a composition material. The soft bags made of synthetic materials or strong weaves are most attractive but can be damaged or pierced if handled roughly. In spite of this warning I find them the most satisfactory luggage.

On overseas flights the airlines weigh almost every piece of baggage, sometimes even those you carry with you onto the plane. The only exceptions are handbags, briefcases (except large, square, or bulging ones), knitting bags, or other lightweight articles obviously for use during the flight—containing baby's diapers, a book or two, embroidery, etc.

You will save an enormous amount of time and irritation if you can confine your luggage to a bag that will fit under your seat or in the overhead compartment of the jumbo jets. You may carry on—and off—any luggage that fits those qualifications and you will avoid the one source of delay the aviation industry has not overcome—the baggage-claim counter. On most large planes you may also carry on small hanging garment bags (if they are not *too* stuffed), and the stewardess will hang them in a special closet.

SECURITY REGULATIONS

In an apparently successful effort to stop airplane hijacking, the government insists that all carry-on luggage be searched. The airports, in most instances, have evolved very efficient systems for doing this, and the delays are remarkably short. However, tempers flare when departure time is approaching fast and you are stuck in a line that seems to be stationary. There is little you can do except leave for the airport a half hour earlier than you used to and be prepared to wait—either before or after the security check. And remind yourself each time you feel your temper rising—"This is far better than ending up in Havana!"

To avoid delays or embarrassment going through security, pack any metal objects in those suitcases that will go to the baggage compartment without being checked. The metal-detection devices that you pass through yourself, and that your carry-on luggage goes through, are very sensitive, and the agents who go through your bags are trained to be overly suspicious. So if you are bringing a machete home to your son, or taking a tool kit to your friend in England, avoid a delay for yourself and those behind you by sending it in luggage other than that which will accompany you to your seat.

ARRIVING AT THE AIRPORT

For overseas flights you are requested to arrive at the airport at least one hour ahead of departure time, as opposed to the half hour required for domestic flights. This provides the extra time involved in checking travel documents other than tickets. The airlines request this much time before departure in order to allow their passengers enough time for the security check.

At the airport your luggage is taken on a cart by a porter and either put in line to be weighed when your turn comes to check in, or on domestic flights, it may be taken directly to the plane. In this event you will receive your claim check directly from the porter. He is tipped a minimum of twenty-five cents for each bag except for small hand pieces. You should make it clear to well-meaning friends who come to see you off that they should not bring presents. They will only be added to your weight allowance, or if you have already been checked in, you may not be allowed to take them onto the plane.

For all long flights, and even some short ones, the passenger agent at the check-in counter has a chart of the airplane from which you may choose one of the available seats. When there is no seat assignment and you prefer a particular location the only thing to do is arrive early enough to stand at the head of the line in the waiting area. In either case you are given a boarding pass with the seat number on it (when seat selection is offered) to be shown at the departure gate and again to the stewardess when you board the plane. If you have no baggage to be checked, you go directly to the departure gate assigned to your flight and check in there. If you have no ticket or reserved space you may purchase it, either at a ticket counter in the main lobby or at the departure-gate counter. Since there are usually "no-shows" on every flight you can often, even without a reservation, be taken on as a "standby." Standby passengers must wait patiently until all those with tickets are aboard, and they are then taken care of in order of their arrival at the counter.

WHILE IN THE AIR

The seats are clearly numbered, but the stewardesses who greets you with a friendly smile when you board will direct you to your chair and assist you with coats and bundles. Get out of the aisle and sit down as quickly as possible so as not to keep those behind you waiting. Coats are hung on a rack in the rear on some planes or folded and laid on the overhead shelf on others. During the trip the stewardesses, when not serving meals or drinks, will do their best to assist you in any way they can. You signal them with a light that you find above your head. They will bring magazines, hand out newspapers, bring food or extra pillows or blankets, or even help care for babies by heating bottles, etc. The steward or stewardess is never tipped, nor is any other member of the crew.

CLOTHING

Be sure that you wear loose, comfortable clothing that is as wrinkleproof as possible. Knits are ideal and pants suits are most appropriate, as they allow a woman to recline as much as possible and wiggle into the most comfortable positions without losing her dignity—or modesty. Remember to take the weather at your destination into consideration. A wool suit with a turtleneck may be just right when boarding in New York, but it will be a disaster when you disembark in Miami.

Men travel in suits, or on vacation trips, in slacks and sports jackets. They are free to remove their jackets and ties and make themselves as comfortable as they can.

On long trips, both men and women should carry light sweaters, as the temperature can be quite low at times. Since many people's feet and ankles tend to swell on lengthy flights you should choose shoes that are not tight to start with. Almost everyone removes his shoes on an overnight flight, so it is wise to take along a pair of warm socks or slippers. On many overseas flights the airline provides "scuffs," but your own warm, comfortable slippers may feel better to you.

I have found it very practical to carry a small overnight bag on overnight flights containing: a sweater, a fresh blouse (I prefer to travel in a slack suit), slippers, brush and comb, one or two paperbacks, a crossword-puzzle book, and some embroidery or knitting.

Having a variety of diversions seems, to me at least, to pass the time more quickly.

BEHAVIOR ON BOARD

When the sign flashes "Fasten Seat Belts," do so promptly. The stewardess has to check on each passenger. Also be prompt in obeying the "No Smoking" signal. When smoking is permitted, only cigarettes are allowed. If your seat is in the "no-smoking" section, don't annoy your neighbors by deciding you would like a cigarette.

No animals are allowed in an airplane cabin except Seeing Eye dogs. If you take your pet he must be in a carrier. His weight is counted as part of the amount of luggage you are permitted. He rides in the luggage compartment if it is pressurized, or in a special compartment if it is not.

The same rules apply in using the washrooms or lavatories on an airplane as on any public transportation. The only difference is that an airline is one of the few places where men and women use the same facilities. You must wait patiently for your turn, and when it comes try to take as short a time as possible. You should leave the washstand and the dressing table in perfect order. When you have finished washing wipe out the basin thoroughly with your used towel and throw it into the receptacle marked for it. Before combing your hair, lay a fresh towel over the washbasin or counter. Leave it there until you have finished your hairdo and put on your makeup. Then gather up that towel and throw it into the receptacle. Complete neatness is a first essential of good manners. Never leave any unpleasant trace of untidiness *anywhere!*

Try to make your trips to the lavatory when meals or drinks are *not* being served. It is impossible to pass the bar cart in the aisle, and the stewardess has to wheel it all the way to the end of the cabin to let you by. If you are in the washroom when the "Fasten Seat Belts" sign goes on, return to your seat as quickly as possible.

There are three habits that are very annoying to the people in the seats behind and in front of you. The first is dropping your seat back suddenly. You have every right to recline, but before you do, glance back and be sure that the passenger behind you is not in the middle of taking a mouthful or leaning over to pick up his newspaper. Unless his tray is down all the time, it is more thoughtful to wait to tip back until he is no longer using it. The second annoyance is slamming the tray into its latch, which jars the person in the seat in front of you. It is quite possible to turn the latch with one hand while holding the tray up with other. It is *not* necessary to slam it hard or repeatedly to make it catch. The third sinner is the person who continually bumps into your seat. There are people who cannot help squirming or swinging their feet when their knees are crossed. If you are one of them request an aisle seat. You can then at least turn your knees toward the aisle, being careful, of course, not to kick anyone passing by. You are also free to get up and release your tension by an occasional walk up and down the plane.

TO TALK OR NOT TO TALK

There is so much informality and friendliness among air passengers that it has actually brought about new rules of traveling etiquette. The old on-the-ground custom of paying no attention to fellow travelers is not observed at all. Those who are willing to talk—and in a plane nearly everyone is—are entirely free to do so. On the other hand, if you wish to be left alone, you can avoid conversation with the explanation, "I'd rather not talk. I'm very tired," or by pointedly burying your nose in a book or magazine and saying no more than "Un-hunh" to conversational gambits.

Most often, conversation starts over a cocktail or when a meal is served. People tend to open their book or newspaper or take out their knitting or their crossword when they first settle down. But when the stewardess comes with drinks or the tray, books or handwork are laid aside, and it is a natural time to start talking. Ordinarily the conversation starts most impersonally, and generally stays that way. "Isn't this a gorgeous flight—look at those cloud formations!" or "I wonder if we'll make up the time we lost waiting to take off," are all you need to determine whether your seat mate wants to chat or not. You may or may not exchange names and information about what you do, where you are going, etc., but women traveling alone should avoid committing themselves too much or they may find the casual encounter more difficult to cut off than they anticipated.

DRINKING ON PLANES

Passengers are limited to two drinks and are not supposed to take additional liquor on board. On a crowded flight, if you know that you will want two cocktails, you should request them when the stewardess takes your order, as she rarely has time to make the rounds a second time. In first class they generally bring the two drinks without being asked.

Occasionally one finds him- or herself seated next to someone who has fortified himself for the trip a little too heavily before boarding. If he becomes obnoxious or if you see someone nipping frequently from a flask or bottle, you should report it quietly to a stewardess. She will take care of the situation herself, or with the help of one of the plane's officers if necessary, and will see that the offender is moved to a seat where he will not bother anyone and can quietly sober up.

OBEYING REGULATIONS

People who travel frequently soon become bored with the required announcements about oxygen masks, life jackets, emergency exits, etc. If you have heard them innumerable times, you don't need to listen, but have the courtesy to be quiet and let other passengers, who may be less experienced than you, hear. The same applies to the captain's announcements about routes, points of interest to be seen from the windows, weather information, etc. Some passengers resent the sometimes "chattiness" of the pilot, but there are always others who welcome it. So again, be quiet, and let the ones who want to listen do so.

You will also make the crew's job much easier and the flight pleasanter for everyone if you obey announced instructions promptly. Put your seat back erect when asked to do so, so the stewardess doesn't have to make a special trip to remind you. Fasten your seat belt when told to and put out your cigarette when the light goes on—not when you've finished it. And finally, don't stand up and start getting your things together as soon as the plane touches the ground. It is a federal regulation that passengers remain seated until the plane stops at the gate, and it is constantly ignored. On a flight I was on recently, the pilot stopped the plane halfway to the gate and announced, "I have asked you to remain seated until we reach the gate. We will not move another foot until every one of you has returned to his seat." Believe it or not, throughout the plane there were cheers and bravos, and I was one of the applauders.

TRAIN TRAVEL

OVERNIGHT TRIPS

Overnight train trips are almost a thing of the past, except for a few businessmen who regularly travel, for example, between Chicago and New York, or perhaps vacationers who don't like to fly and take a train from New York to Florida. However, should you decide, for whatever reason, to go by rail rather than by air, there are a few customs and conditions that you should know and observe.

LUGGAGE

The official rate for a porter who takes luggage from the entrance of a railroad station to a train is twenty-five cents or more for each piece, and an additional tip is optional but expected. In large cities the rates are posted by the checkroom or the porter's stand. Since there are no porters at all in most small cities or towns, restrict your baggage to pieces that can be carried by hand. Large bags will be stacked in the space at the end of your sleeping car, so do not leave anything in them that you might need for the night. Small bags may be kept with you in your own bedroom or roomette. You should send very large bags and trunks ahead by railway express.

IN THE DINING CAR

On a daylong journey there is no need to speak to your companions at the table beyond a possible "May I have the salt, please?" although there is no objection to casual conversation. On a longer journey, if you happen to sit next to or near the same person for a number of meals, it is extremely unfriendly to sit in wooden silence.

Ask the porter in your sleeping car at what times meals will be served. You go at any time within the hours he tells you and you are seated with other passengers if there are no empty tables. There are also snack bars and cocktail bars on many trains. The bar car sometimes has groupings of chairs and tables and can provide a pleasant change from your sleeping car seat. Passengers in the bar car generally do chat with each other casually.

When you go to have a drink or for a meal be sure to take your ticket with you, as the conductor may ask you to show it at any time.

GOING TO BED

Since bedrooms, compartments, drawing rooms, and roomettes all have doors that can be closed, there is no reason not to have a friend or two in for a chat after dinner. But since the partitions between rooms are thin, voices must be kept low, and the porter should be called to make up the bed by ten or ten thirty at the latest. If you wish to have another drink or continue your talk you may go to the club or bar car.

When you are ready to go to bed, you ring for the porter to make up your berth. Then you simply shut your door when he is finished and go to bed. In each of these rooms bathroom facilities are included so that you do not go to the public washrooms at all.

deck games or bridge or likes to dance, the director arranges for games and introduces partners. On the smaller ships the purser, or possibly the chief steward, assumes the role of director.

By the time you arrive at your first port you probably will have made a number of friends. If you especially like someone who was introduced to you or someone who sits next to you on deck or at table, you can go ashore with her or him. If this is not the case, then you may always go along with the general group.

A group of people develops something like a group photograph. At first you see a crowd of faces and none of them stands out. Little by little they take on identity, and more often than not, some inconspicuous person whom at first you hardly noticed is the one who becomes your closest friend.

CLOTHING FOR A CRUISE

Clothing on a cruise ship is much less formal than on a transatlantic crossing. The majority of cruises head for the Caribbean or points south, and cool cottons, shorts, and bathing suits are worn all day. Bathing suits may not be worn in the dining room unless covered with a long shirt, a caftan, or a robe of some sort, but other sports clothes are acceptable at lunch and dinner. Passengers do not dress formally for dinner except for the night of the captain's dinner, and that, as mentioned above, is often a costume party. Women generally wear dressy cottons or silks or pretty pants suits to dinner, and the men wear blazers with shirts and ties. Nights can be cool, even in the tropics, so women should take a pretty sweater and/or stole, which are more appropriate than fur jackets.

Since cruise passengers will be making trips ashore, they should be prepared with comfortable "sightseeing" shoes. Women should have a hat or scarf for visiting churches, and they should wear dresses rather than short shorts for sightseeing tours. Longer shorts and sleeveless shirts are fine, but all clothing should be modest and simple. If you plan to visit elegant restaurants or nightclubs in the big resorts, long skirts for the ladies and summer-weight linen jackets for the men are appropriate although not necessary.

If you are going on a summer cruise to the north, the rules are the same, but you will be comfortable in wool knit slacks and dresses, and a fall-weight coat will be comfortable.

TIPS

There are definite minimum amounts that a passenger is expected to give. If you are traveling first class your cabin steward should receive ten dollars. If you have a steward and stewardess the same amount is divided between them. The dining-room steward receives ten dollars and the headwaiter five. One or two dollars to the bus boy, if there is one, would make him very happy. Lounge and bar stewards are tipped 15 percent at the time they render their services. The chief deck steward receives three dollars, and his assistant, if he has one, one dollar.

Fifteen percent of the amount of the wine bill is given to the dining-table wine steward.

To the bath steward you give a dollar.

All these suggestions for tipping are per person, first class, on a transatlantic trip.

Tips in the cabin and tourist classes are lower, in proportion to the difference in the passage fare. A good general rule for shipboard travelers is to allow approximately 10 percent of their fare for tips. Divide about half of this allowance between the cabin and dining-room stewards and distribute the rest to others who have served you. The same holds true for cruise passengers. They should allot approximately 15 percent of their fare for tipping, divided in the same way described above. Obviously, passengers occupying suites are expected to tip more generously than those in modest accommodations. To thank someone who has taken extra pains to please you, give a more generous tip to show him that you appreciate his efforts.

On no account attempt to tip a ship's officer! Thank the purser as you would any other acquaintance for courtesy. If you consult the doctor on board, he will probably send you a bill for his services. If he does not and you have a real illness, when you leave the ship it is proper to send him the amount that probably would have been charged by your own doctor. If you are ill enough to be hospitalized an extra charge will be added to your fare.

❧25❧ By Automobile, Bus, and Taxi

TRAVELING BY CAR

THE COURTEOUS DRIVER

If every driver would follow the rule "Do unto others as you would have others do unto you," there would be very few accidents on our highways. No one who has a license to drive can fail to appreciate the good manners of the driver who signals his turns, makes his stops smoothly, and gradually pulls into the proper lane well before making a turn. This type of consideration not only shows "good manners" but may actually save the lives of others—as well as his own.

Really fine drivers do exist, and very good ones are not uncommon. This chapter is certainly not for either of these groups, but for the tens of thousands who swarm out on the highways to have their lives saved time and again (though they don't know it) by the experts —or by Lady Luck. If we think seriously of the power in all these machines running freely over our streets and roads and realize that no examination in *driving courtesy* is required of one applying for a license, the wonder is not that there are accidents, but that there are not more.

Courtesy is essential to safe driving. The thoughtful driver constantly considers how his actions will affect those behind, in front of, and beside him, and is alert to what other cars are doing as well. Because of this attitude he is invariably a safe driver. Many men and women whose behavior in all other circumstances is beyond reproach become transformed into bad-mannered autocrats behind the wheel of a car. Even calm and considerate drivers become jittery when exposed to repeated experiences with rude motorists. These otherwise safe and well-mannered people, when impatient and irritated, often become "accidents going somewhere to happen."

A polite driver no more cheats at a red light or stop sign than he would cheat in a game of cards. Often the man who tries to force his way ahead of others in a line of cars would not think of trying to force himself ahead of others in a box-office line—if he accidentally did such a thing he would probably be mortified by his own rudeness. However, let him get behind the wheel of a car, and his good instincts may fly right out the window.

AT TRAFFIC LIGHTS

Always stop for a red light in a position that does not block the crosswalk. In heavy traffic don't enter an intersection unless you are sure you can complete the crossing before the light changes.

It is both illegal and impolite to start up with a rush when the light turns orange in the other direction. But it is equally discourteous to linger lazily after the light has changed, since the drivers behind you will be caught by the next red light.

If you know that there is a right- or left-turn arrow at an intersection, stay out of those lanes when you intend to go straight through, so that you do not prevent others from turning with the arrow.

CASPAR MILQUETOAST

Traffic police are well equipped to deal with those who exceed the speed limit. On many highways there is a minimum limit as well as a maximum, but where there is not, the offender is not always just the fast driver but also the slow! The snail who pokes along thirty miles an hour slower than the other cars is a menace to everyone. He is frequently ill-mannered enough to drive in the left or center lane, causing overtaking cars to change lanes—often too suddenly. If you wish to drive slowly, please stay off the superhighways entirely, or if you must use them have the courtesy to keep to the right where the slower traffic belongs.

OTHER OFFENDERS

Another menace is the "weaver." He scoots back and forth from lane to lane, cutting drivers off, causing them to jam on their brakes or swerve suddenly into another lane. He rarely looks beside or behind him and shows complete lack of consideration for the other motorists on the highway.

When you are on a highway always signal well in advance before you switch lanes or make a turn. Keep an eye on your mirror to be sure that drivers behind you have noticed your signals before you make your move.

Get into the proper lane well before you reach your turn or exit.

There are few people more dangerous on the road than the person who suddenly realizes that he has reached his turnoff or that he needs gas at the service station, and who disregards the cars in the lanes behind him as he cuts through, in front of, or into them in order to reach his destination.

PASSING POINTERS

One of the worst offenders on a two-lane road is the driver who pulls out of a solid line of cars to steal his way forward. Finding himself in sudden danger of a head-on collision, he makes a frantic effort to push his way back into the line—possibly forcing someone off the road or at the very least crumpling fenders.

Of course the one who causes him to take his rash action is also to blame. He is the same Caspar Milquetoast who drives well below the speed limit, this time on a narrow, twisting road through hilly country with a long line of impatient drivers behind him. In their exasperation these drivers take desperate chances, passing too close to a curve or the top of a hill, and the net result is that Caspar is more likely to be involved in a serious crash than if he were to drive a little faster.

A final word about good passing habits: When you have reached that safe stretch of road with adequate visibility, make your move smoothly, quickly, and without changing your mind. And when you are the driver being passed, slow down a little to allow the other car plenty of space to pull back into line ahead of you.

NIGHT DRIVING

There are two very important rules of safety and courtesy to be followed when driving at night. First, be careful to lower your speed in the darkness because you simply cannot see as far ahead in the dark as in daylight, no matter how excellent your headlights. Second, whether your state laws require it or not, dim your lights when meeting other cars at night. Blinding another driver by a blaze of light is not only rude but dangerous. When drivers courteously dim their lights first, they automatically invite others to do the same. If you are driving with lights on low beam, it is reasonable to turn them high momentarily to remind an approaching driver to turn his down, but keeping on your high-beam lights to "get even" with someone who has not dimmed his is both impolite and stupid. After all, you can be the victim of the driver you "blind."

USING THE HORN

If more people realized that the horn, as the voice of the car, is in reality the voice of the driver, there would be less thoughtlessness in its use. If it is necessary to prevent an accident, use your horn, of course, but don't blow it at an individual, a crowd of persons on foot, or other automobiles as if to blast them out of the way. In other words, sound your horn as a warning only in emergencies. Otherwise beep it gently as a polite signal.

I have the greatest sympathy for the man in the following story. His car had stalled in heavy traffic, and although he was obviously trying to remedy the trouble, the driver behind was impatiently honking and swearing at the embarrassed victim. After standing the noise and rudeness for as long as he could, our driver walked back to the other's car and said, "Sir, if you would be kind enough to start my car for *me*, I would be delighted to stay here and blow your horn for *you!*"

PARKING

The two most important parking rules are: First, never take up more space than necessary; and second, never park so close to the car behind or in front of you that he will be unable to pull out. A young man of my acquaintance was so thoroughly irritated by a driver who had done just this that he unscrewed the valve and let the air out of the offender's tires! I cannot truly recommend such drastic actions, but I confess I can sympathize with them.

In addition to those two rules, it is considerate as well as required by law to park as close to the curb as possible. And most important, when the car in front of you obviously wishes to back into a parking space, stop in time to give him room to do it without rushing him by creeping forward, or worse, blowing your horn! It is, of course, an unforgivable sin to sneak into an empty space when another car is about to back in.

In addition, stay within the lines for parking spaces, take care not to block driveways, and park off the pavement on rural roads or when you are forced to pull off a highway. Don't monopolize unmetered parking spaces in busy shopping areas for long periods and don't pull out without carefully looking in all directions. Finally, always look behind you before backing up to make sure there are no pedestrians about to step off the curb.

GETTING INTO AND OUT OF A CAR

The custom of a man's opening the door and assisting a woman into a car is still correct—in fact many women feel slighted if the gesture is not made. However, when the car is parked on a busy street the man should not help her in and then walk into the stream of cars to get in on the other side. In this case he excuses himself for preceding her and slides in from her side. Safety for everyone concerned is far more important than obedience to an old and impractical rule of etiquette. On a wide or lightly traveled street a man enters the car on his own side after first assisting any women into the car on the curb side. Obviously passengers in the back seats should also enter from the side nearest the curb whenever possible.

A man taking a girl on a date, or on any occasion when the woman is dressed up, gets out of the car when they arrive at their destination, goes around, opens the door, and offers the woman a hand if necessary. But on ordinary occasions—a trip to the store, or the beach, or whatever, the woman opens the door and gets out by herself.

DRINKING AND DRIVING

One cannot overemphasize the menace of the drunken driver; certainly there is nothing to be said in his defense, nor could anyone want him to escape the full penalty of the law. But not half enough blame is laid on the exhilarated driver who has had one or two cocktails and cannot be called drunk by any standard. With joyful recklessness he takes chances that he would not think of taking when he has had nothing to drink. Alcohol and gasoline do not mix. If you have had a drink or two and realize that your senses are not as sharp as they should be, *do* have the intelligence to refuse to take the wheel. It is only sensible to ask, when the stakes are so high, that some other man or woman do the driving. Furthermore, any host, seeing that one of his guests is showing the signs of his liquor, should do his best to persuade him to stay away from the wheel.

IN AN EMERGENCY

If in spite of all precautions you have an emergency such as a flat tire or broken fan belt, it is not only essential to your safety but is also courteous to the other motorists to pull well off to the side of the road. Raise the hood and tie a white handkerchief or cloth to your door handle, as this is the universal signal of distress. Any policeman, and often a kindhearted passerby, will stop to offer assistance. On a superhighway stay in your car until help arrives. Walking for help on such a road is dangerous both for yourself and for the cars that must swerve to avoid you.

DRIVERS WE LIKE—AND DISLIKE

The perfect driver is one with whom you never find yourself driving the car. If you are constantly tensing your muscles and pressing your feet on imaginary controls, this is an indication that you are with a poor driver. Rapid accelerations and sudden stops can only mean that the person driving has not been planning ahead and concentrating on his responsibility.

SOME TIPS FOR AUTOMOBILE TRIPS

YOUR CAR AND EQUIPMENT

When starting out on an automobile trip that will take you away from your normal garage or repair shop, make certain that your equipment is in the best possible condition. Tires are the most important item—never start on a trip on which you will undoubtedly be driving at higher speeds than you normally would with worn tires, or if you are likely to find winter driving conditions, without having snow tires put on. Your fuel, oil, brakes, and automatic-transmission fluid should be checked before starting, as well as frequently during the trip. In strange territory you have no way of knowing when you will find the next gas station. Windshield-wiper blades should be replaced if rough or worn, and headlights, turn indicators, and brake lights checked. And of course your car registration and driver's license must be in order and easily available.

AVOID FATIGUE

On long trips it is essential to make frequent stops to stretch your legs, take some refreshment, and allow your engine and tires to cool off. If you are accompanied by a licensed and capable driver you should, of course, take turns at the wheel. A good rule is to stop and change drivers every hundred miles or every two hours, whichever comes first.

If you are stopping at motels along the way, it is wise to make a reservation for the following evening before you set off in the morning. The many chains of excellent motels all over the United States are delighted to help you estimate the distance you will cover and call ahead, free of charge, to one of their member motels to reserve a room for that night. You will find yourself much less tired if you plan to arrive at your destination by four in the afternoon to allow time for a rest, a little sightseeing if there are attractions in the neighborhood, and a leisurely dinner.

TRAVELING WITH CHILDREN

Traveling with children who are old enough to read, write, or play games need not be a problem. By taking along a supply of papers, crayons, or one of the excellent game books that are sold just for the purpose, the time can be made to fly. Verbal games, too, such as "Twenty Questions," or finding the letters of the alphabet on signboards, help to pass the hours. You may find that frequent stops are necessary—young stomachs seem to demand a steady flow of nibbles when motoring—but the stops will help to avoid restless wriggling while in the car.

For little children a mattress laid in the back of the station wagon or a little playpen with a well-padded mat on the back seat is a boon to the parents. The baby is free to move about safely, rather than endure the restraint of a car seat or his mother's lap. Even the older child will enjoy the luxury of being able to stretch out on such a mattress if you can afford to use the space in this way. Usually children will sleep away many hours if they can lie down comfortably.

FOR COMFORT AND SAFETY

It is required by law that all new American cars be equipped with safety belts, and most new models will not start unless the belt is fastened. This has caused considerable resentment, and many people go to great trouble to detach the mechanism so that they need not wear them. However, you are very foolish if you do this. Figures on accident deaths prove that while they do not prevent accidents, fatalities are far less frequent among drivers and passengers wearing properly installed belts or shoulder harnesses. They should be snugly fastened, so that you are not thrown hard *against* the belt by a sudden stop. Not only should the driver use his own belt, but he is correct in asking his passengers to do the same.

It is an excellent idea to keep a pair of sunglasses in the glove compartment of your car, since many people find that prolonged glare can cause severe headaches. If the glasses are always there, you will never be caught unprepared by an unexpected change in the weather.

Your clothing should be loose and comfortable. A girl who is comfortable in slacks or shorts will find that they are excellent for traveling. They allow maximum mobility, and now that there are so many motels available, a woman need not be seen in public until after she has had a chance to wash and change. A man, even though he may be dressed in a business suit, will probably be more comfortable if he removes his tie and replaces his jacket with a loose sweater, or if it is warm, drives in his shirt with the collar loosened.

CAR POOLS

Many thousands of Americans go to work in "car pools." As a practical and economical arrangement the car pool allows the other members of their families to have the car except on those days when it is their turn to provide the transportation.

For people who are about to join a car pool there are several basic rules of courtesy to be observed:

1. Be on time! If you keep the others waiting you may cause them to be penalized for late arrival at work.
2. Don't carry quantities of articles. If you must take a package or two, don't pile them where they will obstruct the driver's view, either directly or in the rearview mirror.
3. Don't open or close windows without asking the permission of the other passengers.
4. Don't bring an extra passenger without asking the driver if there is room. For example, some drivers do not object to three in the front seat, but others might find this a considerable annoyance.
5. Ask the permission of the other riders before smoking. When you do smoke, make sure that a window is opened, if only a little, to allow the smoke to escape.
6. If you are a woman, don't use the rearview mirror to fix your makeup. Carry a small mirror or a compact with a mirror in your purse.
7. If you must carry an umbrella when it rains, shake it well (and your raincoat too) before getting in the car, so that you don't soak your neighbor.
8. If you are not planning to use the car pool let the driver know in advance, so that he does not go out of his way to pick you up or wait for you unnecessarily before continuing his trip.

SEATING IN A CAR

Where people sit in a car may not be a matter of tremendous importance, but it certainly does cause a lot of confusion! The following questions and answers, taken from my column "Doing the Right Thing," cover almost every conceivable problem.

Q. What is the proper way to sit when a girl is driving and she picks up her boyfriend and a girl friend?

A. The girl friend should sit in the middle, and the boy on the side opposite the driver. In this way he can look at and talk to both girls at once rather than talking back and forth. Also, boys' legs are usually longer, and they are not comfortable straddling the hump in the center of the car.

Q. Same situation, but the car has bucket seats?

A. Whichever one the driver picks up first sits in the other front seat. *If they all get in together, the boy should certainly suggest that the other girl sit in front, and she may do so or she may say, "Oh no, you sit up front with Sue."*

Q. *When three women (or three men) are in a car do two sit in the front seat and one in back, or vice versa?*

A. *If all three cannot sit in front, one should sit alone in the back, and the third should sit up front with the driver. Otherwise the driver, who cannot keep turning around to talk, is entirely left out of the conversation.*

Q. *When a young couple have an older person with them—either a mother, a mother-in-law, or a friend—which lady sits in back? Does the relationship make a difference?*

A. *The relationship makes no difference at all. The front seat is considered the most desirable, and it should be given to the older lady. This is especially true in a two-door car. The more agile younger woman can climb into the back much more easily than the older one.*

Q. *When* two *older people ride with a young couple what is the seating arrangement?*

A. *The older people would ride together in the back, unless, again, it is a two-door car and one person would have difficulty getting in and out. In that case the wife of the driver and the more agile of the older people (or the man if they are a couple) would sit in the back.*

Q. *What is the seating order in a car pool of four people? The driver picks them up one at a time.*

A. *In a four-door car the first to be picked up gets in beside the driver, and the others sit in back. In a two-door car the first two get into the back, since it is almost impossible to tip up most front seats when someone is already sitting there. If the first person picked up sits in front, he must get out to let each of the others get in.*

Q. *When three couples go out together what is the best way to sit? All three pairs like to sit next to each other, so how do you decide which couple must split up?*

A. *If the car is very wide and the men very small you could make it "fair" by putting three men in front and three women in back. But this would probably not be the case, and the best solution is for the couple that includes the driver to split up. They can't "bill and coo" anyway, so the wife should not mind joining one of the couples in the back. If you all go out together often, take turns providing the transportation.*

Q. *When two women and two men (married couples) go out*

together, and both men have long legs, is it correct for them to sit in front while their wives sit in back? If so, who makes the suggestion? The driver, his wife, or one of the others?

A. *Since it is the driver's wife who would be giving up the "preferred" front seat she is the one who should make the suggestion. And it is proper—not only are the men more comfortable but the women can get through with their "girl talk" before they reach their destination.*

DON'T BE A FREELOADER

Unless you can afford to share the expenses don't take advantage of a friend or neighbor by continually accepting a "lift." Elderly people who can no longer drive are among the worst offenders. Without meaning to they take advantage of kind friends who do have cars and who frequently offer them a ride. If you are in the position of relying on friends for transportation frequently, *be sure* you can repay them in some way.

Offer to pay for the gas occasionally, or if you ride with them regularly, offer to pay a fixed weekly amount. One lady I heard of arranged with a gas station to make out a "gift certificate" and gave it to a friend who "chauffeured" her frequently. If the driver refuses to accept money for the expenses you can at least offer to buy her lunch on the way, or snacks, or if you can afford it, dinner at a restaurant.

SOME SUGGESTIONS FOR WOMEN DRIVERS

Here is a very practical, helpful list of suggestions for women drivers. Some are matters of courtesy; most are matters of safety. But in driving manners the two go hand in hand.

1. Travel during the day when possible.
2. Stay on the main roads.
3. Don't take shortcuts or unfamiliar roads after dark.
4. Wear a dark hat or scarf over your hair so as not to emphasize that you are a woman traveling alone.
5. Don't stop at roadside parks unless there are three or four cars, campers, or possibly trucks, especially in the evening. These are good signs of trustworthy people.
6. Don't stop after dark unless it is absolutely necessary, and then only at a well-lighted place such as a gas station or restaurant parking lot.
7. Do not hurry.
8. Keep car doors locked.

9. Be sure your car is in good condition and the gas tank full.
10. Drive defensively—as though everyone else is crazy.
11. Slow up if you see a traffic jam ahead. That's a good place for an accident.
12. Don't get angry when someone makes a mistake that doesn't cause an accident. You may be the next one to make the mistake.

With these rules in mind, you should arrive at your destination feeling relaxed and not too tired, even on a long trip.

TRAVELING BY BUS

Coast-to-coast or even city-to-city travel on a luxurious bus is a far cry from the familiar trip from Fifth to Twenty-fifth Street in a city bus. Transcontinental and intercity buses offer comfortable reclining seats, large windows to enjoy the scenery, air conditioning, toilets, and washbasins. Those that do not provide toilet facilities stop with reasonable frequency at bus stops that provide rest rooms, food, occasionally a bar, and best of all, a chance to stretch one's legs.

INFORMALITY ON BUSES

Since bus travel is the least expensive transportation of all, it is very popular with young people and also with the elderly who do not like to fly or are living on small incomes. Both these groups tend to like to chat and enjoy companionship, so the atmosphere on a bus is usually very friendly and relaxed. The same rules apply to talking to your seatmate on a bus as do on a plane. It is quite all right to make an attempt to start a conversation and to carry it on if the response is enthusiastic. But if the other person shows little enthusiasm don't intrude—let him read or sleep or whatever he wishes until, later on, he, perhaps, puts down his book and says, "We're right on time, aren't we?"

Young people in particular love to travel with small radios or tape recorders. If they wish to play them softly they may do so, but if the music is loud enough to annoy anyone their neighbors are quite within their rights to ask that it be turned down.

Seats are not assigned on buses, but the seat you choose when you board remains yours for the duration of the trip. When you get out at a bus stop, it is wise to leave a magazine, book, or something of that nature on the seat to indicate that it is taken.

CLOTHING

There are really no rules about clothing for bus trips. You wear whatever you are most comfortable in. College students and other young people generally travel in their everyday clothes—blue jeans, "cords," T-shirts, or whatever. Older women wear slacks or comfortable dresses, and men (few businessmen travel by bus) wear sports shirts or slacks and sports jackets. Naturally, if you are going directly to a "dressier" atmosphere when you arrive at your destination, you wear whatever is appropriate.

LUGGAGE

Bus lines have a weight limit on luggage—generally 150 pounds—but as on the airlines you may pay extra and take more. Overnight bags, briefcases, and other small baggage can be placed on the rack over your seat, and larger bags are stored in a separate compartment. There is no hanging space for garment bags, so they must go below with the other luggage.

MEALS

Meals are not served on buses but are bought at meal stops, which last thirty to forty-five minutes. Snacks can also be bought at in-between, fifteen-minute "rest stops." Some passengers bring their own food, and if you do, be sure that it is easy to eat and will not make a mess. Sandwiches, fruit, such as pears or apples, cookies, and soft drinks are easy to handle and can be packed in a very small container.

TAXIS

Taxi drivers, especially in New York City, have a reputation for being unfriendly, unhelpful, and rude. Were this true, it would be quite understandable, considering the stresses and strains they work under. Yet I have not found it so. Naturally there *are* rude and unfriendly drivers, just as there are objectionable butchers, bankers, and salespeople. But on the whole I have found taxi drivers willing to go at least halfway to be friendly if you get in with a smile and a "Good morning" or "Hello, nice day, isn't it?" Therefore I suspect that their reputation is not generally deserved, and that often the passengers bring the rudeness on themselves.

When a taxi picks you up, it is wise to glance at the driver's identification card, to be sure that he is "legitimate." If he has a "no-smoking" sign posted, observe it, and if his cigar or cigarette smoke is annoying to you, tell him so—nicely. If he is rude about it you have every right to report him to his company. If he starts a conversation it is your prerogative to respond or not, as you see fit. If his conversation is objectionable—if, for example, he launches a bitter attack against the mayor or starts to regale you with dirty jokes—the best way to put an end to it is to say nothing, and certainly not to encourage him by laughing at his jokes. But if his choice of topics is not offensive to you I recommend that you encourage him, because I have learned many interesting facts and discovered whole new viewpoints from cab drivers.

I stepped into a cab one day and found a shaggy white rug on the floor. Amazed, I asked the driver about it. He said, "You see, it's a great conversation piece! Besides, my riders like it, they're happier, so I'm happier, and it's made my job a lot easier."

On another occasion a friend of mine had been waiting in the rain for some time to get a cab to the train station at rush hour. A taxi with an "off-duty" sign finally stopped, and the driver asked where he was going. "Hop in," he said, "I'm going right by there." When my friend got out and asked how much he owed, the driver said, "Not a cent. I'm off duty but it was right on my way and I was happy to give you a lift!"

Unfriendly? Not all drivers by any means!

TIPPING

Twenty-five cents is generally considered a minimum tip unless the trip is under fifty cents—almost an impossibility today. The quarter is adequate for a fare of up to $1.50, and for higher fares a tip of approximately 15 percent is correct. This is also true when you contract with a driver to make an unmetered trip for an agreed-upon fee.

When a man cannot escort a woman to her home but must send her in a taxi he asks the driver what the fare will be, approximately, and gives her enough to cover it adequately, including the tip. If the woman does not wish him to do this, she may refuse, but he should at least make the offer firmly.

GETTING INTO A TAXI

In spite of the "ladies-first" rule for getting into cars many women—especially when they are wearing short, tight skirts or voluminous long skirts—don't like to slide across the seat. They may, if they wish, ask the man to precede them. This of course means that he must try to lean back across the woman to shut the door, or she

251

must lean out to shut it herself. There is something to be said on both sides. Therefore the man should make the gesture of holding the door for her and helping her in, but if she says, "Please go first," he should do so.

When they arrive at their destination he gets out first if he has entered last, and gives her a hand. If she is nearest the door, he leans over, shoves the door open, and she steps out first.

TIT FOR TAT

If, in spite of your friendly smile, your courtesy, and your adequate tip, the driver growls a nasty remark at you as you leave the cab, you have one means of retaliation. Get out and walk away, leaving the cab door open.

﹫26﹫ *Currency and Language*

The two greatest problems for travelers abroad are language and currency. Lack of understanding of another country's currency can result in painful situations—you may grossly undertip someone who has done you a real service, or you may overpay highly, appearing to be either ostentatious or stupid. But worse than this is the ill feeling and misunderstanding that can result from being unable to communicate with someone who knows no more of your language than you do of his.

MONEY MATTERS

The rates of exchanging dollars for each country's currency vary from time to time, but revised and inexpensive wallet-sized guides may be bought at stationery stores or gift shops and are distributed by many travel agencies, ticket agencies, etc. You may also buy adjustable ones that can be changed to give the current exchange. In any case they are a great help to the tourist who (like me) has great difficulty in equating seventy-five cents with several hundred (or thousand) lire, francs, pesos, or whatever the local currency may be. Whether you carry a computer or not, it is wise to memorize the corresponding sum for such standard amounts as a quarter, a dollar, and five dollars. If you know the amount equal to one dollar it is not difficult to arrive at that corresponding to ten dollars or one hundred dollars. How much more intelligent one looks in the marketplace if he says quickly, "Oh, no—that's too much!" than if he has to pull out a card, find the price and its equivalent sum in dollars, and then start to bargain!

A word about bargaining—in large city stores all over the world the prices are just as firm as they are at Macy's in New York City. Items are often marked or tagged exactly as they are in the United States, and there is no bargaining in such cases.

In small towns or rural marketplaces, however, especially in Latin countries, bargaining is part of the fun of making a sale. Not only is the tourist considered an idiot if he pays the "asking price," but he has ruined the day for the vendor, in spite of the exorbitant amount paid. In some countries like Mexico, which are overrun by tourists, you may at first be told that the price is fixed, but with persistence and a little firmness (an indication that you are about to walk away and forget the whole thing is usually effective) it is sure to be lowered.

In most restaurants in Europe there is a charge on the bill for service. When this is so, it is not necessary to leave anything extra, but if the service has been good most people leave the coins that the waiter brings back in change, or the equivalent of twenty-five to fifty cents. The waiter, aware of this custom, will usually bring your change in denominations that make it correct to leave only the coins on the plate. If there is no service charge, or a very small one, you should tip the usual 15 percent.

THE LANGUAGE BARRIER

For years Americans have been criticized for their ignorance of the idioms of countries in which they not only travel but sometimes live. Not even our diplomats have been required to learn to speak the languages of the countries to which they are accredited. The criticism is justified.

Although people will tell you time and again that it is not necessary to speak a foreign language because "everyone in Europe speaks English," it simply is not so. Outside the cities and areas frequented by tourists, there are literally millions of foreigners who neither speak nor understand one word of English. One cannot stress enough the importance, first, of knowing a few words of the idiom of whatever countries you are planning to visit, and second, of carrying a small pocket dictionary or phrase book with you. It is not necessary, of course, to take a course or buy a self-teaching system, but the following few often-used words and phrases (your grammar need not be perfect—your inflection will indicate a statement, question, exclamation, etc.) will smooth your path in any strange land:

"Yes" and "No."

"Please" and "Thank you." (Most important of all!)

"Hello." "Good-bye." "Good morning." "Good evening." "Good night."

"How much?" and "How much does it cost?"

"The check [or bill], please."

"Please speak slowly."

"I don't speak [whatever the language may be]."

"I don't understand."

"Where is . . . ?" and "How do you get to . . . ?"

"Ladies' room" and "Men's room."

"More, please" and "No more, thank you."

"Beautiful," "Wonderful," "Nice," "Kind," etc. These single words, said admiringly and sincerely about the place or people you are visiting, will warm the heart of the most skeptical native.

All phrase books will give more explicit sentences and questions on many subjects, but the above words should be learned by heart, so that they can be used quickly and easily without having to refer to a book.

On many overseas flights the airline gives out booklets about the country you are flying to. They contain practical information about currency, language, clothing, customs, etc., and are generally excellent. If you have not had time to "study up" beforehand, avail yourself of this opportunity on your flight.

For some reason we all have a natural reluctance to use foreign words if we do not really know the language. This results in a tendency to mumble or else to shout as if your listener were deaf. Obviously neither of these mannerisms helps him to understand you. The best way to make yourself understood is to say a word or phrase slowly and distinctly. Look at the other person and use gestures if they are meaningful. Waving your arms about may mean nothing, but making a writing motion can certainly help the waiter to understand that you are asking for the check.

Nothing pleases a native of any country, including our own, more than the realization that a visitor has taken the time and made the effort to learn a little of the country's language. If we could all remember this we would be far more eager to enter into conversation with foreigners. A great stride would be made toward furthering friendship among all peoples, and we would derive much greater pleasure from our travels.

Anyone who has walked through a little alley in a tiny town on a Greek island and seen the beaming smiles and eager response of the old ladies who sit there in the sun and hear *"Calimera"* instead of "Hello" or "Good morning" will know that this is true.

⊷27⊷ An Audience with the Pope

Any American tourist visiting Rome can be granted an audience with the Pope, for although there are often hundreds of people in a day who wish an audience no one with a proper introduction is denied. Obviously only relatively few can be granted one of the three types of audience that are considered to be personal; group or collective audiences are arranged for the great majority.

Requests by Americans for these group audiences as well as for the personal ones are cleared by the North American College and then sent to the Office of the Master of the Chamber (*l'Uffizio del Maestro di Camera di Sua Santità*), which is in the Vatican. Your request should be mailed well ahead of your departure date, so that you will have your acknowledgment in hand. On your arrival in Rome, your request and the approval you have received should be presented in person or mailed to the monsignor in charge, whose name, and the address, can be obtained from the concierge of your hotel. Each applicant must fill out a form requesting the kind of audience desired and show his credentials, which for a Roman Catholic may be simply a letter of introduction from his parish priest or a prominent layman. The length of his stay in Rome and his address and telephone number are also included on the form so that he can be notified of the day and hour of the audience. Non-Catholics as well as Catholics are granted audiences, but their requests must be arranged through prominent Catholic laymen or members of the Catholic clergy.

The reply, and the invitation if the answer is favorable, will be sent to you within a few days. You may receive a general admission ticket, meaning no reserved seat, or if you are considered sufficiently important, a reserved seat in a special section.

The concierge will also give you any other information you may need about the procedure.

THE GENERAL AUDIENCE

General audiences are held at 11:00 A.M. on Wednesdays at St. Peter's. During the summer months they take place at 10:00 A.M. People without reserved seats should arrive very early if they want a location with a good view. Choice places are often filled early in the morning.

Everyone rises as the Pope appears, seated on a portable throne called the *Sedia Gestatoria,* carried by eight Swiss Guards. At the end of the aisle he leaves the portable throne for a fixed one, and when he sits down the people may be seated also. He delivers a short address, and then everyone kneels as he gives his benediction to all those present as well as to all the articles they have brought to be blessed. The group rises, and if the Pope has time, he greets each person in the special area. The audience is over when he mounts his portable throne and is carried out.

For general audiences it is only required that everybody be dressed in a sober and suitable manner. Women must have their hair covered, must wear black or dark everyday dresses with necklines that are not too low and skirts that are not too short. They may not have bare arms or legs, but pants suits are permitted. Men in the general audience wear business suits and white shirts. In the reserved section some men will be seen in formal daytime wear, and women in long-sleeved black dresses and mantillas, but this is no longer obligatory, and sober, conservative daytime wear is acceptable.

OTHER AUDIENCES

The "private" audience is reserved for cardinals, heads of state, ambassadors, or others in important positions. Another type, the "special," is granted to people of slightly lower rank or to those who have an important subject to present to the Pope. The third type, the *"baciomano,"* is the only special audience to which laymen are invited. At the *baciomano* each visitor comes into the personal presence of the Pope, kisses his ring, and exchanges a few words with him, addressing him as "Your Holiness."

In this third type of audience visitors stand in a single file around the room until the Pope enters. They then kneel and do not stand again until he leaves the audience chamber or makes a sign for them to rise. He passes from one visitor to another, extending his hand so that all may kiss his ring. He also may ask a question and exchange a few words with each. As in the general audience, visitors customarily take with them one or more rosaries or other small religious objects, which are also considered to have been blessed when the visitor has received the papal blessing.

The rules of dress are not so strict as they once were, but even now for a private or special audience many men wear evening dress with tails or a morning coat, and women long-sleeved, high-necked black dresses and veils or mantillas over their hair. However, male visitors who do not have formal clothes with them are admitted in very dark blue or gray business suits. No one may wear any but the most functional jewelry—wedding rings, watches, etc.

NON-CATHOLICS

At a general audience every person present must kneel, rise, and sit at the prescribed time. Non-Catholics, if they do not ordinarily do so, need not make the sign of the cross.

At the *baciomano* non-Catholics on their arrival will be told the proper manner of kneeling and kissing the Pope's ring. If they object to these requirements on the grounds of their own religion, there may be some slight modification. But since the procedures are strictly followed, these people would be wiser to forgo the private audience than to make an issue.

❧28❧ *Representing America Abroad*

As a result of jet travel people at the farthest reaches of the earth have become our neighbors. Every traveler will increase his enjoyment of his trip if he attempts to make friends and exchange ideas with the foreigners he meets. We should try to acquire an understanding of the customs of the countries we visit and never presume that our own behavior is the only pattern to be followed.

The principal rule of conduct, abroad as well as at home, is to do nothing that either annoys or offends the sensibilities of others. Thus it is necessary for us to consider the point of view of all those with whom we come in contact when traveling. We must learn something of the customs that determine the foreigner's attitude if we want to be accepted with warmth and understanding. The best way to learn about the customs of other lands is to read all the books you can find about the people and places you intend to visit.

OUR ATTITUDE

We don't love all the foreigners who come to our shores. We do love those individuals who are appreciative of our country and courteous to us. Plainly then, corresponding manners are expected of us in the countries where we are foreigners.

At first thought it would seem that there could be no difficulties between us and those whose language is the same as ours—especially Canadians, Australians, and New Zealanders, who are said to be so similar to ourselves. But since frictions develop even when there is no language problem careful observance of other people's reactions to the things we do and say would be helpful. It has been said of Americans living abroad not only that they have more money than people of other nations, but that they are careless—and ostentatious —in their manner of spending it. This naturally angers those who are less well off or are more frugal by nature.

To our credit it can be said that we are straightforward; we honor our obligations; we keep our word. But sometimes we make overoptimistic promises, and tact is not one of our virtues. It is necessary, therefore, that we try to remember that it is always the stranger who must adapt himself, just as the visitor does to the ways of the house in which he is a guest.

Our travel attitude serves a dual purpose: It determines, of course, the impression we make on those who meet us, but it also determines the amount of enjoyment we get from our trip. Who enjoys his travels more, the man who goes with an open mind, eager to see the best in each country and forget the inconveniences, or the man who finds it too hot in Spain, broods all day because he had no hot water for shaving, or can't find a hamburger stand to buy his favorite lunch? This may sound ridiculous, but I have lived abroad and many a time I have shuddered and tried to pretend that I was anything but American when I heard the boorish complaints of my compatriots repeated endlessly in a penetrating voice. The complainer was certainly not enjoying his trip, nor was he impressing his neighbors with the charm of Americans.

ENTHUSIASM

You will make yourself thoroughly popular in every part of the world if you show appreciation and enthusiasm for the customs and sights of the country you are in. Of course there will be annoyances—service in many places is less efficient than that to which you are accustomed; neither the food nor the climate may appeal to you, but it is not necessary to voice your disappointments in public. You need not be falsely ecstatic, but you may be politely noncommittal and attempt to find and dwell on the parts of your stay that you *do* enjoy.

NO COMPARISON

Don't compare everything you see with the United States. We may have taller buildings, bigger automobiles, newer supermarkets, and less poverty (and none of this is necessarily true anymore), but because no one wishes to "suffer by comparison," to make such claims is the surest way of alienating your foreign acquaintances. Every country in the world has something to offer that we do not.

Therefore, remember that not everyone necessarily envies us our material wealth—others may prefer a simpler, less complicated existance.

ADAPTABILITY

Life and culture in Northern Europe are more similar to ours than those in Latin countries. In Germany, the Scandinavian countries, and the British Isles we have fewer problems understanding the people, whose way of life differs less from ours. Without exception Latins live in warmer parts of the world. The combination of temperament and the necessity of adapting themselves to hot weather has resulted in a relaxed, unhurried attitude in all things, and *mañana* is the order of the day. This is one of the most difficult adjustments for Americans to make. We are by nature hustlers, and to arrive in a country where no one cares about time, where people arrive for appointments hours late or forget to keep them at all, and where meals are served hours later than we are used to, is quite a shock. Some Americans simply cannot get used to it, and they leave as soon as they can. Others, who are more adaptable, find that the Latin countries have something to offer that is unique. They find it as difficult to return to a clock-watching society as it was to leave it behind in the first place.

MERCENARY AMERICANS

American tourists generally have an ample supply of cash, and they must learn to spend it graciously. The fact is that some of us still don't understand that the payment we make must be in something more than dollars—that is, if we are going to be given more than just what dollars can buy! Dollars, pounds, francs, pesos, lire—yes, all these buy material things, but they don't buy a single gesture of welcome, admiration, or sympathy.

A little thought, a little preparation, and a great wish to learn and understand are the attributes that will reap the reward—the foreigner's friendship.

APPEARANCE

The first thing that the native of another country notices is your appearance. Neatness and modesty are the two most important features. Your clothing may be the least expensive you can find and you may be traveling with only two or three outfits. But if you choose wrinkle-resistant materials as much as possible, unpack your clothes when you arrive and keep them clean (always carry a good spot remover and soap powder) and pressed (use valet service or your own little traveling iron), you will appear well dressed. Clothing should, of course, be appropriate. Good-looking pants suits are ideal for daytime sightseeing. Women should include a "dressy" suit or dress for dining out, and both men and women should take the proper clothes for any sports they intend to participate in. In resorts on the Riviera or Majorca, for example, you may wear the same things you would wear at any American resort—even more daring if you wish—but foreign men and women do not wear shorts or casual slacks except at resorts, in the privacy of their own yards, or for golf, tennis, boating, etc. Tourists show their ignorance and lack of respect for convention if they appear on the street in such attire. In fact, apart from cities in tropical climates, clothing is more formal than in our cities. Men are rarely seen in anything but business suits, and well-dressed women wear conservative suits, dresses, and pants suits. This is not so in the tropics, however, where the women often wear gay sleeveless cottons. The men in hot countries do not wear shirts and ties, but a loose cotton or linen shirt-jacket, worn outside the trousers and sometimes beautifully pleated or embroidered. Women should always carry a head covering, if only a scarf, for some churches ask that heads be covered, and it is only courteous to comply with their requirements.

No matter how you are traveling or for how long, your luggage should be neat and compact. There is no excuse for bags that look as if they'd been with you on a ten-year safari, since durable and lightweight luggage is available at moderate cost. Nothing looks worse or makes a traveler so uncomfortable as broken-down bags and numerous bundles.

Young people who are hiking or biking around Europe wear just what they do at home—generally blue jeans—as do the youth of every nation. They should always have with them, however, one "good" outfit (a dress for the girls; a shirt, jacket, and tie for the boys) for a visit to a private home or a good restaurant, for church, or simply to be ready for the unexpected invitation or event that may require dressing up.

The sloppiness, dirtiness, and indolent attitude of the itinerant "hippie" does little to enhance the reputation of his generation or his country.

GENERAL CONDUCT

The next thing people abroad will notice is your general behavior. Don't attract attention to yourself by talking in a loud voice. Americans have a reputation for being "loud," and it is true that foreigners, Latins especially, are brought up to admire a well-modulated voice. You will be far more attractive to people abroad if your voice carries only to those with whom you are talking. Your actions should be as inconspicuous as your voice. There is no need to gesture wildly because you are trying to speak a strange language—your movements should be natural but dignified. When you see a friend from home across the square or in a crowded restaurant, it is not necessary to shout and wave violently to attract his attention. Approach him quietly and greet him as you would ordinarily do at home.

Don't push ahead of others in lines or crowds. Most Europeans are more polite about waiting their turn than we are, and nothing could be ruder than shoving ahead of someone who is too polite to object.

Above all, don't stare! Of course you are interested when you see a Greek gentleman pull out his worry beads and toy with them, or when a peasant family approaches with mother burdened down with a heavy load while father rides the donkey. But don't stand rooted with your mouth open, obvious surprise or criticism written all over your face. Their customs are natural to them—it is not your place to judge them—and when you are in their country accept whatever you see as normal, storing it away in your memory as an interesting facet of life abroad.

Probably the best piece of advice was suggested to me by a young lady who had just returned from a most successful trip to Europe. She said, "Don't try to be different from what you are at home, but be the same as nicely as possible."

FOOD AND DRINK

Drinking and eating habits are different abroad, but if your table manners are good you will not be criticized because they are typically American. For example, you will not be considered ill-mannered if you switch your fork from your left hand to your right after cutting your meat, but everyone in the room will know that you are from the United States.

Cocktails are not a part of life abroad as they are in our country. Because everyone suspects, thanks to the movies, that Americans drink whiskey and cocktails from morning to night, they are frequently offered to us in private homes, and they are served in bars in all big cities. But beware! They may not taste like any cocktail you have ever had before, and they will more than likely be served lukewarm, possibly with a peanut-sized piece of ice. They may soon cure you of any desire to continue your normal "cocktail habit." It is far better to follow the customs of most foreign countries and take, instead, the delicious local wine or beer served with your meals. There are drinks, alcoholic and nonalcoholic, in each country that are interesting to try at least once. Wines in France, aperitifs in Italy, beer in Germany, and retsina wine in Greece are examples. While you may not enjoy all (or any) of them they are a part of the culture and economy of the country and should be sampled by all tourist visitors. This is true of the many new and strange foods you will encounter, too.

TAKING PICTURES

If you wish to include a citizen of the country in your pictures, have the decency to ask his permission. Although an impoverished farmer may appear unusual or picturesque to you, he may be ashamed of the very costume that to you seems "typical," and the last thing he wishes is to have his poverty recorded and distributed to strangers from another land. Some tribes in Africa believe that the camera is an "evil eye," and in the "bush" one should be sure that pointing the camera at a child will not scare him out of his wits.

In countries where the natives still wear a national costume (which are rare in Europe except on holidays, but common in Africa and the Middle and Far East), the people are accustomed to being photographed by tourists, but it is still polite to ask their permission unless you are just taking a picture of a large crowd.

Even though children may be frightened of you or the camera, their fears can usually be overcome by a smile and perhaps some token—a coin, candy, or gum. In areas where there are many tourists, children will often crowd around you, offering their services as models.

If you happen to see a tourist couple, one of whom is taking a picture of the other, offer to snap the picture for them, so that they may both be in it. This is always greatly appreciated, and we should remember to be thoughtful to fellow travelers as well as to the residents of the country in which we find ourselves.

EUROPEAN AND SOUTH AMERICAN MANNERS

CHAPERONS

Until very recently in Latin countries, no girl or young woman ever went out alone with a man unless he was her husband. Because more and more women are now being sent away to schools and colleges in more liberal societies, standards are slowly changing and the chaperon is becoming a thing of the past. In remote areas and in small towns the daughter's social life is still quite restricted, but in most parts of the world she may go out with a group of friends without an older chaperon. Brothers are considered excellent guardians, and a man wishing to go out with a girl may often arrange a "double date" through her brother.

Both men and women visitors to Latin countries should remember these customs. A man still cannot expect to meet a well-brought-up girl one night and take her out the next. He must be presented to her family, gain their approval, and then arrange, at least on the first few dates, to include mutual friends.

In many countries women do not go out alone after dark. A woman on the street by herself at night is an open invitation to improper advances by any Latin man. In fact he would consider himself at fault if he did not attempt to approach her. Young girls should stay in groups of three or four, and older women must be accompanied by at least one friend.

GRACIOUS MANNERS

The manners of Europeans and South Americans are more elegant than those of Americans. The men bow more deeply, the women always shake hands when introduced, and hand-kissing is still practiced. If you are a woman and you see that a handsome gentleman is about to lean over and kiss your hand, don't giggle or pull away. Accept the gesture for what it is—a compliment to your femininity—and act as natural as you can. European gentlemen not only tip their hats to ladies, they remove them and bow with a flourish. And ladies are always seated on the gentleman's right—except in a theater, when this would place her on the aisle.

Theater ushers, unlike those in the United States, are tipped the equivalent of a quarter for showing you to your seat.

Most Europeans shake hands all around when arriving at and leaving a place, or even when they meet each other on the street. Traveling Americans who adopt this custom will show their awareness and acceptance of local manners.

FLOWERS AND PRESENTS

Europeans, and especially Latins, dearly love to give presents, not only at Christmas or at someone's birthday, but unendingly. Such gifts are often foods baked in their own ovens or flowers grown in their gardens, but they may be anything more trifling or more expensive.

In accepting these, if we cannot speak the language, we bow and smile to show our pleasure in receiving the gift. As soon as possible thereafter we reciprocate with a simple present to prove our courteous intentions when fluency of speech is lacking. Flowers are always sent or taken to the hostess when you are invited to dinner. When you deliver them in person, remove the wrappings before you hand them to the hostess. They are also sent as a "thank you" and to greet visitors. In fact almost any occasion can be called an excuse to send a bouquet.

If it so happens that you cannot speak a word of Spanish or Portuguese, or it may be French or Italian or Dutch, remember that a smile and a genuine handshake will be received with a cordial welcome.

Part Six

PARTIES, PARTIES, PARTIES

᪥29᪥ Seated Dinners

THE SEATED DINNER

One thing is certain, no novice should ever begin her social career by attempting a formal dinner, any more than a pupil swimmer, upon being able to take three strokes alone, should attempt to swim three miles out to sea. The former will as surely drown as the latter.

Introspective people who are fearful of others, fearful of themselves, are never successfully popular hosts or hostesses. If you, for instance, are one of these, if you are really afraid of knowing some one who might some day prove unpleasant, if you are such a snob that you can't take people at their face value, then why make the effort to bother with people at all? Why not shut your front door tight and pull down the blinds and, sitting before a mirror in your own drawing-room, order tea for two?—Emily Post, 1922

Almost any dinner where guests are seated at a dining-room table and are served by someone other than themselves is considered a "formal" dinner today. Of course there are all degrees of formality, depending upon the dress, the table setting, the food served, and the type of service. Emily Post wrote, in 1922, that "it is not possible to give a formal dinner without the help of servants." Yet today the hostess who cooks a perfectly prepared meal and serves it at a beautifully set table is considered to have given a "formal" dinner.

There are "official" formal dinners, which must follow certain rules and are given only by diplomats or people in very high public positions. In those cases rules of protocol and precedence must be rigidly followed, and there are government agencies and special books to help those who are unacquainted with the requirements. For details not included in this book, newcomers to the world of diplomacy can get the information they need through the Office of Protocol in Washington or from the famous *Green Book* published each year with all the current social information a hostess needs to know—names, titles, rules of precedence, etc.

This chapter will deal mainly with the requirements for the sort of formal dinner with which most of us are familiar, and which we enjoy. By taking the suggestions that appeal to you, by eliminating the details that would be difficult for you or seem unnatural to you, and by combining the elements that are suitable to your home and your friends, you can use the information as it should be used—as a guide. Remember always, it is far less important to have matching silver or fine goblets than it is to be a warm, relaxed, and gracious hostess. Self-confidence helps you to be all these things, and a knowledge that you are doing things correctly—to the very best of your ability—will give you the assurance to entertain easily and well.

Whether your dinner party is held in a restaurant, a club, or your own home, and whether there are a hundred guests or eight, the requisites for a successful dinner party are the same. They are:

Guests who are congenial.

Servants (if you have them, or are hiring them for the evening) who are competent and pleasant.

An attractive table—everything in perfect condition: linen pressed, silver polished, glassware sparkling.

Food that is well prepared.

A menu that is well planned and suited to your guests' tastes.

A gracious hostess—one who is welcoming and at the same time enjoys her guests, and/or

A cordial host.

WITH HELP—OR WITHOUT

The first consideration is the size of your party. Eight is the maximum number that can be served comfortably at a sit-down dinner without help. If you enjoy cooking, you may prepare the food for as many guests as you wish, but to *serve* a seated dinner of more than eight efficiently and quickly it is almost essential to have assistance. For a party of twelve to sixteen the services of two people are necessary—one to help at the bar, pass hors d'oeuvres, and serve dinner, while the other cooks. Greater numbers, of course, require more help.

When you are entertaining without help, careful planning is essential to the success of your dinner. If you wish to enjoy the company of your guests you must choose dishes that can be prepared in advance and served with a minimum of last-minute fuss. You need not worry about fancy hors d'oeuvres—salted nuts or "niblets" and perhaps one dip or a good cheese are adequate, and you won't ruin your guests' appetites for dinner.

Because the normal routine of housework must continue along with the added work of preparing for your party try to spread it out over several days. Cigarette boxes may be filled, flowers arranged (being sure to choose those that will last several days), silver polished, and even your table set in advance. *(For details on table settings, see Chapter 38)*. Of course your husband must agree to eat in the kitchen, and the children must be asked to play in other parts of the house, but any chores that can be attended to ahead make the day of the party much more enjoyable. If you have a freezer by all means prepare in advance whatever dishes can be frozen.

THE INVITATIONS

Allowing the butler to invite guests at his own discretion is not quite as casual as it sounds. It is very often an unavoidable expedient. For instance, at four o'clock in the afternoon, Mr. Blank telephones that he cannot come to dinner that same evening. Mrs. Gilding is out; to wait until she returns will make it too late to fill the place. Her butler who has been with her for years knows quite as well as Mrs. Gilding herself exactly which people belong in the same group. The dinner cards being already in his possession, he can see not only who is expected for dinner but the two ladies between whom Mr. Blank has been placed, and he thereupon selects some one on the "Pantry" list who is suitable for Mr. Blank's place at the table, and telephones the invitation. Perhaps he calls up a dozen before he finds one disengaged.

> *When Mrs. Gilding returns he says, "Mr. Blank telephoned he would*
> *not be able to come for dinner as he was called to Washington. Mr.*
> *Bachelor will be happy to come in his place." Married people are*
> *seldom on this list, because the butler need not undertake to fill any*
> *but an odd place—that of a gentleman particularly. Otherwise two*
> *ladies would be seated together.*—Emily Post, 1922

Invitations to very formal dinners may be engraved or written by hand in the third-person style, or they may take the form of a "fill-in" printed invitation. Less formally, they are written on notepaper or on a visiting card or informal. For most occasions, however, the attractive, decorated, fill-in invitations available at all stationers are practical and useful. You may choose either the type made for a special event or those that are designed to be used for any occasion. Telephone invitations are perfectly correct for any but the most formal dinners. They have the advantage of an instant response but the disadvantage of leaving the invitee with no reminder of the time, date, or location of the party.

Invitations to a dinner party should be extended between ten days and two weeks ahead of time. They should be answered at once, according to the implied instructions on the invitation. If the RSVP is followed by an address, the reply should be written—in the third-person form if that is the style of the invitation, by informal note if the invitation is informal. The new bordered or illustrated fill-in invitations, however, do not require the third-person form, even though they may come from "Mr. and Mrs. Jones."

When the RSVP is followed by a telephone number (and perhaps "regrets only") try to respond by phone. If, as sometimes happens, you cannot reach the sender and the time of the party is approaching, it is thoughtful to drop a note in the mail instead.

Nothing but illness, unexpected absence, or an unavoidable accident can excuse the breaking of a dinner engagement. To accept a dinner at Mrs. Franklin's and then call to say you can't make it when you are invited to dine with the Goldbergs is inexcusable. But had you declined the Franklin's invitation in the first place, you would, of course, be free to accept Mrs. Goldberg's invitation or to stay at home. In other words don't accept an invitation if you don't care about it.

If for some reason a guest who has accepted a dinner invitation is forced to drop out at the last moment, the hostess may try to fill in by inviting an intimate friend. She does this by telephone. The one who receives such an invitation is virtually bound by the rules of friendship and good manners to accept if possible.

For information about the style and wording of invitations see Chapter 39.

SELECTING YOUR GUESTS

It is usually a mistake to invite great talkers together. Brilliant men and women who love to talk want hearers, not rivals. Very silent people should be sandwiched between good talkers, or at least voluble talkers. *Silly people should never be put anywhere near learned ones, nor the dull near the clever, unless the dull one is a young and pretty woman with a talent for listening, and the clever, a man with an admiration for beauty, and a love for talking.*

Nor must a "specialist's" subject be forced upon him, like a pair of manacles, by any exploiting hostess who has captured him. Mrs. Oldname might perhaps, in order to assist conversation for an interesting but reticent person, tell a lady just before going in to dinner, "Mr. Traveler who is sitting next to you at the table, has just come back from two years alone with the cannibals." This is not to exploit her "Traveled Lion" but to give his neighbor a starting point for conversation at table.—Emily Post, 1922

When making up her guest list, a hostess must try to invite and put together those who are likely to be interesting to each other. Professor Bugge might bore *you* to tears but Mrs. Entomoid would probably adore him, just as Mr. Stocksan Bonds and Mrs. Rich would probably have interests in common. Making a dinner list is a little like making a Christmas list. You put down what *they* will like (you hope), not what you like. People placed between congenial neighbors remember your dinner as delightful, but those seated next to their pet aversions will need wild horses to drag them your way again.

While a friendly difference of opinion or even a mild argument is often stimulating, a bitter controversy is embarrassing and destructive to good conversation. It is thus safer to avoid seating people next to each other who are deeply involved in, or rabidly opinionated about, opposite sides of a controversial issue.

The lady who is guest of honor sits, of course, on the host's right. She may be the oldest lady present, a girl who has just become engaged, a woman who has just published a successful novel, or simply the wife of the male guest of honor. When there is no particular guest of honor among a group of friends dining together, the hostess might choose the oldest lady or one who has not visited her house for some time to sit on her husband's right. Otherwise she may seat her guests according to whatever arrangement she thinks they will enjoy the most, alternating the men and women and separating husbands and wives. If there is an uneven number of men and women she must space them as evenly as possible. She may keep her place at the end of the table unless doing so puts too many women in a row. Whatever else she may do she still seats the honored guests at her and her husband's right. The lady next in importance sits at the host's left, and her husband, or the man of next importance, on the hostess' left.

The host who holds an official position may have more to say in the choosing of guests than the man in private life. He may, if he is in the diplomatic corps, for instance, be ordered by his government to entertain important visitors, and he may even be told in what way and to what extent he is to do so. He relays this information to his wife, who takes care of details of food, service, etc., as usual, but who follows his suggestions as to the date, what officials must be invited, and other matters important to the specific occasion. When the official list is complete, his wife will, as at any dinner, choose as the other guests those who will be most congenial to the ones who must be invited.

ANNOUNCING GUESTS

Guests are never announced at private dinners. But at large official functions it is often necessary, as even the hostess may not know some of those she has invited. A gentleman follows his wife into the living room. If the butler knows the guests he merely announces the wife's name first and the husband's. If he does not know them by sight he asks whichever is nearest to him, "What name, please?" He or she answers, "Mr. and Mrs. Lake."

The butler then precedes the guests a few steps into the room where the hostess is stationed, and standing aside, says in a low but distinct voice, "Mrs. Lake," and then after a pause, "Mr. Lake." Married people are usually announced separately, but occasionally people have their guests announced as "Mr. and Mrs. Lake."

GREETING THE GUESTS

At very large formal dinners guests are greeted at the door by a butler or maid, and their coats are taken by another maid. The hostess stands in the living room, near the door. As guests enter she greets them with a smile and a handshake and says something pleasant to each. What she says is not important; her expression and manner convey a gracious welcome. She may simply say, "I'm very glad to see you," or "I'm so glad you could come!" No matter what she says she takes their hand with a firm pressure and her smile is really a *smile* of welcome. Her husband, who is circulating and talking to other guests, excuses himself and comes to greet newcomers as soon as he can.

Most dinners, however, are much less formal. The host and hostess stay near the door if possible, or if they happen to be in the living room, they go together to greet their guests when the doorbell rings. If the host is serving cocktails he brings them what they wish or he sees that the waiter or bartender takes their order. The hostess introduces them to the people they do not know.

If cocktails are served, dinner should be planned for at least an hour later than the time on the invitation; twenty minutes later if drinks are not served, to allow late arrivals a moment of relaxation. During this period the hostess may slip out to the kitchen to attend to last-minute details and be sure that her help are having no problems. She should make her absence as brief as possible so that the guests will not feel that she is overburdened.

THE LATE GUEST

Old Mrs. Toplofty's manners to late guests are an exception: on the last stroke of eight o'clock in winter and half after eight in Newport, dinner is announced. *She waits for no one! Furthermore, a guest arriving after a course has been served, does not have to protest against disarranging the order of dinner since the rule of the house is that a course which has passed a chair is not to be returned. A guest missing his "turn" misses that course.*—Emily Post, 1922

Fifteen minutes is the established length of time that a hostess need delay her dinner for a late guest. To wait more than twenty minutes, at the outside, would be showing rudeness to many for the sake of one. When the late guest finally enters the dining room he must go up to the hostess and apologize for being late. The hostess remains seated, and if the guest is a lady she merely shakes hands quickly so that all the men at table need not rise. The hostess should not take the guest to task but should say something polite such as, "I'm so sorry you had such a bad drive but I was sure you wouldn't want us to wait dinner." The latecomer is served whatever course is being eaten at the time he arrives. Of course, if that happens to be dessert the hostess would ask the waitress to bring him a plateful of the main course from the kitchen.

DINNER ENVELOPES

Although they are rarely seen anymore, dinner envelopes are still needed at very formal official dinners, mainly in diplomatic circles. The dinner envelope has a gentleman's name on the outside, and inside, a card with the name of the lady he is to take in and sit beside at dinner. This card just fits in the envelope, which is an inch or so high and about two inches long. When the envelopes are addressed and filled they are arranged in two or three neat rows on a silver tray and put in the front hall. The tray is presented to each gentleman just before he goes into the living room or just after his arrival in the entrance hall.

A practical method of telling each gentleman where he is to sit at a very large table is to choose a small fold-over card instead of the usual single one. His name is on its front fold and his partner's name inside, and below her name in the lower half of the fold is a small engraved diagram showing the table, the location of the door, and their seats.

If it is so big a dinner that there are many separate tables, the tables are numbered with standing placards (as at a public dinner) and the table number is written below the lady's name.

If the gentleman does not know the lady whose name is in his envelope he should make every effort to be introduced, or if necessary, to introduce himself, before dinner.

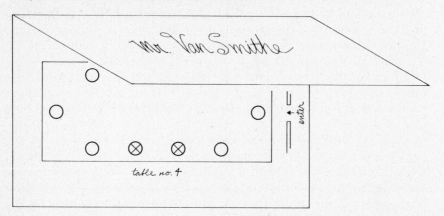

WHEN DINNER IS ANNOUNCED

It is the duty of the butler or waitress, if you have engaged help for the evening, to "count heads" so that he or she may know when all the guests have arrived. As soon as the last person has come in, he notifies the cook. When the cook is ready, the butler, having glanced into the dining room to see that water glasses are filled and the candles lighted, enters the living room, approaches the hostess, and says quietly, "Dinner is served." Or if she happens to be looking at him he merely nods and she says, "Dinner is ready. Shall we go in?" If cocktails are being served, the hostess signals the butler when she sees that the guests will be ready to go to dinner shortly, and he warns the cook. Or the hostess may have told her help in advance at what time she wishes dinner announced.

Occasionally some of the guests are enjoying the cocktail hour so much that they are reluctant to go in to dinner. At a large party, when people have formed several groups, the hostess who does not want her beautiful roast to dry out, or her soufflé to fall, insists that the most amenable of these groups start moving toward the dining room, and the others usually follow. Or she may ask two or three good friends to lead the way.

If the hostess has no objections she may suggest that her guests bring their cocktails to the table. Some will, but most will empty their glasses and leave them. If a guest says, "May I take my drink?" she cannot refuse, but she can discourage others from doing so if she is serving wine or another beverage by simply not making the suggestion.

The host leads the way in to dinner with the woman guest of honor, whom he seats on his right. The hostess is always the last to go into the dining room at a formal dinner unless the President of the United States or a governor (but only in his own state) is present. In these exceptional cases the hostess would go in to dinner with the guest of honor, who would lead the way, and the wife of the President or governor would follow immediately with the host. Unless envelopes have been given to the men (see "Dinner Envelopes," above) the other guests walk in with whomever they are talking to when dinner is announced.

The guests find their own place cards, or if there are no place cards, wait for the hostess to tell them where to sit. Women sit down as soon as they find their places, even though the hostess remains standing until everyone is at his chair. The men hold the chairs for the ladies on their right, who slide in from the left-hand side of the chair. The men do not sit down until the hostess is seated. The male

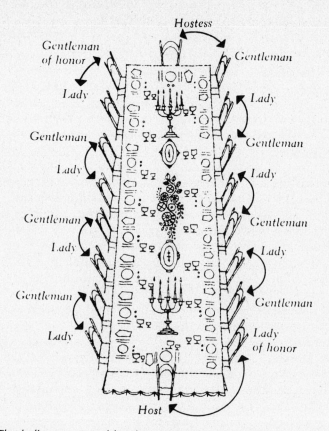

The ladies are seated by the gentlemen indicated by the arrows.

guest of honor, even though he has escorted the hostess in, seats the lady on *his* right, and the man on the hostess' left seats her.

THE PLACE CARDS

Place cards are always used at very formal dinners, and I find them very useful at *any* dinner so large that the hostess cannot easily indicate where everyone is to sit. Place cards are about an inch and a half high by two and a half inches long, usually plain, bordered in silver or gold, or marked with a simple monogram or crest. Decorated cards, while suitable on such special occasions as Christmas or a birthday, are out of place on a formal table. The courtesy title and surname—"Dr. Gooding," "Mr. Ashley"—are used at official dinners except when there is more than one guest with the same surname, in which case "Mr. Russell Albright" and "Mr. Lee Albright," for example, should be used to make the distinction. At a party of friends or relatives first names are used, or if necessary to "differentiate," "Bob P." and "Bob M." *See also Chapter 12 if your dinner involves government officials.*

SEATING PLANS

When you are seating three, five, or seven couples, there is no problem at all. It works out evenly, with the hostess at one end of the table (usually the end nearest the kitchen), the host opposite her, and the men and women alternating on either side. However, when you have multiples of four you must make another arrangement. To avoid seating two women and two men together, the hostess moves one place to the left, so that the man on her right sits opposite the host at the end of the table.

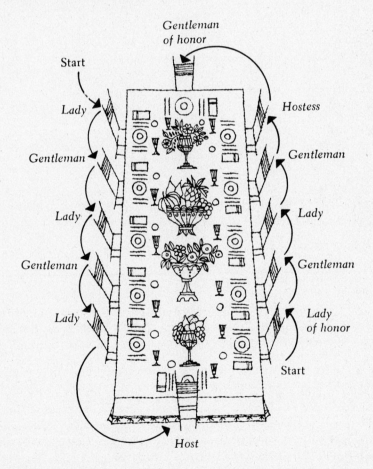

Seating arrangement for a party of eight, twelve, or sixteen. Arrows indicate the order of service.

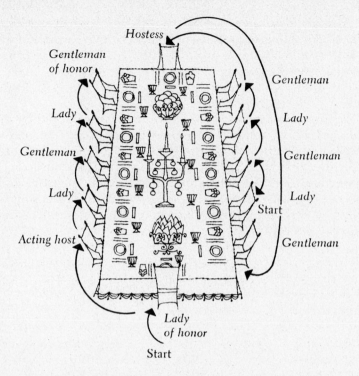

The correct seating arrangement for a group that has a hostess but no host. Arrows indicate the order of service.

Other situations require variations, too, but almost all seating problems can be worked out by common sense and an awareness of which guests will be happiest seated next to certain others.

EXPERT HELP

. . . None but vulgarians would employ a butler (or any other house servant) who wears a mustache! To have him open the door collarless and in shirt-sleeves is scarcely worse!

All house servants who assist in waiting on the table come under the direction of the butler, and are known as footmen. One who never comes into the dining-room is known as a useful man.

In a small house, the butler polishes silver, but in a very big house one of the footmen is silver specialist, and does nothing else. Nothing!
—Emily Post, 1922

As mentioned on page 269, two efficient servants can handle a party of up to sixteen people very nicely. If you wish, however, to have *all* responsibility taken off your hands and to give a dinner truly memorable for its smoothness and elegance, you should hire a butler, a maid, and a cook for a party of more than twelve. We will consider this larger or "special" party first.

If you have live-in help and entertain frequently they will presumably have learned to serve in the way you like best, and as long as they are neat, friendly, and efficient you have no problem. But you are in the minority, and most of us must hire temporary help for the evening when we wish to entertain formally. All cities and most smaller communities have catering services that provide not only servants but excellent meals, either prepared by a cook sent to your home or partially cooked in their kitchens and finished in yours. Specialized employment agencies will provide the help only, if you prefer to do your own cooking. And if there is a permanent cook in your house, she prepares the meal, and only the butler and/or maid are hired for the evening. They serve and also assist the cook with the cleaning up.

When temporary servants are used, the hostess naturally must do most of the advance preparation. She sets the table, arranges flowers, and does all else, so that they will have no other responsibilities beyond the preparation and serving of the meal.

If the meal is to be prepared in your home the cook arrives early in the day, so that after the hostess has given explicit directions as to the food and explained the whereabouts and workings of all the utensils and appliances to be used, there will be plenty of time for the careful preparation of the meal.

The butler and maid come later, but early enough to discuss all details of service with the hostess and to take care of any last-minute polishing or arranging that may be necessary. If cocktails are to be served, the butler sets up the bar, sees that he has all the necessary ingredients, and is ready to serve as each guest arrives. A few minutes before the hour of the guests' arrival the butler and maid put on their uniforms, which should be impeccable. The maid takes her place in the hall to direct the guests or help with their wraps. The butler stands nearby and passes cocktails or simply waits to assist in any way he can. It is the responsibility of the temporary butler, as it would be if he were permanently employed, to see that all runs smoothly. The hostess should be able to devote her attention to her guests.

The butler and waitress ordinarily do not leave until the guests have been ushered out, the last glass washed, and the last ashtray emptied. However, if they are hired on an hourly basis the hostess may specify ahead of time that they may leave at ten or eleven, or whenever she wishes. The cook, however (unless all three work as a "unit"), leaves as soon as the cooking utensils and dinner service have been washed and the kitchen made immaculate.

The method of paying temporary help varies in different localities and also depends on the policy of the agency through which they are hired. Some caterers send a bill for their services and prefer that you do not add a tip. Others send a bill but indicate that you may add a tip. If the help has been hired from an employment agency or by you personally, you simply pay them before they leave at the rate you have agreed upon. In any case, it is most important to establish the method and amount of payment at the time the servants are hired to avoid embarrassment or unpleasantness that may ruin an otherwise perfect evening.

AND EXPERT SERVICE

At a very formal dinner served by a large staff the butler always stands behind the hostess' chair, except when giving one of the men under him a direction or when pouring wine. His duty is to see that everything goes smoothly and he is not supposed to leave the dining room. At a small dinner, when he has no assistant, he naturally does everything himself; when he has a second man or a waitress he passes the principal dishes and the other follows with the accompanying dishes or vegetables.

In any case, whether there are two at table or two hundred, plates are changed and courses presented in precisely the same manner. No serving dishes or platters are ever put on the table except the ornamental compotes of fruit or candy. The meat is carved in the kitchen or pantry; vegetables, bread, and condiments are passed and returned to a side table or the kitchen.

From the time the table is set until it is cleared for dessert, a plate should remain at every place. The plate on which oysters or clams are served is put on top of the service plate, and so is a plate holding fruit or cold seafood in a stemmed glass. At the end of the course the used plate is removed, leaving the service plate. The soup plate is also put on top of this same plate. But when the soup plate is removed, the underneath plate is removed with it, and the hot plate for the main course immediately exchanged for the two taken away.

If the first course is passed instead of being served on individual plates, it is eaten on the service plate. An exchange plate is then necessary before the soup can be served. That is, a clean service plate is exchanged for the used one, and the soup plate then put on top of that.

Although all dishes are presented at the left of the person being served, it is better that plates be removed from the right. If more convenient, however, it is permissible to remove them from the left. Glasses are filled and additional knives placed at the right, but forks are put on as needed at the left.

The only plates that may be brought into the dining room one in each hand are for soup and dessert. The soup plates are put down on the service plates, which have not been removed, and the dessert plates are put down on the tablecloth. The plates of every other course have to be exchanged, and therefore each individual service requires two hands. Soup plates two at a time can be dangerous, as it is while putting down one plate and balancing the other that a mishap can occur. If only one plate of soup is brought in at a time, accidents should not happen. Also, the spoon and fork on the dessert plate can easily fall off unless it is held level. Two plates at a time are therefore not a question of etiquette, but one of the servant's skill.

At one time good service required the removal of each plate the instant the fork was laid down on it, so that by the time the last eater was finished, the entire table was set with clean plates and was ready for the service of the next course. But the protests of the slow eaters were loud and clear, and a considerate hostess now does not have the plates removed until the slowest eaters have finished.

ORDER OF SERVICE

The lady of honor on the host's right is always served each dish first. The butler serves the entrée, followed by the maid with a vegetable. They move around the table counterclockwise, serving the host last. Some hostesses insist that they be skipped and that the dishes be brought back to them after being offered to the host, but I consider this time-consuming and unnecessary. When a dinner is large enough to require two services of each dish the butler serves one to the lady of honor, and the maid, at the same time, passes the other to the lady seated on the man of honor's right. When a single woman entertains, the lady on the acting host's right, or the lady sitting at the opposite end of the table (if that is the way the seating works out), is served first.

Study the diagrams on the preceding pages, which explain seating and service arrangements.

THE HOSTESS IS NEVER SERVED FIRST

The hostess who has herself served first when there is another woman at the table, is acting in the poorest taste. Perhaps in the dark ages the host sampled the food before his guests to prove that he wasn't poisoning them, but that is scarcely necessary today, and the hostess who helps herself to the fresh and untouched dish and lets the others take what she leaves is either unthinking or rude.

FILLING GLASSES

I, personally, like to have the water glasses filled before the guests enter the dining room, but if they are not, the butler goes from guest to guest, on the right-hand side of each, and fills the water goblet as soon as they are seated. He then serves the wine, from the bottle or a decanter, asking each guest, "Wine, sir [or madam]?" All wines are poured at the right of each person and without lifting the glass from the table.

The proper way to serve champagne is from its own bottle with a napkin wrapped around it. The reason for this is to catch all drops —either of wine or of condensed moisture—that might fall, as well as to protect its proper chill from the warmth of hands.

SERVING BREAD

As soon as soup is served, dinner rolls are passed in a flat dish or a basket. It may be an old-fashioned silver bread dish or simply a shallow wicker basket with a fringed napkin laid in it. Several varieties of breads may be served—crescent rolls, melba toast, and rye or whole-wheat crackers, for example—but one kind of roll alone is perfectly acceptable. A guest helps himself with his fingers and lays the roll or bread on his butter plate. *(See Chapter 37.)* Whenever a guest has no bread left at his place, more should be passed to him.

PRESENTING DISHES

Dishes are held flat on the palm of the servant's left hand; every hot one must have a napkin placed as a pad under it. An especially heavy platter can be steadied if necessary by holding the edge of the platter with the right hand, the fingers protected from being burned by a second folded napkin.

Each dish is supplied with whatever silver is needed for serving it. A serving spoon, somewhat larger than an ordinary tablespoon, and a large fork are put on most dishes. Sometimes the spoon alone is used if the dish is not hard to help oneself to. Braised celery, broccoli, spinach *en branche*, etc., need both fork and spoon. There are various special lifters and tongs for asparagus, but most people use the ordinary spoon and fork. With the spoon underneath, the fork prongs turned down hold the stalks on the spoon. Corn on the cob is taken with the fingers, but for a *formal* dinner party corn should be cut off, buttered, seasoned, and served in a vegetable dish. An aspic or mousse should have both fork and spoon, but peas, mashed potatoes, rice, etc., may be offered with a spoon only.

THE SERVING TABLE

The serving table is a halfway station between the dinner table and the pantry. It holds stacks of plates, extra forks and knives, finger bowls (if you are using them), and dessert plates. If the serving table is small or too crowded, the latter can be put on the sideboard.

All dishes of food after being passed may be left on the serving table on a warming tray in case they are needed for a second helping. Or they may be taken to the kitchen and kept warm on the stove.

CLEARING THE TABLE FOR DESSERT

Salad plates as well as the plates used for the entrée are removed before dessert is served. The saltcellars, pepper shakers, unused flat silver, and nut dishes are taken off on a serving tray, and the crumbs are brushed off each place with a tightly folded napkin onto a tray or "silent butler" held under the table edge.

DESSERT SERVICE

There are two methods of serving dessert. One is to put the fork and spoon on a china plate with or without a glass bowl on it, depending on the nature of the dessert. After dessert the finger bowl is brought in on another plate. In the other, more common, service the finger bowl on a small doily, as well as the fork and spoon, are brought in on the dessert plate. The diner puts the finger bowl on the doily above his plate, and the fork and spoon each to its proper side.

When fresh fruit is to be served, it is passed immediately after the dessert or ice cream; and decorative sweets are passed last.

FINGER BOWLS

Before leaving the subject of dessert I want to say a word about finger bowls. One rarely sees them nowadays, and it is too bad. With the number of automatic dishwashers in use, they would scarcely cause much extra work. And what could be nicer than to leave the table with your fingers and lips really clean, as no dry "wipe" can possibly make them? Perhaps, if the current trend toward a search for more elegance continues, they will come back in style. In any case, the finger bowl is less than half-filled with cold water; and at dinner parties a few violets, sweet peas, or rose petals may be floated in it.

This reminds me of a delightful story that one of my daughter's friends told about herself. She was invited for the first time to a dinner at her boyfriend's home. She was somewhat nervous about it because she knew that his family lived on a grander scale than her own. Naturally, she wished to make a good impression and decided to watch carefully and simply copy other guests if she had any problems. Everything went beautifully through the entrée: She chose the right silver, broke her bread before buttering it, and served herself impeccably. Then came the dessert—she thought! A pretty bowl of clear liquid with bits of pink icing or pastry floating in it. Flushed with her success until then, she forgot to look around her, picked up her spoon, and proceeded to eat the rose petals that were floating in the finger bowl!

Fortunately, her sense of humor and that of her boyfriend's family carried her through, and the couple are soon to be married!

A slice of lemon is never used in a finger bowl at a formal dinner. But after broiled lobster at an informal or family dinner lemon in *hot* water is excellent.

AFTER-DINNER COFFEE

Coffee is served in one of three ways:

1. The butler passes a tray of cups, saucers, and sugar; the maid follows with the coffeepot and pours into the cup held in the guest's hand.
2. A tray with filled cups is proferred by the butler to the guests, who help themselves.
3. The tray of cups and sugar (if not too heavy) is held on the servant's left hand. The guest puts sugar into one of the cups and the servant pours coffee with the right hand.

Liqueurs are offered exactly as coffee in the second or third manner. The guests pour their own, or they say, "Cognac," or "Mint, please," and their choice is poured for them.

Cigarettes are arranged and passed on a tray with matches or a lighter.

If the men are separated from the women after dinner, cigars are offered to them on a tray, either neatly stacked or in the wooden box in which they come. There should be a cigar cutter and a lighter with a good strong flame beside them.

SERVICE WITH ONE MAID

One maid cannot possibly do all the preparing and serving of a dinner party of any size, but she certainly can do a great deal toward making it go smoothly and allowing the hostess more time to be with her guests. Before dinner, if she and the hostess have planned well and prepared in advance, she is on hand to take coats from the guests and serve hors d'oeuvres if cocktails are offered. She should attend to as many last-minute details as possible so that the hostess need not leave her guests. When everything is ready she announces dinner, or signals the hostess, who tells the guests that dinner is ready.

If a first course is served, it should be on the table when the guests sit down. The maid removes the plates when everyone is finished and either replaces each one with a hot plate or places a stack of hot plates in front of the host, depending on how the main course is to be served. If all the food is ready in the kitchen she passes it to each guest, the meat first and then the vegetables. If the host is carving and serving at his place she takes each plate as he fills it and places it in front of a guest.

When the maid serves the food directly from the kitchen, she starts on the host's right with the lady who is guest of honor and continues around the table counterclockwise, serving the host last, just as described for a more formal dinner. The order is exactly the same when the maid passes plates that have been filled by the host.

All main dishes are served from the left, and if convenient, removed from the right. Condiments, breads, and sauces are usually passed around the table by the guests themselves, but if the group is not large the maid may pass one or more of them when she has finished with the main dishes. Dishes that hold two or three varieties of condiments and divided vegetable dishes can greatly facilitate serving. There is no reason why a competent maid may not pass two vegetable dishes at the same time, holding one in each hand.

When everyone is served, the maid may remove the serving dishes to keep them warm in the kitchen; or if the dishes have covers, or are of pottery or other heat-retaining material, or if you have an electric hot plate, they may be left in the dining room. When the hostess sees that the guests are ready for another portion she rings for the maid and says, "Mary, would you please pass the meat and rice again?" If Mary is experienced she will bring in the serving dishes without being asked.

While the guests are eating, the waitress neatens up the living room, empties ashtrays, and prepares the dessert and the coffee tray.

When all her guests have finished, the hostess rings and the maid clears the table. Everything is removed except the glasses and the silver for dessert. She then crumbs the table, using a clean folded napkin to sweep the crumbs onto a small plate held below the edge of the table.

Dessert may be brought in from the kitchen already on the plates and placed before the guests in the same order as was the main course. Or the plates may be set before the guests and the dessert passed to each one in turn.

WITHOUT HELP

The ideal solution when one is giving a dinner party with no help is to have the guests serve themselves from a side table or buffet and then seat themselves at the dining-room table. This completely avoids the necessity of passing dishes around the table and makes dining easier and more pleasant for everyone.

However, some hostesses do not have the facilities to do this, or prefer that the food be served at the table after the guests are seated.

For this type of meal start with the main course and provide the equivalent of a first course by serving plenty of substantial canapés with your cocktails. You may also serve cold soup, oysters, clams, or smoked salmon in the living room before going in to the dining room.

When the "cocktail hour" (if you serve cocktails) is over, you leave your guests with your husband; light the candles, fill the water glasses, bring the meat from the kitchen, set the vegetable dishes beside it, and then invite everyone to "Come in to dinner."

When the food is served at the table, your husband carves the roast or serves the casserole. Preferably he also serves the vegetables, but the vegetable dishes may be handed around. If the table is overly crowded he may carve the meat and serve the vegetables at a sideboard. He hands you the filled plates, and you pass them to your guests.

In either case, the first plate is given to the lady on the host's right. When he is serving from his seat at the head of the table he says, "This is for you," since the guest of honor should be served first. The next plate is passed down the table on the right side and is placed in front of his wife, or whoever is seated at the opposite end. The rest of the guests on his right are served in order, working back toward the guest of honor, and the process is then repeated on his left. He serves himself last. Since this procedure can consume considerable time and the food will surely be getting cold it is important that the host or hostess ask the guests to start after three or four people have been served. If the host and hostess forget to do so, one of the guests is perfectly correct in beginning to eat.

When salad is served, it is best that the guests pass the bowl, each one in turn holding it for the person on his right. Dessert may be put on each plate in advance, or you may serve it at the table as your husband did the roast.

In many cases, when the guests see you start to rise to clear the table, some of them will also stand up, saying, "May I help you?" You *must* refuse, telling them, "No, really, it is easier to do it myself," or "Thank you, but we'll just get in each other's way." The only exception to this occurs when you have a daughter, sister, or very close friend at the table and have asked her in advance whether she would mind helping.

In any case, alone or with help, you remove the dishes two at a time, not stacking the dinner plates, although to save time you might be excused for putting a butter plate on each dinner plate. Salt and pepper containers and condiment dishes must be taken off also, but you need not crumb the table. Each time that you take something out to the kitchen you may bring back dessert plates, salad and salad plates, or whatever is needed for the next course. If you wish you may put a dessert plate at each place you have cleared as you return to take the next plate. Or as soon as you have removed your husband's plate, you may have put a stack of dessert plates and the dessert in front of him, and he may serve it while you are finishing the table-clearing. In other words any system that speeds and smooths the changing of courses is acceptable, so that your guests do not feel that you are going to too much trouble.

There is no need to clear the dessert dishes unless your dining table is at one end of your living room. In that case you cannot subject your guests to the unappetizing sight of dirty dishes for the rest of the evening.

At this point, one of your guests is likely to say, "Let's just wash the dishes quickly. It won't take a minute, and we don't mind at all." Even if they are close friends or relatives do your best to dissuade them, or at least limit their efforts to getting a first load of dishes into the dishwasher. If they are only acquaintances you must flatly refuse. After all, you have invited them to your home hoping to make a pleasant break in their routine, and allowing them to do the same unpleasant chores they must do every day at home is hardly the way to make their evening the most enjoyable possible. At the same time the considerate guest will not insist too stubbornly, because the embarrassment it may cause the hostess far outweighs the help that is given.

THE SINGLE WOMAN ENTERTAINS

When a single woman invites guests to a dinner party she may well need to appoint one of her men guests to help her with the mechanics of mixing drinks and serving dinner. He should not be expected to act as a host by greeting or entertaining the guests, but the hostess may ask him to carve meat, serve wine, and otherwise assist her in making the dinner run smoothly.

Unless the man is a relative or close friend, however, this can be an imposition. If possible it is best to hire a maid for the occasion, to take care of the preparation and serving.

AFTER THE MEAL

LEAVING THE TABLE

At the end of the dinner, when the last dish of candy has been passed and the hostess sees that no one is eating any longer, she catches the eye of one of the ladies and slowly stands up. Anyone who happens to be observing also stands up, and in a moment everyone rises and they stroll back to the living room. Years ago the men and women always separated after dinner to have their coffee, cigars, and cigarettes in different rooms. This is still done today in large homes where entertaining is very formal. More often, a host will suggest to his male guests that they remain at the table for a demitasse, brandy, and a cigar. This stems from the idea that many women object to the smell of cigar smoke, and this is often quite true, so there is a valid reason behind the custom. The hostess leads her women guests to the living room, where they have their coffee, liqueurs, and cigarettes. She often suggests, too, that they might like to go to her room and "freshen up," and two or three generally accept. After fifteen or twenty minutes the men rejoin the ladies, and more liqueurs or highballs are offered.

AFTER-DINNER COFFEE

Personally, I prefer that the men and women remain together for their coffee. If they do, the men should either forgo the cigars or ask the ladies' permission to smoke them. If you have help for the evening, the butler or waitress passes after-dinner coffee to the guests from a tray containing the cups of coffee, spoons, and cream and sugar. A good hostess may offer a choice of a large cup or a demitasse and should provide "real" coffee or decaffeinated coffee. When you have no help, you should have your coffee tray prepared in advance, except for the coffee itself. You carry the tray to the living room, set it on a coffee table or other convenient place, and pour the coffee, asking each guest how he wants it. You hand the cups to the guests, who step up when you ask them if they want sugar, milk, etc., or your husband can hand out the cups as you fill them. If you have a small electric hot plate keep the coffeepot warm on that, or you may prefer to serve it in an electric percolator that can be plugged in in the living room after serving the first helpings. Liqueurs are passed while the guests are drinking their coffee.

TAKING LEAVE

It was once a fixed rule that the guest of honor be the first to take leave, and everyone used to sit on and on, no matter how late, waiting for him or her to go. More often than not the guest of honor was saying to herself, "Oh, my! Are these people *never* going home?" until it dawned on her that the obligation was her own!

Today, although it is still the obligation of the guest who sat on the host's right to make the move to leave, it is not considered ill-mannered for any other couple to rise first if the hour is growing late. They simply stand up, say good-bye to the people with whom they were talking and to the guest of honor, and look for their hostess. They chat for a *brief* moment with her and the host, and then offer their thanks and good-byes, and leave.

FOOD AND DRINK

COCKTAILS

Two or three varieties of cocktails should be offered, with the butler or host indicating what they are: "Would you care for an old-fashioned or a martini?" If the bar is well stocked he may ask, "What kind of a cocktail would you like?" There must also be glasses of tomato juice or some other nonalcoholic beverage available for those who prefer something other than liquor. Unless dinner is delayed because of waiting for late arrivals only two cocktails need be served. There is usually wine with the meal, and the smart hostess knows that wine does not mix well with too many cocktails.

MENU SUGGESTIONS

Six courses is the maximum for even the most elaborate formal dinner. They are:

1. Soup *or* fresh fruit cup *or* melon *or* shellfish (clams, oysters, or shrimp)
2. Fish course (*or* on rare occasions, a dish such as sweetbreads instead of fish, and omitted if shellfish is served first)
3. The entrée, or main course (usually roast meat or fowl)
4. Salad
5. Dessert
6. Coffee

Notice that the salad is served between the entrée and the dessert. This is correct in spite of the custom in almost all restaurants of serving it as a first course. Unless you know that a group of friends at a casual dinner prefer it first, salad should be served as stated here, or it may be served with the entrée, on a separate salad plate.

One should always try to choose a well-balanced menu; an especially rich dish is balanced by a simple one. Coquilles St. Jacques (scallops) with a thick cream sauce might perhaps be followed by spring lamb, roast squab, or a filet mignon; broiled fish by a more elaborate meat dish.

Consider the appearance of the food you serve. Avoid a dinner of white sauces from beginning to end: creamed soup, creamed sweetbreads, followed by breast of chicken and mashed potatoes. Combine flavors intelligently. Don't serve all "sweet" dishes: beet soup, duck basted with currant jelly, a fruit salad, and a sugary dessert. In these examples each dish is good in itself but unappetizing in the monotony of its combination.

Menus for a less elaborate dinner are not limited by rules or conventions, but there are certain practical aspects to consider. Try to avoid dishes that require many extra condiments or sauces. Because you probably wish to eliminate extra plates or silver if you are to clean up alone, or with little help, restrict your courses to two or three. If you decide on only two, a main course and a dessert, you may serve more substantial hors d'oeuvres beforehand. To make the serving of dinner less complicated some hostesses serve soup or a fish course, such as jellied consommé, cold salmon, or shrimp, in the living room. If this is done, the host may help his wife by removing the empty plates and ashtrays quickly while she is seating the guests in the dining room. Or else the hostess must excuse herself while the guests are finishing their dessert in order to have the living room neat when they return there for coffee. If there is a maid she should do this tidying up while the guests are eating their main course.

A roast is always delicious, and there is something mouth-watering about watching the meat being carved. If you follow a recipe that calls for it to "repose" (to be removed from the oven after a shorter cooking time than usual and to continue cooking from its own heat), even the gravy may be made before the guests arrive and kept hot in a double boiler. Creamed or curried chicken within a ring of noodles or rice is pretty and saves table space by eliminating an extra dish. Almost any meat-and-vegetable casserole, such as coq au vin or beef in red wine, is ideal. Or you may invite your guests for a special dinner—lobsters flown from Maine, or shrimp cooked in beer and shelled and eaten in the fingers. With these delectable and filling dishes you need serve only a salad, rolls, and dessert.

In recent years an increasing number of men have become interested in cooking, especially in cooking meat on a grill or spit. A marvelous sight and a fine conversation piece is a golden, aromatic roast of beef turning over glowing coals in the fireplace when the guests arrive.

The imagination of the hostess (or host) is really the only limitation on an informal menu. But a word of caution: Don't experiment with a new dish at a party. Try it out at least once on the family so that it will be perfect when you offer it to your guests. And remember, the appearance of a dish is almost as important as its flavor. Chops should be arranged in a pretty design rather than piled in a heap, just as asparagus neatly laid in the same direction has infinitely more appeal than a helter-skelter pile of broken stems.

MENU CARDS

Menu cards are most often seen at official dinners or banquets, but once in a while one sees them at a formal dinner in a private home. Usually there is only one, which is placed in front of the host, but sometimes there is one between every two guests.

The menu card never includes obvious accessories such as celery, olives, rolls, jelly, chocolates, or fruit, any more than it would include salt and pepper or iced water.

CHOOSING AND SERVING WINE

Tradition has always decreed that one particular wine goes with one particular food, but unless the meal is strictly formal there is no reason why the host may not choose any wine he thinks his guests would prefer. Many fine wines now come from American vineyards, and their lower prices have made wine available to almost every family. The two most important considerations in choosing a wine are not the cost or where it came from, but that it complements the food with which it is served and pleases the palates of the people drinking it.

Since wines do have an important place on the menu of most dinner parties let us consider some of them in detail.

Sherry is the first wine offered at dinner, and then usually with a soup that contains sherry in the preparation. In other words it should not be offered with cream of chicken soup or vichyssoise, but it would be an appropriate accompaniment to black bean or green turtle soup. Sherry should be put into a decanter at room temperature and poured into small, V-shaped glasses. It can stand being decanted almost indefinitely without spoiling. Sherry, which is also served at lunch or supper, is often included as an alternate choice with cocktails.

A dry white wine is served with fish or with an entrée and is often the only wine at a women's lunch or at the family dinner table. White wine may be kept in the refrigerator for at least several hours or even days before being used, since it should always be well chilled before being served. The quickest and most efficient way to chill a bottle of uncooled white wine is to place it in a bucket or cooler filled with a mixture of ice and cold water. The actual melting of the ice in the water will cool the wine faster than if it is immersed in cracked ice alone. Drawing the cork and turning the bottle from time to time will hasten the cooling. Unlike red wines a white wine is good to the last drop, and the bottle may be upended when pouring the final glass.

Red wine is normally served with red meats, duck, and game, but at less formal dinners it may be drunk from the beginning of the meal to its close. This would more likely be true with a claret, a light red wine, than with a burgundy, which is much heavier. All red wines should be served at room temperature, and the burgundy may be a degree or two warmer if the vintage is very good. It may be brought to this temperature by being left in a warm spot—never by warming over a burner or flame. The procedure for serving a fine vintage wine is somewhat complicated but should be followed carefully if its excellence is to be appreciated. A day or two before it is to be used, the wine should be removed from the wine cellar or closet. This is done by transferring the bottle into a straw basket as gently as possible, maintaining the bottle in a semihorizontal position. Actually, in the basket it should be tilted 15 or 20 degrees more toward the vertical than it was in the bin, and it is left in this position for a day at least to permit any disturbed sediment to settle. If you do not have a wine cellar purchase the wine several days before your dinner and follow the same procedure. The bottle should be opened an hour or so before serving. At this time, the foil is neatly cut away to prevent the wine from coming in contact with it while being poured. For the same reason a damp cloth is used to wipe the mouth of the bottle, removing any accumulated dirt and grime. The cork is then carefully pulled and placed beside the neck of the bottle in its basket in order that the host or any interested guest may note that it is undamaged. During this hour the bottle is open, the wine is given an opportunity to "breathe" and rid itself of any musty or other unpleasant odor it might have absorbed in the cellar.

It should be served in the basket, with the label showing to permit each guest to note what he is being offered. Caution must be taken when pouring the wine to avoid any "backlash" or bubbling that can result if it is handled carelessly. This would agitate the sediment, which should now be resting in the bottom of the bottle. Finally, it is obvious that the last inch or so should not be poured from the bottle, since this will be murky with sediment.

When a bottle of red wine is so heavy with sediment that the procedure given above will not result in a palatable drink, it may be decanted. Another less legitimate reason for decanting is to prevent a guest whose palate does not tell him otherwise from discovering that he is not being served a particularly high quality wine.

Champagne is, above all other beverages, that of the very special dinner party. When other wines are included, it is served with the meat course, but when it is the only wine it is served as soon as the first course has begun. Its proper temperature depends upon its quality.

Champagne that is not of especially fine vintage is put in the refrigerator for a day and then chilled further by putting it into a cooler with a little salt as well as ice. Occasionally, holding the bottle by the neck, turn it back and forth a few times. In doing this, take care not to leave the bottle in the salt and ice too long, or the champagne may become sherbet. Also, when opening, be sure to wrap the bottle in a towel or napkin as a protection in case it explodes.

An excellent vintage champagne, on the other hand, is packed in ice without salt, which chills it just a little less. Generally, champagne is served in a wide-brimmed glass such as the one shown on the left of the drawing on page 294. Although this is correct, the type of glass on the right is preferred by many connoisseurs. This shape of glass tends to prolong the life of the effervescent bubbles that distinguish this particular wine. The old idea of stirring champagne to remove these bubbles has nothing to recommend it. If you dislike effervescence a good white wine would be a much more preferable drink.

Two types of champagne glasses

Champagne glasses ought to be as thin as soap bubbles. Thick glasses will raise the temperature at which a really good champagne should be served and spoil its perfection. If they must be used, the epicurean thing to do is to chill them in the refrigerator and put them on the table at the moment the champagne is served.

| Flute | German | Alsace | Bordeaux | Burgundy |
| Sherry | | White wine | | Red wine |

Types of wine glasses

Wineglasses should be picked up by the stem rather than the bowl. In the case of white wine and champagne this helps to keep the wine cool, and in the case of all wines, including red wines, it enables you to appreciate the color.

At large dinner parties the butler or maid passes the various wines with the appropriate courses. If help is hired for the evening, the host must make sure that the butler is experienced in serving wine and knows which glasses are used for each variety of wine. The butler watches the guests' glasses carefully and offers to refill them each time he sees that one is empty.

When you have little or no help the simplest way to offer wine is to place the opened bottle on the table in front of the host, preferably on a coaster or wine holder to prevent any drops from spotting the tablecloth. If there are enough guests to require more than one bottle, a second one is placed at the other end of the table and the host asks a man at that end to assist him in pouring. When the first course is served, the host, and his helper when necessary, fill the glasses of the guests at each end of the table. If a maid is present she may pour the wine after she has served the first course. To do this she removes the bottle from the table, serves the lady who is guest of honor, and continues around the table counterclockwise. She serves the host last and replaces the bottle in front of him. Anybody who does not wish wine merely says, "No, thank you," but does not cover his glass with his hand nor turn it upside down. Incidentally, when drinking white wine finish the glass completely, but with red wine it is better to leave a sip in the bottom to avoid swallowing any possible sediment. Those pouring the wine offer to refill a guest's glass whenever it is empty or almost empty.

COFFEE OR TEA WITH DINNER

When the coffee or tea is to be served with the meal, the simplest method is to have the cups on the table when the guests sit down. After the meal is served, the hostess takes the coffee- or teapot and goes around the table filling the cups, starting with the woman on her husband's right. She fills her own cup last. It is not incorrect if she prefers to fill the cups while seated at her place—the guests passing them down the table from hand to hand. But this is inconvenient for the diners, and there is a strong possibility that an accident will occur.

"NO, THANK YOU"

Not so many years ago, when diet fads had not yet come into fashion and the scientific study of balanced rations, vitamins, allergies, and so on was unknown outside the laboratories, it was considered very discourteous to refuse whatever one's host or hostess offered. A well-behaved guest took at least a little of everything passed and ate or drank that little. Today the increasing use of the word *allergic* has been helpful in developing the acceptance of the phrase *No, thank you.* After all, if a guest knows that lobster gives him hives he would be stupid to eat it even though it *has* just been flown in from Maine. Naturally he should explain the reason to his hostess later, so that she will not think it was the quality or the choice of the food that caused him to refuse it.

⊸§30è~ *Buffet Dinners*

There are three great advantages to a buffet dinner that appeal to all of us. First, you can accommodate many more guests than your dining-room table will seat. It is important, however, to restrict the number so that there will be places for everyone to sit down, and also so that there will be room for the guests to move about freely when serving themselves and returning to the living room.

Second, lack of service is no handicap. Because a buffet is truly a "do-it-yourself" party, even the hostess without a maid may spend almost the entire evening with her guests.

And third, it has the informality that most of us so much enjoy. There is something about sitting in one place before dinner, going into the dining room and foraging for yourself, then coming back to the same place or finding a new place, as you prefer, that makes buffet parties so popular. Also, you are free to choose your dinner companions yourself, as you cannot do at a seated dinner. If you have never given a buffet lunch or dinner you can't begin too soon to discover the charm and ease of this delightful form of entertaining.

WITH OR WITHOUT HELP

The duties of a hostess serving a buffet dinner alone are far lighter than those at a sit-down dinner, providing that she has planned carefully and prepared the food well in advance. Just before she announces dinner she must, of course, attend to such details as lighting candles, putting out iced water, and arranging the platters, casseroles, or serving dishes on the table. But the food can be all ready in double boilers or chafing dishes, or if it is to be served cold, in the refrigerator. Thus a hostess' last-minute chores will take her away from her guests only briefly. After eating, the guests take their empty plates back to the dining room themselves, putting them on a side table—not on the buffet or dining-room table from which the food was served—and serve their own dessert. The host and hostess may remove the dessert plates, or the guests may assist. If the dining room has a door, it can be closed, or a screen can be pulled across the entrance once all the plates have been taken out, If, however, the dining area opens onto or is a part of the living room, the hostess should remove the soiled plates to the kitchen while the guests are helping themselves to coffee.

If the hostess has a live-in maid or has hired a waitress for the evening, she has very little to do. If cocktails are served she must watch to see that her guests are ready and then advise the waitress when to put the food on the buffet table. The maid, in turn, signals to her when all is prepared in the dining room. The waitress should remove cocktail glasses and clean the ashtrays while the guests are serving themselves, and she should take out empty plates as they set them down. She may or may not, as the hostess wishes, pass the dishes around for second helpings. Because the guests will not all finish simultaneously, the maid should have adequate time to remove the food from the buffet table and replace it with dessert plates and dessert, or salad and cheese, or whatever is to finish the meal.

After the maid has removed the last of the plates she brings the coffee tray into the living room and the hostess pours. From then on the host takes over the serving of liqueurs and after-dinner drinks, and the maid is free to clean up the kitchen and dining room.

THE INVITATIONS

The invitations may be written on informals, on your notepaper, across the top of the face of your "Mr. and Mrs." visiting cards, or on the attractive fill-in invitation cards available at every stationer's. They are almost never in the formal third-person form. The RSVP is generally followed by your telephone number, and if you wish you may add: (regrets only).

You may telephone your invitations, too, but if you do so ten days or two weeks ahead, you will be wise to send "reminder cards" a few days before the party. *(See Chapter 39, "Invitations and Replies.")*

TYPES OF BUFFET

REAL BUFFET

When guests at a real buffet have served themselves in the dining room, they simply take their plates into the living room (where there are enough chairs for everyone), hold their plates on their laps, and set their glasses on the nearest table. Your guests will be much more comfortable and there will be much less chance of an accident if you set a small table (the folding kind that fit in a rack are ideal and easy to store) by each chair, or at least by each chair not within easy reach of a coffee or side table.

SEATED BUFFET

At this type of buffet your guests may be seated at small tables—sturdy card tables, perhaps—in your living room, dining room, or library. This arrangement is, of course, dependent on your having large enough rooms so that the tables will not be in the way before dinner or while the guests are serving themselves. If you do have the space, most men and many women prefer to be seated in this way. The tables are covered with cloths of almost any color and style. The places are set exactly as for any seated dinner, and since the guests need not carry silver, napkins, or glasses with them, a great deal of space is saved on the buffet table. The guests serve themselves as at all buffets, going for second helpings and removing their empty plates unless there is a maid to do it. If the living room is used for the tables, the hostess must take the tables out after the meal to make room for conversational groups or whatever activity she may have planned. For a bridge party she simply clears the tables and removes the cloths, leaving them ready to be used.

SEMIBUFFET

A pleasant way of serving a small group of friends or a family party is to arrange the food on the sideboard or a side table and set the dining-room table as for a sit-down dinner. Two variations are possible. First, the guests are seated, and the host serves each plate, asking the guests, "Do you like your meat rare or well done?" or "Do you take cranberry sauce and stuffing?" He helps himself last. The hostess passes the plate and serves herself next to last. She should say as she hands the plates around, "Please start, so that your dinner won't get cold." Second, the guests may serve themselves as at a regular buffet and carry their plates to the table while the hostess watches to see whether she may help or whether they have missed any of the sauces or side dishes. Again the hostess serves herself after the guests, and the host is last.

THE INVALUABLE ELECTRIC HOT PLATE

Whichever type of buffet you are serving, the most valuable piece of equipment you can have is one that keeps things hot. I recommend an electric hot plate or tray, because they can be used to heat your plates and keep your meal warm for an almost indefinite period of time. As long as a finished casserole is covered so that it will not dry out, it may be placed on a hot plate an hour or more before dinner and be as delectable when it is served as it was the moment it was taken from the oven. The only exception, of course, is a soufflé, which must be served at once. Furthermore, with an electric appliance on the buffet table, there is no need to take the dishes to the kitchen to be kept warm for second helpings. And finally, it is unnecessary to watch and replace fuel for flame-heated chafing dishes.

THE BUFFET TABLE

The basic principle of buffet table-setting is that only necessary and useful objects are used. Unless there is ample space omit articles that are solely ornamental. Flowers in the center of the table are lovely, of course, but if it is a question of choosing between decorative flowers and edible fruit a centerpiece of the fruit to be served for dessert is preferable.

In the same way, if the table is crowded and candles are not needed to see by, they are better left off. If candles are needed

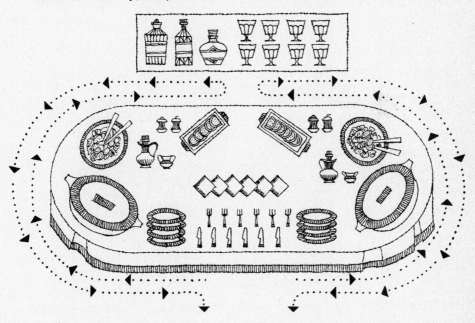

Buffet table in the center of the room

candelabra are better than candlesticks because first, they give better light, and second, they are less likely to be knocked over by a guest reaching for a plate of food.

If the party is large it is better to leave the table in the center of the room so that two lines of guests may serve themselves at once. Then the most important dish is divided into two parts, and one platter or casserole placed at each end of the table. The plates are in two stacks beside them, and the napkins and silver neatly arranged next to the plates. Dishes of vegetables, salads, bread and butter, and sauces and condiments are on each side of the table so that the guests need to pass down only one side—greatly speeding the service and keeping them from turning back and bumping into each other.

If the table is set against the wall, place your plates and main dish at the end that makes for the best flow of traffic. This is usually the one nearest the entrance, so that the guests, after serving themselves, do not have to double back against the people coming in.

The table may be set as formally or informally as you wish. If you use a white damask cloth, silver candelabra, and an elaborate centerpiece, your buffet will appear quite formal. But you can just as well go to the other extreme and use orange pottery dishes on a brown-and-white-checked tablecloth with a bowl of fruit in the cen-

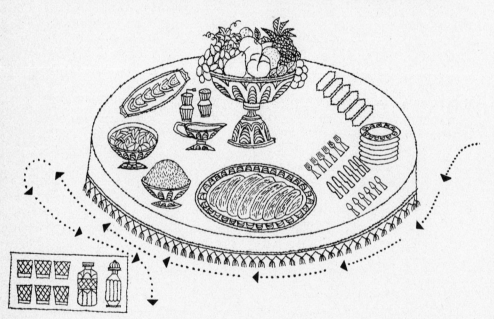

Buffet table against the wall

ter of the table. What makes your table attractive is not the elegance of the utensils and decorations you use, but the combination of dishes, linen, and silver, and the way in which they are arranged.

Color plays an enormous part in the beauty of a buffet table. If you have a copper bowl or kettle to use as a centerpiece, fill it with red and yellow fruit or a combination of fall vegetables—squash, tomatoes, pumpkins for a Halloween or Thanksgiving table. Keep the autumn tints in mind: Use green, red, or russet mats and yellow pottery on a bare table. Or a green or yellow tablecloth is warm and inviting. Bright red napkins and/or china set the tone for an appealing Valentine's Day table, and of course pastel pinks, yellows, or blues are synonymous with springtime.

BEVERAGES

Red or white wine, a punch or other cold drink, iced water, or beer in its cans or bottles, together with glasses, are on the sideboard or a nearby table. If it is a seated buffet water glasses are on the tables and are filled before the guests sit down. Wine glasses should also be at the guests' places, but they are never filled in advance. The host (or a waitress) passes the wine when everyone is seated, or there may be an opened bottle of wine on each table to be poured by the man nearest to it.

If coffee is on the sideboard the guests may serve themselves at any time. Or the hostess, if she prefers, takes a tray set with cups, a coffeepot, cream, and sugar into the living room to serve after dinner.

When there are no individual stands or tables, and guests must put their glasses beside them on the floor, it is wise to use iced-tea glasses or highball glasses because they are steadier than goblets. If the beverage is served with ice in the glass, it should not be put down on a table unless coasters are provided.

THE MENU

It does not matter what foods you choose so long as they are well prepared and easy to eat with fork alone if your guests are not seated at tables. Beyond that, merely use a reasonable amount of common sense in selecting dishes that will be satisfying to the people invited. Don't feed hungry men bouillon, daubs of hors d'oeuvres, samples of fruit salad, and meringues. Food may be lighter for women alone, but for men with good appetites three or four substantial dishes should be provided, at least one of them hot.

"Substantial dishes" would include most meats, fish in a sauce such as Newburg, potatoes, and the heavier desserts. Nearly everything made in a baking dish or casserole is ideal for a buffet meal, not only because it is hearty, but because it is easily kept hot.

There are countless delicious menus to be tried; the only limit is your imagination. If you wish to be very elaborate, or if you have a great many guests, you may wish to serve two main dishes, possibly a lobster Newburg at one end of the table and beef stroganoff at the other. But choose two dishes that will be complemented by the same vegetables and condiments, or you will have more preparation than you can easily handle and not enough space on your table for all the dishes. If you do serve two main dishes, your guests may help themselves to the one they prefer, or they may take a little bit of both. They should remember, however, that it is very easy to overload a plate when there is a variety of tempting dishes. If you are a guest at a buffet don't let your eyes dictate to your stomach, and while you may try as many dishes as you want, take very small portions of each.

Here are some menu suggestions, ranging from an elaborate buffet to a very simple family-type menu. Use any combination that appeals to you, omitting or adding to each menu as you wish.

Veal Scallopini   Roast Turkey
Mashed Potatoes
String Beans with Mushrooms
Cranberry Sauce, Stuffing, Gravy
Buttered Rolls
Fresh Fruit Compote
Cookies
Coffee

Italian Spaghetti and Meatballs or Chili con Carne
Mixed Green Salad
Choice of Roquefort, French, Italian Dressing
French or Italian Bread, Butter
Lemon Ice
Coffee

Hungarian Goulash or Beef and Kidney Pie
Noodles
Glazed Carrots
Green Salad with Mandarin Oranges
Buttered Rolls
Coffee

Curried Lamb or Chicken or Shrimp Creole
Rice Ring
Chutney, Raisins, Ground Nuts
French Bread, Butter
Raw Spinach Salad
Ice Cream and Cake or Cookies
Coffee

For a summer evening:

Cold, Sliced Ham, Turkey, Roast Beef, Lamb, or Cold Cuts
Scalloped Potatoes
Vegetable Salad
Buttered Rolls
Vanilla Ice Cream with Green Mint Sauce
Cookies
Coffee

A good suggestion for a Friday evening, when some of your guests may not wish to eat meat:

Lobster or Shrimp Newburg or Beef Stroganoff
Rice
Green Peas and Onions
Croissants
Caesar salad
Cheese and Crackers
Fresh Fruit (Apples, Pears, Seedless Grapes)
Coffee

THE PARTY ITSELF

The table is set with all the cold foods, the dining-room lights are lighted, and the hot foods are ready to be brought in from the kitchen—or are already on the electric hot plate or in their chafing dishes. Let's go with the host and hostess into the living room and wait for the guests to arrive.

As people enter the room the host and hostess go to the door to greet them and to introduce any who may for the moment find themselves strangers.

When the guests have all arrived and the time allotted for cocktails (if served) is over, the hostess announces that dinner is ready and people in more or less of a queue file around the dining table. The guests go first, urged along by the hostess, if necessary, but whether it is a seated dinner or a buffet the hostess should *never* serve herself first. The women as well as the men help themselves—it is fun to see what there is to eat and to take just what one wants. Sometimes, however, and quite correctly, a man may ask a woman what she would like, fill a plate, and take it to her.

A man seeing a woman sitting without a plate or with an empty one asks her, "Can't I get you something to eat?" or "Would you like more of anything?" If she says, "Yes, please," he brings her whatever it is she would like. But most likely she says, "Thank you, but I'm going into the dining room in a moment."

If people continue to sit and wait to be served, the hostess has to prod them a little, saying, "Please go into the dining room and help yourselves to dinner." If they linger at the buffet, carrying on a long conversation and blockading the table, she should suggest that they take their plates into the other room.

Important item: Have plenty of ashtrays. For a large buffet supper recently, a wise hostess I know went to a ten-cent store and bought two dozen ashtrays. She put them on several steps of her staircase, on the mantel, on every table, on the piano, on the windowsills, and in every space that could possibly serve as a cigarette-parking place.

The only serving detail of importance in a buffet meal is the clearing away of used dishes and the unceasing emptying of ashtrays. If the hostess has help for the evening, every plate is removed as soon as it is put down, and filled ashtrays are constantly replaced. Also, if there are servants they refill the glasses of seated guests from time to time, and the main dishes may be passed for second helpings. The servantless hostess can ask one or two members of her family—or her most intimate friends—to help her take the used dishes to a convenient table or sideboard, from which she can take them to the kitchen as unobtrusively as possible.

~§31§~ Luncheons

Although there are many business lunches given for men only, most "social" luncheons are given by and for women. Of course on weekends or special occasions mixed groups are not uncommon. If men are included in the guest list, the meal is likely to have a stronger resemblance to a dinner, for the menu must be fairly substantial or half the guests will go away hungry.

Again, the type of luncheon you give depends upon the size of your dining room, the number that can be seated at your table, and the help that you will have with the serving. If you have extra rooms or a large enough living room you may set up one or more card tables to increase the number of guests you can accommodate. In this case you seat an intimate friend or member of your own family as hostess at the card table and you sit at the head of the dining-room table. If you are one of those who have a very small dining room, or perhaps no dining room at all, but have a living room or a patio large enough to permit two or three small tables to be set up ahead of time, a luncheon for eight or twelve people, perhaps followed by bridge, is one of the nicest parties imaginable.

THE INVITATIONS

The word *lunch* is used much more often than *luncheon. Luncheon* is rarely spoken, but it is written in books like this one and sometimes in third-person invitations.

Although invitations may be telephoned, an engraved card is occasionally used for an elaborate luncheon, especially for one given in honor of a noted person. If written, a formal invitation to lunch is sometimes in the form of a personal note, but more often on a "fill-in" invitation. It is rarely mailed more than a week in advance. The personal invitation might read:

Dear Mrs. Swift [or Martha]:
  Will you come to lunch on Monday the tenth at half past one?
  I hope so much that you will be able to join us.

  Sincerely [or Affectionately],
  Jane [Kelley]

If Jane's luncheon were given in honor of somebody, the phrase "to meet Paul's fiancée" would be added immediately after the hour. If it is a very large luncheon for which the engraved card is used, "To meet Congresswoman Lawrence" is written across the top.

COCKTAILS

Cocktails may or may not be served before lunch. If they are, they differ a little from those offered before dinner. Although a martini can be offered, sherry, Dubonnet, Bloody Marys, or daiquiris are more usual. As always, there must be tomato juice or plain fruit juice available for those who wish it.

WHEN LUNCH IS READY

When all the guests have arrived and have had time to enjoy a cocktail if it is offered, the butler or maid at a large luncheon notifies the kitchen, goes back to the living room, and approaches the hostess and says quietly, "Luncheon is served." At a simple luncheon, the hostess, after seeing that the table is ready, says, "Shall we go in to lunch?"

If there is a guest of honor, the hostess leads the way to the dining room, walking beside her. Otherwise the guests go in in any way they wish, except that the very young should make way for their elders. Men stroll in with the women they happen to be talking to. If alone, they bring up the rear. Men never offer their arms to ladies going in to lunch—unless there should be a very elderly guest of honor, who might be taken in by the host, as at a dinner.

THE TABLE

Candles are not needed on a lunch table, but are sometimes used as ornaments. They should never be lit in the daytime. The plain white tablecloth that is correct for dinner is not used for luncheon, although colored damask is acceptable. Far more often, the lunch table is set with place mats made in any variety of linen, needlework, lace, or plastic. A runner, matching the mats but two or three times as long, may be used in the center of the table.

The decorations are practically the same as for dinner: flowers or an ornament in the center, and two or four dishes of fruit or candy where they look best. If the table is very large and rather too bare without candles four small vases with flowers matching those in the centerpiece—or any other glass or silver ornaments—may be added.

The places for a large formal luncheon are set as for dinner, with a service plate, a fork, a knife, or a spoon for each course. The lunch napkin, which should match the table linen, is much smaller than the dinner napkin and is not folded in the same manner. Generally it is folded like a handkerchief, in a square of four thicknesses. The square is laid on the plate diagonally, with the monogrammed (or embroidered) corner pointing down toward the near edge of the table. The upper corner is then turned sharply under in a flat crease for about a quarter of its diagonal length; then the two sides are rolled loosely under, with a straight top edge and a pointed lower edge and the monogram displayed in the center. Or it can be folded in any simple way one prefers.

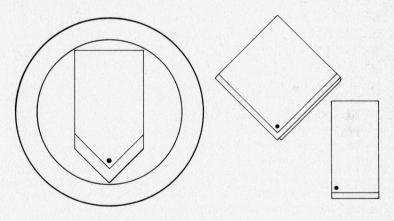

Ways to fold luncheon napkins

If it is a large luncheon, guests are often seated at several card tables, and place cards are used just as they are at dinner.

Card tables are covered with square tablecloths, either white or colored. They may be of any style, but they should, if possible, be exactly alike. It is better to have simple, matched ones than assorted,

307

elaborate ones. A small flower arrangement makes the prettiest centerpiece. *For more details about table settings, see Chapter 38.*

THE SERVICE

If the luncheon is to be formal the hostess will need help, whether her own servants or temporary ones.

The formal service is identical with that of dinner. Carving is done in the kitchen, and except for the ornamental dishes of fruit, candy, and nuts, no food is set on the table. The plate service is also the same as at dinner. The places are never left without plates, except after the salad course when the table is cleared and crumbed for dessert. The dessert plates and finger bowls are arranged as for dinner.

At a simpler luncheon one can serve eight or twelve guests quite easily if the first course is already on the table. The maid may clear the plates from card tables by standing at the corners and taking away one plate in each hand. The main course should be limited to a single dish and salad, or it will take a rather long time to serve, as the maid must pass the food in the usual way, from each person's left. The salad may be all ready in small bowls or plates, which are brought in two at a time and placed on the guests' left. If there is no first course, the salad may already be on the table. Rolls, butter, and iced water and any other beverage should also be put on the table beforehand.

When dessert is finished, the waitress carries the coffee tray to another room and if it is a bridge party readies the tables while the hostess pours the coffee.

If you are serving without the help of a maid you will be wise to make your party a buffet luncheon. The food is set out as for a buffet dinner, on the dining-room table or on any table with sufficient space. For a ladies' luncheon the fare is much simpler than for a dinner. Among a group of eight or twelve women, there are almost always some who are watching their calories, so a delicious but light meal is far more appreciated than one dressed with rich sauces and ending with gooey sweets.

As soon as you announce that luncheon is served, your guests file past the table and serve themselves, taking their plates to the card tables and seating themselves wherever they wish. If you are having a course before the entrée, it should already be on the tables when your guests arrive, and they sit down and finish it before going to the buffet table for the main course. When there is no maid to help, the guests take their empty plates and leave them on a side table as they go to get their next course. While they are helping themselves you may remove the soiled dishes to the kitchen.

The same procedure is followed when the guests are ready for the salad or dessert. When they have finished you ask them to go to another room, or at least to leave the tables and sit on more comfortable chairs to have their coffee. This gives you a chance to clear away the glasses, silver, and cloths from the table, and if bridge is to follow, set out the cards.

THE MENU

Two or three courses are sufficient at any but the most formal luncheon. If you serve many more than that and then move to the bridge table, you will find some of your players falling asleep over their hands! There are five possible courses, and you may select the ones you wish to serve from those listed below:

1. Fruit, or soup in cups
2. Eggs or shellfish
3. Fowl, meat (not a roast), or fish
4. Salad
5. Dessert

The menu for lunch eaten in a private house never consists of more than four courses, and two or three are the general rule.

Melon, grapefruit, or fruit cup, with or without a liqueur poured over it, is a popular first course. The latter may be served in special bowl-shaped glasses that fit into long-stemmed, larger ones with a space for crushed ice between, or it can just as well be served in champagne glasses, after being kept as cold as possible in the refrigerator.

Soup at a luncheon is never served in soup plates, but in two-handled cups. It is eaten with a teaspoon or a bouillon spoon, or after it has cooled sufficiently the cup may be picked up and lifted to the mouth with both hands. It is almost always a clear soup: in the winter a bouillon, turtle soup, or consommé, and in the summer a chilled soup such as jellied consommé or madrilene. Vichyssoise is also popular in hot weather.

There are innumerable lunch-party egg and fish dishes, and they often serve as the main course at a ladies' luncheon. But when men are present, the third course should not be omitted. A second course that is substantial and rich, such as crabmeat au gratin, should be balanced by a simple meat, such as broiled chicken served with a salad, combining meat and salad courses in one. On the other hand, if you serve eggs in aspic, or escargots, first, you could have meat and vegetables, as well as salad and dessert.

While cold food is both appropriate and delicious no meal—except on the hottest of hot summer days—should ever be chosen without at least one course of hot food. Some people dislike cold food, and it disagrees with others; but if you at least offer your guests a hot soup it is then all right to have the rest of the meal cold.

Four of the following menus have been planned with the idea that you can have all the preparation finished in advance. But since the main dish in the last one should be cooked and served at an exact moment, that menu should be saved until a day when you have some help in the kitchen.

Clam or Oyster Chowder with Oyster Crackers
Fruit Salad and Cottage Cheese
Melba Toast
Chocolate Mousse
Coffee

Curried Chicken with Rice Ring
Mixed Green Salad
Baking-Powder Biscuits
Jello Made with Fresh Fruit
Coffee

Little Neck Clams, or Oysters
Cold Sliced Roast Beef, Horseradish Sauce
Potatoes au Gratin
Hot French Bread
Watercress and Tomato Salad
Fresh Strawberries and Sour Cream
Coffee

For that very hot day:

Cold Salmon with Green Mayonnaise Sauce
Sliced Cucumber and Tomato
Protein and White Toast
Lemon Chiffon Pie
Coffee

Fresh Fruit Cup
Filet of Sole Amandine
Spinach Salad with Chopped, Hard-boiled Egg, Tart Dressing
Buttered Rolls
Orange Chiffon Cake
Coffee

Hot breads are an important feature of every lunch—hot crescents, baking-powder biscuits, English muffins, dinner rolls, corn bread, etc. They are passed as often as necessary. Butter is usually put on the butter plate beforehand, and it is passed again, whenever necessary, until the table is cleared for dessert. Preferably it should be served as butterballs, or curls, rather than in squares.

Bread-and-butter plates are always removed immediately before dessert, with the saltcellars and pepper pots.

BEVERAGES

In the winter a wine is often served with lunch. One wine is sufficient, and it should be a light wine such as dry Rhine wine or a claret.

A chilled white wine may also be served in the summer, but iced tea or iced coffee are the usual choices. Iced tea at lunch is prepared with lemon and sugar and sometimes with cut-up fresh fruit or a little squeezed fruit juice. It is poured into the glasses and decorated with sprigs of fresh mint. Iced coffee should be passed around in a pitcher on a tray that also holds a bowl of granulated sugar and a pitcher of cream. The guests pour their own coffee into tall glasses that are half full of ice and accompanied by long-handled spoons. Or if your luncheon is a buffet a pitcher of each should be available close to the buffet table. A bowl of fruit punch may take the place of iced tea or coffee and appears cool and refreshing if it is prepared with floating slices of orange and lemon and is surrounded by glasses or cups adorned with fresh sprigs of mint.

In the winter many hostesses like to have hot coffee or tea served with the meal instead of, or in addition to, serving it later.

A pitcher of iced water should always be in evidence at a buffet, or glasses of water should already be on the table if it is a seated luncheon.

LATER IN THE AFTERNOON

On a hot summer day when people have been playing cards for an hour or more, a tray should be brought in with a large pitcher of iced water and perhaps another pitcher of iced tea and put down on a convenient table. One thing that hostesses frequently tend to forget is that five people out of six long for a cold drink in the afternoon more than anything else—especially after a cocktail or two and a larger-than-usual lunch. Occasionally sandwiches and cookies are brought in as well as the iced tea, but these are not necessary when bridge follows a luncheon.

≈♪32♪≈ Afternoon Entertaining: Teas, Receptions, and Cocktail Parties

TEAS

Afternoon tea at a very large house party or where especially invited people are expected for tea, should include two plates of hot food such as toast or hot biscuits split open and buttered, toasted and buttered English muffins, or crumpets, corn muffins or hot gingerbread. Two cold plates should contain cookies or fancy cakes, and perhaps a layer cake. In hot weather, in place of one of the hot dishes, there should be pâté or lettuce sandwiches, and always a choice of hot or iced tea, or perhaps iced coffee or chocolate frappé, but rarely if ever, anything else.—Emily Post, 1922

Afternoon teas are given in honor of visiting celebrities, new neighbors, to "warm" a new house, for a houseguest, or for no reason other than the hostess wants to entertain her friends.

INVITATIONS

Invitations to an informal tea are almost always telephoned. However, if the occasion is more formal, the invitation is sent on a visiting card or informal. "Jan. 10, Tea at 4 o'clock, [your address]" is written on the face, below the engraved name if you have personalized cards, or in the center if not. When the tea is given in honor of someone, you write "In honor of" or "To meet Jennifer Smithers" at the top.

THE TEA TABLE

At a gathering of this sort, the tea and the coffee (or hot chocolate) are sometimes passed on trays, but far more often the hostess has them poured at a table. Those who have dining-room tables use them as the simplest and most comfortable place from which to serve. However, the tea table may be set up in any room that has adequate space and easy access and exit. The guests should be able to circulate freely without becoming trapped in a corner after they have been served.

Except on a glass-topped table a cloth must always be used. It may barely cover the table, or it may hang half a yard over the edge. A tea cloth may be colored, but the conventional one is of lace or white linen with needlework, lace, or appliquéd designs.

A large tray is set at either end of the table, one for the tea, and one for the coffee.

One tray is used to bring in all the equipment necessary for the proper serving of tea: a pot with boiling water—with a flame under it, if possible—a full pot of tea, tea bags if the tea is not made with loose tea, cream pitcher, sugar bowl, and thin slices of lemon on a dish.

The coffee tray is simpler. The coffee is in a large urn or pot— with a flame under it. A pitcher of cream and a bowl of sugar (preferably lumps) complete the tray. If chocolate is served instead of coffee, there is nothing needed other than the pot of steaming chocolate.

If the trays are carried by a maid the flames under the pots are not lighted before the trays are set down in order to avoid the danger of fire.

The cups and saucers are placed within easy reach of the ladies who are pouring, usually at the left of the tray, because they are held in the left hand while the tea (or coffee) is poured with the right. On either side of the table are stacks of little tea plates, with small napkins matching the tea cloth folded on each one. Arranged behind these, or in any way that is pretty and uncluttered, are the plates of food and whatever silver is necessary. Forks should be on the table if cake with soft icing is served. If the table is not large enough to hold all the plates some may be placed on a sideboard or a small table in a convenient location.

Food for a tea party is quite different from that served at a

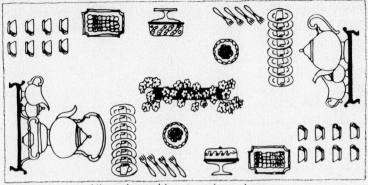

View of tea table as seen from above,
with food distributed around outside edges as shown.

cocktail party. For one thing, much of the food is sweet—cookies, cupcakes, fruit cake, or slices of iced cake are almost always offered. In addition, for those who do not have such a "sweet tooth," tea sandwiches are served. They are small, made on very thin bread, and are usually cold, although in winter there is sometimes a tray of hot cheese puffs, pastry filled with mushrooms, etc. The sandwiches are light and delicate—watercress rolled in thin bread, a cherry tomato sliced on a round of bread, cream cheese on date-and-nut bread, or crabmeat on toast are typical choices for tea-party menus.

NO HELP NECESSARY

Because nothing needs to be passed to the guests it is perfectly possible for a hostess to give a formal tea without help. If she has no maid she sets out the tray with everything except the boiling water before her guests arrive, leaving the kettle on the stove in the kitchen. She greets the guests at the door, telling them where to leave their coats, and when she is ready for tea she fills the teapot from the kitchen kettle and carries it in to the tea table.

MAKING GOOD TEA

The most important part of the tea service is boiling water and plenty of it.

To make good tea, first, half-fill the pot with boiling water, let it stand a moment or two to heat the teapot, and then pour it out. Put in a rounded teaspoonfull of tea leaves or one tea bag for each person. Half this amount may be used if the tea is of superb quality. Then pour on enough *actually boiling* water to cover the tea leaves about half an inch. It should steep at least five minutes (or for those

315

who like it very strong, ten) before additional boiling water is poured on. When serving, pour half tea, half boiling water for those who like it "weak." Increase the amount of tea for those who like it strong. The cup of *good* tea should be too strong without the addition of a little lively boiling water, which gives it freshness.

When tea has to stand a long time for many guests, the ideal way is to make a strong infusion in a big kettle on the kitchen stove. Let the tea actually boil three to four minutes on the range; then pour it through a sieve or filter into your hot teapot. The tea will not become bitter, and it does not matter if it gets quite cold. The boiling water poured over no more than the tablespoonful of such tea will make the drink hot enough.

THOSE WHO POUR

The pouring is usually done by close friends of the hostess. These ladies are asked beforehand if they will "do the honors," and unless they have a very valid reason, they should accept. Sometimes, after an hour, the first two are relieved by two other friends of the hostess.

It does not matter that a guest going into the dining room does not know the deputy hostesses who are pouring. Each person walks right up to the table and says, "May I have a cup of tea?"

The one pouring should smile and answer, "Certainly! How do you like it? Strong or weak? Would you like cream or lemon?"

If the visitor says, "Weak," *boiling* water is added, and according to the guest's wishes, sugar, cream, or lemon. If the guest prefers coffee she asks for it at the other end of the table. If the lady pouring is unoccupied and her momentary guest is alone, she makes a few pleasant remarks; but if there are a number of people around the table she need only smile as she hands each guest her cup.

TEA-PARTY GUESTS

When a tea is given for someone, or to celebrate something special, it is, to some extent, "formal." Women wear afternoon dresses or suits rather than pants suits, hats, if they wish to, and gloves. The latter are removed with the coat, or if it is summertime, before going to the tea table.

When there is a guest of honor, the hostess introduces her to each woman as she arrives. But rather than forming a receiving "line" they stand together near the door and talk for a little while with the arriving guests.

Otherwise, behavior is very informal. You may (and should) talk to anyone there, whether you have been introduced or not. You may return to the tea table as many times as you wish (or your calorie count permits), but you may *not* overload your plate at any one time. When you are ready to leave (and you are not expected to stay until the very end at a large tea) you simply thank your hostess, say goodbye to the guest of honor, and go.

TEA DANCES

An afternoon tea dance occasionally takes the place of a debutante party. It may also be given to honor a birthday or anniversary or to celebrate a holiday.

Invitations are usually written on the hostess' visiting card, on a fold-over informal, or on a "fill-in" invitation.

Since houses with rooms large enough for dancing are comparatively few a tea dance is usually given at a club or in a small ballroom of a hotel. Remember that it is a mistake to choose too large a room, for too much space for too few people gives an effect of emptiness that throws a pall on the party. Also remember than an undecorated public room needs more people than a room in a private house to make it look filled. Although a crush may be unpleasant, it does give the effect of success. Nothing is more dismal than a half-empty room with scattered guests.

The arrangements for a tea with dancing are much the same as for an evening dance. A screen of greens behind the musicians and flowers on the tables form the typical decorations.

Whether in a hotel, club, or private house, the curtains are drawn and the lights lighted as though for a dance in the evening.

Tea, coffee, tea sandwiches, and cakes are served. In addition there is usually a table nearby with pitchers or bowls of fruit juice or punch, and a bar for those who wish stronger drinks.

Guests go to the table and are served coffee or tea. They help themselves to the sandwiches or cakes, which they eat standing at the table, or if there are tables set up for all the guests, they return to the one at which they have been sitting.

RECEPTIONS

The reception today is primarily a state affair, a public or semi-public gathering in honor of a prominent person or an important event. Receptions most frequently take place on the diplomatic or civic level and are handled, like official dinners, by a household staff or a caterer.

However, there are occasions that call for a reception at home, and one that occurs quite frequently is when a groom's parents wish to give a party for their son and his bride. This generally happens when the wedding has taken place in the bride's distant hometown, and the groom's family wants to introduce their new daughter-in-law to their friends.

Receptions are sometimes held instead of cocktail parties because the host and hostess do not serve liquor but do not want to give a tea. In this case a punch, iced tea or coffee, soft drinks, and/or hot coffee and tea may be served.

Receptions are rarely given for women only, so except in the circumstances mentioned above, liquor is almost always served as well as punch and coffee. There may be some tea-type sandwiches offered, but in addition, heartier fare is served, Small meatballs, dips, various kinds of cheese and crackers, and nuts, olives, etc., are added to the menu.

The table for a reception is covered with a floor-length white tablecloth rather than the shorter tea cloth. The table is set with the platters of food, small paper napkins, plates, and forks if necessary. Alcoholic drinks are served from a bar or passed around, and coffee and punch are on side tables from which the guests help themselves.

Since receptions are almost always given in someone's honor, there is generally a receiving line, consisting of the host and/or hostess, guest of honor, and in some cases, various officials of the committee giving the reception.

Receptions—especially official ones—take themselves seriously, and guests are expected to dress and act accordingly.

COCKTAIL PARTIES

In many parts of the country cocktail parties have become the most common form of entertaining, and they can be the answer to a busy housewife's prayer. Along with open houses, barbecues, and picnics they provide a relatively simple answer to the rule that all invitations must be repaid. Their advantages over a dinner party are many in a society in which relatively few households have servants, and in which the cost of hiring temporary help or a caterer is beyond the reach of many. Cocktail parties require little preparation, they are less expensive than a dinner party, they are limited as to time, and you can entertain many more people at once in a small house. On the other hand, no one invited to a cocktail party feels as honored as if he had been invited to dinner, and at a large party the host and hostess cannot spend as much time with any one guest as they would if they were seated at a dinner table. Cocktail parties do provide an excellent opportunity for entertaining new acquaintances, particularly if you also wish to include the people at whose house you met your new friends, and others to whom you want to introduce them.

"PAY-BACK" PARTIES

One of the least attractive customs that I know of is that of giving large "pay-back" cocktail parties. A hostess who has been invited to many parties herself and thinks she has not the time or the energy to give a number of small parties creates one large horror by inviting everyone to whom she is indebted at once. The guests are not chosen for compatibility, there are not enough places to sit down, the crowd is likely to be such that no one can move freely from group to group (or table, or bar), and the noise level reaches such a pitch that it becomes intolerable. If you are a popular guest and incur social obligations with any frequency, make the effort to give small parties from time to time and avoid the necessity of a yearly "pay-back."

JUST COCKTAILS

Cocktail parties may be as large or small, as simple or elaborate as you wish, and the ways of inviting people are as varied as the parties themselves. If the number of guests is small the invitation is almost always by telephone. For a larger party they may be written on your own informal, on a printed fill-in card, or on one of the many attractive illustrated cards sold at stationers for every occasion. *(See Chapter 39 for more on invitations.)*

When there is to be no buffet the time is usually stated: "Cocktails *from* 5:00 to 7:00," rather than "Cocktails *at* 5:00." While "RSVP" is often omitted, thoughtful guests let the hostess know whether or not they are planning to attend the party. If there is an RSVP the telephone number is usually written beside it, as this type of invitation may always be answered by telephone.

At a cocktail party you may serve literally every sort of hors d'oeuvre or appetizer that you think tastes good and looks tempting —as long as it can be eaten with the fingers. You might serve olives or artichoke hearts (either chilled or wrapped in bacon and broiled) or tiny broiled sausages; thin bread rolled around baby hot dogs, skewered, and toasted; or small frogs' legs, broiled, with a garlic dip. Or try this: Hollow out a cabbage, put a can of Sterno in it, and beside it a plate of little frankfurters or bits of tenderloin to be speared on a pick and cooked over the flame. This is sure to be a conversation piece! Don't forget a pile of cocktail napkins—cloth or paper—on the hors d'oeuvres tray. Many hors d'oeuvres are a little greasy, and also, since plates are not used, the napkin may be used to hold an appetizer that is, for a moment, too hot to eat.

Paper napkins should be offered with the cocktails or available on the bar, too, to wrap around the glasses. Especially at a large party, where everyone stands most of the time, it is unpleasant to have to hold an icy, wet glass, and furthermore the napkin prevents drips.

Plenty of coasters are a necessity if you wish to preserve the finish on your tables. Disposable paper ones are fine—just be sure they are in view at every conceivable resting place for a glass.

At a large party extra glasses are essential too. Guests continually put down their glasses and forget where they put them, or leave their empty ones behind when they go to the bar for another drink. You may get very inexpensive glasses—even plastic ones—for a big party, but be sure you don't run out.

WHAT DRINKS TO SERVE?

The two most important things about "what to serve"—whatever you decide on—are to have enough and to have the drinks mixed properly. Phyllis Diller tells a story about a bride who almost lost her husband the first time they entertained. The young lady appeared before her guests with a tray of cocktails. "I hope these martinis are all right," she said. "We ran out of olives, so I just poured a spoonful of olive oil into each glass."

As a general rule a host should count on each guest's having at least three drinks. Since a quart of liquor will provide 21 one-and-a-half-ounce drinks, one bottle will serve approximately seven people.

In the winter, martinis, whiskey "on the rocks," and whiskey in a tall glass with water or soda are the most popular drinks. In warm weather, cocktails mixed with fruit juice or tonic, and vodka, gin, or rum, or tall drinks made from these same ingredients are more often served. But there is an infinite number of other drinks that are offered in different localities, and the host may choose according to his own taste or that of his guests.

Unless you know for certain that your guests all drink alcoholic beverages (and even then, someone may just have gone "on the wagon") you *must* have nonalcoholic drinks available. Tomato or other fruit juices, colas, and ginger ale are all popular substitutes and should always be available. To avoid remarks that may be annoying, a nondrinker may choose ginger ale, which looks exactly like a whiskey and soda.

Never urge a guest to have a drink—or *another* drink—if he has once refused. If as a guest you are pressed further, simply say firmly, "No—really, I can't," or "No thanks—honestly." It is the host's responsibility to see that a guest who has had too much to drink is served no more, and especially that he is not allowed to drive himself home. If his wife is not with him to do the driving, the host either sees that a mutual friend will get him home safely, or calls a taxi, but for the sake of everyone on the roads as well as his own, the inebriated reveler must *not* get behind the wheel of his car.

BARTENDERS AND WAITERS

If you are planning a cocktail party for more than eighteen or twenty people, and if you have no maid in your home, it is wise to consider hiring a bartender for the evening. One bartender can serve between twenty and thirty people very well. If it is a really large party the services of a waiter or waitress as well will make the evening much pleasanter for the hostess. She may prepare the hors d'oeuvres herself in advance, even days ahead if she has a freezer, or she may hire a waitress or caterer who will both prepare and serve the food.

The bartender attends to the drinks in any one of various ways, or he may combine several means of serving. He generally stands behind a large table loaded with ice, bottles of each kind of liquor and soft drink to be served, and every sort of cocktail glass. At a big party it is essential to have two bars or the crush around one will become unmanageable. The guests go to the bar themselves and request the kind of drink they wish. A man usually asks the woman with him what she would like, and she waits at a little distance from the bar while he gives the order to the bartender and brings her the drink. If a group of women are talking together, it is perfectly correct for one of them who wishes another drink to go to ask the bartender to mix it for her, rather than to interrupt a conversation that her husband or escort might be having.

Another method of serving is for the bartender to pass a tray of drinks, already mixed, to each guest as he arrives. He may continue to do this, but it involves using an enormous number of glasses, because a fresh one must be passed each time. Therefore, after the first serving, it is more practical for him to watch carefully for empty glasses, and when he sees one, approach the guest and say, "May I bring you another drink?" The guest replies, "Thank you, I'm drinking bourbon and soda," and hands him the glass to be refilled.

If you have two men to serve drinks, but only one bar, one man acts as a waiter. He may ask each new arrival for his order, go to the bar where the second man (as bartender) mixes the drink, and return with it to the guest. This method is too slow for one man alone, however, especially when a large group of people arrives at the same time.

One important note to remember: Be sure that you instruct the bartender in advance exactly how you like your drinks mixed and insist that he use a measure. If you let him measure "by eye," you may find that your liquor supply is about to run out long before you had planned. Or you may have some unexpectedly boisterous guests on your hands!

WITHOUT HELP

When no extra help is hired for the evening, the host is the bartender and the hostess is the waitress. She passes the trays of hors d'oeuvres once or twice, sometimes with a close friend helping her. The food is then left in a conspicuous spot (on a hot plate or in a chafing dish if the hors d'oeuvres are hot), and the guests help themselves. She must watch carefully and remove trays or dishes even before they are empty. There is nothing more unappetizing than one remaining cold, limp shrimp, or a mayonnaise-smeared platter.

The host-bartender asks each guest as he arrives what he would like to drink. If the choice is limited he may say, "Will you have a martini or bourbon?" rather than "What would you like?" This saves them both from the embarrassment of having the guest request a drink that is not to be had. Also, he may ask the men to refill their own glasses as well as those of any women who wish another drink. He will have much more time to mix with the group and perform his other duties as host if he does not have to spend the entire evening at the bar.

If there are only a few guests the host may hang their coats in a hall closet. If there are more wraps than a closet can conveniently hold, the men and women are asked to put them in separate bedrooms (or in the same bedroom if the house or apartment is small), neatly on the beds. This scheme is far better than having them piled on chairs or banisters in the entry, and furthermore the ladies have an opportunity to comb their hair and freshen up before they appear in the living room.

Either the host or the hostess should stay within sight of the door to greet arriving guests, but they should try to avoid being out of the room where the party is held at the same time. They should not go to the door to greet their guests with drinks in their hands.

WIDOWS, DIVORCÉES, AND SINGLE WOMEN

When a woman who lives alone gives a large cocktail party she should, if she possibly can, hire a man to bartend for her. If the party is too small or too informal to warrant that expense she may ask one of her male guests to take over the duty. If she has invited a single man as her "date" he would be the logical choice; if all the guests are married couples she should ask a relative or one of her closest friends. Of course, if she is an experienced drink-mixer and enjoys doing it, there is no reason why she cannot bartend herself.

OVERSTAYING YOUR WELCOME

Cocktail parties rarely begin—or end—at the hours stated on the invitation. Although the hosts must be ready on time, the guests may—and do—arrive as much as an hour after the start of the party. Invitees who do not drink, or only drink a little, may stop in very briefly out of courtesy and friendship. However, a late arrival should not mean a late departure. Every experienced hostess knows that she must expect some of her guests to linger a half hour or so beyond the indicated time, but that is as much as she should be expected to endure. She may even take steps to hurry the last survivors out. The best way to get guests to leave is simply to remove the liquor and close the bar. Once the guests finish the drinks in their hands and find no more being served, the party will soon be over. As a safety valve, in case there are diehards who linger on regardless, a smart host and hostess make plans to go to a restaurant for dinner after the party with a few friends. This provides the excuse to say, "It was such fun to see you, but I'm afraid we must get going—the Forsythes are waiting for us. . . ."

COCKTAILS BEFORE A DANCE

A pleasant form of entertaining is to have a group of friends for cocktails before a dinner dance or any other function that they would enjoy attending. Invitations are sent out on informals, fill-in cards, or any printed cocktail-party invitation card, but they must state: "Cocktails before the dance at the Black Rock Golf Club, 6 o'clock," as well as the place and date. It is also necessary to add "RSVP," because the hostess usually makes the reservations for those of her guests who wish to go on to the other event.

It is also correct to extend the invitations by telephone, since then the hostess knows immediately how many will be joining her at the club or dance and can make the reservations sooner. An invitation to this type of party should not be accepted if you do not intend to go on to the later party. Unless a hostess specifically says, "Please join us first even though you can't come to the club afterward," it is not up to you to make this suggestion in most cases. Only to very close friends might you say, "We'd love to stop by for one drink, but we are going to dinner at the Browns'."

When you are the guest you must pay the cost of admission, dinner, drinks, and anything else at the later party unless your hostess specifically says or writes that she expects you *as her guest*. If you are not a member of the club involved, you must find out in advance whether you may sign as a member of another club or pay in cash. If neither is permitted, then you must ask your host if you may sign his name and add your initials to enable you to pay him your share when he receives his bill.

COCKTAIL BUFFETS

A cross between a cocktail party and a buffet dinner party, the cocktail buffet is the choice of many hostesses for entertaining all except the smallest and most informal groups. Because there is usually enough food presented that the guests need not have dinner afterward and therefore are expected to linger longer, the invitation frequently states only the hour of arrival. In many sections of the country this is likely to be a little later than a simple cocktail party, often at six thirty or seven. It should be made very clear that the gathering is a "cocktail buffet," so that the guests realize that they will be served some substantial food and need not make other plans for dinner.

The menu may vary from simple to very elaborate, but even the simplest must provide more than just hors d'oeuvres. The least that one can expect is a platter of cold meat—ham, chicken, or roast beef—slices of buttered breads, accompanying dishes such as sliced carrots, celery, olives, raw cauliflower, and possible some sandwiches. This minimum type of buffet may be eaten standing near the table without a plate. The meat can be placed on a slice of bread and eaten like a sandwich, and the raw vegetables picked up and dipped in a sauce if one is served. Often a smoked ham or turkey is placed whole on the table, and when the platters of meat are running low, the host, or any of the guests, may carve additional slices as they are required.

The table should be covered with a tablecloth, and napkins must be available. If there is room a centerpiece of flowers or fruit is attractive, but it is better to leave it off and use a decorated cake (or even one of the main dishes) in the center rather than crowd the table.

For a more elaborate buffet you might include one or more hot dishes, generally casseroles that can be kept warm on an electric hot plate or served in a chafing dish over a flame. In this case, of course, there must be stacks of plates and rows of forks. If the main table becomes too crowded, the hot dishes and plates may be put on the sideboard or on a side table. The main difference between this type of cocktail buffet and a buffet dinner is that only one real course is served, although cookies or cake may be offered with coffee.

If you do not wish to go into the added complication of plates and silver you may choose a hot dish such as bite-sized meatballs or frankfurters, tiny hot potatoes dipped in salt, and hot bread or rolls with a cheese fondue, all of which may be speared with a toothpick. Tacos (Mexican meat-filled turnovers) are hearty and can be bought frozen. Fritonga, a South American mixture of fried bits of meat, banana slices, potatoes, and popcorn, will give you a reputation for originality. Chicken wings dipped in batter and deep-fried are delectable too. Use your imagination and you will delight your guests, but don't experiment on them—try out your new ideas on family or your best friends beforehand!

◆§33◆ Balls and Dances

PRIVATE AND PUBLIC BALLS

Snobbish as it sounds and is, *a brilliant ball is necessarily a collection of brilliantly fashionable people, and the hostess who gathers in all the oddly assorted frumps on the outskirts of society cannot expect to achieve a very distinguished result.*—Emily Post, 1922

There are two fundamental differences between balls and dances. First, while guests at a dance are of approximately one age, those at a ball may go from high-school students to octogenarians. Second, since dances are smaller, the decorations and refreshments are simpler.

Although great private balls have become almost unheard of in recent years, this book would be incomplete if a reference to them were omitted. Besides, the charity and debutante balls that have replaced private ones all over the country are similar to them in terms of customs, rules, and procedures. *For more details on debutante assemblies, see p. 332.*

PLANNING THE BALL

The hostess who gives a private ball must, of course, assume the final responsibility for every aspect of the evening, but fortunately she may enlist the aid of many and various people. The club or hotel where it is to be held will provide the servants, the food, and the drinks; or if the ball is held at home, a caterer will provide the same services. A florist will see to the decorations, and there are social secretaries available who can help her with the lists and invitations. But no matter how much help she is able to amass, the hostess giving a private ball must make the final decisions on all the details that are so important to the success of the party.

A public ball is run by a committee, whose chairman is in some ways comparable to the hostess, but without the full burden of responsibility. Special duties are allotted to each member of the committee: One takes charge of invitations, one of decorations; others are appointed to be responsible for the orchestra, the food, the ticket money, etc. In the following paragraphs, wherever the word *hostess* is used, you may substitute *committee member* if the ball is other than a private one.

The first thing the hostess must do is make an appointment to see the manager of the hotel, club, or any other suitable assembly room and find out which evenings are free. It is important to select an evening not already taken by another hostess or organization in order not to conflict on lists, or in a small town, on the services of caterers, florists, etc.

She then telephones and engages the best orchestra she can for the chosen evening. If it can possibly be arranged, there should be two orchestras so that the moment one finishes playing, the other begins. You cannot give a ball or a dance that is anything but dull if you have poor music.

Having hired the bands and engaged the ballroom and necessary extra rooms, the hostess makes out her list and orders the invitations. They are sent out three to four weeks prior to the ball. Invitations to balls, private or public, are always formal. There are, however, many variations in good taste. *For these forms, and also for less formal invitations appropriate to the smaller dance, see Chapter 39.*

DRESS FOR A BALL

The correct dress for a man going to a formal ball is white tie and tails *(for details see Chapter 69).* Nothing could be handsomer, and men who have these suits welcome the rare opportunity to wear them. However, most men do not own a set of "tails," and rather than rent them for the evening, they wear the less formal tuxedo. Because of the practical consideration of a young man's pocketbook, and the fact that the soft shirt and collar that goes with the tuxedo is so comfortable, "black tie" (tuxedo) is accepted at all balls, even though the invitation says "formal." Only if it actually says "white tie" must one make the effort to rent a tailcoat for the evening.

Women who may live most of their lives in slacks and tweeds go "all out" for a ball. Dresses are always long, sleeveless, and as elegant as one can afford. A ball is also the time to take your best jewelry out of the safe and enjoy it. Pants suits on women are not acceptable unless they are very full and styled to look like a long ball gown. Even the youngest guests must leave their "casual" look behind for the evening and dress up as they never have before. The attraction of a ball *is* that it is very special and very elegant, and every person there should cooperate in appearance, in behavior, and in graciousness to keep it that way.

IN A PRIVATE HOME

ASKING FOR AN INVITATION

> *It is unheard of for a gentleman to "take" a young girl alone to a dance or to dine or to parties of any description; nor can she accept his sponsorship anywhere whatsoever. A well behaved young girl goes to public dances only when properly chaperoned and to a private dance with her mother or else accompanied by her maid, who waits for her the entire evening in the dressing room. It is not only improper, it is* impossible *for any man to take a lady to a party of any sort, to which she has not been personally invited by the hostess.*—Emily Post, 1922

You may always ask a hostess whether you may bring a man who is a stranger to her; extra men are always in demand—the more the better. But it is rather difficult to ask for an invitation for an extra girl, unless the person asking for the invitation is a man, and willing to look after her. In that case the hostess should be delighted to invite her. Invitations are never asked for persons whom the hostess already knows. This is important because if she knows them she will send them invitations if she cares to. It is not at all out of the way, however, for a close friend to remind her of someone who may have been omitted by mistake.

The one who has arranged for the invitation for the stranger should accompany him to the ball and introduce him to his hostess: "Mrs. Norman, I would like you to meet John Franklin, my roommate"; and John should promptly thank her for extending him an invitation. If for any reason the stranger arrives unaccompanied he says, "I believe Bob Stacey wrote you and asked if I might come and join him here. I'm John Franklin."

THE SURROUNDINGS

On those rare occasions when a ball is held at home, there is always an awning and a red carpet down the front steps or walk of the house. A uniformed man at the curb opens the car doors, and there are men hired to park the cars. To protect the hostess and her guests from crashers you are expected to hand in your invitation—or admission card, if you have been sent one—to whoever is receiving them at the door.

All the necessities such as awning, red carpet, coat racks, and ballroom chairs, as well as crockery, glass, napkins, food, and the waiters can be supplied by hotels or caterers.

The room selected to serve as a ballroom should be emptied of furniture. An informal grouping of chairs in a hall or library is a far better arrangement than the stiff row or the wallflower exhibit suggested by the alignment of straight chairs around the dance floor. The floor itself, it goes without saying, must be smooth and waxed.

Decorations for a ball may be as elaborate as the pocketbook and the taste of the hostess allow. When the ball is held during a holiday season—Christmas, for example—the decorations generally are in keeping with that time of the year. Christmas ornaments, a beautifully decorated tree in one corner, red, gold, or green ribbons, and so on, would provide the central theme of a "Mistletoe Ball." Or the hostess might choose a type of decoration that goes particularly well in her house, perhaps Japanese lanterns and Oriental flower arrangements. In any case, some greens behind the orchestra and flowers on the tables and wherever else they are most effective are minimum requirements for a ball.

THE NIGHT OF THE BALL

The hostess must be ready to receive on the stroke of the hour specified in her invitations. If the ballroom opens on a hall or reception room at the head of a stairway she usually receives there. Otherwise she receives in the ballroom near the entrance.

Guests are sometimes announced at private balls as they arrive, but this is rare today. After shaking hands with the hostess, the guests pass directly into the ballroom.

Since the hostess must remain at the door as a solitary "receiving line," or with her guest of honor if there is one, it is up to the host, for a good part of the evening, to see that guests are looked after, that refreshments flow freely, that strangers are presented to partners, that shy girls are not left at the wallflower outposts, and that the older and honored guests are taken care of.

Every man must dance at least once with the hostess, the girl or girls the dance is given for if it is a debutante ball, the hostess of the dinner he went to before the dance, and both girls he sat beside at dinner. If he has brought a girl himself he must of course dance the first dance with her. He must also watch during the evening to be sure that she is not stuck too long with any one partner and he must take her home after the dance. He should not, as is the custom at informal dances for young people, dance with the same girl all evening.

THE USHERS

The hostess who wants to assure the success of her ball chooses a number of young men who are tactful and self-possessed to act as ushers. They are identified by distinguishing boutonnieres as deputy hosts. They are supposed to see that the wallflowers remain wall-bound as little as possible, and they must also try to relieve any young man who has been "stuck" for any length of time.

An usher has the right to introduce any man to any girl without knowing either of them personally and without asking permission. He may also ask a girl (if he has a moment to himself) to dance with him, whether he has ever met her or not. He should also release every stag he calls upon by substituting another, and the second by a third, and so on.

If an usher fulfills all his obligations he has very little chance to spend any time with his own date, so the appointment is a doubtful pleasure.

Even an attractive girl who is a stranger can spend a miserable evening when none of her friends happens to be present and when there are no ushers. Ushers can indeed be useful, and their greatest advantage is that their presence gives courage to many a young man who, knowing he will be rescued, will be willing to dance with a girl he would otherwise avoid.

ASKING FOR A DANCE

When a man is introduced to a girl or sees a friend he wants to dance with, he says, "Would you like to dance?" She replies, "Certainly," or "Yes, I'd like to very much." At the end of the dance, whether it has lasted one minute or twenty, the man thanks the girl, and she returns the compliment.

REFUSING TO DANCE

If a girl is sitting in another room or on the stairs with one man, a second man should not interrupt or ask her to dance. But if she is sitting in a group he can go up and ask, "Would you like to dance?" If she wants to leave the group, she says, "I'd love to," but if she is enjoying herself, she smiles and says, "Not just now, thanks, I'm resting." If she likes him she may add to her refusal, "Come and sit with us!"

To refuse to dance with one man and then immediately dance

with another is an insult to the first one—excusable only if he is intoxicated or otherwise offensive. In ordinary circumstances, if a girl is dancing she must dance with everyone who asks her; if she is not dancing she must not make exceptions.

A girl who is dancing may not refuse to change partners when another cuts in. This is the worst phase of the cutting-in custom; those who particularly want to dance together are often unable to take a dozen steps before being interrupted. Possibly the current custom of dancing only with one's date the entire evening is a reaction against the old idea that to be popular a girl must be constantly cut in on.

CUTTING IN

When one of the stags sees a girl with whom he wants to dance he steps forward and taps the shoulder of her partner, who relinquishes his place in favor of the newcomer. The couple then dances until a third man cuts in.

When cutting in, the following rules must be observed:

1. The partner who was first dancing with a girl must not cut back on the man who took her from him. He can cut in on a third man if he wants to.
2. A man must not continue to cut in on the same man when the latter dances with other partners.

SUPPER IS SERVED

A sit-down supper may be served by the caterer at a very elaborate ball, but a buffet supper that begins at one o'clock and continues for an hour or more is pleasanter and easier to manage. People may serve themselves whenever they feel like it, and small tables are set up so that the guests may sit down to eat. They may sit where they please—with a group making up a table, or a man and his partner may take any two vacant chairs. A woman is always taken in to supper by the man who is her escort. If there is an unescorted girl at the party, the ushers (or the host, if there are no ushers) should see that one of the stags takes her to supper or that she is included in a group.

Suppers are no longer as elaborate as they used to be. Although hot dishes are still served at some balls, many times the supper consists of a variety of sandwiches, platters of cold meats and accompanying dishes. There may be hot drinks such as coffee, chocolate, or bouillon, or bowls of iced fruit punch. And if it is in accordance with the customs of your community and your own taste, and if the guests are of legal drinking age, nothing is more festive than serving champagne at a ball.

At almost all balls there are two or more bars serving liquor and soft drinks throughout the evening. However, until the supper hour no food is in evidence, with the possible exception of bowls of nuts on strategic tables.

When you are ready to leave, you must find the host and hostess and thank them, just as you would at a smaller party. If there is a guest of honor, you should say good-bye to him, or her, also.

CHARITY BALLS

With few exceptions public balls are "charity" balls, given to benefit an organization or a cause. Once you arrive at a charity ball the procedure is identical to that described above unless the invitation includes dinner.

In that case you will receive an invitation, on which the cost is indicated—for a single person or a couple. The committee members and the sponsors organize parties and reserve a dinner table for their own group. The host and hostess doing this generally give a cocktail party first, but their guests pay for their own tickets to the ball. The price very often includes some entertainment—the appearance of a dance company, a famous monologist, or whatever it may be.

Dress is just as formal and elegant as it is for a ball in a private home.

In addition to guests who pay a fee to attend a charity ball, there is an additional group of "sponsors." They have nothing to do with running the ball, but they are people, selected by the committee, who are asked to make an additional contribution to increase the amount given to the benefiting charity. Their names are always listed on the program presented to the guests, and sometimes on the invitations. The names appear with their titles: "Mr. and Mrs. Samuel Cohen," "Mr. Reid Phillips," "Miss Ann Smythe," etc.

DEBUTANTE BALLS

The phrase "presenting a debutante to society" has a quaint flavor and seems to echo a long-outdated social custom. Yet when a young lady is approximately eighteen her parents may want to present her to their friends and acquaintances with a certain degree of formality. For this "coming-out" they have a choice of several forms.

The most elaborate, only possible for parents of considerable means, and becoming rarer and rarer today, is a private ball. Somewhat less elaborate is a small dance. Third is a tea dance. Fourth, and currently the most popular, is the big dance given for, or by, a number of debutantes together. Sometimes it is given cooperatively by a group of parents who get together and share the expense of a single coming-out party for their daughters. In other cases it may be given by an organization that invites a group of girls to participate. Many balls or cotillions of this kind are benefit affairs, handled by a committee representing the sponsoring charity. Thus they serve a double purpose, since the parents of the girls invited to participate are expected to give a substantial donation to the charity involved in return for the privilege of having their daughter presented at this ball. *The correct forms for the invitations and their answers to these functions may be found in Chapter 39.*

THE RECEIVING LINE AT A PRIVATE DEBUT

The debutante's mother—or grandmother, or whoever is giving the ball and "presenting her"—stands nearest the entrance. The debutante stands next to her, and they are the only people who formally "receive." On entering, the guests approach the hostess, who introduces the debutante to those who do not know her. As the hostess shakes hands with each, she turns to the debutante, repeats the name to her, and says, "My daughter," or "You remember Cynthia, don't you?" or merely, "This is Cynthia."

Each arriving guest shakes hands with the debutante as well as with the hostess. If there is a queue of people coming at the same time, there is no need of saying anything beyond "How do you do?" and passing on as quickly as possible. If there are no others entering at the moment, each guest may make a few pleasant remarks.

At a ball, where the guests begin coming at ten or eleven o'clock, the debutante receives for about an hour—or longer if guests continue to arrive. Then she is free to join the dancing. She usually dances the first dance with her father and the next with the young man (or men) she has asked to be her escort for the evening.

The role of the father at a private debut is simply that of the good host at any party. He does not stand in the receiving line, but he stays nearby, greets friends and acquaintances, and sees that everything is running smoothly. He dances the first dance with his daughter, and then he dances with his wife, with the grandmothers if they are present and wish to dance, and then with the other guests, young and old alike.

AT SUPPER

The debutante goes in to supper with her escort. If she is very popular and does not wish to center her attention on one man, an easy way out is to ask a brother or other relative. She makes up her own table, which includes her most intimate friends. It is usually in the center of the dining room, is somewhat larger than the tables surrounding it, and has a card on it saying "Reserved."

THE DEBUTANTE'S DRESS

At a ball, the debutante wears the very prettiest evening dress she can buy. Traditionally it is white and suggests something light, airy, gay, and young. Today, pastel colors or color in the trim is acceptable, but the dress should not be scarlet or a bright blue, and on no account black, no matter how sophisticated or chic the debutante thinks she would look in it. At a multiple debut the girls wear the same color, almost invariably white, but they choose their own style. The mothers of the debutantes wear evening dresses in any color except black.

Although today the young men guests may wear tuxedos to debut parties, the escorts and fathers of the debutantes who are coming out must wear white tie and tails.

SENDING FLOWERS

It is customary in most cities to send a debutante flowers at her coming-out party. They may be bouquets or baskets or corsages, and they are sent by relatives, friends of the family, her father's business associates, and by the young men who are her escorts. These flowers are usually banked as a background for her when she stands to receive.

If she has only one escort she wears the corsage he sends, but if she has two she cannot very well wear both corsages. The best solution is to pin both—and any received from other guests—to a wide white velvet or satin ribbon that is then tied around her wrist. This is kept in place while she receives but must, of course, be removed when she starts to dance. At that time, to avoid favoring one escort, she might pin one corsage to her dress and the other to her evening bag.

DINNER DANCES

Since the times of the year when young people are free to give and attend parties are restricted to school vacations, there are often more girls who wish to come out at private parties than there are evenings available. In many communities two girls whose guest lists overlap agree that one will be presented at a dinner dance and the other at a late dance on the same evening. This is a very convenient arrangement for both families. The parents who go to the expense of serving the dinner know that they need provide drinks and refreshments for only a limited time after dinner. The other family need worry only about a light supper served around one o'clock and the champagne, punch, or whatever they choose to serve for the rest of the night.

The two debutantes attend each other's party, and the one giving the second party leaves, with her escorts, shortly after dinner to help her mother with last-minute arrangements. The dinner dance is usually held at seven thirty or eight o'clock, and the debutante and her hostess receive until dinner is served at eight thirty or nine. The late dance begins at approximately eleven.

SMALLER DANCES FOR DEBUTANTES

The afternoon tea dance to introduce a debutante is similar to that described in Chapter 32, and the small evening debut party needs little comment, because its pattern is precisely the same as the informal dinner discussed later in this chapter. As at every coming-out party the debutante and her mother or hostess stand in line and receive the guests as they arrive.

ASSEMBLIES, COTILLIONS, AND COMMUNITY DEBUTS

To come out as a member of a group and thus eliminate the expense and rigors of a private ball is becoming more and more common. In fact in many large cities mothers apply years ahead to assure their daughters a place on the lists of the most prominent cotillions. While one hears constantly about the decline of the private debut, the cotillion or "mass" debut is gaining in popularity and has spread to every corner of our society. If she wishes, a girl's parents may give a small debut party or tea at home and still present their daughter at one of the assemblies or cotillions.

Customs vary widely in different areas, and because debutante balls are generally planned by knowledgeable people, it is safe to assume that whatever local practices have become traditional and are accepted by the participants are, in that city or town, quite correct.

The debutantes send in the names of their escorts as soon as they have accepted, and the committee then sends the young men formal invitations. The girls are expected to pay for their escorts' tickets if the ball is charity-sponsored. At most multiple debuts the committee does not invite guests, but each debutante's family is allowed a certain number of invitations, and they are responsible for paying for those guests whom they invite. Some committees, however, do invite extra boys—and girls—at their discretion.

There may be entertainment in the form of a dance performed by the debutantes and their fathers or escorts, or nothing more than the formal presentation, by their fathers, of the girls to the committee members who are acting as hostesses. There may or may not be professional entertainment—a singer or dancer, perhaps.

The party may be a dinner dance, but it is more likely to be a late party. When a ball is private, friends frequently give dinner parties preceding it; and when it is run by a committee, the members often have dinners for the debutantes and their escorts. This may also be done by the families of the girls themselves.

Whatever the local traditions these "mass debuts" are a great success. By sharing the costs many families can afford far more elaborate decorations, prettier dresses, and better music than they could otherwise hope to obtain. The debutantes, if they are at all shy, are spared the nightmare of being alone in the spotlight. And any mishaps that may occur seem smaller when the responsibility is divided, whereas sharing a success with friends makes it doubly sweet.

INFORMAL DANCES

Informal dances are held for any number of reasons—to celebrate a graduation, an anniversary, a birthday, a holiday, or simply because the host and hostess and their friends like to dance. Generally the dress is "black tie"—tuxedos for the men and long dresses or evening pants suits for the women. There are also costume parties, for which, of course, fancy dress is specified on the invitations, and young people may get together for a barn dance in their jeans. The rules are, as you can see, quite relaxed, but there are certain points that should be kept in mind to assure the success of your dance.

INVITATIONS

When a dance is given to celebrate an anniversary or a birthday, or is for any reason considered to be somewhat formal, invitations are written on an informal or an engraved or printed fill-in invitation. But in most cases they are sent out on commercial fill-in party invitations with attractive drawings on the outside and spaces for writing time, address, and type of party on the inside. Remember to include at the bottom a hint about clothes. An RSVP with a telephone number beside it is the surest way of having some idea of how many will be at the party. The invitation, too, may be by telephone. *For additional details, see Chapter 39.*

DECORATING FOR A DANCE

When the dance is held in your own home rather than a public room of any sort, the most important thing is good, "danceable" music. Next in importance is a large enough clear space and a floor properly prepared for dancing. If possible all the furniture should be removed from the room, but if not, take out whatever you can and move the rest close to the wall. The rugs should be rolled and put away, and the floor freshly waxed.

Decorations should be gay and imaginative rather than expensive and elaborate. A few flowers placed where they are not in the way—on a mantel, for instance—are sufficient but not very original. For more interesting ideas look through the women's magazines or get one of the many paperbacks that are full of decorating tips. If the party is held during a holiday season, appropriate decorations such as Christmas sleigh bells or valentines on the walls always add a festive note.

OUTDOOR DANCES

If you are fortunate enough to have a smooth terrace or a stone patio, perhaps, beside a swimming pool, an outdoor dance on a summer evening is one of the loveliest ways of entertaining. There should be tables and chairs available for those who are not dancing. The bar, if you are serving liquor, and the refreshments should be nearby.

Plenty of light is important. There must be light for members of the orchestra to see their music, and the bar should be well lit for the benefit of the bartender and waiters. Your guests may be delighted to dance in the moonlight, but when they are ready to sit down, uneven ground or steps may be a hazard if not well lit. The most satisfactory lighting, because it is diffused and has a romantic effect, is achieved by placing floodlights in the trees, with some of them pointed up to reflect off the branches.

THE IMPORTANCE OF GOOD MUSIC

Probably the most important element in assuring the success of any dance is good music. Therefore, although you may save as much as you can on decorations and refreshments, spend as much as your pocketbook can afford on the music. If it is within your means, hire the best orchestra you can obtain, even though you may only be able to afford three pieces. Rhythm, gaiety, and a knowledge of the taste of the age group at the party are the essential qualities that the orchestra must have. If the guests are people in their fifties, they probably will not want to dance the latest teenage fad. By the same token, teenagers would think a party a miserable failure if the orchestra played nothing but foxtrots and waltzes.

If you simply cannot hire an orchestra and are planning to use a phonograph, choose records that are specifically intended for dancing and will appeal to your guests. If you borrow records from your friends—and many people do in such a situation—be sure the owner's name is clearly printed on the label in indelible ink or put on with marking tape.

WHO DANCES WITH WHOM?

Good manners at a dance are the same for young and old alike. Whatever the local customs about cutting in, double-cutting (that is, switching partners on the dance floor), and so on, a man must dance with his hostess, and he must dance the *first and last dances with the lady he brought to the party, whether she be his wife or a date*. The exception is the dinner dance, when he dances first with the ladies seated beside him.

At a dance where the guests are married couples, there may be a few or no extra men, and the only time to change partners may be during the intermission or when the music starts again. At this type of party there are almost always tables to which the couples return between dances. The men are expected to ask the women next to them, their wives, and their hostess to dance. If the hostess is at another table, a man should not ask her to dance until he is sure that all the women at his table have partners or at least that there is a group remaining at the table so that no one woman is left alone.

When the dance is over, every guest must, of course, find his host and hostess, thank them, and say "Good night."

SATURDAY NIGHT AT THE COUNTRY CLUB

In many communities the Saturday-night dance at the local country club has largely replaced small informal private dances. Usually a group of friends will attend a country club dance together after a cocktail party or similar gathering described in Chapter 32. On arriving at the club you ask to be shown to the table that your hostess at the earlier party has reserved. Or since it is likely that you will arrive before her, since she cannot leave her home before all her guests have departed, the guests may gather at a table in the bar until she arrives. If you do go directly to the table, and she has not arranged to have place cards, you should leave seats free at each end or at opposite sides for her and her husband.

Generally, in deciding where to sit, husbands and wives split up, since much of the fun of a dance is to enjoy the company of different people.

As soon as possible a man should dance with the women seated on either side of him. If his wife is one of these two, and the woman on his other side has already been asked to dance, he then asks his wife for the first dance. Otherwise he waits to be sure his wife has a partner and then asks the woman on his other side for the first dance. After dancing with the women on either side of him he should try to dance with as many of the other women at the table as possible, being certain not to forget either his hostess at the cocktail party or his wife! When she gets up to dance, a woman leaves her bag, if it is a small one, on the table, or a larger bag on her chair.

When you make up a group to go to this type of party try to choose couples who like to dance. It is inexcusably rude for the men to go off to the bar or otherwise ignore the women at the table. From time to time a man may of course cut in on a woman he knows who is sitting at another table, but after that particular dance is over he should escort her back to her own table and then rejoin his original group.

At a late party you do not have to stay until the music stops, although do not leave so early that your departure will be construed as breaking up the party. Since people do not always want to leave at the same time, it is far safer to take your own car to the club than to share a ride with another couple. Even though sharing a ride may seem practical and friendly before the dance begins, it can be very disconcerting to have to stay on at a party just because your companions have decided to make a night of it.

~§34~ Other Get-Togethers

ANNIVERSARY PARTIES

Anniversary parties may be given in honor of any anniversary, but the first, fifth, tenth, twenty-fifth, and fiftieth are those most generally celebrated. The parties given for the first three are usually informal, not distinguishable from any other reception except that there would be toasts to the bride and groom, and close friends would bring gifts. The twenty-fifth and fiftieth anniversaries, however, are given much more importance, and certain customs—almost rituals—are followed. Therefore this chapter will deal principally with the latter two.

When it is convenient the party should be given on the actual date of the anniversary. But should the couple prefer to have it on a Saturday night, for example, it is perfectly all right to move it forward or back a few days. If the husband or wife is ill or absent at the time, an anniversary may be celebrated several weeks after the true date. When the illness or the absence is prolonged, it is preferable to celebrate the anniversary the following year. There is no rule that says one must recognize the twenty-fifth rather than the twenty-sixth.

WHO GIVES THE PARTY?

Early anniversary parties are always given by the couple themselves. By the time they reach the twenty-fifth they may well have grown children who wish to make the arrangements, but it is perfectly correct for them to do so themselves if the young people do not or cannot. When a couple do not have children close friends often prepare the celebration. Fiftieth-anniversary celebrations are almost invariably planned by the family of the couple.

340

PLANNING THE PARTY

The party may be held in the home of the couple, in the home of the person planning the party, in a church parish house, or in a room of a hotel, restaurant, or club.

If the party is a dinner or a small reception the guests are primarily family, members of the wedding party, and closest friends. If it is to be a large reception or an open house, the list may include business acquaintances, church and club members, and in very small communities—everyone in town.

INVITATIONS

The form of the invitations depends entirely on the degree of formality of the party. They may range from an informal telephone call to an engraved "third-person" invitation. In between lie the most common forms—handwritten notes, or the necessary information written on a visiting card, an informal, or a fill-in card. Formal invitations for a twenty-fifth anniversary are often bordered and printed in silver; those for a fiftieth, in gold.

For the large open house the invitation may simply be an announcement in the local paper or the church or club bulletin. The dangers in this form of invitation are that more people than the host and hostess expect may appear, or that some who are really wanted may fail to read the announcement or hear of the party. If the only invitation is the announcement in the paper, anyone who reads it may attend, but if invitations are extended personally, only those who receive them may go.

The following are some sample invitations.

When the couple are giving the party themselves:

1950–1975
Mr. and Mrs. Harvey Langdon
request the pleasure of your company
at a reception
in honor of
their silver wedding anniversary
on Saturday, the eighth of December
at eight o'clock
Barrymore County Club

R.s.v.p.
12 Corning Road

On an informal or visiting card (name engraved):

1950–1975
Mr. and Mrs. Harvey Langdon
Cocktail Buffet
March 1 at 6 P.M.
12 Corning Road

R.s.v.p.

When the children of the couple give the party:

Dear Anne [or Mrs. Franklin],
Will you and Joe [or Mr. Franklin] join us for dinner at the Rosemont Club on Saturday, May 4, at 7:00 P.M., to help us celebrate Mom and Dad's twenty-fifth anniversary? Hoping to see you then,

Helen and Bill
[or Helen and Bill Porter]

Or if they have a card printed:

In honor of the
fiftieth wedding anniversary of
Mr. and Mrs. Harvey Langdon

Mr. and Mrs. William Porter
[or "their sons and daughters"]
request the pleasure of your company
on Tuesday, the fourth of July
at seven thirty o'clock
10 Glenwood Road

R.s.v.p.

The newspaper or church-bulletin announcement reads:

Open House
to celebrate the fiftieth anniversary
of Mr. and Mrs. Harvey Langdon. Sunday,
March 4, 4 to 6 P.M., *12 Osborn Road*

REFRESHMENTS

The refreshments depend on the type of party being given. If it is a meal—a luncheon or a dinner—the hostess simply chooses whatever menu she thinks will please the couple and the guests most. Since the later anniversaries attempt to recreate the wedding day to some extent, the food might be the same as that served at the original wedding reception.

If the party is a cocktail party, hors d'oeuvres are served, but a wedding cake should be cut and passed with a round of champagne for toasting the couple before the guests leave.

At an afternoon reception or an open house, the menu varies according to the formality of the party and the pocketbook of the host and the hostess. The refreshments may consist of sandwiches, snacks, and punch, or a complete buffet—cold ham, turkey, sliced fillet of beef, and chafing dishes filled with hot snacks or hors d'oeuvres. Whatever the other food, as close a replica of the couple's wedding cake as can be made is often a feature of the menu.

Drinks may range from tea and coffee at an afternoon reception to wine, champagne, or highballs at an evening affair. Soft drinks should always be available for those who prefer them. Punch made with or without liquor is often served at open houses and other daytime parties. When the family does not object to alcoholic beverages a glass of champagne is the traditional drink for toasts—at any hour of the afternoon or evening. Otherwise the toasts may be made with punch or whatever drinks are available. *For suggested anniversary toasts, see Chapter 5, "Public Speaking."*

DECORATIONS

Decorations need not be elaborate, but the twenty-fifth-anniversary party should feature white and silver ornaments and flowers, and the fiftieth, gold (or yellow) and white. Flowers make the loveliest decoration of all, and the "bride" should always be presented with a corsage.

WITH OR WITHOUT MUSIC

There need not be any entertainment, but a strolling accordion player adds a touch of romance, and he can be asked to play the couple's favorite tunes, wedding music, etc. If the host and hostess wish to hire an orchestra or provide records, dancing will be all the entertainment necessary.

THE RECEIVING LINE

One of the distinguishing features of an anniversary party is the receiving line. Except for a somewhat elderly couple celebrating their fiftieth, the couple stand near the door and greet the guests. Their children may join them in the line, and if the party is given by someone else, that person always heads the line as hostess.

Older couples who tire easily, or who may not be well, may be seated in a central spot—in front of a fireplace, for example. The guests, after greeting the hostess near the door, move on to find the honored pair and offer their congratulations.

OPENING GIFTS

When gifts are brought to the anniversary couple—as they should be, if "no gifts, please" was not written on the invitations—the opening of the packages is a feature of the party. After everyone has arrived, or perhaps after dinner while the guests are enjoying their coffee, everyone gathers around, and the couple open the gifts and thank the donors. One of their children, or anyone they choose to designate, helps by taking care of the wrappings, making a list, collecting the ribbons, etc. The couple do not need to write notes later to those they have already thanked, unless they wish to do so.

For a chart giving anniversary gifts, see Chapter 45, "Anniversaries." For specific gift suggestions, see Chapter 66, "Gifts and Giving."

THE MAIN TABLE

The table should be as much like the bridal table at the couple's wedding reception as possible. The "bride and groom" sit together at the center of a long table or in the places facing the guests if the table is a round one. The "bridesmaids and ushers," if any are present, are seated next to them; their husbands or wives are also included at the table. The couple's children are seated with them, the oldest son on the "bride's" right and the oldest daughter on the "groom's" left. Their husbands and wives, their older children, and brothers and sisters of the couple are arranged in whatever way they will enjoy most.

When the party is given by a married son or daughter of the anniversary couple, the host and hostess sit at either end of the table, or at a round table, opposite the "bride and groom." But the couple always sit together rather than having the "bride" sit on the host's right and the "groom" on the hostess' right as would other guests of honor.

The table is decorated with white flowers, or for a fiftieth anniversary, gold or yellow flowers. If there is room the wedding cake may be in the center of the table, but if it is large it is more convenient to place it on a side table.

PICTURES

Because the event is such a memorable one, all anniversary couples enjoy having candid pictures made of their party. They are generally taken by one of the guests, although a professional photographer may be hired. These pictures, put into an album, make an ideal present for the couple, either for the anniversary itself or for the next Christmas. A picture of the whole family, including children and grandchildren, also makes a perfect anniversary gift.

SWEET-SIXTEEN PARTIES

A sixteenth birthday is a big milestone—really the division between childhood and young adulthood. Therefore it is often celebrated more elaborately than other birthdays, with a sweet-sixteen party. Although there is no rule about it, it seems to be a female prerogative, and few boys have sixteenth birthday parties—even under another name.

Sweet-sixteen parties are usually given by the girl's parents, although a grandmother or aunt could certainly do so, and a group of friends—with the parents' approval—often proposes a surprise party.

Invitations may be telephoned, but they are usually written on decorated, fill-in commercial invitations, which can be found, if you wish, specifically for sweet-sixteen parties. They are almost always sent in the girl's name rather than her mother's. For a mixed party a girl may send invitations to all her classmates—boys and girls—or else may send them to the girls only and write on them, "Please bring a date if you want to." If she knows the date's name she sends him an invitation too. And she must invite enough extra boys to take care of the girls who do not have dates.

All invitations should have "RSVP" on them, followed by a telephone number. Telephoning a response seems easier to phone-prone youngsters than writing a reply, and this will elicit more and quicker answers.

The party is sometimes held in a club or hall if it is large, but more often it is held at home.

Sweet-sixteen parties may be for girls only, and sometimes take the form of a "slumber" party. When they are mixed they are often, but not necessarily, dances. They *can* be almost anything: a brunch, a hayride, a theater party, a weekend house party, or a swimming-pool party, for example.

ENTERTAINMENT

While some groups of young people would rather dance than do anything else, others like more variety at their parties. It is a good idea to break up the dancing with some games. Active games like "Twister," carpet bowls, and Ping-Pong are fine if you have the facilities, but some "mental" games are fun too. Charades give youngsters a chance to "ham it up," and there are many others that are good for a laugh. Put out eight or ten dishes of common substances and see how many the blindfolded guests can identify. Or cut out advertising slogans from magazines and have the young people write down what products they think they advertise. Offer some prizes, and you will find that games—alternating with good music— will make the evening fly.

REFRESHMENTS

If you are serving a meal—luncheon or dinner—the menu should simply be the favorite food of the birthday girl, although nothing so exotic that it will not appeal to the majority of the guests. But for an after-dinner party a hearty snack should be served about 11:00 P.M. A big tray of hamburgers on rolls, a stack of waffles, pizzas, or crisp fried-chicken pieces are sure to make a hit. For a noontime brunch a platter of scrambled eggs and sausages, English muffins, and again, waffles, are popular. Teenagers almost all like sweets, so cakes, ice cream, cookies, fruit punch, and all sodas should be available in quantity.

DRESS

There is no rule—the dress depends on the type of party. The young hostess can help her guests tremendously by specifying on the invitations, "jacket and tie," "jeans," "long skirts," "slacks," or whatever she wishes.

GIFTS

Gifts are expected at a sweet-sixteen party, and they are usually somewhat more elaborate than for other birthdays. Each person who receives an invitation "on his own" should take a present, but when a girl invites a boy to go with her, she selects a gift to be presented from them both.

Look for specific gift suggestions in Chapter 66.

Gifts are opened at the party. If there are just a few guests the packages may be opened as each one is presented, but if it is a big party and lots of people arrive at one time, the gifts are set aside and opened at one time with everyone looking on. The hostess, who thanks each donor as she opens the gift, does not need to write thank-you letters later.

FAREWELL PARTIES

Farewell or "going-away" parties are like any others in most ways, but there are one or two things to be remembered when the move is permanent. First, the guests of honor cannot be expected to reciprocate by giving a party and inviting those who have entertained them. Therefore, more than in other cases, they should do more than say "Thank you," and should show their appreciation by sending flowers or a small gift to their hostess.

If you are planning a party for someone who is leaving town for good, coordinate your efforts with other friends. I know a popular couple who moved away from my hometown recently, and there were *thirteen* parties held for them! By the time the departure date arrived, their exhausted friends could hardly wait for them to go! So if you find that your friends are being overly feted, plan something different—take them to the theater, or a hockey game, or whatever they will miss most in their new locale.

While friends are expected to take farewell gifts to one party, they should not be obligated to take gifts to several. This should be made very clear on the invitations. In choosing a gift try to think of something that will serve as a memento to the ones going away. A picture of their home, of their friends, or candids of the going-away party will be treasured. A subscription to the local newspaper will help them to keep up with news of their old friends. And a gift certificate for a store in their *new* locality will prevent their having to pack one additional item.

BYOB AND BYOF PARTIES

"BYO" means "Bring Your Own"—bottle or food, as the case may be. Such parties serve a real purpose, but they also can and do cause resentment, so one should be very careful in planning this sort of entertainment.

Let's talk first about "BYOB" parties. These are almost invariably given by young people who are on a tight budget and could not possibly entertain a group of friends if they had to provide *all* the refreshments. So they call their friends, invite them over, tell them that they will provide the food and mixes but the guests are asked to bring whatever they want to drink. When a written invitation is sent, all that is necessary is to put "BYOB" in the corner and the rest is understood.

The bottles brought to these parties are *not* intended to be gifts for the host and hostess. They simply make it possible for the group to get together without anyone's incurring an enormous expense. Therefore each couple may initial their bottle and take home any liquor that is left. The bottles are "pooled," however, at the party, and if one couple runs out of Scotch, for example, they are offered some by one of the other Scotch-drinkers.

Guests do not take their own mixers. These are provided by the host, who should also have soft drinks available.

Bring-your-own-dinner or bring-a-dish parties are usually given for much the same reasons as BYOB parties. The host and hostess want to get their friends together and have a good time, but they can't afford to do it all, so they ask everyone to chip in. This is perfectly all right, with a big "IF." That is, *if* it is made clear *when the invitation is extended* that it is a chip-in party. The misunderstandings and resentments occur when a guest accepts an invitation and is *then* told that he or she is expected to bring a casserole or perhaps to contribute ten dollars "toward expenses."

A hostess who arranges this sort of evening is not "giving" the party—she is "organizing" it. There are several ways of doing it. She may call several people and say, "Let's get a group together. We'll all bring one dish, and I'll have a keg of beer on hand." Or she may do it "on her own" by sending written invitations asking each person to provide a specific dish. In this case she would write "Come to a Dutch-Treat Dinner" or a "Chip-in Dinner" at the top. Unless she has specified a dish *and* a bottle, she should provide the liquid refreshments. However she goes about it, the important thing is that she make it quite clear that she is not "giving" the entire party— *before* the guest is trapped. The invitees are then free to refuse the invitation if they are unwilling or unable to contribute.

In spite of the obvious advantages of this type of entertaining, it cannot take the place of the party you truly "give" for your friends. As long as you can afford to provide even the simplest food and drink, a hostess should accept the entire responsibility. She should *never*, for a private party, ask for contributions of money to help defray expenses. The only time this is permissible is when the group—official or unofficial—gives a party to celebrate a special event (a testimonial dinner, for example) or to raise funds for a cause, and either sells tickets or asks for donations. Again the amount requested must be clearly stated on the invitation, and guests should never be asked to contribute—without warning—at the party.

PICNICS

Although picnics can be utterly delightful when well managed, they can be perfectly awful when bungled! Therefore here are a few general directions for the benefit of those who want to have a really outstanding picnic.

WHAT KIND OF PICNIC?

There are several ways of organizing a picnic.

The first is to give the picnic yourself, inviting the guests by telephone. If they accept, tell them the hour, where to meet, and possibly ask them to bring a blanket or backrest if the party is large and you do not have enough for everyone.

Or you may call and say, "Mike and I are trying to get a group together for a picnic Saturday night. We'll bring the steaks, and we're asking each couple to contribute one dish. Would you rather bring dessert or salad?" Others might be asked to bring the condiments, chowder, corn, or the drinks.

Lastly, a group of friends may simply arrange to picnic together, each family bringing their own food and cooking it over a community fire. It is fun to see what the others have prepared, and often there is considerable trading and sharing. "I'll trade you a chicken leg for a lobster claw," or "Do try some of this special steak sauce that Susie taught me to make." This sort of picnic is especially good if children are included, as each mother knows best what her young ones will eat most happily.

TAILGATE PICNICS

Tailgate picnics have come into being with the universal popularity of the station wagon. They are particularly suitable on two occasions. First, if you are making a long trip and do not wish to take too lengthy a break for lunch, you may pull over to the side of the road (preferably in a "rest area" if you are on a big highway, because of the receptacles provided for garbage, etc.), let down the tailgate, spread your picnic out on it, and eat, in no time at all.

The other occasion that has gained tremendous popularity is the lunch before a college football or baseball game. Call your classmate who lives in another town—"How about meeting us at the Number

Two parking lot at the stadium, before the State-Hometown game in October? We'll bring the food, and you bring the drinks, and we'll have a reunion!" Having arranged the meeting place specifically, you load your whole family into the station wagon and enjoy the game and a chance to catch up on all the news of old friends after a sumptuous meal cooked on your folding grill. In fact many of those friends may turn up in the same parking lot. Tailgate picnics have been such a success at colleges that the custom has caught on before professional games too.

The tailgate takes the place of a folding table, and the only other pieces of necessary equipment are the grill and a piece of oilcloth or plastic to lay on the tailgate, which is likely to be dusty or sandy.

Of course, it is not necessary at all to have a station wagon to have a delightful picnic with your friends before a game or at any other time. A folding table and your own ingenuity can more than make up for the lack of a tailgate.

CLAMBAKES

The preparations for a clambake are quite specialized; but if you know how a seaweed oven is made (practically, as well as theoretically), and you have a loyal friend who is willing to spend the whole day helping, nothing is more in keeping with a holiday at the seaside. To be successful, however, you or someone on your beach must have experience in preparing and timing the baking of corn on the cob and potatoes as well as the clams and lobsters. Therefore, since most seashore resort areas have clambake specialists who will do the entire bake for you, it is far wiser for the unpracticed amateur to avail himself of their services.

YOU'RE THE HOSTESS

If you wish to entertain friends by taking them on a picnic, your first task is to consider your guest list very carefully. Nothing is so dampening to the enjoyment of a picnic as the presence of one or more faultfinders who never lift a finger but sit and complain of the heat, of the wind, of a possible shower, of the discomfort of sitting on the ground, or of their personal sufferings caused by mosquitoes or flies. On the other hand, if you select your company from friends who really enjoy picnics, not only will they make everyone forget blowing sand and inquisitive ants or hungry mosquitoes, but most likely they will work like beavers.

Knowing that you have a congenial group and considering the ages and preferences of your guests—whether adults and children or just adults—you now decide whether you are going to provide an already prepared outdoor lunch or supper, meaning that you will take only things that are ready to serve—sandwiches, or cold chicken and salad, and a thermos of liquids, for example—or whether you are going to build a fire and cook.

Next you must choose the location. If you live near the mountains you may decide to climb or drive to a site that has a beautiful view, but if there are children in the party be sure there is a field nearby for games or races, or a stream in which they may swim. It should scarcely be necessary to remind you to select a site that you know something about—because you or your friends have picnicked there before. Be sure that the ground is not swampy, that it is not more mosquito- or ant-infested than anyplace else, and that it is not covered with poison ivy.

If you choose a beach remember to make some preparation to shield both your guests and the food they are to eat from blowing sand. For this nothing is better than some five-foot garden stakes and a few yards of burlap with a wide hem at each end through which stakes are inserted. Thrust the stakes into the sand to form a windbreak. If you are going to be on the beach all day, an umbrella is a must for those who are not well tanned or accustomed to the sun.

If you are giving a large picnic and including a number of people who are not necessarily picnic addicts it is important to select a site that is easy to get to or away from. You may have a Jeep or "beach buggy" that allows you to reach a remote part of the beach with no effort at all, but if not, don't expect your average guest to tramp through miles of soft sand carrying blankets, beach towels, and backrests.

Having made up your mind as to what to eat and where to cook it, you should plan as carefully as you would if you were inviting people to dine with you at home. You wouldn't ask guests to lunch at your house at one o'clock and then not serve until three; nor would you give them fish or chicken that was raw on one side and charred to a cinder on the other. There is no more reason to do this at an outdoor meal than at an indoor one.

HOT OR COLD?

The very simplest type of picnic is a "continental" picnic, straight from the farmers of Europe. It consists of a loaf of bread, a piece of cheese, and a bottle of wine. If the cheese and wine are good and the bread fresh this menu has all the advantages of being delicious and nourishing, requiring no preparation, and costing next to

nothing. However, in spite of the ease of getting together and carrying the ingredients of a continental picnic, most Americans prefer
to expand the menu in varying degrees. Using the three items above
as a base, you may add whatever you wish—fruit for dessert, little
tomatoes as a vegetable, tins of sardines or meats, and so on.

If there are children at the picnic, sandwiches are the most
popular food of all. Peanut butter and jelly still outstrips any other
variety in popularity contests among the very young. Adults and
children alike enjoy meat sandwiches, well-seasoned and with plenty
of mayonnaise to moisten the bread. Don't, however, make the mistake of using too much mayonnaise or too many tomatoes and other
"runny" ingredients, as the sandwiches will turn to mush on the way
to the picnic grounds. Don't attempt to make bread and fillings
separately and let people make their own. The messiest picnic imaginable is one at which knives and plates and bread and butter and
a half dozen jars of jams and meat pastes are all spread around and
flavored with sand or ants.

It is wise to offer a choice of two or three kinds of sandwiches,
and by all means label each variety, especially if they are wrapped
in foil. Wrapping and unwrapping and pulling apart to view the
insides can make a hash of the most beautifully prepared sandwich.

To accompany the sandwich menu offer a selection of potato
chips, pickles, tomatoes, carrot and celery sticks, or jars of potato or
macaroni salad. Cake or cookies or any other dessert that may be
eaten with the fingers (seedless grapes are among the most popular
with all ages) make a perfect ending. Thermos jugs of milk or soft
drinks for the children, and beer, iced tea, or coffee for the adults
complete the meal.

Cold menus may be much more elaborate than sandwiches. In
fact if you have the necessary equipment you may have an entire
buffet spread on a folding table. But most people prefer a simpler
picnic, and the main requirement is that the food be the best of its
kind. Cold fried chicken, or cold boiled lobster, accompanied by
coleslaw or lettuce brought in a damp cloth and mixed with dressing
when the group is ready to eat, bread and butter, and fresh fruit for
dessert make a meal that is truly "fit for a king."

When the nights are cool, or simply because you prefer it, you
may wish to serve a hot dish on your picnic. Again you have a choice
to make. Do you wish to bring a main dish already made in an
insulated container, or do you wish to build a fire and heat your meal
at the picnic site? Stews complete with potatoes and other vegetables, creamed chicken with noodles, roast-beef hash made with

potatoes, or filling chowders are all excellent choices. All keep indefinitely in big thermos jugs or any other well-insulated container.

Many men enjoy cooking meat over an open fire, and they generally have more assistance and suggestions than they need from their male guests. If the host—or the hostess—likes to do it, there is nothing more delicious than meat or fish cooked over coals. Steak, lamb chops, chicken, swordfish, or lobster are all superb when done in this fashion, and hot dogs and hamburgers change from an uninspired meal to a delectable treat. Whole potatoes or corn, wrapped in foil and roasted in the coals, and a mixed green salad make the best accompaniments, along with as many condiments such as mustard or ketchup as you can fit into your baskets. Cold, sliced watermelon, or perhaps fresh strawberries, already sugared, might finish the meal.

Your plates for a "hot" picnic must be more substantial than uncoated paper. Plastic or enameled ones are really the most satisfactory, even though they must be taken home to be washed. Plastic bowls or cups for chowder are far more leakproof and easier to hold than paper cups. As long as you are bringing the utensils for this type of meal, there is no reason not to accompany your main dish with a salad already mixed in a big bowl and breads kept warm by several layers of foil wrapping.

Good strong coffee in a thermos and plenty of beer and soft drinks kept cold in a tub of ice should be on hand for the singing around a roaring fire that should be a part of every evening picnic.

EQUIPMENT

Several items of equipment available at hardware stores, chain stores, or specialty shops are a delight to any picnic enthusiast. Styrofoam containers, which will keep food either hot or cold and weigh almost nothing, are a must. Another excellent item is an insulated, wide-mouthed jug or thermos to carry anything from cold vichyssoise to hot lamb stew.

Portable grills with folding legs are a great help if you are planning to cook, although on the beach you may simply scoop a hole in the sand, put in the charcoal, and lay a grill from your oven across it, resting it on sturdy boards pressed into the sand on either side of the hole.

Charcoal briquettes in a cardboard container save the trouble of taking newspaper or lighting fluid, and they are easier to carry than a large bag of charcoal. All one has to do is touch a match to the cardboard and the fire is started. And one warning—don't try to cook before the flame has died down and the coals have turned white, with a faint red glow here and there.

A two-sided grill, hinged on one end and with a long handle, is wonderful for holding and turning hamburgers, hot dogs, and steaks. It eliminates the danger of the hot dogs' rolling between the rungs of a larger grill into the fire, or the hamburgers sticking and crumbling when they are turned.

A pair of long tongs is useful for arranging coals and for moving anything that is hot. They are ideal for turning corn or potatoes as they cook in the coals and better for turning a steak than a fork, which pierces the meat and allows the juices to escape.

There are many other items that add greatly to the ease of preparing a picnic, and each picnic fan must decide which please him most. In general, choose those articles that are the most compact and lightweight and those that serve several purposes—without being limited either to a sandwich-and-cold-drink picnic or to a cooking picnic, but useful for transporting or preparing either.

A CHECKLIST

Like the perfect traveler, the perfect picnic manager has reduced the process to an exact science. She knows very well that the one thing to do is to take the fewest things possible and to consider the utility of those few.

Fitted hampers, tents and umbrellas, folding chairs and tables are all very well in a shop—and all right if you have a trailer or a station wagon for hauling them. But the usual flaw in picnics is that there are too many things to carry and look after and too much to clean and pack up and take home again.

Therefore people who organize picnics frequently should make up a list of all items that may be needed and check it each time before leaving. All the equipment may not be necessary for every picnic, but a list will prevent the salt or the bottle opener from being omitted!

LEAVING THE PICNIC SITE

No matter where your picnic has taken place, be sure not only to tidy up before you leave so that no trace will be left, but to be careful, while you are eating and opening papers, not to throw them carelessly aside where they will blow out onto the road. Many of our highways have pleasant wayside parks for picnickers, equipped with rustic tables, safe drinking water, and incinerators. On the property of a private owner, the least payment you can make is to be sure that you do nothing that might despoil any of his property.

Most important of all, *never* leave a fire without being absolutely certain that it is out. In the woods water may be poured on the logs until there is no sign of steam, or if you have a shovel or other means of lifting them, the embers may be carried to a nearby pond or stream and thrown in. On the beach a fire should also be put out with water. *Never* cover the coals with sand, as they will retain the heat for hours, and someone walking by with bare feet, unable to see the remains of the fire, may step on the hot sand and receive a terrible burn.

BARBECUES

A barbecue is essentially a cooking picnic in your own yard, but because of the proximity to your house, your menu and equipment may be more elaborate than that for a meal transported in your car.

ARRANGING YOUR DINING AREA

If you have a built-in grill in your yard or patio, you are fortunate indeed, but it is not at all necessary. A portable grill, either one on wheels or the folding variety, serves just as well. There should be a table, or tables, near the fire to hold the food and the plates, cooking utensils, and any other necessary equipment. There must be seating facilities for every guest. If your garden has a wall, or if the patio has steps leading to it, these may be used as seats, but it is thoughtful to provide cushions to cover hard stone or cement. If you do not have enough small chairs that can easily be carried to the yard, it is possible to rent them very inexpensively from a caterer.

SETTING THE BARBECUE TABLE

In setting the table for a barbecue you may give your flair for color and decoration a free rein. Checked or striped tablecloths, those with splashy designs of fruits or flowers, or those with bright red lobsters or colorful chefs' hats are eye-catching and set the tone for a gay party. They may be of cotton or linen if you wish, but plastic ones that can be wiped clean are more practical. Paper napkins in every imaginable color and design are available, but if your cloth is patterned a solid-colored napkin is best.

Disposable plates and cups of paper or plastic, which lighten the hostess' duties, can also be bought in many colors and varieties. Be sure, however, that they are of a sturdy material—plastic or plastic-coated paper rather than the somewhat flimsy cardboard-paper type. If you are serving a hot drink, paper cups must have handles or your guests will have difficulty holding them; and the package should be labeled "for hot drinks," or they will leak. Styrofoam or insulated plastic cups or glasses are ideal in that they do not conduct the heat and at the same time keep the liquid hot.

Hostesses who do not like to use disposable plates have many alternatives. Hard plastic sets of pseudochina come in lovely patterns, and although unbreakable, feel much like real china. Drink containers, too, come in many breakproof materials that are ideal for use outdoors, where uneven ground or stone patios add to the ordinary number of broken glasses.

Flameproof pots and pans in gaily colored enamelware or ironware are very useful to the barbecue cook. What a joy to be able to cook or heat a casserole over your fire and serve it in the same handsome container! This enamelware can also be purchased for individual servings—little casseroles with covers, perfect for hot chowder, stew, meat pies, etc.

Types of centerpieces and decorations are unlimited, but you will receive more compliments if they are appropriate for the meal or the season. For example, Chinese lanterns strung above the table and a centerpiece of gay paper parasols might accompany a Chinese dinner. Or a fishnet tablecloth with colorful felt cutouts of fish is decorative on the table set for a lobster dinner. Half a watermelon, filled with fresh melon balls and other fruits and decorated with sprigs of mint, makes a cool and appealing centerpiece for a hot summer evening. And fresh flowers arranged in a container that fits the barbecue theme are always attractive—yellow daisies, for instance, arranged in a copper kettle.

THE HOST AS COOK

At most barbecues the host is the cook, but this is not a hard-and-fast rule. If he dislikes cooking and the hostess enjoys it, there is no reason why she should not act as chef—and she is almost sure to be deluged with suggestions and assistance from her male guests. But the party will run more smoothly if she is relieved of the duties at the grill and is free to bring the other dishes from the kitchen, to help the guests serve themselves, and to see that everyone is having a good time.

MENU SUGGESTIONS

Rather than discuss menu possibilities generally, I am going to give you some sample menus, all of which may be enlarged upon or changed to fit the tastes of the guests and the hosts. These suggestions are intended as a guide, to show the infinite variety that may be presented at this type of party; they are not in any way meant to be a complete list. In each case the main dish—meat, fish, or fowl—is prepared on the grill. Unless specified, the others are prepared in advance and kept on the stove indoors or brought out to sit on a corner of the grill where the temperature must be neither too hot nor too cold.

The following meal is the least expensive, but always popular —especially with young people:

Hamburgers and/or Hot Dogs
Buttered Rolls
Casserole of Baked Beans
Potato Chips
Celery and Carrot Sticks
Watermelon Slices

This exotic menu calls for more preparation beforehand (pieces of meat or shrimp, mushrooms, tomatoes, onions, and bacon are marinated and threaded alternately on long skewers, ready to be laid on the grill):

Beef, Lamb, or Shrimp "Kabobs"
Rice
Watercress and Tomato Salad
Hot Rolls
Chocolate Eclairs

Especially good for the seashore are:

Grilled Swordfish
Casserole of Scalloped Potatoes
Spinach Salad
Croissants
Fresh Fruit Compote and Cookies or Cake

Spareribs are messy to eat, but delicious. Be sure that your guests are informally dressed for this one:

Spareribs with Barbecue Sauce
Baked Potatoes
Coleslaw
Hard Rolls
Apple Pie with Vanilla Ice Cream

This is the classic barbecue menu:

Sirloin Steak
Potato Chips
French-Fried Onions
Mixed Green Salad
French or Garlic Bread
Assorted Pastries

Beer, any soft drink, and pitchers of milk all go well with the informality of a barbecue. In hot weather, iced tea, iced coffee, and icy sangria are delicious. Pots of coffee should be kept hot on the grill for serving either during or after the meal.

Cocktails may be served, but since the food is hearty, elaborate hors d'oeuvres are not necessary. A few dishes of nuts or potato chips scattered about are sufficient.

A side table loaded with a variety of condiments is a nice idea. As each guest fills his plate (the host usually cuts and serves the meat) he passes by this table and helps himself to ketchup, mustard, relish, sauce, or whatever may be offered.

SOME GENERAL HINTS

Remember to have plenty of light; it is very difficult for the chef to tell when the meat is done if he cannot see it. Floodlights directed up into the trees give a beautiful effect. Gay and colorful Japanese lanterns can be purchased strung on electric wires like Christmas-tree bulbs. Candles give a soft light but must be placed in hurricane lamps to protect them from the breeze. Some candles contain an insect repellent—an excellent idea for a summer night.

Entertainment after the meal depends on your facilities and the preferences of your guests. A lunchtime barbecue may be followed by a swim if you have a pool or are near the beach. If not, you may want to organize a game of softball or badminton. Many adults enjoy a game of catch or touch football on a brisk day. When there are children present, suitable games and races are almost a necessity to keep them out of the chef's way.

In the evening you may dance to records if the patio or terrace has a suitable surface. Or if you have a stone fireplace, build up the fire to a blaze so that the guests may gather round to sing or chat. If you notice your guests shivering or putting on sweaters or coats, you must be prepared to move the party into the house—one of the advantages of having a barbecue in your own yard—otherwise your guests will soon start to leave.

HOUSEWARMINGS

When you have put a great deal of time and effort into making a lovely home you are naturally as eager to show it off as your friends are to see it. The nicest way to do so is to call your friends and ask them to a housewarming. Or you may invite them informally whenever you want. Invitations on informals or commercial fill-in cards are quite suitable too. Because the object of the party is to show your guests the house it is far better to have two or three small parties at which you will only have to make the tour a few times. If you have too many people at once, you may spend the entire time leading groups from one room to another.

A housewarming is generally a cocktail party or a cocktail buffet. It may be as simple or as elaborate as you wish, but it is fun to keep the style of your house in mind when you plan your decorations. For instance, if it is an Early American type, a brown tablecloth set with copper or pewter may be more appealing than lace with crystal or silver.

The guest generally takes a small gift to a housewarming. It need not be expensive, but it is more thoughtful to find something that will be of permanent use rather than flowers, which will only last a short time, or paper napkins, which will soon be used up. An ashtray, a few pretty dish towels or place mats, a framed print for the wall, a brush for the fireplace are a few possibilities.

OPEN HOUSE

An open house is literally what the name implies. The door is open to all those invited at any time between the hours stated on the invitation. Today most open houses are held to celebrate a holiday—New Year's Day, perhaps, or Christmas Eve. They also may take the place of a housewarming.

In very small communities an announcement of the open house is often put in the local paper, and anyone and everyone who reads it is expected to attend if he wishes. When invitations are issued in church or club announcements the host is saved from having to invite the entire membership individually. Personal invitations are generally sent out on informals or commercial cards bought for the occasion.

Because an answer is never expected, refreshments are simple and the sort that may be expanded or not set out all at once. Dips, sandwiches, bowls of nuts, and a punch—rather than individual drinks—are good choices. People drop in to greet their hosts, and friends wish each other a "Happy New Year" or "Good luck to you in your new home." They generally stay no more than a half hour to an hour.

If the open house is to celebrate a holiday the decorations are generally appropriate to the season. At Christmastime the tree would be trimmed and whatever other decorations you might wish to use would be arranged as beautifully as possible. Eggnog is the traditional drink at a Christmas open house. For a Fourth of July party, red, white, and blue streamers, balloons, or bouquets might add a note of gaiety. But if the open house is not held to celebrate any particular holiday no decorations are necessary other than some vases of pretty flowers or greens.

The food and beverages may be arranged on the dining-room table if you have enough plates of cookies or sandwiches so that it will not look bare. If your refreshments are restricted to one or two plates of food and a punch bowl they should be set out on any conveniently placed table in the hall or living room, or on a side table in the dining room. You may wish to surround a bowl of eggnog with holly twigs or a fruit punch with flowers, but otherwise only the attractive arrangement of glasses, little napkins (cloth or paper), and food is necessary to assure the charm of your refreshment table.

BRUNCHES

Brunch—a combination of breakfast and lunch that relies on both breakfast and lunch dishes for its menus, although it is held closer to the usual hour for lunch—is a pleasant sort of informal, even casual, entertaining. It is not unusual to find brunches being given on the day after a large party, especially if there are many out-of-town guests who have come for the "big" occasion. However, no such excuse is necessary if you find the late-morning hours convenient for you and your friends.

In any event informality is the rule. In the country, slacks or simple dresses may be worn by the women, or if the host is having the party beside his swimming pool, people may come in shorts and bring their bathing suits. In the city any daytime clothing—dress or slacks—is correct for a woman, and a man usually wears a sports jacket rather than a business suit.

Invitations may be telephoned ahead of time, but this kind of gathering is so casual that the host often simply says to his friends as they are leaving someone else's party, "Why don't you come over around eleven thirty tomorrow for a late breakfast?" or "Would you all come for a late breakfast after church tomorrow?"

Bloody Marys are often served, as well as martinis and other cocktails. But tomato juice or consommé must also be offered without the liquor for friends who prefer it that way.

The food is arranged on a buffet table less elaborately set than for lunch or dinner, but attractively and conveniently laid out. Breakfast and lunch dishes are combined. For example, a platter of scrambled eggs surrounded by bacon or little sausages may be accompanied by hot rolls, toast, sautéed potatoes, and broiled tomatoes. Or platters of waffles may be served with maple syrup or with creamed chicken for guests who prefer a heartier meal. Pitchers of fruit juice and pots of coffee should be on a table beside the buffet.

COFFEES

Coffees or coffee parties are better known in the South than in the North, but they are becoming more popular all over the country because they offer entertainment for young women during the hours their youngsters are in school.

Coffees may be extremely simple—just a group of neighbors getting together for a cup of coffee and a "Danish" or a doughnut—or they may be an elaborate party held in a club or hotel. The menu is much like that for a tea, ranging from delicate sandwiches to chafing dishes of scrambled eggs, to fresh fruits, to pastries.

Women go to neighborhood coffees in their regular daytime slacks or skirts, but they should not look as if they have just come in from weeding the garden. For large, special coffee parties they dress in "afternoon" dresses, suits, or dressy pants suits.

Invitations are always issued by telephone except to the more formal "coffees," which are generally held in honor of someone or something. In the South coffees are frequently given for brides-to-be, and may or may not be showers.

CARD PARTIES

ON PLANNING YOUR TABLES

In giving a card party, whether of two tables or of ten, the first thing to do is plan the tables carefully. The tables may all be different

—one with good players, another with beginners, one where the stakes are high, another where they play for nothing—but you must do your best to put those who play approximately the same kind of game at the same table. In addition to skill it is important to remember temperament. Don't put people who take their game seriously (and "play for blood") with those who chatter unceasingly and keep asking, "Whose turn is it?" or "What's trump?" If it is a bridge party don't put two men who are the best players in town at a table with one woman who thinks of nothing but the next bright remark she can make and another who is beautiful to look at but who knows nothing about bidding. A man will be delighted to find a pretty woman next to him at the dinner table, but at the card table he hopes for an intelligent partner. In short, one poor player can spoil the whole evening—or afternoon—for the three who play well.

However, when a group of friends play together regularly, and they have approximately the same degree of skill, they may prefer to draw for partners and tables in order to have the opportunity of playing with different combinations of people. They may also move around—changing tables and partners after four hands, two rubbers, or whatever they decide upon. Each player keeps his own individual score. The game is just as much fun but far less "cutthroat" than the conventional play tends to promote.

And now your preparations: It seems scarcely necessary to say that the packs of cards on each table must be fresh and that the pencils laid beside the score pads must be sharp. And yet I have played with grubby cards and kept score on odd little scraps of paper in the most beautiful homes! On each table you leave a slip of paper with the names of the players who are to sit there, or you may simply tell each guest at which table he is to play. At a bridge party, players cut for their seats and partners. It is important to see that each table is comfortably lighted. Poorly placed light that is reflected from the shiny surface of the cards is just as bad as darkness that makes red cards indistinguishable from black ones. If you have any doubt about the light, sit in each place, hold the cards in your hands, lay a few on the table, and see for yourself.

REFRESHMENTS

The kinds of refreshments you offer your card-playing guests depends, of course, on the time of day. While small sandwiches and tiny cakes accompanied by tea or coffee might be suitable when served at four o'clock to a group of women, they would hardly please the men at an evening gathering. Then, if you have not served dinner, a selection of cold meats and cheeses and a variety of breads for do-it-yourself sandwiches, served with coffee and beer around eleven o'clock, would be more appropriate. In either case, however, the food may be attractively arranged on the dining-room table, and having served themselves, the guests may be asked either to return to the cleared card tables or to take their plates to more comfortable chairs in the living room.

PRIZES

If it is customary in your community to play for prizes, then you must select a first prize for the highest score made by a woman and a first prize for the highest score made by a man. At a party of women only, a second prize is usually given. All prizes should be attractively wrapped before being presented. Those who receive the prizes must, of course, open the packages at once and show some evidence of appreciation when thanking the hostess. Needless to say, a considerate person does not show disappointment upon receiving a prize that happens not to please him or her, nor does he "forget" to take it home.

DESSERT CARD PARTY

A dessert card party is a happy compromise for the hostess who may feel that she cannot provide a full luncheon or dinner for her guests, yet wishes to do more than simply invite them to play cards. When the group is small and she has a dining-room table large enough to seat them, dessert may be served in the following way: The dining table is set for the dessert course only. Individual place mats are set with a dessert plate, a lunch napkin on the plate, a fork at the left and a spoon at the right, and a glass of water. While her friends are having their dessert, the hostess pours coffee, and it is handed around the table. After coffee they begin playing on tables already set up in the living room.

If there are more guests than she can seat, the dining table may be set as a buffet, using a tablecloth or place mats or round lace doilies (paper ones will do if you have no lace mats) under the stack of plates and the dishes on which the dessert is served.

The guests serve themselves and take their plates to the living room to eat. The hostess may or may not ask them to sit at the card tables, which have already been set up and readied for bridge. They help themselves to coffee, and if they wish to start playing immediately, they may take their cups with them to the bridge tables.

STAG DINNERS

A man's dinner is sometimes called a stag or bachelor dinner and as its name implies is a dinner given by a man for men only. It usually celebrates some special event or person. It may be a welcome or farewell, or the bridegroom's last party with his good friends before his wedding. Occasionally a man may have a quantity of game that he has shot, or fish that he has caught, and want to share it with his friends.

Nearly always a man's dinner is given at the host's club or in a hotel or restaurant. But if he chooses to give a stag dinner in his own house, his wife (or mother or sister) should *not* appear. For his wife to come downstairs and receive the guests with him is most definitely out of place. No matter how much you may want to say "How do you do?" to your husband's or son's friends—*don't*.

Therefore, if a man does decide he would like to entertain his friends at home, he must discuss his plans and the menu with his wife and help her prepare it ahead of time. She may unobtrusively set out the dishes on a buffet table at the time agreed upon with her husband. After the men have eaten, she may, if she wishes to, remove the plates and clean up. She might also leave the cleaning up until the next day, when her husband can help.

A wife might also prefer to absent herself entirely and go, perhaps, to a friend's house or to a movie. She has every right to do this, but she should see that everything is as ready as it can possibly be in the kitchen and that the house is neat and welcoming.

SURPRISE PARTIES

Years ago, in the days of many servants, surprise parties were often arranged in the home of the guests of honor—with the cooperation of the cook, waitress, or whoever would be involved. The couple were spirited away on some pretext, and when they returned, the house was ready and the guests were hidden inside waiting to shout "Surprise!" as they entered.

Today, very few servantless couples would welcome a group when they have had no warning to prepare their home for a party. An exception might be made when a husband wishes to give his wife a surprise birthday party, or she wishes to surprise him with a party in honor of a special occasion—a promotion, for example. Then, with the help of friends, the one planning the party can arrange it at home.

Otherwise, surprise parties take place at a friend's house or possibly in a club. The couple to be honored are invited for a "quiet" dinner or evening by another couple, and when they arrive their entire circle of friends is there waiting to surprise them.

Such parties always consist of a group of intimate friends and usually take place on John's or Mary's birthday or their anniversary, particularly an early one.

Some caution should be exercised in arranging surprise parties, and thought given to whether the people honored would really enjoy the occasion. For example, a word of warning is necessary for persons who might be inclined to surprise their friends with a party for their golden wedding anniversary. If the "bride and groom" are young for their ages, it is possible that they would like this type of party. But if they were not married in their earliest youth the excitement of too great a surprise might very well have the opposite of happy results.

SINGING, READING, OR DISCUSSION GROUPS

When neighborhood groups include both men and women they usually meet in the evening at a time agreed upon as convenient for everyone. Therefore the hostess has little to say about the hour. But a group of women interested, for example, in reading French together may find that an afternoon or even a morning meeting is the only solution to the problem of family schedules. The convenience of the members carries more weight in such circumstances than any prescribed hour, and even neighborhood custom should not discourage a group from picking their own time or changing it by mutual consent.

Refreshments are usually served after the activity of the meeting, and of course the kind depends on the hour, the preferences of the group, and the inclination of the hostess-of-the-day. Coffee and sandwiches, Welsh rarebit and beer, cider and doughnuts would all be appropriate after an evening gathering. Earlier in the day coffee and rolls or tea and cookies might very well be adequate.

Otherwise there are no rules for such groups—except to be firm with those who don't try to keep in tune or with the gossipers who wander from the topic under discussion.

SEWING CIRCLES

The hostess at whose house a sewing group meets should have a supply of different-sized thimbles, extra needles, and several pairs of scissors and spools of thread. What is sewed depends upon the purpose of the group, which may be to make garments for a nursery, hospital, or other organization. It may have no object other than to meet socially, in which case the members sew for themselves—doing needlepoint, quilting, hooking rugs, even knitting. Sometimes a sewing circle is a lunch club that meets weekly or fortnightly at the houses of the various members. They sew from eleven until about one and then have a sit-down or buffet luncheon. More often coffee and light refreshments, such as coffee cake, cookies, or doughnuts, are served approximately halfway through a session that may run from ten to twelve or from two to half past four.

"FAMILY STYLE"

Mealtime—especially dinnertime—is the one hour of the day that a family can—and should—get together. This is when the youngsters learn the basic elements of good manners—not only table manners but consideration and the importance of participating—that increase the pleasure of being together at mealtime. Therefore, while dinner at home is not a "party" as we generally think of it, every effort should be made to make family meals as entertaining and attractive as possible, while still keeping them relaxed and informal, so that the members of the family look forward to them as the best part of the day.

THE TABLE

In many of today's houses and apartments the pressures of space and expense have caused the formal dining room to disappear. The dining table appears in any one of a number of other places—in an ell or an alcove off the living room, at the end of the living room nearest the kitchen, sometimes in a wide hall, or in the kitchen. The location of the table does not affect its use, however, and even though it may not have the formal surroundings that it did in Grandmother's day, it should be thought of as a pleasant center of family gatherings.

The table itself should be large enough to accommodate the entire family comfortably. A pretty cloth or attractive place mats (in any material that is easily wiped clean or laundered) should always be used, not only to protect the tabletop but also to lend an air of graciousness to even the simplest meal. Although not necessary, a centerpiece is pleasing. With a little help children can arrange a few flowers or make a simple table decoration for some particular holiday or special occasion. Such contributions add to the family's enjoyment of mealtime and help the children recognize the importance of household appointments as well.

Seating arrangements at table depend entirely on the convenience of the family. Most often, when there is no maid, the mother sits nearest the kitchen door with the youngest children who may still need help from time to time next to her. The place opposite hers is the father's. Some families make a tradition of seating a birthday child as the guest of honor would be seated at a formal dinner, a custom that is flattering to the child and at the same time provides practice in the behavior that will be expected of him when he is older.

At large family parties—Thanksgiving or Christmas dinners, for example—it may be necessary to have more than one table to accommodate everyone. In this case Father sits at the head of the dining-room table and Mother at the other table, so that the people sitting there will not feel that they are "beyond the pale."

KITCHEN DINING

Some families, even though they have a formal dining room, prefer the coziness and convenience of the kitchen when dining alone. Many others, as mentioned above, have no dining room. In either case, if space permits, it is most desirable to have an end or corner of the kitchen set apart and furnished or decorated in such a way that children growing up in the home feel the importance of good manners at any table, no matter where it may be. When there is no such space, the ordinary kitchen table must do, but an extra effort should be made to make the room attractive and to make sure that the table is uncluttered and clean.

Even a kitchen table should be nicely set for dinner, with place mats (even though they may be paper doilies), spotless utensils (although they may be stainless steel), and pretty plates and glasses, attractive in color and pattern (no matter if they were bought at the local "five-and-ten").

THE PLACE SETTINGS

The main difference in setting a table for guests and setting a table for the family is that for family a minimum number of utensils is put at each place—only those absolutely necessary for each course. Very often there may be no more than two or three pieces of silver: a fork, a knife, and a spoon or fork for dessert. At a family dinner it is certainly not necessary to have a separate fork for salad, but a salad plate is another matter. Who could wish to have the gravy and salad dressing run together into an unsavory soup, or the salad wilt on a heated plate?

Butter plates and knives are often omitted, and the bread and butter are placed on the edge of the dinner plate, but with the convenience of an electric dishwasher it is far nicer to have a separate plate. This is especially true if the dinner plates are, as they should be, heated, because butter put on them melts at once. Or you may place the butter on the side of the salad plate to reduce the number of dishes.

SERVING

If the family has a maid the meals are served exactly as they would be if guests were present. She may serve from the kitchen, or if the family is large she may pass the plates as the man of the house fills them.

In most households, where Mother is cook and waitress, she fills the plates and brings them to the table two at a time, giving her husband the first one. She may, and should, enlist the aid of any one of the children who is old enough to help her. If the family is small she may remove the dishes herself, but if there are a number of children, those old enough should take their own plates to the kitchen. They should wait until everyone has finished eating.

If the meal is served by the father at the table, the dishes are passed from person to person. The first one filled is sent down the table on the host's right (or counterclockwise) and stops at the mother's place. The others are served in order, working back up the table, first on the right side, then on the left. Aside from the fact that the first plate is not given to the person on the father's right, the order is the same as that described for an informal dinner party.

At large family meals the vegetable dishes, instead of being at the father's place, may be farther down the table. When this is done the person nearest the dish, as soon as he receives his own plate, helps himself and passes the vegetable in the direction of those who already have their meat.

When a person seated at one end of the table asks for something that is near the other end, the person nearest the food requested picks it up and passes it on. If he wishes he may help himself to the dish before passing it to avoid his neighbor's having to send it back again.

᚛35᚜ Showers

A shower is a gathering of friends in honor of someone special—a bride-to-be, a new mother or mother-to-be, a new homeowner, or a new neighbor. It is, in short, a celebration distinguished by the "showering" of gifts on the guest of honor.

The time and setting vary as greatly as the reasons for the party. A morning coffee, a luncheon, an afternoon tea, a cocktail party, or a buffet dinner—all are suitable. A cocktail party or an after-dinner gathering is especially appropriate to welcome a new neighbor or a new homeowner—so that men can attend. A shower may be held on any day of the week that is convenient for the guest of honor, the hostess, and the majority of the guests.

When a shower is to be held for a new mother, even though it may be planned as a surprise, she should be given *some* notice so that she can adjust the baby's schedule and have him (and herself) ready for visitors.

Bridal showers should be held from two weeks to two months prior to the wedding. If the shower takes place too close to the wedding date, it may be very inconvenient for the bride, who has so much to do during those last busy days.

INVITATIONS

Invitations to all showers are almost invariably written on commercial fill-in shower invitations, which are available in an infinite variety of styles. They may also be short personal notes, or in the case of an older woman giving the shower, they may be written on her informal or visiting card. In some cases they are even telephoned or issued in person, as might happen when a girl asks the other girls in her office to a shower.

The name of the guest of honor and the type of gift expected should be included with every invitation. In the case of a kitchen or bathroom shower for a bride, her preference in color should be noted, so that gifts will fit in with her decorating plans. Lingerie-shower invitations should include the bride's sizes.

WHO GIVES THE SHOWER?

Almost anyone who wants to "do something" for someone may give a shower. An old-time resident might give a shower for a new neighbor, even though they barely know each other. A retiring clergyman might give a shower for his replacement, although they've barely met. A cousin or an aunt might give a shower for a new baby, and a "best friend" often gives a shower for the bride. The one rule is that *immediate* family—meaning mothers, mothers-in-law, and sisters—should not, under ordinary circumstances, give showers. This is because it seems very "commercial" and in poor taste for someone so close to the honoree to issue an invitation that, in effect, says, "Come—and give my daughter a present." Somehow it seems much less greedy when the invitation comes from someone less closely involved.

But even then there are *extra*ordinary circumstances. For example, when a bride comes from a foreign country, or even from the other side of our own country, and will be married in her groom's hometown but knows no one there, the groom's sisters might well give her a shower. Etiquette is meant to make life easier—not to impose unnecessary or impractical rules, and when the circumstances warrant it, the "almost" can be dropped and "anyone" may give a shower. It is also perfectly correct for two or three friends to get together and act as cohostesses for a shower. This often happens when the guest of honor is a new mother, or when two or three bridesmaids give a "joint" shower for the bride.

GUESTS

Ordinarily, only close friends and relatives are invited to showers, since the invitation automatically means a gift. Also, showers were traditionally (although this has, unfortunately, changed) sentimental occasions, and only those most intimate with the bride or the person being honored were included. The exception is, of course, the newcomer, in which case the guests are neighbors who want to meet the new arrival, and to make him or her welcome.

No one should be invited to a bridal shower who is not also invited to the wedding. It is extremely presumptuous to ask someone to a shower—meaning she *must* bring a gift—if she is not close enough to the bride or groom or their families to be included on the wedding list. Nor should anyone who does not know the guest of honor be invited, even if she is the closest friend of the hostess. Again, it would be an imposition to expect her to give a gift to someone she has never met.

There is one exception to the above. When a wedding is very small—restricted to family only, and perhaps with no reception—the bride may be given a shower to which are invited friends who would have been included at a larger wedding. The shower, in this case, almost takes the place of the reception, and the shower gifts are given instead of (rather than in addition to) wedding gifts.

Except in the case of surprise showers, or a shower for a newcomer, the guest of honor is consulted about the guest list. This is very important in cases where there may be several showers, because only the person being honored can divide up her list of friends and relatives so that no one is invited to more than one or two. The hostess, however, decides on the *number* of guests, since she will be paying the bills. Bridesmaids, who are generally included on several lists for bridal showers, should be told by the bride not to bring gifts to each one, or they may keep expenses down by giving "joint" presents.

Otherwise there are no rules about who should or should not be invited. Some showers may be restricted to family members only, some to young people only, and others may be a mixture of young and old, friends and relatives, and in the case of evening showers, men and women.

One final word about guest lists. The huge bridal showers that include almost everyone invited to the wedding (which are, unfortunately, gaining popularity) are in the *poorest* taste. The entire idea of an intimate party is lost, and they are no more than a demand for more gifts. As such, they are an unforgivable imposition on those invited.

GIFTS

There are three hard-and-fast rules about shower gifts.

1. The gift is presented to the guest of honor at the shower. It is never sent to her from the store. If, however, the donor cannot attend, she leaves the wrapped package at the hostess' house ahead of time.
2. The gift must be accompanied by a card, so that the guest of honor knows from whom each present comes as she opens it.

3. Presents must be opened at the shower, and each donor thanked personally then and there. The recipient may write thank-you notes later if she wishes, but it is not necessary unless the donor was not there to receive her personal thanks.

Shower gifts should not be elaborate. They should be useful, appropriate, and as original as the donor can make them. Traditionally, shower gifts were handmade for the occasion, and such gifts are still the nicest of all, but unfortunately many of us today do not have the time or the ability to create a handmade gift.

The type of shower, of course, determines the type of gift. At a stork shower, gifts are anything you can think of for a new baby, or for the mother's use in caring for the baby. Gifts for a new-neighbor shower could range from foods to help her provision her kitchen, to plants for her garden, cleaning or cooking utensils, or decorative ornaments for her new home. Invitations to bridal showers invariably specify what sort of shower it will be, and gifts must be in that particular line.

Money-tree showers should be avoided, since the shower gift is meant to be a memento of the giver, and money can hardly fulfill that requirement. In the rare case in which a bride is not going to have a home after her marriage, or perhaps when a new mother is visiting from abroad and cannot carry gifts back with her, a money tree would be acceptable. The guest of honor does not disclose the amounts in the envelopes on the tree.

OPENING THE GIFTS

The present-opening is the high spot of all showers. When everyone—or almost everyone—invited has arrived, the guests are expected to gather round while the guest of honor opens the packages one by one and thanks each giver. As mentioned above, cards should be enclosed, because otherwise each giver must say more or less sheepishly as her present is unwrapped, "That's from me."

A friend (or at a bridal shower, one of the bridesmaids) should sit beside the guest of honor and make a careful list of the gifts and who gave them. This is essential if the honoree plans to write thank-you notes.

In some localities all the presents are delivered to the hostess several days beforehand. She leaves the packages as they are, but puts each in a uniform outer gift wrapping so that the whole stack of packages will be alike. When all are wrapped, the presents are piled on a table in another room or behind a screen, or perhaps in the living room.

DECORATIONS

No decorations are necessary except a centerpiece for your table and an inventive or attractive way of arranging the gifts. For some showers, the hostess gives a gift that holds the other presents, and decorates it appropriately with bows, flowers, or whatever she wishes. Examples: a shiny new garbage can for a new homeowner; a shopping basket on wheels for a city-bound bride; a large picnic basket to hold the canned goods given to a new clergyman's wife; a covered container for disposing of diapers for a stork shower. More specific suggestions for bridal and baby-shower decorations appear below.

The guest of honor and at a bridal shower, the bride's mother and future mother-in-law are often given corsages by the hostess, although this is not obligatory.

REFRESHMENTS

There is no rule about the refreshments served other than that they be appropriate to the hour and to the tastes of the guests. At a morning coffee shower, the hostess may serve no more than doughnuts and coffee cake, or she may serve bowls of fresh strawberries, waffles, or French pastries. Luncheons are generally light, consisting perhaps of a chafing dish of shrimp Newburg, a green salad, and a fruit compote or melon for dessert. At a small informal luncheon shower, the menu might be no more than soup and sandwiches, dessert and coffee. Cocktails may be served or not, depending on the inclination of the hostess and the habits of her guests. If they are served, Bloody Marys and whiskey sours are popular in the winter, daiquiris and "Collinses" in the summer. Wine, too, may be served if the hostess wishes. However, soft drinks or iced tea or coffee should always be offered for the women who prefer not to drink—especially at noon. At a late-afternoon shower, the menu is typical tea fare—sandwiches, cake or cookies, tea, and coffee.

A punch, mixed drinks, and beer are generally offered at evening showers when men are included.

Showers are rarely dinner parties, but they may be "dessert" parties, or they may be held later in the evening. If a substantial dessert is served when guests arrive, no additional food need be offered. But if guests arrive after dinner at home, they should be served a light "supper" later in the evening. This could be as simple as pizzas or hamburgers, or as elaborate as creamed chicken on toast, Mexican chili, or whatever the hostess dreams up.

ENTERTAINMENT

No entertainment is necessary, since the opening of the presents is the "featured entertainment" of the occasion. However, in some areas local custom dictates that games be played, and showers may also be card or bridge parties.

The choice of games is entirely up to the hostess, who knows what is popular in her locality.

Prizes for games should not, as some people think, be handed over to the guest of honor. She has already received a gift from all the guests, and it makes the games more fun if everyone has a chance at the prizes.

"IN ABSENTIA"

When you are invited to a large shower for someone you do not know, or know well, and you refuse the invitation, you do *not* need to send a gift. If, however, the shower is a small and intimate one, and you are a good friend of the guest of honor, you are expected to give a gift even though you cannot attend. You should take the gift, with your card on it, to the hostess' house at some time before the shower takes place. The hostess usually explains to the guest of honor the reason for your absence.

SPECIAL HINTS FOR BRIDAL SHOWERS

DISPLAYING THE GIFTS

Here are two ideas for attractive, inexpensive ways of arranging bridal-shower gifts:

1. Take an old, straight-handeled umbrella and remove the fabric, or buy an inexpensive Japanese paper umbrella and strip the paper off. Spray the frame and a six-inch metal funnel white or pink. Invert the funnel and stick the handle of the umbrella into the small end. Secure it with clay or tape. The umbrella will now stand up. Decorate the spokes and the top with bows, artificial flowers, or whatever your imagination

Two ideas for arranging shower gifts

can devise. Set it on a table and cover the base with flowers, leaves, or crepe or tissue paper. Tie a ribbon to each spoke and tie the other end to a gift. Arrange the packages under the half-opened umbrella so that the ribbons fall in a pretty pattern.

2. Make a hole in the center of a lacy paper doily. Push the stems of fresh flowers through the hole and into a narrow-topped vase, filled with water. Tie a big white satin bow around the stems below the doily and above the vase. Attach white satin ribbons so that they are hidden by the bow, and tie their other ends to the gifts. Arrange the gifts around the "bridal bouquet" so as to hide the vase.

"WISHING-WELL" SHOWERS

In addition to her regular gift each guest is asked to bring something for a "wishing well." These are tiny presents—a spool of thread, a kitchen sponge, a wooden spoon, a can of soap powder, etc. This is explained on the invitation, and sometimes a price limit—perhaps fifty cents—is established.

The hostess usually makes a cardboard replica of a wishing well, and the gifts, wrapped and tied to ribbons, are tossed in. There are no cards on the presents, although at some showers the guests write a poem, which is wrapped around their gift. The bride pulls out the gifts with the ribbons and reads the poems aloud.

The wishing well may be made from a trash can, a laundry hamper, or any round receptacle.

ROUND-THE-CLOCK SHOWERS

At a "round-the-clock" shower, each guest is given an hour of the day on her invitation and brings a present appropriate for that hour. For example, at a bridal shower, if her hour is ten in the morning a guest might bring a dustpan and brush, or if it is six in the evening she might bring a set of four or six cocktail glasses.

RECIPE SHOWERS

This is one type of shower that could well be given by "immediate family," since no money is expended by the guests. It is a lovely idea because it allows the bride's friends to express their love without the commercial connotaton of so many showers.

With every invitation the guests receive a sheet of typing paper and are asked to make up a menu including their favorite recipes.

These papers are collected as they arrive and put into a notebook or recipe folder provided by the hostess. The bride is sure to treasure them—and add to them—for many years.

At some recipe showers, the guests also bring very small gifts—similar to those for a wishing well—in addition to the recipes. In fact the recipe shower could well be combined with a wishing-well shower.

PROXY SHOWERS

On occasion, a shower is given for a bride who cannot be there, generally because she lives too far away. This is perfectly correct, but poses some problems for the hostess who is responsible for sending the gifts on to the bride.

A recipe shower is an excellent solution to this problem, but if gifts are given, it should be specified that they be small, light, and easy to pack and ship.

Gifts, once they are wrapped, should certainly not be opened by anyone except the bride, and yet the best part of a shower is seeing and admiring the presents. The best way to compromise is to ask the guests to bring their gifts unwrapped. The hostess provides wrapping materials, and the guests, after displaying their presents, wrap them themselves. The hostess may offer a prize for the prettiest package. She then packs the gifts into one large box and mails it to the bride.

At most proxy showers, a telephone call is put through to the bride so that she can talk to her friends, or if that is impractical a card or note is made up with short messages from each guest present.

RETURNING SHOWER PRESENTS

Insofar as possible, bridal-shower presents should be returned if the marriage is called off. They are given to the bride with the intent that they be used in her new home, or by the bride and her husband, and these reasons for giving them are gone. Naturally, monogrammed articles, or anything that has been used, cannot be given back, but every effort should be made to return the gifts that are unused.

The easiest way is to mail them, with a note enclosed, saying, "I appreciated your thoughtful gift so much, but since John and I have broken our engagement, I will not be needing it and am returning it with thanks."

If the friends insist that you keep their gifts you may do so. If you become engaged again at a future date, ask the friends who gave you gifts the first time not to do so again, since the original present may still be unused.

STORK SHOWERS

Stork—or baby—showers are best given after the happy event takes place. While the vast majority of babies are born healthy and happily, there is always a faint chance that something can go wrong, and nothing could be sadder for the bereaved mother (or father) than to have to put away or return the unused shower gifts. But once mother and baby have been home for a few weeks, they are ready to "receive," and the mother is eager to show off her pride and joy.

Showers may be given for second babies, but they should be restricted to either *very* close friends and family or to people who were not invited to showers for the first baby. Only if the mother has moved to a new area and has a new circle of friends should she allow anyone to give her a shower for additional babies.

SHOWERS FOR ADOPTED BABIES

It is not only correct, but a nice thing to do, to give a shower for the mother of an adopted baby. It is exactly the same as any stork shower, except that on the invitations you should include the correct size for baby clothes, since the child is not necessarily a "new" baby.

SHOWERS FOR UNWED MOTHERS

Fortunately, the stigma of being "born out of wedlock" is nowhere near as black today as it used to be. Girls who find themselves in this situation frequently need more support and love from their families and friends at this time than they ever will again. Therefore it is perfectly acceptable to give a small shower for an expectant unwed mother, or for one whose baby is already born. For her sake, however, the shower should be restricted to close friends and relatives.

GRANDMOTHER SHOWERS

When a women's club or social organization learns that one of their members is about to become a grandmother the others may wish to give her a "grandmother shower." It is usually held during or at the end of their regular meeting or get-together, with some special refreshments served and a few extra minutes devoted to the opening of the gifts. However, it may be given in the usual way—by a close friend or group of friends of the grandmother-to-be as an afternoon tea or a morning coffee.

The main distinction between a grandmother shower and any other is that the gifts are not for the use of the recipient. Often they are gifts for the baby or the new mother, which are given through the grandmother. They may also be articles to be used by the grandmother when she is caring for the new baby—diaper pins, a bathinette, a teething ring, bibs, etc.

Whatever the arrangements, the grandmother shower is a delightful way to honor a friend and to make the prospective grandmother feel an important part of the coming event.

ᒧ§36ᒫ House Parties and Weekend Visits

Although the day of the great house staffed by a horde of servants is almost gone, the simple house with a relaxed hostess and enthusiastic guests can be the setting for a house party that is just as successful as the elaborate affair of other years.

The size of the house party today is limited mainly by the number of available beds. However, for a hostess who has no help, it is certainly easier to cook, serve, and keep the house in order with two guests than it is with eight, a fact she should remember even after she has counted the beds.

THE INVITATIONS

Invitations are generally telephoned, but if your guests live in another town they may be written:

June 15

Dear Ellie,

John and I are hoping that you and Bob and the children can spend the weekend of the fourth with us in Edgartown. If Bob could leave the office a little early on Friday the second, there is a 6:00 P.M. ferry that would get you here in time for dinner, and there are ferries leaving the island at 5:00 and at 8:00 on Sunday. The fishing should be great, and the children are counting on Sally and Jimmy for the annual picnic. Please come—we have wanted to show you the island for so long.

Much love,
Ann

With the rising popularity of winter sports, more and more people are acquiring lodges in the mountains, and ski weekends are becoming almost an institution in all sections of the country where there are nearby slopes. An invitation might be on this order:

January 4

Dear Joan,
The forecast is for snow and more snow, and Dick and I are hoping that you and Bill will spend the weekend after next skiing with us at Stowe. Come as early as you can on Friday the eighth, and stay until Sunday night so as not to miss a minute of it. The Hortons are coming, too, so maybe you could drive up together. To find us, you turn off Interstate 89 on Route 100, drive exactly three-tenths of a mile past the Standard Church, and we are the house on the right.
No formal clothes, only your ski outfits, and slacks to change into. Plenty of woolies and flannels—it's cold!
We're counting on you, so do say "Yes."

Love to you both,
Barbara

In your letter or on the telephone, be sure to give the details of transportation, or the route if your guests are coming by car. If they will be arriving by public transportation, you must tell them to let you know at what hour they will arrive so that you can meet them at the station or airport.

To make it easier for guests to know what to bring, it is wise to indicate what the activities will be: "We're planning a deep-sea fishing expedition on Saturday," "The Joneses have asked us to a beach picnic on Sunday," or "There is to be a black-tie dance at the club on Saturday."

A ROOM FOR YOUR GUESTS

TEMPORARY ARRANGEMENTS

Most familes today do not have a room in their house that is intended solely for the use of guests. When they wish to have friends spend a night or a weekend (or more) the children are doubled up to vacate a room, or perhaps sent to spend the time with friends. If there is a library or den with a convertible sofa it is put in readiness. In a child's room toys are hidden from sight, some clothes are removed from the closet, sufficient drawer space is cleared so that the guest may unpack his suitcase, and the room is made sparkling clean. If he is to share a bath with other members of the household his towels should, if possible, be hung on a rack in his bedroom, so that children do not inadvertently use them.

The host and hostess should never move out of their own room to give it to their guest or guests. It would cause considerable confusion, since all of their personal belongings are in the closet, in the drawers, and in every other imaginable place. The guest could not help but feel that he was imposing and making everyone uncomfortable, and he would therefore be uncomfortable himself. Even putting the guest on a convertible sofa in the living room, with a screen arranged around it to afford privacy, is preferable to switching everyone about. Of course if a guest is staying only for a night or two, a child, or children (if the sofa makes into a double bed), might be moved to the living room, but they should not be expected to give up their quarters, either, if the visit is an extended one.

UNMARRIED COUPLES

> *It is almost unnecessary to say that in no well-appointed house is a guest, except under certain circumstances, put in a room with any one else. An exception is a man and wife, if the hostess is sure beyond a doubt that they occupy similar quarters when at home.*—Emily Post, 1922

I am frequently asked by parents what they should do when their sons or daughters arrive home with someone of the opposite sex with whom they have been living without benefit of matrimony. Should they put them in the same room, or insist that they sleep separately?

Parents have a right to insist that their own standards be observed in their own home. If they have been brought up to feel that it is morally wrong to sleep with someone before marriage and they would feel guilty or uncomfortable allowing it in their house, they should make that very clear to their children *before* they come home. If the parents have accepted the situation, but do not want to meet it face-to-face, they must wrestle with their own consciences. If the son or daughter says, "Very well then, I won't come home at all," they have an even harder decision. They must decide whether their relationship and continued communication with their child is more important than upholding their standards. I cannot give an answer because it is a very individual matter of conscience—not one of etiquette. I *can* repeat that everyone has a right to insist on certain standards in their own home, and I can add that if you and your children understand each other, and have a good relationship to begin with, they will hesitate to put you in a difficult position and will accept the "rules" you establish for their behavior in your home. My only advice is, whatever you decide, let them know when they call and say, "We're coming home next weekend"—not after they carry their bags upstairs.

AN APPEALING GUEST ROOM

Although it may seem that not a great deal can be done to make a guest room out of one that is used every day, many of the suggestions made in the following section describing the permanent guest room can be adapted—to the comfort and convenience of your visitors.

It is by no means idle talk to suggest that every hostess try her guest room by spending a night in it herself. If she doesn't do this she should at least check the facilities thoroughly. If there is a guest bathroom that is not used frequently, she should check the drains to see that there is no stoppage and make sure that the toilet flushes properly. If a man is to use the bathroom she should see that there is a receptacle for used razor blades and a well-lighted mirror in which he can see to shave. Even though it may be adequate for powdering her nose it would be safer to ask her husband to shave in the guest bathroom and then listen to what he says about it.

There must, of course, be plenty of bath towels, face towels, a washcloth, a bath mat, and fresh cakes of soap for the bathtub and on the washstand.

It is not expected but it is a nice touch to place bath oil, bath powder, and hand lotion in decorated bottles on the washstand shelf and aspirin, Alka-Seltzer, and Band-Aid in the medicine chest. A good clothes brush and a pincushion with both straight and safety pins are always a welcome sight on a bureau or dressing table, and a new toothbrush in the bathroom has saved many a guest a trip to the local drugstore.

Good beds are most important. The mattresses should be firm— many people develop serious backaches from sleeping on a sagging bed. The most desirable arrangement is to have twin beds placed together, possibly with a single headboard. This satisfies both the couple who cannot sleep in the same bed and the couple who are used to a double bed. It also serves perfectly well for two girls or two boys. If there is space, the beds may be pushed apart and a table put between them if the visitors are not intimate friends.

It is nice but not necessary to provide two pillows for each guest, one medium-hard and one soft, so that he may have a choice. Two pillows are also a comfort to those who like to read in bed.

There must be a light at the head of each bed or between the beds—not just a decorative glowworm but a 75- or 100-watt bulb with an adjustable shade that provides good reading light. Each light should, if possible, be so shaded from the other that the occupant of one bed can read while the other sleeps. A reliable clock, with an alarm, is essential, or if you have one, a clock radio is best of all. And in case the visitor has not brought his own reading material, there should be magazines, a few short paperbacks, or a volume of condensed books—chosen more to divert than to strain the reader's attention.

There should be ashtrays on the tables and a wastebasket beside the bureau.

Facial tissues in pretty containers should be placed on the dressing table or beside the beds, and in the bathroom.

If there is a desk in the room, the blotter should be fresh and the calendar up-to-date. A thoughtful hostess puts notepaper and a few stamps in the desk drawer.

The closets should contain wooden clothes hangers with bars or pressure clips for trousers, and plastic hangers for dresses. Thin wire hangers from the cleaner's crease the shoulders of dresses and the knees of pants, and are barely adequate.

The lining in the bureau drawers must be fresh, and everything stored in the top drawer or two by members of the family must be removed to make space for the belongings of the guests. Lightly scented sachet in the drawers is delightful. Everyone loves flowers, and vases of them dress up rooms as nothing else can. Even an uninteresting room embellished with a few wild flowers or a potted plant becomes inviting.

Guest rooms should have dark shades for those who like to sleep late.

If you have no thermos jugs to be placed by the guest-room beds, be sure that there are glasses in the bathroom, or suggest that your guest take a glass of iced water with him when he says good night.

THE HOUSE WITH SERVANTS

When houseguests arrive at a house staffed by a number of servants, the personal maid of the hostess (if she has one—otherwise, the housemaid) unpacks the luggage, putting folded things in the drawers and hanging dresses and the men's suits in the closet. She also sees that the clothes are pressed if necessary.

The breakfast tray is usually carried to the bedroom floor by the butler and handed to the maid, who takes the tray to the guest's room. If there is no butler, trays are carried up by the waitress.

A breakfast set consists of a coffeepot or teapot, a cream pitcher and sugar bowl, a cup and saucer, two plates, one bowl, an egg cup, and a cover. Hot cereal is usually put in the bowl, toast in a napkin on a plate, and eggs and bacon on a plate with a cover. Glasses for fruit juice and iced water complete the tray. The thoughtful hostess who has a morning paper sent up with her guest's breakfast tray deserves a halo. When the visitor breakfasts in the dining room, the hostess sees that the paper is near his place at the table.

When a guest rings for breakfast the maid goes into the room and pulls up the shades. In cold weather she closes the windows and turns up the heat. If the guest wishes a morning bath she goes into the bathroom, spreads a bath mat on the floor and a towel over a chair, and draws the bath. If the hostess has not done so the night before, the maid asks what the guest would like for breakfast at this time.

Anyone breakfasting in the dining room is expected to dress before going down to the table. On some rare and informal occasions the hostess may suggest the night before that dressing gowns are in order, but this is not usually the case in a household with servants.

In the evening the guests' beds are turned down while they are at dinner. The bedspread is removed, folded neatly, and put in a closet or some inconspicuous place. The sheet and blanket are folded back on one side. The guests' nightgowns or pajamas are folded neatly on the bed, or placed on a chair with their bathrobes, and their bedroom slippers are put on the floor beside them. A small tray with glasses and a thermos of iced water is placed on the bedside table.

TIPS

If you have your maid with you, you always give her a tip (about two dollars) to give the cook (often the second one) who prepared her meals and one dollar for the kitchen maid who set her table.—Emily Post, 1922

When you dine in a friend's house you do not tip anyone—ever. But when you go to stay overnight or longer as a houseguest, you are expected to give a gratuity to anyone who has given you personal service—unpacked your bag, pressed your clothes, etc. Two or three dollars would be ample from either a single person or a couple after a one-night visit, but if you spend a weekend five dollars would be more appropriate.

In a large household, where a number of guests are entertained often, the hostess compensates the servants herself for the extra work involved, and thus ensures that they will not object to frequent visitors. Guests are informed about this and do not tip anyone except someone, as mentioned above, who has given them personal service.

You give the maid her tip when she finishes packing your bag, or if you are not there at the time, you look for her when you are ready to leave and give her the money personally. If she is out or unavailable put the money in an unsealed envelope with her name on it and ask your hostess to give it to her for you. It is courteous to enclose a note saying, "Thanks so much for taking such good care of us," or whatever you wish.

THE HOUSEHOLD WITHOUT SERVANTS

When you entertain without help, the more planning and preparation that can be done ahead, the more effortless and pleasant the result. House parties do not generally last for more than two days and nights—at most, three. With the help of a freezer, or even the freezing compartment of your refrigerator, your meals can largely be prepared in advance. A casserole kept warm in the oven can be ready at whatever hour your guests arrive, early or late. A steak cooked on the beach in summer or over the coals of the fireplace in winter, served with potato chips and salad, takes little effort. And you may wish to treat your guests to a dinner in a local restaurant that specializes in foods native to the region. At most summer resorts yacht clubs, hotels, or nightclubs provide dinner and dancing on Saturday night.

For lunches you may prepare the ingredients for a chef's salad, lobster rolls, chowder, and sandwiches ahead of time, ready to be mixed or spread at the last moment.

The one meal that the hostess cannot organize in advance is breakfast. Because one of the joys of a weekend away from home is being able to sleep as late as one wants, a good hostess does not awaken her guests unless there is an activity planned in which they truly wish to participate.

The hostess should get up at an early enough hour to precede her guests to the kitchen. She makes coffee, prepares fruit or juice, and cooks sausage or bacon enough for everyone. This can be kept warm on a hot plate or in a very low oven. She may then put butter, eggs, and frying pan—or pancake batter and griddle—by the stove, bread by the toaster, and an assortment of cereals and milk and cream on the table, which she sets with places for everyone. She may wait for her guests, or she may eat her own breakfast and be ready to help the latecomers as they arrive. If some of the group want to make an early start, to the beach or to ski, for instance, plans should be made the day before. The host and hostess may accompany those who are leaving, as long as everything is left in readiness for those who wish to sleep or relax, and arrangements have been made for their joining the group later on if they wish.

There are many people who get very upset if they do not get breakfast at the hour to which they are accustomed. When you are one who wakes at dawn, and the household you are visiting has the custom of sleeping late on a Sunday morning, the long wait for your coffee can truly upset your whole day. On the other hand, to be aroused at seven on the only day when you do not have to hurry to your office, in order to yawn through an early breakfast and then sit around and kill time with the Sunday paper, is just as trying.

Although he cannot very well appear in the kitchen before the cook has had her own breakfast, the farsighted guest with the early habit can, in a measure, come prepared. He can carry his own little electric water-heating outfit and a package of instant coffee or tea, sugar, powdered milk or cream, and a few crackers. He can then start his day all by himself in the barnyard hours without disturbing anyone. Or, in the servantless household, he may slip quietly into the kitchen and make himself a cup of coffee and a piece of toast to sustain him until the others are ready for a full breakfast. Few people care enough to fuss, but if they do, these suggestions for a visitor with incurably early waking hours can make a great difference to his enjoyment of the entire day.

THE WELCOME HOUSEGUEST

If you go to stay in a small house in the country, and they give you a bed full of lumps, in a room of mosquitoes and flies, in a chamber over that of a crying baby, under the eaves with a temperature of over a hundred, you can the next morning walk to the village, and send yourself a telegram and leave! But though you feel starved, exhausted, wilted, and are mosquito bitten until you resemble a well-developed case of chickenpox or measles, by not so much as a facial muscle must you let the family know that your comfort lacked anything that your happiest imagination could picture—nor must you confide in any one afterwards (having broken bread in the house) how desperately wretched you were.—Emily Post, 1922

The welcome houseguest is, above all else, adaptable.

You must always be ready for anything—or nothing. If the plan is to picnic, you like picnics above everything and prove it by enthusiastically making the sandwiches or the salad dressing or whatever you do best. If, on the other hand, no one seems to want to do anything, you find a book to be absorbed in, or a piece of sewing or knitting, or you walk on the beach by yourself.

Whether it is easy or not, you must conform to the habits of the family with whom you are staying. You take your meals at their hours, you eat what is put before you, and you get up and go out and come in and go to bed according to the schedule arranged by your hostess. And no matter how much the hours or the food or the arrangements may upset you, you try to appear blissfully content. When the visit is over, you need never enter that house again, but while you are there, you must at least act as though you are enjoying yourself.

It is not only courteous but obligatory to give your hostess a gift—or if she has children, to take presents to them. The conventional list of flowers, fruit, candy, or a book is acceptable, but be sure you know of a book she wants, or that she is not on a diet, or that she has no flowers in her garden or fruit on her trees. Some people prefer to send a present after their visit, having made note of something that their hostess would find useful or that would go perfectly in her home.

If you plan to do that, you might arrive with an additional, inexpensive gift to be used during your stay—a bottle of wine, some tomatoes from your garden, a jar of a special marmalade, etc. *For specific gift suggestions, see Chapter 66.*

When you take a gift with you, you give it to your hostess as soon as you arrive. If you send it later, it should be done as promptly as possible. In this case the hostess must write you her thanks—unless of course she lives next door and calls or runs over to thank you when the gift is delivered.

Overnight visits require written thank-you's within a day or two of your return home. The only exceptions are when your hosts are relatives or close friends with whom you visit back and forth frequently, or they are friends or neighbors with whom you travel to their vacation home and back. Even then a call the next day to say,

"We're still talking about what fun the weekend was!" is appreciated.

When you go to visit close friends, especially those who do not have help, you may offer in advance to bring a roast or a casserole to provide one evening's meal. There is no reason why the hostess should not accept such an offer. On an informal weekend, guests feel more comfortable if they can contribute, and it certainly adds to the pleasure of the hostess.

If your visit is for more than two or three nights it is also thoughtful to suggest that you all go out to dinner one evening—at your expense. You should not suggest this on a two-day weekend visit, however, since your hostess will undoubtedly have planned, and possibly prepared, meals for both nights.

If you are going where you are to play golf or ride or take part in other sports be sure you take your own riding clothes, tennis racket, or golf clubs. Your hostess will want to have her things available for her own use, and you will avoid having to use borrowed clothes or equipment that may not fit or may be totally unlike that to which you are accustomed. On the other hand, the hostess who invites her city friends for a weekend of sailing or camping should have extra foul-weather gear, boots, bedrolls, and so on, since her guests should not be expected to buy those things for one weekend's use.

Even should you be staying in a house where there are many servants, remember that each has a share of work to do. If the maid offers to press a dress that has become mussed in packing, accept her offer and later give her a gratuity—but you should not ask this service unless the pressing is really necessary.

If the hostess does her own housework you must make your bed, pick up your room, and offer to help in preparing meals, clearing the table, and cleaning up in the kitchen. You must be particularly careful to keep your bathroom immaculate, especially if you are sharing it with other people. Don't leave a ring in the tub, a rim of dried shaving soap in the basin, hairs anyplace, or dirt on the soap. A wise hostess leaves a sponge on the basin to help her guests leave a clean bathroom. And don't use more than your share of hot water if others are planning to bathe, or use any towels but your own.

The morning of the day you are going to leave, ask your hostess what she would like you to do with your bed linen. She will probably say, "Oh, just leave the beds," but don't! Unless she especially says, "My cleaning woman is coming in later to make up the beds," remove the sheets, fold them, and pull the blanket and spread up neatly so that the bed will look "made." If you make it up with your sheets in place, it is all too easy for a busy hostess to forget, and then turn down the beds for the next guest, only to find the dirty sheets still on. Or if you take her at her word and leave the bed untouched she is almost forced to do something about it after you leave, when she might rather be doing something else. If you are very close friends and a frequent visitor get out fresh sheets and make the bed up for her. But if you are only casual friends your hostess will feel that this is an imposition on you and it will make her uncomfortable.

If you run into other friends in the area and they invite you and your hosts over for a swim or to play tennis, you should never accept the invitation and then relay it to your hostess. It is better to leave the "door ajar" and make a noncommital reply such as, "May I call you back?—I'm not sure about Joan's plans."

OFF TO BED

If you are not needed to make up a foursome at bridge or for any other reason, and you are tired and want to go to bed before your hosts and the other guests do, it is perfectly all right to say to your hostess that you've had a rugged week at the office, or an exhausting trip, or whatever, and would like to say good night. By the same token the hostess who has a baby who gets her up at dawn could explain, "I know Sally will have me up before six, so I'm sure you'll understand if I leave you now. . . ." A host who must keep an appointment at an early hour, might say, "I'll never make that appointment if I don't get to bed, but please feel free to stay up and watch TV as long as you like, and help yourself to a beer. . . ." A good hostess watches for signs that her guests are getting sleepy and saves them possible embarrassment by saying, "Well, do you think it's about time . . . ?"

OVERSTAYING YOUR WELCOME

There is a saying that "unwelcome guests never guess they're unwelcome." It has also been said, less politely, that guests who overstay their welcome are like fish that are no longer fresh! Both statements have an element of truth in them, although most people who are guilty of visiting for too long, or insist on coming when their visit is inconvenient, do not do so deliberately, but because they don't *think*. Because they are enjoying themselves they assume that their hostess is, too.

Popular and sought-after guests *never* stay longer than planned. The length of the visit should be clearly stated by the hostess and interpreted literally by her guests. When you are inviting Aunt Sally for the Christmas holiday your invitation should say something like this: "Dear Aunt Sally, Bob and I—and the children—are counting on you to spend Christmas with us. We could pick you up on Friday the 23rd, and take you back on Wednesday the 28th, and we are making all sorts of plans so you can see the rest of the family. . . ." If from past experience you know that certain guests are apt to try to extend their visit, you should make plans for the day after they are to leave so that you can tell them that if the problem arises.

In short, for both hostess and guest it is far better to end a visit while everyone is still enjoying it.

THE SUCCESSFUL HOSTESS

Never try to make any two people like each other. If they do, they do; if they don't, they don't, and that is all there is to it.—Emily Post, 1922

The abilities of a good hostess are called upon long before the actual start of the house party. They begin with choosing guests who have the same interests and who will enjoy each other's company. There is little pleasure in having one couple who enjoy staying up all night dancing, while the others wish to go to bed early in order to be up at sunrise to go on a fishing expedition.

Arrangements for whatever activities you know your visitors will enjoy must be made ahead of time. If they like tennis be sure that you sign up or reserve a court at a convenient hour, or if you are certain that they would love to go to the dance at your club, don't forget to make a reservation for a table or you may be disappointed when you arrive at the door. Don't try to fill every minute with strenuous projects, however. It is probable that your guests would like some time to relax and visit with you and the other guests, and they may very well have some suggestions of their own about a special landmark they would like to see or a shopping trip to stores carrying merchandise made in the area.

An intelligent hostess has the cleaning, marketing, and as much cooking as possible done in advance, so that an absolute minimum of her time is spent on these chores while her guests are with her.

A host or hostess should never dwell on annoyances of any

kind—no matter what happens. Unless actually unable to get out of bed, they should not mention their physical ills any more than mental ones.

If anything goes wrong with the household the host and hostess must try to keep it from their guests. If, for instance, the stove breaks down, a picnic might be held as though it had been planned that way from the beginning. Should a guest be taken ill the hostess must convince him that he is not giving the slightest trouble; at the same time, nothing should be overlooked that can be done for his comfort.

EXTENDED VISITS

Extended visits are almost entirely restricted to family members—a grandmother, a bachelor uncle, or a widowed parent who comes to stay for a couple of weeks—or more. These visits often take place over a holiday season, and problems arise concerning invitations you receive while your visitor is there. Should you tell the prospective hostess, let us say, that your mother is with you and ask if you may bring her? Should you just go without her? Or must you stay home?

There are several answers. When the invitation is to an open house, a cocktail party, or a church or club festivity, one more guest would cause no difficulty, and you should feel free to ask if you may bring your mother along if she wishes to go. Naturally, your visitor, whoever it may be, should be consulted first. When it is a dinner or luncheon invitation you can say, "I'm afraid we can't come—Mother is staying with us." This leaves it up to the *hostess* to suggest that you bring your mother if she wishes, but there should be no criticism or ill-feeling if she does not. One more person, especially an "odd" woman, could disrupt her entire plan for seating, games, etc. Close friends and other relatives who know that your mother is with you should not invite you without including her in this invitation. And don't forget, your older visitor will be pleased and flattered if you arrange a party or two in your own home, so that she has a chance to see your friends.

When the visit is really a long one, you are certainly free to say occasionally, "Would you mind if we left you for a little while Saturday evening? Some old friends are going to be at the Ponds'." The wise visitor, who wants to be asked again, will obviously say, "Of course not—go ahead. There are some good TV shows on Saturday that will keep me busy."

PETS

Never ask whether you may bring a pet along on a visit. Your host and hostess may be great dog-lovers but they will probably not want a strange dog who may or may not get along with their Fido, and whose manners may or may not be the best. You are putting your hostess in a difficult position if she is not enthusiastic about your request.

If she makes the suggestion, naturally your pet may go But be sure, before you accept on his behalf, that his behavior will be exemplary. You have no right to take a dog that is not perfectly house-trained, chews things, or will not stay off furniture or legs or laps, to anyone else's home.

SERVING YOURSELF

When helping yourself to any food the most important thing is to pay attention to what you are doing and not handle a serving fork or spoon in such a way as to spill food on the floor, the table, your neighbor, or yourself.

Anything served on a piece of toast should be lifted from the platter on the toast. Squab or quail might be lifted, leaving the toast on the plate, but foods such as mushrooms, sweetbreads, or asparagus must remain on the toast. Otherwise, it would be difficult to serve them, and a soggy, unattractive piece of toast would be left on the platter. The toast with its topping is lifted on the spoon and held in place with the fork. If you don't want to eat the toast simply put it to one side of your plate. When there is only a serving spoon and no fork in the dish, you must balance the food with great care.

Gravy should be put *on* the meat, potatoes, or rice, and the condiment, pickles, and jelly *at the side* of whatever they accompany. Olives, nuts, radishes, or celery are put on the bread-and-butter plate if there is one, otherwise on the edge of the plate from which one is eating.

When passing your plate to the head of the table for a second helping, always leave the knife and fork on the plate and be sure they are far enough on not to topple off.

When the host or the "man of the house" fills the plates and sends them around the table, they are started counterclockwise. Each diner on the right side of the table takes the plate from the person on his left and passes it on to the person on his right. If there is a woman guest on the host's right she keeps the first plate, but the second is passed on to the person at the end of the table. The third goes to the person farthest down on the right side, the next to the person on *his* left, etc. When all the people on the host's right are served, the plates are sent down the left side, and the host serves himself last. If the hostess is serving, the same order is followed from her end.

Often "family style" means that the host or hostess serves the meat and the other dishes are passed around with each diner helping himself. These dishes, too, are passed counterclockwise. Men do not offer the dish to the women on their right first, but help themselves when the dish reaches them. They may then, if they wish, hold the dish while the woman next to them serves herself. When someone at the far end of the table asks to have a dish passed to him for a second helping, it is only sensible for someone in between, who also would like more, to say as the dish is passed to him on its way down the table, "Do you mind if I help myself so that it needn't come all the way back?" Naturally you would not do that if there were only one portion left!

At a family meal where Mother knows what, and how much, each member will want, she may serve the plates in the kitchen and bring them herself, or with the help of one or two of the children, to the table. This should never be done when guests are present, however. They should have the prerogative of serving themselves. Exceptions are individual "arranged" dishes, such as eggs Benedict or individual molded salads, which must be "put together" in the kitchen.

REFUSING A DISH

If you are served a food you are allergic to, or especially dislike, and if you are among friends, you may refuse with a polite "No, thank you." Otherwise it is good manners to take at least a little of every dish that is offered to you, which can be spread out on your plate so that it is barely noticeable that you have not eaten much. The old rule that one must not leave anything on his plate is outdated, but it would be wasteful and upsetting to your hostess if you took a large portion and left it untouched. You need not give your reason for refusing a dish, but if it *is* because of an allergy, diet, or other physical cause, you may avoid hurting your hostess' feelings if you quietly tell her your problem, always without drawing the attention of the entire table.

When declining a dish offered by a waiter, you say, "No, thank you," quietly, and in fact a negative shake of the head and "No thanks" more nearly describe the usual refusal.

At a buffet dinner, where there are a number of dishes offered, you need only help yourself to those that appeal to you.

THE SILVER

"FROM THE OUTSIDE IN"

There should never be any question of which silver to use: *You always start with the implement of each type that is farthest from the plate.* This question arises again and again, and the answer is always the same, with one exception. If the table is incorrectly set, and you realize that you cannot use the implement for the course that its position indicates, you must, of course, choose the next one that is appropriate. For example, if the small shellfish fork has been put next to the plate, you would not use the dinner fork for the shrimp cocktail and leave the little fork for the main course, even though they were placed in that order. Otherwise, you assume that the table is correctly set, and starting at the outside, you work your way with each course toward the center.

When you have finished the main course the knife and fork are placed beside each other on the dinner plate diagonally from upper left to lower right. The handles extend slightly over the edge of the plate. The dessert spoon or fork is placed in the same position. If dessert is served in a stemmed bowl, or in a small, deep bowl on another plate, the dessert spoon is put down on the plate when you are finished. If the bowl is shallow and wide, the spoon may be left in it, or on the plate below it, as you wish.

USING THE KNIFE AND FORK

The proper way to use the knife and fork can best be explained by the accompanying illustrations. Study them carefully and you will see that they depict easy and graceful ways of cutting food and bringing it to your mouth.

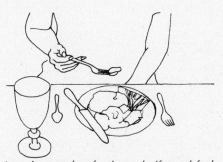

American style of using a knife and fork

The American custom of "zigzag" eating (changing the fork from left to right hand after cutting meat) is perfectly correct, but I feel that it is unnecessarily complicated. Therefore it does not have so pleasing an appearance as the simpler European method of leaving the fork in your left hand after you have cut your meat. You eat the meat from your fork while it is still in the left hand, rather than turning the fork over and switching it to your right hand. Although some people feel that it is "putting on airs" to adopt this "foreign" way of eating, I can see nothing wrong in adopting a custom that seems more practical than your own.

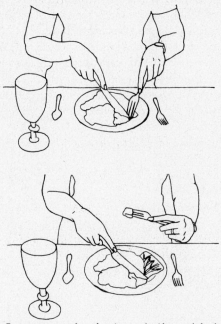

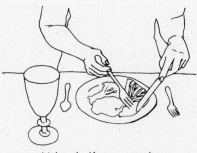

European style of using a knife and fork

Using knife as a pusher

PUSHERS

There is no better pusher than a piece of bread crust. Lacking this, the knife is also correct—if properly used. It is held in the left hand in the same position as when cutting with the right hand, and the tip of the blade helps to guide and push the food onto the fork. It is a natural motion and in no way incorrect.

OTHER THAN THE MAIN COURSE

DESSERT

Dessert may be eaten with spoon or fork or both. Stewed fruit is held in place with the fork and cut and eaten with the spoon. Peaches or other very juicy fruits are peeled and then eaten with knife and fork, but dry fruits, such as apples, may be cut and eaten with the fingers.

Pie is eaten with a fork; if it is "a la mode," the spoon is used also. Ice cream is generally eaten with a spoon, but when accompanied by cake, either the spoon alone, or both the spoon and fork, may be used.

Soft cakes are best eaten with a fork; in most cases it is a matter of dexterity rather than rule. If you are able to eat a plum or ripe pear in your fingers and not smear your face or make a sucking noise, you are the one in a thousand who *may*, with utmost propriety, continue to do so. If you can eat a Napoleon or a cream puff in your fingers and not let the cream ooze out on the far side, you need not use a fork. But if you cannot eat something—no matter what it is— without getting it all over your fingers, you must use a fork, and when necessary, a spoon or a knife also.

SOUPS

Either clear soup or thick soup may be served in a cup with one handle or with handles on both sides. After taking a spoonful or two you may pick up the cup if the soup is cool enough. Use both hands if the cup has two handles, or continue to use your spoon if you prefer.

Clear soups are sometimes served in a shallow soup plate rather than in a cup. When the level of the soup is so low that you must tip the plate to avoid scraping the bottom noisily, lift the near edge in your left hand and tip the plate away from you. Then the soup may be spooned away from you or toward you, whichever is less awkward.

Both soup cups and soup plates should be served with a saucer or plate beneath them. The spoon, when not in use or when the soup is finished, is laid on the saucer when a soup cup is used, but it is left in the soup *plate* rather than on the dish under it.

BREAD AND BUTTER

Bread should always be broken into moderate-sized pieces—but not necessarily single-mouthful bits—with the fingers before being eaten. To butter it, hold a piece on the edge of the bread-and-butter plate, or the place plate, and with a butter knife spread enough butter on it for a mouthful or two at a time. If there is no butter knife use any other knife you find available.

This buttering of bread is not an important rule. There are always commonsense exceptions. For instance, hot biscuits or toast can of course be buttered all over immediately, since they are most delicious when the butter is quickly and thoroughly melted. Bread should never, however, he held flat on the palm and buttered with the hand held in the air. If a table knife is used, care must be taken not to smear food particles from the knife onto the butter.

JELLIES AND JAMS

Jellies and jams as well as butter are spread on bread or toast with a knife, never with a fork, though you do put butter on vegetables and jelly on meat with a fork. A small portion is taken from the container with a spoon and put on the butter plate or edge of the large plate. If no spoon is provided, you must use your own knife. In this case be sure that you wipe all butter and crumbs off it carefully, on the edge of your plate, before touching the jelly in the jar or dish.

GRAVY AND SAUCES

You may sop bread into gravy, but it must be done properly—by putting a small piece down on the gravy and then eating it with your fork as though it were any other helping on your plate. You may put it into your mouth "continental" fashion, with the tines pointed down as they were when you sopped up the gravy. A good sauce may also be finished in this way—in fact to do so is a compliment to the cook.

SALAD

Why one should not cut one's salad in small pieces—if one wants to—makes little sense unless, that is, one cuts up a whole plateful and makes the plate messy. Until stainless steel was invented, a steel knife blade was not usable for salad or fruit, since the metal turned black; but silver-bladed knives have always been used for salads as well as for fruits, and stainless steel is not affected in the slightest by the vinegar in the dressing. So there's no possible reason why anyone should be denied the use of a salad or dinner knife. Anything more difficult than managing leafy salad with a fork alone—especially the fresh, crisp, springing variety—is difficult to imagine. At all events, beware of rolling the fork and wrapping springy leaves around the tines in a spiral. Remember what a spring that lets go can do!

HOT BEVERAGES

Many people today are using mugs instead of cups and saucers for coffee, tea, or hot chocolate. They are pleasant to hold, and retain the heat better than thin china cups. Since saucers are not used with mugs, the problem arises of what to do with the spoon—which should never be left in the mug. Mugs are not proper on a formal table and are rarely seen on any table covered with a damask or lace cloth, so the solution depends somewhat on the table covering. If the mats (or a cloth) are informal, of paper or plastic perhaps, the spoon may be wiped clean with the lips and laid on the mat or on the table beside the mug. If the mats are of fine quality it would be thoughtless to risk staining them. The bowl of the spoon, face down, should be rested on the edge of the butter plate or dinner plate, with the spoon handle on the table.

When dining informally one may use a teaspoon to put a small piece of ice from the water glass into a steaming beverage to cool it slightly. This may only be done, however, with a clean, unused spoon.

Tea bags are naturally placed on the edge of the saucer, but they should be pressed gently against the side of the cup with the spoon to remove excess liquid. Should the tea be served in a glass or china mug without a saucer, you may ask for a dish on which to place the bag. Otherwise you must put it on the edge of the butter or dinner plate, where it inevitably leaks drops of tea into the food on the plate.

In spite of an outdated idea to the contrary, tea that is too hot to drink from the cup may be sipped from the spoon, as may coffee or any other hot beverage.

When coffee slops into the saucer, the best course is replace the saucer with a clean one. This is always true at home, where one may get the replacement oneself, or when dining at a friend's house or in a fine restaurant where one may request the exchange. It is sometimes impossible, however, in some restaurants or in a cafeteria. Rather than drip coffee each time you lift the cup to your mouth, it is permissible to pour the liquid back into the cup and use a paper napkin (if one is available) to dry the bottom of the cup.

ICED TEA OR ICED COFFEE

Iced tea or iced coffee presents the same problem as mugs, so a smart hostess serves a coaster or saucer under the glass. Iced-tea spoons may be left in the glass and held against the rim with the forefinger when drinking. However, this is awkward, and the procedure mentioned above for removing the spoon and resting it on a plate is generally more practical.

SALT IN A SALTCELLAR

If there is no spoon in the saltcellar (a tiny open bowl), use the tip of a clean knife. If the saltcellar is for you alone, you may either use the tip of your knife or you may take a pinch with your fingers. Salt that is to be dipped into should be put on the bread-and-butter plate or on the rim of whatever plate is before you.

If you do not wish to risk insulting your hostess—or the chef, —don't sprinkle salt and pepper over your food before tasting it. Furthermore, it is foolish. When dining out you cannot possibly know how much salt your hostess customarily uses in her cooking.

HOW TO EAT:

ARTICHOKES

Artichoke leaves are always eaten with the fingers; a leaf at a time is pulled off, and the edible portion dipped in melted butter or hollandaise sauce and then bitten off. When the center is reached, the thistlelike part is scraped away with a knife, and the heart eaten with a knife and fork.

ASPARAGUS

By reputation this is a finger food, but the ungraceful appearance of a bent stalk of asparagus falling limply into someone's mouth and the fact that moisture is also likely to drip from the end, cause most fastidious people to eat it—at least in part—with the fork. That is, cut the stalks with the fork to where they become harder, and then pick up the ends in the fingers if you choose. But don't squeeze the stalks or let juice run down your fingers.

Asparagus that has no hard end is eaten entirely with a fork. All hard ends should be cut off asparagus before serving it at a dinner party, since picking up stalks in the fingers is scarcely compatible with formal table manners.

BACON

Breakfast bacon should, when it is limp, be eaten with a fork. But when it is dry and crisp, so that it scatters into fragments when broken by the fork, fingers are permitted.

BUTTER

Every sort of bread, biscuit, toast, and also hot griddle cakes and corn on the cob are buttered with a knife. But corn that has been cut off the cob, or rice, or potato—or anything else on your dinner plate—has seasoning or butter mixed in it with a fork.

CHEESE

Cheese is one food that may be spread with either a knife or a fork. If eaten with a salad with which one is using no knife, a piece of cheese may be broken off and put on lettuce or a cracker with one's fork. Runny or soft cheeses, such as Brie, Camembert, or Liederkranz, are spread with a salad knife or butter knife if there is one. Served as an hor d'oeuvre, cheese is always spread with a knife.

Cheese served with ripe pears (or apples) is a superb dessert. The fruit is quartered, cored, and if you wish, pared. The cheese—a mild Port Salut or Brie are good choices—is eaten with a fork. You may eat the fruit in the fingers, followed by a bite of cheese, or you may cut the fruit into pieces and take a little fruit and a bite of cheese on the same forkful.

CHERRY TOMATOES

Except when served in a salad or other "dish," cherry tomatoes are eaten in the fingers. And they *squirt!* The best thing to do is try to select one small enough to be put in your mouth whole. Even then, clamp your lips tightly before chewing it. If you must bite into a big one, make a little break in the skin with your front teeth before biting it in half.

CLAMS AND OYSTERS ON THE HALF SHELL

Clams and oysters on the half shell are generally served on cracked ice, arranged around a container of cocktail sauce. The clam is speared with the small shellfish fork (or smallest fork provided), dipped into the sauce, and eaten in one bite. Neither clams nor oysters served on the half shell are ever cut up. They may also be eaten by taking a little of the sauce on the fork and dropping it onto the clam, if only a little sauce is desired. Some people enjoy them with nothing more than a few drops of lemon, and lemon wedges should be offered as well as the sauce.

If oyster crackers are served they may be crumpled up in the fingers and mixed into the sauce. Horseradish, too, is mixed into the sauce, or a drop may be put directly onto the shellfish if the diner likes the very "hot" taste.

When clams are eaten on a picnic, when they are opened fresh and served as an hors d'oeuvre informally, or when they are ordered at a clam bar, the shell is picked up in the fingers and the clam and its delicious juice are sucked right off the shell.

CONDIMENTS

Smearing condiments with a knife on food already impaled on a fork is quite unpleasant if more than a small amount is taken. The proper way to manage a quantity of cranberry sauce, dressing, jelly, pickle, etc., is to lift it onto the fork and either eat it as a separate mouthful or take some of it with a small piece of meat on the tips of the tines.

CORN ON THE COB

To attack corn on the cob with as little ferocity as possible is perhaps the only direction to be given, and the only maxim to bear in mind when eating this pleasant-to-taste but not-very-easy-to-manage vegetable is to eat it as neatly as possible. It doesn't matter whether you break the ear in half, or whether you hold it by its own ends or by special little handles. The real thing to avoid is too much buttering all at once and too greedy eating. If you like a lot of butter, spread it across only half the length of two rows at a time. If you take a moderate amount of butter, you can spread it across the whole length of two rows, add salt and pepper, hold the ends in both hands, and eat those two rows. Repeat the buttering and eating until it is finished.

Considerate hostesses should supply small, sharp vegetable knives (steak knives would do nicely) to guests who like to (or must) cut the corn off the cob. Corn served at a formal dinner party should always be cut off the cob in the kitchen and creamed or buttered.

CHICKEN (ROAST OR BROILED), SQUAB, GAME HEN, AND OTHER SMALL BIRDS, AND FROGS' LEGS

At a formal dinner no part of a bird is picked up in the fingers. However, among family and friends and in "family style" or informal restaurants, it is permissible to eat it as follows:

The main body of the bird is not eaten with the fingers. You cut off as much meat as you can and leave the rest on your plate. To eat the small bones, such as joint or wing, or the second joint of a squab, you put the piece of bone with meat on it in your mouth, eat it clean, and remove the bare bones between forefinger and thumb. Larger joints, such as the drumstick of a roast chicken, may be picked up after the first few easily cut off pieces have been eaten.

Frogs' legs are eaten in the same way—according to their size.

CRACKERS OR CROUSTADES WITH SOUP

Croustades, which are very small forcemeat pastries, are scattered on soup after it has been ladled into the plate to be served. Croutons (tiny French-fried cubes of bread) are either floated on the soup or else passed separately in a dish with a small serving spoon so that each person may put a spoonful in his soup. Oyster crackers, as well as any others, are put on the bread-and-butter plate—or on the tablecloth—and dropped two or three pieces at a time into the soup. Larger soda crackers, served with chowders, are broken, and then, a few pieces at a time, crumbled up and scattered over the soup.

FONDUES

Cheese fondue is served in a fondue pot that is kept warm by Sterno heat or by electric heat. It is accompanied by a bowl of bite-sized squares of French bread. A piece of bread is speared on a long fondue fork and dipped into the hot cheese. When coated, it is removed, held over the pot for a moment to drip and cool, and then taken from the fork with the front teeth. Lips and tongue should not touch the fork, as it goes back into the fondue pot for the next bite.

Meat fondue, in which pieces of meat, on the fondue fork, are plunged into very hot oil to cook, is eaten differently. Each diner has a plate onto which he removes the cooked meat to let it cool. It is then eaten with a regular fork while his next piece of meat is sizzling in the pot on the end of the fondue fork.

FRUIT

The equipment for eating raw fruit at table consists of a sharp-bladed fruit knife, a fork, and a finger bowl. In a restaurant, when no knife is given you, it is proper to ask for one.

Raw apples and *firm pears* are quartered, with a knife. The core is then cut away from each quarter, and the fruit is eaten in the fingers. Those who do not like the skin, pare each quarter separately. If the pears are very juicy they must be cut up with the knife and eaten with the fork.

For eating pears with cheese as dessert, see page 407.

Bananas may be peeled halfway down and eaten bite by bite at the family table, but when dining out it is better to peel the skin all the way off, lay the fruit on your plate, cut it in slices, and eat it with a fork.

Berries are usually hulled or stemmed ahead of time, served with cream and sugar, and eaten with a spoon. When especially fine and freshly picked, strawberries are often served with their hulls on and sugar placed at one side of each person's plate. The hull of each berry is held in the fingers, and the fruit is dipped in the sugar and then eaten.

Cantaloupes and *muskmelons* are served in halves, or sometimes quarters, and eaten with a spoon.

Honeydew, Persian, and *casaba* melons are cut into new-moon-shaped quarters or eighths, depending on size, and eaten with either spoon or knife and fork—whichever you prefer.

Watermelon is cut into large-sized pieces or slices and usually eaten in the fingers. If using a fork, remove the seeds with the tines and then cut the pieces with the side of the fork.

Raw cherries and *plums* are eaten in the fingers, of course. The pit of the cherry should be made as clean as possible in your mouth and dropped into your almost-closed, cupped hand and thence to your plate. The plum is held in your fingers and eaten as close to the pit as possible. When you remove a pit with your fingers, you should do it with your thumb underneath and your first two fingers across your mouth, and not with your fingertips pointing into your mouth.

Hothouse grapes are eaten in two ways: One, lay a grape on its side, hold it with the fingers of your left hand, cut into the center with the point of your knife, and remove the seeds. Two, put a whole grape in your mouth, chew it, swallow the pulp and juice, and drop the bare seeds into your almost-closed fist.

With *garden* or *Concord grapes* you press the stem end of the grape between your lips and against your almost-closed teeth, so that the juice and pulp will be drawn into your mouth and the skin left to be discarded.

Little *seedless grapes* are no problem, since they are eaten whole.

Grapes should never be pulled off the bunch one at a time. Choose a branch with several grapes on it and break it off, or if scissors are provided, cut the branch off close to the main stem.

Navel oranges, often served at the table, are rather rough-skinned, firm, and usually seedless. A practical way to eat them is to slice the two ends of the rind off first, and cut the peel off in vertical strips with the knife. You then cut the peeled orange in half at its equator. After this, each half is easily cut and eaten mouthful by mouthful with knife and fork together. Oranges can also be halved, the sections loosened with a curved grapefruit knife, and then eaten with an orange spoon or teaspoon.

A thin-skinned orange, filled with seeds, is more difficult to eat. The best way is to peel it, cut it into eighths, take out the seeds from the center with the tip of the knife, and eat the new-moon–shaped pieces as daintily as you can in the fingers.

Tangerines present no problem because the skin is removed easily and the segments separate readily. But the seeds and fibers must be removed from the mouth neatly with the thumb and first two fingers (fingers above and thumb underneath).

A *freestone peach* or a *nectarine* is cut to the pit, then broken in half and eaten. You can't break a *clingstone* apart; therefore it is eaten whole, or quartered as best you can with a knife. Since most people do not like the fuzz, peaches are almost always peeled before eating.

STEWED FRUIT

Stewed prunes, cherries, etc., are eaten with a spoon. The fruit is put into the mouth whole, and when the meat is eaten off the pit, it is dropped directly onto the spoon from the lips and deposited on the edge of the plate or saucer.

LAMB CHOPS

At a dinner party or in a formal restaurant lamb chops must be eaten with knife and fork. The center, or "eye," of the chop is cut off the bone, and cut into two or three pieces. If the chop has a frilled paper "skirt" around the end of the bone, you may hold that in your left hand and cut the tasty meat from the side of the bone. If there is no "skirt" you must do the best you can with your knife and fork. At the family table or in an informal group of friends, the center may be cut out and eaten with the fork, and the bone picked up and eaten clean with the teeth. This is permissible, too, with veal or pork chops, but only when they are broiled or otherwise cooked without gravy or sauce.

LOBSTER, BROILED OR BOILED

Lobster claws should be cracked in the kitchen before being served, but nutcrackers or clam crackers should also be available for the diners' use. The additional cracking of the claws should be done slowly, so that the juice does not squirt when the shell breaks. The meat is removed from the large claw ends and from each joint with a pick or shellfish fork. The tail meat is pulled out of the shell in two solid pieces—one side at a time. It is then cut into bite-sized pieces with a knife or the side of a dinner fork, and dipped into melted

411

butter if hot, or mayonnaise if cold. The red roe and the green "fat" are not only edible but delectable, and a small bit of one or both may be put on the fork with each bite of meat.

Real lobster-lovers get an additional morsel out of the legs by breaking off one at a time, putting it into the mouth, and chewing up the shell, squeezing the meat out of the broken end. A bit of work, but worth it if you care!

Properly, a big paper napkin (or bib) is provided for the lobster-eater. Finger bowls with hot water and lemon slices should be put at the side of each place as soon as people are finished eating. These are carried away after the dinner plates have been removed.

A large bowl for the empty shells and inedible parts is a necessity. If a receptacle is not provided in a restaurant the diners may, and should, ask for one.

MUSSELS

Mussels, and occasionally clams, may be served in their shells in the broth in which they are steamed. Mussels prepared in this way are called moules marinières. The mussel may be removed from its shell with a fork, dipped into the sauce, and eaten in one bite. But I much prefer to pick up the shell, scooping a little of the juice with it, and sucking the mussel and juice directly off the shell. The empty shells are placed in a bowl or plate, which should always be provided for them. The juice or broth remaining in the bowl may be eaten with a spoon, or you may sop it up with pieces of roll or French bread speared on the tines of your fork.

OLIVES

Eat them with your fingers. Bite off the meat, but don't nibble too avidly around the stone. Remove the stone from your mouth with your fingers. Bite a large stuffed olive in half. Put only a very small one in your mouth whole. When the olive is in a salad, pick it up with your fork and eat it in the same way.

OLIVES, ONIONS, AND CHERRIES IN COCKTAILS

When most of the liquid is gone you may reach into the glass and remove the "garnish" with your fingers. Or you may wait until the glass is drained, and then it is easy to tip it back enough to let the olive or onion or cherry slide into your mouth.

PIZZA

Pizza is cut into manageable wedges with a knife, and then picked up and eaten in the fingers.

POTATOES

Baked potato, whether white or sweet, is usually eaten by breaking it in half with the fingers (cutting a slit with a knife first if necessary), scooping all the inside of the potato onto the plate with a fork, and then mixing butter, salt, and pepper in it with a fork.

Another way to eat baked potato is to break it in half with the fingers and lay both halves, skin down, on the plate. Mix a little butter in part of one half with a fork and eat that. Then mix a little more, and so on, eating it out of the skin without turning it out onto the plate.

A third way—for those who like to eat the skin as well as the inside—is to cut the baked potato into two halves and then cut them again into pieces, a few at a time, of eatable size. If you wish to eat the skins separately, scrape the inside part onto your plate, put the skins on the side of the plate, or on the butter plate, and eat a small piece at a time, exactly as you would bread and butter.

When French-fried potatoes accompany a hamburger, hot dog, or other sandwich, they may be eaten in the fingers. At other times they should be cut into reasonable lengths and eaten with a fork.

SANDWICHES

All ordinary sandwiches, not only at picnics but everywhere, are eaten in the fingers. Club sandwiches and other inch-and-thicker sandwiches are best cut in small portions before being picked up and held tightly in the fingers of both hands, or if literally dripping with mayonnaise they should be served on a plate with a knife and fork. If you are not sitting at a table and you have no knife, you bite into an overlarge and hugely thick piece as nicely as you can, and following the previous advice on eating corn on the cob, attack it with as little ferocity as possible.

SHRIMP

Shrimp as a first course present one of the most difficult problems encountered by the diner. If not too impossibly large each shrimp should be eaten in one bite. But when they are of jumbo size, the diner has no alternative but to grasp the cup firmly with his left hand and cut the shrimp as neatly as possible with the edge of his fork. It is impractical to use a knife because the stemmed shrimp cup will tip over unless held with one hand. At home the problem can be avoided by arranging the shrimp attractively on a small plate— where they can easily be cut with knife or fork—and I see no reason why restaurants should not do the same. Among family and friends it is permissible to spear a large shrimp with your fork and bite off a piece. But you must never dip the remainder back in a bowl of sauce that is being used by anyone but yourself.

SNAILS (ESCARGOTS)

Snail shells are grasped with a special holder, in the left hand, or with the fingers if no holder is provided. The meat is removed with a pick or oyster fork. The garlic butter that remains in the dish is sopped up with small pieces of French bread and eaten with the fork.

SPAGHETTI

Most restaurants (and hostesses) that feature pasta provide guests with a large spoon as well as the knife and fork. The fork is used to spear a few strands of spaghetti, the tips are placed against the spoon, which is held on its side, in the left hand, and the fork is twirled, wrapping the spaghetti around itself as it turns. If no spoon is provided, the tips of the fork may be rested against the curve of the plate.

MINOR DIFFICULTIES

FOOD THAT IS TOO HOT OR SPOILED

If a bite of food is too hot, quickly take a swallow of water. Only if there is no beverage at all, and your mouth is scalding, should you spit it out. And then it should be spit onto your fork or into your fingers, and quickly put on the edge of the plate. The same is true of spoiled food. Should you put a "bad" oyster or clam, for example, into your mouth, don't swallow it, but remove it as quickly and unobtrusively as you can. To spit anything whatever into the corner of your napkin is unnecessary and not permissible.

CHOKING ON MEAT OR BONES

Although we occasionally hear of someone choking to death on a piece of meat the ordinary "choke" or "swallowing the wrong way" is not serious. If a sip of water does not help, but you think you can dislodge the offending bit by a good cough, cover your mouth with your napkin and do it. Remove the fish bone or abrasive morsel from your mouth with your fingers and put it on the edge of your plate. If you need a more prolonged cough excuse yourself and leave the table. In the event that you are really choking, don't hesitate to get someone to help you. The seriousness of your condition will quickly be recognized, and it is no time to worry about manners. Keeping calm and acting quickly might well save your life.

COUGHING, SNEEZING, AND BLOWING YOUR NOSE

It is not necessary to leave the table to perform any of these functions, unless the bout turns out to be prolonged. In that case you should excuse yourself until the seizure has passed. When you feel a sneeze or a cough coming on, cover your mouth and nose with your handkerchief, or if you do not have one, or time to get it out, use your napkin. In an emergency your hand will do better than nothing at all. Never use your napkin to blow your nose. If you are caught short without a handkerchief or a tissue, excuse yourself and head for the powder room.

STONES, BUGS, HAIRS, ETC.

When you get something that doesn't belong there into your mouth, there is no remedy but to remove it. This you do as inconspicuously as possible—spitting it quietly into your fingers. But occasionally you notice the foreign matter before you eat it—a hair in the butter, a worm on the lettuce, or a fly in the soup. If it is not too upsetting to you, remove the object without calling attention to it and go on eating. If it is such that it upsets your stomach (as a hair does to many people) leave the dish untouched rather than embarrass your hostess in a private home. At a restaurant you may—and should—point out the error to your waiter and ask for a replacement. Of course an observant host or hostess will spot the problem when he or she notices that you are not eating something, and will see that the dish is replaced.

FOOD STUCK IN A TOOTH

Toothpicks should not be used at the table, and certainly you should not pick at food in your teeth with your finger. If it is actually hurting, excuse yourself and go to the powder room to remove it. Otherwise wait until the end of the meal and then go to take care of it, asking for a toothpick if necessary.

The same holds true for food caught in dentures. If it is unbearable, you must excuse yourself and go to the nearest bathroom to rinse them.

SPILLS

If you should spill jelly or a bit of vegetable or other solid food on the table, pick up as much as you can neatly with a clean spoon or the blade of your knife. If it has caused a stain dab a little water from your glass on it with a corner of your napkin. Apologize to your hostess, who, in turn, should not add to your embarrassment by calling attention to the accident.

If you spill wine or water at a formal dinner or in a restaurant, try quietly to attract the attention of the butler or waiter, who will bring a cloth to cover the spot. At the family table or at an informal dinner without servants, offer to get a cloth or sponge to mop up the liquid and help the hostess clean up in any way you can.

THE LEFT-HANDED DINER

Left-handed people who are accustomed to the normal place setting have no more trouble than do right-handers. After all, the fork—the most-used utensil—and the butter plate are both on the left. If left-handers are brought up with the table set for them in the usual way—as it should be—there is no problem and no reason to change it for them.

There is, however, a problem of "bumping elbows," so whenever convenient, it is thoughtful to seat a left-handed diner at a corner where his left arm will not bump into the right arm of the person beside him, as they are both eating.

SOME DINING "DON'TS"

While I much prefer to emphasize the affirmative approach to good manners, there are a number of dining rules that are better expressed by the negative. Here are the most important ones:

Don't encircle a plate with the left arm while eating with the right hand.

Don't push back your plate when finished. It remains exactly where it is until the person serving you removes it. If you wait on yourself, get up and carry it to the kitchen.

Don't lean back and announce, "I'm through," or "I'm stuffed." The fact that you have put your fork or spoon down shows that you have finished.

Don't *ever* put liquid into your mouth if it is already filled with food. You might have a little toast in your mouth when you drink your coffee, if it be so little as to be undetectable by others. But a good habit is *never*.

Don't wipe off the tableware in a restaurant. If you do happen to find a dirty piece of silver at your place, call a waiter or waitress, show him the soiled article, and ask for a clean one.

Don't, if you are a woman, wear an excessive amount of lipstick to the table, out of consideration for your hostess' napkin, and also because it is very unattractive on the rim of a glass or on the silver.

Don't crook your finger when picking up your cup. It's an affected mannerism.

Don't—ever—leave your spoon in your cup. Not only does it look unattractive; it is almost certain to result in an accident.

Don't leave half of the food on your spoon or fork to be waved about during conversation. One often sees this done with ice cream, but the coldness is no excuse. One should put less on the spoon and eat it in one bite.

Don't cut up your entire meal before you start to eat; it only makes a mess on your plate.

Don't pile mashed potatoes and peas on top of the meat on your fork—in short, don't take huge mouthfuls of *any* food.

❧38❧ *Table Settings*

THE MOST FORMAL TABLE SETTING

The one unbreakable rule for a formal table is that everything must be geometrically spaced: the centerpiece in the actual center, the places at equal distances, and all utensils balanced. Beyond this one rule you can vary your arrangement and decorations to a wide degree.

TABLECLOTHS

If the tablecloth is of white damask, which is best for a formal dinner, a pad must be put under it. (If you do not have a felt pad cut to the dimensions of your table, a folded white blanket serves very well.) To say that the cloth must be smooth and spotless—in other words, perfectly laundered—is, I hope, unnecessary. Damask is the most conservative tablecloth, suitable in any dining room from English or French style to "contemporary" furnishings. Lace tablecloths are better suited to an Italian room—especially if the table is refectory style. Embroidered or lace-inserted tablecloths are appropriate for low-ceilinged, old-fashioned rooms. Either lace or linen goes over the table without felt or other padding. It is now permissible to use machine-made lace cloths, but only if they are of superb quality.

Whenever a damask or linen cloth is used, the middle crease must be put on so that it is an absolutely straight and unwavering line down the exact center from head to foot of the table. I find that it is usually necessary for me to touch up my cloth with the iron, because the folds made by the laundry are not always as straight and evenly spaced as they should be. If it is an embroidered cloth be sure the embroidery or monogram is right side up.

The tablecloth for a seated dinner should hang down approximately eighteen inches. It should *not* extend to the floor as it does on a buffet table.

No matter how concerned you are about soiling your beautiful—possibly heirloom—damask cloth, *never* cover it with clear plastic. Not only does it have an unpleasant, slippery surface, but the beauty of the cloth cannot possibly show clearly, and you might just as well buy an imitation plastic cloth and keep the other in the drawer! With modern cleaning processes, there are few spots that cannot be removed, and those who are fortunate enough to have lovely table linens should not hide them away, but should use them, for their own enjoyment and to the delight of their guests.

NAPKINS

A truly formal damask dinner napkin matches the tablecloth and is approximately twenty-four inches square. Whether your napkins are that size or not, they are folded in the manner described below.

Very large napkins are folded three times in each direction to make a smaller square. The two sides are then folded under, making a loosely "rolled" rectangle. The napkin is not flattened down completely. Care must be taken so that the monogram shows at the lower left corner of the rectangle, or if the initials are at the center of one side of the napkin, that they appear in the center third of the "roll."

Napkin folded to form a
loosely rolled rectangle

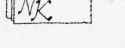

Napkin folded diagonally

Smaller napkins may be folded in the same way, making only two folds to form the smaller square. Or the smaller square may be folded in half *diagonally*, and the two points folded under, leaving the monogram showing in the center point.

Napkins are placed in the center of the service plate with the monogram facing the diner. They are put at the side only when a first course is put on the table before seating the guests. To put the napkin at the side of the empty plate simply in order to display the plate is incorrect for formal table-setting. The old custom of wrapping a roll in the napkin was most impractical and, fortunately, is passé. When the diner flicked open the napkin he generally also flicked the roll right onto the floor.

PLACE CARDS

Place cards may be put on top of and in the center of the napkin, but if unsteady there, they may be placed on the tablecloth above the service plate at the exact center of the place setting.

Although decorated place cards are not inappropriate for a special holiday such as Christmas or Thanksgiving, those for other formal dinners should be plain white, or white with a narrow gold border. Cards for a wedding or twenty-fifth-anniversary dinner may be bordered with silver. Some hostesses have their cards monogrammed in silver or gold, and a family that uses a crest may have the crest engraved at the top. Place cards are generally about two inches long by three quarters of an inch high after folding in half, although they do vary somewhat.

The writing should be large enough to be seen easily by the guests, and at formal dinners titles are always used: "Mrs. James," "Judge Greenberg," "Dr. Phillips," etc. If there are two Dr. Phillipses at the dinner, naturally the cards must read "Dr. John Phillips" and "Dr. Henry Phillips."

For proper titles for government officials and diplomats see Chapter 12.

THE SILVER

> *Don't put any silver on your table if you can't have it cleaned. Infinitely rather have every ornament of glass or china—and if knives and forks have crevices in the design of their handles that are hard to clean, buy plain plated ones, or use tin! Anything is better than yellow-faced dirty-finger-nailed silver. The first thing to ask in engaging a waitress is, "Can you clean silver?" If she can't, she would better be something else.*—Emily Post, 1922

The silver used at a formal dinner should be sterling, or at least should appear to be sterling. Gold is used at the White House, but it is not so appropriate as silver for private parties.

It is not necessary that *all* silver match, although all forks or all spoons or all knives should be of the same pattern. Dessert silver, which is not on the table but is brought in with the dessert plates at a formal dinner, need not match the dinner forks, and after-dinner coffee spoons are frequently entirely different. Knives and forks should match, unless you happen to have a set of knives with crystal or carved-bone handles that may be used with any pattern.

CHINA

China, too, may be mixed, but *all* the plates for each course at one table must match. For example, all the service plates must be of one pattern, although the dinner plates, while matching each other, may be entirely different. Silver butter plates and glass salad or dessert plates may be used with any fine china. The most important consideration is that each item be of the same high quality as the others. It is entirely incorrect, for example, to use heavy pottery salad plates with fine china dinner plates. Just as at a formal table with lovely appointments you should *never* use paper napkins or stainless-steel utensils.

THE CENTERPIECE

The first piece to be put on the table once the cloth is in place is the centerpiece. As its name implies, it must be in the exact center. It must never be so high that the diners cannot see over it, but its length and width are limited only by the size of your table. It can be composed of a wide variety of things—fresh flowers being the most common and surely one of the loveliest. "Cheap" plastic artificial flowers are out of place, but lovely glass or china imitation flowers or fruit are appropriate. Carefully arranged fruit makes a beautiful centerpiece, and ornaments that need neither fruit nor flowers can be effective too. Two of my own particular favorites are a covered china tureen decorated with charming shells and fish, and a pair of large crystal fish, which I use with glass candlesticks.

CANDLES

Candles for a formal dinner should be white, and brand-new. Only if you are skilled with a candle-tip shaper, and there is no evidence of smoke or drips, might a used candle be permissible.

Candles are lighted before the guests come to the table and remain lighted until they leave the dining room. They are extinguished by the waitress or butler.

When the centerpiece is in place, a pair of candlesticks is placed at each end, about halfway between the centerpiece and the end of the table, or candelabra at either end halfway between the places of the host and hostess and the centerpiece. The number of candles depends upon whether the dining room is otherwise lighted or not.

If the candles alone light the table, there should be a candle for each person. You will need two or four candelabra, depending on the length of the table and the number of guests. If there are two candelabra at each end, they are spaced evenly between the centerpiece and the host's and hostess' places. But if the candles are merely ornaments four candles will be adequate for a table of eight. Four is the *minimum* number of candles for a table of six or more, but at a small table set for two or four people, two candlesticks are adequate. Candlesticks or candelabra must be high and the candles as long as the proportion can stand, so that the light does not shine into the eyes of those at the table.

FINISHING TOUCHES

Dishes or compotes filled with candied fruit, thin chocolate mints, or other edible trimmings are put at the corners, between the candlesticks or candelabra and the centerpiece, or wherever there are equally spaced vacancies on the table. They are left there through the entire meal and are sometimes passed around after dessert is finished. Nuts may be put on the dinner table either in large silver dishes or in small individual ones at each of the places, but they are removed with the salt-and-pepper shakers after the salad course. The colloquial description of eating "from soup to nuts" does not apply to a formal dinner. After-dessert "nuts and raisins" belong only on the family dinner table—especially at Thanksgiving and Christmas.

Flowers are also often seen in two or four smaller vases or epergnes, in addition to the larger arrangement in the center.

Pepper pots and saltcellars should be at every place or between every two places. For a dinner of twelve there should be six (and never less than four) salts and peppers. Open saltcellars must be accompanied by tiny silver serving spoons, which sometimes have a gold bowl—gold is not so easily damaged by the salt.

Whether or not the hostess and her husband smoke, she sees that her guests are supplied with ashtrays and cigarettes. A small ashtray is put at each place, and cigarettes are found on the table, either in a small holder in front of each diner or in larger holders spaced evenly about the table. Smokers should follow the usual rules of good smoking manners more strictly at the table than at any other time.

There are some hostesses who prefer that their guests do not smoke until coffee is served, and no ashtrays or cigarettes are placed on the table. When this is so, the guests should have the good sense and courtesy to refrain until after dinner.

THE INDIVIDUAL PLACES

Next comes the setting of the places. The distance between places at the table must never be so short that guests have no elbow room and the servants cannot pass the dishes properly. When the dining-room chairs have very high backs and are placed so close as to be almost touching, it is difficult for even the most skillful server not to spill something on someone. On the other hand, people placed a yard or more apart will find a shouted conversation equally trying. About two feet from plate center to plate center is ideal. If the chairs have narrow and low backs, people can sit much closer together. This is especially true of a small, round table, the curve of which leaves a spreading wedge of space between the chairs at the back even if the seats touch at the front corners. But on the long, straight sides of a rectangular table in a very large dining room, there should be a foot of space between the chairs.

Formal dinner table

The service plates, with the pattern properly positioned so that the "picture" faces the diner, are first put around the table at equal distances—spaced with a string if the person setting the table does not have an accurate eye. The silver is placed in the order of its use, with the implements to be used first farthest from the plate. The

423

salad fork is placed next to the left of the plate, then the meat fork, and finally the fish fork, which will be used first. Just to the right of the plate is the salad knife, next is the meat knife, and on the outside is the fish knife, the cutting edge of each toward the plate. Outside the knives are the soup spoon and/or grapefruit spoon, and beyond the spoons, the oyster fork if shellfish is to be served. Note that the oyster (or shellfish) fork is the *only* fork ever to be placed on the right.

Formal place setting

No more than three of any implement is *ever* placed on the table (with the exception of the oyster fork's making four forks). Therefore, if more than three courses are served before dessert (rare, these days), the fork for the fourth course is brought in at the time it is served. Or the salad knife and fork may be omitted in the beginning and may be brought in when salad is served.

Dessert spoons and forks are brought in on the dessert plate just before dessert is served.

Although for many years butter plates were never seen on formal tables, this rule is rapidly being forgotten. Today there are few people who do not prefer their bread or roll with butter, and the idea of putting a buttered roll, or a dry one for that matter, directly onto the tablecloth is totally contrary to the aims of etiquette. Therefore, no matter how formal the dinner, the use of a butter plate is now correct. The butter plate is located above the forks at the left of the place setting. The butter knife is laid across it, slightly diagonally from upper left to lower right, with the sharper edge of the blade toward the edge of the table.

The wineglasses chosen depend of course upon the menu, but their table-setting arrangement is according to size, so that little ones are not hidden behind large ones. Therefore the goblet for water is

Formal table set for two

placed directly above the knives at the right of the plate; next to it, at a slight distance to the right, the champagne glass; in front and between these two, the claret or red-wine glass, or the white-wine glass; then, either in front of this or somewhat to the right again, the sherry glass. Or instead of grouping the glasses on the table, some prefer to have them placed in a straight row slanting downward from the goblet at the upper left to the glass for sherry at the lower right.

Such an array as this is scarcely ever seen except at a public dinner, which is more properly classified as a banquet. At the private dinner two or three glasses in addition to the goblet are usual—one for sherry, one for a claret or possibly a Burgundy, and one for a light white wine.

THE INFORMAL TABLE

Whether you call your dinner party "informal," "semiformal," or "casual," you have much more latitude in planning your table setting than you do for a formal dinner. There are a few overall considerations that should be given attention, based on your availa-

425

ble space, the style of your home, the theme of your party, and the tastes of your guests. Outside of the restrictions imposed by that list, you may give your imagination and your creativity free rein in setting your table.

TABLE COVERINGS

While there is no reason not to use a white damask or lace cloth for a semiformal dinner, you should add color in the other table appointments to give the table warmth and interest and to take away the formal atmosphere. The color may come in the napkins, the centerpiece, and your choice of china or pottery.

More often, the table is covered with a gaily colored or pat-

Informal table set for six

terned cloth, or with place mats. If you have pretty linen, organdy, or lace mats with napkins that match or complement them, they are ideal for informal dinners, and there are many lovely plastic sets that are appropriate too. Whatever covering you choose, be sure that your centerpiece and china go well with it. Strive for an unusual or individual look that will make *your* table stand apart.

Candles are used on informal tables just as they are at formal dinners, but usually in candlesticks rather than candelabra. They may be of any color that goes well with the tablecloth or mats, but must be high enough so that the flame is above the eye level of the diners. The hostess (sometimes one of the guests helps her) extinguishes the candles as she leaves the table. Some brave souls pinch the flame quickly between thumb and forefinger, but I prefer to cup my hand behind the flame and blow it out!

The centerpiece, too, may show your originality. A Thanksgiving turkey made of a large crooked-neck squash with smaller gourds for neck and head and pineapple leaves for tail feathers makes a real conversation piece. A dried-flower arrangement on a brown tablecloth with orange or beige napkins is stunning. Wide red ribbons crisscrossing a white tablecloth and a centerpiece of large red crepe-paper poppies brighten a winter or Valentine's Day table. In short, don't rely on the usual bowl of flowers—pretty though it is. Look through women's magazines for ideas if you are not creative yourself, and give your dinner guests a happy surprise.

PLACE SETTINGS

As at a formal dinner everything on the table should be symmetrically and evenly spaced. The main difference between the formal and informal place setting is that for the latter there is less of everything. There are fewer courses served, so fewer pieces of silver are set out.

Generally only one—at the most, two—wines are served, so a water goblet and one (or two) wine glasses are all that are necessary. Frequently wine is not served at all, and iced-tea glasses or simply tumblers for water or mugs for beer are used. If bread or rolls are to be served, a butter plate should be used. If you do not have butter plates to match your dinner plates try to buy a set of glass ones. It is less than appetizing to have one's bread or roll get soggy and messy because it has slid into the juice or salad dressing on your dinner plate, or to see the pat of butter on the edge of the warm plate melting rapidly down into your meat and vegetables before you can spread it on your bread.

For more or less the same reason, serve separate salad plates if your menu includes any dishes with gravy. Salad may be put on the same plate with broiled steak or chops or chicken, perhaps, but an unappetizing mess results when it is combined with lamb stew!

The typical place setting for an informal three-course dinner would include:

2 forks—one for dinner at the far left
    one for dessert or salad to the left of the plate
dinner plate—not on the table when guests sit down
salad plate—to the left of the forks
1 knife—next to the plate on the right—for steak, chops, chicken, or game birds, it may be a steak knife
2 spoons—dessert spoon to the right of the knife
    soup spoon at the far right

Notice that the silver to be used last is next to the plate.

1 butter plate with butter knife—if you have them
1 water goblet—or tall tumbler
1 wineglass—if you plan to serve wine
ashtray—if your guests smoke
napkin in the center

If you plan to serve coffee with the meal, the cup and saucer go to the right of the setting, with the coffee spoon on the right side of the saucer.

Service plates are not used at an informal dinner, except under the stemmed glass used for shrimp cocktail, fruit cocktail, etc., and under soup plates. It may be a true service plate, or it may be simply another dinner or dessert plate—whichever size and style is most appropriate.

The dinner plate should not be on the table when your guests sit down, because it should be very warm when the food is served. If you have help, the maid passes the hot plates around before she starts serving. If you are having a seated buffet the stack of warm plates is on the buffet table.

The dessert spoon and fork (or if you prefer, just a spoon) need not be beside the plate. They can be brought in, as at a formal dinner, with the dessert plate, or they can be placed, European style, above the center of the place setting, horizontally, with bowl and tines to the left.

You may use any materials that appeal to you on your informal table. Wooden salts, pepper grinders, pewter plates, wooden salad bowls, ironware, pottery, and stainless-steel "silver" are all fine. However, each item must be in keeping with the others. Don't combine plastic wineglasses with fine bone china, or plastic plates with delicate crystal glasses. You may, however, use wooden salad bowls with pottery or "everyday" china dinner plates, or glass salad plates with stoneware dinner plates. The secret is not in having everything of one design, but in creating, out of a variety of patterns and colors, a harmonious whole.

When your guests arrive at the table, the butter should already be on the butter plates, the water glasses filled, and the wine (if served) in a cooler beside the host or in a decanter on the table. Salad is often served with the main course instead of as a separate one, and as mentioned above, rather than putting a crisp cool salad on a hot plate or one swimming in gravy, a salad plate or a bowl should be set at the left of each place.

Cigarettes, ashtrays, salts and peppers, and condiments in serving dishes—not the jars they came in—must all be in place, conveniently spaced around the table.

If the host is serving the meat and vegetables the stack of warm plates may be in front of him along with the foods to be served and the necessary implements. If there is a course already on the table, however, the hostess or maid must bring the entrée in from the kitchen after the plates have been removed.

A course to be served before the entrée should be on the table when the guests come in to dinner. Long-stemmed glass bowls containing fish or shrimp should have a plate under them. Both are removed to make way for the hot plates of the main course. If your first course is soup the most practical soup dishes are little pots with lids, which will keep the contents hot while the guests are seating themselves.

In some houses the salad-dressing ingredients are arranged in a set of bowls and bottles that, with the salad bowl, are put in front of the hostess, who mixes the dressing herself. A few drops of this or shakes of that, according to the taste of the hostess, lend an excitement to a dressing that can never be duplicated in a store-bought bottle.

The same idea exactly has made certain internationally known restaurants famous—the headwaiter, or the proprietor himself, cooks and mixes something before your eyes. The ducks of the Tour d'Argent, the noodles of Alfredo's in Rome, or Jananese sukiyaki seem to acquire a special flavor by the visible preparation. In short, preparing a dish at the table (which many hostesses think of as a handicap) may easily become a special feature of your hospitality.

LUNCHEONS

There is little to be said about place settings for luncheons, because most of it has been said above. The formality of the occasion decrees the elaborateness of the table, but the utensils used, and the arrangements, are similar to those of the formal or informal dinner.

Luncheon place setting

One exception is candles. Candlesticks with candles in them *may* be used on the luncheon table as part of the decorations, but they should not be lighted during daylight hours. For this reason they are more often omitted. At a late-afternoon tea, when curtains are drawn, candles may be lighted, but *never* at a luncheon in the middle of the day.

Napkins are never as large as the twenty-four-inch dinner napkin. The folding is simple—generally the triangle with the pointed ends tucked under, described above.

White damask tablecloths are not used for luncheons. Place mats are almost invariably used, of lace or organdy if the luncheon is formal. A lace or embroidered tablecloth may be used also, but it should not overhang the table to any degree. *For other than these exceptions, see above, under "formal" or "informal" dinner settings, for correct luncheon settings.*

FAMILY STYLE

Practicality is the keynote in setting the table for family meals.

Seating arrangements at table depend on the convenience of the family. Mother usually sits nearest the kitchen door with young children who may need help nearest her. Father sits at the end opposite her. If there is a male guest he is seated on Mother's right, a female guest on Father's right.

KITCHEN DINING

Some families, even though they have a dining room, prefer the coziness and convenience of the kitchen when dining by themselves.

If space permits, it is grand to have an end of the kitchen set apart, furnished and decorated so that the children feel the importance of good manners at the table, no matter where it may be. In our country's past the kitchen served early settlers as living room, dining room, and cooking area, and certainly from Mother's point of view it was practical. Aside from the convenience in serving, she was right with the family, not only during the meal, but while preparing it. Today, in our servantless homes, many women yearn to end their isolation in a remote kitchen and return to this "family-kitchen" or "country-kitchen" idea. Many houses are being constructed with such a room, and this section of *Etiquette* is becoming far more useful than it was a short time ago.

When you have no such room, nor extra space in the kitchen you have, the ordinary kitchen table must do, but an extra effort should be made to make the room neat and attractive before the family sits down.

Even a kitchen table should be nicely set for dinner—the one hour of the day when most families get together "socially." There should be place mats or a tablecloth (a pretty plastic one is most practical) or even paper doilies; spotless utensils, though they may be stainless steel; and pretty, colorful glasses and plates, even though they were bought at the "five-and-ten."

THE BARE ESSENTIALS

A minimum number of utensils is put at each place—only those absolutely necessary. Since there is usually only one course and dessert, there may be only three pieces of silver—a fork, a knife, and a spoon for the dessert. Of course if you are having soup or fruit first, utensils for those foods must be added. You do not need to bother with separate salad forks, although individual salad bowls should be set out, even at the family table. Butter plates and knives may be

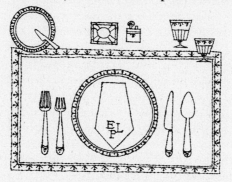

Place setting for family meals

omitted, although if you have a dishwasher the extra plate is more than worth the trouble of putting it in the rack.

TV dinners and other prepared dishes should not be eaten from the containers, but should be spooned out onto warm plates.

Milk glasses should be filled before the meal, or the milk should be served in a pitcher. However, ketchup, jellies, pickles, etc., may be served in their jars if no guests are present. The jars should be on saucers, and each should have its own separate serving spoon or fork on the saucer.

Paper napkins are perfectly correct for family meals. However, if you prefer cloth napkins you may wish to conserve on your laundry by using napkin rings. These, too, are correct for family meals. Each member has his own ring, marked so that he can recognize it. He folds his napkin at the end of the meal and puts it back in the ring, which is removed from the table until the next meal. Napkins should be changed after two or three meals—some families change each morning or evening. Of course if a napkin gets badly soiled, it should not be used again.

Napkin rings are not used by guests, with the exception of a relative or close friend who is making a prolonged visit. Occasionally they are put on a table as part of the decor at an informal party, but the guests do not replace the napkins in them after dinner.

The rings are usually placed at the left of the setting, but they may be put in the center, especially if they are broad, flattened ones.

PLACE SETTINGS

Since no china or silver that will not be used need be placed on the table, the following settings must be reduced to fit your menu.

BREAKFAST

More so than at other meals, there is a wide difference in the tastes of breakfast eaters. Some people, teenage girls especially, prefer to eat no breakfast at all—or perhaps a piece of toast and a glass of milk. Many women take only a cup of coffee and a glass of juice, while others eat a hearty morning meal and watch their calories at lunchtime. Men generally like a more substantial meal, sometimes two or three courses, including fruit, cereal, and eggs. Unlike other meals, breakfast may, and should, be prepared "to order." That is, if daughter Susie truly dislikes eggs she may be given a dish of cold cereal, but Father should not therefore be deprived of his scrambled eggs and bacon.

In setting the breakfast table, Mother puts out just those utensils which will be needed by each person.

A variety of cold cereals, milk, cream, sugar, salt and pepper, and jams or jellies may be placed in the center of the table or on a convenient side table, but whoever is doing the cooking serves the hot food directly onto the plates and places them in front of those sitting at the table. If your table is large enough a lazy Susan or turntable is most convenient and makes each item easily accessible to everyone.

The setting is as follows:

Fork at the left of the plate.

Knife at the right of the plate.

Spoon for cereal at the right of the knife.

Teaspoon for fruit or grapefruit spoon at the right of the cereal spoon.

Butter knife across the bread-and-butter plate, which is to the left and above the fork.

Napkins, in rings or not, at the left of the plates.

Coffee cups with spoons lying at the right of the saucers or mugs, or at the right of each plate if the coffee is served from the kitchen. If it is served by Mother at the table, cups and saucers, mugs, and coffeepot are beside her place.

Glass for milk or water, to the right and above the spoons.

LUNCH

For the busy woman of today, lunch usually consists of a sandwich, a bowl of soup, or a salad. She may eat it at the dining-room or kitchen table or she may bring it to the living room or patio on a tray. When children are home for lunch, it can be served either at the dining table or in the kitchen, according to the preference of the family. If the man of the house has lunch at home, he will probably want a more substantial meal, and the table is set in accordance with the food to be served. In the average household—unless the main meal is eaten at midday, in which case the table is set as for dinner—no more than three courses are ever served for lunch, and even that number is most unusual.

The setting is as follows:

Meat fork at the left of the salad fork.

On the right, a meat knife; and at the right of this knife, a soup or dessert spoon, if necessary.

Butter plate and knife above the fork at the left.

The dessert fork or spoon may be brought in with the dessert plate if you prefer.

Glass for a beverage above the knife.

Napkin at the left of the place setting.

DINNER

If the food is to be passed, the warm dinner plates are at each place on the table when the family sits down, or they are stacked in front of the head of the household if he is to serve. However, many women prefer to serve the plates directly from the stove in order to avoid the use of extra platters and serving dishes. The table setting for dinner is similar to that for lunch:

At the left of the plate, the dinner fork.

At the right, the dinner knife next to the plate, then the soup spoon or the oyster fork or the dessert spoon (if necessary) on the outside.

Glass or goblet for a beverage at the right above the knife.

Butter plate to the left and above the fork, with the butter knife laid on it diagonally from the upper left to the lower right.

Salad plate (if necessary) at the left of the fork.

Napkin at the left of the setting.

Coffee mug or cup and saucer with a spoon at the right. If you are using mugs for coffee during the meal, the spoon goes to the right of the mugs.

THE MEALTIME TRAY

Although few people in the ordinary household are served breakfast on a tray, there are many occasions when a member of the family is ill and must remain in bed for his meals. An attractive tray with a flower in a little vase or a gay napkin and tray cloth can do much to aid a lagging appetite and a sagging spirit. Also, dinner is frequently eaten from a tray taken to the living room or den when a favorite television program is in progress.

For all meals the tray is covered with a tray cloth or if you do not have special tray linen, a doily or place mat of any sort. The setting is the same as the individual place setting at the table insofar as space permits. Because of lack of room, the dessert plate and the coffee cup and saucer are usually brought when the main meal is finished. The dinner plate should be heated. A piece of foil laid over the food will keep it warm while the tray is carried to its destination.

Individual breakfast sets for trays are available and often given as wedding presents. They generally include an egg cup, a cereal bowl, two or three plates and a cover, a coffee cup and saucer, sugar bowl, cream pitcher, and small coffeepot. They come in gay patterns or lovely solid colors and by the very charm of their appearance make the morning more cheerful.

⋖39⋗ Invitations and Replies

YOUR OBLIGATIONS

Wedding and shower invitations, invitations to dances or balls, and invitations to any official function, or one that you pay to attend, carry no obligations. Parties in private homes, whether luncheons, brunches, cocktail or dinner parties, do require a return invitation.

The "pay-back" invitation need not necessarily be "in kind." A bachelor living in a hotel or tiny apartment cannot invite his boss to an elaborate dinner of the kind to which the boss invited him. He must repay, however, by taking his boss to dinner in a restaurant, or perhaps inviting him to a picnic at his beach cottage instead. An invitation to a large cocktail party means only that the next time you entertain in a similar way your host and hostess should be on your list. To be invited to a small dinner party is another matter. This invitation is more personal, more flattering, and should be returned in kind within a couple of months. The same is true of a weekend-visit invitation. Often it cannot be repaid at once, but when circumstances permit, you should invite your host and hostess to visit you. If you have no facilities to repay their hospitality in that way, you should plan to treat them to dinner and the theater, or anything that they would especially enjoy. Wedding invitations should never be used to pay back other social obligations.

One attempt to return the invitation after a dinner party is not enough. If your hosts refuse your first invitation you should try at least once, and preferably twice, more. After that, if you cannot seem to get together, you might well give up, or at least wait until some future date when they will fit into a party you are planning.

You are never, in any way, except according to your own conscience, obligated to accept an invitation. Once having accepted, however, you must go. Nothing can change an acceptance to a regret except illness, death in the family, or a sudden, unavoidable trip.

Furthermore, having refused one invitation on these grounds, you must not accept another more desirable one for the same day. You need give no excuse beyond "I'm afraid we are busy on the thirteenth," and *that* leaves you free to accept anything else that comes along. But if you have refused because you would be "out of town," and then you appear at a party attended by a mutual friend, you can certainly give up any idea of friendship with the senders of the first invitation.

When you are invited to a party and cannot go, you incur a milder obligation to return the invitation. It is not so important as if you had accepted the host's hospitality, but the *intent* to entertain you was there and should be acknowledged by an invitation in the not-too-distant future.

Anyone receiving an invitation with an RSVP on it is *obliged* to reply as promptly as possible. It is inexcusably rude to leave someone who has invited you to a party with no idea of how many people to expect.

Your reply should "match" the invitation. A formal, third-person invitation requires a third-person reply. However, a good friend who wishes to explain her refusal or to express her delight in the invitation may always write a personal note if she prefers. Those who groan at the thought of written replies should stop and think how much easier it is to follow the prescribed third-person form than to compose a lengthier letter!

When the RSVP is followed by a telephone number, do your best to telephone your answer. If you cannot get through to the host after several attempts, do not, however, give up. Rather than no reply at all, he will appreciate a brief note or even a post card saying "We'll be there" or "So sorry, can't make it."

If the invitation says "regrets only," don't send or call an acceptance unless you have something to discuss with the hostess. If there is no RSVP at all, you are not obligated to reply, but it is never *wrong* to do so, and any hostess will appreciate your effort.

When invitations are being sent out, *every* guest should receive one—even good friends and neighbors. They should reply, too, in whatever form is indicated by the invitations.

"THIRD-PERSON" FORMAL INVITATIONS

For information about wedding invitations and announcements, see Chapter 50.

Formal invitations are engraved on white or cream cards—either plain or plate-marked like those for wedding receptions—or they may be written by hand on personal notepaper. There is now a fine printing process called thermography that is also acceptable.

Handwritten invitations are written on plain paper or paper with a very small monogram, but never on paper headed by an address. If the family has a coat of arms, it or the crest may be embossed without color on engraved invitations.

The size of the card of invitation varies with personal preference. The most graceful proportion is approximately three units in height to four in width, or four high by three wide. Cards may vary in size from six by four and a half to three by four inches.

The lettering is a matter of personal choice, but the plainer the design, the safer. Punctuation is used only when words requiring separation occur on the same line, and in certain abbreviations, such as "R.s.v.p." The time should never be given as "nine thirty," but as "half past nine o'clock," or the more conservative form, "half after nine o'clock."

If the dance or dinner or other entertainment is to be given at one address and the hostess lives at another, both addresses are always given, assuming that the hostess wishes replies to go to her home address.

Traditionally, the phrases "black tie" or "white tie" were never used on invitations to weddings or private parties. It was assumed that people receiving formal invitations to these events would *know* what to wear. Today, however, the vast majority of parties are *not* formal, so the hostess who wishes her guests to dress formally must indicate this on her invitations. The phrase "black tie" should appear in the lower-right-hand corner of invitations to proms, charity balls, formal dinners or dances, evening weddings, or any event to which a wide assortment of people are invited.

The replies are addressed to the person, or persons, from whom the invitation comes. The full first name, rather than initials, is used, and the name of the state is also written out in full. A return address should appear on the back flap of the envelope. When a response card is sent with the invitation, it should be used for the reply, rather than a handwritten response.

DANCES AND BALLS

Vouchers or tickets of admission like those sent with invitations to assembly or public balls should be enclosed in invitations to a masquerade; it would be too easy otherwise for dishonest or other undesirable persons to gain admittance. If vouchers are not sent with the invitations, or better yet, mailed afterwards to all those who have accepted, it is necessary that the hostess receive her guests singly in a small private room and request each to unmask before her.—Emily Post, 1922

TO A PRIVATE DANCE

The forms most often used are the following:

Mr. and Mrs. Harold Gilding

request the pleasure of

Miss Sally Waring's

company at a small dance

Monday, the first of January

at ten o'clock

400 Lake Shore Drive

Chicago, Illinois

R.s.v.p.

The expression "small dance" is sometimes used no matter what the size of the ball, but it is not necessary.

If it is a dance for young people, and dates are to be included, the wording is: "request the company of Miss Sally Waring and escort at a . . . ," or "Mr. William Frick and guest."

Note that while "Miss" is not used on wedding invitations, the title is always used on other invitations.

Mr. and Mrs. Harold Gladstone

request the pleasure of your company

at a dance in honour of their niece

Miss Susan Gladstone

Thursday, the twenty-second of December

at ten o'clock

1300 Massachusetts Avenue

Washington, D. C.

When the dance is given for a debutante, her name does not necessarily appear:

Mr. and Mrs. Sidney Colbrook

request the pleasure of your company

at a dance

Monday evening, January the third

at ten o'clock

The Fitz-Cherry Hotel

New York City

Please reply to
Brookmeadows
Islip
Long Island 11751

439

If the address to which replies are to be sent appears on the envelope, or follows "RSVP" on the invitation, the zip code is not included in the body of the invitation.

Mr. and Mrs. James Wellstreet

Miss Deborah Wellstreet

request the pleasure of your company

on Friday, the third of June

at half after nine o'clock

The Hunt Club

Richmond, Virginia

R.s.v.p.

6 Laurel Lane · · · · · · · · · · · · · · · · · Dancing

Richmond, Virginia 23200

There is also another traditional form of invitation to a debutante party, but it is not often used today—the phrase "At Home," whether the party is held at home or not. If there is to be dancing, the word appears, as above, at the lower right.

Mr. and Mrs. Davis Jefferson

At Home

Monday, the third of January

at ten o'clock

Town and Country Club

Kindly send reply to · · · · · · · · · · · · · · · · · Dancing

Three Vernon Square

Rutland, Vermont 05701

INVITATIONS TO A DEBUTANTE ASSEMBLY

An invitation to present the debutante reads:

The Committee of the Westchester Cotillion

invites

Mr. and Mrs. David S. Williams

to present

Miss Penelope Williams

at the Cotillion

on Friday, the ninth of September

at ten o'clock

Shenorock Shore Club

Rye, New York

WHEN THE ASSEMBLY IS TO BENEFIT A CHARITY, OR THE EXPENSES ARE TO BE COVERED BY THE SALE OF TICKETS

These invitations are accompanied by a card stating the amount of the subscription, where it should be sent, etc. Names of the debutantes being presented, the committee, and sometimes the patrons are printed inside the invitation.

The Governors of the Tuxedo Club
invite you to subscribe to
The Autumn Ball
to be held at
The Tuxedo Club
on Saturday, the twenty-second of October
Nineteen hundred and seventy-five
at eleven o'clock
Tuxedo Park, New York

R.s.v.p.

THE INVITATION TO A PUBLIC BALL

The word *ball* is rarely used except in an invitation to a public one—or at least a semipublic one— such as may be given by a committee for a charity or by a club or association of some sort. For example:

The Entertainment Committee of the Greenwood Club
requests the pleasure of your company
at a Ball
to be held at the clubhouse
on the evening of Thursday, the seventh of November
at ten o'clock
for the benefit of
The Neighborhood Hospital

Single Ticket $15.00   *Black Tie*
Couple $25.00

Response cards, lists of patrons, and cards with pertinent information accompany these invitations.

One does not need to refuse this type of invitation. The return of the filled-in response card and the check for the tickets constitute an acceptance.

DINNER INVITATIONS

Private dinners that are formal enough to demand a third-person invitation are rare, but they take place occasionally, and there are many diplomatic, official, or organizational dinners that require formal invitations.

An engraved invitation to a private dinner reads:

Mr. and Mrs. Howard Little
request the pleasure of your company
at dinner
on Saturday, the fourth of July
at half past seven o'clock
Seabreeze
Edgartown, Massachusetts

R.s.v.p.
Box 65
Edgartown, Massachusetts 02539

If the dinner is held in honor of someone, "to meet Mr. Edgar Rice" is inserted before the address, or it may also be written by hand at the top.

THE FILL-IN FORMAL INVITATION

Hostesses who entertain frequently and formally often have a supply of "fill-in" cards engraved that can be used for any occasion.

Mr. and Mrs. George Wentworth

request the pleasure of

Mr. and Mrs. Jonathan Fields'

company at *dinner*

on *Saturday, the second of March*

at *eight o'clock*

44 High Street

Columbus, Ohio 43200

R.s.v.p.

If there is a guest of honor for the occasion, "to meet Mrs. Harold Smythe" is again handwritten at the top.

INVITATIONS TO RECEPTIONS AND TEAS

Invitations to receptions and teas differ from invitations to balls in that the cards on which they are engraved are usually somewhat smaller. The phrase "At Home" with capital letters may be changed to "will be at home" with lower-case letters or "at Home" with a small *a*. The time is not set at a certain hour, but is limited to a definite period indicated by a beginning and a terminating hour. Also, except for very unusual occasions, a man's name does not appear.

An invitation to a tea for a debutante would read:

Mrs. James Town
Mrs. James Town, Junior
Miss Pauline Town
will be at home
Tuesday, the eighth of December
from five until seven o'clock
850 Fifth Avenue

Mr. Town's name would appear with that of his wife if he were an artist and the reception were given in his studio to view his pictures; or if a reception were given to meet a distinguished guest, such as a bishop or a governor. In this case "In honor of the Right Reverend William Grosvenor Ritual" or "To meet His Excellency the Governor of California" would be engraved at the top of the invitation.

Suitable wording for an evening reception would be:

To meet the Honorable George Stevens
Mr. and Mrs. James Town
at Home
Tuesday, the eighth of December
from nine until eleven o'clock
850 Fifth Avenue

INVITATION BY MORE THAN ONE HOSTESS

There is no rule about the order in which the names of two or more hostesses should appear, except that the one at whose house the party will be held is usually placed first. Or if one is a great deal older her name may head the list. The invitation should make very clear where the event is to take place and where the acceptances and regrets are to be sent. For example, if a dinner is to take place at a club or restaurant, the form is this:

Mr. and Mrs. Walter David White
Mr. and Mrs. Henry Edward Black
Mr. and Mrs. Theodore Jamison Gray
request the pleasure of your company
at dinner
Friday, the tenth of November
at half after seven o'clock
at
The Brook Club

R.s.v.p.
Mr. and Mrs. Walter David White
123 Greenwood Lane
Lakeville
Michigan 48036

If, on the other hand, it should be a luncheon to be at Mrs. White's house, the correct form would be this:

Mrs. Walter David White
Mrs. Henry Edward Black
Mrs. Theodore Jamison Gray
request the pleasure of your company
at luncheon
Tuesday, the tenth of November
at half after one o'clock
123 Greenwood Lane
Lakeville, Michigan 48036

R.s.v.p.
Mrs. Walter David White

INVITATION SENT BY AN ORGANIZATION

An example of this type of invitation:

The Alpha Chapter
of
Beta Chi Delta
requests the pleasure of your company
at a reception
on Monday, the twenty-third of February
at four o'clock
at the Beta Chi Delta House
2 Campus Row

INVITATION TO A COMMENCEMENT

Each school, college, and university follows its own established customs for commencement week. *(See Chapter 44.)*

Of the varying forms of invitation to commencement exercises sent, the following is the most usual:

The President and Faculty
of Hotchkiss College
request the pleasure of your company
at the Commencement Exercises
on Wednesday morning
the twentieth of June
at eleven o'clock
in the Sterling Gymnasium

HANDWRITTEN INVITATIONS

When the formal invitation to dinner or luncheon is written instead of engraved, plain white or cream notepaper or paper stamped with the house address or the husband's crest is used. The wording and spacing must follow the engraved models exactly. The invitation must be written by hand—it may not be typewritten.

> *Mr. and Mrs. John Kindhost*
> *request the pleasure of*
> *Mr. and Mrs. Robert Gilding Jr's*
> *company at dinner*
> *on Tuesday, the sixth of December*
> *at eight o'clock*
> *The Englewood Field Club*
> *R.s.v.p.*

Or it may be worded:

> *Request the pleasure of your company*
> *at dinner*

If the return address does not appear on the back flap of the envelope, it must be written under the RSVP.

A formal invitation should never be written like this:

> *Mr. and Mrs. J. Kindhost request*
> *the pleasure of Mr. and Mrs. James Town's*
> *company at dinner on Tuesday*
> *etc.*

For wedding invitations, see Chapter 50.

446

SEMIFORMAL INVITATIONS

VISITING-CARD INVITATIONS

For an informal dance, a tea to meet a guest, or any other semi-formal occasion, a lady may use her ordinary visiting card. *(See Chapter 11 for their style and form.)* Because the U.S. Postal Service will not accept envelopes smaller than three by four and a half inches, a size at least this large should be ordered for visiting cards or other small-sized cards. These larger envelopes, being thinner but of the color and texture of the cards, need not look unmatched.

The following examples are absolutely correct in every detail —including the abbreviations. They should be written, if possible, in black ink:

> *To meet*
> *Miss Millicent Gordon*
>
> Mrs. John Kindhart
>
> *Tues. Jan. 7*
> *Dancing at 9 o'ck.*
> 1350 Madison Avenue

> *Wed. Jan. 8.*
> *Bridge at 2. o'ck.*
>
> Mrs. John Kindhart
>
> *R. s. v. p.*   1350 Madison Avenue

INFORMALS

The use of informals (small folding cards, described in Chapter 11) for invitations is correct and practical. If the card is engraved with your name, the invitation is written in this way:

Cocktail Buffet

Mr. and Mrs. Allen Burns

Sunday, June 9th
6:30 o'clock

10 Haverstraw Rd.

If the card is monogrammed or unmarked, the invitation takes the form of a brief note and must include your name, since the recipient may not know by whom it was sent. If the card is going to a close friend the signature need be only the first name; but if there should be any question whether the receiver knows from which "Lucy" the invitation came, it is safer to include the last name.

June 6

GBT

Dear Sally,
Could you and Jim
join us for a barbecue
dinner on Sat. June 12th ?

Lucy Brooks

9 Holly St.

If you prefer, on all informal invitations it is correct to put "Regrets only," followed by your telephone number or address, instead of the RSVP.

SEMIFORMAL FILL-IN CARDS

A relatively new, and very popular, form of invitation is a fill-in card, but unlike the "formal" fill-in, it is printed rather than engraved, colorful, and comes in a variety of styles. The printed lines follow the wording of the formal third-person invitation, and you may either order them with your name already printed on them, or you may buy them unpersonalized and fill in your own name.

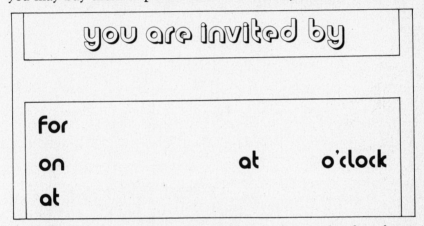

The cards are usually bordered and printed in a bright color on a white background, or they may be beige bordered in brown, yellow bordered in green, etc. The printing is apt to be modern and stylized, rather than traditional. Even though the wording is "third-person" these are *not* formal invitations and need not be answered as such. A brief note, a telephone call (if the number appears in the invitation), or your own informal with "So sorry, must regret the 17th," is all that is necessary.

INFORMAL INVITATIONS

With the exception of invitations to house parties, those sent to out-of-town guests, and those requiring a certain amount of formality, the invitation by note is almost a thing of the past. On informal occasions, the attractively designed and decorated fill-in invitations sold for every sort of entertainment are widely used. Many of these are charming and in the best of taste. The telephone is also a perfectly acceptable means of extending an informal invitation, and nothing need be said about the correct form beyond a reminder that you should be perfectly clear about the date and hour and leave your guests in no doubt about what is intended. If you feel that a written invitation is needed, that is certainly never incorrect. However, as is true with more formal invitations, the informal one should not be typewritten unless the sender is truly unable to write by hand.

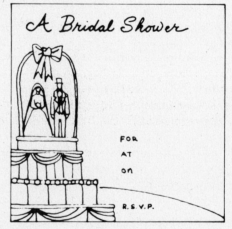

REMINDER CARDS

When invitations have been telephoned, extended verbally, or sent out several weeks in advance, it is never a bad idea to send your prospective guests a written reminder of the occasion.

You simply write on a visiting card, informal, or notepaper: "To remind you—Wednesday 10th, 7:30."

To expected houseguests, one might write:

Dear Helen,
Just to remind you that we are expecting you and Dick on the
sixth.

Love,
Muriel

ANSWER CARDS

It is regrettable that it is necessary to write this section at all, but the custom of sending "answer cards" with invitations to debut parties and subscription dances is so widespread that it must be discussed.

This custom has arisen out of sheer necessity. Years ago, even teenagers would not have thought of appearing at a party without having answered the invitation. Also, years ago, when parties were given in houses with large staffs, it was not so important for the hostess to know the exact number of guests she might expect. Both costs and service were more flexible than they are today, when parties are served and food prepared by catering services that must know the exact quantity of food to be sent and number of waiters to be hired.

Therefore, while the lack of manners that makes the sending of these cards necessary is deplorable, I recognize the problem of the hostess who sends them. It must be admitted that it seems the only way to obtain the answers.

An answer card is usually small and engraved in the same style as the invitation, with a box to check that indicates whether the invited guest will attend or not. It is not wise to have a box saying, "Number that will attend," since some of the recipients may take that to mean that children, houseguests, or anyone else may be included.

Mr. Allen Fordyce

☐ accepts

☐ regrets

Friday, January second
Columbus Country Club

Invitations to private parties often include a self-addressed, stamped envelope with the card. Subscription-dance committees may send the envelope, but generally do not stamp it, as they are more concerned with costs. Another arrangement is to enclose a self-addressed, stamped postcard.

Etiquette has been made so simple for the receivers of these invitations that they can hardly fail to answer them. Having returned the card, they should not send a formal reply as well, as the hostess or committee undoubtedly is keeping a filing box and does not wish to receive the answers in a variety of shapes and sizes.

MAPS

If you live in the suburbs or country, and the location of your home or the club or hall where the party is to be held is unfamiliar to some of your guests, it is most helpful and courteous to draw a map of the best route to the place, have it reproduced, and enclose it with your invitations.

RECALLING AND REQUESTING INVITATIONS

A CHANGE OF PLANS

If invitations have to be recalled because of illness or for some other reason, the following forms are correct. They are always printed instead of being engraved—there being no time for engraving. In an emergency the message may be handwritten or given by telephone.

> *Owing to the sudden illness of their daughter*
> *Mr. and Mrs. John Huntington Smith*
> *are obliged to recall their invitations*
> *for Tuesday, the tenth of June*

When an engagement is broken after the wedding invitations have been issued:

> *Mr. and Mrs. Benjamin Nottingham*
> *announce that the marriage of their daughter*
> *Mary Katherine*
> *to*
> *Mr. Jerrold Atherton*
> *will not take place*

ASKING FOR AN INVITATION

One may never ask for an invitation for oneself anywhere. Nor does one ask to bring an extra person to a meal unless one knows it is a buffet at which one or two unexpected people could make no difference.

When regretting an invitation you may always explain that you are expecting to have weekend guests. Ordinarily the hostess-to-be says, "I'm sorry!" But if it happens that she is having a big buffet lunch or a cocktail party she may say, "Do bring them. I'd love to meet them."

Single men and women should not ask if they may bring dates to parties, especially if there is to be dancing. The hostess may well have planned on a good ratio of men to women, and if four or five men all ask to bring extra girls—or vice versa—the balance could be totally upset. If a hostess *wants* her guests to bring dates she should make that clear in her invitation.

Requests for invitations are almost always telephoned, so that the invitee's situation can be explained, and the hostess can also explain her "Of course" or "I'm afraid I have too many men already."

REPLIES

The form of acceptance or regret depends upon the form of the invitation received, for the degree of formality or informality is generally the same. The exception is this: If you receive an invitation to a dance, or perhaps a wedding invitation, from a good friend, and you cannot accept, you may well feel that the impersonal third-person reply is too formal and unfriendly. Because you want to explain your refusal, and perhaps extend your best wishes to the guest of honor or the bride, you would prefer to write a personal note. Do it. Just as the personal note is the most flattering kind of wedding invitation, it is also the friendliest type of reply under special circumstances. However, on most occasions, for acceptances and when there is nothing special to say, the "reply-in-kind" rule holds.

On the telephone, of course, there are no problems, but for the handwritten answer there are formulas that should be used. Once learned, the formal reply is the easiest to write, because no changes or embellishments are necessary other than in the names and the dates.

Your reply is always addressed to the person or people from whom the invitation came. If it is from "Mr. and Mrs. Arthur Smith" your reply goes to "Mr. and Mrs. Arthur Smith," even though you know that Mrs. Smith alone is keeping the records.

THE FORMAL ACCEPTANCE OR REGRET

Whether the invitation is to a dance, a dinner, or whatever, the answer is identical, with the exception of the pertinent word—that is, the following form may be used with the substitution of "a dance," etc., for "dinner."

Mr. and Mrs. Donald Lovejoy
accept with pleasure
the kind invitation of
Mr. and Mrs. William Jones Johnson, Jr.
for dinner
on Monday, the tenth of December
at eight o'clock

Also used, but not quite so formal, is this form:

Mr. and Mrs. Donald Lovejoy
accept with pleasure
Mr. and Mrs. Johnson's
kind invitation for dinner
on Monday, the tenth of December
at eight o'clock

Note that in the first form the full name, including "Jr." when appropriate, must be used, whereas in the second, "Mr. and Mrs. Johnson's" is sufficient.

When the wording of the invitation is:

Mr. and Mrs. Harvey Bullock
request the pleasure of your company, etc.

your reply may also say:

. . . accept with pleasure
your kind invitation for . . .

454

The formulas for regret:

Mr. and Mrs. Timothy Kerry
regret that they are unable to accept
the kind invitation of
Mr. and Mrs. Harvey Brent Smith
for Monday, the tenth of December

Mr. Sidney Hartford
regrets that he is unable to accept
Mr. and Mrs. Worldly's
kind invitation for dinner
on Monday, the tenth of December

"Monday, December the tenth," is sometimes used, but the wording above is better.

In accepting an invitation you must repeat the day and hour so that any mistake can be rectified. But if you decline an invitation it is not necessary to repeat the hour.

TO MORE THAN ONE HOSTESS

If the names of two or more hostesses appear on an invitation, the reply is addressed to the one at whose house the party is to take place; or if it is to be at a club or hotel, to the name and address indicated below the RSVP. (Without such indication you must address it to all of them at the hotel or club.)

When you write your answer you repeat the entire order of names that appears on the invitation, even though the envelope is addressed only to the name following the RSVP, or the first name on the list of hostesses.

Mrs. Donald Lovejoy
accepts with pleasure
the kind invitation of
Mrs. White and
Mrs. Black and
Mrs. Grey
for Tuesday, the tenth of November
at half after one o'clock

COMBINATION ACCEPTANCE AND REGRET

It is entirely proper for a wife or husband to take it for granted that either one alone will be welcome at a general wedding reception and to send an acceptance worded as follows:

Mrs. John Brown
accepts with pleasure
Mr. and Mrs. Smith's
kind invitation for
Saturday, the tenth of June
at eight o'clock
but regrets that
Mr. Brown
will be unable to attend

If it were the wife who could not attend, the wording would merely transpose the "Mr." and "Mrs."

TO AN ORGANIZATION

Miss Mary Jones
accepts with pleasure
the kind invitation of
The Alpha Chapter
of
Beta Chi Delta
for Monday afternoon, February twenty-third

TO A COMMITTEE

If the name of the committee or its organization is very long or complicated, you may write your reply in the following form:

Mr. and Mrs. Geoffrey Johnson
accept with pleasure
your kind invitation
for a Ball
on Saturday, the first of January

SEMIFORMAL REPLIES

ON VISITING CARDS AND INFORMALS

The reply on a visiting card is simply this:

sitting near each other. If, however, you notice that one of your neighbors is left with no one to talk to, common courtesy dictates that you should either include him in your conversation or turn at a break in your discussion to talk to him for a while.

The unbreakable rule is that you must at some time during dinner talk to both your neighbors. You must; that is all there is to it!

Even if you are placed next to someone in whom you have little interest, consideration for your hostess and the other guests demands that you give no outward sign of your dislike and that you make a pretense, at least for a little while, of talking together.

There are other more flexible rules, too. A popular guest does not talk at length about himself, he is not didactic but listens to his neighbors' point of view, and he does not (at length, at least) "talk shop."

"Shop talk" can dampen any party unless everyone there is involved in the same business, sport, or hobby. Have you ever been to a party on a Saturday night, where most of the men had played golf that day? If you were not an ardent golfer yourself, you might as well have stayed at home with a good book! In short, any guest who talks continually about one subject, regardless of the listener's interest, can only be classified as a bore.

AT THE START OF THE MEAL

At a small dinner women wait until the hostess is ready to seat herself before they sit down, unless she says, "Please sit down. I have to bring in another dish." At a large formal dinner, however, men help the women on their right to be seated as soon as they get to the table.

If there is a cold first course already on the table, you must wait for the hostess to pick up her fork or spoon before you start. However, after four or five guests have been served a hot course one of them should pick up his fork and start to eat, even though the hostess may have forgotten to say, "Please start."

SMOKING AT THE TABLE

At a truly formal dinner cigarettes are passed at the end of the salad course, if they are not already on the table. But there are numberless people who light their own cigarettes the moment they are seated at the table—and when young Mrs. Nicotinic lights her cigarette before laying her napkin across her knees and greets the man beside her from behind a veil of smoke, everyone else at the table feels free to follow her example. To stop this practice a hostess has no choice except to avoid putting ashtrays on the table—a clear indication that she would prefer that her guests wait until the cigarettes are passed. Since no guest can know his hostess' wishes until the table is in sight, he should always put out his cigarette before going in to the dining room, and when there are no ashtrays in sight he should refrain from lighting up.

SECOND HELPINGS

At formal dinners guests should not ask for second helpings. If dishes are passed a second time, anyone is free to help himself, even though others do not. At an informal dinner a guest may say to his hostess, "Is there more of that chicken? It is just delicious," and the hostess passes it to him or asks the maid to pass it around. If only one person takes a second helping, a considerate hostess will take a little too, so that her guest will not feel he is responsible for holding everyone up.

DIETERS AND TEETOTALERS

Dieters and teetotalers should never feel it necessary to eat anything that is injurious to their health or contrary to their moral standards.

If you are, for example, a vegetarian, you need not feel obliged to taste the roast. In most cases don't mention it to your hostess when you accept the invitation, because she will feel obliged to change her menu or prepare something special for you. You may tell her privately when you arrive, saying, "I am a confirmed vegetarian and I just wanted to tell you so you'll know why I'm not eating the meat." Or you may take a very little meat and leave it on your plate, since no one is required any longer to leave his plate clean. If you are concerned that your dietary restrictions will result in your not getting enough food you can always fortify yourself with a snack beforehand. If you know that *nothing* will be served that you can eat, as sometimes happens with Orthodox Jews, who eat only strictly kosher foods, you might better discuss it with your hostess beforehand. If it is a formal "public" dinner you might have to refuse the invitation, but if it is a "friendly" occasion you can tell the hostess you will bring a little dish for yourself, prepared according to your restrictions.

Teetotalers should not necessarily feel that they must refuse cocktail parties or dinners where liquor will be served. *Many* people do not touch alcohol, and there is nothing wrong whatever with saying, "No, thank you." If you are a teetotaler for moral reasons and disapprove of drinking in general, you should refuse invitations to homes where liquor is served, but you should do so without sermonizing or expressing your disapproval. However, if you do not drink yourself but enjoy the company of your friends who do, accept their invitations happily. Every good hostess has soft drinks of some kind available, but if you are worried about it, take a bottle or two of your favorite soda along. Leave it in the car unless you find that there is literally nothing you can drink in the house.

HELPING YOUR HOSTESS

No matter how much you want to help, or to keep your hostess company, don't follow her to the kitchen and chatter away while she is making her last-minute preparations.

When she rises to pass something, or to clear the table, don't jump up to help unless she has asked you to beforehand. You'll probably only get in her way. However, it can only be a help if you wish to offer to pass the cups around when she serves coffee after dinner.

At a dinner served by a maid (or butler) guests never try to help by handing her empty plates, stacking dishes, etc. An exception is a large restaurant table where the waiter cannot reach some of the places. In that case one of the guests, or the person beyond his reach, may take the plate from him and put it in its place. Guests do not talk to servants at a formal dinner other than to say "No thank you" or possibly to request something that the hostess is not aware of. Of course if you know a servant well and have not see her (or him) before a small dinner, you would greet her briefly when she passes something to you, saying, "Good evening, Mary—nice to see you," or whatever you wish.

Even though a hostess has no help, do not insist on clearing the table and washing the dishes. If the dinner is formal, or you are somewhat of a stranger, you should not even make the offer. At a more casual dinner you may ask, "Can't we help clean up?" but if your hostess says, "No, I'd really rather do it later," don't pursue it. Only when you are dining with closest friends or relatives, whose kitchen and habits you know well, should you try, unobtrusively, to get one load into the dishwasher.

AFTER DINNER

Guests do not put their napkins on the table until their hostess does. When she rises to signal the end of the meal, they do not prolong their conversation, but rise and go wherever she indicates.

If games are suggested after dinner, no matter how you feel

about them, try to look as though you think it's a fine idea and help you hostess to organize the group. Very often, especially if the guests do not have a great deal in common, entertainment that a hostess would ordinarily avoid can be the means of pulling a party together and making a delightful evening out of what started out as a very dull one.

DEPARTING

Once you have decided that it is time to go—GO! Nothing is more irritating than the guest who gets her coat, says good-bye to the other guests, and twenty minutes later is still standing in the open door giving last-minute words of wisdom to her hostess.

Try to be sensitive and aware of the people around you. Most hostesses are reluctant to try to "speed the parting guest," so make an effort to observe when your hosts—and others at the party—begin to look tired, and make the move to break it up yourself. When there is a guest of honor, it is supposedly his or her obligation to leave first. But many of them do not know this, and furthermore thay may be having a better time than some of the other guests and not want to leave as early. So, fortunately, that old rule is obsolete, and with the exception of when the President of the United States is present, guests at a large party may leave whenever they wish. They should, however, remain for at least one hour after dinner, as it is hardly complimentary to the hostess to "eat and run." At a small party a couple should not leave long before anyone else seems ready to go, because their departure is very apt to break up the party.

It is a good idea for husbands and wives to agree on approximately the time they think they should go home before they go to a party. Of course the hour would be subject to change if they were both very bored, or both having a wonderful time, but it would help to avoid the problem of one feeling very tired while the other gets a "second wind." Should one wish to stay on longer than the other, they must settle their argument quietly between themselves and not embarrass other guests and their hostess by having a loud argument.

If you have gone to a party in someone else's car, it is up to them to decide when to go home. You may, of course, say quietly to them, "We're ready whenever you are." But if you think there is a chance that you will want to go home earlier than the others, you will be wise to try to get to the party on your own.

GIFTS FOR YOUR HOSTESS

When a party is given especially for you, you should send flowers to your hostess beforehand. Other guests need not do this, although a few flowers sent later as a thank-you for a very special evening are alway appreciated. Ordinarily, however, neither a gift sent later nor a note is necessary, and your verbal thanks when you leave is enough. A phone call the next day to say how much you enjoyed the evening is *always* welcome.

I am, however, constantly asked about taking a gift of food or wine to your hostess when you go to a party. As far as food goes, I do not recommend it *unless* you consult with your hostess first. It is very disconcerting for a hostess who has planned a light dessert to follow a hearty meal to feel that she must serve a rich cake or a sugary pie brought by one of her guests. A box of candy or other food that can merely be passed after dinner or kept for another occasion is far more acceptable but not necessary at all.

The custom of taking wine as a gift to a small dinner party (one bottle only serves four, or possibly six at the most) is becoming very widespread. It is not too expensive or elaborate and has the advantage that if the hostess does not wish to serve it at once because she has planned another type of wine or a different beverage, she need not do so. If your gift goes well with her meal, and she feels it would be more popular than whatever she had planned on serving, she should certainly offer it, but no guest should ever feel insulted if his hostess says, "Thanks so much, but I already have white wine chilled and I'd like to save this red wine for the next time we have steak."

It is better not to take a gift at all to a larger or formal party —especially if you do not know the hosts well. It may not be customary among their friends, and you will only embarrass your hostess and other guests who have not brought a gift.

OVERNIGHT GUESTS

The entire guest situation may be put in one sentence. If you are an inflexible person, very set in your ways, don't visit!—Emily Post, 1922

Since hostesses for weekend parties or house parties have to do more planning than dinner hostesses it is essential that prospective guests answer the invitation promptly. If it is a telephoned invitation, don't say, "I'll have to find out about thus-and-so. I'll let you know next week." If you can't give a definite answer or promise one within a day or two, it is better to refuse. Let the hostess fill your place with someone else. You may, of course, say, "May I call you back tomorrow?" or "on Monday," or whatever, but never leave it indefinite or until a day or two before the weekend. Written replies, too, should be sent promptly, and should include the time of your arrival and your means of transportation: "Dear Joan, What a wonderful invitation. We plan to drive up by car, and should arrive about 7 o'clock Friday (the 12th). Can't wait to see you. . . ."

Guests who are coming and going by public transportation should have their return reservations confirmed. No matter how successful the house party, it should end when the hostess expects it to (which should be made clear in her invitation), and no guest should overstay his welcome because he suddenly finds there are no spaces left on the Sunday-night plane.

For other specific suggestions for houseguests and weekend visitors, see Chapter 36; for gifts for hostesses, Chapter 66.

IF YOU WANT TO BE ASKED AGAIN. . .

The perfect guest not only tries to wear becoming clothes but tries to put on an equally becoming mental attitude.—Emily Post, 1922

Any party—whether of four hours' duration or a whole weekend —will be a success if the guests are enthusiastic, congenial, and considerate. If they are none of these, there is nothing the hostess can do to save the occasion. So, while it is her responsibility to try to choose guests who will have fun together and cooperate to make the party a success, it is the guests' responsibility to help her.

Here are some of the things that you can do, or should not do, to be a welcome guest:

Leave your bathroom neat—*especially* if you are sharing it with someone else. This means that you fold towels neatly, use only those allotted to you, and don't use them for chores such as polishing your shoes. You wipe shaving-soap rings off the basin and rings off the bathtub, and you don't leave your cosmetics or shaving equipment spread all over the available space. Finally, you leave the toilet seat— and preferably the lid too—down.

At a dinner party, if there is a hamper in the powder room, wipe off the basin with your hand towel and put it in the hamper. Otherwise fold it loosely so that others will know it has been used.

If you borrow a book from your hosts, don't "dog-ear" it (turn the pages down). Find a piece of paper or something similar to use as a bookmark. Don't go home with a book you have started, without your host's permission. If he does suggest that you take it home, return it promptly unless he tells you explicitly that he does not want it back.

Wipe your feet carefully if it is muddy or wet outside, and keep them on the floor whatever the weather. No hostess is happy with a guest who stands on the upholstered furniture to reach something, or who lies back and puts his feet on the bed, the sofa, or an easy chair. If you need to reach something, ask your hostess for a stool, or find a kitchen chair that cannot be harmed. If you want to put your feet up, take your shoes off and remove the spread from the bed.

Speaking of furniture, don't tip chairs back on their rear legs if you value your hostess' friendship.

Use coasters for your drinks and ashtrays for your cigarettes.

If you do burn a table or a rug, break an ornament, or snap the back legs off the chair, don't "hide" the damage. Apologize at once and arrange to replace the item if possible or to pay for repairs if not. If it is a substantial amount perhaps your insurance policy will cover it.

Remember that very wise adage, "Neither a borrower nor a lender be." Try to take everything you need with you. But if you *must* borrow, return the article as soon as you no longer need it—in as good, or better, condition than when it was lent to you.

If you use the telephone for a long-distance call be sure to pay for it. You can

ask for the charges and pay your host in cash.

use a credit card if you have one.

reverse the charges.

charge the call to your house number.

In any case do not monopolize the telephone.

Finally, don't give orders to children or to servants in anyone else's home. *For information about tipping servants, see Chapter 36.*

⊸ᴈ41ᴈ⊸ Tips for Hosts and Hostesses

Tips on how to give a successful dinner party or weekend house party are thoroughly discussed in Chapters 29 and 36. This chapter is concerned with common problems of all sorts confronted by hosts and hostesses—and how to handle them.

UNINVITED GUESTS

"Drop-in," or unexpected, visitors, if you can judge by the mail I receive, cause as much confusion and ill-feeling as anything else I know of. People are thrown completely off-balance by the arrival of someone they have not expected—especially when it happens, as it often does, at the most inconvenient times.

Other than the normal requirement of being courteous to *any* visitor, you have no actual obligation to an unannounced visitor. If you are not busy and have no other plans, naturally you should ask him to stay, and entertain him as you would any guest.

But when he arrives just before mealtime, you have several choices. If you are having a stew or a meal that will stretch, and you value his friendship, ask him to join you. If the meal cannot possibly feed an extra person (or two, if the visitors are a couple), explain that you were about to eat and could he—or they—stop by later? He may say that he has already eaten, in which case ask him to sit down with you and have a cup of coffee or some after-dinner drink.

If guests arrive uninvited when you have other plans for the evening, say so. Your first obligation is to the people with whom you have made the plans. Tell the visitors that you are so sorry but the Joneses are expecting you for dinner (or whatever), and ask them to call you the next time they are in your neighborhood—thereby hint-ing that you would like some advance warning. Or if you wish, make a definite date to get together with them soon.

Of course, if your "plan" was just to run over to your sister's for a cup of coffee, and the drop-in visitors are your oldest friends whom you have not seen for years, you will undoubtedly want to call your sister and postpone your date until another evening. If she knows the guests too, you might ask her if you may bring them along, but you should not do that without warning her.

The same holds true when visitors "drop in" when you already have invited guests. You may ask the unexpected callers to have a drink or a cup of coffee if you are just sitting and chatting, but if you have invited a couple to play bridge, for example, your obligation is to them. Continue the game, asking the newcomers if they would like to join you and "kibitz." Only if the invited guests *insist* on stopping the game should you do so.

SINGLE WOMEN

Although single women are far less reluctant to go to a party by themselves than they used to be, there are still many—especially older women—who hesitate to do so. Either they feel left out of the generally marriage-oriented conversations or they are nervous about going and coming home by themselves.

Thoughtful hostesses are aware of this and ask a couple who pass near the single woman's home on the way, to pick her up and to take her home. And you, if you have one or more single friends, will be showing real consideration if you ask them to go with you to parties to which they are also invited.

LINGERING GUESTS

When a hostess feels that a party has passed its peak, but a few diehards don't seem to be ready to go home, what can she do? Must she sit and suffer or can she "speed the parting guest"?

She can, and she should.

The first, and usually the most effective, way to end a party is to close the bar. The host may offer "one last nightcap," and then—quite obviously—put the liquor away. The hostess may, more subtly, glance at her watch or hide a yawn. If these measures don't work, you can drop a broader hint. You might say, as Johnny Carson once suggested, "Would you mind dropping the kids off at school on your way home?" Or more seriously, copy Peg Bracken's story about the kindly professor who said loudly to his wife, "Well, my dear, don't you think it's time we went to bed so these good people can go home?"

When one of your guests makes a tentative suggestion that it is time to go home before you want the party to break up, you should make that clear, too. It is far friendlier for a host to say, "Oh, don't go—it's Saturday night, and we can all sleep late tomorrow morning," than to jump up and bring in the coats the minute someone says, "Well, it's getting late. . . ."

A house-party hostess may perfectly properly go to bed before her guests. All she need do is say something like this: "If you all don't mind, I'm going to bed because the baby will be crying for her bottle by six . . . but stay here as long as you want and help yourself to a beer or whatever you want. Just turn out the lights when you go up. . . ."

LIQUOR PROBLEMS

No gentleman goes to a lady's house if he is affected by alcohol. A gentleman seeing a young man who is not entirely himself in the presence of ladies, quietly induces the youth to depart. An older man addicted to the use of too much alcohol, need not be discussed, since he ceases to be asked to the houses of ladies.—Emily Post, 1922

Hosts who are doing their own bartending frequently run into a problem with their guests who want to mix their own drinks. Although the guests may simply be trying to be helpful, they often are more hindrance than help, especially if the host feels they are apt to be heavy-handed in pouring their drinks. Without being insulting, the host can hardly tell his friends to stay out of the bar. But he can control the situation somewhat. He can go to the bar *with* the men, and ask them to get out the ice or the mix or whatever while he pours the liquor himself. He can avoid having more than one bottle of any liquor in evidence. He can make it very obvious that he uses a jigger to pour drinks, and he can *hand* the jigger to his friends before they pour themselves.

When it becomes obvious that one of the guests has had too much to drink, the host or the person tending bar should not serve him more liquor. He may become insulted and abusive, but that is preferable to having him become more intoxicated.

The host is responsible for seeing that a drunken guest is taken home. He can ask a good friend to take him, he can go himself if the inebriated person's home is close by, or he can call a cab, give the directions, and pay for it. The man's car keys should be taken away if he is not willing to go with someone else. If he has reached the stage where he is about to pass out, two or three of the men should get him to a bed, and he should remain there overnight. If the offender has a wife or a date with him, the host and hostess should offer her accommodations too, or see that she gets safely home.

UNEXPECTED GIFTS

Although this subject was discussed in Chapter 40, it is worth mentioning from the hostess' side of the fence.

When a dinner guest arrives with an angel-food cake, or an apple pie, without having warned you in advance, you are put "on the spot." There is undoubtedly an obligation to serve it—to share it with the other guests. This is fine—if you have no dessert made, or if it could be served in addition to your dessert. But if you do have a very special dish ready to offer to your guests, the unexpected gift, like unexpected guests, need not be given priority. You are quite free to say, "Thank you so much—it looks wonderful. But I had promised a specialty of mine for tonight, so may I keep this to enjoy tomorrow?" Guests who have not "cleared" their intentions with their hostess beforehand should never be hurt when their gift is not served at the dinner. After all, they presumably made it for their hostess' enjoyment, and she should feel free to use it as she wishes.

Sometimes you may be given two or three cakes, or boxes of candy, or whatever. In this case it would be unreasonable to cut into, or open, all of them, so choose the one that seems to go best with your meal and appeal most to your friends, and offer that one.

The same rules apply to a gift of wine. If it goes with your menu, and you do not have another beverage planned, or another wine chilled, serve it. Otherwise thank the donor and tell him how much you will enjoy his gift at another meal.

SELECTING PRIZES

Hostesses at bridge parties, game parties, or any party where prizes will be given, face a problem. It is difficult to pick out something that will be appreciated when you don't know who will be the receiver. As one reader wrote to me, "I have just added another 'This is darling—what is it?' item to a drawer filled with bridge prizes. Each has seemed a great prize to an anxious hostess, but too often it's just another gadget to the winner." Here are two or three good-for-anybody ideas. A small potted plant (even one from your supermarket), which can be thrown out or planted outside when it stops blooming. A bottle of wine or sherry. If the recipient doesn't drink it herself, there will be members of her family, or visitors, who do. A box of really "good" candy. If the recipient is on a diet, she can use it as a gift to one of her nondieting friends.

These ideas may not be startlingly original, but they are infinitely better than the ornament that doesn't go with the style of your home, or the scarf that doesn't match any of your clothes.

THE HOSTESS' RECORD BOOK

One of the best ideas I can offer a hostess who entertains at all frequently is to keep a notebook in which you record the names of the guests at your parties, the dates the parties were held, and the menus you served. With this record, you will not serve the same people the same veal tarragon three times in a row, nor invite the Joneses every time you invite the Smythes. In addition you can make a note of foods that some of your friends particularly like or dislike, or to which they are allergic.

Part Eight

SPECIAL OCCASIONS

ᜒ42ᜒ The New Baby

BEFORE THE BABY COMES

When a baby is on the way—especially a first baby—friends and relatives rally round to help the expectant mother in any way they can, and to cheer her through the tedious months of her pregnancy.

Friends give showers, mothers who no longer need their bassinette or high chair fix them up and lend them, and others whose pregnancy is past lend maternity clothes.

For these favors no concrete repayment is expected. However, it would be courteous and friendly of the new mother to invite her shower hostess for lunch with one or two friends, or perhaps to take her and her husband out to dinner. A small gift such as a potted plant or a box of homemade cookies would show your appreciation for the baby furniture or the clothes, although a gift is not obligatory. The one requirement is that when you are finished with the maternity clothes they be returned to the lender (if they are still wearable) or passed on to another friend who is pregnant. The one who lent the clothes first may well say, "Keep them or give them away—I wore them until I was sick of the sight of them!" but she *might* be looking toward another pregnancy herself, and she should have the chance to refuse to take them back.

THE BABY'S HERE!

The first announcement of the birth of a baby is usually made to friends and relatives as soon as the proud father or delighted grandparents can get to the telephone. Sometime before the blessed event actually takes place, or immediately thereafter, the parents may, if they wish, visit a stationer's and select an announcement card to be sent to their friends, and those of the grandparents, who are close to the family. After the birth and as soon as the name is determined, the father notifies the stationer, and in a few days the cards are ready.

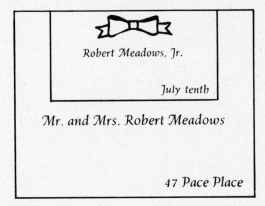

One of the nicest types of birth announcement consists simply of a very small card with the baby's name and birth date on it, tied with a pink or blue ribbon to the upper margin of the "Mr. and Mrs." card of the parents.

A large variety of commercially designed announcement cards with space for the baby's name, date of birth, and parents' names to be written in by hand are also available, and as they are much less expensive they are very popular. Some are in the best of taste, but those which include unnecessary data and foolish phrasing or coy designs are better left on the rack. Other parents design their own announcements, and if you have the talent these cards are the nicest of all.

To announce the birth of twins, have both their names printed on the small card, and if they are a boy and girl, use pink and blue ribbons. Or have a card printed, saying, "Mr. and Mrs. Harvey Smith announce the birth of twins," or "twin sons," followed by the names.

Our Baby Has Arrived

The arrival of a birth announcement carries *no obligation*—it does not mean that the recipient need send a gift. Parents sometimes hesitate to send cards for fear that that will be the reaction, and there will always be people who think it does require a gift. But they are wrong, and this should not discourage new parents from taking this pleasant way to let friends know about the happy event.

It *is* thoughtful, however, for those who receive announcements to send a note of congratulation to the new parents. Depending on your relationship, your message may be sentimental or humorous. Few of us could top the advice sent to a new mother by Arlene Francis: "Don't take any wooden nipples."

Announcements are sent for second and third (and additional) babies just as they are for the first.

ANNOUNCEMENT OF ADOPTION

It is a fine idea to send a card announcing an adoption to your friends and relatives. A card such as this will bring reassuring comfort to the child later on, should he or she ever doubt his place in the hearts of the family who chose him.

> *Mr. and Mrs. William Foster*
> *have the happiness to announce*
> *the adoption of*
> *Mary*
> *aged thirteen months*

Or if announcements are sent during the legal proceedings, the wording may be changed:

Mr. and Mrs. William Foster
have the happiness to announce
the arrival of
Mary,
born December fifteenth, 1975

If you choose to use a commercial birth announcement for your adopted child, choose one in which you can easily insert the words *adopted* or *adoption* in the wording, and one appropriate to the child's age. In other words don't select a card with a picture of a stork with a baby in its mouth to announce the arrival of your two-year-old adopted son. Again, if you can design a card appropriate to the situation, that will be the best announcement of all. One of the nicest I've ever seen was this card sent by a family who already had a son and a daughter.

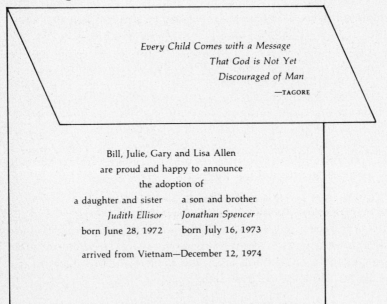

Every Child Comes with a Message
That God is Not Yet
Discouraged of Man

—TAGORE

Bill, Julie, Gary and Lisa Allen
are proud and happy to announce
the adoption of

a daughter and sister a son and brother
Judith Ellisor *Jonathan Spencer*
born June 28, 1972 born July 16, 1973

arrived from Vietnam—December 12, 1974

A SINGLE WOMAN'S ANNOUNCEMENT

When a mother and father are divorced before a baby's birth, the mother may, for a variety of reasons, wish to send out announcements. It is still a happy event for her, in spite of her marital situation. She does not, since she is no longer married, use "Mr. and Mrs." She should use whatever name she plans to be known by—probably

"Mrs. Mary Johnson." A widow would use "Mrs. James Johnson." In most cases, however, the new mother would prefer to write personal notes in which she could explain her new status as well as the baby's birth.

There are, today, some women who have no desire to get married, but wish to give birth to and raise their own child. There is no longer the stigma that used to be attached to the unwed mother, and if this is her choice and she is happy with it, she certainly may send announcements. Again, she uses the name and title she goes by ("Miss" or "Ms.") if the cards are printed; otherwise she, too, writes personal notes.

OFFICE ANNOUNCEMENTS

The picture of the puffed-up father strutting around offering cigars to everyone in sight is a thing of the past, but men should announce the happy event the first time they are in their office after the birth. They may, if they happen to smoke cigars themselves, pass a box around, but it is no longer the "expected" thing it used to be. In addition to a man's verbal announcement to his co-workers, his wife should send written announcements to his boss and to those closest to him in the office.

NEWSPAPER ANNOUNCEMENT OF BIRTH

In the week following the birth, the father may send a release to the local newspapers announcing the event: "Mr. and Mrs. Robert Meadows of 202 Park Avenue, New York City, announce the birth of a son, Robert, Jr., on July 10, 1968, at Doctors' Hospital. They have one daughter, Jane, four. Mrs. Meadows is the former Miss Mary Gilding." Or: "A daughter, Mary Jane, was born to Mr. and Mrs. John Phillips of 19 Maple Avenue, Hillsdale, on February 9 at St. Joseph's Hospital. Mrs. Phillips is the former Miss Mary Star of New Haven, Connecticut." The same announcement may be sent to the editor of the church newsletter or bulletin.

CHOOSING A NAME

It is nice for a name to have some significance, perhaps because of its original meaning or because it is traditionally carried by some member of the family. A child may also be named for a highly respected national figure or a beloved friend. However, many names are chosen simply because the parents like them or they are euphonious with the last name.

Many Christian first sons are given exactly the same name as their fathers, and "Jr." is added to distinguish between father and son. Or a child may be named for his father but given a middle name different from that of the parent. The name of a Roman Catholic baby, by canon law, must include the name of a saint. Although he may be called by any diminutive, his baptismal certificate must record the saint's name as the baby's first or middle one. Most Jewish babies are traditionally named for a deceased relative, and thus the name of a loved one is perpetuated.

Parents should be careful to avoid giving the baby a name that will be a handicap because it is too long or difficult to pronounce. Simple or biblical names will go well with most family names.

OTHER CONSIDERATIONS

Think of the nicknames that may evolve from the name you choose. "Bob," "Betty," or "Nick" are surely unobjectionable—if not very original—and they are certainly preferable to "Belly" for Belinda, "Leggy" for Allegra, etc.

A name that does not clearly indicate the owner's sex can be a constant source of embarrassment and irritation. Frances or Francis, Marian or Marion, Lynn or Lynne, are in this category. Unless you have strong family reasons for doing so, stay away from these ambiguous names for your child.

Sometimes the combination of first and last names can be a disaster. Pity the poor children whose parents thoughtlessly (or perhaps out of a perverted sense of humor) blighted their lives with these names: "Ophelia Legg," "Flora N. Forna," or "Ura Nicholsworth."

Initials, too, should be given some thought. Avoid combinations that could be used as a not-so-nice nickname—PIG, NUT, etc. For example, I doubt that the late senator Robert A. Taft had many articles marked with his initials.

Finally, if you have an unusual or complex last name, a simple, short first name would be the best choice. But if you are a Smith or a Brown, a more unusual first name will help to distinguish your child from all the other 579 Browns in the telephone book.

PRESENTS AND VISITS

Anyone who wishes to send a gift to the baby may do so. It may either be addressed to the parents at home or brought with you if you visit in person. It is thoughtful to bring something for the new mother too—cologne (if she uses it), a book, or perhaps a plant or flower arrangement.

Since the average stay in the hospital after a normal birth is no more than three or four days, and visiting hours and numbers of visitors are limited in most maternity wards, the majority of people who want to see the new mother and child must wait until they return home. If you do plan to visit in the hospital, call the mother first and find out during which visiting hours she expects to have few, or no, visitors. Later, when she is home, call to find out what time will be most convenient so that you do not interfere with naps, feedings, etc. Friends *should* do the calling first—they should not expect the busy new mother to call all her friends and relatives to say, "We're ready for visitors."

THANKS FOR PRESENTS

If a friend arrives at the hospital or the house with a gift for the baby, and the mother thanks her warmly at the time, she need *not* then write a note. However, when gifts are sent or delivered when she is not at home, a note—or a phone call to close friends—is in order.

The note may be handwritten, or on a thank-you card with a personal message. It should be signed with the mother's name, *not* the baby's. Everyone knows the baby can't say "Thank you" himself, and cards that say, "Baby . . . thanks you . . .," are painfully "cute."

CHRISTENINGS AND OTHER RELIGIOUS CERE-MONIES

TIME OF CHRISTENING

At one time it was required that a baby in the Roman Catholic or High Episcopal church be baptized on the first, or possibly the second, Sunday after its birth. In the Catholic church the baptism still takes place when the baby is very young—usually not over a month old—and always in the church or baptistery. In Latin countries babies are often baptized in the hospital, within a day or two of their birth. In Protestant churches the average age for christening is from two to six months, although in some denominations or under special conditions, children may not be christened until they are several years old. In all churches the mother should be present if she is able.

CHRISTENING INVITATIONS

Usually, christening invitations are given over the telephone —or to out-of-towners, by personal note.

Dear Jane,
We are having Karen christened on Sunday at 3:00 in Christ Church. Would you and Bob come to the ceremony at the church, and join us afterward at our house?

Love,
Sally

Or a message may be written on the "Mr. and Mrs." card of the parents, or on an informal, saying simply, "Karen's christening, St. Mary's Church, Jan. 10, 3 o'clock. Reception at our house afterward." All invitations to a christening should be very friendly and informal.

THE CHILD'S CLOTHES

The baby's christening dress is provided by the parents, not the godparents. It is often one that was worn by the baby's mother, father, or even one of his or her grand- or great-grandparents. Everything the baby wears on this occasion should be white, although this is merely a custom and not a church requirement. The traditional christening dress is long, made of sheer, soft material with lace and hand-embroidery trim, and worn with delicate long petticoats. It is not necessary to go to the expense of buying a traditional christening dress if there is no family heirloom; any long, or even short, plain white dress will do. However, some very pretty christening dresses are available in the new miracle fabrics, which are quite inexpensive.

In Protestant churches, when the children are older, little girls wear white dresses even though they may be well past the baby stage. Little boys, however, do not have to wear white suits. An Eton jacket, dark blue with matching shorts, is appropriate for very little ones, and older boys may wear a dark-blue or dark-gray suit.

WHAT THE GUESTS WEAR

The guests at a christening wear what they would wear to church. The mother wears a colored dress; she should not wear black on this occasion. According to the custom in her church, she may, or may not, wear a hat or a veil.

THE CHURCH CEREMONY

The clergyman, of course, is consulted about the place and hour for the christening before the guests are invited. The ceremony may take place at the close of the regular Sunday service, the guests remaining after the rest of the congregation leaves. Roman Catholic parishes generally schedule baptisms for a specified time on Sunday afternoons, and the parents make an appointment at the rectory in advance. If a large number of guests are invited to attend a Protestant christening, it is best to choose a weekday and an hour when the church is not being otherwise used. Some churches, due to pressure of time and work, are scheduling "mass" baptisms at which a number of children are baptized during one ceremony following the Sunday service.

The godmother, holding the baby in her arms, stands directly in front of the clergyman. The other godparents stand beside her, and relatives and friends nearby, or at their places in the front pews.

The godmother holding the baby must be sure to pronounce his name distinctly; in fact if the name is long or unusual it is wise to print it on a slip of paper and give it to the clergyman beforehand, because whatever name he pronounces is fixed for life. More than one baby has been given a name not intended for him. The godmother states the given name or names only, and not the surname.

In the Presbyterian church and others that do not require godparents, the father holds the baby and gives his or her name. There is no separate service—it is done during or immediately after the regular Sunday service.

As soon as the ceremony is over, the baby, the relatives, and the friends go to the house of the parents or grandparents, where a reception is usually arranged.

Baptism is a sacrament of the church, for which no fee is ever required. A donation, however, is presented in an envelope to the clergyman after the ceremony, commensurate with the elaborateness of the christening.

A HOUSE CHRISTENING

If the family is very high church or the baby is delicate and its christening therefore takes place when it is only a week or two old, the mother is carried into the drawing-room and put on a sofa near the improvised font. She is dressed in a becoming negligé and perhaps a cap, and with lace pillows behind her and a cover equally decorative over her feet. The guests in this event are only the family and the fewest possible intimate friends.—Emily Post, 1922

If permitted by the church to which the baby's parents belong, the house christening is a most satisfactory ceremony—because a baby whose routine has not been upset by being taken to a strange place at an unusual hour is more apt to be good.

The arrangements for a house christening are quite simple, the only necessary decoration being the font. This is always a bowl—usually of silver—put on a small, high table.

Most people prefer to cover the table in a dark fabric such as old brocade or velvet—a white napkin suggests a restaurant rather than a ritual and is therefore an unfortunate choice. Flowers may be arranged around the bowl in a flat circle, the blossoms outside, the stems toward the center and covered by the base of the bowl.

At the hour set for the ceremony, the clergyman enters the room, the guests form an open aisle, and he takes his place at the font. The godmother, or the father if there are no godparents, carries the baby and follows the clergyman; the other participants walk behind, and they all stand near the font. At the proper moment the clergyman takes the baby, baptizes it, and hands it back to the godmother or father, who holds it until the ceremony is over.

After performing the ceremony the clergyman, if he wears vestments, goes to a room that has been set apart for him, changes into his street clothes, and then returns to the living room as one of the guests.

THE CHRISTENING PARTY

The only difference between an ordinary informal reception and a christening party is that the latter features christening cake and "caudle." The christening cake is generally a white "lady" cake elaborately iced. A real caudle is a hot eggnog, drunk out of little punch cups. But today champagne or punch is usually substituted for the caudle, and those who have an aversion to punch are often offered a highball or a soft drink.

Guests eat the cake as a sign that they partake of the baby's hospitality and are therefore his friends, and they drink the punch to his health and prosperity. But by this time hopefully the young host or hostess is peacefully asleep in the nursery.

Gifts are usually taken to the baby, since those invited are presumably very close to the family.

JEWISH CEREMONIES FOR THE NEWBORN

On the eighth day after birth, in the ceremony known as *brith milah*, a boy is initiated into the Jewish covenant between man and God. The circumcision is accompanied by a religious ceremony during which the boy is named. After the ceremony, which may take place in a special room in the hospital, there is a light collation. The guests drink to the baby's future and toast the parents, grandparents, and witnesses. Relatives and close friends are invited to the *brith* by telephone or informal note. They dress as they would for a service in a synagogue, and both men and women customarily wear hats.

Girls are named in the synagogue on the first Sabbath after birth, when the father is called up to the Torah. Sometimes the naming is postponed until the mother is able to be present. In some Reform congregations boys are also named in the synagogue (in addition to being named at the *brith*) when both parents are present, and a special blessing is pronounced by the rabbi. The mother may be hostess at the reception following the service. Friends and relatives may be invited to attend the religious service during which the baby will be named.

The ceremony of redemption of the firstborn, the *pidyon ha-ben*, which takes place only if the firstborn is a boy, is performed when the baby is thirty-one days old. According to ancient custom described in the Bible, the firstborn son was dedicated to the service of God. It became customary for a *cohen* (a descendant of the priestly tribe) to redeem the child from his obligation, entrusting him to the care of his father for upbringing in the Jewish faith. The *pidyon ha-ben*, consisting of a brief ceremony and a celebration, is held in the home. Informal notes of invitation are sent about ten days beforehand to close friends and relatives.

GODPARENTS

If your faith requires godparents they should be asked and their consent obtained before the day of the christening is set. They may be asked to serve when the baby's arrival is announced to them, and in some cases they are asked even before the birth. In Protestant practice, there are usually two godfathers and one godmother for a boy, two godmothers and one godfather for a girl. A Catholic baby has one godparent of each sex, who must be Catholics, too. (Catholics are not allowed to serve as godparents for children of other faiths.)

It is perfectly correct to send a note if the godparent lives at a distance, or he may be asked by telegraph: "It's a boy. Will you be godfather?" Those who live nearby are asked by telephone.

If a godparent is unable to be present, a proxy acts for him or her at the ceremony, the consent of the real godparent having first been given. It is considerate for the real godparent to send a note to the clergyman authorizing the proxy.

One must never ask any but a most intimate friend to be a

godmother or godfather, for it is a responsibility not to be undertaken lightly and also one difficult to refuse. Godparents are usually chosen from among friends rather than relatives, because one advantage of godparents is that they add to the child's stock of "relatives." But when a child is born with plenty of relatives who can be called upon in time of need, godparents are sometimes chosen from among them.

The obligation of being a godparent is essentially a spiritual one; therefore the godparent should be of the same faith as the parents. The godparent is supposed to see that the child is given religious training and is confirmed at the proper time. Beyond these obligations he is expected to take a special interest in the child, much as a very near relative would do. He remembers his godchild with a gift on birthdays and at Christmas until the child is grown—or perhaps longer if they remain close. Godparents who live far away and have lost contact with the child and his or her parents need not continue to give presents after the threads of friendship have broken.

If there are other children in the family, the godparent might choose a gift that could be enjoyed by *all* of them, but he need not give individual gifts to the others. Each of them has his *own* godparents to take care of him.

Godparents do not, as is sometimes thought, have any obligation to give financial assistance or to adopt children who lose their parents. This responsibility is the guardian's—not the godparent's. Naturally, since they are—or were—close to the parents, they will offer to help in any way they can, but their actual obligation is spiritual only.

At the christening, godparents give the baby as nice a present as they can afford. The typical gift is a silver mug or porringer, inscribed, for example:

> *Robert Meadows, Jr.*
> *December 5, 1975*
> *From his godfather*
> *John Strong.*

Other typical presents are a silver fork and spoon, a silver comb and brush set, a government bond, or a trust fund to which the donor may add each year until the child is grown.

ꞏ§43§ꞏ *First Communion, Confirmation, and Bar Mitzvah*

FIRST COMMUNION

First Communion for a Catholic child takes place when the young-ster is six or seven. It is the first occasion on which he actually re-ceives the Host, and is an important event in his religious life. The child goes through a simple course of instruction, to learn both the meaning and the ritual, and his class takes First Communion together.

Although some families celebrate the occasion with elaborate festivities, most, because of the youth of the participants, restrict the celebration to relatives and perhaps a few close friends. These attend the service, and if they are also Catholics, participate in the Mass. The little girls wear white dresses, some with elaborate veils and headpieces, and in other congregations, simpler white costumes. The boys wear dark suits with white shirts and ties.

Usually a small party is held for the young celebrant at the parents' home, or the family may go to his favorite restaurant for a dinner party.

Immediate family members give meaningful gifts of a lasting nature.

CONFIRMATION

Catholic children are generally confirmed when they are eleven or twelve, Protestants a year or two older. However, if one was not confirmed as a child, it may be done at any age, and there is a special confirmation for those who change their faith.

The candidates for confirmation in all faiths undergo a period of instruction. Those who complete these lessons satisfactorily are confirmed by a bishop or other high church dignitary in the manner of a graduating class. The service, which in the Protestant church is held at a regular Sunday service, and which in the Catholic church is separate from the regular Mass, is attended by members of the families and close friends of the young people.

Some churches hold an informal reception after the ceremony, at which the parents and friends may have a chance to meet and chat with the visiting churchman who performed the confirmation.

Afterward the family and a few friends usually gather at the house for lunch, and those who wish to, give the newly confirmed youngster a gift. This is often of a religious nature—a Bible with his name engraved on it, a prayer book, a gold cross, a medal, or a charm of a religious nature are appropriate choices.

Catholic girls wear white dresses and sometimes a short veil. Some Protestant clergymen request that the girls wear white, but most only ask that they wear simple, modest dresses in quiet colors. This is up to the discretion of the minister. In both Protestant and Catholic churches, the boys wear dark-blue or dark-gray suits.

Confirmation is a religious occasion rather than a social one. It is the moment when the young person himself confirms the vows that were made for him by his godparents at the time of his baptism. It is a thoughtful and serious event and therefore is celebrated joyfully—but with restraint.

BAR MITZVAH

For a Jewish boy the ceremony that compares to the Christian confirmation is the Bar Mitzvah. There is a corresponding ceremony for girls of thirteen in some Conservative and Reform congregations, the Bat Mitzvah. The following paragraphs might apply to either a Bar Mitzvah or a Bat Mitzvah, but the girls' ceremony is not so widely celebrated—nor so elaborately—as the boys'. In the Orthodox and Conservative branches, and in some Reform congregations, the Bar Mitzvah takes place on the first Sabbath (Saturday) after the boy becomes thirteen. As in the Christian church, candidates have undergone a period of religious instruction prior to the ceremony. Other Reform congregations have replaced the Bar Mitzvah with a "confirmation" service at which both boys and girls are confirmed, sometimes at an older age than the traditional thirteen. A Jewish boy's Bar Mitzvah or confirmation celebrates his acceptance as an adult member of his congregation.

The Bar Mitzvah differs from the Christian confirmation in that, in addition to being a deeply religious occasion, it is always celebrated socially as well. It is one of the most important events in the boy's life, and the family generally bends every effort to make it as wonderful an occasion as they can. The religious ceremony, which takes place on Saturday morning, may be followed immediately by a gathering in the social rooms of the synagogue. This is open to any member of the congregation who wishes to offer his congratulations.

The party—luncheon, dinner, or reception—that follows later in the day usually includes all the close friends of the parents as well as friends and classmates of the boy. Only those who receive invitations may attend.

Invitations may be engraved in third-person style if the party is formal; they may be handwritten notes or they may be telephoned if it is not. Often many more people are invited to the reception than can be accommodated at the synagogue, so the invitation must be quite explicit as to the hour, the place, and the occasion. It must, like other invitations, be acknowledged promptly, and in kind.

For the ceremony, guests wear the clothes that they ordinarily choose for a religious service. And if the party is a luncheon, they go directly to it without changing. If the celebration is later in the day, they change into clothes more appropriate for an evening party. If the affair is formal or "black tie," this should be specified on the invitation. Otherwise the women wear cocktail dresses or long skirts and the men wear dark suits.

Everyone invited to a Bar Mitzvah is expected to send, or take, a gift. Something of a permanent nature to serve as a reminder of the occasion is most appropriate, but gifts of money are also acceptable. A piece of jewelry, such as a tie clip is typical, as well as a wallet, a leather desk set, a book on a favorite hobby—the list is limitless.

The boy must, of course, write thank-you letters promptly for each and every gift.

The reception itself is just like any other. Dinners and luncheons may be sit-down or buffet, and the party may be held at home or in a club, hotel, or restaurant. There may or may not be an orchestra, but if many young people are invited, they will enjoy dancing after the meal is over.

~⁊44⁊~ Graduation

INVITATIONS AND ANNOUNCEMENTS

Attendance at schools and colleges has grown so fast that the facilities of these institutions cannot handle the crowds of parents and friends who would like to attend the graduation festivities. Years ago graduates could invite their entire families, and often friends, too. Today almost every educational institution limits the number of visitors each student may invite—often to no more than four. The invitations are usually provided by the school, but if they are not, the parents or the graduate himself may write them, have them printed, or issue them by telephone. The graduate and his (or her) family must select the recipients very carefully so that there will be no hurt feelings. If, for instance, both sets of grandparents would like to be included, the ones who receive the invitations must be chosen with great tact. The choice might be made on the basis of which ones live closest, or are better able to travel. If there are no valid reasons for choosing one over another, names might be drawn out of a hat—perhaps the fairest solution of all. Whatever the reason, those not invited must be convinced that the choice is fair and not guided by preference, and the ones who do not attend the ceremony should be included at any other festivities that take place.

The restriction on the number of invitations allowed has led many people to send graduation announcements. This is all right as long as the list is restricted to close family, who would otherwise be invited to the ceremony, and to friends of long standing. These announcements are intended only to spread the good news and *should* carry no obligation at all. But the current rage for giving gifts for every occasion has made announcements appear to be a request for yet another donation. So the list should include only those who would *want* to send presents, or you may write at the bottom, "No gifts, please."

The announcements are generally printed formally, but if the graduate is creative there is no reason why he should not design and make his own. Many young people prefer to do this or to buy informal illustrated cards, feeling that it seems more natural to them and less foreign to their life-style.

When the school distributes announcements, as some do, the graduate's name is filled in the appropriate space in black ink, or he may have visiting cards printed and enclose these with the announcement. A male graduate uses "Mr." on his card; a girl uses "Miss." A married student uses her married name on the card of announcement, but if she is sending any to schoolmates or to people who do not know she is married she may add "(Susan Crow)" under the married name.

If for any reason a student does not graduate with his class, but must make up a credit or take an exam over, he may not send out his announcements at the time his class graduates, even though they have been printed. He should keep them and may write in a new date and send them when he has met the necessary requirements. Those who complete their courses and "graduate" at midterm or anytime other than the normal end of the school year, also send their announcements and celebrate the event then—not the preceding or following June.

GRADUATION PROGRAMS

Because the activities differ widely in each of our thousands of schools and colleges, no definite schedule for commencement week can be given. Graduation or commencement programs at the high-school level are much the same as at colleges, but on a modified scale. The senior-class dance is most likely to be attended by the graduates and their dates only, although at some preparatory schools the graduates' families are invited too. For many years senior parties were informal, but there is a decided trend back toward more formal parties, including "black-tie" dress, flowers for the girls, and receiving lines. There may be a class play or a varsity game attended by parents and dates, or there may be nothing other than the graduation ceremony itself.

Although college and university commencement-week festivities start for the students a week or more in advance of the actual graduation day, the events to which families and friends are invited take place only on the last day or two before commencement. These events usually consist of any or all of the following: a senior-class play—generally a comedy or review that sometimes involves the class history, attended by everyone; fraternity, club, or class parties, to which the graduates' dates are invited; special events peculiar to a particular college, such as torchlight parades or barn dances. Finally, the baccalaureate service and the commencement exercises, which are attended by every guest, complete the festivities.

MAKING RESERVATIONS

It is essential in this day of large college classes for the graduates to make reservations for their families well in advance of graduation day. Because many hotels and inns have no rooms left to reserve by the time Christmas vacation arrives, it is well to think of this during the fall term, especially if the college is in a small town that does not have too many accommodations. Parents should find out how many guests each senior may have and then consult with their son or daughter as to whom he or she wishes to invite. If the graduate has a fiancé or a serious boy or girl friend, the graduate makes a reservation for him, too.

THE SENIOR'S DATE

The male senior's date, unless she has friends in town with whom she wishes to stay, stays in the same hotel or motel as the graduate's family. She attends the events at which the students are separated from their guests—the baccalaureate service and commencement exercises, for example—with his parents. Male dates of female graduates accompany the family to these events, too, although they do not *necessarily* stay in the same lodgings.

If the senior's family cannot attend, he may ask the parents of one of his friends whether his date may go with them to the exercises, so that she need not sit alone. He should, if possible, find a room for her near the same family.

CLOTHING

Clothing varies with the activities planned, of course, but it is much the same as for similar social events elsewhere. Guests are usually sent a program well in advance, either by their son or daughter or by the college, and can determine then what may be needed.

Since most graduations take place in June and it is apt to be very warm, mothers and girl friends will look prettiest and be most comfortable in cool summer dresses for the baccalaureate and commencement services. A dress with a matching jacket or sweater is an ideal choice, in case it does turn cold or damp. Naturally, if any of the parties are formal, the men attending must wear tuxedos, and the women long dresses or evening pants costumes.

Hats are not required at either the baccalaureate service or commencement, but if you wish to wear one it is perfectly correct. Since those behind you will want to have a clear view of the proceedings you should either choose a close-fitting hat or remove it as you would in the theater.

PRESENTS

Graduation presents are unlimited in variety, but the closer the giver is to the graduate, the more elaborate the gift. Parents may give a fine watch, jewelry, an automobile, or even a trip to Europe. If these gifts are beyond their means, anything that is lasting and of the best quality that they can afford is always appreciated. A nicely bound book on a favorite subject, for instance, or a good pen-and-pencil set can be a source of much pleasure.

For other specific gift suggestions, see Chapter 66.

THANK-YOU NOTES

A note of thanks, written by hand, must go to everyone who has not been at the commencement or been thanked in person. This note need not be long, but it should express appreciation and be written as promptly as possible.

Dear Aunt Mary,

I can't thank you enough for the check you sent me, which will be such a help toward my summer in Europe. I'm looking forward to seeing you in the fall to tell you all about the trip.

With much love,
Jane

Or:

Dear Uncle Jim,

Thank you so much for the pen-and-pencil set. Mother must have tipped you off that I really needed them! I was disappointed that you couldn't make the graduation, but I'll drive down to see you and thank you in person as soon as possible.

Thanks again,
Bill

GIFTS FOR OTHER GRADUATES

Although it is not obligatory it is a very nice gesture for parents of a graduating senior to have small gifts for his (or her) roommate and closest friends.

GRADUATION PARTIES

Parties are frequently held to celebrate high-school graduations, but rarely for college graduations. Occasionally a young man or woman's family will give a small dinner or a reception when he or she receives a graduate degree, but in most cases the graduation gift is the only special acknowledgment of the occasion. This section, therefore, is primarily devoted to high-school graduation celebrations.

Invitations should be sent out at least three weeks ahead if you wish to be sure that your particular friends will be there. Several other members of the class may be planning parties, too, and some may have selected the same night you have. If your class is not too large it is wise to try to talk to other seniors and coordinate your plans so that not everyone chooses graduation night, or the following Saturday, for the parties.

The gay, illustrated invitations available at all stationers are ideal for the occasion, since very few of these parties are "formal." Write at the top, "In honor of Sue's graduation," because your parents—rather than you—give the party. You may write "RSVP" at the bottom, followed by a telephone number, or you may prefer to write "Regrets only." Either of these impose easier or fewer obligations on your friends than "RSVP" followed by an address. If your party is to be catered, so that you must know the number of guests coming, and you know that people in your group are slow to reply, you may enclose a response card.

There are very few "rules" about graduation parties—your party should be whatever you and your friends enjoy most. It may be a dance at home or in a club or hall, it may be a dinner party at home or in a restaurant, or it may be an after-dinner party, a barbecue, or a picnic. Your guest list may be made up mostly of relatives if you have a large, close-knit family, or it may be all your classmates and only enough adults to organize the party and help with the food, drinks, etc.

It may be held on graduation night, or anytime thereafter, but it should *not* be held before you have received word that you are to graduate. If you are having many adults, choose a Friday or Saturday night, so that they will not have to go home too early in order to be ready for work the next day.

Although relatives would undoubtedly bring gifts to a small, intimate party, guests at a big celebration should not be expected to bring presents. If a few do, the boxes should be unwrapped somewhat privately with only the donors present, so that other guests will not feel that they were remiss in not giving a gift too. Or the presents may be set aside and opened after the party, for the same reason. If everyone brings gifts they should all be opened at one time with the guests sitting around and watching.

Whatever type of party you plan, you and your mother should stand near the door and greet the guests. This is not a formal receiving line, but the party is in your honor, and the guest of honor, whatever the person's age, should always be standing where the arrivals can greet and congratulate him or her.

If the party is a seated family dinner, you (if you are a girl) sit on your father's right; a boy would sit on his mother's right—the places "of honor." You may choose who sits on your other side, and where the other guests sit. If, at a larger party, there are a number of small tables, you should feel free to choose the people you want to sit with you. You may want your parents there, or you may prefer to sit with a group of your best friends.

Otherwise graduation parties are just like all others, and are generally great successes because the occasion is such a happy one.

◦§45◦ Anniversaries

Anniversary parties are discussed in Chapter 34. However, there are many considerations other than the celebration itself, and this chapter answers the questions that are frequently asked.

REMEMBERING ANNIVERSARIES

It takes a very remarkable person to remember all the anniversaries and birthdays that he should—especially if he has a large family. Here are three suggestions to help you:

1. Make a chart of twelve squares—one for each month of the year. Label them January, February, etc., but do not put Monday, Tuesday, and so on down. Then, in each square, note the appropriate dates, occasions, and names. In the square marked January, you might list:
   12th—Anne's birthday
   17th—Fred and Sue's anniversary
   This chart is good forever and should be hung by your desk, your bulletin board, or wherever it will be noticed.
2. At the beginning of the year take a regular calendar and fill in all the anniversaries and birthdays you want to remember on the appropriate days. Each January spend a few minutes transferring the notations to your new calendar.
3. At the beginning of each month, address cards to the people you will want to send them to that month. Have them stamped and ready to go, and keep a list of the dates they are to be mailed on top of the pile. Again, keep the pile in a place where you will be sure to notice it.

Incidentally, couples who divorce and subsequently remarry each other, celebrate the anniversary of their *first* marriage, counting their twenty-fifth as twenty-five years from that date and forgetting the intervening years of separation.

ELDERLY COUPLES

Some couples who are celebrating their fiftieth anniversaries are so elderly or infirm that they must be given special consideration. They should not be asked to stand to greet their guests, but should be seated in a central spot where people can pass by comfortably to offer congratulations. In most cases it is best to plan to have the party in their home, or perhaps in the home of one of their children, rather than in a restaurant or hall.

If the couple is not up to any party at all, a lovely thing to do is to arrange a card shower. A daughter or'son sends out cards saying that the parents' anniversary will be celebrated by a card shower, and would the "guest" attend by sending a card. No other gift is expected, but the couple will be delighted with the messages of love and congratulations carried in the cards.

Some couples who marry late in life may feel that they will never reach their golden anniversary and ask whether they may have a big celebration on their thirty-fifth or fortieth. Of course they may! There is nothing "magical" about the fiftieth, and a couple may celebrate any anniversary they choose to. It is tradition only that makes the fiftieth the "big" one.

WIDOWS AND WIDOWERS

Even though you want someone who has lost his or her mate to know that you haven't forgotten their anniversary, you should not send a congratulatory card. The nicest thing you can do for people who are recently bereaved, if you live close enough, is to take them out to dinner, or have them to your home that day. This will give them something to look forward to and keep them from being lonely and sad.

For those farther away, to whom you have always sent a card, write a letter instead. You need not mention the bereavement or the anniversary other than to say, "We want you to know we are thinking of you today."

When one member of a couple is ill, or perhaps in a nursing home, the other will not feel like celebrating alone. But family and friends can make it a special occasion in the same way mentioned above—by taking him or her out to dinner, or having a few close friends for dinner in their home.

GIFTS

Specific gift suggestions will be found in Chapter 66.

Information on opening gifts at anniversary parties is discussed in Chapter 34.

Gifts are almost always taken to a couple celebrating an early anniversary because they are usually in need of household articles of every sort. But when a couple have been married twenty-five years or more, they probably have all the material things they can use. If they wish, it is perfectly correct to say "No gifts, please" on the invitations. Guests receiving those invitations should *not* take gifts to the party, since this is embarrassing to the anniversary couple, and to those guests who abided by the request. Very close friends or relatives, who really wish to give the couple a remembrance, and perhaps know of something they especially want, should take their presents to the couple's home at some time before the party.

No one giving a twenty-fifth-anniversary party should *ever* write "No silver" or "No silver gifts, please." That is simply a clear hint that while the couple do not want silver they *do* expect other gifts.

Nor is it ever proper for a hostess to request a gift of money for herself, so a couple giving their own anniversary party cannot, in good taste, suggest to their friends that they would like gifts of cash. But when a relative or friend is giving the party and knows of something the couple long for, the hostess may enclose a note with the invitations explaining that the couple being honored want, for example, to go on a cruise, and if the guests would like to help make it possible, would they, instead of bringing a gift, send a small check to the "Anywhere Travel Agency." If the travel agency does not feel it can handle money sent in this way, the hostess may have the contributions sent to her, and also would, of course, keep the amounts secret. In any case she would then make up a packet of folders, tickets, boat plans, and a card signed by all the guests, to be presented at the party. In this way the couple would not know the exact amounts contributed, and the mercenary aspect would be missing—replaced by the joy of knowing that the gifts would be truly appreciated.

Although in most circumstances I consider gifts of "pure" money in poor taste, a fiftieth anniversary can be an exception. The idea of giving is, of course, to please the recipient, and it is undeniably true that many older couples, perhaps living on a small pension or social security, appreciate cash more than gifts, which they neither need nor have room for. For them, a "money tree" is acceptable and practical.

The person giving the party sends a note with the invitation saying something on this order: "We are planning a money tree for Mother and Dad, and if you would like to add a twig, please send whatever you wish to me at the above address." An artificial tree or a dry branch is hung with rolled-up bills or checks, tied with gay ribbons, and the cards are collected separately to be given to the anniversary couple.

For couples who might resent gifts of money, and in fact do not want personal gifts at all, there is yet another solution. A card is enclosed with the invitation, reading, "In place of gifts, please, if you wish, send a contribution to Mother and Dad's favorite charity—the 'XYZ Research Foundation.' " The check may be sent with a note saying, "Please accept this contribution in honor of the fiftieth anniversary of Mr. and Mrs. John Doe."

When gifts are given they need not necessarily be of the traditional material allotted to each anniversary. But many people feel that it is more meaningful if they are, and the following list has been modified to include modern materials in some cases. When an article of the original material cannot be purchased, something similar but not identical may be chosen—for example, a stainless-steel or pewter platter instead of a silver one would be acceptable (and perhaps preferred) on a twenty-fifth anniversary. For all anniversaries a lovely flower arrangement or a plant that can be set out in the couple's garden is always appropriate.

Here are the traditional anniversary gifts:

1.	Paper or plastics	12.	Linen (table, bed, etc.)
2.	Calico or cotton	13.	Lace
3.	Leather or simulated leather	14.	Ivory
4.	Silk or synthetic material	15.	Crystal or glass
5.	Wood	20.	China
6.	Iron	25.	Silver
7.	Copper or wool	30.	Pearls
8.	Electrical appliances	35.	Coral and jade
9.	Pottery	40.	Ruby
10.	Tin or aluminum	45.	Sapphire
11.	Steel	50.	Gold
		60.	Diamond

MARKING GIFTS

Gifts of silver are still often given on twenty-fifth anniversaries. A couple's children, for example, may get together and give their parents a beautiful silver tray, a bowl, a coffeepot, etc. These gifts should be marked to commemorate the occasion. The two simplest and most satisfactory forms are:

1950–1975
to
Mom and Dad
from
Jane and Rick
Helen and Bill

or:

To Mom and Dad
on their twenty-fifth anniversary
from
etc.

Once in a while, the children giving a party for their parents present mementos of the occasion to all the guests. These gifts, too, are monogrammed. There are several choices, depending on relationships and costs. If it is not too expensive it is nice to have silver, leather, or glass marked with the anniversary couple's name and the date. The articles for their sons and daughters might be engraved:

Mom and Dad
October 10
1950–1975

and those for friends:

Jean and Harry
October 10
1950–1975

If this is impractical or too expensive, simple mementos such as paper match boxes or coasters could be marked and distributed:

JSP and HTP

or:

Jean and Harry Porter
October 10
1950–1975

A "CONFERENCE CALL"

A lovely gift to a couple whose children are scattered and far away is a "conference call." The person giving the party can arrange with the telephone company to connect the lines so that all members of the family can talk together at an appointed hour. This could, in many cases, be the most wonderful gift the couple receive.

REAFFIRMATION OF MARRIAGE VOWS

Some couples want to reaffirm their marriage vows on their twenty-fifth or fiftieth anniversaries. They may have—insofar as it is feasible—a duplicate of their entire wedding ceremony, or they may have only a simple repetition of the vows. As many members as possible of the original wedding party gather for the service. If there are children they sometimes stand with the couple, or if the best man and maid of honor are present they may stand and the children sit in the first pew.

The "bride" should not wear her wedding dress, nor should the couple and attendants walk up the aisle or otherwise try to reenact the wedding. Women wear dresses appropriate to the hour of the day, and men wear business suits in the daytime and either suits or tuxedos, whichever is indicated, in the evening.

After the service, everyone may be invited to the couple's home for a reception, and a replica of the wedding cake may be served as dessert, or with coffee and champagne. Toasts by members of the "wedding party" and the couple's children are in order.

❧46❧ *Funerals*

As a person becomes of age, or decides that he should make a will, he must also consider how and where he would like to be buried. These wishes may be put into his will, and while they are not irrevocable, the family will naturally give them every consideration. If he does not include them in his will, he should at some point discuss the question with those closest to him so they will be able to arrange for the type of burial that he would have chosen himself. He may also leave a note giving burial instructions with his personal papers.

If his parents have a plot in a cemetery, he should know whether there is space for him (and his wife, if she wishes) to be buried there, or he should think about purchasing a plot for himself and his own family. If he wishes to be cremated the law requires that his nearest relatives give permission, and in many states the deceased must have expressed this desire in his will. Therefore he should make his desires very clear in a signed and sealed letter, to "be opened in the event of death," addressed to his wife (or husband, if we are speaking of a woman), his children, and his brothers or sisters.

Although few people like to think of death in personal terms, it is wise for the head of the family, at least, to have a space set aside in which he keeps a copy of his will and the name of the attorney who drew it up, a deed to a burial plot if he has one, a list of the location of safe-deposit boxes, mortgages, bank accounts, etc., and any personal instructions he may wish to leave in case of his death. The other members of the family should know the location of these papers and something about their contents. The small amount of effort necessary to put such a sensible precaution into effect is nothing compared to the help it can be to a stunned and confused family at the time of death.

IMMEDIATE STEPS

At the actual time of death, when the bereaved feel baffled and alone, etiquette performs a most valuable service by smoothing the necessary personal contacts and making sure that the last rites will be performed with beauty and gravity.

At this time it is of immeasurable help if a very good friend is willing to take charge of the funeral arrangements. The persons closest to the deceased may be in such an emotional state that it is impossible for them to make rational decisions, and they may rush, or be pushed, into situations that they later regret. If no such friend is at hand, then decisions must be made by a relative, possibly one who is not of the immediate family, a nephew or a cousin, perhaps. This lot often falls to a son of the deceased, however, and he must exercise strict self-control.

NOTIFYING FAMILY AND CLOSE FRIENDS

If members of the immediate family are not already present, the first act of someone at the bedside of the deceased is to notify them. At the same time one or two intimate friends whose capability and sympathy can be counted on should be alerted.

Members of the family and other close friends should be called on the telephone. Relatives, even though they live at some distance, should also be called, but if expense is a factor, friends and more distant relatives may be notified by telegram.

THE DEATH CERTIFICATE

The death certificate is filled out and signed by the physician in attendance at the time of death. If the death was sudden or caused by an accident, or if for any other reason there was no doctor in attendance, the county medical examiner or coroner must be called in to ascertain the cause of death and sign the certificate. This must be done immediately, because no other steps can be taken until the death certificate is properly signed.

NOTIFYING AN ATTORNEY

The next step is to notify an attorney, preferably the one who drew up the will of the deceased. If neither he nor anyone in his firm is available, then any other attorney who is reputable—perhaps one who has been retained by another member of the family or one who is a personal friend—may be called.

THE FUNERAL DIRECTOR AND THE CLERGYMAN

The next most immediate matter is that of selecting a funeral home. If the family belongs to a church or synagogue, they may call the office, which will give them all the information about the funeral directors in the area and probably recommend one who will suit their needs. The family doctor can also provide this information.

The funeral director will come to the house as soon as possible after he is called and remove the body to the funeral home. Whoever is in charge for the family discusses all the arrangements with him at that time, telling him how elaborate a funeral the relatives wish or can afford and how the details that the funeral director will enumerate are to be handled. The type of casket must be chosen as well as any floral arrangements for the casket or for the church which the family wants to have. If the service is to be held at the funeral home or in the home of the deceased, the day and hour may also be settled. If it is to be held in a church, the clergyman must be consulted immediately to fix the time. If the family is not affiliated with a church, the funeral director or a friend can recommend a clergyman of any faith the family chooses to perform the service.

NEWSPAPER NOTICES

Paid notices of the death should go to both morning and evening papers in a large city, and to the local paper (daily or weekly) in towns or suburbs. The notice should be written out and carefully read to the editor over the telephone. Most large city papers call back to check the veracity of the notice. In some cases the funeral director makes the call for the family, whose representative tells him what they wish the announcement to say. They usually contain the date of death, names of the immediate family, hours and location where friends may call on the family, place and time of the funeral, and frequently, a request that a contribution be given to a charity instead of flowers being sent to the deceased.

A man's notice might read:

MILLER—*Paul B., on December 17, 1975. Beloved husband of the late Mary Stuart Miller. Devoted father of Catherine Miller Sutphen, Frederick and John Miller. Friends may call at 636 Jones Rd., Englewood, N.J., on Friday, December 19, 2–5. Funeral service Saturday, December 20, 11:30* A.M., *Christ's Church, Englewood.*

The word *suddenly* is sometimes inserted immediately after the deceased's name to indicate that there had not been a long illness, or that the death was by accident.

Instead of "Friends may call at [private address]" the phrase "Reposing at the Memorial Funeral Home" is commonly used.

A woman's notice always includes her given and maiden name for purposes of identification. The same is true when married daughters and sisters are mentioned.

COHEN—*Helen Weinberg, on May 13. (Beloved) wife of Isaac, loving mother of Rebecca, Paul, and Samuel, (devoted) sister of Anna Weinberg Gold and Paul Weinberg. Services Thursday, May 14, 2 P.M., at Star Funeral Home, 41 Chestnut St., Pittsburgh. In lieu of flowers, please send contributions to the United Jewish Appeal, or your favorite charity.*

The deceased's age is not generally included unless he or she is very young, or the age is needed to establish further identification. It is usually added after the names of young children.

Daughters of the deceased are listed before sons, and their married names are used.

Occasionally the notice reads "Funeral private," and neither time nor place is given. Very intimate friends are given this information, either by telephone or on the personal card of the relative or friend in charge: "Sam's funeral will be at Christ Church, Monday at eleven o'clock." Others are not expected to attend.

If the person who has died was prominent in any way, it is probable that the newspapers have a file on him, and in the case of an older person, an obituary already written. The information that they have should be checked by someone who is acquainted with the facts so that no errors will be made in the published articles. If the paper has no obituary file, the family may submit one, but it is the option of the editors to decide whether they wish to print it or not.

"IN LIEU OF FLOWERS"

When "in lieu of flowers" appears in the death notice, everyone except a most intimate friend or relative is expected to follow the suggestion. The family has it put in because they honestly feel the contribution will help them to feel that some good has come from their loss, and thus they are comforted. A check is sent to the charity with a note saying, "This donation is sent in loving memory of Mrs. Roy Haskell, of 10 Park Place, Mount Vernon." The address of the sender should appear on the note. The charity sends him an acknowledgment, which serves to let him know his contribution has been received, and is also for his use in claiming a tax deduction. The charity also sends a notice of the contribution to the family of the deceased. The charity's acknowledgment to the sender *in no way* takes the place of a thank-you note from the bereaved family—one of whom must write in person to express their appreciation.

Occasionally a notice reads, "Please send a contribution to your favorite charity." You are free to choose whichever one you wish, but it is thoughtful to select one that might also mean something to the bereaved family.

When you write a condolence note to a bereaved person or family you may, if you wish, mention that you have sent a contribution as they requested. This will ensure that they know of it in case the charity is lax in sending notices to the family or an error has been made.

The amount of the contribution is, of course, up to you. However, you should *not* give less than you would have paid for a flower arrangement, and in view of the tax deduction you should really give more.

If no "in lieu of" appears in the notice, you should send flowers, since it indicates that the particular family feels they would derive the most comfort from the beauty of the flowers, and this is surely their prerogative.

Although people may not want a mass of flowers at the funeral, a lovely plant or flower arrangement may always be sent to the family a few days after the burial as an indication of your continuing sympathy and love. Sometimes friends do this instead of funeral flowers or contributions; others do it in addition to one or the other. Cards accompanying these flowers or plants should not mention the recent loss, but may simply say, "With love from us all."

Gifts of cash should never be sent directly to the family in place of flowers or a charitable contribution. However, a group—fellow employees, club or lodge members, or just neighbors—may take up a collection for a bereaved person who is in financial difficulty. This is a generous gesture and can be a great help in defraying funeral expenses.

SENDING AND RECEIVING FLOWERS

If there is a notice in the papers requesting that no flowers be sent, you send none. Otherwise they are addressed to "The funeral of Mr. James Snow," either at the funeral home or at the church. When you did not know the deceased, but only his close relatives, flowers may be sent to them at their home. An enclosed card, on which you write, "With deepest sympathy," or if appropriate, "With love and sympathy," is addressed to "The family of Mr. James Snow," or to the one you know best.

If you hear of the death sometime later, you may still send flowers to the family of the deceased at their home. In fact, these flowers, arriving after the confusion and misery of the first days, are often appreciated more than those which arrive promptly.

To avoid confusion, whoever is making the arrangements for the family should appoint one person to take charge of flowers, and he or she must carefully collect all the accompanying cards that are sent to the house or funeral home. This person writes a description of the flowers that came with the card on the outside of each envelope if this has not been done by the florist or the funeral director. The cards are delivered to the bereaved family after the funeral. For example:

Large spray of Easter lilies and greens
Laurel wreath with gardenias
Long sheaf of white roses—broad silver ribbon

Without such notations the family has no way of knowing anything about the flowers that people have sent. Moreover, these descriptions are invaluable when writing notes of thanks.

If some friends have sent potted plants or cut flowers to the house, their cards are also removed and noted for later acknowledgment.

If the family is Protestant, one or two women friends go to the church an hour before the time set for the service to help the florist or someone on the church staff arrange the flowers and to collect the cards. Their duty is mainly to see that those sent by relatives are given a prominent position. Moving about and arranging heavy wreaths and sprays is difficult for novices, and the florist is capable of doing a more effective job than amateurs.

Flowers are never sent to the funeral of an Orthodox Jew. Nor are any flowers except those sent by the immediate family permitted in Catholic churches, although they may, of course, be sent to the family at their home.

Therefore, when a Catholic dies, friends of any faith may send a "spiritual bouquet" (a Mass said for the deceased) to a Catholic family. Any priest will make arrangements for the Mass and accept the donation. A card is sent to the family, stating the time and place of the Mass and the name of the donor.

THE CLOTHING FOR BURIAL

The person who has been put in charge of arrangements, with the help of someone who may know of the deceased's special preferences or a favorite piece of suitable clothing, delivers the clothes to the funeral director, who will specify what clothing is needed. Members of some faiths, Orthodox Jews among them, still prefer to bury their dead in shrouds, but most religions have no restrictions on clothing for a burial. Dresses should be in solid, subdued colors, of a style that might be worn to church. Young girls are usually buried in white, and children in their Sunday-school clothes. Men are also dressed as for church; generally the family chooses a dark suit. Wedding rings are usually left on, but other jewelry is removed.

EMBLEM OF MOURNING ON THE DOOR

It is very rarely done anymore, but if the family wants to indicate that there has been a death in the house, the funeral director may hang streamers on the front door: white ones for a child, black-and-white for a young person, or black for an older person. Flowers are, of course, most beautiful and the choice of those who can afford them. Usually they are ordered by the family directly from their own florist, but quite possibly the funeral director orders them. White flowers are used for a young person, and purple for someone who was older.

Any emblem is removed by a member of the funeral establishment before the family returns from the services.

THE ROLE OF FRIENDS

Immediately on hearing of the death, intimate friends of the deceased should go to the house of mourning and ask whether they can be of service. There are countless ways in which they can be helpful, from assisting with such material needs of the family as food and child care, to sending telegrams, making phone calls, and answering the door. When you hear of the death of a less intimate friend, you call at the home or funeral parlor according to the directions contained in the newspaper notice. At the house, if you have visiting cards, you leave one with "With sympathy" written on it. At a funeral home you sign the register and offer the family your sympathy in person. If, by chance, you do not see them, you should write a letter to the family at once. Telephoning is not improper, but it may cause inconvenience by tying up the line, which is always needed at these times for notifying members of the family and/or making necessary arrangements.

HONORARY PALLBEARERS

The member of the family who is in charge sometimes asks six or eight men who were close friends of the deceased to be the pallbearers. This may be done when they come to pay their respects, or by telephone or telegraph. When a man has been prominent in public life, there may be eight or ten of his political or business associates as well as six or eight lifelong friends. Members of the immediate family are never chosen, as their place is with the women of the family.

There are almost never any pallbearers at the funeral of a Christian woman, but in the Jewish faith both men and women may have pallbearers.

One cannot refuse an invitation to be a pallbearer except for illness or absence from the city.

Honorary pallbearers serve only at church funerals. They do not carry the coffin. This service is performed by the assistants of the funeral director, who are expertly trained. The honorary pallbearers sit in the first pews on the left, and after the service leave the church two by two, walking immediately in front of the coffin.

USHERS

Ushers may be chosen in addition to, or in place of, pallbearers. They serve at women's funerals as well as those of men. Although funeral directors will supply men to perform the task, it is infinitely better to select men from the family (not immediate family) or close friends, who will recognize those who come and seat them according to their closeness to the family, or according to their own wishes.

When there are no pallbearers the ushers sit in the front pews on the left and march out ahead of the coffin as pallbearers would. If there are pallbearers the ushers remain at the back of the church.

AT THE FUNERAL HOME

More often than not, the body of the deceased remains at the funeral home until the day of the funeral. In that case some members of the family receive close friends there, at specified hours, rather than at home. The hours when they will be there to accept expressions of sympathy should be included in the death notice in the newspaper. People who wish to pay their respects but who do not feel that they are close enough to intrude on the privacy of the bereaved may stop in at any time and sign the register provided by the funeral parlor. Their signatures should be formal, including their title—"Dr. and Mrs. Harvey Cross" or "Miss Deborah Page," and not "Bill and Joan Cross" or "Debbie Page"—in order to simplify the task of anyone helping the family to acknowledge these visits. Close friends who feel it is unfriendly to sign "Mr. and Mrs." may use their first names but must put "Mr. and Mrs. William Cross" in parenthesis after "Bill and Joan Cross." A visitor who sees and personally extends his sympathy at the funeral home need not write a note of condolence, unless he wishes to write an absent member of the family. Those who merely sign the register should, in addition, write a note. The family need not thank each and every caller by letter, but if someone has made a special effort or if no member of the family was there to speak to him, they may wish to do so.

The visit to the funeral home need not last more than five or ten minutes. As soon as the visitor has expressed his sympathy to each member of the family, and spoken a moment or two with those he knows well, he may leave. If the casket is open, guests are expected to pass by and pay their respects to the deceased, but if this is too difficult or repugnant to someone, he need not do so. Unless one's religion has specific requirements, the question of whether or not the coffin will be open is entirely up to the family. The funeral director will follow their instructions.

In general, visitors should follow the religious customs of the bereaved family when they make their visit. However, they need never do anything that is contrary to their own faith. For example, if there is a crucifix over the coffin of a Catholic, a Jew need not kneel, and a Protestant need not cross himself. An attitude of respect and sincerity can be indicated by standing a moment with bowed head and saying an appropriate prayer silently.

In speaking to members of the bereaved family, who are generally seated (the men may prefer to stand) in a different part of the room or even in another room adjacent to that where the coffin lies, what you say depends entirely on your relationship to the family. Acquaintances and casual friends need say no more than "I'm so sorry" or perhaps "He was a wonderful person." Closer friends might ask whether there is anything they can do to help or say that "We are going to miss John so much, too." Visitors should not ask about the illness or the death, but in some cases widows or widowers feel a need to talk about it. If they do bring the subject up, their friends should offer as much comfort as possible by listening and discussing it.

In reply to visitors' comments, the family members need say only "Thank you for coming," or "Thank you so much," or "You're very kind."

Visiting friends who happen to meet at a funeral home greet each other just as they ordinarily would. If a stranger is present, and introductions are made, the response is the usual one—"I'm very glad to meet you." Naturally, laughing and giggling are in very poor taste, but a short chat about subjects other than the unhappy reason for the meeting is perfectly correct.

Visitors should not smoke when they pass by the coffin, nor in the same room where the coffin is lying, unless the bereaved family are smoking in another part of the room. If the relatives are receiving in a separate room, which is often furnished as a living room, visitors may smoke. However, if the family members are not smoking, visitors should ask if it would bother them before lighting their cigarettes. In most cases the visits are so brief that there is no need (or excuse) for smoking until the call is over.

WHO ATTENDS THE FUNERAL

All members of the family should find out when the funeral is to take place and go to it without waiting to be notified. If the newspaper notice reads "Funeral private," a friend does not go unless he has received a message from the family that they wish him to come. If the hour and location of the service are printed in the paper, that is considered an invitation to attend. It is entirely up to you to decide whether you knew the deceased or his family well enough to wish to be at his funeral. But it is certainly heartless not to go to the public funeral of a person with whom you have been closely associated in business or some other interest, to whose house you have often been invited, or whose family are your friends.

A divorced man or woman may go to the funeral of the ex-wife or ex-husband if cordial relations have been maintained with the family of the deceased. He or she may make a brief visit to the funeral home, and may go to the church service, sitting in the rear and not attempting to join the family. If the deceased had remarried, and there was bitterness and ill feeling, the former spouse should not attend, but should send flowers and a brief note of condolence.

CLOTHING

It is no longer considered necessary to wear black when you go to a friend's funeral unless you sit with the family or have been asked to be one of the honorary pallbearers. However, you should choose clothes that are subdued in color and inconspicuous.

FUNERAL SERVICES

AT THE CHURCH

Some people find the church funeral most trying because they must leave the seclusion of the house and be in the presence of a congregation. Others find the solemnity of a church service—with the added beauty of choir and organ—helpful.

As the time appointed for the funeral draws near, the congregation gradually fills the church. The first few pews on the right side of the center aisle are usually left empty for the family and those on the left for the pallbearers, but this may be reversed if the vestry or waiting rooms are on the left.

Friends enter the church as quietly as possible, and if there are no ushers, they seat themselves wherever they wish. Only a very intimate friend should take a position far up on the center aisle. Acquaintances seat themselves in the middle or toward the rear of the church.

The trend today is to have the casket closed. Protestants may follow their own wishes. At a Catholic or Jewish service it is obligatory that the casket be closed.

At most funerals the processional is omitted. The coffin may have a floral piece or a blanket of flowers on it. In some churches it may be covered with a pall of needlework, or for a member of the armed forces, it may be draped with the flag. The coffin is placed on a stand at the foot of the chancel a half hour before the service. The family usually enters through the door nearest the front pews.

However, if the deceased is very prominent, or if the family wishes a processional, it forms in the vestibule. If there is to be a choral service, the minister and choir enter the church from the rear and precede the funeral cortege. Directly after the choir and clergy come the honorary pallbearers, two by two; then the coffin; and then the family—the chief mourner first, walking with whoever can offer the most comfort to him or her.

Usually each woman takes the arm of a man. But two women or two men may walk together, according to the division of the family. For example, if the deceased is one of four sons and there is no daughter, the mother and father walk together immediately after the body of their child, and they are followed by the two elder sons and then the younger, and then the nearest woman relative. It is important that the people in deepest grief should each be placed next to the one whose nearness may be of the most help to them. A younger child who is calm and soothing would be better next to his mother than an older one who is more nervous.

At the chancel the choir takes its accustomed place, the clergyman stands at the foot of the chancel steps, the honorary pallbearers take their places in the front pews on the left, and the casket is set upon a stand previously placed there for the purpose. The actual bearers of the casket walk quietly to inconspicuous stations on the side aisles. The family and pallbearers occupy the front pews; the rest of the procession fills vacant places on either side. The service is read when everyone is seated. Upon its conclusion the procession moves out in the same order it came in, except that the choir remains in its place.

If the family wishes, one of the male relatives may stop at the back of the church to thank those who have attended the services. He need say nothing more than "Thank you for coming," with perhaps a special word for close friends, but the gesture will certainly be warmly received.

Outside the church the casket is put into the hearse. The family enters automobiles waiting immediately behind, and the flowers are put into a covered vehicle (far preferable to an open car parading through the streets). Flowers are sometimes taken by a different route and placed beside the grave before the hearse and those attending the burial service arrive.

AT THE HOUSE

Many people prefer a house funeral. It is simpler and more private, and it eliminates the necessity for those in sorrow to face people. The nearest relatives may stay apart in an adjoining room where they can hear the service yet remain in seclusion.

Years ago there seldom was music at house funerals, because at that time nothing could substitute for the deep, rich tones of the organ. Now, however, phonographic recordings of organ and choir music are excellent and readily available and may be used as a beautiful addition to a house funeral.

Arrangements are usually made to hold the service in the living room. The coffin is placed in front of the mantel, perhaps, or between two windows, at a distance from the door. It is usually set on stands brought by the funeral director, who also supplies enough folding chairs to fill the room without crowding.

At a house funeral the relatives can either take their places near the casket or stay in a separate room. If the women of the family come into the living room, they wear hats or veils, as they would in a church.

All other women keep their coats on if it is cool. The men, if they are wearing overcoats, keep them on or carry them on their arms and hold their hats in their hands.

Only a very small group of relatives and intimate friends goes to the cemetery from the house.

AT THE FUNERAL HOME OR CHAPEL

In recent years the establishments of funeral directors have assumed a new prominence. There is always a chapel in the building, actually a small and often very beautiful nonsectarian church. There are also retiring rooms and reception rooms where the families may remain undisturbed or receive the condolences of their friends.

Services are conducted in the chapel just as they would be in a church, although sometimes there is a private alcove to one side so that the family need not sit in the front pews.

THE BURIAL

If the burial is in the churchyard or within walking distance of the church, the congregation may follow the family to the graveside. Otherwise those attending the funeral, wherever the services are held, do not go to the interment. The long line of vehicles that used to stand at the church, waiting to be filled with mere acquaintances, is proper only for a public personage.

CREMATION

Many people whose religions allow it, prefer the idea of cremation to burial. The service is exactly the same as that preceding a burial. The family may, or may not, as they wish, accompany the body to the crematorium. If they do, a very short service is held there also. However, many ministers incorporate the burial prayers into the funeral service, thus eliminating any need for the family to go to the crematorium.

The ashes are later delivered to the family to be disposed of in any way that the deceased would wish (as long as it is not contrary to any law). Often, however, the urn is deposited in a building or section set aside in the cemetery or churchyard, and sometimes it is buried in the family plot.

A MEMORIAL SERVICE

In some circumstances—if, for instance, the deceased has died in a far country or perhaps drowned at sea or simply because the family prefers it—a memorial service is held instead of a funeral.

Notice of this service is put in the obituary column of the paper, or in a small town, relatives and friends may be given short lists of their own nearest neighbors whom they are asked to notify.

If the service takes place very shortly after the death, the service is very much like an ordinary funeral service. If it takes place much later, however, it is more often very brief. In general outline: Two verses of a hymn are sung, short prayers follow, and a very brief address is given about the work and personality of the one for whom the service is held. It is closed with a prayer and a verse or two of another hymn.

Usually, no flowers are sent except a few for the altar. On those occasions when flowers are sent, they are arranged as bouquets and stand on the altar or on either side of the chancel.

DONATING YOUR BODY TO SCIENCE

If you wish to donate your body for scientific research or use, you should notify the institution that will receive it when you make the decision. Your wish should also be made clear to your family, and they should notify the funeral director immediately after your death, since special embalming processes will be used to preserve the body properly for the research. The funeral director will notify the state anatomical committee and the institution that will receive the body. After the special embalming, the body is prepared for the funeral in the usual way.

If the situation is such that the body must be delivered to a hospital immediately after death (for an organ transplant, for example), the funeral service is held without the body, or the family may prefer to have a memorial service.

The procedures are exactly the same as for any funeral, except that there is no trip to the cemetery or crematorium.

AFTER THE FUNERAL

The custom of having a roaring wake after the funeral service often helps those who are accustomed to it to get their minds off their tragedy, but others feel that it shows neither sadness nor respect for the deceased. However, it is a time-honored tradition among some ethnic groups and in some localities, and where this is so, wakes are beneficial and therapeutic to those who participate. If some friends or mourners resent the seeming gaiety, they should stop in and pay their respects to the bereaved family, but they need not stay to drink or take part in the "festivities."

In most cases a quiet luncheon or reception at the home of one of the relatives takes the place of a real wake. If it is held at the house of the immediate family, other relatives and close friends often provide the food. Members of the family who may not have seen each other for some time have a chance to talk, and it provides a meeting place and a meal for those who have come from out of town.

Because the mourners from out of town undoubtedly will be leaving shortly after the funeral, the will is often read right after the luncheon, or at least that same afternoon. If this is not possible for any reason, it should be done within the next day or two at the latest. It may be read either in the home of the deceased, or if more convenient, in the office of the lawyer in charge.

FEES AND DONATIONS

No fee is ever asked by the clergyman, but the family is expected to make a contribution in appreciation of his services, and they should do so. The amount may be anything from ten dollars for a very small funeral service to one hundred dollars for a very elaborate one. A check may be presented to him either before or after the funeral, or it may be mailed a day or two later with a personal note thanking him for his services.

A bill rendered by the church office includes all necessary charges for the church.

ACKNOWLEDGMENT OF SYMPATHY

When impersonal messages of condolence mount into the hundreds, as may be the case when a public figure or perhaps a prominent business executive or a member of his family dies, the sending of engraved or printed cards to strangers is proper:

> *The Governor and Mrs. State*
> *wish gratefully to acknowledge*
> *your kind expression of sympathy*

or:

> *The family of*
> *Harrison L. Winthrop*
> *wish to thank you for*
> *your kind expression of sympathy*

If such cards are used, a handwritten word or two and a signature must be added below the printed message *when there is any personal acquaintance with the recipient.* In no circumstances should such cards be sent to those who have sent flowers or to intimate friends who have written personal letters.

Perhaps as the result of the use of cards in these rare but permissible cases, a most unfortunate practice has sprung up. Some funeral directors supply printed cards, and the mourner feels that he need only sign his or her name to them. This is a poor return, indeed, for beautiful flowers or even a sincere and comforting note. The bereaved may use these cards if he wishes, but he *must* add a brief personal note below the printed message.

A personal message on a fold-over card is preferable to any printed card, and it takes but a moment to write "Thank you for your beautiful flowers" or "Thank you for all your kindness."

If the list is very long, or if the person who has received the flowers and messages is really unable to perform the task of writing, some member of the family or a near friend may write for her or him: "Mother asks me to thank you for your beautiful flowers and kind message of sympathy." No one expects more than a short message of acknowledgment, but that message should be *personal* and written by hand!

Acknowledgments should be written for all *personal* condolences, for flowers, for Mass cards, for contributions, and for special kindnesses. They need *not* be made for printed condolence cards with no personal message added, or for calls at the funeral home.

Letters must also be written to the honorary pallbearers and those who may have served as ushers.

MOURNING CLOTHES

During the past fifty years no changes in etiquette have been so great as those in the conventions of mourning. A half century ago, the regulations about dress were definitely prescribed according to the precise degree of relationship of the mourner to the deceased. One's real feelings, whether of grief or comparative indifference, had nothing to do with the outward manifestation one was expected to show as a sign of respect for the dead.

A greater and greater number of persons today do not believe in going into mourning at all. There may be a few who believe that great love should be expressed in rejoicing at the rebirth of a beloved spirit instead of selfishly mourning one's own earthly loss. It is certain, however, that the number who can actually attain this spirit are few indeed. Most of us merely do the best we can to keep occupied, to make the necessary adjustments, and to avoid casting the shadow of our own sadness on others. The sooner we can overcome our grief and turn our thoughts to the future, the better. Because mourning is a continual reminder of the past, it can only delay the wearer's return to a normal life.

A WIDOW'S MOURNING

> *The young widow should wear deep crepe for a year and then lighter mourning for six months and second mourning for six months longer.*
> —Emily Post, 1922

A widow of mature years used to (and in some Latin countries still does) wear mourning for life. However, today deep mourning for a year is considered extreme, and for even six months is very rare.

The young widow, if she wishes to wear mourning for a short time, might wear black for one season. When summer changes to winter, or winter to summer, her new wardrobe should consist of more cheerful clothes, although she may stick to subdued shades for another few months if she wishes. Black clothes are never appropriate in the country, and ordinary sports clothes should be worn, provided they are of an inconspicuous nature.

A woman *never* remains in mourning for her first husband after she has decided that she can be consoled by a second. But it would be inappropriate to welcome the attentions of a new suitor while still in mourning.

MOURNING FOR BUSINESSWOMEN

Since mourning is the outward evidence of a personal frame of mind that has no place in the impersonal world of business, deep mourning that attracts attention is as unsuitable in an office as a black uniform would be on a soldier. Inconspicuous mourning—black or gray dresses with white trim in winter, or white with a little color in the trim in summer—would be most appropriate.

But if a woman arrives at her office a day or so after the death of a close relative in the clothes she ordinarily wears, no one looks askance.

MOURNING FOR MEN

It is correct, but rather unusual nowadays, for a man to go into mourning for a few weeks or months by the simple expedient of putting a black band on his hat and on the left sleeve of his clothes. Also, in the city he wears black shoes, gloves, socks, and ties, and white instead of colored shirts. In the country a young man continues to wear his ordinary sports clothes and shoes and sweaters without any sleeve band.

The sleeve band is from three and a half to four and a half inches in width and is of dull cloth on overcoats or winter clothing and of serge on summer clothes.

But a sleeve band on business clothes may appear to be an implied bid for sympathy, which most men want to avoid. Therefore it is best that they go to the office with no evidence of mourning other than a black tie and black socks, if anything at all.

THE BEHAVIOR OF THE FAMILY AFTER THE FUNERAL

As soon as possible after the funeral the life of the family should return to its normal routine. There are many things that must be attended to at once, and while these may seem like insurmountable chores to a grieving husband or wife, the necessity of having to perform them and in so doing to think of others rather than oneself, is in reality a great help in returning to an active life.

The return of the close relatives of the deceased to an active social life is up to the individual. If he or she is not wearing mourning, he may start, as soon as he feels up to it, to go to a friend's house, to a movie, play, sports event, classes, or meetings. He may wish to avoid large gatherings for a time, but little by little he increases the scope of his activities until his life has returned to normal. A man or woman may start to have dates when he or she feels like it, but for a few months these should be restricted to evenings at the home of a friend, a movie, or some other inconspicuous activity. After six months any social activity is permissible. One year is generally considered the appropriate "waiting period" before remarrying, but there are many valid reasons for shortening that time. It is up to the people involved, but they should, in making their decision, consider the feelings of their ex-in-laws, their children, and others close to them.

Those who do choose to wear mourning do not go to dances or other formal parties, nor do they take a leading part in purely social functions. However, anyone who is in public life or business or who has a professional career must, of course, continue to fulfill his duties. The fact that many women have gone into business or are following careers is another cause of the lightening of mourning and the shortening of its duration. In sum, each year the number increases of those who show the mourning in their hearts only by the quiet dignity of their lives.

CHILDREN

On no account should children be put into black at any time. They wear their best church clothes to a funeral, and afterward, whatever they ordinarily wear.

Very small children under five or six should perhaps not be taken to funerals. Older children should be seated with their family, close to someone who can give them the most comfort.

Many people are uncertain about whether children who have lost a parent should participate in their usual school activities and after-school entertainments. The answer is "Yes." They should take part in sports and in school concerts or plays. However, older children may not wish to go to a purely social party within two or three weeks, or even longer, after the death of a parent. The normal routine of a small child should not be upset—more than ever he needs to romp and play.

DISPOSITION OF POSSESSIONS AND HEIRLOOMS

No one can possibly foresee which of the children will want or need each piece of furniture or tableware in the home, and include all the instructions for dividing up such articles in his will. However, thoughtful parents can help their children immensely by writing a letter, which although not binding, will serve as a guideline, and which members of the family will be glad to follow. Since it is not binding, as a will is, the suggestions can be ignored if circumstances have changed since the letter was written. But it is most helpful to survivors who hardly know where to begin, if they have a word from the deceased along these lines: "I would like Sally to have the dining room table, since she has a room big enough for it. James needs a sturdier sofa, so I would like him to have the chintz sofa from the den," and so on. A mother may allot jewelry in the same manner.

If this has not been done, the most practical method is to call a family council. Each member should list his choices in order. They draw straws to decide who gets first choice, second choice, etc., and then continue around in turn. Toward the end, when there may be wide inequities in the value of the remaining items, the person choosing the lesser might be given a second choice. Where two people have chosen the same article in the same "round," they might agree to draw straws again. An effort should be made not to break up sets of china or matching furniture.

These situations can be a real disaster, but if they are handled sensibly, unselfishly, and unemotionally, they can serve to draw family members closer together than they have ever been before.

THE GRAVE AND THE GRAVESTONE

For most of us the gravestone we choose for our loved one is the only permanent memorial that will exist. Therefore, it, and the inscription on it, should be chosen with great care. The worst mistake one can make is to rush into ordering an ornate stone with sentimental carvings and a flowery inscription, which may later seem in poor taste or objectionable. For example, one might wish in the emotion of the moment to write something about the deceased being "the only love" or "the greatest love" of the spouse. This could conceivably cause considerable anguish to a future husband or wife.

The wisest course is to choose as handsome and appropriate a stone as one can, and refrain from ordering terribly ornate decorations. Almost invariably, the simplest constructions—be they monuments, buildings, or any work of art—are those which endure and continue to please forever. The inscription, too, should be simple and sincere. "Beloved husband of" expresses true devotion without excluding other members of a present, or future, family. Titles are not used for either men or women, with some exceptions. A man who spent his life at sea might wish to have "Captain Ahab Marner" on his stone, and the names of men of high military rank or on active service are generally preceded by their titles.

The relationship of wife and husband is usually included, although not necessarily. Today, no other legend or information usually appears, and perhaps it is too bad. Years ago, most interesting poems and inscriptions were written for loved ones. My particular favorites are three gravestones in New England. The center is inscribed (let us say) "Captain Cyrus Miller." Next to him lie the remains of "Elizabeth, his wife." And on the stone next to her, the legend reads, "Sarah, who should have been!"

Today, however, a typical inscription reads

1900–1968
Helen Jones Schaeffer
beloved wife of
John Simon Schaeffer

Whatever you choose, remember that you must consider the feelings of the living. While a memorial is, in part, a solace to the bereaved, it is something that will be seen and shared with others. Surely the one who has died would not want a memorial that could ever be anything but an honor to him and a pleasure to those he leaves behind.

In cemeteries where it is permitted, some people plant a veritable flower garden around a grave. Others prefer to have only grass and to bring fresh flowers or potted plants regularly as an evidence of their continuing love. This can become quite a chore, however, as the first grief diminishes, because garden flowers need constant care or they become a straggling weed patch in short order. A very satisfactory solution is that of using evergreen shrubs and ground cover, which look beautiful all year round with little attention.

OTHER MEMORIALS

Many bereaved families wish to make a material gesture to honor their dead. For the very wealthy this may take many forms, from the building of a monument to the donation of a piece of equipment to the hospital that cared for the deceased. This type of memorial does not need a great deal of discussion in this book, because its very nature requires that it be considered carefully, and because time will be required for extensive planning before it can be done. The advice of other people will be involved, and that will put an automatic restraint on those who might otherwise be overcome by their emotions.

Part Nine
WEDDINGS

~§ 47 ~ Engagements

Courtship is a time of excitement and fun, but as it progresses and as the couple find themselves more and more attracted to each other, it also becomes a time of serious consideration. At some point, the girl begins to think, "This is the man I want to marry—I wonder if he feels the same way about me?" And the man is asking himself similar questions. Their conversation becomes more personal and more serious, and they start to "sound each other out." Very often the man never actually says, "Will you marry me?" They agree to marry through a sort of understanding and acceptance of each other that has grown with their deepening acquaintance.

During this preengagement time, it is very important that young people not avoid the company of others. While the evenings when they are alone are surely their favorite ones, it is essential for them to get to know each other's friends. A marriage in which either partner is incompatible with people who have always been part of the other's life has one strike against it to begin with. This is even more true of the couple's families. Each should be entertained in the home of the other so that they may see the surroundings and the family to which they will be expected to adjust. Although it may not be possible if either or both of the families live in another area, an overnight or weekend visit can be helpful in making the decision as to whether to propose and whether to accept if the proposal comes. The family who are to entertain the young people should be advised beforehand what the situation is by their son or daughter, in order to avoid embarrassing their guest.

Dear Mother,

   May I bring Sally Foster up for the night next Saturday? We have been seeing a lot of each other, and I'm eager to have her see Waterbury, and to introduce her to you.

Love,
Jim

Or:

Dear Mom,

   I've met a most attractive man, Jerry Boyd, from Syracuse, and I'm very eager for you to meet each other. So I wondered if it would be convenient for us to spend next weekend with you and Dad.
   Please let me know as soon as you can.

Love to you both,
Sue

The parents receiving such a note or a telephone call are prepared to meet their possible son- or daughter-in-law, but should realize that unless they are told otherwise when the couple arrives, the engagement is still in the future.

THE BRIDEGROOM TALKS TO HER FATHER

As soon as he and she have definitely made up their minds that they want to marry each other, it is the immediate duty of the man to go to the girl's father or her guardian, and ask his consent. If her father refuses, the engagement cannot exist.—Emily Post, 1922

Shortly after the couple decide that they want to get married, the man should arrange to talk to his future father-in-law. He no longer asks for his consent, although if the bride's father does have objections this is the time when he should express them. In most cases, however, the parents are happy that their daughter has found someone she loves, and the conversation is simply a discussion of the couple's plans and the man's prospects. The bridegroom does have an obligation to explain to his future father-in-law, not necessarily how he will support his wife, as used to be the case, but how, between them, they will be able to get along. He should also, at this time, be quite frank about other obligations he may have if he has been married before, health problems that might have an effect on the marriage, etc. The future bride often joins her fiancé and her father after a little while, and together they work out their plans. If the young man is still in college or graduate school, or if his salary is inadequate, the father may offer some financial help to be paid back later, or whatever they agree to. Or the bride may explain to her father that she plans to work for a time. In any case, at the conclusion of the talk, if all goes well, the engagement is "official."

In the event that, for whatever reason, the girl's mother and father refuse to approve of the marriage, she then is faced with the problem of changing her "Yes" to "No" or "Wait a while," or else marrying in opposition to her parents. An honest young woman who has made up her mind to marry in spite of her parents' disapproval tells them that her wedding will take place on such-and-such a day, and that she hopes they will be there. If the parents care about their future relationship with their daughter, they will swallow their feelings and attend. They will gain nothing, and very possibly lose their daughter for good, if they refuse.

THE PARENTS BECOME ACQUAINTED

Years ago, one of the most unbreakable rules of etiquette was that the parents of the groom should call on those of the bride as soon as their son made the engagement known to them. But the custom of "calling on" anyone formally has long since passed—replaced by the informal meeting, usually arranged by telephone.

It is still the parents of the groom who should make the first move to become acquainted with the bride-to-be's family. If they live in the same town, the young man's mother calls the girl's mother and tells her how happy she and her husband are about the engagement. She suggests that they get together as soon as possible for coffee, cocktails, dinner, or whatever she chooses.

If they live in different cities, it is up to the groom's parents to write—or call if they wish—first. A visit should be arranged between the families as soon as possible, and whichever one can travel most conveniently should make the trip.

If for any reason the man's family does not contact the parents of the girl, her father and mother should be very careful not to permit an oversight or lack of knowledge to develop into a situation that may cause great unhappiness, and should make the first move themselves. The important thing is that this time should be a happy one for the young couple and that both sets of parents should act with spontaneity and in a spirit of friendship.

The girl, too, must try to understand and accept the attitude of her future family (whatever it may be), and she must *not* stand inflexibly upon what she considers to be her own family's rights. The objective that she should keep in mind is the happiness of the relationship between her future in-laws and herself.

In the event that the bride's parents are divorced, the groom's mother and father should get in touch with each of them, calling first the one with whom the bride is, or has been, living. When a groom's parents are divorced, the one with whom he makes his home should contact the bride's parents. If he lives alone, however, it is entirely possible that neither his mother nor his father will think of making the move, so the bride's parents should be prepared to break the ice. They should, of course, arrange to see the divorced parents separately, usually meeting the mother first and the father shortly thereafter.

THE ENGAGEMENT RING

It is doubtful that the man who produced a ring from his pocket the instant that the woman said "Yes" ever existed outside Victorian novels. In real life it is both correct and wise for *him* to consult *her* taste. The fiancé first goes alone to the jeweler, explains how much he can afford, and has a selection of rings set aside. He then brings his fiancée to the store and lets her choose the one she likes best.

She might choose a traditional diamond ring, or she might prefer a ring of more important size with her own birthstone. If there are family heirlooms to be chosen from, the man may show them to his fiancée and have her selection set to her taste.

Today many girls choose to use semiprecious stones, beside which a tiny diamond loses some of its appeal.

An aquamarine is first choice as a solitaire diamond's substitute. Amethysts, topazes, and transparent tourmalines are all lovely as selections for an engagement ring. But if a birthstone seems more appropriate these are the traditional choices:

JANUARY—*Garnet*. (Its rather dark glow makes a pleasing engagement ring.) The *zircon*, a white, crystal-clear stone, makes a very attractive ring and closely resembles a diamond, particularly when square-cut and kept brilliantly clean. But because it does look like a diamond, there is a chance that a bride might fear that people will feel she is trying to fool them into thinking it really is a diamond. There is also a beautiful steel-blue variety.

FEBRUARY—*Amethyst.* (A big one with a square cut is effective.)

MARCH—*Aquamarine* first, then *bloodstone* or *jasper.* (A square-cut aquamarine is very popular and a really beautiful substitute for a diamond.)

APRIL—*Diamond.* (The stone of stones, but very expensive.)

MAY—*Emerald.* (Also very costly if perfect in color and without a flaw.)

JUNE—*Pearl.* (Nothing is more becoming to a young girl with lovely skin.)

JULY—*Ruby.* (Of very high value when of the desirable pigeon-blood color.)

AUGUST—*Sardonyx, peridot* (a rare and beautiful stone), or *carnelian.*

SEPTEMBER—*Sapphire.* (A favorite engagement ring of the past and always beautiful.)

OCTOBER—*Opal.* (The opal is believed to be the stone of good fortune for those born in October, but unlucky for those not born in this month.)

NOVEMBER—*Topaz.*

DECEMBER—*Turquoise* or *lapis lazuli.*

The engagement ring is worn for the first time in public on the day of the announcement. In the United States it is worn on the fourth finger (next to the little finger) of the left hand, although in some foreign countries it is worn on the right hand. It is removed during the marriage ceremony and replaced immediately afterward, outside the wedding ring. *An engagement ring is not essential to the validity of the betrothal.* Some people confuse the engagement ring with the wedding ring and believe the former is as indispensable as the latter. This is not the case. The wedding ring is a requirement of the marriage service. The engagement ring is simply evidence that he has proposed marriage and that she has said "Yes!" A man may give his fiancée a ring no matter how many times he has been married before.

Countless wives have never had an engagement ring at all. Others receive their rings long after marriage, when their husbands are able to buy the ring they have always wanted them to have. Some brides prefer to forgo an engagement ring in order to put the money it would have cost toward furnishing their future homes. A daughter may wear her deceased mother's engagement ring, but not her wedding ring.

A WIDOW'S OR DIVORCÉE'S ENGAGEMENT RING

When a widow becomes engaged to marry again, she stops wearing her engagement ring from her first marriage, whether or not she is given another. She may continue to wear her wedding ring, if she has children, until the day of her second marriage. She and her new fiancé must decide together what they wish to do with her old engagement ring. If she has a son she may wish to keep it for him to use someday as an engagement ring for his future bride. Or the stones may be reset and used in another form of jewelry—by herself or her daughters.

A divorcée does not continue to wear her engagement ring on her "wedding" finger, and she may, if she wishes, have the stones reset into another piece of jewelry.

IF SHE GIVES HIM AN ENGAGEMENT PRESENT

It is not obligatory for the girl to give the man an engagement present, but she may if she wishes.

The more usual presents include such articles as a pair of cuff links, a watch band or a key chain, or if he smokes, a cigarette lighter. Probably because the giving of an engagement ring is his particular province she very rarely gives him a ring.

ANNOUNCING THE ENGAGEMENT

PERSONAL ANNOUNCEMENT

Shortly before the engagement party or newspaper announcement the woman and man write to their relatives and their closest friends to tell them of their engagement. If the news is to be announced at a surprise party they ask them not to tell anyone else. This is so that those closest to them will not read of it first in the newspapers. The relatives who receive notes should telephone or write the bride as soon as they receive the news.

In case of a recent death in either immediate family, the engagement should be quietly announced by telling families and intimate friends and without a big party. The announcement in the newspaper serves to inform other acquaintances.

THE FORMAL ANNOUNCEMENT

The formal or public announcement is made by the parents of the bride-to-be. This is done at the engagement party and/or publicly through the newspapers. Sending engraved announcements is not in good taste.

NEWSPAPER ANNOUNCEMENTS

Copies of the newspaper announcement of the engagement with all the pertinent information are sent by the bride's parents to the society editors of the papers in which it is to be printed. You may include a picture if you wish. If you live in the suburbs of a large city or in a small town, a copy should be sent to the local paper (which may be a weekly). Others go to the paper of your choice in the nearby city and to the paper suggested by the bridegroom's family in their locality.

The announcement should be sent to the papers a week or more in advance of the date on which you wish it to appear, and that date should be clearly stated so that the announcement comes out simultaneously in all the papers. If the couple wish to keep their engagement a surprise until it is announced at an engagement party, the newspaper announcement should appear on the day following the party. Otherwise it may be printed on whatever day the families choose, with the party held shortly afterward. Many people think it important to have it appear in the Sunday paper, probably because more people read the society page on Sunday than they do on weekdays. But there is a far better chance of having all the information printed, and the photograph used, on a weekday, when the demand for space is not so pressing. If your local paper is a weekly, the date given the other papers should coincide with the day on which it is published.

The usual form is as follows:

Mr. and Mrs. Herbert Coles Johnson of Lake Forest, Illinois, announce the engagement of their daughter, Susan [Bailey Johnson —optional] to Dr. William Arthur Currier, son of Mr. and Mrs. Arthur Jamison Currier of Atlanta, Georgia. A June wedding is planned.

Miss Johnson was graduated from Bentley Junior College. She made her debut in 1970 at the Mistletoe Ball in Chicago, and in May will complete her nurse's training at Atlanta General Hospital. Dr. Currier was graduated from the Hill School, Yale University, and the Yale Medical School. He completed his residency at the Atlanta General Hospital and is now in practice in that city.

In unusual situations the information as to schools and employment remains the same, although the identification of the bride and bridegroom and their parents may vary.

WHEN ONE PARENT IS DECEASED

The announcement is worded the same whether made by the mother or father of the bride.

Mrs. Herbert Coles Johnson announces the engagement of her daughter, Susan, to Dr. William Arthur Currier. . . . Miss Johnson is the daughter also of the late Herbert Coles Johnson. . . .

WHEN THE BRIDE IS AN ORPHAN

The engagement of an orphan is announced by the girl's nearest relative, a godparent, or a very dear friend. If she has no one close to her, she sends the announcement herself:

The engagement of Miss Jessica Towne, daughter of the late Mr. and Mrs. Samuel Towne, to Mr. Richard Frost of Savannah, Georgia, is announced.

This form may also be used if her parents live very far away or if she has, for some reason, separated herself completely from her family.

IF THE PARENTS ARE DIVORCED

The mother of the bride usually makes the announcement, but the name of the other parent should be included.

Mrs. Martha Farnham announces the engagement of her daughter, Cynthia. . . . Miss Farnham is the daughter also of Mr. Henry Farnham of Worcester, Mass. . . .

IF THE PARENT WITH WHOM THE BRIDE LIVES HAS REMARRIED

Mr. and Mrs. Samuel Harvey announce the engagement of Mrs. Harvey's daughter, Jane Barber Cutler, to. . . . Miss Cutler is the daughter also of Mr. David Soames Cutler of Menlo Park, Calif.

IF DIVORCED PARENTS ARE FRIENDLY

On occasion divorced parents may remain good friends, and their daughter's time may be divided equally between them. If this is true they may both wish to announce the engagement.

Mr. Gordon Smythe of Philadelphia and Mrs. Howard Zabriskie of 12 East 72nd Street, New York City, announce the engagement of their daughter, Carla Farr Smythe. . . .

IF THE BRIDE IS ADOPTED

If the bride has been brought up since babyhood by her foster parents and uses their last name, there is no reason to mention the fact that she is adopted. If she joined the family later in life, however, and has retained her own name, it is proper to say:

Mr. and Mrs. Warren La Tour announce the engagement of their adopted daughter, Miss Claudia Romney, daughter of the late Mr. and Mrs. Carlton Romney. . . .

OLDER WOMEN, WIDOWS, AND DIVORCÉES

A woman of forty or more, even though her parents are living, generally does not announce her engagement in the newspaper, but instead calls or writes her relatives and friends shortly before the wedding. An older widow or divorcée announces her second engagement in the same way, although the engagement of a young woman marrying for the second time may be announced in the newspaper.

Occasionally a situation arises in which the parents of the groom would like to announce the engagement. For instance, when a man in the service becomes engaged to a girl from another country, her parents may not have the knowledge or means to put an announcement in the paper in his hometown. Rather than announce it in their own name, the groom's parents should word the notice:

The engagement of Miss Gretchen Strauss, daughter of Mr. and Mrs. Heinrich Strauss of Frankfurt, Germany, is announced, to Lt. John Evans, son of Mr. and Mrs. Walter Evans of. . . .

When there has been a recent death in either family, the announcement may be put in the newspaper, but a big engagement party is not held.

No announcement should *ever* be made of an engagement in which either member is still legally married to someone else—no matter how close the divorce or annulment may be.

THE ENGAGEMENT PARTY

The bride's family usually gives the engagement party. However, if they cannot afford it, or if the bride's parents are dead, or perhaps live far away, the groom's family may do so. They should not make the first announcement—that should be done by the bride's family regardless of who gives the party. But as soon as that is done, the groom's family is free to give the party celebrating the announcement.

The guest list is unlimited, but the majority of engagement parties are restricted to relatives and good friends. Occasionally—and it is not improper—the party is a huge open house or reception, including all the friends of both families.

Although the engagement party may be of any type that the bride and her mother prefer, it is most often a cocktail party or a dinner. The news may be told by the girl herself, or by her mother as the guests arrive and find the fiancé standing with their hostess. There is no formal receiving line, but his presence beside the family, being introduced as the guests arrive, needs no further explanation.

Perhaps, if the party is a dinner, the engagement is announced by the bride's father, who proposes a toast to the couple. Little announcing is necessary by the time dinner is served, however, when the young woman is wearing a shining ring on the fourth finger of her left hand.

To those who ask about using a novel way to announce an engagement, it can be said that there is really no logical objection to whatever may be pleasing to you. Whether you let a cat out of a bag with your names written on a ribbon around its neck, float balloons with your names printed on them, display a cake decorated with the couple's initials inside two hearts, or use place cards in the form of telegrams containing the announcement, there is not a rule in the world to hamper your own imagination.

THE TOAST

This is the conventional announcement made by the father of the bride-to-be at a dinner: After seeing that all glasses at the table are filled, the host rises, lifts his own glass, and says, "I propose we drink to the health of Mary and the young man she has decided to add permanently to our family, Tim Baldwin."

For other appropriate toasts, see Chapter 5, "Public Speaking."

Everyone except Mary and Jim rises and drinks a little of whatever the beverage may be. They congratulate the young couple, and Tim is called upon for a speech. He must stand and make at least a few remarks thanking the guests for their good wishes.

When the party is given on the evening of the day of the newspaper announcement—or later—the engagement is never proclaimed to the guests as a surprise. The news is "out," and everyone is supposed to have heard it. The guests congratulate the bridegroom and offer the bride-to-be wishes for her happiness, and her father and everyone else who wishes to, propose a toast.

Presents are rarely taken to an engagement party (except possibly by someone from out of town who may see the engaged couple only on this occasion), because only intimate friends or relatives are expected to give gifts, and other guests might be embarrassed. Should some friends arrive with gifts, the bride should open them in private with only the donor present, rather than make a display of them in front of those who did not bring anything.

ENGAGEMENT PRESENTS

A bride-to-be generally receives a few engagement presents, given either by her relatives, her intimate friends, or those of her parents, godparents, or by members of her fiancé's family as a special welcome to her. It is never necessary for other friends to give engagement as well as wedding presents. However, if one wishes to do so, the gifts are usually table linen, towels, bed linen such as a set of sheets and pillow cases, or an ornament for the home such as a china figurine or an artificial flower arrangement. They are most often directed particularly toward the bride's pleasure, and if they are monogrammed, her *married* initials alone are used, unless the present (cocktail glasses, for example) is definitely for both.

THE WEDDING RING—OR RINGS

Shortly before the wedding, it is not only customary but important that the bride go with the groom when he buys the wedding ring. One reason is that since she may not intend to take it off—ever—she should be allowed to choose the style she prefers. No ring could be in better taste than the plain band of yellow or white gold or platinum.

If the bridegroom wishes to have a ring the bride buys a plain gold band to match hers but a little wider—or it may be any type of ring he prefers and she is able to buy. A man's wedding ring, like a woman's, is worn on the fourth finger of his left hand.

The wedding ring may be engraved with whatever sentiment the bridegroom chooses. On the broad rings of many years ago, it was not unusual to have a quotation of twenty-five letters or more, as well as initials. Today, however, only the initials and date are usually engraved.

Handcrafted rings of intricate design are popular too, and are sometimes made by the couple themselves. These can be very beautiful and are more meaningful than the most expensive diamond-studded band.

THE LENGTH OF THE ENGAGEMENT

A long engagement is invariably a strain on all involved. The ideal duration is from three to five months, which allows time for the wedding arrangements to be made and for the couple to come to know each other very well. If one or both are finishing school, they may want to be engaged during the last year so that they do not have to become involved in more social life than they wish. Or if a man is overseas with the armed forces and his fiancée wishes everyone to know that she will not be going out with other men, then it is right and proper to announce the engagement some time before the wedding. Nonetheless, it may be a somewhat trying period. The young people, trying to see as much of each other as possible and at the same time continue studying or working, are often exhausted. The bride has the added time-consuming responsibilities of planning the wedding, and her mother, who may be left to make the arrangements almost alone, is also in a difficult position. Therefore, unless there are good and sufficient reasons for a long engagement, a shorter one ensures that the bride, the bridegroom, and their families will arrive at the wedding in good health and a happy frame of mind.

THE BROKEN ENGAGEMENT

In the unfortunate event of a broken engagement, the ring and all other gifts of value must be returned to the former fiancé. Gifts received from relatives or friends should also be returned with a short note of explanation:

Dear Sue,

I am sorry to have to tell you that Jack and I have broken our engagement. Therefore I am returning the towels that you were so sweet to send me.

Love,
Jane

A notice reading: "The engagement of Miss Sara Black and Mr. John Doe has been broken by mutual consent," may be sent to the newspapers that announced the engagement.

If the man should die before the wedding, his fiancée may keep her engagement ring. If it happens to be an old family heirloom, and she knows that his parents would like to have it remain in the family, she would be considerate to offer to return it. She may keep any gifts that were given her by friends.

BEHAVIOR OF THE ENGAGED COUPLE

Somewhere in Massachusetts there is still a "whispering reed," and through its long, hollow length lovers supposedly whispered messages of tenderness to each other while separated by a room's length and the inevitable chaperonage of the fiancée's entire family. At the opposite extreme is the engaged couple of today who persist in embarrassing everyone around them with constant displays of their emotion. While most people look kindly, and perhaps even enviously, at young couples strolling hand in hand or with their arms around each other, greater intimacies don't elicit the same reactions. Furthermore a public display of private emotions can't fail to make those emotions less meaningful and to destroy the one-to-oneness of the relationship.

There are few places in the world today—and none in the United States—where engaged couples may not spend as much time alone together as they wish. Society as a whole has not accepted the attitude that to indulge in sexual relations before marriage is right, and couples that do so overtly are opening themselves to criticisms that could even lead to a breakdown in their relationship. Each couple must decide on this question for themselves, and they must take into consideration the effect it may have on their parents, themselves, and society in general. With the freedom and opportunity open to all couples today, admittedly, temptation is very difficult to resist. Therefore every girl, engaged or planning to be engaged, should consult a physician for information about birth control. Statistics prove that far too many girls today "have to" get married, and unplanned pregnancy is a poor basis for a good marriage. A young couple owe it to themselves as well as their families to practice restraint and discretion during their engagement.

The couple may open a joint bank account in order to deposit checks they receive as gifts. Either may draw on it, but only when the money is to purchase something for their future home or their "joint" use.

It is unnecessary to say that an engaged man shows no marked interest in other women. Often it so happens that engaged people are together very little because he is away at work, lives in another city, or for other reasons. Rather than sit home alone, he or she may, of course, go out with their friends, but they must avoid going out with any man or woman alone.

THE HOPE CHEST

Years ago, most mothers started making and embroidering linens for their little girls' future trousseau almost from the time the child was born. Today with little leisure time and less knowledge of the art of sewing, mothers go out and buy their daughters an "instant" trousseau when they become engaged. Hopefully the current rage for sewing, crewel work, embroidering, and crafts of all sorts will see a return of the handembroidered towels or the beautiful handsewn lingerie of earlier times. My daughter is fortunate to have a skilled mother-in-law who presented her with beautifully mono-grammed sheets as an engagement gift—a present that could never be duplicated by machine.

Since there had to be a place to keep the lovely linens they had worked so hard over, those early-day mothers bought for their daughters trunks or boxes in which to store the articles until the girls married. These were known as hope chests. Today, parents rarely buy a hope chest for their daughter before she becomes engaged, since there is nothing to put in it. But when the time comes, and the sheets, towels, table linen, etc., are piling up, it is the prerogative of the bride's family—not her fiancé's—to provide the hope chest. It is not a necessity—a closet shelf or an empty bureau drawer or two will do just as well, but a good-sized chest, perhaps a carved Chinese chest or a lovely-smelling cedar chest, will be treasured by the bride long after the contents have been removed to other places.

THE HOUSEHOLD TROUSSEAU

A trousseau, according to the derivation of the word, was the "little truss or bundle" that the bride carried with her to the house of her husband. Today, extravagant trousseaux are dwindling to items of actual requirement, and in fact few linen closets would hold the old requirements. The modern bride will be adequately equipped to start married life with the items below.

Of course she could get along perfectly well with far less, especially if she has a washing machine and dryer readily available. However, the following list is a good one for a bride to "aim for." The practical bride will select wrinkle-resistant materials, except possibly for a few "special" top sheets.

BED LINEN (amounts are for *each* bed)
> 6 sheets for master bed (2 fitted lower sheets)
> 4 sheets for guest bed (2 fitted lower sheets)
> 4 pillow cases (for each single bed; 8 for double bed)
> 1 blanket cover
> 2 quilted mattress pads
> 1 lightweight wool blanket for summer
> 1 electric blanket (dual control for double bed) or 2 heavyweight wool or wool-blend blankets
> 1 comforter (if no electric blankets)
> 1 bedspread

BATH LINEN (quantities are for each bathroom)
> 6 large bath towels
> 6 small towels to match
> 6 washcloths to match

    6 hand towels for powder room

    1 shower curtain

    2 bath mats

    Extra hand towels and washcloths for part-time help

KITCHEN

    6 sturdy dish towels

    4 dishcloths or 2 sponges

    4 potholders

    Remember that terry-cloth towels are very practical because they don't wrinkle. Linen towels rumple the moment they are used.

TABLE LINEN

    1 damask tablecloth, white or pastel color, to fit your dining-room table. Or if you prefer, embroidered linen or lace.

    12 dinner napkins to match

    2 or 3 yard-and-a-half-square linen tablecloths for bridge tables; matching napkins optional

    1 or 2 sets of linen place mats with matching napkins

    12 linen or cotton napkins in a neutral color that will go with any odd place mats that you may be given

    2 sets (4 to 6) plastic place mats with smooth, hard surface, or treated paper mats for everyday use

    1 set (6 or 8) plastic, straw, or any attractive place mats of a more elaborate design for use at informal parties

    Optional, but very useful—large monogrammed paper napkins

    Cocktail napkins, paper or cloth

A damask cloth is very useful for any buffet setting because, with a felt pad under it, every inch of space is available—which is not the case with the bare table spaces if mats are used. An embroidered linen cloth or one of lace is also practical with the addition of a heatproof mat under any exceptionally hot platter or dish.

Small place mats of linen with or without a runner to match are most practical. No matter how pretty your plastic mats may be, linen or lace ones always make your table a little dressier.

You should try your best to have cloth napkins to use with your tablecloths or linen mats. They need not be of the same fabric so long as they are appropriate. Paper napkins are so attractively made today that they can be used to solve the laundry problem very practically, but they *are* informal and should be used only with other casual table appointments.

If your dining room is very small, or if you have none at all, it may be practical to set up two or three sturdy bridge tables with tablecloths. The color should, of course, go well with the colors in your room.

MARKING LINEN

Linen embroidered with a monogram or initials is very decorative, and it makes a lovely gift for a bride who, later in life, may never bother (or be able to afford) to order monogrammed sheets or tablecloths.

Years ago, when Muriel Barbara Jones married Henry Ross, not a piece of linen or silver in their house was marked otherwise than "MBJ." But because this proved a confusing and senseless custom, when articles are acquired after a girl becomes engaged, it is now recognized as more practical to mark everything with the bride's future initials: "MJR," or simply "R." The single letter with some decorative work around it looks better than two simple letters. Naturally, things that are monogrammed *before* an engagement must be marked with the girl's maiden initials.

Long tablecloths are marked on either side of center, midway between the table center and the edge. Small square tablecloths are marked at one corner, midway between the table center and the point. Square monograms look well set in line with the table edge; irregular ones look best at a corner.

Very large damask napkins are marked in the center of one side, smaller ones in one corner—cross-cornered usually, but sometimes straight. To decide about the place for marking the napkins, fold the napkin exactly as it is to be folded for use and then make a light pencil outline in the center of the folded napkin.

Sheets are always marked with the base of the letters toward the hem—when on the bed, the monogram is right side up and can be read by a person standing at the foot of the bed—and it is put at half the depth at which the sheet is turned back. Pillowcases are marked halfway between the edge of the case and the beginning of the pillow.

Towels are marked so that the monogram is centered when they are folded in thirds and hung on the rack.

The monogram should be in proportion to the size of the piece. If it is too small, it will look skimpy; if too large, it is overly conspicuous.

CHOOSING CHINA, GLASS, AND SILVER

Before her wedding invitations are sent out, a bride may, if she wishes, go to the gift shops or department stores in her neighborhood, or anywhere that she knows her friends will be shopping, and select those patterns of glass, china, and other items that she would like to receive as wedding presents. All stores of this type are prepared to cooperate with the bride in keeping a record of her choice, and this is an immeasurable help to those selecting gifts.

CHINA

Today stores are filled with such entrancing sets of pottery and china—thick, thin, plain, or decorated—that the problem is not to find sufficiently attractive table decorations but to choose one from among the many available. There is, however, one item of important advice. Keep in mind the subject of replacements. Any pattern not easily replaced means that breakage will leave you helplessly handicapped. It is always wise to ask if a pattern is in open stock. Remember, too, that soap-bubble-thin glass or glass that is very finely chased or cut naturally goes well with porcelains, whereas the heavier glassware is best suited to pottery.

Let us consider a few general principles that apply to a table set entirely with china. The one requirement is that the pieces be in harmony, meaning that they have some matching detail—such as a repeated note of color. In other words dinner plates of one variety, bread-and-butter plates of another variety, a centerpiece of another, dishes for sweets of another would look like an odd-lot table unless the individual pieces were closely allied. Therefore, if you have highly decorated dinner plates, use glass or silver salad or butter plates, rather than plates of a different pattern.

Whether you decide on decorated china or plain is your own choice. All white china of the same color and texture need not match in pattern or shape, but it would be unpleasing, for example, to use translucent milk glass with opaque white earthenware. The tastefulness of china in any other plain color necessarily depends upon the color of the cloth or table upon which it is to be set.

The following lists are what the bride should *basically* have to start out with. If her funds are limited and if she is not given enough dinner and dessert plates, for instance, to complete six or eight settings, she may add a piece or two as often as she can, completing one place setting at a time rather than buying two or three more dinner plates and still having an incomplete setting.

FOR EVERYDAY USE:

1 complete set of 4 or 6 place settings of inexpensive china, pottery, or unbreakable plastic ware—which now comes in most attractive patterns. This set should include:
dinner plates
dessert plates (may also be used for salad)

cereal dishes (used also for soup, puddings, canned fruit, etc.)

cups

saucers

cream pitcher and sugar bowl

2 platters

2 vegetable dishes

FOR ENTERTAINING:

The bride may choose between:

1. A complete service of fine matching china for 6 or 8 place settings. Each place setting should include:

   soup cup (two-handled, for both clear and cream soups)

   saucer

   dinner plate

   salad plate

   butter plate

   dessert plate

Optional:

   cups and saucers

   cream soup plates

   cream pitcher and sugar bowl

   platters and vegetable dishes

   demitasse cups

   gravy boat

   sauce bowls for hollandaise, mayonnaise, etc.

2. Odd sets of 6 or 8 dinner plates and dessert plates and additional items in any pattern she chooses.

If the bride prefers variety to a single set of china she must choose her accompanying items carefully. Glass, silver, pewter, and easy-to-care-for stainless steel may be combined with any china to make a charming dinner table. To go with the odd dinner and dessert plates the bride will need:

   6 or 8 glass, pewter, or silver butter plates

   6 or 8 glass salad plates (the cresent-shaped ones are pretty and take up less space on the table)

   12 cups and saucers in any pattern

   6 or 8 demitasse cups and saucers in any pattern (or in glass)

   2 platters and 3 vegetable dishes of silver or stainless steel

   1 cream pitcher and sugar bowl—silver, glass, stainless steel, or pewter

Other essential items that may be of any material or style that the bride prefers are:

4 salts and peppers—silver, glass, pewter, wood, china, or a
   combination of silver and wood, or salt and pepper dishes

1 salad bowl and servers—wood or glass

1 bread dish—silver or wicker

1 gravy or sauce boat—silver, pewter, or china

3 condiment dishes—glass, china, or pottery

1 water pitcher—any material

8 or 12 fingerbowls—optional, but nice for formal entertaining.
   May also be used to serve fruit compote, ice cream, etc. (see
   below)

silver or china tea service

1 silver coffeepot, or a presentable coffee maker (stainless steel,
   glass, etc., whether an electric one or not) that may be brought
   from the kitchen for serving after-dinner coffee

8 deep dishes for serving ice cream with sauce or a "runny"
   dessert (glass dishes are best—they look very pretty on a plate
   with a colorful pattern showing through)

6 or 8 tiny dinner-table ashtrays—china, glass, or silver

enamelware pots and casseroles, in place of china serving dishes
   (invaluable to a busy bride, as dishes may be cooked and
   served in the same utensil)

GLASSES

Glasses are so easily broken and good glass so expensive to replace that a bride who wishes to have a matching set for any length
of time should have far more than she actually needs to start out with.

In order to save her good glass for entertaining, she should have
for the everyday use of herself and her husband and for casual drop-
in visitors:

8 "kitchen glasses" or tumblers

6 juice glasses

6 old-fashioned glasses

6 stem cocktail glasses (may also be used for wine)

6 iced-tea or highball glasses

Beyond this, she should have, depending on the amount and
type of entertaining she intends to do, but preferably no less than
a dozen:

goblets

wineglasses

liqueur glasses

sherbet glasses

highball glasses

stem cocktail glasses
old-fashioned glasses

Since the chances are that not all the guests at a party will request the same type of drink, this should be adequate for quite a large party. Also, she may bring out her plainer cocktail and highball glasses if necessary.

SILVER

A large amount of silver is neither so desirable nor so fashionable as it used to be. In fact many brides request that rather than silver they be given pewter or stainless steel, both of which require little care and are more durable. However, although the bride may ask for a set of stainless-steel eating utensils for daily use, nothing can replace a set of beautiful sterling flat silver on the dinner-party table. There are innumerable patterns; the bride whose home is "traditional" may choose one of the older, more ornate patterns, and she who lives in a modern house or apartment will probably prefer a very plain design. Each has its advantages. The modern, undecorated piece is easier to clean, but it also shows wear and tear more quickly and is sometimes dulled by scratches. Whichever the bride chooses, she should remember that it is probably the silver she will use all her life, and possibly her children after her. It is therefore safer to select a pattern that is neither too severely modern nor so ornate that it easily appears outdated.

As with china, it is wiser to complete one place setting at a time than to have twelve forks and no knives with which to cut the meat. If the bride is getting her china and silver a place setting at a time, she will simply start out with smaller parties. They will grow as her implements permit, and this is not necessarily a disadvantage. A girl who has had little practice in party-giving will do far better to start out with two or four guests and enlarge her group as her experience increases.

The necessary silver for one place setting is:
1 large fork
1 large knife
1 small fork
1 small knife
1 dessert spoon
1 teaspoon
1 butter knife

In addition—and these items need not be in the same pattern as the above list:

    oyster forks
      3 serving spoons (tablespoons in the chosen pattern may be
        used)
    2 serving forks
   12 after-dinner coffee spoons
    2 gravy or sauce ladles
    4 extra teaspoons (for sugar, condiments, etc.)
Optional—and often received as wedding presents:
    salad or fish forks (broad tines)
    sugar tongs
    butter server
    ornamented spoons for jellies or jams
    cake knife
    pie server

If the flat silver is monogrammed, either a single letter—the initial of the groom's last name—or a triangle of letters is used.

When Jane Ross marries Henry Cranmore, the silver may be engraved with the bride's married initials:

$$J\,R$$
$$C$$

Or with the last-name initial above and their two first-name initials below:

$$C$$
$$J\,H$$

Any initialing should be simple in style. Elongated Roman goes well on modern silver, and Old English is best on the more ornamented styles.

A wedding gift of silver may be marked if the giver is absolutely sure that it is something the bride truly wants and that no duplicate will arrive. However, generally it is safer to leave it unmarked so that it can be exchanged if desired.

If a man is a "Junior," the "Jr." is added when his initials alone are engraved on anything in a straight line, as, for example, on a tray or cigarette box. "Jr." is not used when the initials form a design, as on flat silver.

ADDITIONAL PRACTICAL EQUIPMENT

It is not necessary to list the ordinary pots, pans, utensils, and gadgets for your kitchen. The variety and number are limited only by the space you have to store them, and the type and amount of cooking you plan to do. The following items, however, are particularly useful, and should be included in your kitchen equipment if at all possible:

> 4 wooden or plastic trays (for meals enjoyed in the living room, or for a meal eaten in bed)
> electric hot plate (the most valuable appliance in my household!)
> electric blender and/or mixer
> electric oven-broiler or "toaster-oven" (if your stove is inadequate)
> kitchen scales
> folding steps (for reaching high kitchen shelves)
> a wok (if you like Chinese cooking)
> fondue set
> chafing dish

⤳48⤳ *Planning the Wedding*

A wedding, be it large and elaborate or small and simple, is one of life's most important occasions—beautiful, meaningful, and traditionally the bride's day of days. However, brides and their families should realize that without the groom and *his* parents there would be no wedding at all, and it should be his day as well as hers. There is an old saying, "A man never knows how unimportant he is until he attends his own wedding." When that is true the chances are he will soon be attending his own divorce. Marriage is a partnership, and from the beginning all major decisions should be made by both partners.

The groom's family, too, should be consulted and informed about all that goes on, insofar as is possible. However, if the bride's family is giving the wedding, as is usually the case, it is their prerogative to make final decisions, taking the feelings of the groom's family into consideration.

Above all, the wedding plans should comply with the wishes of the young couple. It is *their* day—not their parents'. It is sad to see a mother and her daughter at swords' points at the very time that should be the happiest in their lives. Two areas are generally the most sensitive—the formality of the wedding and its size. The life-style of most young people today is far more relaxed and informal than that of their parents, and they want their weddings to be informal too. And a great many young people want small, private ceremonies, while their parents, having planned and saved for years for a huge celebration, want to make the most of the occasion for social, and even at times business, reasons. To quote the *Catholic Digest*, "One of the queerest things about modern life is the number of people who are spending money they haven't got for things they don't want, to impress the people they can't stand the sight of."

PLANNING THE WEDDING

	FORMAL	SEMIFORMAL	INFORMAL
BRIDE'S DRESS	Long white gown, train, veil optional	Long white gown, veil optional	White or pastel cocktail dress or suit or afternoon dress (sometimes, very simple long gown)
BRIDESMAIDS' DRESSES	Long or according to current style	Long or according to current style	Same type of dress as worn by the bride
DRESS OF GROOM AND HIS ATTENDANTS	Cutaway	Sack coat	Dark business suit
BRIDE'S ATTENDANTS	Maid and matron of honor, 4–10 bridesmaids, flower girl, ring bearer (optional)	Maid or matron of honor, 2–6 bridesmaids, flower girl, ring bearer (optional)	Maid of honor, 1 or 2 children (optional)
GROOM'S ATTENDANTS	Best man, 1 usher for every 50 guests, or same number as bridesmaids	Best man, 1 usher for every 50 guests, or same number as bridesmaids	Best man, 1 usher if necessary to seat guests
LOCATION OF CEREMONY	Church, synagogue, or large home or garden	Church, synagogue, chapel, hotel, club, home, garden	Chapel, rectory, justice of the peace, home, garden
LOCATION OF RECEPTION	Club, hotel, garden, or large home	Club, restaurant, hotel, garden, home	Church parlor, home, restaurant
NO. OF GUESTS	200 or more	75–200	75 or under
SERVICE AT RECEPTION PROVIDED BY:	Caterer at home, or hotel or club facilities	Caterer at home, or club or hotel facilities	Caterer, friends and relatives, or restaurant

	FORMAL	SEMIFORMAL	INFORMAL
FOOD	Sit-down or semibuffet (tables provided for bridal party, parents, and guests); hot meal served; wedding cake	Buffet. Bridal party and parents may have tables. Cocktail buffet food, sandwiches, cold cuts, snacks, wedding cake	Stand-up buffet or 1 table for all guests. May be a meal or snacks and wedding cake
BEVERAGES	Champagne. Whiskey and soft drinks may be served also	Champagne or punch for toasts. Whiskey and soft drinks (optional)	Champagne or punch for toasts; tea, coffee, or soft drinks in addition
INVITATIONS AND ANNOUNCEMENTS	Engraved	Engraved	Handwritten or telephoned invitations; engraved announcements
DECORATIONS AND ACCESSORIES	Elaborate flowers for church, canopy to church, aisle carpet, pew ribbons, limousines for bridal party, groom's cake (given to guests in boxes), engraved matchbooks or napkins as mementos, rose petals or confetti	Flowers for church, aisle carpet, pew ribbons, rose petals (other items optional)	Flowers for altar, rose petals
MUSIC	Organ at church, choir or soloist optional; orchestra for dancing at reception	Organ at church, choir or soloist optional; strolling musician, small orchestra, or records for reception; dancing optional	Organ at church; records at reception optional

There must be compromises, of course, but the important thing for everyone to remember is that the people who should be happiest of all with the wedding plans are the bride and groom. Even though her mother and father are "picking up the tab" they should be doing it for their daughter's pleasure, and not as an excuse to impose on the couple the type of wedding that *they* think it should be.

There are so many details involved in even the simplest wedding that careful planning and preparation are essential if everyone is to enjoy the day itself. For a large wedding, expert help of all kinds should be arranged for well in advance. Without adequate preparation Father may be irritated, Mother jittery, the bride in tears, and the bridegroom ready to cancel the whole thing. This chapter and those that follow are dedicated to helping you avoid such needless unhappiness.

Let it be said at the outset that the following discussion of wedding plans will be based on the most elaborate wedding possible. Very few will want or be able to have such an affair, but only by including every detail can the complete pattern be given. Then you follow as many of these suggestions as you find pleasing and practical for you.

THE RESPONSIBILITIES, FINANCIAL AND OTHERWISE

A big, fashionable wedding can total several thousand dollars, whereas a lovely, simple one can be given for under $500. A schedule of approximate costs follows, but remember that the prices listed will vary considerably depending on the area you live in, the type of music or food that you choose, and, of course, rising prices must be taken into consideration. Furthermore, you may substitute one expense for another. If you choose to borrow cars to transport the wedding party, for example, you may apply that expense toward more elaborate beverages or flowers.

TOTAL WEDDING BUDGET

TYPE OF WEDDING	$500–$750 INFORMAL OR FORMAL	$1,000– $1500 SEMIFORMAL	$2,000– $3000 FORMAL	$5,000+ FORMAL
Number of Attendants	1 or 2	2–4	4–6	6–8
Number at Reception	50	100	150–200	300+
Place of Reception	Home or in church facilities	Home, club, or restaurant	Club or hotel	Club or hotel

TOTAL WEDDING BUDGET *(Continued)*

TYPE OF WEDDING	$500–$750 INFORMAL OR FORMAL	$1,000– $1500 SEMIFORMAL	$2,000– $3000 FORMAL	$5,000+ FORMAL
Type of Reception	Stand-up reception	Buffet at home or club, sit-down in restaurant	Buffet or sit-down	Buffet or sit-down, depending on number
Refreshments	Sandwiches and snacks, punch, liquor	Sandwiches and hors d'oeuvres	Cold buffet menu, liquor and champagne	Hot meal, liquor and champagne
ITEMS TO BUDGET:				
Wedding Dress and Accessories	$125–175	$200–250	$300–400	$500
Invitations, Announcements, etc.	$50–75	$50–150	$200–250	$350
Flowers, Attendants at Church and Reception	$50	$50–60	$100–200	$350
Music (Church and Reception)	none or $20 for organ	$50–100	$120–350	$450
Transportation for Bridal Party to Church and Reception	none	none–$50	$100–200	$200
Photographs—Formal and Candids	$50–125 (or none)	$100–150	$200–300	$350
Bridesmaids' Gifts	$10–20	$20–40	$80–120	$150
Reception (Food, Beverages, Wedding Cake, Catering Service)	$200–250	$450–600	$750–1000	$2,400
Contingency Fund (Awning, Tent, Sextons Fee, etc.)	$20–35	$80–100	$150–180	$250

The inclusion of the chart above does not mean that a lovely wedding cannot be given for less than $500. Actually, it is perfectly possible to have a beautiful and memorable wedding for $350, or even less. To illustrate, I will describe a wedding and reception that I attended recently. The ceremony took place in the evening in a small chapel decorated with two vases of white flowers. The couple received on the church steps, and then the wedding party (a maid of honor and best man) and the thirty-five guests went to the bride's home. Whiskey and soft drinks were offered, but no hors d'oeuvres. At eight thirty a buffet dinner was served, consisting of shrimp New-burg, sliced roast beef, salad, bread and rolls. There was a handsome wedding cake on display, which later served as dessert. At the time the bride and groom cut the cake, one round of champagne was passed to drink a toast to their happiness.

The house was very simply decorated with vases of greens and flowers from the family's garden.

The bride could not afford to buy the wedding dress she wanted, but she was fortunate to be able to borrow one. If this had not been possible she would have worn the prettiest dress she owned, as did her maid of honor.

The bride and groom issued the invitations by telephoning, eliminating that expense.

The total cost of this wedding was $350. The expenses were as follows:

Food	
10 lbs. shrimp	$37.00
9 lbs. roast beef (eye round)	16.00
Cream	2.00
Salad	10.00
Rolls and bread	7.00
Miscellaneous	10.00
Wedding cake	35.00
Beverages	
Whiskey, 6 bottles	38.00
Mixes, soft drinks	10.00
Champagne (domestic), 8 bottles	40.00
Catering help—cook and bartender	75.00
Flowers—church, table centerpiece, bride's and maid of honor's bouquets, corsages, and boutonnieres	70.00
Total	$350.00

Had the hostess been able to do the cooking herself, and had the host wished to serve the drinks, the cost of the help would have been eliminated. Other costs could have been lowered too. A friend might have provided the wedding cake as a gift, and the champagne was not essential. The floral centerpiece could have been replaced by an ornament or less expensive paper flowers or figures. Corsages for the mothers of the couple were not necessary, although they were much appreciated. At the wedding described above, friends took pictures at the reception and gave them to the bride as wedding presents. Extra china, glasses, and silverware were lent by relatives and neighbors.

No important element of a large and elaborate wedding was missing. The details were reduced only in amount or elegance. Even though this wedding was planned and given in less than ten days' time, it will be remembered as a lovely occasion by everyone there. The bride will always know that she had as beautiful a ceremony and reception as if she had planned and prepared three months in advance, and spent ten times the amount of money that she did.

DIVISION OF EXPENSES

TRADITIONAL EXPENSES OF THE BRIDE AND HER FAMILY

The invitations to ceremony and reception, and the announcements.

The service of a bridal consultant if desired.

The trousseau of the bride, consisting not only of her clothing but of her household linen and her hope chest.

Floral decorations for the church and reception, bouquets for the bride and bridesmaids, corsages for the bride's mother and grandmother, and a boutonniere for the father of the bride. In some American communities it is customary for the groom to provide the bouquet carried by the bride. In others it is the custom for the bride to send boutonnieres to the ushers and for the groom to order the bouquets of the bridesmaids. But in most areas the bride's as well as the bridesmaids' bouquets are looked upon as part of the decorative arrangements, all of which are provided by the bride's parents.

The choir, soloists, and organist at the church, and the fee to the sexton. Some churches send a bill covering all these services; if not, they must be paid for separately.

The orchestra at the reception. This may mean twenty pieces with two leaders, or it may mean one violinist or a phonograph.

Transportation for the bridal party from the house to the church and from there to the reception, if rented limousines are to be used.

All expenses of the reception, including: rental of the club or hall, the caterer's or restaurant bills, food, beverages (including liquor and champagne), wedding cake, and flowers.

The bride's presents to her bridesmaids. They may be quite elaborate or carefully selected trinkets of negligible cost.

Hotel accommodations for the bride's attendants if they cannot stay with relatives, friends, or neighbors.

Formal photographs of the bride in her wedding dress, and candid pictures taken the day of the wedding. If a bridesmaid or usher or guest wishes to have a wedding photograph, she or he may properly order and *pay* for a print from the photographer, as may the groom's family.

Awnings, a tent for an outdoor reception, and a carpet for the church aisle if not provided by the church.

The bride's present to the groom if she wishes to give one.

The groom's ring if it is to be a double-ring ceremony.

The services of a traffic policeman, if necessary.

THE BRIDEGROOM'S EXPENSES

The engagement ring and wedding ring.

A wedding present to the bride—jewelry if he is able, always something for her to keep forever.

His bachelor dinner—if he gives one.

The bride's bouquet, where local custom requires it, and in any case, a corsage for her to wear when they go away.

The marriage license.

A personal gift to his best man and to each of his ushers.

Even if his attendants' suits are rented, he gives his best man and each usher his wedding tie, gloves, and boutonniere.

Boutonnieres for his father and himself.

The clergyman's fee. Clergymen do not charge a regular fee, but a donation is expected, and it should be in accordance with the circumstances of the family and the elaborateness of the wedding. It may vary from ten or fifteen dollars for a private ceremony to a hundred dollars or more for a large one.

Hotel accommodations for his attendants, if necessary.

All expenses of the honeymoon.

The groom's parents pay for: the rehearsal dinner (not obligatory but customary); their own transporation and lodgings (unless they stay with friends or relatives).

BRIDESMAIDS' EXPENSES

Bridesmaids pay for their own dresses and accessories. In a case where this would impose a real hardship, the bride might offer to help, but ordinarily she does not.

Transportation to and from the site of the wedding, but the bride pays all their expenses while they are there.

A gift to the couple.

A share of the "joint" present from all the bridesmaids.

Participation in showers, including one, or possibly two, shower gifts.

The maid of honor usually gives one of the showers herself, although other bridesmaids may be co-hostesses.

USHERS' EXPENSES

Rental of wedding clothes, if necessary.

Transportation to and from the site of the wedding, but all other expenses are paid for by the groom.

A gift to the couple.

A share of the ushers' "joint" present.

A share of the expenses of a bachelor dinner, if given by the ushers.

EXCEPTIONS

Whether a wedding is to be large or tiny, tradition decrees that the reception must be either at the house of the bride's parents or other relatives or close friends, or else in rooms rented by her family. The groom's family may give entertainments of whatever description they choose for the young couple after they have returned from the honeymoon, but the wedding and reception—however simple they may be—are supposed to be furnished by the bride's family.

There are circumstances, however, when it would be ridiculous not to break this rule. If, for instance, the bride were without family, or came from another country, the reception might perfectly well be held in the house of the bridegroom's parents.

Then, in certain localities and among some ethnic groups, it is customary for the groom's family to share in the expenses of the reception, often paying for the liquor and other beverages. When this is an accepted practice—traditional to that particular group of people—it is perfectly correct.

Furthermore, because we have a much more open and practical attitude toward money today than when earlier etiquette books were written, it is no longer considered an insult for the groom's family to offer to "help out," simply out of thoughtfulness, or perhaps to allow the young couple a bigger reception than the bride's family alone could afford. The main point is that the offer should come from the groom's family, and it should *not* be a request on the part of the bride's.

The question of *why* the bride should pay the expenses comes up so often that I would like to comment on it. The traditional argument—that the groom will assume all the expenses for the rest of their lives—no longer holds water. Most brides contribute for many years to the family income, sometimes a larger proportion than do their husbands.

However, there is a *good* reason why the bride and her family should, when possible, "give" the wedding and reception. It is far more practical and less complicated for *one* family to make the plans and decisions—hopefully with the approval of the other, of course. It is still the bride who cares most about the details of the wedding and is willing to assume the responsibility for them. Few grooms would want to be bothered, or would have the time and interest necessary. Therefore it is natural that the bride's parents should be the host and hostess for the occasion. And as in entertaining of any kind, it is the host and hostess who assume the expenses and make the arrangements. Therefore, (in most cases) because of their position as host and hostess, it is best that the wedding be planned and paid for according to the means of the bride's family, even though it may mean that it is not as large or elaborate as the groom's family might wish.

WHEN, WHERE, AND HOW BIG?

As soon as the couple decide approximately when they want to get married, the bride must find out on exactly which day her church or synagogue and the clergyman who is to perform the ceremony will be available. If it is to be a large wedding she must also coordinate the time that the church is free with the time at which the caterer or hotel or club will be available.

Next the couple must decide on the precise time of day that will be best for the ceremony. Religion, climate, local custom, and transportation schedules may be important factors, as well as the bride and groom's plans for their wedding trip. Also, due consideration should be given to the convenience of a majority of the relatives and friends who will want to come.

In the South most weddings are held in the evening when the heat of the day is over, although that is not so important a consideration as it once was since the advent of air conditioning. Many Catholic weddings that include a Nuptial Mass are held at noon. Protestant weddings most often take place in the late afternoon. This is the most satisfactory time if an evening reception is planned, because it can follow the ceremony immediately. A noon wedding leaves an awkward gap between ceremony and reception, which guests are somewhat at a loss to fill, unless, of course, a luncheon reception is held.

Remember, too, that if the reception comes at a customary meal hour, substantial food is usually provided. In this case the number of guests invited to the reception may be restricted by the expense.

Having settled upon a day and hour, the bride and groom next determine the number of guests who can be provided for, considering the type of reception intended, the size of the bride's house or club, and the amount that her family can afford to spend.

The number of guests invited to the ceremony is unlimited—determined only by the size of the church, chapel, or synagogue.

THE WEDDING LIST

Four lists are combined in sending out wedding invitations: The bride and the bridegroom each make a list of their own friends, in addition to the list of the bride's family and that of the groom's family.

The bride's mother discusses with the groom, or if possible with his mother, how the list is to be divided between them. If the families are old friends and live in the same community, the invitations should be divided more or less equally between them. At least half of the names on the two lists would undoubtedly be the same, and therefore each family would be able to add several more in place of those which are duplicated. But if they have never known each other well, and their friends are unknown to each other, each list would have to be limited to half the total.

On the other hand, if the groom's people live in another place and not more than a few will be able to come, the bride's mother will be able to invite as many people as will result in the total number of spaces available. Both mothers may risk being a little overliberal because there are always a few who, having accepted, are then prevented for one reason or another from coming.

When some refusals are received, the bride's mother may send out additional invitations to replace those guests, up until two and a half weeks before the wedding.

It is most important for future harmony that the family of the out-of-town groom estimate *realistically* the number of guests who will make the trip to the wedding. When the bride's mother tells them the total number that can be invited and how many acceptances she expects on her side, they should make every effort to stay within the total. It is up to the out-of-town family to respect the requests of the bride's family in this matter, as they may not be aware of the limitations of space or expense that are factors in the number of invitations to be sent.

INVITATIONS TO THE RECEPTION

Invitations to the reception do carry an obligation—the receiver is expected to send a gift. Therefore mere acquaintances, old friends with whom the bride's or groom's family has lost touch, and people who live too far away to attend should *not* be included on the list. They should, instead, receive an announcement, or possibly an invitation to the church only, neither of which carries any obligation.

The clergyman who performs the ceremony (and his wife) should be sent an invitation to the reception. If they are not acquainted with one family or the other, they may not wish to attend, but it would be discourteous not to include them on the list.

The groom's parents should receive an invitation simply because they generally enjoy them as mementos of the occasion. They need not acknowledge the invitation unless they have had no contact with the bride's family. Bridal attendants are also sent invitations, to have as mementos.

When a bride knows that one of her attendants or one of the guests is engaged, she should, whether she knows the fiancé(e) or not, send him (or her) a separate invitation. If she does not know the name, and cannot get hold of a guest to find out, she may write on her attendant's invitation: "We would be delighted to have you bring your fiancé."

If the parents of the attendants are acquainted with the bride or groom, they should receive invitations. Otherwise it is not necessary.

Youngsters who cannot be included at the reception are often delighted with an invitation to the church ceremony.

People in mourning should be sent invitations, even though they may not feel like attending.

Couples to whose weddings the bride and groom were asked should be invited if their wedding was of a commensurate size.

WHEN CHILDREN CANNOT BE INCLUDED

Very often it is impossible for the young children of friends and relatives to be included at the reception. It is the prerogative of the bride and groom to make this decision, but it is somewhat awkward to enforce. Although parents *should not* assume that an invitation addressed to "Mr. and Mrs." means "and family," they often do. If the bride has reason to suspect that a number of uninvited children will appear, she must take steps to prevent it. She cannot write on the invitations "No children," which would seem very discourteous and cold. She can, however, enclose a brief note with the invitations to relatives and close friends with children, explaining that she could not include the youngsters, and why. She may also talk to friends and relatives, asking them to spread the word for her. Having done this, she must make no exceptions—other than her brothers and sisters and those of the groom.

CHURCH INVITATIONS AND ANNOUNCEMENTS

Invitations to the church or announcements may be sent to the entire list of personal acquaintances, and often to business associates of both families—no matter how large the combined number may be or whether they will attend or not. People in mourning are included, as well as those who live miles away, for the invitations to the ceremony and announcements carry no attendant obligation.

At a typical wedding, friends are asked to the reception as well as to the church. If the wedding is to be in the house or is otherwise small, so that only families and close friends are invited, announcements may be sent to all uninvited acquaintances.

LODGING FOR OUT-OF-TOWN GUESTS

If the groom lives far enough away from the bride so that his family and attendants cannot return home after prewedding parties and the wedding itself, the bride (or her mother) makes arrangements for their lodging. The groom's mother must, as soon as possible, tell the bride's family exactly how many of their relatives will definitely attend the wedding. Friends and neighbors of the bride, if they possibly can, offer accommodations for bridesmaids and ushers and occasionally (especially if they happen to be acquainted with them) for the immediate family of the groom. But aunts, uncles, cousins, and friends stay at nearby hotels, inns, or motels to avoid imposing on strangers. If the bride's family or some of their close friends are members of a club that has guest accommodations, it is an ideal solution for grandparents or older relatives, who can be provided with all services and meals when they are not attending wedding festivities.

Some weeks before the wedding the bride's mother reserves the necessary number of rooms in the best hotels or motels nearby, or if there is a choice she may send pamphlets or brochures (adding her own recommendation) to the groom's family. They select the one that appeals to them and make their own reservations or ask her to do so. In either case, unless the bride's family is very wealthy and that of the groom can barely pay for its transportation to the marriage, the cost of the accommodations is paid by those using them.

ORDERING THE INVITATIONS

As soon as the wedding lists are complete, the bride-to-be and her mother go to the stationer's to decide on the invitations. Details such as size and texture of paper and style of type and print are considered.

While true engraving is beautiful, and is almost mandatory for a very formal wedding, there are far less expensive methods of simulating engraving (thermography), which are pleasing and entirely suitable for almost all weddings. The invitations should be "in keeping" with the wedding. If the wedding is to be traditional, the invitation should be in the third-person, traditional form. If the couple are being married on the beach at dawn, with an informal brunch afterward, the invitations might well be a poem written—and illustrated—by the couple themselves.

For the wording of wedding invitations and announcements, see Chapter 50.

CHOOSING THE ATTENDANTS

At the average wedding there are generally two to six bridesmaids and ushers, in addition to a maid of honor and/or a matron of honor, and a best man. Even though it is sometimes difficult to make a choice, there should not be two maids of honor or two matrons of honor. When one of two good friends must be selected, the other serves as a bridesmaid. There may also be one or two flower girls, one or two ring bearers, and pages. Young relatives who are between the ages of ten and sixteen (approximately) can serve as junior ushers or bridesmaids. There need not be an even number, since it is perfectly all right for one junior usher or one junior bridesmaid to walk alone in the procession.

The bride's attendants may or may not be married, but whether they are "matrons" or not, they are always known as "bridesmaids"—not "bridesmatrons." It is best not to choose a girl who is too obviously pregnant, however, as her condition cannot help but detract from the appearance of the wedding party. The bridesmaids should be reasonably close to the bride in age. Much older relatives or friends might help serve at the reception or have other "duties," but they should not be numbered among the bride's "maids."

Although the bride need not have any bridesmaids she must have one attendant or maid of honor. The picture of her father or the best man holding her flowers while she and the groom exchange rings is, to say the least, ludicrous!

There should not be more bridesmaids than ushers in the wedding party, but there are often more ushers than bridesmaids. In deciding on the number of attendants a good rule of thumb to follow is "one usher for every fifty guests." The number of bridesmaids may then be chosen accordingly.

The bride's closest sister is almost always asked to be maid (or matron) of honor. If she has no sister near her age, she chooses her best friend, or perhaps a cousin. The groom selects a brother or good friend for a best man, and some grooms ask their fathers to stand up with them. Wherever possible both the bride and groom should invite friends in whose weddings they have served.

As ushers and bridesmaids are chosen from relatives or very close friends, the invitation to serve is extended in person or by telephone. If they live far away they are asked by telegraph or note. They should be contacted as soon as the engagement is announced, to allow plenty of time to choose replacements if someone must refuse. However, unless there is a very good reason, no one should ever turn down the honor of being an attendant, especially as a maid or matron of honor. If the problem is one of expense, this should be explained to the bride or groom honestly. He or she will probably be able to help with transportation costs, to assist with the purchase or rental of the costume, or otherwise help to defray expenses, so that the friend will be able to accept. If at the last moment one of the ushers or bridesmaids is forced to withdraw, the bride or groom may ask another friend to fill in. Friends should not be offended by this, but rather, flattered that they are considered close enough to be called on in an emergency.

RELATIVES OF THE BRIDE AND BRIDEGROOM AS ATTENDANTS

Unless attendants are limited to one or two, a brother of the bride is usually asked by the groom to be an usher. The bride returns the compliment by asking the sister of the groom who is nearest her own age to be bridesmaid.

When the homes of the bride and bridegroom are at such a great distance apart that none of the groom's immediate family can make the journey to the wedding, it is not unusual for him to choose (if he has no brother) his father or even stepfather as his best man. In such situations the ushers are chosen from among the friends of the bride.

MARRIED ATTENDANTS

It is entirely correct for a married man to act as usher, or for a married woman to be either matron of honor or a bridesmaid. Neither the wife of the first nor the husband of the second need be asked to take part. The one not officiating is, of course, invited to the wedding and sits at the bridal table. It is unusual for a husband and wife to be attendants at the same wedding, but if they are both close friends of the bride and groom there is no rule against it.

THE BRIDE'S ATTENDANTS

MAID AND/OR MATRON OF HONOR

The maid or matron of honor's most important duty is to act as a consultant and assistant to the bride. She should take as many duties and as much responsibility off the shoulders of the bride as possible—especially on the wedding day. She walks just in front of the bride in the procession (unless there are flower girls and ring bearers), she holds the bride's flowers during the ceremony, and she also hands the groom's ring to the bride if it is a double-ring ceremony. She helps the bride adjust her train and veil when she turns to leave the church. If there happen to be a maid *and* a matron of honor, the maid takes precedence and is in charge of the flowers and the ring at the altar.

She signs the wedding register as the bride's witness.

The maid of honor stands on the groom's left in the receiving line and sits on his left at the bridal table. She may or may not make a toast to the couple. She helps the bride change into her going-away clothes and helps the bride's mother put her wedding dress away. Although it is not obligatory she usually arranges to give a shower for the bride, with or without the help of the bridesmaids.

She is also in charge of choosing the gift that will be given to the bride from all the bridesmaids together, and collecting the money to pay for it.

BRIDESMAIDS

Bridesmaids have few specific duties other than forming the procession, and if the bride wishes, standing in the receiving line. They also act as "deputy hostesses" at the reception.

Any of them may give a shower, or they may all give one together. They also may entertain the bride and groom in any other way they wish.

They are responsible, as mentioned under "Expenses," for paying for their own costumes, and also for seeing that they are properly fitted and that they have the necessary accessories. It is unfortunate but true that occasionally a girl has to refuse the joy of being in the

wedding party because a complete bridesmaid's outfit costs a sum
that neither she nor her parents can provide. But it is also true that
seldom is the bride herself in a position to pay for six or more sets
of dresses and accessories even if she wishes to make an exception
to the rule. Therefore the bride who has a conscience tries to choose
clothes that will not be too expensive. Department stores as well as
specialty shops offer enchanting ready-to-wear models that can be
ordered to fit almost any budget. Ideally the bride should choose a
model that will be useful to the bridesmaids after the wedding.

JUNIOR BRIDESMAIDS

Junior bridesmaids are young girls, generally between eight and
fourteen, who are too big to be flower girls and too young to be
regular bridesmaids. They attend the rehearsal, of course, and usually the rehearsal dinner (for a little while, at least), but are not
necessarily included in other festivities.

FLOWER GIRLS

Flower girls used to scatter petals before the bride, but more
often today they simply carry old-fashioned baskets of flowers, or
bouquets. They walk directly in front of the bride unless there is a
ring bearer, in which case the flower girl precedes him.

Flower girls are usually young relatives of the bride or groom,
although sometimes the bride chooses the daughter of a close friend.
The little girl should be between four and seven years old. Unless
a child is unusually self-possessed, a two- or three-year-old is unreliable at best, and older children look foolish as "flower girls."

The flower girl's dress is paid for by her family. It should be
similar to the bridesmaids' dresses, but modified in style, if necessary,
to be more becoming to a child.

Flower girls must attend the rehearsal, of course. Whether they
go to some of the showers and the rehearsal dinner—for a short
time—depends on their age and the wishes of their parents.

RING BEARERS

Ring bearers, like flower girls, should be between four and
seven.

The ring bearer carries the ring on a firm white velvet or satin
cushion. If it is the real ring, it should be fastened on the cushion by
a single thread, and the best man should be aware of this. It is actually
safer to have a facsimile on the cushion, while the best man carries
the real ring safely in his pocket.

OTHER SMALL ATTENDANTS

Train bearers, as the name implies, hold the bride's train. They, too, must be very little boys and dressed in white. Unless they have rehearsed their part thoroughly, the train trailing smoothly by itself is really safer than a train in the hands of small children whose behavior is apt to be uncertain. Pages, too, are small boys who walk in the procession, but do nothing else.

A boy who is too big to be a ring bearer and too young to be a junior usher can be made responsible for running the ribbons along the ends of the pews. When there are two boys one takes the right side of the aisle, the other one the left, and they stand beside the front pews during the ceremony.

Remember, when planning your wedding party, that no matter how charming and cute they are, the presence of too many children is distracting. Even when they are well behaved (and sometimes they are not!) they may steal the show from the bride.

DUTIES OF THE GROOM'S ATTENDANTS

THE BEST MAN

No matter how small the wedding, the bridegroom always has a best man, just as the bride has a maid of honor. In civil ceremonies, before a justice of the peace, the best man and maid of honor are replaced by two "witnesses." This is required by law. Generally the closest brother of the groom is best man unless he is a great deal older or younger. But this is not an unbreakable rule. When the groom has no brother he would probably choose his closest friend; or if deciding upon this is difficult, he perhaps chooses a cousin, or a brother of the bride. Frequently a son who is very devoted to his father will ask him to serve as best man.

At some point before the wedding, the best man consults the ushers about a "joint" present for the bride and groom, and he is responsible for ordering it and collecting the money. He presents the gift to the groom, usually at the rehearsal dinner.

The duties of the best man vary with the circumstances—the plans for the wedding and the honeymoon, the amount of time he has free to place at the groom's disposal before the ceremony, and so on. The important thing is that he relieve the groom of as many details and as much responsibility as possible. Any or all of the following suggestions will smooth the groom's way and add to the couple's enjoyment of their wedding day. The best man should take care of as many of these situations as he possibly can.

He may help the groom pack for his honeymoon, and he sees that the clothes the groom will change into after the wedding are packed in a separate bag and taken to where the reception will be held.

He makes sure that the groom is properly dressed and perfectly groomed. It is his job to get him to the church on time, too.

He is responsible for the wedding ring and must be sure that the groom gives him the ring before the ceremony, to be kept in his pocket until it is time for it to be placed on the bride's finger. If there is a ring bearer who will carry the actual ring, the best man sees that it is carefully attached to the cushion.

In Christian ceremonies he enters the church with the groom and remains at his side during the entire ceremony, producing the ring at the proper moment. In Orthodox and Conservative Jewish ceremonies he precedes the groom in the wedding procession. Ordinarily he walks out with the maid or matron of honor immediately behind the bride and groom. If he does not walk out with her, however, he leaves through a side door while the procession goes down the aisle. He quickly goes around to the front of the church to give the groom his hat and coat. Sometimes the sexton takes charge of the groom's hat and coat and hands them to him at the church door as he goes out. But in either case the best man always hurries to see the bride and groom into their car, which should be waiting at the entrance to the church. If a chauffeur is not present to drive the newlyweds to the reception, the best man performs this duty too.

He signs the wedding certificate as the groom's witness.

The best man is responsible for giving the clergyman his donation on behalf of the groom. He may do it before the ceremony while they are waiting to enter the church, or if he is not driving the bride and groom to the reception, he may return to the vestry immediately after the recessional to deliver the envelope.

The amount may be from ten to twenty dollars for a very simple ceremony, fifty dollars for an average wedding with perhaps four attendants, one or two hundred (or more) for a very large wedding.

If the donation is given in the form of a check, it is made out to the minister himself rather than to the church.

If the father of the bride has reason to suspect that the circumstances of the groom or his family do not permit them to make a contribution commensurate with the elaborateness of the occasion, he may, if he wishes, make an additional contribution on his own later.

At the reception the best man does not stand in the receiving line but mingles with the guests and helps the bride's family in any way he can. When the bride and groom sit down at the bridal table, he sits on the bride's right, and it is his responsibility to make the first toast to the newlyweds. He reads aloud any telegrams or messages that have been received and keeps them to be given to the couple later. He is the first man to dance with the bride after the groom, her father, and her father-in-law.

When the bride and groom are ready to leave the reception he helps the groom change and takes care of his wedding clothes. He makes sure that the groom has his tickets, his money, his credit cards, his car keys, and anything else that he will need. He escorts the groom's family to the room where their son is dressing, for their farewells.

The best man is also in charge of whatever transportation the couple plans to use to leave the reception. If it is by car he has the car hidden—with the newlyweds' honeymoon luggage already in it—to protect it from practical jokers. If they are using the car to get to a station or airport he often drives them there himself. In any case he leads the couple through the waiting guests to the door, and when they have pulled away in a shower of rice or rose petals he may breathe a sigh of relief and join the rest of the wedding party in a final celebration.

The best man selects and collects the money for the ushers' "joint" present to the groom.

THE USHERS

The ushers are chosen from among the relatives and good friends of the groom and are usually of more or less the same age. If the bride has brothers who are contemporaries, they are generally included. One who is experienced or close to the family is appointed head usher. He is responsible for seeing that the others get to the church at the appointed time, assigning them to special aisles if the church is large, and designating the ones who will escort members of the two families. He himself escorts the bride's mother in and out of the church, unless she has a son among the ushers, or she prefers to walk out with her husband.

As mentioned above, there should be one usher to every fifty guests (approximately), and they are responsible for seeing that the guests are all seated before the ceremony starts. Two ushers are assigned to putting the white carpet down the aisle just before the procession starts, and two others lay the ribbon along the ends of the reserved pews after the occupants are seated.

Ushers do not stand on the receiving line, but they do sit at the bridal table when there is one.

They are expected to contribute to a "joint" gift to the groom.

JUNIOR USHERS

Junior ushers are between ten and fourteen years old. They dress like the other ushers and walk behind them. Sometimes, when there are two junior ushers, they are appointed to be in charge of the white carpet or the ribbons.

PLANNING THE CEREMONY

Shortly after the future bride and groom announce their engagement they get in touch with their clergyman. If the bride is not in the town where the wedding is to take place, she writes to him and arranges for an appointment at the first opportunity. If possible, bride and groom should go together, because many important decisions will be made at this first conference. If the groom is not present, the bride's mother may accompany her. If the marriage is to take place in the bride's own church there are few difficulties, but if the couple are not affiliated with a church there may be complications. The bride and her fiancé, if they want a religious ceremony, must decide on which church they would prefer and ask the clergyman if he would officiate. If they are not able to find a minister who can do so, they must settle for a civil ceremony.

A Protestant marrying a Catholic must be prepared to present a birth certificate and a baptismal certificate from his own church, and the birth certificate will be required in all churches. The bride should find out just what papers will be necessary when she calls to make the appointment.

The matters that should be discussed with the clergyman are:

The service itself—whether it will be the traditional service, or whether the bride and groom plan to write all or part of their service themselves.

Whether the congregation will be seated or will stand throughout the ceremony.

Whether the couple will kiss after the ceremony.

Whether photographs may be taken during the service.

Whether there are restrictions in that particular church as to dress.

Whether candles may be used or not.

The clergyman's recommendations on the size of the wedding party and the number of guests, relying on his judgment and experience.

When the couple are not being married in the bride's own church, she may wish to have the clergyman from her home parish officiate. Or perhaps she or the groom has a relative or godparent who is a minister, and they would like him to marry them. This can be arranged quite easily, with the two clergymen participating in the service. On some occasions the clergyman of the church where the wedding takes place turns the service over to the visitor completely, but this is unusual. The donation is still given to the "host" minister, and an additional "gift" is given to the one who officiates, which may be either money or a "concrete" gift—perhaps a small wedding picture of the bride and groom in a good leather frame. Naturally, if the visiting clergyman is a relative or personal friend, the gift is more appropriate than the money. His expenses would, of course, be paid by the bride's family (or the groom's, if he came at their request).

The church organist is also consulted about the couple's choice of music. If they plan to have a visiting soloist or musician, this, too, must be discussed.

Finally, the sexton is the one who can give the bride and groom the information they will need about carpets, canapés, dressing facilities, candles, etc. He will also tell them what the church charges will be for each of the items.

In planning the service, the bride and groom must decide whether they want a traditional wedding or not. If they do, there are certain rules to follow. The bride is given away by her father, the procession is formed in a specific way, the service is taken from the prayer book, and so on. These customs are long established and very beautiful, but they do not allow for very much individuality. When the couple feel that they want their wedding to be less stereotyped and more "their own" they may incorporate many untraditional acts and words. For example, some Christian brides are adapting the ancient Jewish custom of having both their mother and their father walk down the aisle with them. This is surely not "traditional" in the Protestant church, but the thought is lovely, and why should it be criticized if everyone is happy with the plan? Many other ceremonies include the bride's mother by having her join her husband in saying "We do" when the minister asks, "Who gives this woman . . . ?" So, assuming that no one is hurt by the plans the couple make, and that both families are informed and approve, many of the variations we see today are so beautiful, and enhance the wedding service so much, that they may become the traditions of the future.

PLANNING THE RECEPTION

The bride and her mother make most of the plans for the details of the reception. If it is to be held at a hotel or club, the staff prepares the food and beverages and serves them. The manager will arrange for flowers and decorations, some of which may be kept on hand for such occasions. All details of the menu, the service, the seating, and other facilities are discussed with the manager well in advance.

When a large wedding reception is held at home, the services of a caterer are indispensable. He will provide the food and drinks, china, glasses, silverware, tables, chairs, linen, favors, and complete service. The arrangements are all made through the head of the service or his agent, and a contract should be signed in advance.

THE ELABORATE, SIT-DOWN RECEPTION

When the reception takes place at home, the caterer brings all the equipment, and the necessary people to set it up, the morning of the wedding. Additional help may arrive later, but well before the hour of the wedding.

In the country a tent is erected on the lawn the day before the wedding. Under the tent there is a platform surrounded by small tables, and at one end a large one is reserved for the bridal party. A second table, called the "parents' table," is reserved for the immediate families of the bride and groom, the clergyman, and a few special friends.

Place cards are put on the bridal table and the parents' table, but they are not necessary on the small tables. All the guests, except the few placed at the reserved tables, sit with whom they like. Sometimes they do so by prearrangement, but usually they sit where they happen to find friends.

The menu is limited only by the preference of the bride and groom. There may be bouillon or vichyssoise, lobster Newburg or oyster cocktail. The main dish might be beef stroganoff with wild rice, sweetbreads and mushrooms, or creamed chicken in pastry shells.

Any variety of vegetable, aspic, or salad may be served.

Dessert is usually ice cream or sherbet accompanied by little cakes or cookies, and slices of wedding cake.

At this type of reception the traditional beverage has always been champagne. However, many people also offer other liquors, and soft drinks or punch must be available. For families who do not wish to serve any alcohol a fruit punch is the best choice.

THE BUFFET RECEPTION

For the stand-up, or buffet, reception a long table is set in the largest room of the home or club. It is covered with a plain white damask cloth. The centerpiece is generally a bowl of white flowers. Piles of plates (preferably white, or white and gold), stacks of napkins, and rows of spoons and forks are symmetrically arranged on the table. This table should be situated so that the guests pass on directly to another table to help themselves to food, or if there is room, the plates of food may be arranged on the same table. Even though it is not a seated dinner, there is a table for the bridal party and one for the parents. There are also a number of tables with cloths and centerpieces, but no place settings, to which guests may carry their plates from the buffet.

The wedding cake is the feature of the buffet, placed at the center of the table with the centerpiece of white flowers behind it or two floral pieces flanking it. If space is limited, the cake may be nearby, on its own small round table. There are usually two or three cold dishes and at least one hot dish served, with appropriate accompaniments. There should also be finger rolls and sandwiches, substantial yet small enough to eat easily.

There may be dishes filled with fancy cakes or "petits fours" chosen for looks as much as taste. There may also be compotes of peppermints, caramels, and chocolates. Ice cream is the typical dessert, served with a slice of wedding cake.

Liquor and soft drinks are served from a bar or a table arranged as a bar. Glasses of champagne are passed around to the guests on trays.

A VERY SIMPLE RECEPTION

A simple home reception that takes place after a noon or evening wedding should provide a substantial luncheon or dinner, as the case might be. But a reception held after an afternoon wedding need not include a meal and can be, in fact, very simple. All that is required is a beverage with which to drink the newlyweds' health, and

advance. The bride and groom may give the leader a list of pieces they would like to have played, but they should consider the tastes of *all* their guests and alternate louder popular music with the more sentimental music enjoyed by their parents.

It is by no means necessary to go to this extent. For smaller, less formal weddings a trio or piano and violin, or even a phonograph, can easily provide music for a small dance floor—possibly one room of the house—cleared for the occasion.

If there is to be no dancing, a wandering guitarist or accordionist playing the music chosen by the couple makes a happy background for toasts and conversation and adds tremendously to the gaiety of the occasion.

THE WEDDING PICTURES

THE FORMAL PHOTOGRAPH

Sometime before the wedding, often at the final fitting of the bridal gown, the photographer takes the formal wedding pictures of the bride. If photographs are to be sent to the newspapers, they must be taken well in advance to allow time for choosing the ones to be used, the final printing, and mailing to the papers two to three weeks before the wedding day.

A small print of this formal picture in a silver frame, with or without date and the initials of the couple engraved on it, makes a charming present from bride to bridesmaid.

CANDID PHOTOGRAPHS

If the candid shots on the wedding day are to be taken by a professional, he must be engaged far ahead of time, especially if the wedding is to be in June. Amateur photographers are often almost as well equipped and skillful as professionals, and if you are fortunate enough to number one of these among your friends, he will surely be delighted to record the event. He cannot, however, provide as complete coverage as a skilled professional. If an amateur covers the entire day and uses quantities of film, the bride's family must certainly pay for the supplies and the printing, which, especially if color film is used, can be exorbitant. But if he uses a roll or two at the reception of his own volition and not at the specific request of the bride, this is not necessary, and often camera enthusiasts present these pictures as a wedding present to the bride.

A candid album starts with the bride's leaving the house before the wedding and continues through the day—her arrival at the church with her father (or whoever is giving her away), the wedding party's departure from the church after the ceremony, the bridal party and receiving line at the reception, shots of the bride dancing, the guests, the toasts, the cutting of the cake, throwing the bouquet, and finally, the departure of the happy pair on their honeymoon.

Pictures of the actual ceremony taken with flashbulbs are in very poor taste because they detract from the solemnity of the service. The cameraman should be informed of this beforehand. But once the service is over and the bridal procession is coming down the aisle, the camera may start to work, and pictures of the radiant bride and groom who suddenly realize that they are "Mr. and Mrs." are often among the best souvenirs of all.

Members of the bridal party who wish to have duplicates of the wedding pictures for their own scrapbooks may have them made at their own expense.

The bride's family are under no obligation to give a set of wedding pictures to the groom's family. They should, however, show them the proofs and arrange for them to order those they want, *at the groom's family's expense*. However, if the bride's family can afford it and the groom's cannot, it would be a thoughtful gesture to send five or six of the best pictures to the groom's parents, especially if they could not be at the wedding. They might also arrange to have a tape made of the ceremony and the toasts at the reception to be sent to parents or grandparents who were unable to attend.

THE NEWSPAPER ANNOUNCEMENT OF THE WEDDING

Most newspapers—and all those in large cities—require that information about weddings be sent in *at least* three weeks before the wedding. If they do not receive it by then, it will simply not get into the paper at all. The applications for announcements to appear in the Sunday papers are so numerous that only a small number can be accommodated. Therefore a bride who wants to ensure that her notice will appear, may send it with a note requesting that it be published on the Monday or Tuesday after the wedding if space is unavailable on Sunday.

The best course in the large cities is to call the newspaper and ask the society editor what the requirements are and what information the paper will want. Many newspapers provide their own form to be filled out, which is very helpful. In smaller towns the bride simply makes up her announcement as she would like it to appear, and sends it in. It should be clear, concise, and legible—typewritten, if possible.

If she wishes a picture to be published, she encloses a glossy five-by-seven or eight-by-ten-inch black-and-white print, unfolded. The newspaper will use it if there is space.

When a family wishes to make an announcement sometime later, after an elopement, for example, they send a brief notice to the newspaper including the place and date of the marriage, and the present location and perhaps employment of the bride and groom. It can be published whenever the paper has room for it.

The information that should be sent to the newspaper for an ordinary announcement is:

Bride's name and address
Her parents' names and their address
Bridegroom's name and address,
His parents' names and their address
Time of ceremony
Place (church, synagogue, etc.) and location of reception
Who will give the bride away—relationship to the bride
Maid of honor
Bridesmaids
Flower girl
Ring bearer
Best man
Ushers
Description of the bride's costume
Wedding trip
Future residence
Bride's schools
Bride's profession
Groom's schools
Groom's profession

Some city newspapers also print information about the careers or professions of the couple's parents. I consider this in poor taste and irrelevant to the occasion.

Announcements of second marriages are also sent to newspapers, but they are much shorter. They include the names of the couple and usually their parents' names, the location and date of the wedding, and the names of previous spouses. They generally indicate whether previous marriages ended by divorce or death. There may also be a mention of the profession of the husband and/or wife, and the place they are now living.

A typical announcement of a first wedding reads:

Miss Harriet Forest Young was married on Saturday, [January 17, optional], to Mr. George Boardman, at the Woodlawn Presbyterian Church. The marriage was performed by the pastor, Mr. Havelock Lewison, assisted by the groom's uncle, Dr. Maurice Stone.

The bride is the daughter of Mrs. Jackson Young and the late Mr. Young of this city. She was given away by her godfather, Mr. William Sutton. Her grandparents are Mr. and Mrs. Franklin Young of Georgetown, Virginia, and Mrs. Clay Jones and the late Mr. Jones of Salt Lake City.

Mr. Boardman is the son of Mr. Robert Boardman, Jr., of Atlanta, Georgia, and Mrs. Anson Parrish of Chicago, Illinois. His grandparents are Mr. and Mrs. Robert Boardman of Atlanta, and the late Mr. and Mrs. John Felch of Huntington, L.I.

Mrs. Boardman wore an Empire gown of marquisette, with insets of Alençon lace. Her long veil of Alençon lace, a family heirloom, was held in place by a crown of stephanotis. She carried a bouquet of stephanotis, roses, and lily of the valley.

Miss Honey Young served as her sister's maid of honor. Bridesmaids were Miss Nancy Young, another sister of the bride, Miss Helen Perry, and Mrs. Gordon Black.

Mr. Boardman's best man was his cousin, Robert Upton. The ushers were Philip Wells, Henry Simms, and Peter O'Malley. Twin brothers of the bride, Thomas and Michael, served as junior ushers.

Mrs. Boardman graduated from Northland School and Wellesley College. She is employed at the Citizens' National Bank of Providence.

The bridegroom was graduated from Peabody Prep in Holyoke, Massachusetts, and Brown University. He is also employed by the Citizens' National Bank.

After a wedding trip to England, the couple will live in East Providence.

Most large papers no longer include information about the costume of the bride. But small local papers do so when possible and sometimes even report on the costumes of the bridesmaids.

THE BRIDE'S TIMETABLE

In order to coordinate all the plans discussed in this chapter, the bride should have a definite schedule or timetable to follow. The list below is based on the time necessary to plan and prepare a large wedding. But even those of you who are getting married simply and on short notice will find a list helpful in organizing the procedures that will be necessary for the success of your wedding.

THREE MONTHS AHEAD OF THE WEDDING

1. With your bridegroom, decide what type of wedding you will have, whether it will be formal, semiformal, or informal, and if it will be held at a church, club, hotel, or home. Be sure to consult your family, whose expenses will be affected by the type of wedding you choose.
2. Decide the hour of the ceremony and the type of reception to follow. Remember, the degree of formality in your wedding ceremony should be matched in your reception.
3. Decide on the date of the wedding. Find out when your clergyman is free to perform the ceremony, and when the church or chapel is available. Visit your clergyman with your fiancé to discuss personal matters as well as wedding details. At this time, you should inquire about any restrictions as to the time of year, day of week, musical selections, floral decorations, or style of wedding clothes. You might also check with him on the rental fee for the church, the organist's fee, whether the church chimes may be used, whether a candlelight service is permissible, whether the social hall is available that day for a reception, and whether arrangements for a policeman or parking attendant may be made through the church secretary.

   Before confirming the church date, be sure that the club, caterer, or hotel selected for your reception can accommodate you and your party at the proper time. Engage their services at this time.
4. Decide how many guests and attendants you will have. The bride should have at least one attendant—her maid or matron of honor. The groom always has a best man.
5. Select your attendants. The bride and groom usually ask their attendants to serve in their wedding at the time the engagement is announced or shortly thereafter.
6. Compile your wedding lists for the church, reception, and

577

announcements. Where the guest list is limited, the bride's family may tell the groom's family how many guests they may invite.

While drawing up your invitation lists for the ceremony and reception you may compile a special list of people to receive announcements only. Remember, guests at house weddings are always invited to the reception as well as the ceremony, while for church weddings the number of guests may vary for the ceremony and reception. Announcements are sent only to friends who are *not invited* to the wedding or reception.

7. Order your wedding invitations and announcements, and if you wish, personal stationery for wedding-gift thank-you notes.
8. Order your bridal gown, select gowns for the bridesmaids, and urge the mothers to get together to choose their clothes.
9. Set a date with your photographer for your bridal portrait and engage him for candid pictures of your wedding.
10. Engage the orchestra for the music at the reception.
11. If the wedding is to be at home, make arrangements for cleaning, painting, redecorating, if necessary.
12. Start to shop for your household and personal trousseau.

TWO MONTHS AHEAD OF THE WEDDING

1. Make your medical, dental, and beauty-shop appointments at appropriate times.
2. Select gifts for your bridesmaids and the groom if you intend to give him one.
3. Set the date for your bridesmaids' luncheon if one is planned.
4. Register your wedding-gift preferences in your local stores.
5. Order the floral decorations for the church or ceremony, the bride's and bridesmaids' bouquets, and the reception decorations, after getting an estimate from your florist.
6. Select your wedding music with the help of your church organist.
7. Make transportation arrangements for limousines or privately driven cars to take the wedding party and both sets of parents to the church. For a large church wedding, a policeman or parking attendant should be hired to help direct traffic and parking.

8. Arrange for fittings for your bridesmaids. Have their shoes dyed in one lot.
9. Have your formal wedding portrait taken.
10. Make lodging arrangements for attendants and out-of-town guests.

THE LAST MONTH BEFORE THE WEDDING

1. Address and mail invitations so that they are received at least three weeks before the wedding. Prepare announcements to be mailed the day after the wedding.
2. Set up your gift display shelves or table if you plan to display your wedding gifts.
3. Record all wedding gifts and mail your thank-you notes as soon as each gift is received, for as long as you possibly can keep up with the flow.
4. Select your wedding ring and your groom's if he is to have one.
5. Make the arrangements for moving into your new home, if necessary.
6. Prepare a list of things you will need for your honeymoon and begin to pack them in your luggage.
7. Set aside everything you will use and wear on your wedding day and keep it together, in one place; check the bridesmaids' apparel and accessories to be sure their costumes are complete.
8. Make the final arrangements with your caterer, florist, photographer, church secretary, or sexton.
9. Send announcements and glossy prints of your wedding portrait to newspaper society editors.
10. Write out place cards for the bride's table, if there is to be one.
11. Change your name on all important papers: driver's license, personal bank account, social security records, insurance policies, etc.
12. Try and relax and enjoy this most important day of your life!

❧49❧ *Clothes for the Bridal Party*

No matter how strong the trend may be toward a "new look" in weddings, statistics show that over 90 percent of the three million girls who get married every year in this country choose traditional wedding gowns. To me, this proves their good sense, because there is no other costume so flattering, romantic, and becoming as the long white dress and veil. It can—and should—be adapted to current styles and to the individual wedding, and should be as becoming as possible to the wearer. But to discard a time-honored, beautiful costume in favor of a fleeting fad or something that is superchic and "in," is a mistake. Any extreme style may be very "in" now; tomorrow it will be gone. When your daughter looks at your wedding pictures twenty years from now, would you rather have her say, "They certainly wore funny-looking clothes in those days!" or "Mom, you certainly were a beautiful bride!"

THE BRIDE'S COSTUME

THE DRESS

The bride who is being married for the first time almost always chooses a gown of white or off-white. Touches of pastel color in the trim are delightful, and pastel silk under white marquisette or organdy creates a soft and beautiful effect.

The traditional and most formal bridal material is satin, but few brides wish to wear such a warm material on a summer day. Therefore, although satin is a favorite choice for fall and winter, other materials have become more popular for the rest of the year.

Other suitable fabrics for autumn and midwinter weddings are brocade, velvet, and moiré. In the spring, lace and taffeta are lovely, and in midsummer, chiffon, organdy, marquisette, cotton, piqué, and linen. An infinite variety of synthetic materials has added to the bride's choice for every season.

Mature brides may wear long gowns of simple design. Tulle, organdy, etc., are not good choices, as they look too "frilly" and youthful. It is very important that a bride in her forties or over choose a dress in off-white or a pastel color, particularly if the dress is of satin. An accent of blue or pink or ivory is far more becoming to the older woman's skin.

The length of the train of the bride's dress depends somewhat upon the size of the church. In a large church the train can be very long; in a small chapel, short. A moderately short train extends one yard on the ground. The length of the train also depends to some extent on the height of the bride. Many girls prefer to have no train at all.

In the case of an informal marriage ceremony, such as a civil ceremony before a justice of the peace or a second marriage when there is not to be a large celebration, the bride chooses the prettiest dress she has or can afford to buy that will be appropriate to whatever the couple plan after the wedding ceremony. If a few friends are gathering to wish them happiness she wears an afternoon or cocktail dress or suit. If they are leaving on a wedding trip directly following the ceremony, she may be married in the suit or traveling dress.

BORROWING A WEDDING DRESS

On rare occasions a wedding dress is borrowed rather than purchased. The wedding may take place on such short notice that the bride does not have time to find a dress that is becoming to her, or finances may prevent her from buying the one she wants. If she is fortunate enough to have a relative or close friend who offers to lend her her own wedding dress, there is no reason why she should not accept.

She must, of course, take extraordinary care with it and return it freshly cleaned and in perfect condition. The bride should also express her appreciation with the loveliest gift she can give.

THE VEIL

The face veil is rather old-fashioned and is usually omitted. The long lace veil falling down the back from a mantilla or the veil of tulle reaching to the waist at the back is far more popular.

If the bride does choose to wear a veil over her face coming up the aisle and during the ceremony, it is always a short, separate piece

DRESS FOR BRIDAL PARTY AND GUESTS

	MOST FORMAL DAYTIME	MOST FORMAL EVENING	SEMIFORMAL DAYTIME
BRIDE	Long white dress, train, and veil; gloves optional	Same as most formal daytime	Long white dress, short veil optional; gloves optional
BRIDE'S ATTENDANTS	Long dresses, matching shoes; gloves are bride's option	Same as most formal daytime	Same as most formal daytime
GROOM, HIS ATTENDANTS, BRIDE'S FATHER	Cutaway coat, striped trousers, pearl gray waistcoat, white stiff shirt, turndown collar with gray-and-black-striped four-in-hand, or wing collar with ascot; gray gloves, black silk socks, black kid shoes, top hat or none	Black tail coat and trousers, white piqué waistcoat, starched-bosom shirt, wing collar, white bow tie, white gloves, black silk socks, black patent-leather shoes or pumps, or black kid smooth-toe shoes; top hat or none	Black or charcoal sack coat, dove gray waistcoat, white pleated shirt, starched turndown collar with four-in-hand tie, gray gloves, black, smooth-toe shoes; black or gray homburg, or none
MOTHERS OF COUPLE	Long or short dresses, hat, veil or hair ornament; gloves	Usually long evening or dinner dress; dressy short cocktail permissible; veil or hair ornament if long dress; small hat, if short; gloves	Long or street-length dresses, head covering, gloves
WOMEN GUESTS	Street-length cocktail or afternoon dresses—colors are preferable to black or white; head covering, gloves	Depending on local custom, long or short dresses; if long, veil or ornament—otherwise, small hats; gloves	Short afternoon or cocktail dress
MEN GUESTS	Dark suits, conservative shirts and ties	If women wear long dresses, tuxedos; if short dresses, dark suits	Dark suits

	SEMIFORMAL EVENING	INFORMAL DAYTIME	INFORMAL EVENING
BRIDE	Same as semiformal daytime	Short afternoon dress, cocktail dress, or suit	Long dinner dress or short cocktail dress or suit
BRIDE'S ATTENDANTS	Same length and degree of formality as bride's dress	Same style as bride	Same style as bride
GROOM, HIS ATTENDANTS, BRIDE'S FATHER	Winter—black tuxedo; summer —white jacket; pleated or piqué soft shirt, black cummerbund, black bow tie, no gloves; black patent-leather or kid shoes	Winter—dark suit; summer— dark trousers with white linen jacket or white trousers with navy or charcoal jacket; soft shirt, conserva-tive four-in-hand tie. Hot climate—white suit	Tuxedo if bride wears dinner dress; dark suit in winter, lighter suit in summer
MOTHERS OF COUPLE	Same as semiformal daytime	Short afternoon or cocktail dresses	Same length dress as bride
WOMEN GUESTS	Cocktail dresses, gloves, small hat or veil	Afternoon dresses, gloves; head covering for church optional	Afternoon or cocktail dresses, gloves; head covering for church optional
MEN GUESTS	Dark suits	Dark suits; light trousers and dark blazers in summer	Dark suits
GROOM'S FATHER:	He may wear the same costume as the groom and his attendants, especially if he is to stand in the receiving line. If he is not to take part, however, and does not wish to dress formally, he may wear the same clothes as the men guests.		

about a yard square. Mounted on a foundation, it need merely be put on the bride's head in front of her headdress. It is taken off by the maid of honor when she gives the bride's bouquet back to the bride at the conclusion of the ceremony, or if it will not destroy the headdress, it may simply be thrown back over the head.

Heirloom veils of lace are very beautiful, but they limit the bride's choice of gown. They are no longer white, and the dress must be of ivory or ecru to match. If ivory is becoming to the bride and she is happy with the color, that is fine, but she should never be made to feel that she *has* to wear her grandmother's veil, if it means she cannot have the white marquisette gown she has always dreamed of.

THE BOUQUET

The bridal bouquet is most often made up of one or more varieties of white flowers, but it may also consist of pastel flowers if her dress is pastel or has color in the sash or trim. The flowers may also be mixed, with soft colors complementing the shade of the bridesmaids' dresses and bouquets.

Whenever possible, for reasons of economy, it is wise to choose flowers that are in season or do not have to be shipped from far away. All brides should consult their florists and ask their assistance in making their choice.

The flowers should, to some extent, reflect the formality of the wedding. With a very elegant gown, a cascade of flowers, made up of camellias, gardenias, and orchids, mixed with lily of the valley, or by themselves, is most appropriate. Roses, daisies, and old-fashioned mixed bouquets, with or without a lace border, are better with simpler, bouffant dresses. With a "severe" style of dress, a single flower —a calla lily or a single rose, perhaps—can be striking. The bride may also carry a white prayer book, with or without flowers attached to the cover.

She should consider the texture of her dress as well as the style. Camellias and gardenias, with their dark-green, shiny leaves, are particularly beautiful with satin. Daisies, sweet peas, or stephanotis is better with cotton or piqué. Tulle, marquisette or organza is complemented by "frillier" flowers—chrysanthemums, carnations, daisies, or stock.

Tall girls should consider large, long-stemmed flowers, such as anthuria, lilies, or gladiolus. Smaller blossoms arranged in a compact bouquet or short cascade are best for the petite bride.

With all these considerations in mind, it becomes obvious that it is important that the bride order her own flowers, whether or not her groom is paying for them.

A bride being married in a civil ceremony, or for the second time, in a home ceremony, may carry a single bouquet complementing her dress. Or she may wear a corsage on her dress (most young women do not like to do this, but many older women do) or pinned to her purse or prayer book.

SHOES AND GLOVES

The bride's shoes are of white satin (if the gown is satin) or peau de soie. She should be sure that they are comfortable because not only does she walk up the aisle in them, but also she has to stand in them at the reception. Pumps are more appropriate than open sandals.

If she chooses to wear short, loose gloves she merely pulls one glove off at the altar so that her ring can be put on. But if she wears elbow-length or longer gloves, the underseam of the wedding finger of the glove is usually ripped open, and she need only to pull the tip off to have the ring put on. I find this unattractive, and wasteful, and prefer that no gloves be worn at all.

JEWELRY SUITABLE FOR THE BRIDE

If the bridegroom has given the bride a piece of jewelry as a wedding gift, she wears it if she possibly can, even though it may be composed of colored stones. Otherwise she wears neutral-colored jewelry such as a pearl necklace or possibly a pin of pearls or diamonds—sometimes given to her by the groom's parents or a grandmother.

MAKEUP

If the bride customarily wears makeup, naturally she will wear it for her wedding, but applied skillfully and in moderation. Nothing could be more inappropriate than the bride and her attendants coming down the aisle of the church made up as though they were in the chorus line of a musical comedy.

THE NEW LOOK

There is a trend today toward much less elaborate wedding dresses, for a number of reasons. Many weddings take place out-of-doors—on a hilltop, on a beach, or in a garden—where a simple peasant style is most appropriate. Girls who are making their own living are very practical and look for dresses that can be modified slightly and used later as dinner dresses. There is a renewed interest in sewing and embroidery, and many brides are making their own dresses. Any or all of these considerations lead to simpler styles —easier to make and easier to use.

It is surely more appropriate to be married on a hilltop in cotton piqué or a peasant-style dress than in satin with a lace veil. The surroundings must be considered in choosing the dress, as well as the cost and the taste of the bride. But whatever you choose, remember that a wedding is a most serious occasion and should be regarded with the respect it deserves. Simplicity and informality are fine— poor taste is not. Everything about the wedding should be beautiful, because a good marriage *is* beautiful. Therefore, no matter how much of a "nature child" the bride may be, she should not downgrade her marriage by going barefoot. Aside from the possible danger of stepping on a piece of glass or a sharp stone at the wrong moment, very few bare feet are pretty. Furthermore, they are dirty, and a set of gray, calloused toes sticking out from below a long skirt cannot help but ruin the whole effect. Sandals might be the bride's choice, to go with a "peasant" costume or Indian sari, but whatever the style, any shoes will be better than none at all!

THE BRIDEGROOM AND HIS ATTENDANTS

The bridegroom (with the help of his fiancée) plans his clothes according to the formality of the wedding, the season, and the type of dress the bride will wear. The best man, the bride's father, and the ushers wear similar outfits.

The following are the correct costumes for traditional weddings:

1. FORMAL AND SEMIFORMAL WEDDING, DAYTIME (before six o'clock)

Black or charcoal-gray cutaway coat, or for semiformal wedding, black or gray sack coat

Pearl-gray waistcoat, double-breasted

Gray-and-black-striped trousers or black trousers with white pinstripes

Stiff white collarless shirt for cutaway; soft white collarless shirt for sack coat

Detachable wing or stiff fold-down collar for cutaway; starched fold-down collar for sack coat

Gray or silver-gray ascot or tie, plain or striped, for cutaway; black-and-gray-striped tie for sack coat

Plain black kid shoes and black silk socks. Shoes should be freshly polished and have new soles and heels. Bridegrooms should blacken the soles of their shoes with waterproof shoe dye, so that when they kneel at the altar their shoes look dark and neat. (Be sure no prankster has painted "Help me" on the soles.)

White boutonniere

Gray gloves. They should be as light gray as possible

If worn, silk hat with cutaway; black homburg with sack coat. More often, no hat at all

2. INFORMAL WEDDING, OR CIVIL CEREMONY (The bride wears a suit or daytime dress.)

Dark-blue or dark-gray suit

White soft shirt

Four-in-hand tie in conservative stripe or small pattern

Black socks and oxford shoes

White boutonniere

No gloves

3. MOST FORMAL WEDDING, EVENING

Full dress (tailcoat, stiffly starched white shirt, wing collar, white bow tie, white waistcoat)

White evening gloves

White boutonniere

Black kid or patent leather plain-front shoes or pumps

Black socks, silk or lisle

Top hat, if hat worn at all

4. LESS FORMAL EVENING WEDDING (should not be worn for afternoon weddings)

Dinner coat (black tuxedo), with matching trousers; in hot weather, a white dinner jacket

White shirt with piqué or pleated bosom, attached collar, or plain white soft shirt

Black waistcoat or cummerbund

Black silk bow tie

White boutonniere

No gloves

Black socks, silk or lisle

Black fine kid or patent leather plain-front shoes or pumps

5. SUMMER DAYTIME WEDDING IN COUNTRY

> Either dark-blue or gray jacket with white flannel, linen, or
> synthetic trousers, or white jacket with dark-gray trousers
> Plain white shirt
> Dark four-in-hand tie, neat pattern
> Black shoes and socks
> No hat
> No gloves

Just as the dark suit and white shirt are no longer the only acceptable clothing in a business office, so have clothes for grooms and their attendants become less prescribed. A new long-tailed jacket—a cross between a sack coat and a cutaway—is popular for semiformal weddings, and ushers frequently wear colored shirts, ruffled or plain, to match the bridesmaids' dresses. These innovations are interesting and lively, but should be avoided when all other elements of the wedding are strictly traditional.

The groom tells his ushers what they will be wearing and which rental agency will provide the clothes. They are expected to have their measurements taken well in advance of the wedding date. If some live out of town, the groom writes to them and asks them to send their measurements to him or to the store. The men pay for the rental of the suits, but the groom presents them with the gloves and ties.

The groom and best man do not wear gloves during the ceremony, which simplifies the business of putting on the bride's ring. The ushers do wear gloves with cutaways or sack coats, but not with tails or tuxedos.

Almost more than anything else, it is essential that the clothes fit properly, each attendant should go for a fitting a day or so before the wedding. He may pick up his suit then, or go back if there are last-minute adjustments to be made. As soon as possible after the wedding, the best man or the head usher (or anyone who will still be in town) should return the clothes to the store.

For help in coordinating the clothes of the bridal party, study chart pp. 582–583.

WHEN THE GROOM IS IN THE SERVICE

When our nation is not officially at war, military regulations ordinarily allow a member of the armed forces to choose whether or not he wears his uniform when he is off the base or off duty.

Therefore officers and enlisted men—with their fiancées' help—may decide whether they wish to be married in uniform. A professional serviceman will undoubtedly choose to wear his uniform, and since his friends are probably regular servicemen too, they will also be dressed in uniform. A reserve officer or enlisted man has a more difficult decision. If his ushers are chosen from among his civilian friends he must decide whether to give the wedding party a coordinated appearance by dressing in civilian clothes himself or to ignore the look-alike question to show his pride in his service by wearing his uniform. Very often the wishes of his bride, who may feel very strongly one way or the other, will settle the problem for him.

Whatever the groom chooses to do, the ushers should be dressed alike. If some are civilians and some are servicemen, those in the service should be asked to conform to the civilians on that occasion, since it cannot be the other way around.

THE BRIDESMAIDS' COSTUMES

The costumes of the bridesmaids are selected by the bride. She may consult her maid of honor or the bridesmaids if they live nearby, but she does not if they live at a distance, and in any case the final choice is hers alone. It is indisputable that six girls almost certainly will have six different opinions, so it is generally safer for the bride to make the selection by herself.

Since her attendants pay for their dresses in most cases, the bride has an obligation to them to consider the price very carefully. She should also try to select dresses that can be used later, either as they are or with some modifications. She must consider the sizes and shapes of her attendants and try to select an easy-to-wear style and a color that will be becoming to all and unflattering to none.

She does not buy jewelry for the bridesmaids, but suggests to them what might look best—a strand of pearls, a gold chain, or whatever it might be.

When a bride has only one or two attendants she may choose to make their dresses herself. They should offer to pay for the material—which would cost far less than a finished dress. If she refuses the offer they should not insist, since she may get great pleasure out of making these "gifts" for her friends.

The bride picks a headdress that will be the most becoming to the majority of the girls. If some have long straight hair and others have short curly hair, a simple bow pinned at the back of the head is perhaps safest. Wide-brimmed "garden" hats are flattering to almost everyone too. She may ask the girls with long hair if they would mind wearing it up for the occasion, but she does not tell them how they "must" wear it.

Bridesmaids' dresses are always identical in texture and style, but not necessarily in color. For example, the first two might wear deep red, the next two a lighter rose, and the next two a still lighter color, while the maid of honor would be in palest flesh-pink. All-white bridesmaids' dresses tend to detract from the bride's costume, but when color is added in the sash or trim, or in the flowers the girls carry, an almost all-white wedding can be entrancing, especially in a garden with a background of dense greens.

The material for the bridesmaids' dresses should complement the material of the dress of the bride. In other words, if the bride chooses austere satin, the bridesmaids should not be dressed in organdy or ruffled lace. They should also match the bride's dress in degree of formality and to some extent in style.

The dress of the maid or matron of honor is usually different from that of the bridesmaids. It is similar in style but different or reversed in color. For example, for an autumn wedding the bridesmaids might wear deep yellow and carry rust-and-orange chrysanthemums, and the maid of honor might wear rust and carry yellow chrysanthemums. Occasionally her dress is identical to the others, but her flowers are quite different.

Since the bridesmaids' backs are often turned toward the congregation during the ceremony, the backs of the dresses should be interesting and pretty. The hemline should be an inch or more above the ground, so that there is no chance of the wearers' tripping on the church or chancel steps.

Whether or not the girls wear gloves is a matter of the bride's preference. If they are particularly becoming to the costumes, short white gloves are most appropriate in the daytime, as are full-length kid gloves in the evening, but gloves are not necessary at all.

The bride should ask her attendants to get their shoes well ahead of time, and to give or send them to her. She then has them all dyed at the same place and at the same time, so they will be identical in color.

Headdresses may be anything from the big leghorn hat mentioned above to a wreath of artificial flowers, a mantilla, or a simple bow. Becomingness to the majority of the bridesmaids and appropriateness to the style of the dresses are the main considerations. Since a headdress of real flowers will inevitably droop in time, this is the one area where artificial flowers are acceptable.

The bridesmaids almost always carry flowers—most often falling sprays held in front of them, or sheaves that they hold on their outside arms. Those walking on the right side hold them on the right arm with the stems pointing downward to the left, and those on the left hold their flowers on the left arm with stems toward the right.

To achieve an old-fashioned appearance, bridesmaids sometimes carry muffs in winter, or in summer, round bouquets, or flower-filled baskets or hats made into baskets by tying their wide brims together with ribbons. These are carried with both hands directly in front.

Since nothing about a wedding should be artificial, fresh flowers only are used for the decorations and the bouquets. The only exception—as mentioned above—might be those worn as wreaths or hair ornaments by bridesmaids and flower girls.

YOUNG ATTENDANTS

Flower girls may be dressed in quaint, old-fashioned dresses with bonnets, or they may be dressed in clothes similar to those of the bridesmaids but in a style more becoming to a child. They usually wear small wreaths of artificial flowers on their heads, but some wear no headdress at all, or have ribbons or flowers braided into long hair. They carry small bouquets or baskets of flowers, although they no longer—as a rule—strew them before the bride.

Very small boys—ring bearers, pages, or train bearers—wear white Eton jackets with short pants. When they are a little older they may wear navy-blue suits instead. If the boy's suit is white the shoes and socks are white; if it is navy, he wears navy socks and black shoes.

Junior bridesmaids wear dresses exactly like those of the older bridesmaids, although they are sometimes of a different color. Their flowers may be, but are not necessarily, different from the others.

Junior ushers dress in the same style of clothing as the other ushers.

THE MOTHERS OF THE BRIDE AND GROOM

The bride's mother should be the first to decide on what she will wear—how long, what style, and what color. She should then tell the groom's mother what her decision is, so that the latter may plan her costume accordingly. The bride and her mother may go so far as to *suggest* to the other mother what they think might be becoming to her—they may *not tell* her what she is to choose. It certainly looks more attractive—makes a prettier "picture"—if both ladies are dressed similarly, especially since they stand together in the receiving line. But if the groom's mother feels uncomfortable in the type of clothing chosen by the bride's mother, or knows that it is unbecoming to her, she should feel free to select a dress in which *she* will feel attractive and happy.

The elegance of the dresses should be keyed to the elaborateness of the wedding. The length is a matter of taste, but long skirts and dresses are so much in style today that they are considered appropriate for any wedding from noon on. And long dresses may vary greatly in formality—from pretty shirtwaist tops and skirts to brocade evening gowns.

The dresses of the mothers should not be of the same color as those of the bridesmaids. They should not try to look like members of the wedding party. Nor should they both be wearing the same color. The shades should be carefully chosen to go with the overall colors of dresses and flowers, and so that the two mothers' dresses will not "clash" with each other. Prints are youthful-looking and pretty for a summer wedding, but if one mother chooses a print dress, the other should wear a complementary solid color. Neither mother should wear black. If one is in mourning, she should wear off-white, gray, or lavender, to avoid any suggestion of sadness on this happiest of days.

Both mothers should wear gloves, which are kept on while they are in the receiving line. They should also wear something on their heads—whether a small artificial-flower arrangement, a hat, a veil, or a bow.

As a rule, the mother of the bride leaves her wrap in the vestibule with those of the bridesmaids. However, if she knows that the church is likely to be cool, and if she has an attractive fur piece, she carries or wears it. Otherwise someone may put a light wrap in the pew for her before she herself comes up the aisle. In other words the bride's mother should not wear or carry anything that might spoil the effect of her dress.

THE FATHERS OF THE COUPLE

There is no hard-and-fast rule governing the clothes of the bride's father, but since he will be escorting his daughter down the aisle behind the ushers, the party will have a more unified appearance if he elects to wear the same outfit they do. And in fact he almost invariably does dress like the other men.

At a formal wedding the bridegroom's father may, and generally does, wear the same type of clothes as those worn by the bride's father. He has, however, no official part in the ceremony and therefore may wear a dark suit if he is more comfortable in informal clothes.

The question sometimes arises whether a mother may wear the same dress for the weddings of two or more of her children. Of course she *may*, if her budget is limited, but if it is at all possible to buy a new dress, the children who marry later will appreciate her looking as stylish and as special for their weddings as she did for the first.

✍50✍ *Wedding Invitations, Announcements, and Replies*

It is most important that all elements of a wedding be in keeping with each other if the whole is to have a smooth and harmonious atmosphere. If you are having a formal, traditional wedding, your invitations should be traditional too. If you are being married on a beach at dawn with a buffet breakfast to follow, your invitations might be a poem illustrated with shells or Terns. I have seen many such beautiful, original invitations, and they were beautiful partly because they fitted in with the rest of the wedding plans. The invitation sets the tone of the ceremony, and if you have decided on a traditional wedding, you should use the formal, engraved or thermographed, "third-person" style invitation. Since these must, to be in good taste, follow a prescribed style, whereas the informal, personalized invitation may be whatever the sender wishes, this chapter will deal primarily with the traditional invitation. Later, however, you will find some suggested wording for invitations to a "new-look" wedding.

Invitations to, and announcements of, a formal wedding are worded and engraved exactly as they have been for countless years. They are worded in the third person, and acceptances or regrets are written by hand in this same form. The words must be placed on specified lines and centered as evenly as possible. Names of hosts belong on the first line, the "request the honour of" on the second, the name of the guest on the third, and so on. "Honour," on formal wedding invitations, is always spelled with the "u."

Invitations to most formal weddings consist of an invitation to the church ceremony, a "pew card" for those who will be seated "within the ribbons," sometimes a response card, and an invitation to the reception. But many variations are possible and perfectly correct, as we shall see.

When a guest is expected to attend the church service only, the invitation to the reception is not enclosed.

If the wedding is to be in a very small church or chapel and the reception in a very big house or club, then many invitations to the reception will be sent and only a few to the ceremony.

If both the church ceremony and the reception are limited to a small number who are sent handwritten invitations or are given oral invitations, then engraved announcements in place of invitations of any kind may be sent to the friends who could not be included, as well as to acquaintances.

The invitations to a large wedding are sent three to four weeks beforehand; those to a simpler wedding can be mailed as late as ten days before the wedding day.

THE STYLE OF THE INVITATION

Correct invitations to any wedding, whatever its size, are engraved (or thermographed) on the first page of a double sheet of heavy paper, ivory or white, either plain or with a raised margin called a plate mark or panel. The invitation may be about five and a half inches wide by seven and three-eighths inches deep, or slightly smaller, and it is folded once for insertion into its envelope. Or it may be about four and three-eighths by five and three-fourths inches and go into the envelope without folding. Separate invitations to the reception are engraved on small stiff cards, appropriate to the size chosen for the invitation to the church.

The engraving may be in whichever lettering style the bride prefers among the several offered her by the stationer. In general the simplest styles are in the best taste. Shaded Roman, Antique Roman, and Script are all excellent choices.

Should the family of the bride's father have a coat of arms, this is one time when it is proper to have it (or just the crest) embossed without color at the top center of the sheet. When the invitations are sent out by the bride's mother alone, a coat of arms is not used. If the family has no coat of arms, the invitation bears no device of any kind.

RULES FOR CONVENTIONAL WORDING

1. The invitation to the marriage ceremony always reads: "requests the honour [spelled with a *u*] of your presence. . . ."
2. The invitation to the reception, when not simply a card saying "reception following the ceremony," reads: "requests the pleasure of your company. . . ."
3. No punctuation is used except commas after the day of the week or periods after abbreviations such as "Mr.," "Jr.," "St. John's," etc.
4. The date of the wedding is spelled out rather than written as a numeral: "Saturday, the second of September." If a long street number is included, numerals may be used.
5. The time of the wedding is "four o'clock"—never "four P.M." Half hours are written "half after four" rather than "four thirty" or "half past four." The hour given is the time at which the actual ceremony begins.
6. No words are capitalized except those that would be ordinarily—people's names and titles, place names, names of day and month.
7. "Doctor" is written in full, unless the name to follow is very long. "Mr." is *never* written "Mister," but "Jr." may also be written as "junior," although the former is preferred.
8. Invitations to Roman Catholic weddings may replace the phrase "at the marriage of" with "at the marriage in Christ of." "And your participation in the Nuptial Mass" may be added below the groom's name.
9. The address of the church is not included if it is in a small town or city. In larger cities, where not everyone may be acquainted with the whole area, it should be included.
10. The year is not included on wedding invitations but usually is on announcements because in some circumstances they are sent long after the wedding takes place.

IN WHOSE NAME?

The person who addresses and mails the invitations, and whose name is at the top of the invitation, is *the person giving the wedding and/or reception*. Since it is almost always the parents of the bride who pay the expenses and act as hosts, it is almost always they who send out the invitations, and *their* name that appears.

Mr. and Mrs. Robert McCullogh
request the honour of your presence
at the marriage of their daughter
Pauline. . . .

If for some reason the groom's family gives the reception, the name of the bride's parents should be on the church invitation, and that of the groom's parents on the reception invitation. In such a case, each family is responsible for sending the invitations carrying its own name. If they divide the expenses equally, and both families act as hosts, the invitations should be in *both* names, but the bride's family is generally responsible for sending them. In the case of divorced parents only the name of the parent giving the party appears, unless, again, they are sharing the responsibilities, in which case both names appear, whether one has remarried or not.

The name of the groom's family—unless, as mentioned above, they are giving, or sharing equally in, the reception—does not appear, because all invitations are issued by the people giving the party or whatever it may be. Unlike announcements, on which the groom's parents' name may appear, the invitation is not intended as a source of information, but strictly, as the word implies, to ask people to attend the wedding.

For wordings in these situations, see page 610.

THE INNER ENVELOPE

Although the use of two envelopes for wedding invitations is an age-old tradition, there are several valid arguments against it today, and I believe that it should be up to the bride to decide what she wants to do.

The tradition probably goes back to the fact that many, many years ago, when invitations were delivered by hand, they were politely left unsealed. Later, when all letters began to be delivered by mail, these same unsealed envelopes were simply inserted in a larger one that could be sealed.

A more practical reason for two envelopes is that names of children can be listed on the inner envelope. Otherwise those to be invited must either be sent a separate invitation, or their names must all appear on the outer envelope, which, if there were many, would be quite confusing.

However, writing the names on the inner envelopes takes considerable time, and few people today can hire a social secretary or someone to do it for them. Brides, who are usually working, have little extra time to spare.

Furthermore, we are all conscious of the need to save our forests, and we are constantly asked to restrict our use of paper. Above all, costs have risen so drastically that we must try to cut down on the expenses that do not seem absolutely necessary.

Therefore I cannot help but recommend that those who are pressed for time, or money, simply eliminate the inner envelope.

For those who wish to maintain the tradition, here is the proper procedure: The inner envelope has no mucilage on the flap and is addressed to "Mr. and Mrs. Brown" with neither first name nor address.

The names of young children who receive their own invitations are written on the inner envelope, "Joan, Robert, and Frederick," and inserted in an envelope addressed to "Miss and the Messrs. Greatlake," or "Miss Joan Greatlake" and (below) "Robert and Frederick Greatlake." When the outer envelope is addressed to "Mr. and Mrs. Robert Jones and family," the inner envelope is addressed:

> *Mr. and Mrs. Robert Jones*
> *Karen, Sue, Ford, and James*

Close relatives may be addressed as "Grandmother," "Aunt Sue and Uncle George," etc.

THE OUTER ENVELOPE

Wedding invitations are always addressed to both members of a married couple, even though only one of them is personally known to the bride and groom.

No abbreviations should be used, either in the name of the addressee or the address. "Street," "Avenue," "New Jersey," "Maryland," are all written out in full. The middle name of the recipient may be omitted, but if it is used, it too should be written out. Only if the name is very long might an initial be used.

A daughter's name may be written below her parents'—"Miss Helen Truehart," or "The Misses Truehart." Boys and girls over twelve or thirteen, however, are more correctly sent separate invitations.

When every member of a family under one roof is included in the invitation, the envelope may be addressed:

> *Mr. and Mrs. Joseph Truehart and Family*

Young brothers or young sisters can also be sent "joint" invitations addressed to "The Misses Truehart" or "The Messrs. Truehart."

STUFFING THE ENVELOPE

An envelope-sized invitation is inserted in the inner envelope, folded edge down, with the engraved side toward the flap. An invitation designed to fit an envelope half its size will require a second fold, which should be made with the engraving inside. This is then inserted, folded edge down, into the envelope. With the unsealed flap of this filled inner envelope away from you, insert it in the mailing envelope. If the invitation is folded, all insertions (such as the reception card or pew card) are placed inside the second fold with the type facing the flap of the envelope. If the invitation is not folded a second time, the cards are inserted in front of it (nearest you), with the reception card next to the invitation and any smaller cards in front of that.

Engravers generally use tissue sheets to protect the pages from the fresh ink. These tissues may be removed, but many stationers recommend that they be kept to prevent the ink from smearing.

INVITATIONS TO GUESTS UNKNOWN TO THE BRIDE OR GROOM

A girl guest may ask a bride if she may bring her fiancé (not a date) to the wedding, if it will cause no inconvenience. If the bride has plenty of invitations, she obtains the man's name and address and sends him a separate one. If she has no more left, or cannot get his address, she may write his name below that of his fiancée on the inner envelope and enclose it in the outer envelope, which is addressed to the girl only. This would also be done if the bride tells some of her friends to "bring an escort."

When an unmarried friend of the bride or groom is living with a member of the opposite sex, a single invitation may be sent to them addressed to Miss Joan Morrow and Mr. Peter Finch.

USHERS AND BRIDESMAIDS, AND GROOM'S PARENTS

Although it is obviously unnecessary, it is thoughtful to send invitations to all members of the bridal party as mementos. This is true also for the groom's parents. These invitations are addressed exactly as they are to the other guests, but, of course, require no reply.

RETURN ADDRESSES

There are three excellent reasons for placing a return address on a wedding invitation, and so far as I know, no valid reason for omitting it, other than an outdated "rule." First, the U. S. Postal Service requests that all first-class mail carry a return address. Second, it provides the wedding guest with a definite address to which to send a reply and a gift, if no address other than that of a club or hotel appears on the invitation. Third, it ensures that the bride will know if the invitation did not reach the destination, and gives her an opportunity to check the address of the recipient, or to cross him off her list.

The practice of stamping the address without ink on the back flap is somewhat helpful, but many people never notice it and discard the envelope before they think to look for the information there. Therefore, regardless of the many years in which it was considered in bad taste to put the return address on the envelope, I believe that it is time to change the rule, and I recommend that all stationers, at the request of their customers, put a legible return address on the back flap of the envelope (rather than in the front-upper-left corner, since it would be impossible to engrave through the double thickness of the envelope.

WORDING OF INVITATIONS

The following wording is correct for all weddings of any size:

Mr. and Mrs. Charles Robert Gilbert

request the honour of your presence

at the marriage of their daughter

Pauline Marie

to

Mr. John Frederick Hamilton

Saturday, the twenty-ninth of April

at four o'clock

Church of the Heavenly Rest

New York

WEDDING AND RECEPTION INVITATION IN ONE

When every guest is invited to both ceremony and reception, the invitation to the reception is included in the invitation to the ceremony.

Mrs. Alexander Hughes

requests the honour of your presence

at the marriage of her daughter

Barbara

to

Mr. James Town, junior

Tuesday, the twenty-first of October

at three o'clock

Church of the Resurrection

Ridgemont, Ohio

and afterwards at the reception

31 Meadow Lane

R.s.v.p.

ENCLOSURE INVITATIONS TO A RECEPTION FOLLOWING THE CEREMONY

The invitation to the reception following the church ceremony is usually engraved on a card to match the paper and engraving of the church invitation. If the latter is folded for the envelope, then the card is a little smaller than half the full size of the invitation. If it is to go with the smaller invitation that does not fold, it may be from two and one-half to three inches high by three and one-half to four inches wide.

When more people are invited to the church than to the reception, the cards are, of course, only inserted in the envelopes going to those invited to the reception. The most commonly used form is this:

> *Reception*
> *immediately following the ceremony*
> *Essex County Country Club*
> *West Orange*
>
>
> *The favour of a reply is requested*
> *Llewellyn Park, West Orange*

INVITATION TO THE RECEPTION ONLY

When the ceremony is private and a big reception follows, the invitations to the ceremony are given orally or by personal note, and invitations to the reception are sent out separately. The size and style of these invitations are exactly the same as those to the wedding itself.

> *Mr. and Mrs. John Huntington Smith*
> *request the pleasure of your company*
> *at the wedding reception*
> *of their daughter*
> *Millicent Jane*
> *and*
> *Mr. Sidney Strothers*
> *Tuesday, the first of November*
> *at half after twelve o'clock*
> *55 Clark Lane*
> *Hillsdale, Long Island*

R.s.v.p.

The forms R.s.v.p. and R.S.V.P. are both correct. In diplomatic circles the capital letters are the correct form.

A RECEPTION FOLLOWING A HOUSE WEDDING

When the reception follows a house wedding, it is not necessary to send any sort of separate invitation as it is assumed that those attending the wedding will stay on.

A WEDDING IN A FRIEND'S HOUSE

Invitations are issued by the parents of the bride even though the wedding takes place at a house other than their own. The names of the parents at the head of the invitation means that *they* are giving the wedding (and probably assuming all expenses) but not in their own house.

Mr. and Mrs. Richard Littlehouse
request the honour of your presence
at the marriage of their daughter
Eleanor
to
Doctor Frederic Robinson
Saturday, the fifth of November
at four o'clock
at the residence [or home] of Mr. and Mrs. James Sterlington
Llewellyn Park
West Orange, New Jersey

R.s.v.p.

SPECIAL SITUATIONS

WHEN THE BRIDE'S MOTHER IS WIDOWED OR DIVORCED

If the bride's mother is giving the wedding alone:

Mrs. Bernard Jones [if a widow; Mrs. Mary Jones or Mrs.
Maiden-Name Jones if divorced]
requests the honour of your presence
at the marriage of her daughter
Helen Jeffrey Jones
etc.

The wording is the same when a divorced father is giving his daughter's wedding, except, of course, for the "Mr." and "his daughter" instead of "her daughter."

WHEN THE BRIDE HAS A STEPFATHER

When the bride's own father is not living and she has a stepfather, or her mother has divorced and remarried, the invitations are worded:

> *Mr. and Mrs. John Huntington Smith*
> *request the honour of your presence*
> *at the marriage of her daughter [or: their daughter]*
> *Mary Alice Towne*
> *etc.*

WHEN THE BRIDE'S DIVORCED PARENTS ARE FRIENDLY

When the bride's parents are divorced, the wedding invitations are issued in the name of the parent who pays for and acts as host at the reception. However, in the event that relations are so friendly that they share the expenses and act as co-hosts, both names should appear on the invitation.

> *Mr. and Mrs. Henry Smith [the bride's mother and husband]*
> *and*
> *Mr. and Mrs. Robert Doe [the bride's father and his wife]*
> *request the honour of your presence*
> *at the marriage of*
> *Mary Doe*
> *to*
> *Mr. William Hughes*
> *etc.*

The bride's mother's name, whether she has remarried or not, appears first. If neither parent is remarried the wording would be:

> *Mrs. Jones Doe*
> *and*
> *Mr. Robert Doe*
> *request the honour of your presence*
> *at the marriage of their daughter*
> *Mary*
> *etc.*

WHEN THE BRIDE IS AN ORPHAN

It is important to remember that ordinarily "Miss" or "Mrs." are not used before the bride's name, but there are exceptions.

If the bride has no relatives and the wedding is given by friends, the wording is:

Mr. and Mrs. John Baxter
request the honour of your presence
at the marriage of
Miss Elizabeth O'Brien
to
Mr. John Henry Fuller
etc.

If she has brothers or sisters, the oldest one customarily sends out her wedding invitations and announcements in his or her name. If another relative has taken the place of a parent, his or her name is used. When the bride is living with a married brother or sister, and that couple plans to give the wedding, the invitations go out in their name:

Mr. Saul Silverman
requests the honour of your presence
at the marriage of his sister
Molly
etc.

or:

Mr. and Mrs. Saul Silverman
request the honour of your presence
at the marriage of their niece
Sarah
etc.

When a bride has no relatives, or her parents have refused to sanction the marriage, or for some other reason she chooses to send out the invitations in the name of herself and her groom, the wording is:

The honour of your presence
is requested
at the marriage of
Miss Elizabeth Franklin
to
Mr. Arthur Coleman
etc.

WHEN THE BRIDE IS A YOUNG WIDOW

Invitations to the marriage of a young widow are sent in the name of her parents exactly as were the invitations for her first wedding, except that her name, instead of being simply "Priscilla," is now written "Priscilla Banks Loring," thus:

Doctor and Mrs. Maynard Banks
request the honour of your presence
at the marriage of their daughter
Priscilla Banks Loring
to
etc.

THE YOUNG DIVORCÉE

A divorcée's second marriage ceremony is usually restricted to family and close friends, often with a larger reception following. She generally issues the invitation to the ceremony by note or word of mouth. However, if she did not have a church wedding the first time, and perhaps it is her groom's first marriage, she may want to send engraved invitations. The form is exactly the same as that shown above for a young widow.

A more mature woman, or one whose parents are dead, may send out her own invitations:

The honour of your presence
is requested
at the marriage of
Mrs. John Kerr Simons
to
etc.

This same woman would drop the "John" and use "Mrs. Kerr Simons" or "Mrs. Thelma Simons" if she were a divorcée.

The fact that the groom has been divorced does not change the invitation to, or announcement of, his new bride's marriage.

WHEN THE BRIDE HAS A PROFESSIONAL NAME

If the bride uses a professional name or a "stage" name, she probably has friends whom she would like to invite but who might not recognize "Pauline Marie Oldname." The invitations may therefore have her professional name engraved in very small letters and in parentheses under her Christian name.

𝕻𝖆𝖚𝖑𝖎𝖓𝖊 𝕸𝖆𝖗𝖎𝖊
(𝕻𝖆𝖙 𝕭𝖔𝖓𝖉)

𝖙𝖔

𝕸𝖗. 𝕵𝖔𝖍𝖓 𝕱𝖗𝖊𝖉𝖊𝖗𝖎𝖈𝖐 𝕳𝖆𝖒𝖎𝖑𝖙𝖔𝖓

This is most practically done by having the name (Pat Bond) added to the plate after the order for regular invitations has been completed. As many invitations as are to go to her professional friends can then be struck off with this addition.

MILITARY TITLES

On the wedding invitations, the name of a bridegroom whose rank is below Lieutenant Commander in the Navy or Coast Guard or Major in the Army, Air Force, or Marine Corps, is given this way:

John Strong
Ensign, United States Navy

Officers of those ranks or above have the title on the same line as their names, and the service below:

Colonel John Spring
United States Air Force

Although "j.g." or "junior grade" is usually used with "Lt." in the Navy, the Army title of "Lt." is not usually preceded by "1st" or "2nd."

Reserve officers *on active duty* use "Army of the United States," or "United States Naval Reserve" below their names.

All titles used to be written out in full, but today "Lieutenant Commander" is usually reduced to "Lt. Commander," "Captain" may be written "Capt.," etc.

Noncommissioned officers and enlisted men in the regular forces may use their titles or not, as they prefer. A private might simply have his name engraved:

John Phillip Jones
United States Air Force

A noncommissioned officer might prefer

Henry Smith Gordon
Corporal, United States Army

High-ranking regular officers who are retired continue to use their titles and include their service on the line below with "retired" following the service.

General George Harmon
United States Army, retired

The name of the bride who is on active duty in the armed forces is engraved:

marriage of their daughter
Alice Mary
Lieutenant, Women's Army Corps

When the father of the bride is a member of the armed forces, either on active duty, a high-ranking retired officer, or one who retired after many years of service, he uses his title in the ordinary way:

Colonel and Mrs. James Booth
request the honour, etc.

OTHER TITLES

Medical doctors, dentists, veterinarians, clergymen, judges, and all other men customarily called by their titles should have them included on their own wedding invitations, and on the invitations to their daughters' weddings.

Holders of academic degrees do not use the "Dr." unless they are always referred to in that way.

Women use their titles only when the invitations are issued by themselves and their grooms.

The honour of your presence
is requested
at the marriage of
Dr. Susan Moore
and
Mr. Willard Copeland

Otherwise, she is ". . . their daughter Jane."

The bride's mother preferably does not use the title "Dr." on her daughter's invitation. If she and her husband feel strongly that she should, the wording has to be: "Dr. Henry and Dr. Mary Smith request . . ." or "Mr. Henry and Dr. Mary Smith . . ." Both phrases appear awkward on a formal invitation.

THE DOUBLE-WEDDING INVITATION

Mr. and Mrs. Henry Smartlington

request the honour of your presence

at the marriage of their daughters

Marian Helen

to

Mr. Judson Jones

and

Amy Caroline

to

Mr. Herbert Scott Adams

Saturday, the tenth of November

at four o'clock

Trinity Church

The elder sister's name is given first.

It is unusual but not unheard-of for two brides who have been long friends—or who are cousins, but with different names—to have a double wedding.

The wording of such invitations must necessarily include the surnames of both parents and brides:

Mr. and Mrs. Henry Smartlington
and
Mr. and Mrs. Arthur Lane
request the honour of your presence
at the marriage of their daughters
Marian Helen Smartlington
to
Mr. Judson Jones
and
Mary Alice Lane
to
Mr. John Gray
etc.

WHEN THE BRIDEGROOM'S FAMILY
GIVES THE WEDDING

When the bride comes as a stranger from a distance, without her family, or for various other reasons, the bridegroom's family may give the wedding and send the invitations in their name. This is the only other case where the title "Miss" is used.

Mr. and Mrs. John Henry Pater
request the honour of your presence
at the marriage of
Miss Marie Mersailles
to
their son
John Henry Pater, junior
etc.

Announcements, but not invitations, might be sent from their home by her own family.

INCLUDING THE BRIDEGROOM'S FAMILY
IN THE INVITATION

On occasion the bridegroom's family, even though the bride's parents are alive and nearby, share in, and even pay for the major part of the reception, which is sometimes held in their home. When this occurs, it seems only fair that their names should be included on the invitation, since they are actually co-hosts. The wording would be:

Mr. and Mrs. Charles Goodman
and
Mr. and Mrs. George Gonzalez
request the pleasure of your company
at the wedding reception of
Julia Goodman
and
Roberto Gonzalez
etc.

A separate invitation to the wedding ceremony should be sent in the name of the bride's parents.

In some foreign countries it is customary for the groom's family to be included in the wedding invitation also, and the invitation is a double one—in the name of the bride's family on the left inside page and the groom's parents on the right. This form is sometimes followed by these nationalities here in the United States, and in many ways is a thoughtful and friendly custom.

Mr. and Mrs. Bruno Cairo	*Mr. and Mrs. Roberto Conti*
request the honour of your presence	*request the honour of your presence*
at the marriage of their daughter	*at the marriage of their son*
Julia	*Francisco*
to	*to*
Mr. Francisco Conti	*Miss Julia Cairo*
etc.	*etc.*

PERSONAL INVITATIONS

The most flattering wedding invitation possible is a note personally written by the bride. Even though she is sending engraved invitations to most of the guests, she may, as a special gesture of affection, send a few handwritten ones to those she cares most about.

Dear Aunt Jane,

Dick and I are to be married at Christ Church at noon on Thursday the tenth. We hope you and Uncle Dick will come to the church and afterward to the reception at the Woodlawn Country Club in Peapack.

With much love from us both,

Affectionately,
Helen

This type of note is also written when the wedding is to be very small, or when it is held on short notice. In these circumstances telephone invitations are also perfectly correct.

WHEN THE BRIDEGROOM IS ABOUT
TO RECEIVE A DEGREE

When the bridegroom is a medical student at the time the invitations are sent, but will be a graduate by the date of the wedding, his name should be written with his title—"Doctor John Jones." This would hold true for any man in a profession in which the title is ordinarily used.

WHEN THE WEDDING DATE IS CHANGED

It happens on occasion that the date of the wedding must be changed after the invitations have already been engraved. To order a new set of invitations would involve an enormous and unnecessary expense. Instead, the bride may enclose a small printed card saying,

611

"The date of the wedding has been changed from . . . to . . . ," or if the number of guests is small, she may write the same information on a small card by hand. If the invitations must go out before cards can be printed, she may also neatly cross out the old date and insert the new by hand.

WHEN A WEDDING IS POSTPONED INDEFINITELY

When a wedding must be postponed indefinitely after the invitations have been mailed, it is necessary to send the news out as fast as possible. If it is possible to have cards printed in time, that is the best solution. If not, the bride and members of her family and bridal party who can help must send out handwritten notes at once. The wording, depending on the cause, would be:

> *Owing to the sudden death of*
> *Mrs. Henry Miller*
> *the marriage of her daughter*
> *Sarah*
> *to*
> *Mr. Robert Sage*
> *has been postponed*

or:

> *Mr. and Mrs. John Fordyce*
> *regret that*
> *due to a death in the family*
> *the date of*
> *Susan Fordyce's wedding*
> *must be indefinitely postponed*

ENCLOSURES

CARDS FOR RESERVED PEWS

To the family and those intimate friends who are to be seated in specially designated pews, a card (approximately two by three inches) may be enclosed, with "Pew No." engraved and the number filled in by hand. The style matches that of the invitation.

The more usual and less expensive custom is for the mother of the bride and the mother of the bridegroom each to write on her personal visiting card the number of the pew that each member of the family and each intimate friend is to occupy.

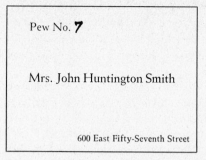

Pew No. **7**

Mrs. John Huntington Smith

600 East Fifty-Seventh Street

A similar card for a reserved enclosure consisting of a certain number of front pews—although for no special pew—and inscribed "Within the ribbon" may be enclosed with the invitations. Or "Within the ribbon" may be written on a visiting card and included with the invitation.

Pew cards are often sent or given in person after acceptances have been received, when the families of the bride and groom know how many reserved seats will be needed.

AT HOME CARDS

If the bride and groom want their friends to know what their address is to be, an At Home card is included with the invitation. These cards follow this form:

> *At home [or: Will be at home]*
> *after the fifteenth of November*
> *3842 Olympia Drive*
> *Houston, Texas 77000*

The card is approximately four by two and one-half inches, slightly smaller than the reception card.

Many people receiving these cards, however, put them away, intending to enter them in an address book or file. Later they come across the card, only to find they have entirely forgotten *who* would be at home at 3842 Olympia Drive after November 15. Even though the couple are not married at the time the invitation is sent, in the interests of helpfulness and practicality, these cards should be engraved:

> *Mr. and Mrs. Howard*
> *will be at home*
> *etc.*

RESPONSE CARDS *(See Chapter 39.)*

When it seems necessary to enclose response cards with wedding invitations, a self-addressed envelope is included, either stamped or unstamped, depending on the state of the bride's finances.

Since people tend to think that their children are invited, even though the invitation is addressed to "Mr. and Mrs. George Harper," it is very unwise to put "No. of people" on the card. Although the bride may intend the recipient to fill in "one" or "two," Mr. and Mrs. Harper may well think it means that the whole family is included. The best form for the wedding response card is:

M—— . . . .
—— *accepts*
—— *regrets*
Saturday, May 7th

Because the return envelope is addressed to the bride, no address is necessary under the RSVP.

MAPS AND TRAVEL INFORMATION

It is very helpful, if the wedding is in the country, or in an area unfamiliar to some of the guests, to have a small map drawn to enclose with the invitations going to friends unfamiliar with the location. The map should include the best approaches to the church and/or site of the reception from every direction.

For those who may be coming by plane, train, or bus, it is also thoughtful to make up a schedule of the arrivals and departures that would best fit in with the hours of the wedding and reception.

INVITATIONS TO A BELATED WEDDING RECEPTION

A belated wedding reception is frequently held some time after the ceremony—perhaps after the honeymoon, or on occasion, even later, when the couple returns after an extended absence. Although the party is held to celebrate the wedding, a true "wedding reception" immediately follows the ceremony, and the invitation for the belated reception omits the word "wedding."

These invitations may be formally engraved as follows:

Mr. and Mrs. Henry Peterson
request the pleasure of your company
at a reception
in honor of
Mr. and Mrs. Floyd Smith
on, etc.

If you prefer to send a less formal invitation, you may write the necessary information on an informal and at the top write "In honor of" the young couple.

UNCONVENTIONAL INVITATIONS

As discussed at the beginning of the chapter, invitations to weddings that make no pretense of being traditional may be as original as the bride and/or her parents can devise. They should, however, be dignified, attractive, and sincerely reflect the sentiments of the bride, the groom, and their families.

Illustrated is a very simple example, written in the bride's hand.

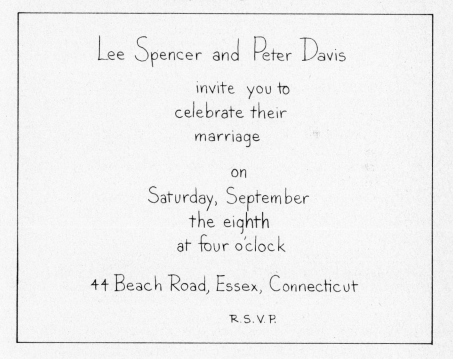

Lee Spencer and Peter Davis

invite you to
celebrate their
marriage

on
Saturday, September
the eighth
at four o'clock

44 Beach Road, Essex, Connecticut

R.S.V.P.

Another, from the bride's parents, is far more elaborate, and might be sent for a semitraditional formal wedding:

Our joy will be more complete

if you can share in the marriage of our daughter

Sarah Fitzgerald

to

Mr. Bayard J. Caldwell

on Friday, the twenty-seventh of June

at half after eight o'clock in the evening

at Christ's Church

Princeton, New Jersey

We invite you to worship with us, witness

their vows, and join us for a reception at

the Princeton Inn. If you are unable to

attend, we ask your presence in thought and

prayer.

Mr. and Mrs. Robert Hampton

(or: Jean and Robert Hampton)

R.s.v.p.
7 Walden Lane
Princeton, New Jersey 08540

I consider this a very lovely and meanful invitation, and in the best of taste.

There are many other possibilities, and prospective brides should explore them, keeping in mind that they should be appropriate to the other plans for the wedding.

INVITATIONS TO A GROUP

Very frequently a girl who is about to be married is faced with the problem of what to do about inviting her co-workers, or perhaps her sorority sisters, or fellow members of any club or organization. May she invite just her special friends, or must everyone be included, and how should the invitations be issued? Taken from recent questions and answers in my newspaper column, "Doing the Right Thing," here are a number of alternatives.

Q. I work in an office and am very friendly with a few of the people. Is it proper to invite those with whom I am friendly to the wedding and reception and to post an invitation just to the wedding for the rest of the office? Or does each get an invitation personally?

A. You may post an invitation to the church ceremony in your office and send individual invitations to those who will be invited to the reception. You may also issue the reception invitations by word of mouth, but be sure you do not do so within hearing of those who are not included.

Q. I work for a government agency having a total of nine clerical and professional staff members. I plan to be married in June and I had originally intended to send only two invitations, one to my supervisor and the other to my closest friend. However, I'm afraid that some may be offended if they are not also invited. Individual invitations would obligate them to send a gift. Would it be "correct" to send them a joint invitation? I feel this would enable anyone who wanted to send a gift or to attend to do so.

A. Since your office is a small and closely knit unit, you are right not to send invitations to only two of your fellow workers. It would be perfectly acceptable in your situation to send a single invitation as you suggested. Those who attend will undoubtedly send gifts, and those who do not will give you a present or not, as they choose.

Q. One of the secretaries in my office was planning to be married and rather than send out individual invitations, she placed an invitation on a central bulletin board with numerous names listed. You had to check to see if your name was included to know whether or not you were invited to the wedding and reception.

I feel it was improper not to send individual invitations, since the whole office force was not included—only a select few.

A. It is correct to post a "blanket" invitation only when *everyone* in an office is invited. Although it is *always* preferable to send individual invitations, there are occasions, when the office force is very large, when time and expense prevent doing that. But when the invitation is posted, it should never be a partial list—that is most unfair to those who are not included.

Q. I am a member of a college sorority and would like very much to have my sisters attend my wedding. However, there are ninety members and I cannot afford to send all ninety invitations. Of course, many of them would not attend. At the same time, I don't want to ask only a few, because the reception area is large enough for many guests.

I could send a blanket invitation, but I am afraid many of them would not consider it as a serious invitation, and besides, I have to know how many will be attending the reception.

What would be the best thing to do?

A. The very best thing to do would be to send individual invitations to each girl in your sorority. However, there are valid reasons for modifying this rule, and the additional expense of ninety invitations might certainly be considered one of them. I would suggest that you post an invitation addressed to the whole sorority on the bulletin board. If you are afraid that some girls will not take it seriously enough to give you an answer, put a paper beside it with a note asking those who plan to attend to sign their names.

In a large office, or an organization such as the sorority mentioned in the last letter, there is sure to be a bulletin board or central spot where names, messages, etc., are posted. One of your wedding invitations, open, should be posted there, with "To Members of the Staff," or "To All Sorority Sisters," written at the top. Since there is no envelope addressed to "Mr. and Mrs.," or to "Miss Jones and fiancé," a note must be placed beside the invitation stating that husbands and wives (and fiancés or dates if you wish) are invited. Many will not attend, but they must be included in the invitation.

To ensure that the staff or club members know that you really hope they will come, and also so that you will know how many to plan for, post a paper headed, "If you can come, please sign here, and indicate if your husband or wife will be with you."

In a small office of, perhaps, ten or twelve people, your invitation may simply be passed around. Each person would be expected to RSVP individually, but if they do not, you are free to ask after a week or so, "Are you going to be able to come?"

ANNOUNCEMENTS

It is never obligatory to send announcements, but I recommend it highly, because they serve a very useful purpose. Since they carry *no obligation* they are far more practical than invitations when sent to people who would like to know about the wedding, but who are not close enough to the families to be expected to send a present.

Announcements, therefore, should be sent to:

Old friends who have been out of touch with the bride's or groom's family for a long time.

Business associates, clients, etc.

People who live too far away to be able to attend the wedding.

Closer friends who cannot be included when the wedding and reception lists are limited.

Although, as I said, no one who receives an announcement is obliged to send a gift, he certainly is free to do so if he wishes. Therefore, when a wedding is restricted to a very few, many of those who receive announcements *will* send a gift, just as they would had they received an invitation, but the often-resented obligation is not there.

Announcements are ordinarily sent out immediately after the wedding takes place—either the same day or the day after. However, they may be sent out up to a year later to announce a marriage that took place in secret. The wording is exactly the same as if it had taken place the day before.

CORRECT STYLE AND WORDING

The form of the wedding announcement resembles the form of the wedding invitation in almost everything except wording. The notepaper, the styles of engraving, the use of a crest, the two envelopes if desired, the manner of addressing the envelopes are all the same. *(See pages 595–598.)*

Announcements have traditionally been sent in the name of the bride's parents. They usually are responsible for buying and mailing them, having received a list from the groom's family—just as they do the wedding invitations. However, because of the work involved, the groom's mother may offer to address and mail *her* announcements, even though the bride's mother orders them.

In many cases the bride's family prefers to send invitations and no announcements, but the groom's family wants to send announcements. They are free to order and send them themselves, but they should be worded as though they came from the bride's family. Only if the bride's parents are dead may the announcement be in the name of the groom's family, and even then it is more often in the name of the bride and groom themselves.

In spite of this traditional "rule," I feel—and recommend—that the family of the groom *be included on the announcement with that of the bride.* Today, the attitude toward marriage is one of "joining" rather than "giving" the bride to the groom, and furthermore the purpose of an announcement, unlike an invitation, is to give as much information as possible. Surely the names of the groom's parents are an important part of the pertinent information! The inclusion of their names is not only informative but also indicates their approval and joy in the marriage.

Therefore, while this is the correct traditional wording:

Mr. and Mrs. John Fairburn

have the honour of

announcing the marriage of their daughter

Madeleine Anne

to

Mr. George Burns Fellowes

Ensign United States Navy

Tuesday, the twenty-seventh of March

One thousand nine hundred and seventy-five

Washington, D. C.

I prefer, when agreed upon and appropriate:

Mr. and Mrs. Howard Carter James
and
Mr. and Mrs. Stanley Holmes Seaburn
announce the marriage of
Nancy Lynn James
and
Stanley Holmes Seaburn, Jr.
Saturday, the second of July
Trinity Church
New Milford, Connecticut

620

Note that while most wedding invitations use the phrase "The marriage of their daughter . . . *to* . . ." the announcement often reads, "The marriage of . . . *and* . . ." This is especially true when, as above, both sets of parents appear on the announcement.

Since "Nancy Lynn James" is not preceded by "Miss," neither should "Stanley Holmes Seaburn, Jr.," be preceded by "Mr." If *to* were used in place of *and*, however, the "Mr." would be used, just as it is on a wedding invitation.

Three forms of phrasing are equally correct: "have the honour to announce," or "have the honour of announcing," or merely the one word "announce." Although "Tuesday, April 24, 1975," is not incorrect, the use of "Tuesday, the twenty-fourth of April," on one line, and "One thousand nine hundred seventy-five," or "nineteen hundred and seventy-five," on the next, is most formal.

The variations in wording necessitated by special circumstances (when the bride has a stepfather, or professional name, etc.) correspond to the variations in wedding invitations. Here are some examples:

Announcements for a young widow's or divorcée's second marriage are the same as for a first wedding:

Mr. and Mrs. Maynard Banks
announce the marriage of their daughter
Priscilla Banks Loring
etc.

The announcement of the second marriage of a widow of maturer years reads differently:

Mrs. William Phillip Hoyt
and
Mr. Worthington Adams
announce their marriage
on Monday, the second of November
One thousand nine hundred and seventy-five
at Saratoga Springs
New York

A divorcée, too, may, with her husband, announce her own marriage:

> *Mrs. Strong Brooks [or: Mrs. Mary Brooks]*
> *and*
> *Mr. Robert Hanson*
> *announce their marriage*
> *on Saturday, the tenth of May*
> *etc.*

The bride who is an orphan, or whose parents do not approve of the marriage, and the bridegroom may announce their own marriage this way:

> *Miss Elizabeth Orphan*
> *and*
> *Mr. John Henry Bridegroom*
> *announce their marriage*
> *etc.*

When the wedding is given by a relative or friend the announcement reads:

> *Mr. and Mrs. John Baxter*
> *announce the marriage of*
> *Miss Susan Murray*
> *[or: their niece, Miss Susan Murray]*
> *etc.*

In the rare event that the announcement is made by the groom's family, the wording is similar to that for an orphan:

> *Mr. and Mrs. Hubert Schenck*
> *announce the marriage of*
> *Miss Jeanette Leroi*
> *and*
> *Mr. John William Schenck*
> *etc.*

"At home" notices *(see page 613)* may be included in announcements, or the couple's address may be engraved in the lower-left-hand corner.

The parents of a bride whose wedding is not traditional, including "original" invitations, should compose announcements in a similar vein. An appropriate announcement to be sent for the same wedding as the invitation on page 616 would be:

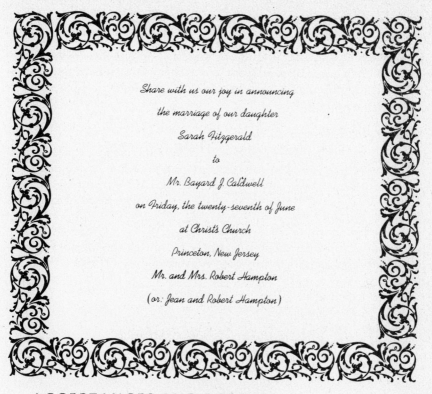

Share with us our joy in announcing

the marriage of our daughter

Sarah Fitzgerald

to

Mr. Bayard J. Caldwell

on Friday, the twenty-seventh of June

at Christ's Church

Princeton, New Jersey

Mr. and Mrs. Robert Hampton

(or: Jean and Robert Hampton)

ACCEPTANCES AND REGRETS

INFORMAL REPLIES

Wedding announcements require no acknowledgment, although many people thoughtfully send a note or congratulatory card in reply.

Invitations to the marriage ceremony do not necessitate an answer, unless the invitation has arrived in the form of a personal note. In that case it should be answered at once, also by handwritten note.

Replies to the new, informal type of invitation described on page 615 need not be in the traditional third-person style. If the invitation is in a semiformal style as in the example on page 616, the answer might be written in that form, with the wording varied to fit the phrasing of the invitation. For example:

We will be happy
to share your joy
and participate in
the marriage of your daughter
Sarah Fitzgerald

> *on Friday, the twenty-seventh of June*
> *Anne and Howard Jones*

Other, less formal invitations may be answered by a short personal note, or even by telephone when that seems most appropriate. All invitations, no matter what the style, should be answered *as promptly as possible.*

TRADITIONAL REPLIES

The traditional third-person form of reply seems to baffle and dismay many people, but actually, once learned, it is far simpler than any other. There is no reason to give excuses or regrets, and the only change in wording is the name of the person who issued the invitation and the date.

The formal reply should be written on plain or bordered, monogrammed, or unmarked letter paper or notepaper in appropriate ink. The lines should be evenly and symmetrically spaced on one page.

The wording is:

ACCEPTANCE

> *Mr. and Mrs. Robert Gilding, Jr.*
> *accept with pleasure*
> *Mr. and Mrs. Smith's*
> *kind invitation for*
> *Tuesday, the first of June*

REGRET

> *Mr. and Mrs. Richard Brown*
> *regret that they are unable to accept*
> *Mr. and Mrs. Smith's*
> *kind invitation for*
> *Tuesday, the first of June*

The alternative form is equally acceptable:

> *the kind invitation of*
> *Mr. and Mrs. Roger James Smith*
> *for Tuesday, the first of June*

This form is preferable if "Mr. and Mrs. Smith" is followed by "Jr."

⋖§51⋗ *All About Wedding Gifts*

WHEN YOU ARE THE GUEST

YOUR OBLIGATIONS

Having sent your acceptance—or your regrets—you should next turn your thoughts to whether or not you will send a gift to the bride.

If you are not an intimate friend of the bride or groom or of their families and if you are not invited to the wedding reception, you need not send a present, unless you know that there is to be no reception. Of course, a gift always may be sent if you wish to, whether or not you receive any invitation at all. Obviously, the more personal the invitation the greater the obligation to send a gift. An invitation by written note definitely indicates that you are considered an especially close friend, and you will therefore certainly want to send a present. And you must always send a present to one who is marrying into your immediate family.

It used to be considered obligatory to send a gift, even though you could not attend the wedding. This is still true when the principals are friends whom you see from time to time, or who live nearby. In the days when that "rule" was made, people did not move around as they do today, and invitations were sent *only* to those within a reasonable distance. Today people often send invitations to their entire list of acquaintances (perhaps using a Christmas card list), not thinking about the obligation they impose. So, if you live in California and receive an invitation to a wedding in New Jersey from people you haven't seen in ten years, *don't send a gift*. If you are a customer, a client, or a patient of someone you meet *only* professionally, and you have never met the bride or groom, *don't send a gift*. The bride's parents *should* have sent you an announcement instead of an invitation—carrying no obligation—and the fact that they were thought-less excuses you from "having to" send a present.

This does *not* mean that you should not send a gift to a bride whose family you will see in the near future, even though you are at a distance when the wedding takes place. For example, the daughter of people you see every summer at your vacation home, who has grown up with your children, gets married in December. The fact that you are hundreds of miles away does not relieve you of the responsibility of sending a gift, if you receive an invitation to both wedding and reception. If you don't, you will surely receive a cool "reception" yourself when you meet next summer.

"JOINT" GIFTS

Engaged couples may give a "joint" gift—one gift from both of them.

Others who may do this are:

The "staff" or co-workers from an office, unless they have each received a separate invitation.

A girl and her "date," when the invitation has indicated that she may bring an escort. In a sense he is *her* guest rather than the bride and groom's, so he should not be obligated to give a gift to someone he does not know. Therefore she would select and pay for a gift to be given from them both. He may offer to pay a share of it if he wishes to.

A boy and *his* "date"—the same as above.

WHEN AND WHERE GIFTS ARE DELIVERED

Gifts are generally delivered to the bride's home before the day of the wedding. They may be delivered in person, or they may be sent directly from the store where they were purchased. Those sent by mail or from a store are addressed in the bride's maiden name. When gifts are sent after the wedding takes place, they are addressed to "Mr. and Mrs. Newlywed" at their new address, or in care of the bride's mother.

When you do not know the bride's address and it does not appear on the invitation, either under an RSVP or on the envelope flap, it may be very difficult to discover where presents are to be sent. If you have no way of getting her address, or her family's, the only solution is to send gifts and responses in care of the club, hotel, hall, or whatever is given as the site of the reception.

In some localities and among certain ethnic groups it is customary to take your gift to the wedding reception rather than send it ahead of time. Checks are usually handed to the bride and groom as you go through the receiving line, but gift packages are placed on a table prepared for them, as soon as you arrive. If there is a large number of presents, the bride and groom do not open them until a later date, so that they will have time to enjoy the other festivities. If there are only a few, however, they should open them after the receiving line breaks up. One of the bride's attendants should help, disposing of wrappings and keeping a careful list of the gifts.

CHOOSING THE GIFT

There is no "formula" to determine the amount you should spend on a wedding gift. The size or elaborateness of the wedding should have nothing to do with the amount you spend or give. Your decision should be based on a combination of two things—your affection for the bride, the groom, or their families, and your financial capability. No one should ever feel that he must spend more than he can afford; not only is it impractical, but it is ostentatious and therefore in poor taste. On the other hand, one should not give a "piddling" gift to a bride whose family are old friends. That would surely make you look "cheap." Having set the appropriate amount you want to spend in mind, you must think carefully about what the bride might most like or need, taking *her* situation into account. If she and her groom are young, poor, and have few possessions of their own, a practical gift is indicated. If they come from wealthier families who have or will provide them with all the basic necessities, something purely ornamental, which they might not buy for themselves, is a better choice.

Remember this: Even though the young couple are going to be living in the simplest manner, in the tiniest apartment for the present, someday they will have a larger place and the surroundings to use more elegant things. Although your gift of a silver serving dish may not be exactly what they need right now, it is something they can put away for that later day. Couples moving to larger apartments or houses have tremendous expenses to begin with, and having a supply of wedding presents to be brought out and enjoyed, and which will save them additional expense in furnishing the home, is a real thrill.

When a bride has registered her choices of gifts at a neighboring store (or stores) you will be wise to avail yourself of this assistance, especially if you do not know her, or her tastes, well. You are under no obligation to select anything from her list, especially if she has not chosen items within your price range. However, you will do well to study her selections whether you buy one of them or not. They will indicate to you the style, the materials, the colors that she likes, and you will be able to select something that you are reasonably sure will please her.

Typical wedding presents include almost anything ornamental or useful for the furnishing of a home or the setting of a dining-room table. Naturally, the less you know about the future living plans of the bride and groom, or their tastes, the more necessary it is to choose a gift that can be used by anyone living anywhere.

Here is a list of gifts in various price ranges, which would be usable in almost any style of home:

Set of folding tables on rack	Carving set
Mirror for entry or hall	Wooden salad bowl
Crystal vase	Large pepper grinder
Planter	or salt-and-pepper sets
Electric hot tray	Framed print or photograph
Lamp	Wastebasket
Set of glasses	Hors d'oeuvres tray

Items of the silver or china selected by the bride.

Unless you know that your gift is something the bride wants, and that it will not be duplicated, it is safer not to have it monogrammed or marked. The exceptions are articles of her selected pattern of silver, or monogrammed glasses she has asked for. Other gifts that are improved by monogramming are leather or silver cigarette boxes, leather picture frames, silver trays, etc. These would be articles she would not be likely to exchange, since she can always use more than one.

MONEY AS A WEDDING PRESENT

The custom of giving money as a wedding present is a long-established tradition in Jewish communities and among various other groups. And at those weddings where most guests give presents, close relatives and intimate friends of the bride's or groom's parents sometimes prefer to give money. To set maximums or minimums on a sum given as a gift is against every principle of etiquette. The sum you give is *in no way* supposed to help pay for the wedding and should never be based on the presumed "cost per head." In some groups it is accepted and expected that one gives five or ten or twenty dollars as a gift. If this is the custom in your area, you must go along with it or risk criticism. Otherwise, for anyone to say "You must give thus-and-so" is entirely wrong.

A check given before the wedding is made out in the bride's

maiden name, or if the couple have opened a joint account, it may be written to both the bride and groom. Occasionally a grandparent or godparent may intend a gift especially for the groom, and he may make the check out to him alone. A check to be presented at the reception may be made out to the bride's married name or to the couple jointly.

Bonds or shares of stock also make wonderful wedding gifts because of their lasting and (hopefully) increasing value. If sent before the wedding the bond is in the name of the bride alone. If it is a government bond, it is made out to "Miss Emily Johnson"; registered bonds and securities are made out to "Emily Johnson" or "Emily L. Johnson." After marriage all bonds and securities given to the couple are made out to "Albert C. Foster and Emily J. Foster."

PRESENTS FOR A SECOND MARRIAGE

Whether you are asked to the reception or not, there is no necessity for sending a present when both members of the couple have been married before. However, special friends and perhaps close relatives usually do send presents to someone being married for a second time, especially if the bride's first marriage was an elopement and/or she never furnished a home. When one of the couple has not been married before, his or her friends will most probably wish to send gifts.

PRESENTS FOR ELOPERS

A person receiving an announcement of an elopement, either in the name of the parents or without their names, is in no way obligated, nor even expected, to send a present. If, of course, out of love or affection for either the bride or the groom or their families, one wishes to give them something, it will be an especially appreciated gesture.

DELAYED PRESENTS

If for some reason your present is not sent until after the wedding, a note should accompany it, giving the reason for the delay. Late presents are sent to "Mr. and Mrs. Newlywed" at their own new address. If you do not know their address, they may be sent in care of the bride's family.

PRESENTS FROM THE BRIDEGROOM'S FRIENDS

You seldom send a present to the bridegroom. Even if you are an old friend of his and have never met the bride, your present is sent to her—unless you send two presents, one in courtesy to her and one in affection to him. Rather often friends of the bridegroom do pick out things suitable for him, such as a decanter or a rather masculine-looking desk set, which are sent to her but are obviously intended for his use.

CARDS WITH PRESENTS

If you have visiting cards, one is practically always enclosed with a wedding present. If you are married, your "Mr. and Mrs." card is used. Sometimes nothing is added, but usually you write "Best wishes" or "All best wishes for your happiness" above the engraved names. If you have no visiting card at hand, write the same message on a blank card provided by the store, and sign it. Even though you are older than the bride you sign it "John and Mary Friendly" —never "Mr. and Mrs. Friendly." Friends of the same age simply write "John and Mary."

Contemporaries of the bride and groom, or older friends who are close to them often cross out the "Mr. and Mrs." and write "Bob and Helen" just above.

WHEN YOU RECEIVE NO ACKNOWLEDGMENT FOR A GIFT

If after several months you have not received a thank-you note from the bride, you need not hesitate to write her and ask whether your present ever arrived. You must word your letter carefully, not implying that you are criticizing her for not writing, but making it clear that you only wish to know what happened so that you may send another gift if the first was lost in the mail. She, too, may have been wondering why a present from you had never arrived, and your letter will serve to clarify the situation for you both. And if she has not thanked you through laziness or thoughtlessness, she deserves the embarrassment your letter will cause her!

WHEN YOU ARE THE BRIDE

Just before or immediately after your invitations are mailed, you should go to the local stores where you would like to register your choice of gifts. You and your groom should select your china, silver, and glassware patterns, so that they may be registered, too. Your choices should cover a wide range of prices, and as much variety in types of gifts as possible, to allow your friends more leeway in picking a gift.

Then, when someone asks you what you would like, you need

only say, "I've listed a number of choices at the Gift-in-Hand. They'll be glad to show you the things on my list." If your friend cannot get to the stores where you are registered, or there are no appropriate stores in your area, you should answer the same question with a generalization rather than mentioning a specific item. "We prefer stainless steel or pewter to silver," or "We're planning to furnish our apartment in a very modern style." or "Our living and dining room will be Early American," will help your friend make a choice, without committing her to paying more or less than she wants to.

You may *never* make any mention of a gift on your invitation. Even though you know some of your friends can't afford to give you one, you must call or write them and ask them not to, rather than writing "No gift, please," on their invitation (as can be done in other circumstances). Wedding guests expect to give gifts, and usually want to, even though they spend a minimum amount or make the gift themselves. Unless you *know* they will not resent the implication that they cannot afford it, you should not even suggest "No gift." Nor should a bride indicate on her invitation that she would prefer money to a gift. No matter how legitimate the reason, you must spread the word through friends and relatives rather than have the request come from you.

YOUR GIFT-REGISTER BOOK

As soon as the invitations are out you should get a book to keep a list of the gifts as they arrive. Specially designed books are sold in all degrees of cost and varieties of design. Although you may use any lined notebook and make the columns and heading yourself, an attractive bride's book serves not only as a record, but as a lovely memento of the wedding. The usual form is this:

NO.	DATE REC'D.	ARTICLE	SENT BY	SENDER'S ADDRESS	WHERE BOUGHT	THANKS SENT
3	7/2	Salad bowl	Mr. and Mrs. George White	11 High Street, New Haven	Altman's	7/2
4	7/3	8 fruit plates	Aunt Susan	Long Mile Road, New Canaan	Holloway Gifts	7/4

Sheets of numbered stickers come with the book. One is placed on the bottom of each gift as it arrives, and the corresponding number is written in the book. Only one sticker goes on each set of things—on one plate of a set of eight, for example.

THE BRIDE'S THANKS

In return for the joy of receiving the presents, there is a correspondence task that the bride may not evade. On a sheet of notepaper—not an informal—in her own handwriting, she must send a separate letter for each present she receives. If humanly possible, she writes each letter of thanks on the day the present arrives. If she does not, they will soon get ahead of her, and the first weeks of her marriage will be taken up with note-writing. A note of thanks is also sent to those who send congratulatory telegrams on the day of the wedding. There is no excuse for not having all thank-you notes written within three months of the wedding—at the most.

It is not possible to overemphasize the rudeness of the bride who sends a printed or even an engraved card of thanks with no personal message added. If you prefer a card that says "Thank you," or has a poem or message on it, choose one that is simple and dignified, and then add your own note, mentioning the specific gift and how you feel about it or intend to use it. Since you *must do this* in any case, it seems foolish to go to the expense of buying cards that come to much more than a box of plain notepaper.

Many brides order paper with their maiden initials on it to be used before their marriage, and other paper with their married initials for afterward. Any of the papers described in Chapter 6 are appropriate, whether plain or bordered, white or a pretty color.

Since most wedding gifts are sent to the bride it is she who writes *and* signs the thank-you note. It is not incorrect to sign "Fran and Bob," but it is preferable to sign "Fran" and include your husband in the text: "Bob and I are so delighted with . . . etc."

Thank-you notes for gifts from married couples are often addressed to the wife only, on the premise, I suppose, that it was she who selected and bought the gift. However, when the present comes from "Mr. and Mrs." or "Hal and Donna," I feel that it is warmer to send your thanks to "Mr. and Mrs." or "Hal and Donna." However, it is equally correct to write; "Dear Mrs. Hancock, I want to thank you and Mr. Hancock so much. . . ."

Every note, no matter how short (and it may be very short), should include a reference to the present itself. While you need not lie about your feelings about the gift, you must try to make some comment that shows your appreciation of the thought and effort spent in choosing it. When you have received a ghastly pincushion covered with sequins and fake flowers, you need not say it is "lovely" or "pretty." But it *can* be "unique," "a conversation piece," or even "interesting." After being sure it is on display the first time the donor comes to your home, you can put it away and hope that its absence will go unnoticed.

SAMPLE THANK-YOU NOTES

TO FAMILY FRIENDS

Dear Mr. and Mrs. Knight,

The clock-radio you sent John and me is just exactly what we needed. Now perhaps I will be able to get him up in time to catch the 8:03 in the morning!

We look forward to seeing you both on the 10th, and in the meantime, thank you so very much.

Affectionately [or: Sincerely],
Cora (Bailey)

Dear Mrs. Hopkins,

John and I want you to know that the mirror you sent fits—exactly—in the space over our hall table. It looks as though it were made for it! And of course John is delighted with the picture of the old Nassau Hall at the top.

We hope you will stop by just as soon as we get back from our honeymoon, to see how lovely it looks. Many thanks from us both.

Linda Sperry

FOR A GIFT OF MONEY

Dear Uncle Henry,

Your check came as the most welcome surprise! John and I were wondering how we would possibly afford a sofa, and now you've made it possible. We are going to select one this week.

We do hope you are going to be able to get to the wedding, and we look forward to seeing you there. Until then, many, many thanks for the check—

With much love,
Betsy

THANK-YOU CARDS WITH THE COUPLE'S PICTURE

There has been something of a fad lately for sending thank-you cards with a picture of the bride and groom at the wedding attached. It is a nice idea, and makes an attractive keepsake, but there are drawbacks.

The problem is one of time. At least a couple of weeks will have elapsed by the time the photographer has gotten the proofs to you, you and your groom have selected the one you want, and the final prints are delivered. Therefore it may be some time after the wedding before the thank-yous can be mailed. However, if you wish to send pictures, you may take several steps to hasten the process. You may ask the photographer to select one good picture and print it immediately, eliminating one whole step. Of course you should see and approve the first print before he makes the entire order.

You should write your notes as the gifts arrive, having asked the photographer, who supplies the cards and envelopes also, to give them to you ahead of time. They may be addressed, stamped, and ready to go, so that all you need to do when the finished pictures arrive is slip them into the slots, or attach them in the indicated way. Even though two or three weeks have passed, your thank-yous will not be later than many others written and mailed after the honeymoon.

These cards, like all others, must carry a personal note.

ACKNOWLEDGMENT CARDS

In unusual cases, such as the hurried marriage of a bridegroom who is unexpectedly transferred to a foreign country, or the marriage of a person of such prominence that the gifts arrive in overwhelming numbers, a printed acknowledgment, *always* followed later by a note of thanks, is permissible. Even then it seems pretentious because it implies that so many presents were expected that special preparations were made in advance to take care of the avalanche.

There is no reason why a bride should not have every thank-you note written within three months. Even those who receive hundreds of presents can accomplish the chore by determining to write a set number each day. The donor who does not receive a note within three months can only think either that the gift was lost or that the bride is most unappreciative.

If circumstances demand it, however, the engraved note reads:

Miss Joanne Carter
[or Mrs. John Franklin,
if the notes are sent after the wedding]
gratefully acknowledges the receipt of
your wedding gift
and will write you a personal note at
the earliest possible date

Quite frequently the bride and groom are away at college, or are working at a distance from where the wedding will be held, and where the gifts will be sent. Because the RSVP gives the bride's mother's address, the presents are sent there, too. Even though the mother may open the gifts and send the bride daily lists, so that she can keep up with the thank-you notes, there can be considerable confusion and delay. Therefore in this case I would recommend this thoughtful solution, suggested to me recently. The bride's mother has cards printed (they need not be engraved), saying, "This is to assure you of the safe arrival of your thoughtful gift. Mary and John will express their gratitude when they have received it from my custody." Although Mary will have a lot of letter-writing to do when she gets back from her honeymoon, her notes will be more sincere, because she will have seen the gifts herself.

DISPLAYING THE GIFTS

Nothing could be nicer than displaying your wedding gifts, showing your appreciation and delight in them.

If your reception is to be at home, they should be in a room easily accessible to all the guests. If they are only to be seen by friends who drop in before the wedding, they may be in a back bedroom, a basement playroom, or anywhere you have room for them.

Gifts are never displayed at the club, hotel, or hall where a

reception is held. In this case relatives and friends are invited to the home beforehand, specifically to see the gifts.

Furniture is removed from the room chosen for the display, and tables—or sawhorses with smooth boards across them—are set up around the walls. They are covered with plain white cloths—either damask or linen tablecloths or sheets. The sides are usually draped with net or tulle caught up here and there with bows and ribbons, and possibly artificial flowers. The ribbons and flowers may be white or they may be in a color to match the color scheme of the wedding. The sheet or cloths should hang down to the floor so that boxes for the presents on display may be hidden underneath.

To do justice to the kindness of the people who have sent gifts, you should show your appreciation by placing each one in the position of greatest advantage. Naturally, all people's tastes are not equally pleasing to the taste of the bride—nor are all pocketbooks equally filled. But very valuable presents are better put near to others of similar quality—or others entirely different in character. Colors should be carefully grouped. Two presents, both lovely in themselves, can completely destroy each other if the colors are allowed to clash.

When the wedding gifts are numerous and valuable it is a good idea to hire a policeman or detective to guard the house while everyone is at the wedding and reception. Thieves have been known to watch for just such an opportunity and to pull up with a "caterer's" truck and make a clean sweep while the bride and groom are exchanging their vows.

Sometimes china is put on one table, silver on another, glass on another, but I think a more attractive arrangement can be made by combining textures and shapes. Pieces that "jar" when appearing together must be placed as far apart as possible and perhaps even moved to other surroundings. A "cheap" piece of silverplate should not be left among beautiful pieces of sterling, but should be put among china ornaments or other articles that do not reveal its lack of fineness by too direct comparison. To group duplicates is another unfortunate arrangement. Eight salad bowls or six gravy boats in a row might as well be labeled: "Look at this! What can she do with all of us?" They are sure to make the givers feel a little chagrined, at least.

SHOULD CARDS BE DISPLAYED?

There is no definite rule as to whether or not the cards that are sent with the gifts are removed. Some people prefer to leave them on, which certainly saves members of the family from repeating many times who sent this and who sent that, especially if the bride has received as unusual number of presents. On the other hand, other brides feel that it is a private matter between themselves and the giver and do not wish the world to know how elaborate a gift someone was or was not able to send, or perhaps wish to avoid odious comparisons!

DISPLAYED CHECKS

Ordinarily it would be in very bad taste to display gifts of money. But because it would not be fair to a generous relative or intimate friend of the family to have it supposed that he or she sent no gift at all, it is quite proper to display checks with amounts concealed. This is done by laying them out on a flat surface one above the other so that the signatures alone are disclosed. The amount of the one at the top is covered with a strip of opaque paper, and then a sheet of glass laid over them all, to prevent curious guests from taking a peek.

You may also write on plain white gift enclosure cards "Check from Mr. and Mrs. Harold Brown" and display such cards neatly.

EXCHANGING WEDDING PRESENTS

Some people think it discourteous if the bride changes the present chosen for her, but they are wrong. A bride may exchange all duplicate presents, and no friends should allow their feelings to be hurt unless they have chosen the present with a particular sentiment. You should never, however, exchange the presents chosen for you by your own family or by your groom's unless you are specifically told to do so.

Whether or not you mention the exchange to the donor depends on the circumstances. If she (or he) is a close friend, and will be in your house frequently, you will probably wish to tell her. Or if you do not know where a present was purchased, you must ask the one who gave it and tell her why, if you wish to exchange it. But if the gift came from a mere acquaintance, or someone far away, it is perfectly all right to simply write and thank her for the present she sent, making no mention of the exchange.

Gifts are never returned to the donor, *except* when a marriage is canceled or immediately annulled.

When a gift arrives by mail, broken, you should immediately look at the wrapping to see if it was insured. If so, notify the person who sent it at once so that he or she can collect the insurance and replace it. If it is not insured, you must decide whether to call attention to it or not. If it is a very special gift from a very special person, you should probably do so. But if it is a small present from someone you barely know, it could be an imposition to mention it, as he would undoubtedly feel he had to buy you something else.

When the broken gift is delivered directly from the store, you should take it back as soon as possible. All reputable stores will be happy to replace merchandise that arrives damaged. You need not even mention it to the donor, as it is unnecessary to bother him about it at all.

GIFTS FOR ATTENDANTS

FROM BRIDE TO BRIDESMAIDS

Either at the bridesmaids' luncheon shortly before the wedding or at the rehearsal dinner, the bride gives each bridesmaid her present. The typical gift is a bracelet with a monogrammed disk, a pin, or other jewelry, and according to the means of the bride, may have great value or scarcely any. The gift to her maid or matron of honor may match those given the bridesmaids or be slightly more elaborate. If it is something that can be engraved, such as a small silver picture frame, the date and the initials of the bride and groom or the bridesmaids' initials commemorate the occasion.

FROM GROOM TO USHERS

The bridegroom's gifts to his ushers are usually put at their places at the bachelor dinner—if one is held. If not, they are presented at the rehearsal dinner or just before leaving the church. Silver or gold pencils, belt buckles, key rings, wallets, billfolds, and other small and personal articles are suitable. The present to the best man is approximately the same as, or slightly handsomer than, the gifts to the ushers.

THE BRIDE AND GROOM EXCHANGE PRESENTS

He is a very exceptional groom who is financially able to take his fiancée to the jeweler and let her choose what she wants. Instead, the bridegroom goes shopping alone and buys the handsomest piece of jewelry he can afford.

The bride need not give a present to the groom, but she usually does if she can. Her gift is something permanent and for his personal use—ranging from cuff links to a watch or ring.

RETURNING WEDDING GIFTS

When wedding plans are canceled, gifts that have already been received must be returned. If it is an indefinite postponement but the couple intend to be married as soon as possible, the gifts are carefully put away until the time the ceremony takes place. If there is doubt as to whether it will take place at all, the bride after six weeks to two months must send back the gifts so that the donors may return them.

~§52§~ Events Before and After the Wedding

THE PARTIES BEFORE THE WEDDING

THE BRIDESMAIDS' LUNCHEON

In many American communities the bridesmaids give the bride a farewell luncheon (or it may be a tea) in addition to the regular showers.

There is no special difference between a bridesmaids' luncheon and any other lunch party except that the table is more elaborately decorated, often in pink and white or the bride's chosen colors for the wedding. The bride may give her bridesmaids their presents at this time, and if they are giving her a single present from all of them, this would be the occasion for the presentation.

THE BACHELOR DINNER

Bachelor dinners are not held so often as they used to be, especially if the ushers are scattered far and wide or if they, as well as the groom, are working until the day before the wedding. If there is a dinner it is generally held in the private dining room of a restaurant or in a club.

Popularly supposed to be a frightful orgy, the bachelor dinner, even years ago, was in truth, more often than not, a sheep in wolf's clothing. As a matter of fact, the orgy was merely a gathering of young men—dedicated to the idea of getting the groom roaring drunk for the last time—at which the principal activities were singing and breaking glasses. A boisterous picture, but scarcely a vicious one! Especially as a lot of the cheapest glassware was provided for the purpose.

The breaking habit originated with drinking the bride's health and breaking the stem of the wineglass so that it "might never serve a less honorable purpose." This highly impractical custom is never so far as I know, practiced today. The only remaining tradition is that toward the end of the dinner the bridegroom rises, holds his glass aloft, and says, "To my bride!" The men rise, drink the toast standing, and that ends the party.

Aside from toasting the bride and possibly some more-than-usual reminiscing, the bridegroom's farewell dinner is exactly like any other stag dinner.

Bachelor dinners used to be given by the groom's father, but that is rarely so today, unless he also happens to be the best man. Instead, the ushers generally get together to organize the party, or it may be hosted by the groom's fraternity brothers or co-workers.

SHOWERS

For a full description of bridal showers, see Chapter 35.

PARTIES FOR OUT-OF-TOWN GUESTS

In order to take care of out-of-town family and guests who may arrive two or three days before the wedding, and also to relieve the bride's parents of extra meals and housework, friends of the family frequently give luncheons and dinners for the early arrivals as well as members of the wedding party who live nearby. Invitations should be sent a week or so after the wedding invitations go out, even though replies are not yet in. Receiving the invitation to the party may jog the memories of those who have forgotten to answer the wedding invitation. These parties are likely to be much less formal than the actual wedding festivities and may be given at home, in a club, or in a restaurant. In warm weather they may be in the form of an outdoor barbecue or swimming party; in the winter a sleigh ride or skating party could be organized for the young people, and a cozier fireside buffet for their elders. Whatever the party, the attendants, the families of the couple, their own close friends, and friends of their parents may be included. To make it clear that it is not a shower, it is permissible to write "This is not a shower!" or "No gifts" on the invitations.

LUNCHEON BEFORE THE WEDDING

A small luncheon for the bridal party may be held on the day of the wedding, again to relieve the bride's mother of extra responsibility. It is usually given by a relative or a friend of the bride's family and may be as simple or elaborate as the host and hostess wish. The bride and groom may not even attend. There is an old superstition that the bridegroom should not see his bride before the ceremony on the day of the wedding—but this is an outmoded idea, and they usually come for a short time, probably not together, but each with his own family.

A PREWEDDING RECEPTION

Occasionally a wedding and reception are so small that only family and a few close friends are invited. In order to include those friends who cannot be on the wedding list, the bride's family may give a party a few days before the wedding, or on an earlier weekend when both bride and groom are in town. This party provides an opportunity to introduce the groom to the family friends, and serves as a substitute "reception."

Invitations should be sent ten days or two weeks ahead of the party, or they may be telephoned. If an informal or invitation card is used, "To meet John Bullett," or "In honor of Jane and John," should be written at the top.

The party, like any reception, may be a buffet or sit-down dinner or a cocktail buffet. Soft drinks and beer should be available as well as mixed drinks. The parents of the bride stand near the door with their daughter and her fiancé, to make sure that all the guests meet the couple as they arrive. The groom's parents, if present, should also be introduced to all those they do not already know.

There should not be a wedding cake or other wedding-reception standbys, since the wedding has not yet taken place.

THE REHEARSAL

The only people who attend the rehearsal are the bride and groom, their attendants, and the bride's parents. Since the groom's parents have no active part in the ceremony, there is no reason that they should be present. If they *do* attend, having been urged to do so by the bride, they should be observers only and not complicate decisions by expressing their opinions—unless asked.

Although most of us are familiar with the traditional marriage service, we do not realize the number of details that go into its planning if all is to go smoothly on the day of the wedding. Therefore it is essential that the bride, the groom, and all the attendants listen carefully and give the clergyman their full attention. When the service is *not* traditional, and has been composed by the couple themselves, even more care must be taken in the rehearsing, since it is unfamiliar to those who will participate.

DRESS AND MANNER

People taking part in the rehearsal or attending as observers should remember that they are in a church and dress accordingly. The girls should wear dresses rather than slacks or shorts, and the men should wear jackets and ties except on a hot day, when a neat sports shirt would be acceptable. One clergyman I know, quite justifiably sent two bridesmaids home to change from shorts to skirts to preserve the dignity of his church and the ceremony.

In manner as well as dress, the bridal party should recognize the importance of the occasion and attend the rehearsal seriously, and make every effort to make the ceremony flawless. This means that they arrive on time, listen to instructions carefully, and avoid horseplay of any kind.

Years ago it was supposed to be bad luck for the bride to take part in the rehearsal, and her role was played by a stand-in. Fortunately, we are no longer so superstitious, and today the "rehearsal" bride is the "real" bride. Although the clergyman tells the couple the order in which the words of the service come and what their responses will be, the actual service is not read, and they do not repeat the responses or vows.

The organist is present at the rehearsal so that the pace and spacing can be practiced. The order of the procession is established, and the attendants walk up the aisle two or three times until all goes smoothly.

The bride and groom decide how they would like the attendants to stand at the chancel. However, they should ask for the minister's advice about this, since he will know from past experience what looks best in his church.

The manner of pairing off and leaving the chancel is arranged, but it is not necessary to practice the recessional, since the bride and groom lead off at their own pace (not running so fast that the congregation can hardly get a glimpse of them) and the others follow at a natural walk.

THE REHEARSAL DINNER

The wedding rehearsal is generally held in the late afternoon of the day before the wedding. It is almost always followed by a dinner party, which has come to be known as the "rehearsal dinner." Because of complications in the clergyman's schedule or the inability of some of the attendants to arrive by that afternoon, the rehearsal must sometimes be held later—either after the dinner or the following morning. But the party is held in spite of that, and is still the "rehearsal dinner."

It has now become an accepted custom all over the country, although it is not obligatory, that the parents of the groom give this party. This is an extremely nice gesture—a slight repayment to the family of the bride for all the courtesies extended throughout the wedding activities to the family of the groom. If they come from another city they may ask the mother of the bride to reserve a room in a club or restaurant for the dinner and consult with her on the number of her family who should be included so that they can make the reservations in advance. They contact the manager by telephone or by letter to make the preliminary plans. Then, when they arrive for the wedding, they go at once to see the facilities and make the final arrangements. If the groom's family does not, or cannot, give the rehearsal dinner, it is arranged by some member of the bride's family or by a close friend.

THE INVITATIONS

Invitations are generally written on informals or fill-in cards, or they may be simply handwritten notes. They may be telephoned, but since there are often out-of-town guests, the written invitation serves as a reminder of the time, address, etc.

Rehearsal dinner for
Pat and Bob

Mr. & Mrs. John Goodfellow

Friday, June 6th, 7:00 P.M.
Short Hills Country Club

RSVP
1700 Low Street
Short Hills, N.J. 07078

or:

Dear Joan [or: Mrs Franklin],

John and I are giving a rehearsal dinner for Pat and Bob on Friday, June 6, at 7:00 P.M. It will be held at the Short Hills Country Club, and we hope you and Bill [Mr. Franklin] will be with us. We will look forward to hearing that you can come.

Affectionately [Sincerely],
Doris [Goodfellow]

1700 Low Street
Short Hills, New Jersey 07078

THE GUESTS

All the members of the bridal party (with the exception of very young flower girls, pages, or ring bearers), the immediate families of the bride and groom, and out-of-town relatives who have arrived for the wedding are invited. If facilities and finances permit, a few very close friends are often included, expecially those who come from a distance. If the clergyman is a personal friend, or comes from out of town, he and his wife should also be invited.

Husbands, wives, and fiancés of the attendants go to the rehearsal dinner, but "dates" are not included.

THE SEATING

For a large dinner a U-shaped table makes an ideal arrangement. The bride and groom, the bride seated *on his right*, sit at the outside of the base of the U with their attendants beside them. The best man sits beside the bride, the maid of honor beside the groom. If there are many in the bridal party, some are seated opposite the bridal couple. The bridegroom's parents—or whoever are host and hostess—sit at either end of the U. The mother of the bride is seated on the right of the groom's father, and the bride's father sits on the groom's mother's right. Other members of the party are seated along the arms of the U in whatever way seems to make for the most congenial dinner partners. Grandparents are seated near the parents, and younger people may be grouped together.

At a smaller dinner a rectangular table is best. The bride and groom sit together at the center of the one long side, their attendants beside them, and opposite them the host and hostess at either end and other guests between.

DURING THE DINNER

The rehearsal dinner makes a perfect occasion for the presentation of the couple's gifts to the bridesmaids and ushers. In return, the attendants' gifts are often presented at the same time by the maid of honor and the best man, accompanied by a short speech or toast.

The host—generally the groom's father—makes the first toast, welcoming the guests and making some remarks about his happiness at the forthcoming marriage. This is followed by a return toast by the bride's father, and by numerous toasts proposed by the ushers and anyone else who wishes to get to his feet. *(For sample toasts see Chapter 5).*

The attendants' toasts, while sentimental to some extent, may be filled with ancedotes and jokes about past experiences of the bride and groom. Sometimes the bridesmaids make up a poem to be read, and limericks fit the bill well. One young man, after an exposé of some of the groom's collegiate shenanigans, ended his toast: "So here's to my ex-roommate and his new roommate."

ENTERTAINMENT AND DECORATIONS

Music and dancing are not at all essential, and many rehearsal dinners offer no more than the meal and a pleasant gathering. Others are far more elaborate. A strolling violinist or accordionist may play romantic background music, or there may be a full orchestra and after-dinner dancing.

The bride and groom generally leave at a reasonable hour to try to get a good night's sleep, but the guests may stay on to enjoy the festivities until the small hours if the host suggests it. Ushers and bridesmaids should remember that they have a responsibility to fulfill the next day, and refrain from either overindulging in champagne or staying so late that they look exhausted.

Decorations are simple. No matter how large the party may be, bowls of flowers, the number depending on the size of the table, make the only ornamentation.

THE MENU

Rehearsal dinners usually start with a short "cocktail hour," giving the families a chance to chat, and strangers to meet. Cocktails may be served, but punch and soft drinks are offered to those who do not drink. Hors d'oeuvres are as simple or elaborate as the hosts wish.

When the wedding is large and formal the style of rehearsal dinner is too, and the meal compares to that of any formal dinner. There are usually three or four courses: soup (consommé, vichyssoise, turtle soup, etc.); an entrée of filet mignon, a roast, guinea hen, or whatever appeals to the bride and groom; a salad, which may be served with the entrée or as a separate course; and dessert. However, such an elaborate and expensive menu is in no way necessary. If the wedding is informal and non-traditional, the menu might range from lasagne to Mexican chili to barbecued hamburgers. The setting would be different too, of course, and these choices would be more appropriate when the setting was an outdoor barbecue or a buffet in the family gameroom.

Wine is usually served with dinner, with a round of champagne for the toasts. Or champagne may be served through the entire meal. To accompany the less formal menus, beer, iced tea, sangria, or whatever appeals to the couple, should be the choice.

ENTERTAINING AFTER THE RECEPTION

In some areas it is an accepted practice that the bride's family invite out-of-town guests home for dinner or a late snack after the reception. But unless it is customary in your community, it is not necessary or expected. The bride's parents have had as much or more than they can do already, and are not expected to do further entertaining—unless they wish to.

Occasionally a few close friends are asked to dine with them, possibly because they have not had time to visit during the prewedding hours, or possibly because the bride's family simply does not yet wish to be alone to face the inevitable letdown of their daughter's departure.

In cases where some of the out-of-town friends and relatives cannot leave before the next day, a relative of the bride's family may help out by inviting them to an informal dinner when the wedding festivities are over early.

THE GROOM'S PARENTS' CELEBRATION

More frequently the bride and groom are married in her hometown, and the friends of the groom and his family, who live far away, cannot attend. His mother and father, in order to introduce their new daughter-in-law to their friends, give a "reception" for them the first time they come to visit after their honeymoon. It is not, however, a "wedding reception."

The invitations are generally "fill-in" cards or informals, with "In honor of Betty and Hank" written in at the top. Since they do not come from the bride's family they should not be inserted with the wedding invitations or announcements. They should be mailed separately, ten days or two weeks before the date of the party.

As there was a wedding reception at the time of the marriage, this second reception does not attempt to compete with the first. There is no wedding cake, and the bride and groom and their attendants do not wear their wedding clothes.

The party can be as elaborate as the groom's parents wish, but it is usually a tea or a cocktail buffet. The host and hostess stand at the door with the newlyweds and introduce the bride to everyone who has not met her. Her parents should be invited, but they should not be made to feel that they *must* attend, especially at a great distance.

The tea or buffet table is covered with a white or pastel cloth, and the flowers may be similar to those at the wedding. Beverages consist of mixed drinks, punch, and soft drinks. Beer may be served, but champagne is rarely offered, unless one round is served for toasting the couple. The toast is offered by the groom's father, and welcomes the bride to his family. There may be either an orchestra for dancing or a strolling musician, or neither. If wedding pictures have been completed, they should be on display.

❦53❧ *The Wedding Ceremony*

BEFORE THE WEDDING

For everyone except the bride and groom the wedding day flies by. No matter how early the parents are up and making last-minute preparations, there never seems to be enough time. And no matter how complete the advance preparations, there are inevitably crises to be solved. But through all this activity the bride and groom—who are almost forgotten in the excitement of straightening out every detail—find that the hours crawl by. Those whose weddings are at noon are often in better shape than those who have to "kill" the long hours until five or six or eight!

The bridesmaids dress in one place—either at the bride's home or in a dressing room at the church. The former allows the bride to be more relaxed, knowing that her attendants are ready on time, and having their company and support, but the latter has the advantage that their dresses do not get crushed in the car going to the church, or dampened by a possible shower. If they dress at the church, an aunt or good friend of the bride's mother should be there to see that everyone's costume is complete and in order.

The bride dresses early, assisted by her maid of honor (the maid of honor might dress at the house even though the others dress in the church) and her mother, who should be ready even earlier in order to have time to help her daughter. Her bouquet, those of her attendants, and the corsages for her mother and the grandmothers are delivered to the house and are distributed there. The corsage for the groom's mother is sent to her where she is staying or is given to her at the church.

The bridesmaids and everyone else at the house admire the bride and make sure that she has forgotten nothing. One of them asks if she has "something old, something new, something borrowed, and something blue." Perhaps she has borrowed a beautiful lace handkerchief of her grandmother's to tuck up her sleeve, her dress is new, her veil is old, but she has forgotten to put on the blue garter her bridesmaids gave her. Her father produces a shiny new penny to serve as "a sixpence in her shoe," and she is ready.

DRIVING TO THE CHURCH

When it is time to go to the church, the cars are waiting. The bride's mother drives away in the first, usually alone. She may, if she chooses, take her younger children or one or two bridesmaids with her; but she must reserve room for her husband, who will return from church with her. The maid of honor, bridesmaids, and flower girls follow in as many cars as may be necessary.

The bride's car leaves last, timed to arrive at the church only a minute or two before the ceremony is to start. She drives to the church accompanied only by her father. This same car stands in front of the church until she and her husband—in the place of her father—drive to the reception. If limousines are not rented to transport the bridal party, close family friends are asked to act as "chauffeurs."

MEANWHILE, AT THE CHURCH

Forty-five minutes to an hour before the time of the ceremony, the ushers arrive at the church, having dressed at their homes or wherever they are staying. The head usher is responsible for seeing that they all get there on time. Their boutonnieres, sent by the groom, should be waiting in the vestibule unless the best man has distributed them beforehand. Each man puts one in his buttonhole and puts on his gloves.

Those of the ushers who are the most likely to recognize the closest friends and members of each family should be assigned to the center aisle, if there are so many invited that the side sections will be used. Relatives of the bride and groom would, for instance, be chosen for this aisle because they should be best able to recognize and look out for their own family's best friends.

According to tradition the parents of the bride and the groom were not to be seen until they walked down the aisle to their pews. However, at several weddings my husband and I have attended in recent years, the groom's parents were outside the church, greeting and chatting with arriving guests. This was especially nice for the friends who had come from their (the groom's parents) town and knew very few of the bride's guests. We were so impressed with the friendliness of the act that we did it ourselves at our son's wedding and were amazed at the pleasure our friends expressed at finding us outside the door. Having expected to arrive at a strange church (not even sure it was the *right* church) amid a sea of strangers, they really appreciated our welcome, and I highly recommend the idea to other parents of the groom.

RESERVED PEWS

The parents of the bride always sit in the first pew on the left, facing the chancel; the groom's parents in the first pew on the right. If the church has two aisles, her parents sit on the left of the right aisle, and his on the right of the left aisle, so that they are both in the center section of the church. *(See page 657.)*

Behind these front pews several pews on either side of the center aisle are reserved for the immediate families of the couple. The people to sit there may have been given or sent pew cards *(see Chapter 50)* to show their usher, who otherwise might not recognize them or know where to seat them. Sometimes pew cards are not sent, but the ushers are given a list of guests to be seated in the first few pews, and those people should mention to the usher that they are to sit in a reserved pew. People seated in this way are said to be "in front of the ribbon." Formerly a ribbon was actually put across the aisle behind them and raised at one end by the usher to allow guests to pass into the reserved section. Now, however, these special pews are designated by a bouquet or white bow on the end, and the aisle is not closed. Just before the procession starts, a ribbon is laid over the ends of the pews parallel to the aisle, starting with the *back* pew and ending at the last reserved pew. This task is assigned to two of the ushers, who are also responsible for removing it after the ceremony. The families are escorted out first and leave for the reception quickly, while the other guests must wait until the ribbon is removed.

The reserved pews should be "evened up" when one family needs a goodly number and the other very few. Let us say the bride needs seven pews and the bridegroom three (as often occurs when he is from a distant part of the country and few of his family or friends can be present). Then the ushers should be told that behind the first three pews those with pew cards are to be seated evenly on both sides.

SEATING DIVORCED PARENTS

THE BRIDE'S PARENTS DIVORCED BUT FRIENDLY

Because it is obviously better for the children when friendliness rather than bitterness exists between divorced parents, most couples who separate today try to maintain at least a civil relationship. If this has been possible, not only the bride's parents but also her stepparents (if one parent—or both—has remarried) are present at the church and reception.

Her mother and stepfather sit in the front pew. If her mother has a "second" family, those stepbrothers or stepsisters are seated in the second pew. The bride's grandparents, aunts, and uncles on her mother's side are seated behind them. The bride's father (after escorting her up the aisle) sits with his wife and their family in the next pew.

WHEN THEY ARE NOT FRIENDLY

In the entire subject of etiquette, there is perhaps no situation that brings more unhappiness than the wedding of a daughter whose parents are divorced and bitterly estranged. This is especially true for the bride who loves her father and his family as much as her mother and her family, because in most cases, unless she has always lived with her father, the wedding is given by her mother.

It is true that she drives with her father to the church, walks with him up the aisle, and has him share in the marriage ceremony. After giving his daughter away, he sits in the pew behind the immediate family of her mother. His second wife sits with him if the bride wishes, but if there is great bitterness involved, the stepmother sits farther back in the church with a relative or friend. If the relationships are truly impossible, the father may see no more of his daughter on her wedding day, because he will avoid unpleasantness by not going to the reception at all. But if he is sent an invitation, both he and his ex-wife should make a great effort to "bury the hatchet" for that day, to make it as happy as possible for their daughter.

THE WEDDING GIVEN BY THE BRIDE'S FATHER

When the wedding is given by the bride's father and stepmother while her own mother is also living, it is usually because the daughter has made her home with her father instead of her mother.

The bride's own mother sits in the front pew with members of her second family, if she has remarried. If all the parents are friendly, her husband joins her there, but if there is bitterness, he sits farther back. The father gives the bride away and then takes his place in the second pew with his present wife and their family.

SEATING DIVORCED PARENTS OF THE BRIDEGROOM

Even if they have remained on friendly terms, it would be in bad taste to seat divorced parents together. The groom's mother and whomever she would like to have with her should be given the first pew on the bridegroom's side of the church, and his father and others of his family are seated in the second pew.

THE GUESTS ARRIVE AT THE CHURCH

The ushers show all guests to their places. An usher offers his *right* arm to each lady as she arrives, whether he knows her personally or not. If the vestibule is very crowded and several ladies arrive together, he may give his arm to the oldest and ask the others to follow. More often, he asks them to wait until he can come back or another usher is available.

The usher does not offer his arm to a man unless he is quite old and it is obvious that he needs assistance. If the older man is accompanied by a younger, the latter follows so that they can be seated together.

The ushers ask those guests whom they do not recognize, or who may be friends of both bride and groom, whether they wish to sit on the bride's side—the left—or on the groom's side—the right. If they fail to ask, the guest may offer the information: "I am a friend of Mary's—may I sit on her side?"

If the usher thinks a guest belongs in front of the ribbons even though she fails to show him a pew card, he asks, "Have you a pew card?" If she has, he shows her to her place. If she has none, he asks which side she prefers and gives her the best seat vacant in the unreserved part of the church.

Ushers are not supposed to escort guests in total silence, even when they are strangers. A few casual remarks are made—in a low voice, but not whispered or solemn. The deportment of the ushers should be natural, but dignified and quiet, for they are in church. They should not trot up and down the aisles in a bustling manner; but at the same time they must be swift and efficient, in order to seat everyone as expeditiously as possible.

The guests without pew cards should arrive early in order to find good places. It is an unwritten law that those who make the effort to get there in time to have a place on the aisle, from where the "view" is decidedly better, need not move farther into the pew to make space for later arrivals. The latecomers slide past those already there and make the next-best place available.

Just as the reserved pews are divided more or less evenly, so should the rest of the church be. Nothing looks sadder than the bride's side filled to the back, and a mere handful of people scattered along the aisle on the groom's side. As soon as the bride's side is reasonably full, ushers should say to guests, "Would you mind sitting on Jim's side? There are much better seats still free there."

A NEW LOOK IN USHERING

There is an increasing feeling among wedding guests that it is incompatible with the concept of marriage for a woman to be escorted down the aisle by an usher while her husband trails along behind—like the proverbial "fifth wheel." The alternative is to have the usher lead the husband *and* wife, walking together, to their pew, and "usher" them both into it. Personally I am in favor of this. I think it is much more in keeping with the spirit of the occasion to have husbands and wives walk together.

Those who want their weddings to be strictly traditional must have the ushers escort the ladies in the time-honored way. But if you are more interested in the meaningfulness than the tradition, I see no reason not to instruct your ushers to escort or lead both husband and wife, as they would at a Sunday service. Instead of offering an arm to the lady as a couple arrives, the usher would simply look at both of them and say, "Please follow me."

THE LAST FEW MINUTES

THE BRIDEGROOM WAITS

In a Christian ceremony the bridegroom and his best man arrive at the church and enter the side door about fifteen minutes before the wedding hour. They sit in the vestry or in the clergyman's study until the sexton or an usher comes to say that the bride has arrived. They then wait for and follow the clergyman to their places.

At many Jewish weddings the bride (and sometimes the groom also) receives the guests in a room in the synagogue before the ceremony takes place.

THE LAST FIVE MINUTES

The groom's mother and father enter the church five or ten minutes before the ceremony is to start. As the bride's mother drives up, an usher hurries to tell the groom of her arrival, as the bride and her father should be close behind. Grandparents and any brothers or sisters of the bride or groom who are not to take part in the wedding are now taken by ushers to their places in the front pews. No one is seated after this except the parents of the bridal couple.

The groom's mother goes up the aisle on the arm of the head usher and takes her place in the first pew on the right; the groom's father follows alone and takes his place on the aisle. The same usher or a brother or cousin of the bride escorts the bride's mother to the first pew on the left. When the bride has a stepfather who is not giving her away, he follows her mother and the usher in the same manner as the groom's father.

If the bride's mother is uncomfortable sitting alone in the front pew until her husband joins her after giving their daughter away, she may ask her parents or another close relative to sit with her. They would be escorted in immediately before the mother of the groom.

When the bride or the groom has no parents the closest relatives—grandparents, sisters or brothers, or an aunt and uncle—would be given the first pew. A bride who is an orphan chooses a guardian or perhaps the person who is giving the wedding to sit there. Whoever is chosen is ushered in last, since that person represents the bride's parents.

If a carpet is to be laid, it is already arranged in folds so that two ushers may now pull it quickly down the aisle. At the last moment the white ribbon is draped over the ends of the pews from the back of the church to the nearest reserved pew on each side of the center aisle. Having done this, the ushers return to the vestibule and take their places in the procession. The beginning of the wedding music should sound just as they return to the foot of the aisle.

To repeat: No person should be seated after the entrance of the mother of the bride. Nor must anyone be admitted to the side aisles while the mother of the bride is being ushered down the center one. Her entrance should not be detracted from by late arrivals scuttling into their seats behind her. Guests who arrive late must stand in the rear or slip unescorted into a back pew.

THE BRIDE ARRIVES

At a perfectly planned wedding, the bride arrives exactly one minute after the hour in order to give the last arrival time to find a place. This is too much to ask in today's heavy traffic, however, and I can only point out that it is better for the bride to arrive five minutes early than five minutes late. If she has a few minutes to spare, she waits in the vestibule or a convenient room. At the appointed hour the procession forms in the vestibule, and a signal is given to the groom and the clergyman that everything is ready.

THE WEDDING CEREMONY

The sound of the music chosen for the processional is the cue for the clergyman to enter the church, followed by the bridegroom and the best man. The clergyman goes up the steps to the chancel and turns to face the congregation. The groom stops at the foot of the chancel steps and takes his place at the right side of the aisle, as indicated in the diagram. His best man stands on his left, slightly behind him. They turn toward the procession coming down the aisle.

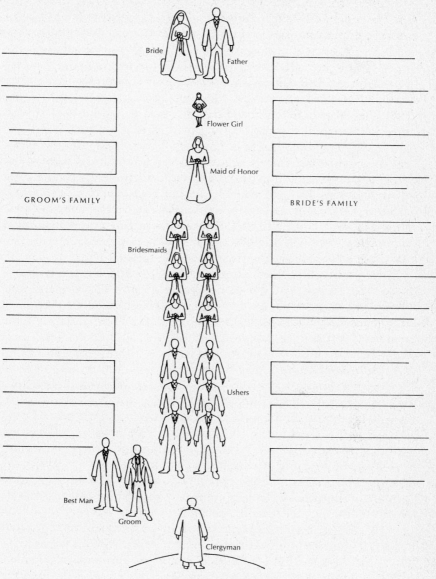

Bride

Father

Flower Girl

Maid of Honor

GROOM'S FAMILY

BRIDE'S FAMILY

Bridesmaids

Ushers

Best Man

Groom

Clergyman

The Procession

WEDDINGS ❧

THE PROCESSION

The procession is arranged according to height, the two shortest ushers leading. Junior ushers walk behind the adults. Junior bridesmaids come next, if there are any. If not, the bridesmaids come directly after the ushers, two and two, also according to height, with the shortest in the lead. If there are only two or three, they walk singly. After the bridesmaids, the maid or matron of honor walks alone; flower girls follow, then the ring bearer, and last of all, the bride on the right arm of her father. If there are both maid and matron of honor, the maid of honor immediately precedes the bride.

The space between each couple or individuals should be even—approximately four paces apart. The attendants should walk slowly and steadily, and the "hesitation step," which used to be obligatory, is rarely seen as it tends to make the pace uneven or jerky. Posture is most important too. At the rehearsal the attendants should be reminded to stand straight and tall, as nothing looks worse than a bridesmaid or usher slouching down the aisle.

The bride (unless she has page boys who carry her train) always brings up the rear, walking on her father's *right*. This position puts her on the proper side to join her groom, and it is the honorary position, as well as being traditional and correct. If her father is dead, a brother, an uncle, a godfather, or a close family friend takes his place. In some instances, when the bride is a foreigner and has no one coming to the wedding, she may ask the groom's father to be her escort. In any case the escort should be a male. Even though both parents walk with their children in Orthodox and Conservative Jewish weddings Christian tradition decrees that the father is the one who gives his daughter to her husband. This may be a changing custom, however. In Protestant ceremonies the mother is often included in the response to "Who gives this woman . . ." when the father replies, "Her mother and I do." I have had an increasing number of inquiries as to why mothers should not walk with their daughters—either with their husbands as in the Jewish procession, or in his place if he is dead or they are divorced. I can only say that it is not customary—or traditional—and if you wish your wedding to follow the accepted "rules," a man should be chosen as the bride's escort. If he is not a close relative, however, it is not his prerogative to actively give the bride away, but that of her mother. She says, from her place in the front pew, "I do," when the minister asks, "Who gives this woman?" Traditionally, the bride who has no father or close male relative walks up the aisle alone.

When a bride has a father *and* a stepfather, there is often a question as to which one gives her away. If she has remained close to her father, *even though she lives with her mother and stepfather,* it is her *father's* right to give his daughter away. If, on the other hand, her father has lost contact with her entirely, and her stepfather has, in fact, brought her up, then her stepfather would assume the father's role. She should never be escorted by both men.

A CHURCH WITH TWO AISLES

In a church with two main aisles the guests are seated according to aisles and not according to the church as a whole. All the seats on the right aisle belong to the bride's family and guests. The left aisle belongs to the bridegroom.

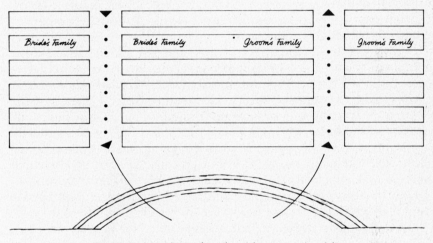

Arrangements in a church with two main aisles

The bride's mother is seated in the front pew at the left of the bride's aisle—exactly as she would be in a center-aisle church. On the other side of the church the bridegroom's mother occupies the front pew on the right of the groom's aisle.

For the processional the bride's (right) aisle is chosen because people naturally turn to the right rather than to the left. After the ceremony the bride and groom come down the groom's (left) aisle. The aisles are necessarily chosen in this way so as to place the immediate families in center pews. If the bride's mother were to choose the left aisle, this would seat her in a side pew instead of a center one.

However, if the church is very large and the wedding small, the right aisle alone may be used. Then the bride's family sits on the left of this aisle and the groom's family on the right, while the marriage takes place at the head of this aisle.

THE CEREMONY STARTS

As the music for the processional starts, and the first ushers step forward, the mothers rise and turn to watch the procession as it comes down the aisle. The rest of the congregation follows their lead. Everyone remains standing until the clergyman asks the congregation to be seated—usually after an opening prayer or address. When the ushers reach the foot of the chancel they divide. In a small church the first two go up the chancel steps and stand at the top, one on the right, the other on the left. The second two go a step or two below the first. If there are more, they stand below. Chalk marks made on the chancel floor can be a great help to little children in remembering their positions.

In a big church the ushers go up farther, standing in front of the choir stalls with the line sloping outward so that the congregation may see them better. The bridesmaids also divide, half on either side, and stand in front of the ushers. The maid of honor's place is on the left at the foot of the steps, opposite the best man. Flower girls stand beside or behind the maid of honor, and the ring bearer stands next to the best man. In some cases the bridesmaids line up on the left side and ushers on the right, rather than dividing. The bride and groom make the final decision on what they think looks best, but they should take advantage of the clergyman's experience and recommendations, since he has seen many more weddings than they.

As the bride approaches, the groom steps forward to meet her. She lets go of her father's arm, transfers her flowers to her left arm, and gives her right hand to the groom, who rests it on his left arm. If this is uncomfortable for either, they may stand hand in hand or side by side. They are then facing the altar.

In a Protestant ceremony her father remains by his daughter, on her left and a step or two behind her. The clergyman stands a step or two above them and reads the betrothal. When he says, "Who giveth this woman to be married?" the father steps forward. The bride turns slightly toward him and gives him her right hand, which he puts into the hand of the clergyman and says distinctly, "I do," or "Her mother and I do." Frequently the bride gives her father a brief kiss at this point to indicate her gratitude and affection. He then takes his place next to his wife at the end of the first pew on the left. The clergyman, holding the bride's hand in his right one, takes the

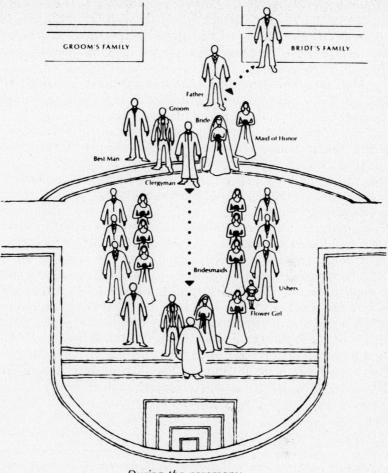

During the ceremony

bridegroom's hand in his left one and very deliberately places the bride's hand in the bridegroom's.

When the bride has neither father nor any very near male relative she may choose to walk up the aisle alone. At the point in the ceremony where the clergyman asks, "Who giveth this woman to be married?" her mother remains where she is standing in her place at the end of the first pew on the left and says very distinctly, "I do." There is no rule against her going forward to take the place of the bride's father, but this would be unusual.

In a Roman Catholic ceremony the father of the bride joins her

659

mother in the front pew as soon as the bride is joined by the groom. He does not give his daughter away.

Some clergyman signal the guests to be seated as soon as the members of the bridal party are in their places. Others wait until this point in the ceremony.

The clergyman turns and walks toward the altar, before which the rest of the marriage is performed. The bride and groom follow, the fingers of her right hand on his left arm.

The maid or matron of honor moves forward too, until she stands behind the bride, slightly to her left. The best man takes the corresponding position behind the groom and to his right. The flower girl and ring bearer follow, also, still in the same relative positions. The bride hands her bouquet to the maid of honor, and the bride and groom plight their troth.

When it is time for the ring, the best man produces it from his pocket, or from the ring bearer's cushion, the minister blesses it, and the groom slips it on his bride's finger. Since the wedding ring must not be put outside the engagement ring the bride wears the engagement ring on her right hand during the ceremony. Afterward she puts it back on her left hand, outside her wedding ring.

When it is a double-ring ceremony the maid of honor gives the groom's ring to the bride after she has received her ring from the groom. The ring is blessed, and the bride places it on the groom's finger, saying, as he did, "With this ring I thee wed." The ceremony proceeds with a blessing and a prayer, and the clergyman pronounces the couple "man and wife."

AFTER THE CEREMONY

At the conclusion of the ceremony the minister congratulates the new couple. The organ begins the recessional. The bride takes her bouquet from her maid of honor, who then lifts the face veil, if one is worn. If they have decided to do so, the couple kiss. With her bouquet in her right hand, the bride puts her left hand through her husband's right arm, and they descend the steps, followed by the flower girl and ring bearer and the maid of honor walking with the best man. Then the bridesmaids and ushers pair off and follow two by two. If it is winter, one of the ushers or the best man will have put the groom's coat in the vestibule before the ceremony so that he need not go back to the vestry or waiting room for it, and someone has the bride's coat ready for her at the door.

The bridesmaids and ushers may walk out in pairs, as they entered, but that arrangement lacks the symbolism of their arriving

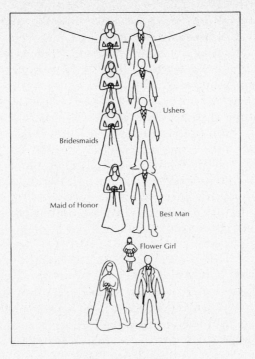

The recessional

separately, like the bride and groom, and leaving together, after the marriage has taken place.

The photographer, who remains at the back of the church during the ceremony, can now snap away the happy couple as they come back down the aisle. He should never be permitted to take pictures during the ceremony, as the clicking and flashing is distracting and detracts from the dignity of the proceedings.

The automobiles are waiting at the entrance in the reverse order from that in which they arrived. The best man helps the newlyweds into the bride's car, and it leaves first; next come those of the bridesmaids; next, that of the bride's mother and father; next, that of the groom's mother and father. If limousines have not been hired, the best man acts as chauffeur for the bride and groom.

To return to the church for a moment: As soon as the recessional is over, the ushers return to escort to the door all the ladies who were in the reserved pews, according to the order of precedence; the bride's mother first, then the groom's mother, then the other occupants of the first pew on either side, then the second and third pews, until all members of the immediate families have left the church. If

661

the bride's and groom's mothers prefer to walk with their husbands, they may do so, following the usher who has come to escort them. At most weddings only the two mothers of the couple are escorted by the ushers, and the husbands or escorts of the other ladies walk out with them. Meanwhile other guests wait until the ribbons along the ends of the pews are removed by the two previously designated ushers, and then go out by themselves. The best man hurries back to the vestry and if he has not done so before the ceremony, gives the clergyman his fee *(see page 563)*. If an altar boy has assisted in the ceremony, he offers him a small "tip" of a dollar or two.

As soon as the ushers have escorted the family out and removed the ribbons they, too, hurry to the reception in order to be on hand for the photographs. Their cars or means of transportation should be in a convenient place so that they will not be held up by departing guests.

A RECEIVING LINE AT THE CHURCH

When there is no reception, or when many of the guests at the church are not invited because it is to be a very small, family reception, the bride and groom may greet their friends at the church. Instead of going directly to the cars they form a line in the vestibule, on the steps, or outside the door. The line consists of the bride's mother, the bride on the groom's right, and the bridesmaids. The groom's parents may stand between the bride's mother and the newlyweds if they are from out of town and this is the only opportunity to introduce them to friends and relatives of the bride.

This is never done if there will be people at the reception who are not invited to the church. However, it may *take the place of* a line at the reception when all the guests invited to the reception are also at the church.

Since most clergymen do not approve of pictures being taken during the service (and the bride and groom should not encourage the photographer to do so), some couples go back into the church when the pews are empty to reenact parts of the service for the benefit of the photographer. This is perfectly all right as long as they do not insist on pictures of each and every step in the ceremony. It is *most* inconsiderate to keep the guests who have gone on to the reception waiting for a long time, especially if there is no comfortable place for them to sit or stand. Therefore pictures in the church should be restricted to half a dozen or so—one or two of the procession, one of the bride's father giving his daughter away, the exchange of rings, the kiss at the end, etc.

JEWISH WEDDINGS

Whether Orthodox, Conservative, or Reform, marriages may not take place between sundown Friday and sundown on Saturday. Therefore most Jewish weddings take place on Saturday evening or Sunday. There are also holy days, and most of the days between the second day of Passover and the holiday of Shabuoth, during which Jews may not marry. These restrictions and many others, some of which are dictated by individual rabbis or local custom rather than Rabbinic law, should be thoroughly discussed with the rabbi who is going to perform the ceremony.

Jewish weddings are often held in synagogues, but both service and reception may be held in halls, clubs, restaurants, or hotels. Frequently the bride and her family, and sometimes the groom too, receive their guests in a private room before the ceremony.

Jewish brides and their attendants wear the same clothes as those described in Chapter 49. The only exception is that at Orthodox and Conservative weddings attendants as well as guests wear yarmulkes. These are always available at the back of the synagogue for Christian guests. At a very formal wedding male members of the bridal party wear top hats.

The Reform service is very much like the Christian service. The processional and recessional are the same, and the bride is escorted by her father. The service is in English, and there is no *huppah*. The bride and groom do, however, adhere to the Jewish tradition of drinking wine from the same cup, and to certain other parts of the Jewish service.

The Orthodox and Conservative ceremonies are quite different. The ushers lead the procession, followed by the bridesmaids. Next comes the rabbi, then the groom, walking between his mother and father. The maid of honor follows them, and the bride, between her parents, comes last. Orthodox brides are always veiled. The marriage takes place under a canopy called a *huppah*. This canopy used to be held over heads of the principals as they walked down the aisle, but today it is fixed in place at the front of the hall or synagogue. The canopy is usually a richly ornamented cloth, although it may be made of, or decorated with, flowers.

The bride and groom, the maid of honor, and the best man—and, if there is room, the parents—stand under the *huppah*. The rabbi faces them, standing by a table covered with a white cloth, on which there are two glasses of wine.

The Orthodox service is mostly read in Hebrew, although certain parts are in English, or the native language of the couple. The rabbi blesses the wine and gives it to the groom. He takes a sip and hands it to the bride. A document in Aramaic is read, giving the pledge of fidelity and protection on the part of the groom and indicating the bride's contribution to the household. The groom places a plain gold ring on the bride's right index finger, which she removes to the conventional forth finger, left hand, after the ceremony. He repeats, "Thou art consecrated unto me with this ring, according to the law of Moses and Israel." The rabbi then addresses the congregation about the sanctity of marriage. Finally, after the Seven Blessings are given, the couple drinks from the second glass of wine, and the goblet is broken, symbolizing the fact that one must never overlook, even at the height of happiness, the possibility of misfortune.

The recessional is led by the bride and groom. They are usually followed by the two sets of parents, the maid of honor with the best man, the rabbi, and the bridesmaids and ushers.

The reception after a Jewish wedding is like that following a Christian marriage, except that more importance is given to the "feast." It is usually as lavish as the bride's family can afford. A blessing is always said over the food.

ROMAN CATHOLIC WEDDINGS

When a Roman Catholic wedding is to center around a Nuptial Mass it often takes place between eight and twelve in the morning. Today, however, Nuptial Masses may be held in the afternoon, so many Catholics are now married at that time. Other Catholic marriages do not include a Mass and may be held at any hour. When this is the case the couple go to take Communion together earlier in the day. The ceremonies may take place at any time of the year, but no nuptial blessing is given during Lent or Advent without special permission from the bishop.

Catholic marriages are proclaimed by banns. The banns, an announcement of intention to marry, are usually proclaimed from the pulpit three times or are published in the church calendar prior to the wedding. The couple should therefore complete church arrangements well in advance.

The bride's father escorts her up the aisle but does not give her away. After leaving her with her groom, he steps into the front pew with his wife.

Other details, such as whether the bride and groom and best man and maid of honor, or the whole bridal party, are permitted within the altar rail, are determined by individual church practice. As some churches have strict rules about procedure, it is essential that the couple ascertain the restrictions in advance and be guided by them.

The maid of honor and best man are usually Catholics, although exceptions have been made. The other attendants may be of any faith. They are instructed how to genuflect and other necessary procedures at the rehearsal. Catholics, incidentally, may serve as attendants in non-Catholic weddings.

An acolyte generally assists the priest at a Mass and may hand him the ring or help with the bride's train. The best man gives him a small gift of a dollar or two on behalf of the groom.

Since the wedding ceremony in conjunction with a Nuptial Mass is a lengthy procedure the wedding party is usually seated. The bride and groom are seated on two chairs before the altar, and the attendants sit in the choir stalls, or possibly in the front pews, in which case the parents sit in the second pews. The maid of honor and best man stay with the bride and groom and are also seated on special chairs. The procedures other than those connected with Communion and the Mass are the same as those described for a Protestant wedding.

When a Catholic and non-Catholic marry, there is no Mass. Today, with the relaxation of strict rules and with ecumenical practices accepted, interfaith marriages often comprise elements of each faith, and both priest and minister officiate. The arrangements for these marriages must be very carefully discussed and planned, of course, but the change in attitude has made interfaith weddings far easier to plan, and much happier events.

~§54§~ Wedding Receptions

PHOTOGRAPHS

As soon as the bride and groom and all the attendants have arrived at the place where the reception is held, the formal pictures of the bridal party are taken. Although this may cause some inconvenience to guests who arrive from the church very quickly it is the only possible time. If it is put off until later, the bridesmaids' costumes and hairdos will not be so fresh and neat, and the newlyweds and their parents may be showing the strain of having stood in the receiving line.

The photographer should be told in advance to be as quick as he can, and the attendants should be asked to hurry to their places without delay so that the receiving line may be formed as soon as possible.

Pictures are taken of the bride and groom with the bridesmaids, with their ushers, and with the entire wedding party. They are photographed with each set of parents, and with both. If either bride or groom has stepparents, they are included in the photographs, too. However, a parent who has remarried does not appear with his or her new spouse in the *same* picture with the ex-mate, even though they are all friendly.

The bride's family orders and pays for the wedding pictures that they want themselves. The groom's family are shown the proofs, and they, too, select as many as they would like. The bride's mother places their order, but the bill is sent to the groom's parents. The attendants may also order and pay for pictures they would like to have. The bride's family may, of course, *give* the parents of the groom an album if they wish to, but with the cost of professional photographs what it is today, few could afford to do so—nor should they.

THE RECEIVING LINE

As soon as the pictures are taken, the bridal party forms the receiving line, in whatever room or location provides the best "flow." The bride's mother stands at the beginning of the line to greet the guests and to introduce them to the groom's mother, who stands next to her. Then come the bride and groom, with the bride on the groom's right. The maid of honor stands next, and finally the brides-maids, if they are to take part. In order to speed up the procedure of going through the line, and because both guests and bridesmaids find it difficult to think of anything to say to so many strangers, I, personally, am in favor of leaving the bridesmaids out of the line. The two fathers may join the line if they wish, but they need not do so and usually prefer to mingle with the guests. If the groom's family comes from another town, however, his father may well join the line so that he may be introduced to relatives and friends of the bride and her parents. If he does stand in line, so should the father of the bride. Flower girls and ring bearers never stand in the receiving line.

Divorced parents do not stand in the receiving line together. If the bride's mother and stepfather are giving the wedding, she alone or both are in the line—but not the bride's father. If her father and stepmother are giving the wedding, they, as host and hostess, stand in line, and the bride's mother is merely an honored guest. If neither has remarried, only the bride's mother should be in the line unless he is giving the reception. In that case the estranged wife would not act as hostess, but the godmother of the bride, or an aunt, or even a very close family friend would receive in her place. When the groom's parents are divorced, his mother joins him in the line, and neither his father nor his stepfather need be there, which eliminates all complications.

At very large formal weddings there may be an announcer, who stands next to the bride's mother and asks each guest quietly for his name as the guest approaches. He then repeats the name aloud. This can be very helpful when the wedding is so large that the bride's mother does not know a number of the people invited by the groom's family.

The guests shake hands with the mother of the bride and groom, and either shake hands with or kiss the newlyweds, depending on their relationship with them. They tell the bride how beautiful she looks and wish her happiness, congratulate the groom, and pass on to say "Hello" to the maid of honor, and the bridesmaids if they are in line.

The bride's mother is responsible for introducing each guest to

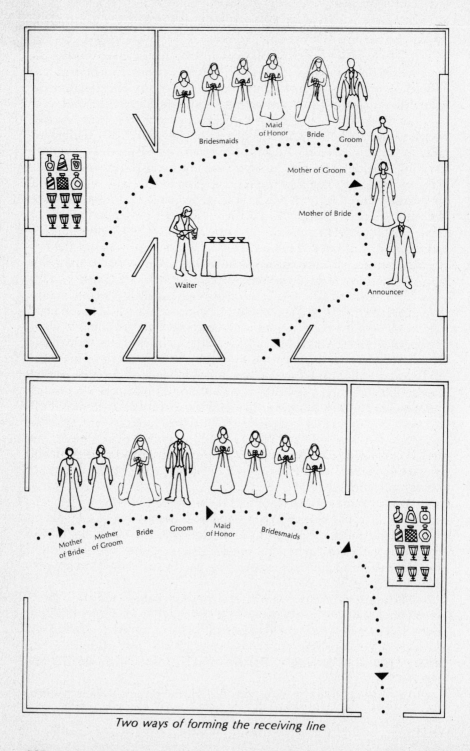

Two ways of forming the receiving line

the groom's mother (and father) and, when necessary, to the bride. She (the bride) then turns and introduces her new husband to the guest. The groom, naturally, leans forward to introduce his wife to *his* friends when he sees them approaching. However, long conversations are out of place, since they delay everyone behind, so remarks other than greetings and introductions are kept to a minimum.

The bride and groom need say no more than "Thank you," "I'm so glad to see you," etc., to the guests. The bride, if she remembers what a guest sent as a gift, might mention how much she liked it, but this does not take the place of her thank-you note.

There is a trend today toward eliminating receiving lines entirely—especially at small weddings. And it is true that they are, for the most part, somewhat boring, tiring, and stiff. In spite of that, at a large wedding they provide the only means for all of the guests to offer their congratulations to the couple, who otherwise might never get to speak to some of their friends at all. Therefore I think they are a "necessary evil" at a large wedding. At a small one, where there are few (or no) introductions necessary, and where the bride and groom can circulate and spend a little time with all their guests, the reason for the line is eliminated. But if the bride decides not to have a receiving line at her wedding, she must be sure that the groom and his family meet everyone there. To do this she and her new husband, and her parents, should stand near the entrance to greet the guests as they arrive. The groom's parents should remain nearby, so that she can introduce them at once to anyone who has not already met them.

Because even the best-planned receiving line involves a lengthy period of standing for all but the first guests to arrive, it is thoughtful to have beverages and a tray of hors d'oeuvres passed to those just getting into line. They may take their glass of champagne—the usual offering—with them until they near the receiving line. A table should be placed in a convenient spot so that the guests can easily put down their empty glasses. If possible, a few tables with chairs should be placed near the entrance to the room where the line forms. If the wait is going to be long, a waiter can be posted near the door to suggest that late arrivals take a glass of champagne and sit at one of the tables until the line reaches a more reasonable length.

A waiter is always standing near the end of the receiving line to offer champagne or punch or whatever beverage is being served to those who have passed through. They take a glass and move on to the next room, the tent, the lawn, or wherever the rest of the festivities are to take place.

THE GUEST BOOK

Although it is not obligatory many couples like to have their guests sign a register or guest book, to be kept as a permanent memento of their wedding day.

The book is placed on a table covered with a white cloth, near the entrance. A relative or friend of the bride is asked to take charge. As the guests arrive and join the line she reminds each one (or one member of each couple) to sign the book. Unlike a register at a funeral home, the names will not be used as a list to whom notes must be sent, so guests may sign in any way they wish, although last names must be included. Young contemporaries of the bride and groom will undoubtedly sign "Beth and Bob Hanson," while older couples who do not know the bride personally might sign "Mr. and Mrs. John Wilson." If a space is provided for "remarks," they should be sentimental or serious rather than joking. "May you always be as happy as you are today," or "The most beautiful wedding I've ever seen," are typical entries.

THE BRIDE'S TABLE

When the last guest has passed through the receiving line, or perhaps after the bride and groom have mingled with their guests and danced, the bridal party is seated at the bride's table. It is a rectangular table set against one side or end of the room, and the bride and groom sit at the center of the long side, facing out so that the guests can see them. No one is seated opposite them. The bride sits on the groom's right, with the best man on her right; the maid of honor sits on the groom's left; and the bridesmaids and ushers alternate along the same side of the table. Husbands, wives, and fiancés of the attendants also sit at the bride's table. If there are too many people to fit along one side, the table should form a "U," so that they may sit at the two arms rather than obstruct everyone's view of the bride and groom. The bride or her mother has put place cards on the table earlier in the day.

The wedding cake is sometimes used as a centerpiece on the bride's table, but since it is usually quite tall and tends to hide the bride and groom from the guests, the cake is more often placed on a small round table at one side or a little way in front of the bridal table. Flowers almost always form the centerpiece, and if the table is long, two more arrangements are placed near either end. Although the tablecloth is always white the flower arrangements may be chosen to complement the color of the bridesmaid's dresses.

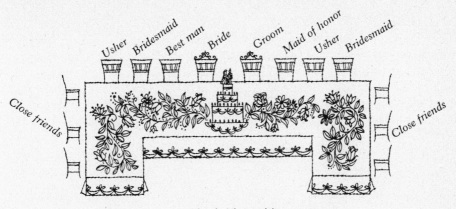

The bride's table

Whether or not the other guests serve themselves "buffet style" the meal is always passed by waiters to those at the bridal table.

WITH NO BRIDAL TABLE

Many couples prefer to wander about and mingle with their guests rather than being seated at a formal table. There should always, however, be a table reserved for the bride and groom and their attendants so that they are assured of a place to sit down and rest their feet.

The newlyweds may go to the buffet table just as the other guests do, or in some cases a waiter fills a plate and brings it to them where they are seated. The bridesmaids and ushers need not all sit with the bride and groom at the same time but may go to dance or see their own particular friends as they will. However, at some point the best man must round them all up and bring them together to join him in a toast to the couple. The attendants should also gather around when the bride and groom cut the cake.

THE PARENTS' TABLE

The table of the couple's parents differs from other tables only in its larger size and the place cards for those who have been invited to sit there. The groom's mother always sits on the right of the bride's father, and opposite them the groom's father is on the right of the mother of the bride. The other places at the table are occupied by grandparents and godparents. If there are more grandparents than the limited space can accommodate, a separate table should be arranged for them and their close friends nearby. Although they have

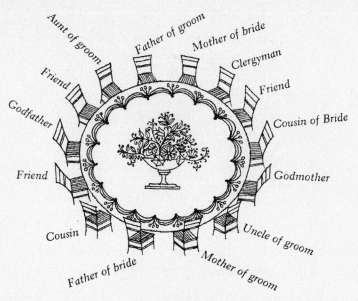

The parents' table

no official part in the wedding, they should at all times be treated as honored guests.

At some receptions there are separate tables for the parents and relatives of the bride and groom. I find this very unfriendly and contrary to the atmosphere of "uniting" that a wedding should create.

The parents' table is the only one other than the bridal table where place cards are used. Other guests sit wherever they wish, joining friends or introducing themselves to strangers already seated at a table.

Divorced parents of the bride or groom are never seated together at the parents' table. If they are reasonably friendly, the parent giving the reception will invite the other, but will seat him or her at a separate table. Stepparents are included at the parents' tables, assuming that they get along with their stepchild—the bride or groom. If there has been great bitterness, it is best that the parent who is not giving the wedding, and his spouse, not attend the reception at all even though they go to the marriage ceremony. If the bride or groom insists, the father or mother might come for a short time, but to avoid possible unpleasantness his or her spouse should tactfully stay away.

A MASTER OF CEREMONIES

I find the custom advocated by many caterers and wedding specialists of having an announcer or "MC" most unfortunate. These individuals run the wedding like a circus—the ringleader announcing each event and herding people about as he might at a sideshow. The charm and intimacy of a private party is destroyed. In certain localities the wedding party and the parents are introduced as they walk into the hall. Where this is the custom, that is fine, but the introductions may be made by the orchestra leader or perhaps the headwaiter, who may also make any other *necessary* announcements. It is totally *unnecessary* to hire a master of ceremonies to "run" the wedding, making the whole affair seem commercial and overorganized.

A bridal consultant, who sees that things run smoothly, can be a great help. But her presence should be almost unnoticed, and she should do her "organizing" behind the scenes.

THE TOAST TO THE BRIDE AND GROOM

At a sit-down bridal table, champagne is poured as soon as the party is seated. The glass of the bride is filled first, then that of the bridegroom, and then on around the table, starting with the maid of honor at the groom's left. The best man proposes a toast to the bride and bridegroom. It is usually a very short toast, and somewhat sentimental. All except the bride and groom rise, raise their glasses, and drink the toast. Then the groom stands and replies with thanks and a toast to his new wife. Other toasts may be offered by anyone who cares to propose one. At a large reception only those at the bridal table join in the toasts, but at a small one all the guests may join in drinking together to the couple's health and happiness. *For suggestions as to the wording of these toasts, see Chapter 5, page 55.*

DANCING AT THE RECEPTION

If a regular sit-down dinner is to be served, the first course is passed shortly after the bridal party sits down, and the dancing does not start until after dessert has been eaten. However, if the reception follows an afternoon wedding, and the meal is not to be served until a little later, there would be some dancing before the bridal party goes to its table. At a buffet reception the bride and groom may start the dancing as soon as they have had a chance to recover from standing in the receiving line.

All the guests watch and applaud while the bride and groom dance the first dance. Her father-in-law asks her for the second dance, and then her father cuts in. The bridegroom, meanwhile, dances with his mother-in-law and then his mother. Next, the bride's father asks the groom's mother to dance, and the groom's father asks the bride's mother. As the groom dances with the maid of honor and the ushers with the bridesmaids, the guests may start cutting in, and dancing becomes general. Insofar as possible, all the male guests try to get a dance with the bride.

CUTTING THE CAKE

At a sit-down bridal-table dinner the cake is cut just before the dessert is served, so that slices can be passed with the ices or ice cream. If there is no bridal table, the cake is cut later, often just shortly before the couple leave the reception.

The bride, with the help of the bridegroom, cuts the first slice from the bottom tier with a silver cake knife. Sometimes she cuts two slices, one for her groom and one for herself, and they each feed the other a bite of these slices. After this the cake is removed from the table, and the tiers are separated and cut into slices and passed to the guests. The bride and groom and the bridal party are served first. The small top layer with its decoration is set aside for the bride and groom to keep. The groom's cake, which has been put into individual boxes, is taken home by departing guests as a memento. *(For a complete description of the bride's cake and the groom's cake, see Chapter 48, page 569.)*

THE MENU *(For menu suggestions, see Chapter 48, pages 567–568.)*

THEY'RE OFF!

Sometimes the bride and groom continue dancing or chatting for so long that those who had intended to stay for the "going away" grow tired and leave. Therefore the wise bride and groom depart before either they or their guests are too exhausted. When they decide it is time to go the bride signals to her bridesmaids, who all gather at the foot of the stairs. About halfway up, she throws her bouquet, and they all try to catch it. In order to show no favoritism she turns her back and throws the bouquet over her shoulder. The one who makes the catch is supposed to be the next married. If the bride has no bridesmaids, she collects a group of friends and throws her bouquet to them. If there are no stairs, she throws the bouquet from whatever spot is most convenient. The bridesmaid who catches the bouquet keeps it.

Sometimes if a very close relative is too ill to attend the wedding, the bouquet is sent to her.

The bride goes upstairs, followed by her mother and her bridesmaids, who stay with her while she changes into her traveling clothes. The groom goes to the room reserved for him and changes into the clothes that the best man has ready for him. His immediate family, as well as hers, has gradually collected to say good-bye. Any that are missing are sent for. The bride's mother gives her daughter a last kiss. The bridesmaids and ushers hurry downstairs to have plenty of paper rose petals ready, and everyone knows they are on their way. A passage from the stairway and out the front door, all the way to their automobile, is left free between the guests, whose hands are full of confetti or petals.

Preceded by the best man, they run down the stairs, out through the hall, into the car, and they're off!

Many young couples devote a good deal of thought and planning to making their going away unusual and dramatic. Every sort of departure has been tried—on skis, in sleighs, on horseback or in horse-drawn carriage, and even in a helicopter! But the most memorable I have ever seen took place when the reception was held at a yacht club on a beautiful June evening. The bride and groom left on a handsome boat polished and shining with all flags flying. They pulled away from the pier while the horns of other boats tooted, and a carpet of rose petals floated on the water. It was truly an ending never to be forgotten by the bride and groom or by any who were there to see them go!

A THOUGHT FOR THE BRIDEGROOM'S PARENTS

At the end of the reception and as soon as she is in her traveling dress, a considerate bride sends a bridesmaid or someone else out into the hall and asks her husband's parents to come to say good-bye to her.

It is very easy for a bride to forget this act of thoughtfulness and for a groom to overlook the fact that he should bid his parents good-bye before leaving the room where he has dressed. Many a mother and father, seeing their son and new daughter rush past without even a glance, have returned home with a let-down feeling and an ache in their hearts. One might say, "How stupid of them! Why didn't they go upstairs?" But often the groom's parents are strangers; they may have met their new daughter only a few days or weeks before the wedding; and if by temperament they are shy or retiring, they hesitate to go upstairs in an unknown house until they have been invited to do so. So they wait, feeling sure that in good time they will be sent for. Meanwhile the bride forgets; and it does not occur to the groom that unless he makes an effort while upstairs, there will be no opportunity in the dash down to the car to recognize his parents any more than anyone else.

GIFTS BROUGHT TO THE RECEPTION

In some areas it is traditional for guests to bring their wedding gifts to the reception rather than send them to the bride ahead of time. A table is made ready for the packages, and each guest leaves his present there as he arrives. In some localities the gifts are opened at the reception; in others they are opened when the bride and groom return from their honeymoon.

When gifts are opened at the reception, great care must be taken that each one is listed properly so that the bride will have an accurate record for her thank-you notes. One of the bridesmaids should be assigned to keep this list and to collect the cards or see that they are kept in the bride's book. Another helper should be appointed to collect and discard the wrappings.

When there is a great number of gifts, I feel that the bride and groom will enjoy them more, and will also have more time to enjoy their friends and the other festivities, if they do not try to open them at the reception. But when most of the gifts have been sent, and only a few are brought to the reception, there is no reason why they should not be opened.

At Jewish weddings, and among some other ethnic groups, it is customary to present a check as a wedding gift. This is usually handed to the bride in an envelope as the guest goes through the receiving line. The bride sometimes has a white silk or satin purse hanging on her arm into which she puts the checks, or there may be a prettily decorated box or basket for them on a table near her. The envelopes are not usually opened until later.

BELATED RECEPTIONS

It sometimes happens that a couple get married privately, far from home, perhaps where they are at college, or even in another country. If they return home shortly after their marriage, the bride's family may wish to give them the reception they did not have after their wedding. The reception may include all the trimmings of the ordinary reception following the wedding. If the bride wore a wedding gown for the ceremony, she may wear it again at the reception, so that her friends and relatives may see how she looked, and feel more a part of the marriage. Invitations may be engraved, in the form shown on page 615.

In the unfortunate event that the bride's family does not give their approval to, or wish to participate in, the wedding, the groom's family, if *they* approve, may want to give a reception shortly after the marriage takes place. They may do so, but it should be kept simpler than it might otherwise be, and invitations should be by word of mouth or personal note. This is so that they will not appear to be criticizing the bride's parents by flaunting their own approval, thus widening the breach between the bride and her family.

RECEPTION AT THE CHURCH OR SYNAGOGUE

A reception held in the social rooms of the church or synagogue, or in the parish house, offers a fine solution to the girl who lives in a very small house or apartment, and who cannot afford to pay for a hall or hire a caterer. In some rural areas where elaborate facilities are not available, all receptions are held in the church hall.

Some large churches and synagogues provide all the services that a caterer would. They necessarily charge a price per head that includes all the accessories such as china, glasses, silver, linen, etc., and in some cases they even have a cooking staff to provide the meal. Fruit punch or soft drinks are served in most churches, but synagogues and some Christian churches permit the serving of alcohol.

Most parishes have a record player for the use of their young members, and it may be used for background music or dancing.

Because the church fees are so very small, especially if the food is provided by the bride's family and friends, more guests can be invited to a church reception in many cases than could possibly be included otherwise. Even more important, the warmth and intimacy of the familiar surroundings lend an atmosphere of happiness and dignity that could never be duplicated in a public restaurant.

RECEPTIONS IN RESTAURANTS

If possible, it is best to choose a restaurant that can provide a private room for the reception. Otherwise the party is apt to become a public spectacle and object of curiosity for the other patrons.

Although some large receptions are held in the private "ballroom" of the restaurant, most restaurant receptions are small ones. A restaurant is often chosen for dinner after a civil marriage, or a marriage attended only by the families and a few friends.

It is up to the couple to find out ahead of time what facilities are offered, and to order or reserve exactly what they wish. It is also best to order the meal ahead of time. This avoids any question of how costly a meal the guests should order and eliminates any complications in paying the check. The bride and groom may order wine or champagne for the group, and the guests may order cocktails and pay for those themselves if they wish. Or the hosts (the bride and groom, or her family) may pay for all the liquor. There should always be a wedding cake, no matter how simple, and there are always toasts to the newlyweds. Otherwise the party is much like any other restaurant dinner, and unless the restaurant has a dance orchestra the couple leave when dinner is over.

~§55~ *Special Weddings*

HOUSE WEDDINGS

The bride-to-be and her fiancé do not always choose to be married in church—for any number of perfectly good reasons. A house wedding requires as much attention as any other, for it should be as perfect in its way as the loveliest church ceremony.

A house wedding usually involves somewhat less expense but a good deal more work for the bride's family than does the church wedding. Of course, if a caterer is hired, the expense may be as high and the work as little as if it were held in a church or hotel. It also has the disadvantage (which may also be an advantage!) of limiting the number of guests. The ceremony is exactly the same as it is in a church, except that the procession advances from the stairs or hallway through an aisle of white ribbons or stanchions to the improvised altar. Chairs for the immediate families may be placed within a marked-off enclosure, but if the room is small, space is merely kept free for them to stand in.

In the country a house wedding may be performed in the garden, with the wedding procession under the trees, and tables set out on the lawn. Alternate facilities should be prepared in the house in case of rain, especially along the Atlantic seaboard where the weather is all too likely to spoil everything.

When the couple's faith requires that they kneel during the wedding ceremony, a cushioned bench is provided for their use. It is often backed by an altar rail. The bench is usually six or eight inches high and between three and four feet long; at its back, an upright board on either end supports a crosspiece of the altar rail. It can be made in the roughest fashion by any carpenter or amateur, since it can be hidden under leaves and flowers or a drapery of some sort.

Either end of the altar rail is usually decorated with a spray of white flowers.

At a house wedding, the bride's mother stands at the door of the room in which the ceremony is to be held and receives people as they arrive. But the bridegroom's mother takes her place near the altar with the rest of the immediate family. The ushers are purely ornamental, as no one is escorted to seats. The guests simply stand wherever they can find places behind the aisle ribbons. Just before the bride's entrance her mother goes forward and stands in the front row on the left.

In a house the procession usually starts from the top of the stairs. In an apartment it starts in the hall or a room off the living room. The wedding music, provided by a small orchestra, piano, or records, begins, and the ushers come in two by two, followed by the bridesmaids, exactly as in a church, the bride coming last on her father's arm. There are seldom many bridal attendants at a house wedding—two or three ushers, and the same number of bridesmaids—unless the house is immense. The clergyman and the groom and best man have, if possible, reached the altar by another door. If the room has only one door, they go up the aisle a few moments before the bridal procession starts.

At an even simpler wedding, the clergyman enters, followed by the bridegroom; the bride then enters with her father, or alone; and the wedding service is read. The bride and groom should each have one attendant, however, and they simply step forward and join the couple standing before the clergyman.

When there are no garden flowers to be had, a suitable background can be made by hanging a curtain of wine-red or deep-green velvet or any other plain fabric across a flat wall space. Against this, the colorful clothes of the bride's attendants (if she has any) and her own white dress and veil are effective. The refreshments may consist of nothing but ginger ale or fruit juice, wedding cake, and a few varieties of sandwiches placed on a small table covered with a white cloth.

One round of champagne is often served in addition to punch and soft drinks for the traditional wedding toasts.

The chief difference between a church wedding and a house wedding is that the bride and groom do not take a single step together. The groom meets her at the point where the service is read. After the ceremony there is no recessional. The clergyman steps aside, an usher removes the prayer bench, if there is one, and the bride and groom turn where they stand and receive the congratulations of their guests. The bride and groom kiss before they turn to receive their guests because it is against the tradition for anyone to kiss the bride before her husband does.

There may be a bride's table set up in the dining room, but more often there is a buffet table, and the bride and groom mingle with their friends, moving from one group to another. If the house is very large, or the reception is held in the garden, tables with centerpieces of flowers and cloths to complement the color of the bridesmaids' dresses are set up. The guests get their food from the buffet and sit at whatever table they wish, or wherever they find a free chair. In this case, as at a reception in a hall or club, there is a table reserved for the bridal party, and often one for the parents and their special guests.

Everyone invited to a house wedding ceremony stays on for whatever type of reception is held. It may be no more than punch and wedding cake, or it may be a complete meal and dancing, but there is a single guest list and no one goes to the first part without staying for the second.

The bride may wear the conventional long wedding dress for her home wedding, or she may prefer to wear a cocktail dress or even a simpler afternoon dress. The man wears the appropriate corresponding clothing as described in Chapter 49.

EVENING WEDDINGS

All through the South, and sometimes in the West, many weddings are celebrated at eight or nine o'clock in the evening. The reason for the evening wedding in the South is, of course, that the heat of the day has passed, and the coolness of the evening lends itself better to festivities and to dancing.

The details are, in general, the same as those for the morning or afternoon. In large Southern cities the bride and bridesmaids may wear dresses that are perhaps more elaborate and more "evening" in type, and the bridegroom and ushers wear full evening clothes. Guests, both men and women, dress in evening clothes.

At simpler ceremonies, especially in smaller communities, the guests wear exactly what they would wear to evening service in church—a good dress and hat for a woman and a dark daytime suit for a man.

Because of the lateness of the hour a full meal is not often served. Refreshments consist of sandwiches, cake, champagne or punch, and frequently coffee.

THE EARLY-MORNING WEDDING

Among Roman Catholics an eight-o'clock morning wedding is not unusual, and other couples choose to be married at dawn on a beach or a hilltop. The beginning of the new day is symbolic of the beginning of·a new life. Still others choose the early morning because they must catch a plane or ship that leaves early in the day.

The bride wears a simple daytime dress, usually the one she will go away in. She might possibly wear a veil, either falling to the hem of her dress or of finger length. However, I feel that a small hat or a hairband is more appropriate. She may carry a bouquet of moderate size or a prayer book or wear a corsage. She wears no gloves. Her attendants wear the simplest sort of morning dresses. The groom and his best man wear business suits or light-colored trousers and blazers. A reception follows the ceremony, featuring a breakfast or brunch menu. There might be fruit, coffee, and hot biscuits, a chafing dish of scrambled eggs, and creamed chicken or chipped beef. A round of champagne may be served for toasts, and Bloody Marys are frequently offered.

Occasionally the reception is held later in the day. This is not too satisfactory, however, because out-of-town guests may be at a loss for something to do or a place to spend the intervening hours.

MARRIAGE AT THE RECTORY

Couples who do not wish to, or cannot, be married in church, but whose clergyman can perform the ceremony, are sometimes married in the rectory.

The bride and bridegroom go together and are met at the parsonage by the members of their families and any friends who have been invited. The clergyman takes his place, and the service is read. Afterward those present congratulate them, and that may be all. Or they may go to the house of the bride or of a witness or to a restaurant to have lunch or dinner together. At such a marriage the bride rarely wears a white wedding dress and veil, but it is entirely proper for her to do so if she chooses—especially if there is to be a wedding dinner at someone's home afterward.

When the bridal party goes to a restaurant for a meal following the ceremony, it is usually paid for by the bride and groom, or the bride's parents. On occasion, however, the six or eight people present agree ahead of time to "give" the party for the newlyweds.

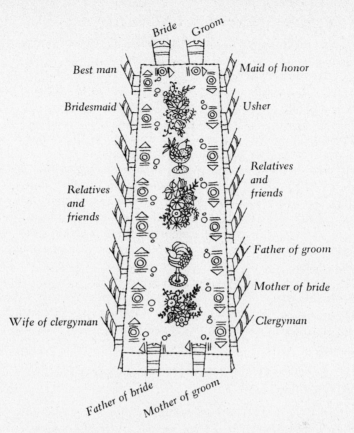

Small seated lunch or dinner following a simple wedding

CIVIL MARRIAGES

The general procedure is exactly the same as that for a marriage at the rectory. However simple and informal the plans, there are always two guests, either relatives or friends, who act as witnesses as well.

The traditional wedding dress and veil are not suitable in the circumstances, but the bride will certainly wish to wear the prettiest daytime dress or suit she has or can afford to buy.

A restaurant dinner or small party at home usually follows the ceremony.

THE BLESSING OF A CIVIL MARRIAGE

When a couple has been married in a civil ceremony, and have had the approval of their church, they may later wish to have a religious ceremony held in a church or chapel to bless that marriage. There is such a service in the *Book of Common Worship.* It is similar to the marriage service, except that the minister says, "Do you *acknowledge* [rather than *take*] this woman . . ." and makes other appropriate changes. No one, of course, gives the bride away, nor does the groom give the bride her ring again.

It is a lovely ceremony and most satisfactory for those who wanted but could not have a religious wedding originally.

The service is attended only by the family and closest friends, and there are no attendants. It is, after all, a blessing rather than a celebration of the marriage. The bride wears a street dress, and the groom, a dark suit. She may carry a bouquet or wear a corsage. There may be music, and the altar is decorated with flowers.

If a reception follows the ceremony, it may be as simple or as elaborate as the couple wish. Presuming the blessing takes place shortly after the civil marriage, the reception may have all the trimmings of any other wedding reception.

RELIGIOUS CEREMONY FOLLOWING A CIVIL MARRIAGE

Many couples who are married in a civil service wish to remarry later in a religious ceremony. This is perfectly proper—in fact a desirable thing to do. Both wedding and reception (if one was *not* held after the civil marriage) can be exactly like that of any other wedding, with one exception. The bride should not wear a veil—the traditional symbol of this "virgin bride"—but she may wear white—the symbol of purity.

If a long time has elapsed between the two ceremonies, so that the couple can no longer be considered bride and groom, the ceremony should be very simple—limited to family and close friends. The reception, too, should be intimate—a dignified celebration reflecting the religious aspect of the occasion.

ELOPEMENTS

To elope, according to the dictionary, is to "run away from home with a lover," but to most of us an elopement means that a young couple has run off and been married without the consent of the girl's parents. I suspect, however, that many such marriages have had a quiet parental blessing; for some reason, financial or otherwise, the family felt that a big wedding would be impossible.

When the bride's parents have approved before the marriage or when they have decided after it to make the best of what has happened, they send out the announcements in their name. Should the parents be unalterably opposed, however, and wish the world to know it, they do not send out the announcements. The newlyweds, if they wish, send them out themselves. *(See Chapter 50.)*

If the bride's mother and father give a belated reception sometime after the marriage, it is generally an informal affair attended by close friends and relatives. This is often done to introduce an out-of-town bridegroom. The invitations are telephoned or sent on informals. If written, they should include the bride's married name— "In honor of Mr. and Mrs. Harvey Kirk, Jr.," or "In honor of Nancy and Bill." If the parents are truly enthusiastic about the marriage and wish to show it, they may give a much more formal reception, including a wedding cake, engraved invitations, etc.

THE DOUBLE WEDDING

Most double weddings involve two sisters. The two bridegrooms follow the clergyman and stand side by side, each with his best man behind him. The groom of the older sister stands nearer the aisle. The ushers—half of them friends of the first, and the others friends of the second bridegroom—go up the aisle together. Then come the bridesmaids of the older sister followed by her maid of honor, who walks alone. The older sister follows, holding her father's arm. Then come the bridesmaids of the younger sister, her maid of honor, and last, the younger bride on the arm of a brother, uncle, or other close male relative.

The first couple ascend the chancel steps and take their place at the left side of the altar rail, leaving room at the right side for the younger bride and her bridegroom. The father stands just below his older daughter. The younger daughter's escort takes his place in the first pew.

The service is read to both couples, with the particular responses made twice. In a Protestant ceremony the father gives both brides away—first his older daughter and then the younger. Then he takes the place saved for him beside his wife in the first pew.

At the end of the ceremony the older sister and her husband

turn and go down the aisle first. The younger couple follow. The bridesmaids and ushers of the first sister pair off and follow; the attendants of the second walk out last.

Each couple should have the same number of attendants. All of the ushers should be dressed alike. The bridesmaids' dresses, while not necessarily all the same, should harmonize.

"ATTENDING" EACH OTHER

It is not usual, but it is quite possible, for each bride at a double wedding to serve as maid of honor for her sister. Each in turn holds the other's bouquet during her sister's ceremony.

But the wise bridegroom, if he dispenses with a best man and uses the services of his brother groom, keeps his own bride's ring in his own waistcoat pocket.

SEATING THE PARENTS AT THE CHURCH

One difficulty of a double wedding is the seating of the parents of the two bridegrooms, who must either share the first pew or draw lots for the occupation of first or second. This question they must decide for themselves.

Occasionally the brides are cousins, in which case the front pew on the bride's side must be shared by both mothers, the older sitting in the aisle seat.

THE RECEPTION FOR A DOUBLE WEDDING

If the brides are sisters, there is only one hostess—their mother. Therefore she (and her husband if he wishes) stands first in the receiving line. Next to her is the mother of the older sister's husband, and then the older sister and her groom. The younger sister's mother-in-law comes next, and then the younger couple. Both maids of honor follow them, but since there are so many in the line, the bridesmaids should be excused. The three mothers could stand together at the head of the line, but if the two grooms' mothers stand next to their own children, they are in a better position to introduce their new daughters-in-law to their special friends.

At a sit-down wedding reception the seating of the bridal parties depends on the numbers. If there are many attendants, it is best to have two tables, next to or facing each other, and arranged in the usual way. If, however, there are not too many in the parties, they may be seated at the same table. One couple would be placed at either end of the same side, or if they prefer, opposite each other at the center of each long side. The bride always sits on the right of the groom. The maid of honor in either case would be on the groom's left and the best man on the bride's right. The other attendants would alternate—either on the same side of the table as their newlywed couple, or at the same end where their particular couple is seated.

In the rare case when the couples are serving as each other's honor attendants, they could sit together at the center of a long table, since there would be no need for spaces to be left on either side for the best man and maid of honor.

Each couple should have their own wedding cake. They cut the cakes one right after the other so that each may watch the other perform that ceremony.

All three sets of parents should be seated together at the same table. It is up to the bride's mother to discuss with her daughters' new mothers-in-law how many other relatives should be included with them.

In all other ways the reception is identical to that of a single wedding.

MILITARY WEDDINGS

The only way in which a military wedding ceremony differs from a civilian one is the arch of swords through which the bride and groom pass at the end of the ceremony. This only occurs when the bridegroom is a commissioned officer. As soon as the service is over, the ushers line up on either side of the aisle at the foot of the chancel steps, and at the head usher's command, "Draw swords!" hold their swords up (blades up) in such a way as to form an arch. The couple pass through, and at the command, "Return swords!" the ushers return them to their sheaths. They then turn and escort the bridesmaids down the aisle.

On a nice day the arch may be formed outside the entrance to the church. In this case the ushers quickly leave by a side door and rush around to the front of the church to form the arch. Only the couple themselves pass through.

Should there be some civilian ushers in the party, they line up also and merely stand at attention while the arch is formed.

AN OLDER COUPLE'S WEDDING

The weddings of couples in their fifties, sixties, or seventies should be just as happy as those of much younger people, but they are necessarily a little different. In many cases one or both members have been married before, but that makes little difference in the arrangements.

The bride has only one attendant unless she has a young daughter or granddaughter who might act as a flower girl. Her maid of honor should be a contemporary, unless her own daughter serves in that position. The groom has a best man, and if there is to be a large number of guests, he may also have an usher or two to seat them.

The older bride is not given away, except when an adult son assumes that honor. She walks down the aisle unescorted, or walks in with the groom through a side door.

The mature bride should not choose a white wedding dress, since pure white is very unflattering to an older person's skin, and the conventional styles are not becoming or appropriate to one of her age. She may wear either a long or short dress in any style or color that is attractive on her. If she wears any veil at all, it should be small and should not cover her face. Her groom would ordinarily wear a dark business suit, but he might, if the wedding were to take place in the evening and she was wearing a long dress, wear a tuxedo. The attendants would wear the same style of clothing as the bride and groom.

Their reception may be as small or as large as they wish. The traditional cake and champagne are served, and toasts are offered by the best man and members of the couple's families.

Unless the wedding is very large, invitation is usually by word of mouth or personal note. If engraved invitations are sent, they are in the name of the couple themselves, in the form found on page 605.

THE INDEPENDENT BRIDE

The girl who lives by herself, works, and is organizing and giving her own wedding, has very special problems. She must limit the activities connected with the wedding, and she must make her plans well in advance, since she will only have evenings and weekends to carry them out.

She will be wise to use all the aid and services that are available. A bridal consultant at a reputable store can save her hours by showing clothes by appointment and by coordinating dresses, flowers, and other accessories. If she is having the reception in her home, she should do her best to hire a caterer, or at least one or two people to prepare food, serve, and wash up. If she cannot afford that, she should have friends enlisted to help her, or her wedding day will find her exhausted and hysterical.

Even though she may be having several attendants and a number of guests, the working girl should not let her friends plan too many parties. Showers should be limited to one or two, and other parties should be restricted to one a weekend so that the time for her preparations will not be too curtailed.

If she works in a small office, she may well want to invite all of her co-workers, but in a larger organization she need invite only her closer friends if her list must be restricted. She *should* invite her immediate superior and his or her spouse. If the wedding is large and more formal, each co-worker should be sent an invitation. If that is impossible, a single invitation may be sent to the whole office. *(See Chapter 50, page 618.*

A single thank-you note may also be sent for a "joint" gift sent by the whole staff, but if the bride can possibly do so, individual notes are infinitely nicer. If she does send a single thank-you, she should offer her verbal thanks to each individual when she returns to the office.

She should remember that all wedding invitations, whether personal or "blanket," include husbands and wives. Therefore the single girl who is limited either by money or by space should refrain from inviting more than the close friends she can easily accommodate.

SECOND MARRIAGES

The second marriages of widows and divorcées are similar in most respects, but there are certain differences that should be noted, and they will be pointed out in the following paragraphs.

A widow, in most cases, should wait a year or more after her husband's death before remarrying. This is simply a matter of showing respect for his memory, and because she is at least mentally "in mourning." Also, she should not rush into a marriage that might seem attractive to her just because she is lonely. A divorcée, on the other hand, may marry the day her divorce becomes final, although she, too, is risking an unhappy marriage "on the rebound." No matter how certain a man and a woman are about their plans to marry they may *not* announce their engagement before one or the other is legally divorced from the first mate. A girl may accept, *but never wear,* an engagement ring while her "fiancé" is still—if only for another day or two—another woman's husband.

EXPENSES

When a young woman whose first marriage ended after a very short time, or who, perhaps, eloped or had no "real" ceremony the first time, remarries, her family usually gives the wedding and pays the expenses just as they would for a first marriage. If, however, their daughter has had one large and expensive wedding, they should in no way feel obligated to give her another. They may help as much as they want, of course, but the wedding should impose no strain on their budget. In most cases the bride and groom plan and pay for the major part of the wedding themselves.

THE CEREMONY

The wedding service itself is exactly the same as that of a first wedding. But the surroundings, to be in the best of taste, should be simpler, and very dignified. The bride (unless, as mentioned above, she had no bridesmaids for her first wedding) has only one attendant—her maid of honor. The groom has a best man and as many ushers as may be necessary to seat the guests.

A widow or widower may have his or her young children stand as junior attendants. A divorcée's children may also be in the wedding if their father has completely severed connections with them. If they are close to him, however, his approval should be given before they act as attendants, since to stand with their mother against their father's wishes would put them in the position of being disloyal to him.

Children should, however, attend their parent's marriage, unless there is great resentment of the new husband or wife. They will adjust to the new family situation much more readily if they feel they are part of the formation of that family.

A young widow or divorcée may be escorted down the aisle by her father, but a more mature woman usually walks alone, preceded by her maid of honor. At a private ceremony there is no procession at all, and the couple merely enter together, usually from a side door, and walk behind the clergyman to the chancel.

THE BRIDE'S DRESS

Neither a widow nor a divorcée should wear a veil at her second wedding, since it is the symbol of virginity. Wearing white, the symbol of purity, is another matter, but since a second marriage should not try to be a replica of a first, it is best to choose another color—a pastel, or perhaps white lace over a colored underskirt.

A young groom who has not been married before may well wish to see his bride in a "bridal gown," even though she is widowed or divorced. To please him she may wear a long white "bridey" dress with color in the sash or trim and carry a bouquet of mixed colors rather than all white. She may wear a bridal hat or headdress, but not a veil. Her attendant's dress matches the style of her own, and her groom's costume is also dictated by hers. He may wear the semiformal sack coat with striped trousers if she wears a long dress, or a business suit if she is in a cocktail dress or suit.

WHEN THE MARRIAGE CANNOT TAKE PLACE IN CHURCH

Some faiths do not allow second marriages to take place in the church if either party has been divorced. In some cases the clergyman is permitted to perform the ceremony in the bride's home; in others he may not officiate at all, and if the couple wishes a religious ceremony they must find a clergyman from another faith to perform it. There are situations when a civil marriage is the only possibility, but it may always be followed by as elaborate a reception as the couple wishes.

The procedure for a second marriage performed at home is exactly the same as that described on page 679.

THE RECEPTION

While simple receptions are usually preferred—especially if there was an elaborate one following the bride's first marriage—there is no rule that they must be small. If the groom has not been married before, the couple may want to have all the "trimmings" for the benefit of his family and friends. In any case the reception, which is, after all, simply a party to celebrate the marriage, may be as large or as small as everyone concerned wishes. At a large reception there is a receiving line so that everyone may meet the groom; at a simpler party the line is not necessary. Although there is no rule about such details as monogrammed matchboxes, napkins, etc., they are usually omitted, but a wedding cake is always a feature.

INVITATIONS AND ANNOUNCEMENTS

Since the majority of second marriages are quite simple and the guest list is restricted to family and close friends, invitations are usually issued by phone, or to those at a distance, by personal note. If, however, a large reception is planned after a small ceremony, engraved invitations may be issued to the reception only, in the form found on page 602, but adding the bride's last name.

Both bride's family and groom's family may send engraved announcements to as many people as they wish, although, as for a first marriage, they are usually sent in the name of the bride's parents. *(See page 621.)*

Announcements of a second marriage may also be sent to the newspaper. They are similar to those of a first marriage except that there are no details about attendants or the bride's dress. The name of the former spouse and previous marital status of both bride and groom are usually included.

A typical announcement might read in part:

The wedding of Mr. and Mrs. Herman Berg took place on January fourteenth at the Third Congregational Church, Binghamton, N.Y. Mrs. Berg is the former Nancy McLeod Corey. She is the widow of Mr. Jonathan Corey of Sioux Falls, Iowa. [Or: Her first marriage to Mr. Jonathan Corey terminated in divorce.]

The announcement may then go on to mention the occupation of Mr. Berg (and Mrs. Berg, if applicable), and where they will be living. In some papers that are not pressed for space, the parents of the couple may also be mentioned.

When a widow or divorcée remains very close to the parents of her first husband there is a question about whether or not to invite them to her second wedding. Since they are fond of her they are undoubtedly delighted that she has found happiness and that the children (if any) will have a stepfather, but at the same time it may be hard for them to see someone taking the place of their son. The bride should tell them personally that she would love to have them at the wedding, but that she understands if they would find it sad or uncomfortable to be there, and leave it up to them.

GIFTS

Although family members usually give a gift to a bride being married for the second time, friends, other than those closest to her, need not do so. If it is the first marriage for the groom, his relatives and friends will surely *want* to give them gifts. Although it is not in good taste to put "No gifts" on a wedding or reception invitation, the word should be spread by family members and good friends that the couple certainly do not expect gifts from friends invited to the reception—especially if they have attended a previous one for the bride.

UNWED MOTHERS AND PREGNANT BRIDES

I am frequently asked whether a bride who had a child before her marriage, or one who is about to, should wear a bridal gown and have an elaborate wedding. The answer is not an easy one. It depends on the bride's own feelings, her honesty, and how much she cares about what other people think or say. The last is, perhaps, less important, and yet few of us do not have some desire to conform and to be thought well of.

As discussed above, under "Second Marriages," the veil is the accepted and traditional symbol of virginity. Therefore unwed mothers and pregnant brides should *not* wear a veil. This in no way brands them as different, because many other brides do not choose to wear veils in any case.

The white dress is another matter, and the bride must think carefully. If she does not feel that what she has done is a mistake or wrong in any way, then she is "pure" in heart and may wear white. She may modify the virginal effect by adding color to the trim and in her flowers or by choosing a definite off-white. She will still look as "bridey" as can be but she will be less open to criticism. A very obviously pregnant bride should not wear a wedding gown, which would look utterly incongruous. Although the attitude toward unmarried mothers is far more liberal than it used to be, a large majority of our society does not approve of that order of events. Many people feel that if the sanctity of marriage and the family unit is to be preserved, the established standards of behavior in that regard should be maintained.

Because this is so, these marriages should be kept relatively simple so that the couple does not appear to flaunt their situation in society's face. The bride may certainly be given a shower or two, as long as they are restricted to intimate friends. There may be attendants, a reception, photographs, and newspaper announcements. Invitations follow the rules for any wedding. In sending out announcements after the wedding, the date is never falsified—even when a baby is to arrive six or seven months later. Most people will have forgotten the wedding date, and it is better to be honest than to try to hide what can't be hidden.

When announcements are sent by the bride's parents the indication that they have accepted and are happy about the marriage can be a great help to the bride and groom, who may be going through a very traumatic experience.

In fact the understanding of the bride's parents is terribly important. It can be disastrous if they force a girl to marry a boy she is not really in love with, just to "make an honest woman of her." A marriage carried out on that basis is almost surely headed for divorce. But when the girl and boy are truly in love and *want* to get married, their parents' support will bring the two generations closer than they have ever been before.

Above all, it should be remembered that this is a *happy* occasion, and one to be celebrated. The fatherless child is getting a father, and the mother will have his support and help in bringing up her baby. Whatever her problems and mistakes have been, they are on the way to being over. So, the wedding should be dignified, beautiful, and in quiet good taste, and the reception should match it—with gaiety and an air of celebration added.

THE NEW LOOK IN WEDDINGS

There is, unquestionably, great beauty and meaning in many of the time-honored traditions associated with weddings. And yet, for so many years, weddings were stereotyped—one exactly like the other except for the faces and the color of the bridesmaids' dresses. Today, with so many couples wanting to do their own thing—to make their weddings more meaningful and more personal—there is a new freshness to the marriage ceremony.

Often the newness is in the actual location of the wedding. It may take place on a beach, on a sailboat, on a hilltop, or in a formal garden. The service may be quite traditional, or it may be written by the couple themselves. The bride may wear a beautiful white bridal gown while the groom wears a velvet Edwardian suit. Or even though the ceremony is held in a church or chapel, the principals may be wearing Mexican or Indian dress—perhaps because they met on the Yucatán peninsula or at the Taj Mahal. The meal at the reception could be Mexican chili and tacos or curry and saffron rice, far more appropriate to the occasion than filet mignon or creamed chicken—more traditional menus.

In deciding to have any or all of the possible innovations in their marriage, the couple should consider several questions. Will it have the approval of their clergyman? Will their parents be very unhappy? Are they doing it because it *really* means something to them, or only to cause a sensation? Will the innovations they want uphold the dignity and seriousness a marriage merits?

While the final decisions should, of course, be up to the couple, "no man is an island," and if they care about their future relationships with their parents, they must consider their feelings too. For example, a soon-to-be bride asked me recently if she *had to* walk up the aisle with her father. Although she loved him, she, as an ardent

Women's Libber, resented the fact that a man should "give her away." I cannot help but feel that her desire to take that stand for her independence was not nearly so important as the hurt she was inflicting on her father.

A wedding should be great fun for everyone, but marriage is a serious step and should be treated with the dignity and respect it deserves. Fun, yes, but childishness, publicity-consciousness, irreverence, and ostentation should *have no part in it*. Not long ago I read a newspaper account of a wedding, which I will repeat: "After the ceremony the couple joined their eighty guests for a competitive buffet reception of games, including Pop the Balloon, Pin the Tail on the Donkey, and Spin the Bottle."

Was that a wedding reception or a toddler's birthday party? This sort of thing downgrades the entire meaning of marriage, and to me, is an insult—not only to the marriage but to the intelligence of the guests.

I also feel that since a marriage is certainly a "special" occasion, everything connected with it should be at least a little "special" too. This includes the clothing of the bridal party and the guests. To suggest on the invitation (as was further reported in the same news item) that the guests come in any clothes, including jeans, certainly does *not* add to the specialness. Naturally, at an informal outdoor wedding the men would not be expected to wear suits or shirts and ties and sports jackets if they are contrary to the life-style of the particular group. But they *should* change out of their everyday clothes into neat, clean slacks, turtlenecks, sports shirts, or whatever to them is "special" clothing.

As mentioned above, the bride may choose any *style* of clothing she likes. But it should be modest, beautiful, becoming, and have a certain dignity. Bare feet are neither beautiful nor dignified. Very few people have pretty feet, nor is it possible to keep bare feet clean. The sight of calloused, smudged toes, whether sticking out from under a peasant dress or a more classic wedding gown, is simply not attractive. Admittedly, conventional pumps would be equally inappropriate with many wedding costumes, but sandals, no matter how "skimpy," are preferable to totally bare feet.

INNOVATIONS I LIKE

Following is a description of various innovations I have seen or heard of that seem to me especially appealing—and in good taste. Some are so widespread that they are scarcely "innovations," but I am frequently asked by brides and their mothers whether they are acceptable.

I hope this list may suggest to you several ideas that will give your wedding a new look and make it very "special."

CHANGES IN THE SERVICE ITSELF

Addition of a favorite poem or passage to the ceremony. In the novel *Love Story,* Erich Segal included, as part of Jenny and Oliver's wedding service, a sonnet by Elizabeth Barrett Browning.

> *When our two souls stand up*
> *erect and strong,*
> *Face to face, silent, drawing*
> *nigh and nigher*
> *Until the lengthening wings*
> *break into fire. . . .*

The first "innovation" to be widely accepted—the optional changing of the word *obey* to *cherish.* The word *obey* was eliminated in the Presbyterian Book of Worship over twenty-five years ago, but it is still included in the services of many faiths, and the change to *cherish* must be requested.

Vows written by the couple themselves, either in addition to or replacing the traditional ones. I particularly liked one of Tiny Tim's vows, although his marriage on TV, witnessed by millions, did not last. This vow could well be incorporated into everyone's service: "I will be slow to anger and quick to forgive."

A new Catholic service changes the promises the couple makes from "until death us do part," to "I promise to be true to you in good times and bad," a far more realistic vow.

In many cases the guests are expected to participate too. So that they will know when, and what their responses should be, programs are prepared and handed out as the guests arrive.

CHANGES IN CLOTHING

While nothing can ever be prettier and more romantic than a traditional wedding gown, there are varieties in the clothing of *all* of the bridal party that are most attractive and appropriate for the new-look, outdoor wedding:

Color in the bride's costume—in the trim of her dress, her headdress, her flowers.

Printed bridesmaids' dresses rather than solid colors.

"Picture hats" for brides as well as bridesmaids.

Styles, as discussed above, which are untraditional but reflect a special meaning to the couple. Peasant dresses, representing the simpler life, are the most popular, but the national costumes of many different countries can be adapted beautifully, from the American Indian dress to the Japanese kimono.

The groom and his attendants would certainly look out of place dressed in sack coats or tuxedos when the bride and her attendants are dressed unconventionally. To give their clothes a new look too, their shirts may match the color of the bridesmaids' dresses, their suits may be "Edwardian," or they too may be dressed in a national costume. Men's clothiers, to satisfy those who are looking for something "in between," have evolved a sack coat with long tails. It is worn with ordinary shirt and tie, and does provide a look that is more formal than a suit jacket or sack coat but less formal than a cutaway.

THE MUSIC

It is scarcely necessary to mention that the traditional wedding march has been replaced by any number of selections more religious in nature. This is a matter that every couple planning to be married in church must discuss with the organist. Those who will be married outdoors usually have a friend who plays and/or sings their selections or music that he has composed especially for the ceremony. Guitars are so often played that they are almost "traditional," but recorders, flutes, harps—almost anything—have been used to provide the music too. Some real nature lovers prefer to let the sounds around them provide the only music—the song of birds, the roar of the surf, the sound of the wind in the pines—or of the guests singing.

INVITATIONS

The new look in invitations is the handwritten and -decorated invitation made by the couple themselves. There is no rule as to the wording—they may say whatever they wish, in poetry or prose. *For a semiformal invitation, sent by the bride's parents, see page 616.*

THE PARENTS' PART

In answer to the clergyman's question, "Who giveth this woman . . . ?" the bride's father includes her mother by saying, "Her mother and I do."

The bride stops as she is leaving the church and gives a flower from her bouquet to her mother and to the groom's mother. The groom kisses the two mothers and shakes hands with the fathers.

The bride places the flowers from the altar on the grave of a deceased parent after the reception. The bride who told me about doing this said that in the few moments at her father's graveside she felt that she had received his blessing.

One bride had flowers delivered to her ailing grandmother at the moment the service was taking place, letting her know that she was in their thoughts.

SURROUNDINGS

I am very much in favor of outdoor weddings when it is possible and practical. Any place that offers beauty and privacy, is accessible, and has special meaning for the bride and groom is appropriate, provided their faith permits. Our church has a very beautiful enclosed garden, and my daughter and her husband chose to be married there rather than inside the church.

Many couples may simply prefer to be married in the familiar surroundings of their own home—however small. This too is most appropriate. One lovely wedding I attended was held in a tiny New York apartment. The young minister, saying that "a marriage affects the whole community, and therefore I feel that the community— represented by you—should have a part in the marriage," asked the thirty or more guests to form a circle and hold hands. The bride and groom, their parents, and the minister formed a part of the circle. The service was traditional except that the maid of honor and the best man passed bread and wine around the circle as a simple "Communion." The best man, a poet, read a poem he had composed for the couple. Although we, the older guests, felt a little strange at first, we came away feeling that it had been a particularly beautiful wedding, and that we truly had taken part.

THE RECEPTION

Champagne used to be an essential part of the wedding reception. Today it is usually only one beverage of many offered, or it is omitted entirely. Brides and grooms tend to offer, instead, the beverages (and the foods) they know that their friends will like. Beer, wine, Bloody Marys, whiskey, and all manner of soft drinks have become not only acceptable but as popular as the traditional champagne.

The receiving line is often omitted. Most new-look weddings are not so large and certainly not so "structured" as traditional weddings. The bride and groom, using the time they would have spent standing in line, circulate among the guests. The advantage of a receiving line is that everyone there has a chance to offer happiness and congratulations to the bride and groom. Therefore, if no line is formed, the couple *and* their parents must make a special effort to talk to each and every guest. If there are many strangers present, it is perhaps best to have a line so that they will all be sure to meet the member of the couple they do not know. But when the group is small, and most *do* know the couple and each other, I am very much in favor of dispensing with the rather boring (and exhausting) receiving line.

Instead of traditional favors such as paper matches with the couple's initials, boxes of groom's cake, etc., one couple wrote me that they had written a message to their guests thanking them for coming and adding to their happiness, and had it printed on small cards and distributed to their friends with the slices of wedding cake. It was a nice thought, and the cards served as a sentimental memento of the wedding.

⊷56⊷ Wedding Guests

"THE HONOUR OF YOUR PRESENCE . . ."

As soon as you receive an invitation, to the ceremony and reception or to the reception only, and see that it includes an RSVP, you must reply at once. It is both inconsiderate and impolite not to do so. Remember that the family will have to make definite preparations for every guest who has failed to send a refusal just as they do for those who accept. Failure to reply causes extra trouble *and* expense.

As the wording suggests, it is an "honour" to be invited to a wedding, and anyone so honored should have the common decency and good manners to sit down and write his answer in person. However, when you receive an invitation accompanied by a response card you should use the card for your reply. The sender has undoubtedly organized a system for filing the returned cards, and a handwritten answer on notepaper would not fit in with the cards. If you feel this is too impersonal, or you wish to explain why you cannot attend, enclose a personal note but fill out the card too to keep the record straight.

"AND FAMILY"

An invitation reading "and Family" includes each and every member of the family living under the same roof—and this means every child from walking and talking age (at about two) up to great-grandparents. Married daughters or sons who live in their own houses are not included because if invited they are sent separate invitations.

In general, however, you should not take small children unless you are willing to look after them. Well-behaved children are very welcome at a wedding, but children out of hand can be most annoying to everyone and detract from the solemnity of the occasion.

Above all, you may *never* take a child to a wedding unless he is specifically invited—either by name on the inner envelope of your invitation, by his own invitation, or by the "and family" on your envelope.

"AND GUEST"

If your invitation has "and escort" or "and guest" on it, you are obviously intended to bring a friend of your own choosing. However, you should let the bride know if you intend to do so, giving her the name and address of your friend. Although it is not absolutely necessary she *should* then send your "date" an invitation.

Single, "unattached" girls should not assume that they may take an escort. Steady dates or fiancés are usually invited, and if not, the female guest may ask the bride if she may bring her fiancé, and the male guest may do the same. Otherwise a wedding is not a "dating" occasion. Single men and single women should have no reluctance about attending alone. They will find other friends there, and as a matter of fact a wedding reception is apt to be a good place to meet other "singles."

WHAT THE GUESTS WEAR

The choice of clothes naturally depends on the size and formality of the wedding, the location, the time of day, and the custom of the community.

In the city or at any formal or semiformal wedding, women wear afternoon or cocktail dresses or dressy suits. The men wear suits, but they no longer are restricted to white shirts.

In the country or in the summertime, either light suits or slacks with solid-color blazers are acceptable. Wild-patterned slacks and sports coats are not in good taste for a formal church wedding, but are fine for outdoor and "new-look" weddings.

Women guests do not wear long dresses to daytime ceremonies, but long skirts and blouses are popular for early-evening receptions. Although they are not appropriate for mature women, dressy "evening pants" may be worn to afternoon and evening receptions by young girls.

As a general rule, at a formal evening wedding the women wear evening dresses, with a scarf over their shoulders in church. They do not wear hats (unless required by their church), but do sometimes wear hair ornaments. At a simpler wedding in the evening or during

the day, they wear afternoon dresses, with small hats or hair ornaments.

When not going to the reception one chooses clothes that are
habitually worn to church.

Children always wear their best party clothes.

Those in mourning should lighten it on this occasion by changing
to lavender or white, or a subdued color. Or they may brighten their
costumes by adding a touch of color in trim or accessary rather than
casting a pall of gloom with unrelieved black.

Wedding guests do not wear corsages unless they are "honored"
guests such as a grandmother or godmother of the bride or groom.

Unless it is very hot, women wear gloves to the wedding, but
it is no longer obligatory to keep them on to go through the receiving
line.

AT THE CHURCH

On entering the church you go to the back of the center aisle
and wait until one of the ushers comes up to you. If you are a member
of either family or a very close friend of the bride or the groom, you
tell him your name. If you have been sent a pew card, you show it
to him. At a wedding without pew cards he may ask your name and
look on his "in-front-of-the-ribbons" list in order to seat you. If you
say nothing to indicate that you should be seated in front, he will ask
you whether you are a friend of the bride or of the groom, in order
to seat you on her or his side of the aisle. In any case a lady puts her
hand on the inside of his proffered arm, and he escorts her to a seat.
A man alone walks beside the usher, or if he comes with a woman,
he follows the usher and the woman unless there is room for the
three of them to walk abreast. As discussed in Chapter 53, page 653,
many people object to the husband or escort tagging along like this,
and I hope that brides and grooms will start to instruct their ushers
to say "Please follow me" to a couple, who may then walk together,
with the wife on her husband's right.

When two women arrive together, one enters with the first
usher to reach her, and the other waits for another usher. If a large
crowd arrives at once, however, they may walk in side by side, with
the usher preceding them.

If you arrive at the church late, after the bride's mother has been
seated, you should slip quietly into a rear pew. If the procession has
formed in the vestibule, you may either go to a side aisle or wait until
they have all entered the church before seating yourself on the

center aisle. Occasionally someone attends a wedding to which he or she has not been specifically invited. This is not wrong, if the person has a good reason for being there, but he too should sit at the back and not allow himself to be ushered in—taking a space that would otherwise be filled by an invited guest.

If you arrive early enough to be seated on the aisle, you need not move over and give your choice place to later arrivals. Either stand or swing your knees to the side to let them pass by. Even though a woman enters the pew before the man she is with, they may switch places so that she (if she is shorter) may have the aisle seat and see the procession with an unobstructed view.

At a wedding it is all right to smile and nod to people you know—even to talk in a low voice to a friend sitting next to you. But when you find yourself among strangers you just sit quietly until the processional starts.

When you are in a church of a religion other than your own observe those in front of you: Stand if they stand, kneel if they kneel, and sit if they sit—as long as it is not contrary to your beliefs.

When the service is over and the recessional has passed by, those in the pews farther back must wait in their places until the immediate families in the front pews have left. If you wait until those around you start to leave, you will be sure of not making any mistake.

FROM CHURCH TO RECEPTION

When you are invited to the reception—if it is to follow the church ceremony—you are expected to go directly from the church to wherever the reception is to be held. But do give the bridal party a little while to arrange for wedding pictures and form the receiving line. No provision is ever made for taking any of the guests from the church to the house. You go in your own car, with a friend, or if the distance is short, you walk.

AT THE RECEPTION

When you arrive at the reception you leave your coat in the dressing room or checkroom and take your place at the end of the queue waiting to go through the receiving line. Should there be an announcer you give him your name with your title—"Mrs. Harry Zuckerman," "Miss Susie Smythe," or "Dr. James Bernard"—and he repeats it to the bride's mother, who, as hostess, is first in the line. Ordinarily, if you are a stranger to her, you shake hands, introduce yourself, and she says she is so glad you could come, or something of that nature. She then introduces you to her husband, if he is in line, and you pass on to say "Hello" to the groom's mother, who is presumably the one whose list you were on. She introduces you to the bride (and groom, if necessary) and you wish the bride happiness, and congratulate the groom. When you are a friend of the bride or her mother you say a word or two about how lovely the ceremony was, and she then introduces you to the groom's mother. You shake hands with each of these people as you speak to them.

Close friends of either sex often kiss the bride and some female relatives and good friends of the groom may kiss him too. But most, like the male guests, simply shake his hand and offer their congratulations.

Even if you know both of the mothers very well, there is no time to say more than perhaps something such as "What a lovely day Mary and John have for the wedding!" or "How beautiful Mary looks!" There is, however, one real rule: Do not launch into a conversation about yourself, how you feel, what happened to you yesterday. Your remarks should be confined to the young couple themselves or their wedding.

Above all, be brief in order not to keep those behind waiting longer than necessary. If you have anything particular to tell the bridal party, you can see them later when there is no longer a line.

In the excitement of the day the bride and groom may easily forget the names even of their best friends, and they are quite likely not to remember Great-Aunt Jennifer, who last visited ten years ago. Therefore it is thoughtful for a guest (even a distant relative) to mention her name even though she thinks that the couple knows her. Never choose this moment to play "Guess who I am?" as some inconsiderate people do.

If you have been invited to bring a friend who is unknown to the bride and groom, you should introduce the friend to them both, as well as to their mothers.

You say a few words to any of the bridesmaids with whom you are acquainted. Otherwise you walk on with a smile and perhaps a "Hello" if you happen to be looking directly at one of them who looks at you. But there is no chance, nor need, to stop and really talk to those you do not know.

The bride's father sometimes stands beside his wife, but he usually circulates among his guests just as he would at any other party where he is host. Therefore you speak to him either on your arrival or whenever you encounter him acting as host.

Although the groom's father is actually a guest it is certainly courteous—especially if he is a stranger—to introduce yourself and tell him how well you like his son or his new daughter-in-law, or best of all, both.

If you are alone you look around for friends of your own after going through the line. If you see no one you know, the best thing to do is to make your way to wherever refreshments are being served. You ask the bartender to serve you a drink, or you help yourself to whatever food you want if there is a buffet. You can linger and nibble as long as you like or just sit down and watch people. And you may speak to anyone else who is alone and looks willing to be spoken to.

A SIT-DOWN BREAKFAST

If you are a stranger at a sit-down reception, you have no alternative but to join a group of people whom you do not know. You may either sit down at an unoccupied table and let others join you, or you may approach a table where several people are sitting and say, "Do you mind if I sit here?" or "May I join you?" It is helpful to identify yourself too: "I'm Sarah Barnes, an old friend of June's mother."

WHEN YOU MAY LEAVE THE RECEPTION

When you want to leave a large reception you just do so. It is not necessary to attract attention to your going if it means you will distract the bride's mother from her duties in the receiving line or from her other responsibilities; but if the line has broken up, you should find her and thank her just as you would for any party. If you know the bride or groom well and they are not involved with a special wedding event such as cutting the cake, you should also bid them good-bye and wish them *bon voyage.*

Part Ten

GOOD MANNERS
FOR EVERY DAY

⋗57⋖ Calls and Visits

FORMAL CALLS

*Etiquette absolutely demands that one leave a card within a few days
after taking a first meal in a lady's house; or if one has for the first
time been invited to lunch or dine with strangers, it is inexcusably rude
not to leave a card upon them, whether one accepted the invitation
or not.*—Emily Post, 1922

The custom of making formal calls is no longer a part of our lives.
But there are circumstances in which even those most indifferent to
social obligations must call and leave their cards: In Washington
members of diplomatic or military circles exchange calls. Members
of the military or the diplomatic service arriving at a new post call
on their superiors. Calls are exchanged between officers on military
posts. Each of the services publishes its own books and pamphlets
on military etiquette, which thoroughly cover the subject of these
special calls.

AT THE DOOR

Today, when a maid who knows you opens the door, she simply
says, "Please come in. Mrs. Franklin is in the living room"; and if you

know the way, you walk in by yourself. Or she may say, "Mrs. Franklin is upstairs. I'll tell her you're here." If you are unfamiliar with the house, she should show you to the living room to wait while she takes the message. When the visitor is not known to the maid she says, "May I tell Mrs. Franklin who is calling?" and the guest simply gives her name.

It is certainly not necessary to have a visiting card to pay a call. If the person on whom you are calling is home and greets you herself, she obviously knows that you have made the effort to see her. If no one is home you may leave a note in her mailbox: "So sorry to have missed you, Sally." If she does not know you well, you sign it "Sally Brown."

When the door is opened by a maid who tells you that Mrs. Franklin is not at home or cannot see you, you may ask for a pencil and paper and leave her a note or ask the maid to tell her that you have called.

When you are ready to leave, the maid should stand with the front door open until you get into your car, or if you are walking, until you have reached the sidewalk. It is bad manners ever to close the door in a visitor's face or while she is still going down the front steps.

CALLS THAT EVERYONE MUST MAKE

CALLS OF CONDOLENCE

Calls of condolence should be made as soon as possible after hearing of the death of a friend or a member of a friend's family. If the friends are very close, you will probably be admitted to speak to them; and if you are, you should offer your services to help in any way that you can. If they do not need anything, you offer your sympathy and leave without delay. *For further details, see Chapter 46, "Funerals."*

When you are not well acquainted with the family and do not wish to intrude on their privacy you may leave your card with "With deepest sympathy" written across the top. Visits of condolence need not be returned.

Rules for calling at the funeral parlor are also found in Chapter 46.

CALLING ON A FRIEND WHO IS ILL

"Making calls" brings to mind one subject that certainly is at one time or another in the thoughts of all of us. This is the occasional visit we must make to a hospital when members of our families or our close friends are ill. The same general rules apply to visiting a sick person at home, although if he is well on the way to recovery they may be slightly relaxed.

The whole routine of a hospital is highly organized and kept in smooth running order by the doctors and nurses and staff. When visiting a friend in the hospital we should try to make our presence there fit into an orderly pattern so that the hospital's staff can do its best for the patients.

Far too often visitors are thoughtless and careless. One should think of the problems that a visitor makes under the busy, crowded hospital conditions of today. Courtesy to nurses and the other hospital personnel, quietness of manner and approach in the hospital buildings, avoidance of asking for special attention from busy people, are obvious requirements—and above all, we must not act in any way that will be tiring or harmful to the patient we are visiting. We must make our visits short and friendly, leaving our small gifts without fuss or any expectancy of more than a simple thank you for them. We must not engage the patient in long discussions nor ask questions about his or her illness that properly are in the sphere of the doctor and the nurse. We must time our visits so that the patient becomes neither tired nor anxious and of course we must always follow the rules as they are given to us by the staff. A surgeon I know claims that visitors kill more patients than do operations, certainly an overstatement but one with more than a kernel of truth. Here are a few dos and don'ts that may be helpful for visitor and patient.

Don't bring as your gift foods such as chocolates or cakes that the patient may not be permitted to have, unless you have first checked with his physician or nurse.

Don't talk about his illness in front of the patient. Ask for the necessary information quietly, from those who are competent to give it, out of the patient's hearing and sight. Also, remember that floor nurses are not allowed to answer certain questions. If one of them says to you, "You will have to ask Dr. Smith about that," you need not feel that she is hiding information from you or that she is being deliberately unfeeling; it is a hospital rule, and she has no choice.

Don't worry a patient about anything that you feel might upset or disturb him. The fact that Bobby is failing algebra, or the dog had a disastrous fight with the neighbor's cat, is not news calculated to improve the mental outlook of the patient. In any case he or she can do nothing about your problems. The best thing you can do, if you wish his speedy return home, is to bring him cheerful, encouraging news that will make him want to get there quickly.

Remember that the average patient is not his normal self and the burden of good behavior is on your side, not his. He may show little enthusiasm for the things that usually interest him, or he may react overexcitedly to a minor incident. If he does either, simply tell yourself that this reaction is only temporary and change the subject to a safer one. But it is up to you to lead the way.

Don't overstay your welcome. Visit briefly, cheerfully, and leave the patient rested and encouraged. Make up your mind before you arrive that you will stay no more than fifteen or twenty minutes, and stick to it, no matter how much your friend may beg you to stay. If other visitors arrive while you are there, leave sooner so that they may have their share of the patient's time without overtiring him. Nothing is more exhausting to a person in bed than to have to try to follow a conversation among several people who may be seated on all sides of the room. If it is possible, when two or three people are present, stand or put your chairs on the same side of the bed.

If, possibly because of the shortage of nurses in many hospitals, the doctor or a member of the family asks you, as a close friend, to stay with the patient, do not let him feel that he must entertain you or even talk. Take a book along, attend to any simple things he may wish you to do, and settle yourself where he may know that you are there, but at the same time indicate that you are quite happy to have an hour or two in which to enjoy your book quietly.

FLOWERS ARE "GOOD MEDICINE"

Flowers, according to Dr. George Jacobsen, professor of psychiatry at the University of Miami Medical School, can be "good medicine" for people in hospitals.

He says, "Sick people, especially those in hospitals, definitely respond to tender, loving care. Flowers mean that someone cares for them—that someone loves them. That's an important incentive to get better."

Whenever it is possible, bring flowers in their own container and let them be of a size that can easily be handled. Hospitals are invariably short of (or do not provide) containers, and it is an additional chore for the nurses to have to hunt for a suitable vase. Florists know this, and if you mention that your purchase is to go to a hospital, they will arrange the flowers in inexpensive (sometimes even disposable) containers at no additional charge.

Patients often prefer potted plants to cut flowers. They are easy to care for, last longer, and can be taken home by a member of the family if more space is needed for those that arrive at a later date. There they continue to give the patient many further moments of

710

pleasure. Plants, as opposed to cut flowers, continue to live and thrive, and this, too, seems to encourage some patients who identify with the living plant, and therefore, with life.

Don't think that the hospital routine has been devised to bedevil you as a visitor, or the patient himself. It is only part of a long-range plan carefully worked out to serve everyone in the best way possible. Limited visiting hours, early meals, and rules governing smoking may seem unreasonable to you, but you must remember that they have not been made just for the benefit or your sister Susie, who may have nothing more than a broken leg, but rather for the sicker patients, who without a carefully planned routine and the best possible conditions for rest and quiet, might not recover at all.

SEMIPRIVATE ROOMS AND WARDS

The number of private rooms in every hospital has been greatly decreased, partly because of the shortage of nurses, partly because they are too costly for most people, and partly because there always seems to be a need for more hospital beds than exist. The vast majority of hospital patients today find themselves in semiprivate rooms or larger wards.

The rules governing visitors to these rooms must be stricter than those for visitors to patients in private rooms. Your friend may not object to cigarette smoke, but it may cause the man in the next bed to have a coughing attack which could be the worst thing for him. Therefore, if it is allowed at all, it is essential to ask the others nearby if it will bother them if you smoke. And please, cigarettes only! Cigar and pipe smoke can actually cause nausea in many people.

Voices must naturally be kept lower, not only for privacy's sake, but in order not to disturb the other sick people who may badly need their rest.

If you are going to the snack bar or restaurant to bring a dish of ice cream or a candy bar to your friend, it is only thoughtful to ask the other person in a semiprivate room if you can bring him anything at the same time. This would not be necessary in a larger ward, unless one of the patients actually asked you to do an errand for him.

If there is a television set in the room—and this rule applies between patients as well as visitor and patient—do not turn it on without asking the other's permission and consulting him as to his choice of program. Unless he shows real enthusiasm, keep the volume very low.

If another patient in a room wishes to rest, draw the curtains between the beds to give him as much privacy and quiet as possible.

On the other hand, if he and your friend have become friendly, include him in the conversation and your visit will be doubly appreciated.

TIPPING

The question of tipping the nurses may arise, but its answer is simple—don't. It is perfectly proper, however, to bring a box of candy or the like that can be shared by all the staff caring for the patient. The package should be left with the nurse on duty at the desk nearest his room, with a word or two to the effect that "this is for all of you who have been so nice."

CALLS OF CONGRATULATION

When a new mother comes home from the hospital, relatives and friends are expected to call to see the baby. It is customary to take a gift at this time, although the present may also be sent later, after the visitor has had a chance to see what might be needed.

Prospective visitors should always call the young mother to find out what time would be convenient. Not only is she busy with the feedings, baths, etc., at certain hours but she will also be able to suggest a time when the baby is apt to be awake.

Good friends should also go to see a bride on her return from the honeymoon, in the evening or on weekends if she is working. And when a man marries a girl from a distant place, friendliness demands that his friends and neighbors visit her as soon as they get home.

CALLING ON A NEW NEIGHBOR

When strangers move into an established neighborhood it is courteous and friendly of the residents nearby to call on them. The newcomers wait for old residents to issue the first "formal" invitation to a meal, but if contact has been established casually through gardening activities, through children, or in the laundry of an apartment house, the new arrival could further the acquaintance by suggesting the other's child come over to play, by inviting the neighbor to join her for a soft drink, or by asking advice on stores, doctors, etc. These openings may well lead to an invitation to dine at the older resident's home, after which the newcomer may reciprocate with any form of entertainment.

If you are planning a visit to a stranger who has come to live in your neighborhood, telephone to be sure it's convenient. But if you are passing by and you find her planting flowers along her walk, say, "Hello—I'm Nancy Jones. I live in the brick house across the street."

The new neighbor says, "Hi, I'm glad to meet you." She may also invite you into her house for a soda or a cup of coffee, and you sit for a few minutes and talk.

You need only stay for ten or fifteen minutes on this first visit, unless your hostess says, "Oh, do stay a little longer," or "Let's have another glass of iced tea." Then you may stay for a few minutes longer if you wish, or reply, "I'm sorry, but I can't today. Do come and see me soon!" She says, "Thanks, I'd love to," you both say, "Good-bye," and that's all.

RETURNING A FIRST VISIT

People who are old friends pay no attention to how often or how seldom one goes to see the other, unless there is an illness, a death, or a birth in the family. Nor do they ever consider whose turn it is to invite whom. But first visits should be returned with considerable punctuality—especially after a *first* invitation to lunch or dine. The casual "first visit" described above allows the newcomer to "drop in" on her neighbor but not to issue a formal invitation to lunch or dinner. To do that too soon makes the newcomer seem "pushy," and older residents may tend to resent being pushed into intimacy too quickly.

INFORMAL VISITS

There is no need to discuss the casual visit between very close friends. There are no rules at all except those which might be set up between them. For instance, one might say, "Give me till ten o'clock to pull myself together before you come over." Or they might agree to take turns making sandwiches for lunch while the babies are napping. Whatever they may enjoy, it is a personal matter, and etiquette requires only that they be considerate to each other and offend no outsiders.

There are, however, many visits made between less intimate friends that are not at all in the category of the formal call. Friends making or receiving these informal visits should know and follow certain rules.

CHILDREN AND PETS

Unless they are specifically invited it is best, if possible, to leave children—and pets—home when you visit friends. This is not always practical, however, and couples with young children should think carefully about their visiting manners.

A smart housewife who knows that she will have young visitors from time to time—whether children of friends, nieces, nephews, or grandchildren—makes preparations in advance.

She removes breakable articles and those which might be dangerous from low tables. She shuts the doors to rooms she wishes to make "off limits," and she sees that doors to cellar steps and low windows are tightly closed. Then, when safety precautions are taken care of, she checks her supply of recreational materials. A basket or sack of simple toys—coloring books, blocks, comic books, wind-up cars, and many others—goes a long way toward making the visit enjoyable for both mother and hostess. And of course this same clever lady has a supply of cookies and milk or soft drinks ready to fill in when the novelty of the toys wears off.

The mother herself can make her child a welcome guest in many ways. She should not take him visiting until he learns the meaning of "No." She also may bring a basket of his favorite toys to keep him occupied. And above all, she should set herself a time limit for her visit, knowing that no toddler has a very long span of concentration. Her call should end well before that limit is reached.

Pets, no matter how well behaved at home, should not be taken along on visits unless they are invited. Fido may be irresistible to you, but to your hostess who has new rugs or upholstery, or who may be allergic to dog hairs, he may be anything but a welcome visitor. Even if he *is* invited, do not take him if he does not mind and is not housebroken. The dog who jumps on people and on furniture, who will not "sit" or "lie down" when told, and who will not come when called does not in any way enhance the pleasure of the visit.

THE UNEXPECTED VISITOR

No one, with the exception of closest friends and immediate family, should ever be an "unexpected visitor." Formal calls are never "unexpected" because in the stratum of society where they are made there are always servants to announce a visitor or say the person being called upon is not at home. In military circles, since the hours for calls are strictly prescribed, the callers are always welcome. While occasionally an unannounced "drop-in" works out well, more often it is most inconvenient to the one visited. She may have previous plans, her hair may be in curlers, her child may be sick, she may be in the middle of preparing dinner, or she may simply be resting or relaxing. The sight of an eager visitor at the door, neatly dressed and ready for an hour or two of conversation, is rarely an undiluted pleasure.

Therefore do not make a visit without making your intentions known, and agree to a time convenient for both of you. It may be done by a telephone call, or if you live some distance away, by a note. In the latter case it should be written far enough in advance so that there is time for a reply. It should not say, "We are coming on Saturday, etc.," but rather, "If you and John are free Saturday, may we drop by . . . ?"

When you are on the receiving end of one of these unannounced visits you have every right to carry on with any previous plans you might have made. If Aunt Sally arrives unexpectedly from three hundred miles away, and you had been planning to go to a church supper, you might suggest that she go along with you. If, however, you are expected at the Howards' for bridge, you simply ask her to make herself at home until your return. You should, if possible, find something in the refrigerator or the cupboard that will serve as a snack or light meal. But you need not make yourself late for your appointment by taking the time to prepare a full dinner, although you should get out the ingredients for her if she wishes to do so herself.

When the visitor is a friend or acquaintance from nearby, you merely say quite frankly, "I'm terribly sorry, but we were just leaving for dinner at the Hornsbys'. Could you come back another time?" *And make the future date definite then and there.* "Another time" left at that means little, but a firm invitation proves that you would really enjoy a visit at a more convenient moment. If your earlier plans were such that they could be carried out on another day, it would, of course, be more polite to postpone them and stay at home with your visitor.

If by chance you are just about to start your dinner when a couple drop in, you must try to make the meal stretch to include them. If they say, "Oh, no thank you—we've just eaten," pull up a chair for them, offer them a cup of coffee or a cold drink, and ask their forgiveness while you finish your meal. No one who drops in unannounced can expect you to postpone your meal to let it get cold while you visit or to produce two more portions unexpectedly.

This whole subject of drop-in visits is a sticky one. It causes more ill-feeling, hurt, and misunderstanding than almost any other single area of etiquette. This is true of both the visitor and the visited. Because the questions are so varied and relate to so many aspects of drop-in visits, I am putting the rest of this chapter into question-and-answer form, based on the letters I have received in the last few years. I believe they cover the most common problems and will help you to find the right way to handle unexpected visitors—and still remain friends!

TELEVISION

Q. We do not accept invitations to a certain friend's home, nor invite them to ours, because they have become TV sports nuts. They insist on watching every event, whether we want to or not. Ordinarily when we have company we turn off the TV so that we can talk, and we would rather our friends did the same when we visit them. Am I looking at this incorrectly?

A. No, you are not. TV is a wonderful thing, but not when it destroys sociability and our desire to communicate. It should never be allowed to take the place of friends. Sitting dumbly and staring at the "tube" is scarcely stimulating to an exchange of ideas and opinions. When you ask your friends over, make it clear that you have plans other than watching TV. When you are invited to their home, be frank. Tell them you'd love to see them, but you honestly don't care about watching the football game. If they say, "Oh, we *had* planned to watch it," just reply, "Okay, let's make it another time, then."

Q. When a friend of my wife's drops in to chat with her in the evening, must I drop my book, turn off the TV, or stop whatever I am doing to talk with them?

A. You should not be expected to join their "hen party," but you *should* come to an agreement with your wife before it happens again. You should have the courtesy to greet her friend and chat for a few minutes. Then you are free to excuse yourself to go back to your book, or if you were watching TV on your only set, *they* should grant you the consideration of going to another room to talk.

Q. When friends walk in, uninvited, and my husband and I are right in the middle of a good TV program, must we turn it off at once?

A. No. Turn it down while you greet them and then say, "We're watching a great movie about Henry the Eighth. Will you join us? It will be another half hour or so. Then we can visit or play a little bridge . . . etc." or "We're right in the middle of a really exciting hockey game. Why don't you sit down and watch it with us?"

Since the visitors were unexpected, they should not expect you to give up what you were enjoying to entertain them.

PRIVACY

Q. Recently a friend dropped in on the spur of the moment. She went through every room in the house—stuck her head in every nook and cranny—even the kitchen cabinets and the oven. I'm not a bad housekeeper, but I felt uncomfortable. Was this proper etiquette? How do you handle someone like that?

A. Your friend was very rude. If it happens again, sit yourself down firmly in the living room and ask her to sit down too. If she asks to see the house, say, "Sorry, it's not in shape today—another time." Surely she wouldn't have the gall to snoop by herself if you remain where you are!

Q. I have a neighbor who comes over frequently and walks in without knocking. She is a warm, friendly person, but this irritates my husband no end. He says we have no privacy. How can I let her know without hurting her?

A. If your neighbor is as friendly as you say, she will understand if you say, "We love to have you drop in, but you've startled John a couple of times, so would you mind giving us a warning knock?" Or you might lock your doors for a week or two, explaining that you are nervous about leaving the house open. This may establish a habit of ringing the bell.

Q. When should the front door of a house be used? Our drive leads to the back door, and I am continually embarrassed by people coming in through the kitchen, which is not in order, while the rest of the house is in readiness for the visitor. How can we persuade people to take the path around to the front door?

A. When you invite your visitors over, or when they call to say they are planning to drop by, say to them, "Please come around to the front door; we'll have the light on for you."

You may also try locking your back door for a while. Although some people will stay there and knock, most will assume you cannot hear them from the front of the house and will go around.

When uninvited guests *do* walk through your messy kitchen, just don't worry about it. No one can be expected to have every room in the house picked up all the time, and besides, the chances are they won't notice the dirty dishes anyway—especially if you don't leave the lights on!

Q. May a man sit in his shirt sleeves—on a hot night—when visitors drop in?

A. Unless your guests were invited in advance, I see no reason why a man should jump into a coat when they appear at the door. If one of the visitors is a man, ask him to take *his* coat off too, and everyone will feel more comfortable.

POSSESSIONS

Q. Is it in poor taste to ask people to use the doormat when they come in with wet or muddy feet?

A. Visitors *should* have the sense to wipe their feet without being told. But if they don't, drop a hint. Say pleasantly, "Would you mind giving your shoes an extra wipe—I've just had the rug cleaned" or "I've just waxed the hall," or whatever is appropriate.

Q. We have a carved leather table from Peru that stains easily and permanently when wet glasses are put down on it. We put out coasters, but our guests often do not seem to see them. We value our possessions, but we value our friends too. How can we tactfully make them aware of the damage they are doing?

A. No one will criticize you for taking reasonable precautions to protect your table. When you see someone about to put the glass down, push a coaster toward it and say, "Would you mind using a coaster—this table stains so quickly." Say it loudly enough so that others nearby will take the hint too.

Q. I get very annoyed at people who sit on my upholstered furniture with their feet tucked up under them. What can I do about this habit?

A. You can't do much at a formal party, but I doubt it would happen on that type of occasion anyway. When it is just a group of girls (I've never seen a man do this) who are good friends, you can say, "Why don't you take your shoes off? I'm trying to keep that chair from having to be recovered for a while."

Q. Why don't guests ever use the guest towels I put out instead of the family towels?

A. I suspect it is because the family towels are larger. Men, especially, have trouble drying their hands on the little "trifles" known as guest towels. If you buy a few medium-sized terry-cloth hand towels and put them near the sink—on a rack or folded in a pile—I suspect that your problem will be solved.

Q. When you use a guest towel in someone's powder room what are you supposed to do with it if there is no hamper?

A. Leave it on the towel rack unfolded, so that it it is obvious it has been used. When a hostess gives a large party she should get a supply of good quality paper hand towels if she does not have room for a hamper for used cloth towels. The paper towels can be thrown into a small wastebasket, which can surely be fitted into the powder room somehow.

FOOD AND DRINK

Q. I dropped in on a friend last week, and we visited for over an hour. There was a bowl of mixed candies and nuts on a table beside me. She didn't pass them or suggest that I take one, and although I was hungry I was embarrassed to help myself. Would I have been rude to do so?

A. Not at all. When nuts or candy are right there it is because they are meant to be enjoyed. Your hostess just wasn't thinking or she would have offered you one. Next time get up and say, "Those candies look delicious—may I try one?"

Q. Last night friends dropped in after dinner and I offered them a cup of coffee. The lady said, "I can't drink coffee at night, but I'd love a cup of Sanka." I didn't have any decaffeinated coffee and was embarrassed. Wasn't she rude to put me on the spot like that?

A. You were wrong to some extent. So many people prefer caffein-free coffee that everyone should try to keep some on hand and offer it when serving coffee. But your guest would have been far more tactful if she had said, "I can't take coffee, thanks—it keeps me awake," leaving *you* the alternative of offering something else.

Q. Should a small child ask the hostess for something to eat or drink when his mother has taken him along on a drop-in visit?

A. Unless the visit is to be a long one, the child should be told *ahead of time* not to ask for snacks. A thoughtful hostess will *offer* him something, but if she doesn't, it may be because she has nothing in the larder, and it will only embarrass her if either the child or his mother brings it up.

PARKING FEES

Q. I live in an apartment house with a garage. The parking goes from $1.50 for one hour to $4 for twenty-four hours. It is impossible to park in the city streets near us. When friends come to see us, should I offer to pay their parking fee, or is it their responsibility?

A. You are not obligated to pay the parking fee. Automobile owners know that there are parking costs in every city and should accept it as a small expense in return for a pleasant evening.

AH-CHOO!

Q. Don't you think it is the height of ignorance and thoughtlessness for people with bad colds to drop in on friends, spreading their germs all over the house? They always say, "Oh, I'm not contagious anymore," as they cough and sneeze and drip away! They also have been known to say they were feeling so awful that they had to get out and get their minds off their aches and pains!

A. I thoroughly agree! Cold sufferers should keep their coughs, their sneezes, their drips, and their misery at home. To spread their cold just because they are bored with their own company *is* the height of inconsiderateness.

THE VISIT ENDS

Q. Our apartment is at the end of a long hall. When guests are leaving I close the door behind them right away. My husband thinks we should keep the door open until the guests enter the elevator. Who is right?

A. Your husband is right. Not infrequently elevators operate erratically, and to be sure that your guests are safely on their way, you should watch from your open door until you see that the elevator has stopped for them. Then give a final wave if they look back, and shut your door.

Q. Our house is fifty or sixty feet from the street. When our guests leave should we walk down the path to their car with them and wait at the curb until they drive off? Or do we just say good-bye at the door?

A. If the weather is good, walk out to the car with your friends and stay there until they drive off. If it is rainy or cold, say good-bye at the door. If it is not *too* cold, leave the door open until they reach their car; then wave a last "good-night" and shut the door.

WHEN YOU DROP IN

Q. When you drop in on a friend in the afternoon and find her playing bridge, what should you do? When this happened to me I was already in the house and had my coat off before I saw what she was doing.

A. Even though the hostess urges you to stay, don't. It will inevitably put a "damper" on their game, and you will feel like a fifth wheel. When you drop in on someone and find her and her guests occupied with anything other than a general conversation, make up any excuse you can think of and leave as quickly as you gracefully can.

Q. The other night my husband and I went for a walk after dinner and decided to drop in on a neighbor. To our embarrassment, she was having a small party. She urged us to stay, but I said we couldn't, and we went home. My husband thinks I was very unfriendly. Do you?

A. Not *very* unfriendly, but a little. If the people there were all friends of yours and if they had *obviously finished dinner*, you might have stayed for a little while, since you were "urged" to do so. This would not be so if the group were playing bride or any game that requires a certain number of players.

~§58§~ *On the Telephone*

When you talk on the telephone, whether in your home or in an office, the quality of your voice and your ability to express yourself clearly and concisely are of utmost importance. The person at the other end of the line cannot, after all, see your facial expressions or gestures, and the impression he receives must depend entirely on what he hears.

The telephone is designed to carry your voice at its natural volume and pitch. It is not necessary to shout. In fact raising your voice, especially during a long-distance call, will only distort it. The telephone transmitter should be held about one inch from your lips and the earpiece close to your ear. Speak clearly and distinctly, with the same inflections that you would use in a face-to-face conversation. If you must put the telephone down during the conversation, do it gently, and when you hang up, do not slam the receiver down. The person at the other end may still have the phone close to his ear, and the sudden sharp bang can be quite deafening.

THE BUSINESS TELEPHONE

ANSWERING THE OFFICE PHONE

When telephone calls go through a switchboard the operator usually answers the ring by giving the name of the company only. Some firms, however, feel that a more friendly impression is made on the caller by the greeting "ABC Company, good morning," or "Good afternoon, ABC Company."

When the call goes directly through to an office or has been transferred by the switchboard operator, it should be answered promptly. The person answering should identify himself and his department: "Mr. Hugo, accounting department." If answering for someone else, as a secretary does, she should give her employer's name as well as her own: "Mr. Carlson's office, Miss Norton speaking." If her employer is not in, or if she wishes to protect him from unnecessary calls, she should then offer to help the caller if she can or if she cannot, to take a message: "He's not available at the moment. May I take a message?" or "He's out of the office just now. May I have him call you?" or "He's attending a meeting this morning. Could I help you?" If he is in his office she asks, "May I tell him who is calling?" Any of these phrases should elicit the necessary information without the abruptness of "Who's calling?" But if the caller is evasive she may have to ask for his name more directly: "Who is calling, please?" is sometimes necessary.

PLACING A BUSINESS CALL

When placing a call be sure that you have the correct number. A wrong number wastes your time and that of the person who answers the call.

As soon as your call is answered, you must identify yourself; and unless the person you are calling knows you well, you should also name your organization: "This is Mr. Kramer of the Hobbs Company. May I speak to Mr. Hughes?"

A salesman does not ordinarily announce himself as Sam Jones to the operator or secretary who answers. Correctly he says, "This is Mr. Jones of the Hi-Fly Company." But when he reaches the man he is calling, he omits the "Mr." and uses "Sam."

A woman in business follows the same rules.

All names must be given as explicitly and as clearly as is humanly possible.

A very discourteous telephone habit is that of the businessman who tells his secretary to call Mr. Jones and then is not waiting to take the call. For example, the secretary dials the number, a voice announces, "A. B. Jones Company," and the secretary says, "Mr. Frank Brown is calling Mr. Jones." Promptly Mr. Jones says, "Hello, Frank," but instead of hearing Frank's voice he hears a secretary explain, "Mr. Brown is busy on another wire. He'll be with you in a moment." Mr. Jones listens good-temperedly a few seconds—and less patiently for more seconds. Mr. Brown is evidently unaware that seconds seem minutes to a busy person listening to a dead receiver.

Initiating a call on a second line after putting in a call on the first shows nothing but rudeness to someone who, having been called to the telephone, is then asked to wait!

The correct form for a wife calling her husband at his office is, "This is Mrs. Jones. Is Mr. Jones in?"

THE TELEPHONE IN THE HOME

"HELLO" CORRECT AT HOME

The best way to answer a house telephone is still "Hello." "Yes" is abrupt and sounds a bit rude, but "This is Mrs. Jones's house" leaves the door standing open wide, and "Mrs. Jones speaking" leaves her without a chance to retreat.

This is not nonsense. It is a really important aspect of modern telephone etiquette. In all big cities telephones are rung so persistently by every type of stranger who wants to sell something to Mrs. Householder, to ask a favor of Mrs. Prominent, or to get in touch with Mr. Official (having failed to reach him at his office) that many prominent people are obliged to keep their personal telephone numbers unlisted.

THE CALLER GIVES HIS NAME

I cannot emphasize strongly enough how helpful and courteous it is to give one's name as soon as the person at the other end answers your call. *What* name you give depends on how well you know, or are known to, the person who answers. But if your call is a legitimate one and you therefore have no reason to hide your identity, *give your name at once.* Here are some of the ordinary forms:

To a maid or secretary: "This is Mrs. Franklin. Is Mrs. Harvey in?"

To a child who answers: "This is Mrs. Franklin. Is your mother in?"

When you recognize the voice answering: "Hello, John. This is Helen. Is Sue there?"

When the person you are calling answers: "Hi, Sue, this is Helen," or "Hello, Mrs. Brooks. This is Helen Franklin."

When a man calls a woman on a business matter: "Mrs. Franklin, this is George Forester," or "George Forester at the Home Oil Company."

An older person calling a younger one says: "This is Mrs. [or Mr.] Bailey."

A young person calling an older man or woman says: "Hello, Mrs. [or Mr.] Knox. This is Janet Frost."

WHO IS CALLING, PLEASE?

Unfortunately not everyone does give his name, and he may simply respond to your "Hello" by saying, "May I speak to Mrs. Franklin?" or "Is Mrs. Franklin in?" In this case the person who answered—especially if he recognizes the voice—may simply say, "Just a moment, please," if the call is for someone else, or "This is Mrs. Franklin," or "This is she." Most people, however, prefer the person who answers to ask who the caller is before coming to the phone. It used to be considered rather "snoopy" if a maid said, "May I tell her who is calling?" or a child said, "Who is this, please?" But with the widespread use of the phone today, and the variety of reasons for calls, a slight warning is often very helpful to the person being called. For example: Mrs. Franklin is upstairs when the telephone, which is downstairs, rings. It is the president of her club, asking how many people have accepted the invitation for the Christmas dance. If her daughter, who answers, doesn't get the caller's name, Mrs. Franklin runs down, answers, runs back up to her desk to get her lists, and back down again. If her daughter had said, "Mom, it's Mrs. Harrison for you," Mrs. Franklin would have taken the lists down the first time.

So, if it sometimes seems a little rude to ask the caller's identity, it stems from the caller's rudeness in not identifying himself.

When a woman or a child is alone in the house, it is not a matter of courtesy—it is a matter of safety. Many calls are made just to find out whether a house is empty, or whether there is a man or an adult at home. If the woman or child who answers does not recognize the voice that asks for "Mr. Householder," she (or he) *must* say, "Who is this, please?" Then, if the name is unfamiliar and the caller does not further identify himself, she does *not* say, "He's not home." She says instead, "He's busy just now" or "He's not available just now—may he return your call?" "Not available" is an excellent excuse for a child to give when his parents are out because it is true and yet it *implies* that they are there but can't come to the phone for the moment. Under no circumstances should children ever admit that they are alone in the house.

INVITATIONS BY TELEPHONE

There are no rules about what you say to a friend when you call to invite him or her to a party, but there are a couple of things you should consider. You should never start out by saying, "Hi, Mary. What are you doing Saturday night?" or "Are you busy Sunday afternoon?" This maneuver puts Mary in the embarrassing position of saying "Nothing" and then not being able to refuse after being told that she is being asked to dine with the Borings or to play golf with the Shanks. On the other hand, if she answers, "I have an engagement," and is then told that she would have been invited to something she likes very much, it is disappointing to be unable to go. A young woman who says she "is busy" and is then told, "Too bad you can't come, because John Brilliant was looking forward to meeting you," cannot change her mind and say, "Oh, then I'll get out of my dinner somehow and come." To do so would be thoroughly rude to everyone concerned.

Therefore when issuing a telephone invitation, start right out with it: "Hi, Mary, we're having a few people in Saturday night for dinner and bridge. Can you and Hank come?" Mary is free to accept, knowing it is just what she would enjoy Saturday night, or to say, "I'm so sorry but we are busy Saturday," if she hates to play bridge.

In responding to a telephone invitation, it is very rude to say, "I'll let you know," unless it is immediately followed by an explanation, such as 'I'll have to ask John if he has made any commitments for that weekend" or "We have tickets for the high-school play for that night, but perhaps I can exchange them for two on Friday." Without this definite sort of reason, "I'll let you know" sounds as though you are waiting for a better invitation to come along before saying "Yes."

FOUR IMPORTANT DON'TS

When you get a wrong number, don't ask, "What number is this?" Ask instead, "Is this Main 2–3456?" so that you can look it up again or dial more carefully the next time.

Don't answer and then say, "Wait a minute," and keep the caller waiting while you vanish on an errand of your own. If the doorbell is ringing and you can't listen at that moment, say, "I'll call you back in a few minutes!" And do so.

Don't let too young a child answer the telephone. A lot of the caller's time is wasted trying to make the child understand a message and relay it to the right person. If there is a long silence, there is no way of knowing whether the child is hunting for Mother or playing with his dog.

Don't hang up before letting the telephone ring at least six times. Nothing is more irritating than to rush down from the attic or out of the bathtub to answer and find that the caller has hung up.

TERMINATING TELEPHONE CALLS

Under ordinary circumstances the person who originates the call is the one who terminates it. This is not a matter of great importance, but it is helpful to know if a call seems to be dragging on and getting nowhere. The caller simply says, "I'm so glad I reached you—we'll be looking forward to seeing you on the seventh. Good-bye," or any other appropriate remark.

The person who places the call is also the one who calls again when you are cut off in the middle of a conversation.

We have all been trapped on the telephone by a long-winded caller—a determined salesman, perhaps, or a loquacious friend. When you have made several tentative efforts to end the conversation, which have been completely ignored, you may take more aggressive measures. At the first pause, or even interrupting if necessary, you may say, "I'm terribly sorry, but I simply must hang up—the baby's crying," or "My bath is running over," or even "I'm late for an appointment now."

Another occasion on which a call should be terminated quickly is when the person who receives it has a visitor—either in a business office or at home. It is very inconsiderate to carry on a long chat while your visitor tries to occupy the time and avoid listening to your conversation. When you answer the phone and find it is not a call that can be terminated in a moment or two, you should postpone it for a more convenient time. At home you might say, "Joan just dropped in for a visit, so may I call you back in a little while?" The businessman could say, "I have a customer with me at the moment. If you will give me your number, I'll call you back when I am free."

In either case be sure that you do return the call as soon as you can.

On the other hand, if you are making a call that you know will take a considerable time, or if you want to settle down for a nice long chat, it is a good idea to say to your friend, "Is this a good time to call?" or "Have you a few minutes to chat?" If more people did this there would be fewer complaints about the "nuisance" and "invasion of privacy" of telephone calls.

LONG-DISTANCE CALLS

When making a long-distance call, remember not to shout—amplifiers on the circuits will step up your voice all the way. On some overseas calls, it is also important to wait for the other person to finish speaking before you start. It can be a one-way-at-a-time circuit, and if both speak at once, both are shut off until one or the other stops talking.

Keep on the tip of your tongue what you have to say, and say it promptly. If you have several things to say, write them down and read them off.

If you call long distance often, a telephone timer is a must. It is a small second-counting gadget that rings a bell before each three minutes. If you are making a personal call and the person on the other end of the line likes to talk on and on, when you put in your call you may ask the operator to interrupt when the three minutes are up. But in these days of direct dialing, you will do well to have a timer—even a three-minute egg timer—at hand, for you may never have a chance to speak to the operator.

INFORMATION, PLEASE

It is quite true that the telephone operator who answers when we dial Information is prepared to answer our questions, but it is not at all true that she can be expected to overcome our lazy carelessness.

Strangely enough, it is not our oldest generation who find it difficult to read the small print in the telephone book (a small magnifying glass near the telephone will help the farsighted). On the contrary, investigation by the telephone company has found that the numerous unnecessary calls made to Information, which at times literally cripple service—especially in our cities—are made by the young. If for some reason you have to ask for a number, and it is one you think you will call again, write it down.

ON A PARTY LINE

The usual number of families sharing a party line is four, and the maximum ten. When you realize that while one person is talking no outside call can reach any other person on that line, it is obvious that each one must show consideration for the others.

Ordinarily, when you find the line in use, you hang up for three minutes before signaling again. In an emergency it is permissible to break in on a conversation and call out clearly, *"Emergency!"* and then, "Our barn is on fire," or "Johnny's had an accident," or whatever it is. But unless everyone on the line hangs up, your telephone is cut off.

Callers on a party line should limit their calls to five minutes—ten at the very most.

During the Vietnam War a soldier tried to say a few last words to his wife just before his plane took off for Saigon. For fifty minutes the long-distance operator repeatedly received a "busy-wire" signal. At the last moment he remembered that while the operator is not permitted to cut in on a busy wire, her supervisor can. He quickly asked for the supervisor and briefly explained the situation to her. Calling it an "emergency" she cut in, announced a long-distance call for Mrs. Soldier, and asked those talking to hang up, please, so that she could receive it.

OBSCENE CALLS

The best way to handle the occasional obscene call is to hang up immediately. Don't give the caller the satisfaction of hearing you become upset, or even responding. If, as sometimes happens, the call is repeated as soon as you hang up, leave the receiver off the hook for a little while. If the caller is a youngster looking for a laugh, or a random-number-picking pervert, he will soon give up when he keeps hearing the busy signal.

If you are subjected to such calls regularly, you should, of course, notify the telephone company. They can, and will, in serious cases, try to trace the calls.

There is also another effective remedy that will discourage the occasional caller. Keep an ordinary police whistle by the phone, and as soon as you hear the first obscene word, blow a hard blast right into your speaker. That caller will drop you from his list of victims there and then.

PAYING FOR YOUR CALLS

ON A NEIGHBOR'S TELEPHONE

Today almost everyone has his own telephone, but sometimes, especially in resort areas, there are people who become embarrassing and expensive nuisances by using a neighbor's telephone over and over again, not only for local calls but for long-distance ones too.

Those who live in a town where local calls are not charged for individually or who seldom use their allotted number of calls may find frequent use of their telephone annoying, but not an added expense, unless long-distance calls are made. Where the system is such that even a local call is charged for, it should be just as correct to present an itemized bill for the charges on your telephone bill as it would be to present a bill for eggs or chickens, which you would never hesitate to do.

For an occasional local call, you might let it go; but for a telephone borrower who makes many long-distance calls, it is simplest as well as most accurate to show him the toll list so that he can check his calls and pay you the total. Local calls that are charged for individually will also be listed on the bill and should be shown to the person who made them.

Try to avoid making calls from a busy doctor's (or other) office, but if you must do so, pay the nurse for the call or use a telephone credit card.

BY VISITORS AND HOUSEGUESTS

Many visitors forget to offer to pay for their calls. The definite rule is this: Should a houseguest be obliged to make a local call or two, he would not ordinarily offer payment for it, but it is absolutely required that he pay for every long-distance call. Moreover, this is the only way in which a houseguest can feel free to telephone as often as he or she may want to. One way the guest can pay is to call the operator as soon as he has finished speaking and ask for "the toll charge on 212–468–9121." The necessary amount should be left with a slip, giving the date and the number called. If it is a substantial amount, he should add the tax. Or if a visitor has used the telephone a great deal during a long stay, the complete list of calls or telegrams with the amounts of each and their total should be handed to the hostess and paid for when he leaves. This is not humiliating, and no matter how rich the host may be, this debt must be paid.

An even more satisfactory way is to charge the call to your own home number. This may be done even though you do not have a telephone company credit card. The operator may or may not call your home and ask whoever is there if he will accept the charge. You must, of course, warn those at home in advance in case she does. This system saves you the annoyance of finding correct change or cash to pay your hostess, and saves her the inconvenience of a larger bill. If you have a telephone credit card, by all means use that.

One additional note about houseguests: They should not answer the phone while visiting unless they say, "Would you like me to answer?" or the hostess says, "I'm in the tub—would you take that call, Sue?"

A TELEPHONE COURTESY TEST

If it interests you to know how good your telephone manners may be, the number of times you can answer "Yes" to the following questions will give you your rating. If every one is "Yes," you deserve not merely a crown, but a halo!

1. Do you make sure of the correct number so as not to risk disturbing strangers by "calling from memory"?
2. Do you make sure that your conversations with busy people are as brief as possible?
3. When calling intimate friends who do not recognize your voice, do you resist playing the game of "guess who?" and announce yourself promptly?
4. Do you try to time your calls so as not to interfere with the occupations of those you call most often?
5. Do you make business calls well before the close of office hours, especially if calling a person you know is a commuter?
6. In a business office do you explain to personal friends inclined to talk at length that you will call them after hours?
7. Do you treat wrong-number calls as a mutual inconvenience and answer, "Sorry, wrong number," in a tone of polite sympathy instead of showing ill-tempered annoyance?
8. On a dial telephone do you always wait for the dial tone?
9. When the number you are calling is not answered quickly, do you wait long enough for someone to lay aside what he or she may be doing and to reach the telephone? It is very annoying to have been disturbed just to pick up the telephone and find the caller has hung up.
10. When making a number of calls on a party line do you space them so that others on the line may have a chance to use their telephones?

☜59☞ For Those Who Smoke

There is no question that smokers cause more distress to nonsmokers than vice versa. Therefore the burden of courtesy falls on the smoker—who must make sure that he is not offending anyone when he smokes his cigarette.

There are so many nonsmokers today that whenever a smoker is surrounded by or is with people he does not know he should ask, "Do you mind if I smoke?" This would be true at a large dinner, on a train, at a business meeting; in short, anyplace where the people in close proximity might be bothered by the smoke. People who are asked that question should feel free to say, "I'm sorry, but smoke really does make me feel sick," or whatever is the case. The smoker who was polite enough to ask the question must also be polite enough to respect the answer.

Some people hesitate to speak out, and say, instead, "Go right ahead." The smoker is certainly free to do so, but if he notices any hesitancy or shying away, he might ask, "Are you sure?" or even wait until later to light up.

In any case there are some rules and some suggestions that will make smoking safer, more tolerable for the nonsmokers, and pleasanter for the person enjoying the cigarette.

JUST A REMINDER

In the following places there is almost always a "no-smoking" sign posted, but just in case you don't notice it you should be constantly aware that smoking is not permitted in the following situations:

One may not smoke in a church or during any religious service or ceremonial proceeding.

731

One may not smoke in a sickroom at home unless the patient himself is smoking or unless he specifically says that his visitor is welcome to smoke. In a hospital, smoking is not permitted except with a doctor's permission in a private room, or in the waiting rooms or solariums on each floor. Even though ashtrays are in evidence in a doctor's waiting room, it is thoughtful to ask if others waiting object to smoking.

One may not smoke or carry a lighted cigarette when dancing. It is not only unattractive—it is very dangerous.

Smoking is forbidden on local buses and on some coaches or sections of cars on the railroad. There are "no-smoking" sections on all planes.

Smoking is permitted in the mezzanine or loge seats in some movie houses, and only in certain designated sections in the main orchestra. Whether it is allowed at all depends on local and state ordinances.

Smoking is forbidden in museums and at galleries, although some have designated areas where it is allowed.

Legitimate theaters do not allow smoking in the theater proper. It is usually allowed in the outer lobby, and those who wish to smoke during the intermission go there to do so. It is perfectly correct for a man who wishes to smoke to leave a lady who doesn't, but he should hurry back and not leave her too frequently.

Smoking is forbidden in all department stores and in many smaller stores.

To these restrictions should be added those in business offices (regulated by the rules of each firm). Finally, one should always consider the customs of the community which he may be visiting or the prejudices of the people with whom he comes in contact.

WHEN GUESTS SMOKE

When I am asked by a hostess how she can protect her possessions from careless smokers, my answer is that hospitality need never be helpless. It is true that after a guest has burned a hole in the upholstery or a groove on a table edge, nothing can be done about it, except that the guest should insist on paying for whatever repairs are necessary. But when a hostess sees a smoker pick up a coaster or an antique bowl to use in place of an ashtray, she can certainly take it away and put an ashtray in its place. She need say nothing or she may smile and say, "Let me give you this," as though she were thinking of the smoker's convenience.

The sensible solution for the wise hostess is to see to it that there is an ashtray within easy reach of every seat that may be occupied by a smoking guest. A thoughtful hostess, even one who does not smoke herself, will see that there are cigarette boxes with fresh cigarettes in them and a lighter that is filled and that works—or plenty of matchboxes—for the comfort of her smoking guests. Ashtrays should be reasonably large and have a wide lip or groove to hold a cigarette.

Whether it is proper to smoke at table depends upon the setting of the places. If each place is set with an ashtray, naturally people may smoke as soon as they choose. However, in the houses where cigarettes are not on the table or where they are passed only after dessert, it is bad manners to light one's own cigarette and smoke throughout the meal.

Cigars are passed only after dinner, usually when the ladies have left the dining room.

A WORD TO THE NONSMOKING HOSTESS

I receive a great many letters from women wanting to know if they must put up with people smoking in their houses. Here is my answer:

A hostess' first obligation is to make her guests as happy and as comfortable as possible—in short, to give them a good time.

Many nonsmokers do not realize how much their friends who are "hooked" on the smoking habit need their cigarettes and how unhappy they would be without them. Therefore, whatever you feel personally about smoking, as a hostess it is not your place or your duty to submit your friends to a smokeless evening. If you feel more strongly about the smell of smoke in your home or the cigarette butts in your ashtrays than you do about your friendship with certain people, you should not ask those people to your house, or you should wait until summer when you can entertain them outdoors.

SMOKING "DON'TS"

It is unforgivable to lay a cigarette (or cigar) on the edge of a table or other piece of furniture. Forgetting it and letting it burn a charred groove on a table edge or a mantel is the inevitable result of putting it down on the wrong place to begin with. Find an ashtray to lay it on—or ask for one.

Don't strike a match toward someone—the head may fly off and cause a painful burn.

Never press a cigarette out without being sure that the object pressed on is intended for that purpose. Cigarettes put out against lamp bases, ornaments, and the like may mar or destroy objects of value. And potted plants do not thrive on unburned cigarette butts!

Lighted cigarettes should not be thrown into fireplaces unless a fire is already burning. If the fire is laid, a roaring blaze when it is not wanted may result, and if it is not, remains of cigarettes or unburned filter tips look dreadfully messy in a freshly swept fireplace. Never toss a cigarette out the window—it may land on an awning or the top of someone's new convertible parked outside.

Don't throw filter-tipped cigarettes on a lawn or terrace where the fireproof, rainproof tip will remain until someone rakes or sweeps it away. And worst of all!—never leave a lighted cigarette in the ashtray to burn itself out, making even the other smokers present ill from the smell.

Don't smoke in close proximity to infants—especially on trains, planes, etc.

If there are no ashtrays on the tables in waiting rooms or offices, wait until your visit is over to "light up."

Don't smoke in a car unless you have the permission of the other occupants.

Never throw a lighted cigarette out of a car window. Millions of acres of our forests have been destroyed through this kind of carelessness.

Don't let your smoke drift into anyone else's face. If you are the victim of a thoughtless smoker, you are perfectly free to say, "Would you mind holding your cigarette on the other side? The smoke is blowing right into my face."

If you are a pipe smoker, don't tap out the ashes on delicate glass or china ashtrays. Find a good solid one—preferably of metal.

Cigar smokers, because so many people dislike the smell, must be especially careful. Don't leave cigar butts in ashtrays. They *do* smell, and they *are* unattractive. Unless you see that someone is prepared to remove the ashtray when you have finished smoking, try to find another means of disposing of the cigar butt—into a lighted fire, down the toilet, anywhere, as long as it is out of sight.

A FEW HINTS ON SMOKING MANNERS

All smokers should carry their own cigarettes. Even though a hostess has filled her cigarette boxes, she will appreciate the guest who does not depend entirely on her supply.

When you are about to smoke you should offer a cigarette to the people next to you or in your immediate group, but you need not pass them farther afield. And a warning to the ladies: The female cigarette "sponge" is no more popular than the male.

A man should light a woman's cigarette if he is close to her but not if he is on the other side of a table or if it would be awkward in any way. As far as that goes, a woman should do the same for a man if she is the one who has the lighter or match close at hand.

When you are in a restaurant with a hurricane lamp or candle on the table, you may use it to light a cigarette. Don't remove the chimney of the hurricane lamp. Just pull it toward you and hold your cigarette over the top. The intense heat there will light it quickly.

Speaking of candles, a burning candle on a table absorbs cigarette smoke. This tip should help hostesses who want their smoking guests to enjoy themselves but don't want a smoke-filled room.

At a formal dinner you should not light a cigarette from a candle or candelabra. It is all right to do so, however, in informal surroundings.

⤳60⤫ In Clubs

A club is an organization composed of persons who have gotten together for their individual convenience or pleasure. Its membership, whether composed of men or women or both, may be limited to a dozen or may include several thousand, and the procedure of joining may be easy or difficult, according to the type of club and the standing of the would-be member.

Membership in athletic associations, YM or YWCAs, health clubs, and many other organizations may be had by walking in and paying dues, and many golf "clubs" are as free to the public as country inns. But joining a private club is a very different matter. To be eligible for membership in such a club, you must have among the members friends who like you enough to be willing to propose and second you and write letters for you; furthermore you must not be disliked so much that a member might raise a serious objection to your company.

JOINING A PRIVATE CLUB

There are two ways of joining a club: by invitation and by application. To join by invitation sometimes means that you are invited when the club is started to be one of the founders or charter members. If you are a distinguished citizen you may at the invitation of the governors become an honorary member; or in a small or informal club you may become an ordinary member by invitation or at the suggestion of the governors that you would be welcome. A charter member pays dues, but not always an initiation fee. An honorary member pays neither dues nor initiation fees; he is really a permanent guest of the club, or a temporary one—as in the case of a mayor, for example, who may be an honorary member just for the duration of his term in office. A life member is one who after paying his dues for twenty years or so in a lump sum is thereafter exempted from dues even if the annual dues should be greatly increased in later years or he should live to be a hundred.

To join an established club by application is quite different. Let us suppose that Jim Ordway has decided that he would like to join the Shoreside Club. Since, presumably, he would not wish to join unless he had friends among the members, he would discuss it with the closest of them, Bill Parks, and ask, "Would you be willing to put me up?" Bill would probably reply that he would be delighted and would suggest Ron Krebbs as a seconder.

It must be remembered that a man has no right to ask anyone who is not really one of his best friends to propose or second him. It is an awkward thing to refuse in the first place; in the second, recommending someone involves considerable effort and on occasion a great deal of annoyance, to say nothing of responsibility.

Very often the suggestion to join comes from the member, who remarks one day, "Why don't you join the Shoreside Club? It would be very convenient for you, the food is excellent, and I know you'd like most of the members."

Whatever way the decision is made, Bill Parks informs the club secretary that he is proposing Jim Ordway as a member, and at the proper time Jim's name is posted—meaning that it appears among a list of nominees put up on the bulletin board in the clubhouse. In many clubs a list of proposed names is also sent to each member. It is then the duty of Bill and Ron each to write a letter of endorsement to the governors of the club, to be read by that body when they hold the meeting at which Jim's name comes up for election. Such a letter might read:

> *June 10, 1975*
> *Arbor Lane*
> *Madison*
> *Connecticut 06443*

Board of Governors
The Shoreside Club
New Haven, Connecticut

Dear Sirs:
I am delighted to propose Mr. James Ordway for membership in the Shoreside Club. I have known him for many years and consider him qualified in every way for membership.
He is a graduate of Wesleyan University, class of 1961, where he was president of Delta Psi and secretary of the senior class. He

*is a member of the Center Club in New York City. He is vice-president
of the firm of Jones, Fairbanks, & Co.*

*I know that Jim would be a great addition to our membership
and hope that you will agree.*

> Yours very truly,
> **William Parks**

In most clubs the number of members is limited by the bylaws.
Therefore there may be a waiting list, necessitating a considerable
delay before Jim's name comes up for consideration. Before making
a decision as to which clubs you wish to join, find out about the length
of waiting time and discuss the possibilities with your sponsor.

Bill Parks must also select, with Jim's help, the required number
of friends who are members of the club (but not governors) and ask
them to write letters endorsing him. Furthermore, the candidate
cannot come up for election unless he knows several of the governors
personally so that they can vouch for him at the meeting. Bill and
Ron must therefore take Jim to several governors and personally
present him.

At many clubs the governors set aside an hour on several weekend afternoons before elections for meeting candidates at the clubhouse. Or a large reception may be held, attended by the governors,
the candidates, and their sponsors.

In all but very rare instances events run smoothly; the candidate
is voted on at a meeting of the board of governors and is elected.
A notice is mailed to him next morning, telling him that he has been
elected and that his initiation fee and his dues make a total of so
much. The candidate at once draws his check for the amount and
mails it. As soon as the club secretary has had ample time to receive
the check, the new member is free to use the club as much or as little
as he likes.

Any member who knows anything definitely objectionable
about the candidate should write a letter voicing his criticism to the
board. One or two such letters (called blackballs) are enough in some
circumstances, and especially in very exclusive clubs, to disqualify
the prospective member.

In the unfortunate event that a candidate is "blackballed," the
governors do not vote on him at all, but inform the proposer that
the name of his candidate had better be withdrawn, which is almost
invariably done. Later on, if the objection to him is disproved or
overcome, his name may again be put up.

The procedure described above is essentially the same for any
private club—city or country, for men or for women.

THE NEW MEMBER

The new member usually, though not necessarily, goes to a club for the first time with his proposer or his seconder, or at least with an old member, who briefs him on unwritten information: "They always play double stakes at this table, so don't sit at it unless you mean to." "There's an unwritten rule that we never walk on the grass in the circle." "The roasts are always good, and that waiter is the best in the room." And so on.

A new member is given or should ask for a copy of the club book, which contains, besides the list of members, the constitution and the bylaws or "house rules," which he must study carefully and be sure to obey.

He should also show his appreciation to his sponsor and seconder by more than just a casual "thanks." He should write a letter to each, and if it is practical, entertain them at his home, at his new club, or with an evening of dinner and the theater—depending on his means.

COUNTRY CLUBS AND YACHT CLUBS

Country clubs and yacht clubs vary tremendously in both characteristics and expense. It is as difficult (or more so) to be elected to some as to an exclusive city club, and yet there are hundreds of others where it is only necessary to know a member or two and have them vouch for your integrity and decent behavior.

MUNICIPAL CLUBS

There are also an infinite number of golf, tennis, beach, and sailing clubs run by municipalities and counties and states. The only requirements for joining these clubs are that you live in the town (or county or state) that sponsors the club and that you can afford to pay the dues and fees. Anyone moving to an area that offers these facilities may request an application-for-membership blank at the town or state offices and join by paying the initiation fee. In "public" clubs of this sort membership is renewed each year. The facilities in many are excellent, and they provide a welcome means of enjoying your leisure time for far less money and in a more simple and integrated atmosphere than the private club affords.

PRIVATE COUNTRY CLUBS

Different clubs offer different types of membership. At some country clubs you might join as a "golfing member," using only the golfing facilities; at another you might be a "house member," using only the restaurant and facilities of the clubhouse. Or it may depend on where you live—the ordinary members of a club might be resident, meaning that they live or have their offices within fifty miles of the club, or nonresident, living beyond that distance and paying smaller dues but having the same privileges.

Many country clubs have, however, one type of membership unknown to city clubs. People taking houses in the neighborhood or vacation visitors in a resort are often granted "season privileges"; that is, on being proposed by a member and upon paying a season's subscription, temporary householders are accepted as transient guests. In some clubs this membership may be indefinitely renewed; in others the member must come up for regular election at the end of three or six months' or a year's time.

Because they are, almost without exception, family clubs, the atmosphere in country clubs—whether they feature golf, tennis, or sailing—is informal. Members feel free to talk to anyone without an introduction, golf foursomes and tennis matches are set up by comparative strangers, and sailing crews are made up of people who meet casually at the bar.

During the week most country clubs belong to the women and children. Mothers bring their toddlers to spend the day at the pool or on the beach, while the older ones are kept busy with "day-camp" activities—tennis lessons, sailing races, lifesaving courses, etc. In the evening, when the men arrive for a cooling swim, and on weekends, the premises belong primarily to the adults.

Young children should not be "turned loose," even on weekdays. A mother or baby-sitter should always be with them to see that they don't dig holes in the lawn, dump dirt in the pool, or throw sand over the sun-worshipers. If parents take their children to the club on weekends, they should see that they are reasonably quiet, reasonably well dressed, and that they stick to the parts of the club that are intended for their use. In other words they are not welcome on the golf course (unless playing *golf,* of course), in the bar, or in the formal dining rooms, except when they are with their parents.

GUESTS IN CLUBS

While there is no limit on bringing guests to the restaurants of most clubs—in fact they welcome the added revenue—your common sense should dictate the frequency. If one person returns with you again and again, it is inevitable that you *and* he will be criticized: "If Joe likes our club so much, it's about time he became a member."

Also, when a member couple invite guests to play tennis or paddle tennis they are using a court that might otherwise be shared with another member. While everyone is happy to see outsiders enjoying the club facilities no one likes to be told time and time again, "Sorry, there are no courts—the Joneses and their guests are signed up."

When you do invite guests to your club they should be people who are compatible with the membership. No matter what your particular feelings are about politics, race, or religion, you should not make your club the place to launch a crusade. If you don't like the limitations or policies of a particular club and are not willing to abide by them, don't join it!

Most clubs that have residential facilities will extend club privileges to a stranger—one who lives beyond a specified distance—for a varying length of time determined by the bylaws of the club. In some clubs guests may be put up for a day only; in others the privilege extends for two weeks or more. Many clubs allow each member a certain number of visitors a year; in others visitors are unlimited. In some city clubs the same guest cannot be introduced twice within the year. In country clubs members usually may have an unlimited number of visitors. When these are golf or tennis players the host is responsible for greens fees or court charges. If the guest wishes to repay his host, the matter is settled between them in private.

As a rule, when a member requests club privileges for a friend, he takes him to the club personally, writes his name in the visitors' book, and introduces him to those who may be present at the time. If for some reason it is not possible for the host to take his guest to the club, he asks the secretary to send him a card of introduction:

> *February 4, 1975*
> *12 Fuller Street*
> *Ellicott City*
> *Maryland 21000*

Secretary
The Town Club
Baltimore, Maryland

Dear Sir [or: Dear Mr. Jones]:
    I would appreciate it greatly if you would send Mr. A. M. Stanton, of Wilkes Barre, Pennsylvania, a card extending the privileges of the club for one week.
    Mr. Stanton is staying at the Carlton House.

> *Yours very truly,*
> *Henry Bancroft*

Note the degree of formality. One does not write "Dear Jim" because this is not a personal letter but a formal request to be put on file.

The secretary then sends a card to Mr. Stanton:

> *The Town Club*
> *Extends its privileges to*
> *Mr. Stanton*
> *from Jan. 7 to Jan. 14*
> *Through the courtesy of*
> *Mr. Henry Bancroft*

A guest who has been granted club privileges behaves just as he would in a private home. He does not force himself on the members, nor does he criticize the personnel, rules, or organization of the club.

MEN'S CLUBS

A gentleman does not bow to a lady from a club window; nor according to good form should ladies ever be discussed in a man's club!
—Emily Post, 1922

While the bastion of the all-male club is falling before the onslaught of Women's Lib, there are still many clubs that have managed, in practice if not in theory, to remain strictly "for men only." As residences for men who travel frequently or bachelors who do not wish to live alone, or simply as places where men may have the opportunity to enjoy the company of other males, they provide a valuable service.

As in all clubs a man should be sure before joining that the members are people he will find congenial and the facilities are what he wants and needs. If he is going to spend considerable time in his club, he should take an active part in its activities. If he has strong feelings about how it should be run, he should get himself elected or appointed to its board and not sit back and criticize those who are doing the running. The more a man is involved with his club the more pleasure he will derive from it.

Good manners in clubs are the same as good manners elsewhere —only a little more so. A club is for the pleasure and convenience of many people; it is not intended as a stage setting for a star or clown or monologist. Few other places require greater self-restraint and consideration for others. In every good residential club there is a reading room or library where conversation is discouraged. There are books and easy chairs and good light for reading by day and night, and it is an unspoken rule that someone who is reading or writing is not to be disturbed or interrupted.

It is courteous for a longtime member, on noticing a new member or a visitor—especially one who seems to be rather at a loss—to go up and speak to him. In the dining rooms of many clubs there is a large table, sometimes known as the social table, where members who are lunching alone may sit and where the conversation is general. All join in, whether they are friends or total strangers.

Today most men's clubs have a dining room to which ladies as well as men who are not members are admitted. If they don't, they usually have an occasional "ladies night" when wives and friends are welcome. Ladies' nights may occur as often as once a month or as rarely as once a year.

When a woman gives a lunch or any party in the "open" dining room of a men's club, she waits for her guests in the lobby, entrance hall, or if there is one, the reception room. As her guests arrive they join her and wait with her until everyone is there.

All men's clubs have private dining rooms where members can give dinners that include nonmembers, either men who are local residents but who do not belong to the club or men who are merely visiting the city.

WOMEN'S CLUBS

In every state of the Union there are women's clubs of every kind: social, political, sports, professional. Some are housed in enormous and elegant buildings designed especially for them; others have no clubrooms at all. Very few women's clubs are residential, with the exception of some city chapters of large national organizations such as the Junior League or the Federation of Women's Clubs.

Although some clubs are purely social most are involved with charity work of some sort, whether actually participating, or in fund-raising. Many, such as the Junior League, support a variety of enterprises. Others, such as the "Twig" organizations found in certain communities, all work for one cause—such as the local hospital.

There are thousands of other clubs built around special interests. The Garden Club of America and the Federated Garden Clubs have enormous memberships, some branches including a few males. There are bridge clubs, sewing clubs, newcomers' clubs, exercise clubs—almost any activity you can name has a woman's club dedicated to it.

There are private, purely social clubs in many cities that are essentially like men's clubs. Membership is limited, exclusive, and prospective members are "put up" or invited—just as described above. Some of the charity-supporting clubs such as the Junior League and the Twigs are exclusive too, in that one must be invited to join and the application must be approved by the membership or by a membership committee. Some require that prospective members have done some work or had experience in the particular area of interest of the club. This is also true of many garden clubs.

To join any of the nonprivate nationwide clubs such as a garden club, the League of Women Voters, or a chapter of the Women's Club, a prospective member writes to the secretary for information and an application form. Or she may accompany a friend to a meeting and talk to the secretary there. Her application must be approved by a committee, but assuming that she meets the requirements for membership she is accepted without further ado. Dues to these organizations are low but must be paid promptly as in any club.

When a woman's club has regular meetings, is headed by officers and a board, and keeps minutes, parliamentary procedure should be followed. All women becoming officers of a club should read Chapter 5 of this book and study *Robert's Rules of Order.*

Most meetings of women's clubs are preceded or followed by a coffee, lunch, or tea. If there is a speaker or guest of honor, he or she is introduced to as many members as possible by the president, although there is rarely a formal "line." Luncheons featuring authors are popular, and after short talks by the guests of honor during lunch, their books are on display and can be purchased.

Although most members of clubs know each other, there are always some who do not, especially if the membership is large. During the social part of the meetings everyone talks to everyone else, introducing themselves or not, as they wish.

When a woman's club is large and official enough to have its own stationery, the officers' names are listed with title: "Secretary, Miss Jean Foster," "President, Mrs. Henry Saber," etc. Married women use the normal social form—their husband's name. The exception is a professional woman in a professional club. In that case she would use whatever name she is known by in her field.

TIPPING IN CLUBS

Tipping is not expected in private clubs where the staff is maintained year round. Instead, members are usually asked to give a contribution to a "Christmas Fund for Employees." Most members who use a club regularly do give an additional Christmas "gift" of five or ten dollars to employees who have given them special service. But waiters, locker-room attendants, launch boys, etc., are not tipped from day to day.

When a club meets at a restaurant or hall, or uses any public facilities, the help are tipped as they would be by any patron.

If you use the facilities of a club of which you are not a member for a party or meeting, you add approximately 15 percent to your payment to be divided among the waiters and other employees. In some cases, however, a service charge is added to the bill.

Guests of members do not tip unless they have been staying at a residential club. In that case they would tip when they leave as they would at a fine hotel.

RESIGNING FROM A CLUB

Failure to pay one's debts or objectionable behavior is cause for expulsion from any club.

If a man cannot afford to belong to a club, he must resign before his bills are overdue. If later on he is able to rejoin, his name is put at the head of the waiting list; if he was considered a desirable member, he is reelected at the next meeting of the governors. But a man who has been expelled—unless he can show that his expulsion was unjust—can never again belong to that club. In fact it would probably be difficult for him to be elected to any other equivalent club, since his expulsion from one will almost certainly come to the attention of another considering him for membership.

When one wishes to resign from a club it is necessary to write a letter of resignation to the secretary well before the date on which the next yearly dues will be due. The letter would read something like this:

November 7, 1975

Mr. James Conlon
Secretary, River Club
Kansas City, Missouri

Dear Mr. Conlon,
    It is with great regret that I feel I must resign from the River Club. Due to my severe arthritis, I can no longer avail myself of the facilities as I did, and I feel that my membership should be filled by someone who can use it and enjoy it.

Would you please present my resignation at the next meeting of the governors?

Sincerely,
Robert Hopkins

16 Watkins Rd.
Kansas City, Missouri 64100

or:

Dear Mr. Conlon,
I have just been informed that I am to be transferred permanently to Ottawa, and therefore must resign from the River Club. It is with great regret that I must ask you to present this resignation to the board.

Sincerely,

ᘒ61ᘒ In Business

Small offices or businesses, consisting of fewer than a dozen people, all of whom know each other well, are, naturally, informal. They make their own rules as to dress, use of first names, social customs, etc. Since everyone involved knows, or quickly knows, the office habits, it is not necessary to discuss the "little" business firm in this chapter. All that is required is that the normal courtesies be followed and that the personnel treat each other with thoughtfulness, courtesy, and understanding.

Whether big or small, every successful executive knows how important etiquette is, both in managing his office and in dealing with other businessmen. No one can ever tell when a knowledge of it may be to his advantage, or when the lack of it may suddenly tip the scales against him.

The more important the executive, the greater courtesy he shows to those with whom he works and to those with whom he does business. A president of a large industry, in fact, chooses his assistants partly because of their tact and good manners. Except in an industry whose image is "arty," such as the theater, or "mod," such as magazines for young people, those in any positions of authority try by their clothes and their manner to project an aura of conservatism, reliability, and courtesy. Men and women whose good manners at home and in their social life are natural to them instinctively use the same good manners in their offices. It is more difficult perhaps for someone who has been brought up in a family where the struggle to survive overshadowed the need to be "polite," but he, too, can learn the necessary forms of courtesy by observation and practice. And it will be to his advantage to do so. Very few men—or women—have risen to the top in their professions—and stayed there—without good manners' becoming an integral part of their characters.

THE BUSINESS "GENTLEMAN"

Whether president of the company or a lowly salesman, the courteous businessman makes every visitor feel there is nothing in the day's work half so important as what his client has come to see him about. If he knows his time is short, he instructs his secretary to come in a few minutes before the hour is up and remind him, "I'm sorry, Mr. Phillips, but your appointment with the traffic committee is due." Mr. Phillips uses up most of the last few minutes bringing the conversation to an unhurried close, so that the visitor leaves with the impression that the subject he has introduced has become of great interest to Mr. Phillips.

This is neither sincerity nor insincerity, but merely bringing social knowledge into business dealing. To make a pleasant and friendly impression is good manners and equally good business. The fact that this is understood by modern businessmen is shown by the importance they give to public relations. A less experienced man might show his eagerness to be rid of his visitor, offending him by showing his impatience.

When visiting another firm, executives and salesmen alike show the same courtesy they would in a social situation. They give their names clearly to the receptionist and present a card to be shown to her employer. They wait patiently if they cannot be seen at once, and they do not bother the employees with conversation in order to pass the time. Once admitted, they present their business as concisely and clearly as possible, to save valuable time for both themselves and the man they are seeing.

Although I firmly believe that some of the ordinary "social" courtesies between men and women can be maintained to a large extent in an office, it would be time-consuming and impractical to insist on others. For example, a businessman does not rise when his secretary comes into his office unless she is new and he is meeting her for the first time.

Neither does he rise when a co-worker of either sex approaches his desk. However, he does stand for his superior or for a much older person, whether a man or a woman. He rises when a client or customer comes into his office, and if the visitor is a man, offers his hand. A woman client should offer *her* hand first, but this is not a hard-and-fast rule and some men feel that their offered hand is a sign of welcome. When a man walks into a woman executive's office he waits for her to offer her hand and doesn't sit down until she asks him to.

When a woman enters a room where a conference is in progress, the men at the table rise if the group is small. If there are a great many men present, only those on either side of her seat need rise.

Men who are used to practicing the social amenities at home do so in the office too. Therefore the well-mannered man opens heavy doors for women in the office and allows them to go through first, whether they are his superiors or members of the stenographic pool. Nor does it hurt a professional man's image to help a woman in his office with her coat, to carry a heavy suitcase for her, or to make any of the other nice gestures that he would make in the "outside" world.

He need, never, however, give her special consideration in business dealings because of her sex.

A sensible executive who wishes to go far in his company does not become "involved" with a woman in his office unless they are both free to do as they please. Office gossip is a dangerous weapon, and anyone on his way up, or already at the top, can find it quickly turned against him. Even the man who is unmarried and fancy-free is wiser to look outside the office for his romance. Office love affairs do occasionally blossom into permanent relationships, but more often they serve to distract, frustrate, and impair the senses and the efficiency of the people involved.

A married executive is asking for nothing but trouble when an occasional lunch with his secretary or an attractive co-worker becomes a regular thing. And a single man should refrain from causing trouble by asking a married employee to go out with him. A little mild flirting, an occasional "mixed" lunch, preferably not as a twosome, help to lighten the inevitable boredom of day-to-day business. But the minute the situation seems to be getting the slightest bit serious or out of hand, the intelligent businessman will cut it off right there.

Husbands and wives who work together in business must try to be as impersonal and businesslike as possible during their working hours.

WOMEN IN BUSINESS

Women have come to stay not only in every branch of business but in every profession as well. Women are the successful heads of many offices, and there are very few businesses that do not have women of all degrees of importance in every department.

The ideal businesswoman is accurate, orderly, quick, and impersonal, whether she is a typist or the top executive of a large firm. Here the word *impersonal* means exactly that! Her point of view must be focused on the work in hand, not on her own reactions to it and not on anyone's reactions to her. Perhaps one of the hardest battles a career woman must fight is to convince her male employer and associates that her job does not play second fiddle to her family. Until recently it was assumed that a woman should take care of the home while her husband worked for what made it possible to keep that home. And it is undeniable that a mother's presence is more important to a baby or a sick child than a father's. Therefore it is difficult at times for a woman to divorce herself from her problems at home to devote herself wholeheartedly to her problems at the office. But to be successful, and to have it recognized that she can pull her own weight as well as a man, the married executive must organize herself so that she can do just that. In general it is wiser for a woman to start her career when her children are past the baby stage, or to take a leave of absence for a few years while she gets her family started. I realize that this will be unacceptable to a great many feminists, but I believe that it is the only approach that *is* acceptable to Mother Nature. And once a woman has passed this period and can devote herself to her job, she is in a position to compete with anyone—man or woman.

Therefore at the very top of the list of women's business shortcomings is the inability of some to achieve this impersonality. Mood, temper, jealousy, especially when induced by a "crush" on an employer or a fellow worker—these are flaws of many women in business, and a source of annoyance in the office where they work.

In spite of all this, a woman should not try to hide or downgrade her femininity. There has always been and always will be a difference between the two sexes—and *"Vive la différence!"* Women who think that they can compete better with men by trying to be masculine are totally mixed up. While a career woman has no business trying to gain an advantage by using her sex, she should not disregard the *natural* advantages it gives her, either. Men have far more respect and admiration for a *feminine* woman who handles a job well than one who does the job but looks and acts like a misplaced male.

A woman who goes into an office because she hopes to meet romance in the form of her employer, or at least to rise quickly because of her physical charms, has plain business and show business mixed up. Much as a man may admire a pretty or magnetic or amusing woman in his leisure hours, in his work hours he wants someone to help him with that work. The more help she can give him, the more he values her, and the more salary he is willing to pay.

Women who work must learn not to waste their employers' time. Employers know that the effect on morale of a ten-minute coffee break more than makes up in increased efficiency for the actual loss in time. No employer, however, will stand for a coffee-break atmosphere throughout the working day. During working hours women should avoid wasting time in idle chitchat, which only interrupts the office routine and is a very unbusinesslike habit.

Neatness, appropriateness, and modesty are the three most important requirements for a businesswoman's clothes. Low-cut necklines, skintight knits and thigh-high miniskirts have no place in an office. A woman whose appearance distracts the men from their work—even though they enjoy being distracted—will not last long in her job.

Most large offices have their own rules about length of skirts, pants suits, stockings, etc., and of course the woman who wants to keep her job must abide by them. In general personnel departments are quite liberal, requiring only that cleanliness, neatness, and modesty be observed by all employees.

Women sometimes object to working for another woman on the grounds that female executives are less kind, less generous, more unreasonable, and more emotional than men. This may have been true years ago, but the competition has become too keen, and women executives can no longer afford to indulge themselves in that way. Therefore many women today make better employers for women than men do because they understand their problems better, and there is no longer the challenge and jealousy between women that there used to be. Also, thanks to Women's Lib, there is a definite increase on the part of women to side together and stand together, providing a bond between employer and employee.

THE PRIVATE SECRETARY

The function of the private secretary is to complement her employer's endeavor and not make any intrusions that would be more likely to impede than help.

Needless to say, a secretary must not betray the secrets of her employer. His business dealings must be regarded as professional secrets. No matter how inconsequential they may seem to her, it would be inexcusable for her to divulge them.

She makes his appointments, sees that he is reminded of them, protects him from unwanted calls and visitors, handles small details without bothering him, and in general attempts to relieve him of all time-consuming chores. He is thus free to concentrate on his more important business.

She should not be expected to do personal chores for him—buy

Christmas presents, pay household bills, etc.—unless she offers to do so on her own. She should, however, take care of personal correspondence that is connected with the business, such as addressing Christmas cards to clients, and of course, she attends to personal calls and messages at his request.

A business school will train a secretary to know everything she can that will be of service to her employer, but to know as little as possible about the things that are not her concern. When sorting his mail she leaves unopened the obviously private letters—envelopes addressed by hand on stationery not suggestive of business or with *personal* written on the envelope. When she opens his other letters and arranges them in whatever order he prefers, she should, if there is confidential material included, clip a sheet of blank paper at the top of each pile or put the mail in a manila folder, so that visitors or others who have access to his office will not have the contents of letters displayed before them.

When a secretary enters a man's office to take dictation, she should take a chair and place it near enough to hear him easily. Where she sits depends very much on the office—where the light comes from and where she can best hear his voice.

In the outer office she does not rise to greet visitors unless they are known to her personally or are important customers. She greets strangers pleasantly and receives their cards or their names, to be taken or called in to her employer. When visitors leave she may get their coats for them, and in the case of an older person, may help him on with his coat.

She does not rise when members of the same company stop at her desk on business.

IN UNCONVENTIONAL SITUATIONS

The young woman who is a private secretary to an executive may sometimes be required to stay late in the evening working with him alone. Or if the nature of his business or profession requires that he take long trips to distant cities, she may accompany him on these purely business trips, although that happens less frequently since the advent of the portable tape recorder. In any case she is entirely free from criticism in these circumstances—unless she gives cause for it herself.

In preparing for a trip she makes whatever reservations are necessary. She makes her professional relationship to her employer quite clear in her letter or telegram, and the hotel will give them accommodations on separate floors or at some distance from each other. It would be a mistake to put herself in another hotel, since the reason she is going is to be available whenever her employer needs her.

If she should by chance find herself shown into a room adjoining that of her employer, the question of what to do depends somewhat upon the type of man he is. She may accept the situation, or if she has reason to suspect he might take advantage of it, she goes down to the desk and tells the clerk that her room is not convenient and tries to get another.

A private secretary traveling with her employer will frequently lunch with him or have dinner with him in hotel dining rooms or restaurants. If one or both are married, they should not go to nightclubs or bars unless there are clients or associates with them. When there is no time to spare she may have to eat in his rooms where they are working. In other words she takes eating alone or eating with him as incidental to convenience.

THE WELL-RUN OFFICE

An employee, whether man or woman, should take as much pride in helping to keep up the tone of the office he works in as he takes in his own efficiency. A company in which everyone contributes to a spirit of enthusiasm and participation is a happier place for both employer and employee.

Do not bring your personal problems to the office. You may rest assured that nine times out of ten no one is interested. Leave them at home, or if you must, discuss them with a friend during lunch.

In the offices of many large companies the executives call their employees "Miss [or Mrs.] Jones" rather than "Mary." The employees, in turn, always call the executives by their last names; for example, "Mr. Smith." There are, however, varying degrees of formality in business organizations. A majority, perhaps, of offices today tend to be more casual than formerly. Some employers feel that in a more relaxed atmosphere employees will be more efficient, more reliable, and more loyal. The ranking executive determines the degree of formality in his office. He may prefer to be on a first-name basis with his staff, and the informality in no way implies a too-familiar relationship.

The newcomer in an office need only keep his ears open for a day or two. He will soon find out what the custom is, and he must go along with it if he is to "fit in." A wife follows her husband's example and uses the same name for his secretary that he does.

Some men have a tendency to call all the women in the office
—or at least those in lower positions than they themselves occupy
—"Honey" or "Dear" or something similar. An occasional woman,
usually a very young one or a considerably older one, may think this
habit "cute" or flattering, but my mail indicates that most dislike it
intensely. I do not think as some do, that it is intended to label a
woman as an inferior or a "sex object," but I *do* think it indicates
laziness about learning names and a lack of awareness of the woman's
feelings. "Honey," "Dear," and so on are endearments that belong
to a wife or girl friend and should be confined to that kind of relationship. When a woman is annoyed enough to make an issue of it she
should say, "My name is Mary, not Honey, and I really prefer to be
called Mary, if you don't mind."

Personal messages over the telephone are at times unavoidable,
but long, chatty conversations not only are out of place but also waste
time that does not belong to the employee. Telephone "chatter"
annoys other people in the office who can't help overhearing your
discussion of the movie you saw last night. Personal calls that interfere with the routine of office procedure, either incoming or outgo-
ing, are inexcusable except in genuine emergencies.

Discourage visits from your family and friends at the office. Your
baby brother may be a most enchanting child, but his place is not
in the office where you work.

Don't be a borrower. Constant requests for a cigarette, a dime
for a candy bar, the use of a comb, etc., will make you thoroughly
unpopular. If it is absolutely necessary on occasion, make sure that
you repay the lender promptly or return the borrowed article in
perfect shape.

OFFICE GIFTS

Gifts from a firm to its employees are usually in the form of a
bonus or a proportion of one's salary. It is not necessary to write a
note of thanks for such a bonus because it is not in the nature of a
personal gift. At Christmas a man gives his personal secretary a
present. Candy and perfume are conventional if they have not
worked together for long, but if she has been his secretary for some
time, he generally chooses a more substantial present. A pocketbook,
a pretty pin, a piece of luggage, a silk scarf, are all gifts that any
woman would appreciate.

Occasionally employees give presents to their employers, but
this is not common. If a girl does decide to give her boss a present,

it should not be too personal, and if he is married, the gift should be something for husband and wife. It is very nice if all the girls in an office get together to give a "joint" present to a popular employer. If one of the members of the office staff gets married, or if a baby is born, then the other employees may all contribute and send a gift. They may also send flowers to a funeral as a group. Some large offices have a regular fund for these occasions, and each employee is asked to make a yearly contribution. A committee usually collects contributions and makes an appropriate selection. No one should feel obligated to contribute more than he can afford—or anything at all if he does not wish to do so. People who do participate should all sign the card that accompanies the gift.

Giving gifts to one's fellow workers who are also personal friends should always be arranged for out of office hours.

SOCIAL AMENITIES

A man who is new in a company or who has been transferred to another branch does not entertain his employer until he has first been entertained. Shortly afterward, it is fitting that the newcomer and his wife return the compliment in some way. *It need not be "in kind."* If the employer takes a young executive and his wife to an expensive restaurant for dinner, for example, the young couple are not expected to entertain him in the same way. They might, instead, invite the couple to a simple buffet supper, including another couple or two if they wish.

If the employee has known his superior for some time, he might invite him over as he would any friend without waiting to be "asked first." Also, if he should be giving a large party—an open house or housewarming, perhaps—including other members of the office staff, it would be nothing short of insulting to leave his employer out.

The most important thing for a young wife to remember in entertaining her husband's boss is that he knows her situation and her means, and she need not "put on the dog." She and her husband should do their best to relax and act naturally and to make the evening as pleasant as possible for their guests. The hosts' aim is to have their guests go home thinking, "What a charming, friendly couple—we're lucky to have them with our company!"

When a salesman or executive entertains a client or customer the latter is under no obligation at all to repay the invitation. The sale or deal that may result is all the "thanks" the host hopes for.

A young employee who calls his older boss "Mr. Franklin" in the office continues to do so socially unless Mr. Franklin suggests that he call him "Bob." Contemporaries, however, even though one is employer and one employee, would be more apt to use each other's first names outside the office. Husbands and wives of office personnel use the same names that their spouse uses for his or her business associates.

BUSINESS INVITATIONS

Although it is perfectly all right for a man to ask one or a number of his co-workers to a party, the invitation should be seconded by his wife. If she does not know the names and addresses of her husband's associates, he should ask for that information when he issues the verbal invitation. The wife should then telephone or send a written note or invitation to the wife of her husband's associates, or if the employee is a woman, to her and her husband. Husbands (or wives) should never make social plans with their business acquaintances without letting their wives (or husbands) know. It is very embarrassing to have to say the next day, "Jim, we'll have to put off that dinner—Helen had already made plans for next Saturday."

CONVENTIONS AND TRIPS

Whether or not a wife accompanies her husband on business trips or goes to meetings and conventions with him is often a matter of choice. Of course, wives are expected at many conventions, and their expenses are paid by the company. But when a man goes on a sales trip or something of that nature, his wife should not expect to be "invited" unless they are in a position to pay her expenses themselves. When two men travel together, one wife should not go unless the other does too.

A wife who attends a convention or meeting at the company invitation has no obligations at all, other than to make herself pleasant and attractive and a credit to her husband. A charming wife can do a great deal toward furthering her husband's interests if she is interested, attentive, and takes a positive part in the various functions, whether she enjoys them or not. No written thanks are necessary, but a word of appreciation to whoever is in charge of the arrangements is simple courtesy.

JOB INTERVIEWS

Anyone applying for a job of any importance should have a personal resumé ready for the interviewer. A resumé should include:

Name, address, phone number

Schools attended, grades completed

Degrees or certificates awarded

Courses relating to job being applied for

Interests or hobbies if at all pertinent

Past working experience

Names and addresses of at least three people who would be willing to give a reference. Clergymen, teachers, previous employers, and family friends are all good people to include.

The applicant should ask their permission to use their names.

Once the interview is arranged—by telephone or letter—the applicant should arrive promptly. Nothing will hurt your chances more than keeping the interviewer waiting.

You should be dressed conservatively, appropriately, and above all, neatly. If you are a woman, remember that you will be judged more for your appearance of seriousness about the job than for your glamour.

Try to remember the interviewer's name, and even though he is younger than you, call him "Mr." unless he asks you to do otherwise.

Unless there is an ashtray on his desk, don't smoke.

Go by yourself—not with a group. Even though there may be several openings, you will do better to stand out on your own, rather than as just one of the crowd.

Be prepared—know as much as you can about the position and the company, but don't hesitate to ask questions. But start with "What are the opportunities ahead of me?" rather than "How much vacation will I get?"

Let the interviewer "lead" you—don't regale him with unsolicited information.

Put on your "company" manners. Shake hands when you leave and thank him for his time. Even if you don't get the job this time, a short note following the interview will keep you in his mind when the next opportunity opens up.

OFFICE PARTIES

Christmas parties at which all the personnel let down their hair, get roaring drunk, and land in all sorts of trouble, are almost a thing of the past. So many companies received such bitter complaints from the wives and husbands of their employees, and there were so many accidents on the way home from the "brawls," that they have eliminated the parties entirely. However, each year a few letters come in after the holidays from hurt or irate wives.

If your husband's company does not invite wives or husbands to the Christmas party, there is little you can do but grin and bear it. But if it is one of an increasing number of firms that have tried to solve the problem by inviting husbands and wives, you have to make a decision. Many women write that they go—out of self-defense —and have a miserable time. Their husbands (and it could be wives too) spend the whole time dancing and joking with their co-workers, while the "little woman," who may know only one or two other people, sits and twiddles her thumbs. If a discussion with your husband—after you have cooled off—and a reminder of it before the next party, do no good, I can only suggest that you stay at home with a good book. If you do go, make up your mind to have a good time without your husband. There will be other women like you there; rather than sit alone, join them, introduce yourself, and find out a little about the company personnel. People who look as though they are enjoying themselves, attract *other* people, and you may even find you can compete with the cute secretary your husband is dancing with.

SALES ETIQUETTE

The technical aspects of salesmanship are much too specialized to be discussed by anyone who has not learned the subject at first-hand and practiced it with success—success measured by satisfactory sales slips, and best of all, an increasing number of customers who ask for Mrs. Keen or Miss Patient when they come again to buy. A salesman or saleswoman can be very helpful, but he or she can also be a nuisance.

THE RETAIL SALESWOMAN

First let us take the point of view of a customer, since this is something that we all know from personal experience. We surely do not all agree as to the type of saleswoman we like or dislike. A clever saleswoman must have different methods with different customers. After all, if customers were identical, perfect salesmanship would not be the difficult accomplishment it is. It is quite possible for methods that are unendurable to some of us to be acceptable to others.

Really great saleswomen have acquired not only a thorough knowledge of the commodities they sell but an equally expert ability to appraise the customers to whom they sell. It is essential to know, for example, whether a customer likes to be "dearied" or "madamed" (a habit I find particularly objectionable!) or chatted to about every topic under the sun, whether she is one who likes to have her mind made up for her, or whether she is one who, knowing exactly what she wants, prefers to have her own questions answered intelligently without any unasked-for advice.

The saleswoman whom an intelligent customer is certain to like—and return to—is one who listens to what the prospective buyer says and tries to give her what she wants, instead of trying to sell her what the store seems eager to be rid of.

For example, if you asked for something the store couldn't supply, the ideal saleswoman would listen attentively to what you said and answer, "I am very sorry, but we have nothing at all like that in the color you want; I could give you something in a small pattern of yellow," and then with some enthusiasm she would ask, "Have you time to let me show it to you?"

You are pleased because the saleswoman has shown herself eager to help you find what you want. When she brings the article, you are inclined to like it because, though you know it is not just what you want, you are sure it is not going to be thrust upon you. And the possibilities are that if you can make it do, you will take it. And even if you do not, you will certainly come back to that saleswoman another time when you are looking for something else.

Of all the varieties of poor saleswomen the worst is the one who simply brushes aside what you say you want and blandly spreads before you something that is exactly what you have explained to her you do *not* want. At the same time she tries to force you to like it by extolling its beauties or its bargain values, and caps it all by telling you that Mrs. Gotrocks thinks this is exquisite!

Then there is the saleswoman who says about something you have asked for, and which you know *is* available, "They don't make that anymore," or even worse, "Oh, those are not in style this year!"

I do not think that anyone likes the "hard sell" or that it ever pays in the long run. One wonders how many customers who have been high-pressured into buying what they did not really want or into spending more than they could afford have thereafter avoided not only that particular salesperson but that particular store as well.

INCONSIDERATE CUSTOMERS

A salesman or -woman is, so to speak, at the mercy of any customer who is rude or unreasonable for as long as that customer takes to make—or not make—the purchase. Moreover, an unjustifiably irate customer can make a complaint about the salesperson, which, whether deserved or not, can cause the loss of his job.

The following letter, written to me several years ago, describes an attitude that, if more prevalent, would make shopping *and* selling pleasanter for everyone involved:

Dear Mrs. Post,

For the past few years I have been working as a salesgirl in a department store. Recently after I had spent some time waiting on a particularly unpleasant woman, a new salesgirl asked me how I managed to keep my temper under such trying conditions. I explained that it isn't difficult to be pleasant for a short period of time. This relationship between an unkind and important customer and myself was over in a few minutes, and how much better it was that one of us retained her composure, instead of having two women shouting at each other!

In fact, most of our lives, our daily contact with other persons is on a "short-term" basis. Aside from our families and friends, the people with whom we do come in contact will only share with us a smile and a few pleasant words. Isn't that a wonderful way to practice love of neighbor—with kindness, consideration and graciousness.

Surely we could all, remembering the fleetingness of a sales transaction, keep ourselves under better control for those few minutes than we sometimes do!

As a guess, one might say that the average customer can be at her worst and cause the greatest strain on a saleswoman in a ready-to-wear clothing department. And what a careless customer often does to the merchandise is scarcely believable. Perhaps she smears the dresses with lipstick as she pulls them on or off, or tears them in her haste or sheer carelessness. She may pull off a button, rip out the hem, or stretch the slacks she is trying to squeeze into. Rarely does she think *she* did the damage. And in the end she orders nothing, or perhaps she buys several articles and then returns everything looking still more shopworn the next day.

Another form of inconsideration is shown by people who go shopping ten minutes before closing time. The salespeople have had a long day and have routine chores to do before they can leave.

Nor is it fair to expect favors from friends who are salesgirls, but who are not in a position to give below-cost prices or to put other customers aside and spend their time in gossiping. Finally, although it is hard to believe it, there are women who, with no thought of buying anything, will go into a dress department solely to pass an hour or so with a friend who is paid at least in part by commissions on the dresses she sells—and not on the ones she shows.

Is the customer always right? It would not seem likely. Unfailing patience and good temper are qualities required of every saleswoman, whereas there is nothing to restrain the ill humor or unreasonableness of a customer—except her own good manners.

⋖62⋗ In Games and Sports

The basic requisite for good manners at any game table or sports area is that age-old quality *sportsmanship,* and the quality that more than any other gives evidence of true sportsmanship is absence of any show of temper. After all, if you can't take sports with grace and good temper, you shouldn't go in for them. Cursing your faults or your luck, excusing, complaining, and protesting against unfairness won't get you anywhere—except in trouble. To hide your ill humor is the first rule of sportsmanship. This does not mean that you may never—by expression or gesture—show either satisfaction or chagrin. It simply means that at all times your emotions are under control.

The next rule is always to give your opponent the benefit of the doubt. Although the particular point in question may seem very important at that moment, never argue with the umpire. If he rules a line ball on the tennis court is out, it is out. Do not turn toward the spectators with an expression that says, "He must be blind!"

Another shortcoming of an unsportsmanlike player is his practice of understating his ability before a match. It is a commonplace occurrence to hear a man who is actually perfectly satisfied with his skill say, "I am not much of a player," or "I know I'll be terrible today—I've got a 'bad' arm!" He is not necessarily being dishonest; he may be motivated by a subconscious effort to create admiring surprise if he plays well and to save face should his game be off. The only time a player may justifiably declare himself unskilled is when his poorer play would be a source of annoyance to a group of competitors beyond his class.

One last example of bad sportsmanship is the person who complains of illness after losing a match: "I had such a pain in my side [or knee, or back]! I don't know how I ever got through the game!"

Sportsmanship can be acquired by following a few simple rules: Keep your mind on the game, not on your feelings. If you win, don't at once begin to consider yourself a star. A gloating winner is detested even more than a bad loser. But when you lose, don't sulk, or protest, or long-windedly explain. If you are hurt, don't nurse your bruises. Get up and good-naturedly get ready for the next play. This is playing the game—and it is good sportsmanship.

It is worth teaching your children these rules, and the way to teach them is to play games with them. They will learn not only sportsmanship, but also tolerance, patience, and cooperation. Of course *you* must set the example. It is up to *you* the parents to show your children how to be modest winners and philosophical losers.

CARD PLAYERS, PLEASANT AND UNPLEASANT

Bridge is probably the most popular "mixed-company" card game, but many of the same rules of good manners apply to players of gin rummy, hearts, poker—mixed or stag—or any other game.

Irritating mannerisms should always be recognized and avoided like the plague. If there is one thing worse than the horrible postmortem, it is the incessant repetition of some jarring habit by one particular player. A common offense is that of snapping down a card as it is played, or picking it up and trotting it up and down the table.

Other pet offenses are drumming on the table with one's fingers, making various clicking, whistling, or humming sounds, massaging one's face, scratching one's chin with the cards, or holding the card one is going to play aloft as though shouting, "I know what you are going to play! And my card is ready!"

Many people whose game is otherwise excellent are rarely asked to play because they have some such silly and annoying habit. Don't spoil your chances for many a pleasant evening by allowing yourself to be unaware of those habits.

PLAYING FOR MONEY

The intelligent card player makes it a rule never to play for stakes that it will be inconvenient to lose. Failure to observe this rule has been responsible for more bad losers than any other reason, and a bad loser is about as welcome at a game table as rain at a tennis match. Of course there *are* people who can take losses beyond their means with perfect cheerfulness and composure because they are so imbued with the gambler's instinct that a heavy turn of luck, in either direction, is the salt of life. But the average person is equally embarrassed at winning or losing a stake that matters, and the only answer is always to play only for what one can easily afford.

Because of this every hostess owes her guests protection from being forced into playing for stakes that can embarrass them. This is more important for a male guest than for a woman. A woman usually feels free to say, "I'm sorry, but I never play for more than so much." But a man sometimes feels that his refusal is an embarrassing confession of financial failure—a position into which no good hostess should ever put him. If you know that people coming to your house, for instance, play together often, nothing need be said; but if you invite strangers to play with others who play for certain stakes, you should say when you invite them, "The Smiths and Browns and Robinsons are coming. They all play for a cent. Is that all right?" The one invited can say either, "I'm sorry. My limit is a tenth of a cent," or "They must be way out of my class! But ask me again when you are having people who play for less."

CONTRACT BRIDGE

This book is not intended to teach you how to play bridge, only the courtesies connected with the game. Therefore the following paragraphs are only for those who know the basic ways and means of making or setting a bid.

A trick that is annoying to moderately skilled players is to have an overconfident opponent (who may be a better player than they are) throw down his hand, saying, "The rest of the tricks are mine!" Often it is quite possible that they might not have been his if the hand had been played out. If they feel that they are poorer players, the others are not likely to challenge the move, even though they feel that their rights have been taken away. This is a foolish habit to get into, because if the defenders can show any possible sequence of play that will give them a trick, they have every right to claim it—and should do so.

If luck is against you, you will gain nothing by sulking or complaining about the awful cards you have been holding. Your partner is suffering just as much in finding you a "poison vine" as you are in being one—and you can scarcely expect your opponents to be sympathetic. You must try to look perfectly cheerful even though you hold nothing but poor cards for days on end, and you must on no account try to defend your own bad play. When you have shown poor judgment the best thing you can say is, "I'm very sorry, partner," and let it go at that.

Always pay close attention to the game. When you are dummy

you have certain duties to your partner, so do not wander around the room or look into your opponents' hands. If you don't know what your duties are, read the rules until you know them by heart and then—read them all over again! It is impossible to play any game without a thorough knowledge of the rules that govern it.

Don't be offended if your partner takes you out of a bid and don't take him out for the glory of playing the hand. He is just as anxious to win the rubber as you are. It is unbelievable how many people really seem to regard their partners as third opponents.

There are certain conventions that should be observed in regard to cutting the cards, shuffling, etc. The person opposite the dealer is responsible for shuffling the deck for the next hand. After shuffling, he places it on his *right* side. The deal moves around the table clockwise, so that when it is time to deal the next hand, the deck is pushed directly across the table to the right side of the person who is to deal it. The person who dealt the last hand cuts the cards. He picks up roughly half the pack and places it beside the bottom half, on the side nearest the new dealer. He (the new dealer) picks up the bottom half and places it on top of the top half. The deck is then ready to be dealt.

And one last word to the semienthusiast: If you really don't like bridge and don't want to devote your full attention to the game—don't play it. Nothing is more irritating to people who do want to play seriously than to find themselves at the table with a "fourth" who prefers to spend the evening chatting about clothes, sports, politics—or anything else, other than bridge.

VARIOUS SPORTS

There are fixed rules for playing every game—and for conduct in every sport. The details of these rules must be studied in the books of the game, learned from instructors, or acquired by experience. And if you tend to get annoyed or bored with the number of rules there seem to be, remember this: If there were no rules, there could be no competitive sports at all.

Above and beyond the "rules" there are certain "manners" that must be observed too. In many cases they are as traditional and as important to the practice of the sport as are the rules of play.

It would be impossible to discuss good manners in every game played by sports-loving Americans. Nor is it necessary, as most are governed by a combination of very strict rules and common courtesy.

I have chosen four sports, however, in which good manners

beyond the rule book are most important. They are boating, tennis, golf, and skiing. I have chosen them for three reasons. First, because of the enormous number of people who enjoy them. Second, because their popularity has increased so tremendously in very recent years that there are more people who do not know the rules. And third, except for tennis, adherence to the rules of etiquette is essential for safety when enjoying the sport.

BOATING

If you are the proud owner of a new boat, be it sail or power, and especially if it is your first venture in ownership, you must learn thoroughly and completely the rules of safety on the water. These rules and regulations can easily be obtained from the United States Coast Guard, and there are many excellent books available on all aspects of boating. After complying with the rules affecting other boats, the captain may establish the routine for his own boat in as rigid or as relaxed a way as he wishes. But since there are certain procedures that have come to be regarded as most correct and most practical, every guest should be acquainted with these conventions before accepting an invitation to go cruising.

On all but the most elaborate yachts or houseboats, space is very limited. Therefore one takes along as few clothes as possible. If you are going on an extended cruise, you must find out where and in what circumstances you will be going ashore. You may attend receptions, cocktail parties, or dances in five different ports; but remember that because the people ashore will not have seen you in the other ports, and the people on other boats understand the space problem, the same outfit will serve for several trips to shore. Most captains keep foul-weather gear on their boats, but before you sail be sure that he has enough, and if not, bring your own.

If you are a smoker you must remember to throw your match or your cigarette overboard to leeward—the side away from where the wind is coming from.

Some cruises, for example the New York Yacht Club cruise, do not allow laundry to be hung on deck. All participants should find out the regulations and plan their wardrobes to last the number of days between ports where a laundromat can be found.

Although many boat owners do not object to hard shoes on board, it is only polite to find out how your captain feels. If he does object, carry your party shoes in your hand until you reach shore, where you may change into them. Remember that regular rubber soles are slippery. If you are to be on board a boat that will be "heeling" (tipping with the wind) or one small enough to pitch about in a rough sea, you should have grooved, nonskid sneakers especially made for sailors.

All clothing must be packed in canvas bags or duffel bags, never in a hard suitcase. The latter is impossible to stow away, whereas the canvas ones can be squashed into a minimum of space.

If cruising on a luxurious yacht, you treat the crew exactly as you would the servants in a house on land. They should be regarded with friendliness and respect, and if a steward has taken care of you and your clothing, you may leave him a tip, just as you would a chambermaid, before going ashore.

Other rules are simply those of good manners anywhere. Remember that the skipper is boss, and as much for safety as for politeness, his word is law. He, after all, is the one who knows the limits of his boat and also the capabilities of his guests or crew, and he has planned for the greatest enjoyment (and in racing, the greatest chance of success) that he possibly can.

As the proud new owner of a yacht—whether a houseboat, a cabin cruiser, or a sleek yawl or sloop—you must observe certain rules of courtesy, both in harbor and at sea. Some are interrelated with safety, and others are just plain good manners—designed to make boating more of a pleasure for you and everyone else. Here are some of the things a considerate—and popular—skipper does:

He doesn't warm up his engines more loudly and for longer than necessary when he is getting off to an early start.

He observes the "no-wake" signs, especially when passing close to boats tied up at docks.

He is careful not to spray neighboring boats when hosing down his decks at a marina.

He keeps the noise level reasonable at evening festivities on his boat and sees that they do not go on too late, when tied up close to other boats.

He gives trolling fishermen a wide berth so as not to cut their long lines.

He slows down when passing small fishing boats at anchor, so as not to rock them or scare away the fish.

He cuts holes in both ends of drink cans, and knocks the bottoms out of bottles before throwing them overboard.

Unless absolutely necessary, he does not discard any trash that might float at sea, but keeps it in plastic containers to be disposed of on shore.

He keeps ship-to-shore telephone conversations as short as possible and remembers that everything he says can be heard by everyone else on the circuit.

Because of the close community living on board a boat, consideration for the other people with you is of utmost importance. Before you make any move, ask yourself if you will disturb one of the others, and try to be constantly aware of the special habits and likes and dislikes of your fellow cruisers.

TENNIS

Good manners on the tennis court are generally the rule, but one does see enough violations of etiquette to make them worth mentioning. More often than not tennis is a partnership game, and one cannot, as he can in golf or skiing, play alone. Therefore the most important rules of etiquette are those which deal with considerate manners between players.

First of all, never question the ruling of the linesmen or referee. You may think your ball landed "in" by a foot, but he is in a better place to see each line, and his decision must be final.

If your ball bounces out of your court and into the occupied court next to you, wait until those players have finished the point. Don't call "Ball, please," or dash over to retrieve it while their ball is still in play.

Change sides on every odd game if the sun or wind give an advantage to one court. This is a requirement in tournament play, and even in a friendly game the offer should be made.

Children and beginners should not sign up for courts (at many clubs they are not allowed to) on weekends or other days that are the only ones on which the businessmen can play. If those happen to be the only times available to the novice as well, he should arrange to play early in the morning or late in the afternoon.

When you arrive at the hour for which you have signed up and find the players on the court are playing what are probably the last points, wait patiently without pacing, bouncing balls, or glaring at them. In fact it is polite to say, "Go ahead and finish. We don't mind waiting a few minutes." And when you are the one on the court, don't try to finish if you are not near the end of a set. Never finish out more than the game you are playing, and if that does not end the set, leave the court anyway.

At the end of a match it is not necessary to hop over the net as the players do in the movies, but do go up to the net, and shaking hands with your opponents, congratulate them for the good game if they won, or thank them for the excellent match if they lost.

White is still the basic color for tennis clothing. It is not actually required anymore, however, except at certain formal clubs and in some tournaments. Clean, neat, modest shorts or dresses, whether all white, a soft color, or a combination of both, are correct on every court in every locality.

Clothing for the tennis court is fully described in Chapter 70.

GOLF

Golf was originally considered (and with reason) a rich man's game. Today, however, with the appearance of the thousands of public courses that eliminate the necessity of joining an expensive club, millions of people are enjoying the game. For those who have recently started to play, there are—above and beyond learning to hit the ball correctly—some important rules of etiquette to be learned.

Golf places a particularly severe strain upon the amiability of the average person, and in no other game, except possibly bridge, is serenity so essential. No one who is easily ruffled can keep his eye on the ball. In a race or other test of endurance a flare of anger might even help, but in golf it is safe to say that he who loses his temper is almost certain to muff his shot and lose the match.

Golf players, of course, know the rules and observe them; but it sometimes happens that casual strollers walk out on a course to watch the players. If they know the players well, that is one thing, but they have no right to follow strangers. A diffident player is easily put off his game, especially if those watching him are so discourteous as to make audible remarks. Those playing in tournaments expect an audience, and therefore erratic and nervous players ought not to sign up for tournaments—certainly not two-ball foursomes where they will handicap a partner.

Let us consider those rules which help to eliminate danger on a crowded golf course.

Never, under any circumstances, hit your shot until the group ahead of you is out of range. On weekends there is generally a starter on the first tee who will tell you when to drive, but if not, you *must* wait until those who teed off before you have hit their second shots and are definitely beyond the limit of a drive. And this rule is followed on every one of the eighteen holes. The only exception occurs when the group ahead feels that they are holding you up and signals to you to "go through." In this case, at least wait until they have moved to the edge of the fairway, and also be sure that they are all watching your ball in case it should go astray.

If you hit a wild shot that goes toward a player on another fairway, or if someone appears unexpectedly from behind a bush where he was searching for a ball, shout "Fore!" at the top of your lungs. Although he will not have time to locate your ball in flight and dodge, your shout will generally cause him to throw his arms over his head and possibly avoid serious injury.

On a blind hole (a hole where the green is not visible from where you are hitting), send a caddy or another player to the point at which he can see the area where your ball may be expected to land. If there are still other golfers in range, he holds up his hand to signal you to wait, and then, when it is safe for you to hit, waves and steps to the edge of the fairway.

While waiting on a tee for your turn to drive, look around before taking a practice swing. Not only may you hit someone with your club, but if you are swinging toward someone else you may blast him painfully with bits of stone or turf from the ground. This is true while playing other shots as well—your caddy or companions may be closer behind you than you think—and it is always safer to look before you swing.

In addition to these rules affecting safety on the golf course, there are many that add to the pleasure of the player and the orderly progression of the game.

Never speak, rattle your clubs, or move when another player is making his shot. This is especially true on the green, where intense concentration is required, but it can be disturbing on any part of the course. Even though you may think you are far enough away from the player whose turn it is to hit, the wind may carry a sound right to him, or he may catch your movement from the corner of his eye in the middle of his backswing.

One matter of convention rather than etiquette should be mentioned because it is important to the smooth functioning of the twosome or foursome: The person whose ball is farthest from the pin, or hole, plays first. Around the putting green there are certain golf rules that apply to special situations, but in an informal match the ball farthest from the hole is played, even though it is not on the green, or putting surface. A player whose ball stops close to the hole has the option of "putting out," or tapping it in, to save the time involved in marking the spot, moving his ball, waiting for the others to play, replacing the ball, and then sinking the putt.

A foursome is obligated to allow a twosome to "go through," or pass them, if there is an empty hole ahead of them. This "if" is important, because when there are players directly in front, the twosome will be prevented from moving on, there will be a pileup of six or more players on the same hole, and those behind will have an even more lengthy wait. In the case of a foursome following a foursome, or a twosome following a twosome, the first one obviously holding up the second, it is very rude of the slower one not to allow the others to go through.

It is customary for the player who has had the lowest score on the previous hole to "tee off," or drive, first on the next hole. If two or more are tied for the "honor," as this privilege is called, the one who had the lowest score on the last hole on which there was a difference plays first. In the case of teams, all members of the team that won the last hole go first and usually keep the same order no matter which one of them had the low score.

The final three rules relate to the proper care of the course. It should hardly be necessary to say that divots (pieces of turf dug up by the club head) should be replaced, but if one walks over a course after a busy weekend, it becomes apparent that golfers' education has been sadly neglected in this area. Equally important is the need for repairing the little pits made in a soft green by a high approach shot.

After playing a shot out of a trap (or bunker), the player must see that his caddy rakes the sand to eliminate his footprints and the hole made by his club. If he has no caddy, he must do it himself. In the event that there is no rake by the trap, he should do his best to smooth the sand with the head of the club.

In addition to these rules, all golfers will continue to enjoy the sport more and more if tempers are restrained and everyday rules of courtesy are observed.

SKIING

The number of people who have recently become enthusiastic about skiing in winter makes this sport comparable to golf in the summer, and as in golf, many of the rules of etiquette for skiers have developed from a need for safety regulations. In fact, on the ski slopes, except for the ordinary rules of good behavior and consideration for others, almost all the etiquette is derived from an effort to eliminate dangerous situations.

Never ski alone. Even the most expert skier in the world can have an accident—in fact the best skiers may have the most serious falls, as a result of their speed—and cold and emptiness are no respecters of skill if one falls on a lonely trail when no one knows his whereabouts.

Never ski on a closed trail. The commonest reason for blocking it off is that it is considered too dangerous for skiing at the time. Some daredevils, thinking that nothing is too difficult for them, are occasionally tempted to ski a trail that has been marked "Closed." First and foremost, this is foolish, as the ski patrols have no obligation to patrol that slope and in case of accident the skiers are far from help. Second, the trail may be closed in order to keep the snow in condition for a time later in the season or for a special competition. In the latter case using the trail indicates a lack of consideration for the management of the area as well as for the skiers who are to use it when it opens.

Never ski on a trail or slope that is too difficult for you. All ski areas mark their trails "Novice," "Intermediate," or "Expert," or possibly a combination of two—"Novice-Intermediate." If you have been skiing only a short time, don't assume that because in other sports you are as good as your friend Sally, who has been on the slopes since she was three, you are capable of accompanying her to the top of the mountain to try the new expert trail. Not only are you likely to break a leg, but you will infuriate the true experts who are entitled to use the trail and who will hardly appreciate rounding a curve at high speed only to find a novice "snowplowing" down the middle of the trail in front of them.

The other side of the coin must be mentioned too. If you are an expert, high-speed-loving skier, stay off the novice and intermediate slopes as much as possible. There is no need to make them more crowded than they ordinarily are, and nothing is more terrifying to a beginner than a hurtling skier rushing past him or even, as I have seen so often, running over the tips of his skis or actually knocking him down.

Skiers cannot be put on little tracks labeled "10 mph," "20 mph," "40 mph," and so forth, however, and there are certain to be occasions when a faster skier must pass a slower skier on a narrow trail. In order to warn him (or her) that he is about to pass, he calls "Track, right" or "Track, left," indicating that he will pass on that side, thereby warning the slower skier to pull to the other side—or at least not to make a sudden turn toward him as he passes.

If, because of a miscalculation, or for any reason whatever, you do knock another skier down, STOP! Apologize and make absolutely sure that he is not injured before you continue on down the hill.

If he appears to be having difficulty in regaining his feet, it is only common courtesy to go back to assist him. If he is unable to move or get up or is in pain, do not fly off hysterically looking for help, but stay with him, doing whatever you can to make him more comfortable, such as undoing his harnesses, until another skier approaches. Then, and only then, having asked the new arrival to stay with the injured person, should you go as fast as you possibly can to the nearest ski patrol. Never try to move the fallen skier. If he is suffering from a broken bone you may cause a much more serious injury if you move him incorrectly. The ski patrol are trained to do this and will have the proper equipment with them when they arrive.

Remember that the mountain may be very large, and it is very difficult to find another person at any given time. When you are a member of a group of family or friends it is wise to set a specific place and time at which to meet for meals, to go home, or just to "check in."

Otherwise, good manners for skiers are simply a matter of employing consideration for others at all times. Don't ridicule the novice even jokingly, and don't boast of your own skill. When the line waiting for the lift is long, don't shove ahead of those already waiting, but take your place patiently and cheerfully. If you are skiing alone, offer to pair up with another "single" on the double lifts, so that no chair goes up unoccupied. If you are with a group, don't hold the better skiers up by insisting that they wait for you, and if you are one of the more expert skiers, don't insist that the beginners accompany you where they are not capable of staying in control.

Skiing is a wonderful sport, both for physical thrills and for the social life that is a part of it. But more than in almost any other sport, consideration of others and good manners are essential to the enjoyment and safety of everyone.

৶63৶ *Artists, Entertainers, and Celebrities*

When we meet a performing artist or a distinguished lecturer or a celebrity of any kind, ordinary good manners and common courtesy SHOULD cover the situation, but only too often they don't. The forms of impoliteness may cover a very wide range—from the debutante's mother who shows no consideration for the musicians hired to play for the debut to the lion-hunting hostess who invites a celebrity to dinner, not because of any genuine feeling of friendship for him, but merely because of a misguided wish to impress her other guests.

WHEN THE ARTIST IS HIRED

Apart from the courtesies that every hostess offers to friends, acquaintances, or strangers when they are admitted to her house, there are rules that apply particularly to professional artists who are hired to entertain.

Unless their presence is to be a surprise, all entertainers should, of course, be admitted at the front door.

Musicians who play at a dance or at a wedding reception necessarily arrive before the guests, and they are shown to a room where they may leave their coats or change, and then to the place where they are to play. They should be greeted briefly by whoever is in charge of arrangements. Refreshments should be taken to them at the times that fit in best with their programs.

Soloists or actors who are to make their entrance on a stage should be shown to a dressing room and then to a convenient and comfortable spot to await the hour of their performance. They should be greeted as soon after their arrival as possible by the host or hostess (or master of ceremonies). Whether they meet the guests after their performance or not depends upon their personality and their wishes. When musicians or actresses or actors are especially charming or talented, or both, guests will almost surely ask to meet them, and the true professional is usually delighted to comply.

A real celebrity, whether a star in the entertainment world or a notable person who is to lecture, is usually the guest of honor at a private party and treated as such in every particular. Unless the party is given in honor of someone else, the guest performer sits on the hostess' right at dinner. When he is hired strictly as an entertainer, the host is delegated to greet the celebrity upon his arrival and to show him to wherever he is to wait until it is time for his entrance. The host remains with the artist or speaker until the hostess appears, greets the celebrity, conducts him to the room where he is to perform, and introduces him to the audience. At the end of the program, the hostess stands beside him and introduces those of her guests who wish to meet him. When this "ceremony" is over, the hostess may ask him to stay on and enjoy the party, or he is free to leave if he wishes.

In whatever category an artist belongs, there is a certain purely business matter-of-factness to the situation of a professional's fulfilling an engagement. He goes prepared to do his job to the best of his ability and at the close of his performance he receives the sum that has been agreed upon. Whether in addition to this he has a delightful evening or a trying one is, as far as his business contract goes, beside the point.

WHEN THE ARTIST IS A FRIEND

For obvious reasons, the hostess who considers that professional friends' talents are assets to which she has proprietary rights, is intolerable. Do you know Mrs. Hi Wayman, who invites Mr. Barry Tone or Mr. Hit Show to dine on Sunday evening? After dinner she coyly announces that she just knows that Mr. Tone will be delighted to sing, or Mr. Show will *of course* do that sensational scene that packs the theater to bursting every night in the week!

It is sometimes true that an entertainer can, or possibly must, refuse to do his act on the plea that his professional contracts prohibit his performance. But at an informal dinner at which one or two other entertainers have contributed their part, it can be embarrassing to refuse because it seems inconsiderate to those who are eagerly looking forward to it. But actually it is unfair to expect someone to return the courtesy of a little food and pleasant companions with an entertainment commercially valued at possibly thousands of dollars. And even if he is not at or near the top of his profession, remember that your guest is not a trained poodle to be shown off for the entertainment of your other guests.

FAVORS TAKEN FOR GRANTED

The unthinking casualness with which people ask favors of their professional friends is quite incredible. One would not think of going to a butcher and asking to be given a steak, nor to a flower shop and ask to be given a plant, and yet the friends of a professional artist will think nothing of asking for a sketch or a portrait. The work of every professional in his livelihood. If he gives to one person how can he refuse to give to another—and who will want to buy what is given so freely?

Another example, which occurs even more frequently: The barest acquaintances of an author think nothing of asking him for his books. Apparently many people imagine that books grow like daisies in the field and that an author need merely pick them at random. Doctors and lawyers are constantly asked for professional advice by people they meet casually in the houses of their friends. In many cases they are delighted to help someone they care for, but when they are asked to give advice that should only be afforded in an office, a conventional "I'm sorry" should be respected so that they are not forced into a position that makes them appear ungracious.

If a man (or a woman) plays a musical instrument well—for pleasure only—his friends can perfectly well ask him to play at a party. But even amateur musicians should not be asked to provide a background accompaniment to chatter. No thoughtful hostess would invite artists to play or sing and then make no effort to preserve a courteous silence during their performance.

AUTOGRAPHS

The number of people who recognize the celebrity on the street and the number who wait outside the stage door to get his autograph are one of the measures of his success. Rudeness or impatience with these fans can only have an adverse effect on his popularity, and therefore most entertainers or professionals whose success depends on their public image are willing to be watched, followed, and hounded for their signatures. The greater the degree of friendliness and tact with which they submit to these annoyances, the greater their success with the public.

By respecting the fact that their idol cannot defend himself against invasions of his privacy without alienating people, his fans should confine their efforts to the times when he expects to sign their books and otherwise fulfill his obligations as a public figure. When a prominent person is in his home or dining with friends, even though he may be in a public restaurant, shopping, seeking relaxation in a sport or a hobby, or otherwise attempting to lead a normal life, he should be allowed his privacy.

⊷64⊷ *With the Handicapped*

It is probably true that a majority of the people in the world have little contact with those unfortunate persons who are handicapped or disabled. If we have a cripple of any sort in our homes, or in the home of a relative or friend, we quickly become accustomed to the situation and learn how to act so as to be of the most help to him and to those around him. Should the disabled person be a member of our own family, we make every effort to learn all that we can about his problem, to seek professional advice, and to make his life, as well as our own, as normal as possible. This chapter, therefore, is devoted to people who meet the handicapped only from time to time and who, in making an effort to be helpful, may go about it in the wrong way, through a lack of knowledge. Their intentions may be the very best, but an act of kindness tendered in the wrong way may be a cause of much embarrassment and even actual harm to the very person they are trying to help.

There are certain rules that apply to your behavior in regard to all handicapped people, and by far the most important is this: NEVER stare or indicate that you are conscious that the person is different from others in any way. People who are getting themselves about in wheelchairs, who have mastered the use of crutch or brace, or who can manipulate a mechanical hand dexterously, take great pride in their independence and approach to normalcy. The last thing they wish is to be reminded by curious or overly solicitous persons that they have not achieved their goal. An offer of help to a man in a wheelchair who must navigate a steep curb in order to cross the street, or an arm proferred to a lady with a cane and a leg brace who is trying to get down a railless set of steps is, of course, in order. But before grabbing the wheelchair or seizing an arm, ask politely if, and in what way, you can be of assistance.

Another important rule is never to make personal remarks or ask personal questions of one with an obvious disability. If he wishes to talk about the accident that caused it or discuss his condition, let him introduce the subject, but never, never pry into his feelings or his clinical symptoms—subjects that he may be doing his best to forget.

DEAFNESS

There are, of course, all degrees of deafness, from partial loss of hearing in one ear to the more unusual extreme of complete deafness, which cannot be helped even by a hearing aid. It may only be necessary to speak a little more distinctly to one who is partially deaf or to repeat a remark that he may have missed. If you know that the hearing loss is in one ear, it is considerate to sit on the side of his good ear in movies, restaurants, or any other place where you may not face him. In the case of total hearing loss, the only means of contact is visual—through lip-reading—so the rules are quite different from those applying to someone with partial hearing.

You must speak distinctly and reasonably slowly.

Don't use exaggerated mouth movements. Distorted lip motions may confuse him, as he has been taught to read normal lip movement.

It is useless to shout to attract his attention. If he is not facing you, tap him gently on the arm or shoulder.

Be patient in talking to him and willing to repeat or make your statement in words that are easier for him to understand.

Encourage him to participate in family and social activities. Persons with severe handicaps tend to withdraw into themselves; this is not good for them and upsets their family and friends. A little extra urging and enthusiasm over their presence can make the handicapped feel much more like leading a normal life. On the other hand, try to be sensitive to their reactions, because too much pressure can have the opposite effect from that desired.

Between the slightly deaf and the totally deaf fall the many thousands with intermediate degrees of the disability. The first thing to be recommended for them is that they wear a hearing aid. There is no more stigma or embarrassment in this than in wearing glasses, and the family and friends of the hard-of-hearing who are reluctant should do their best to encourage them to overcome their hesitation. Once persuaded, they will find that their life will attain a normality they never thought possible. Here are some rules that should be observed for conversation with the partially deaf:

Don't raise your voice or shout—a hearing aid is probably adjusted to the normal tone of voice.

Call the person by name to attract his attention.

As with the more severely handicapped, be patient—willing to repeat if necessary. And if you must repeat, don't shout or appear annoyed. This will only embarrass him and make it harder for him to understand.

Don't exclude him from conversation, but try to place him so that he can see you or the group. Even normal people read lips unconsciously, and seeing your lips is a great help to one handicapped by partial deafness.

If you are one of those handicapped by deafness yourself, a few of the following suggestions may add to your comfort and that of your friends:

DO wear a hearing aid—they are now made in such a way as to be almost invisible, and even if they weren't, loss of hearing is no more "shameful" than loss of sight, and few people refuse to wear glasses.

Having gotten a hearing aid, use it! A strained expression of concentration, a constant "What did you say?" and answers that make no sense may cause you to appear inattentive or stupid. Keep your hearing aid turned on and gain the admiration of your friends for so capably overcoming your handicap.

With or without your aid, do listen attentively and concentrate on what people are saying. Even people with normal hearing miss many remarks through inattention.

Look at the people talking to you—their expression and their lips will help you to "hear" them.

Don't take advantage of your impairment by trying to arouse sympathy. There is no justifiable reason for sympathy—with a little extra effort a deaf person can lead a perfectly normal life.

BLINDNESS

The most important thing to remember when coming in contact with someone handicapped by blindness is that in every other respect he is probably exactly like you. His other faculties are in no way impaired, and compensating for his handicap, they may be more sensitively developed than yours. His interests and his way of life may be much the same as yours. He certainly has a problem to overcome that a sighted person does not face, but it is a problem with which one can learn to live, and most blind people have done so with considerable success.

Therefore the cardinal rule is this: Treat the blind man as you would any other person. Talk to him, in a normal voice, about the same subjects that would interest your other friends, including blindness, if it should come up. Don't avoid the use of the word *see*. A blind person uses it as much as anyone else. There is no reason to show surprise at his ability to dial telephone numbers, light cigarettes, dress himself, or perform any of the other daily chores that we all do. He has simply made a little more effort to learn to do them by touch or sound.

Aside from your attitude, there are several specific suggestions that will make your contacts with a blind person more pleasurable to you both.

When you are with, or pass by, a blind person on a street corner, you are perfectly correct in asking if you can help him to cross; but never grasp his arm or try to give assistance without first asking whether he wishes it or not. If he does, let *him* take *your* arm, which will give him far more confidence than being propelled forward by you. If he should ask you for directions, be sure to use left and right from his viewpoint—the direction he is facing.

If you go to a restaurant with a blind person, do not hesitate to read him the menu, including the prices if the occasion demands. You certainly may tell him quietly where the salt and pepper are and help him to the sugar and cream if he wishes. You may tell him how the items on his plate are arranged and help him cut his meat if necessary. But much of this he will prefer to do himself if you simply locate the food for him.

When he visits your home lead him to a chair and then just place his hand on the arm or back. If he is staying with you for any length of time, remember to tell him where the furniture is, inform him if anything is rearranged, and keep doors completely—never halfway—open or closed.

When taking him to a strange place, tell him quietly where the furniture is located and who is present. And before you leave him alone be sure that he has someone to talk to—one thing he cannot do (unless he is among good friends whose voices he recognizes) is single out a person who would, from his appearance, be congenial.

When there is a blind person in a room you have just entered, make your presence known and tell him, if he does not recognize your voice, who you are. Tell him also when you leave, so that he will not be left talking—to himself.

Last of all, if the blind person has a Seeing Eye dog, do not attempt to play with or distract the dog in any way. His attention must remain fully on his master, whose safety and well-being may depend entirely on his strict adherence to his training.

LOSS OR PARALYSIS OF A LIMB

While loss or paralysis of a leg is a tragic thing it does not necessarily affect the crippled person's relationship to others. If he is in a wheelchair he may need help in certain situations, but if he walks on crutches or has an artificial leg he undoubtedly leads a reasonably "normal" life with just a few limitations—which may not even be obvious to those around him.

Loss—or paralysis—of an arm is in some ways more difficult. If the arm is paralyzed, it may not "show" at all, and the cripple suffers agonies of embarrassment thinking that people are criticizing him for not helping them with heavy packages, lighting cigarettes, or whatever it may be that he cannot do. A person to whom this happens must be made to realize that there is nothing to be ashamed of in his condition, and to face up to it openly. Rather than sit back and let himself be thought rude, he must teach himself to say "I'm sorry. I can't help you—I've got a bad arm."

Perhaps the most common difficulty occurs when someone who has lost a right hand, or has an artificial one, is introduced to someone else. What to do next is up to the injured person; he may simply smile and say "Hello" without offering a hand, he may offer an artificial right hand, or he may offer his "good" left hand.

The person being introduced to him—if he recognizes the problem—lets the handicapped person take the lead. If the latter offers his left hand, the other takes it with *his* left, which is less awkward than using the right. If an artificial hand if offered, naturally the other person would shake it as he ordinarily would—saying nothing and showing no surprise—if possible.

If by chance, the non-handicapped person does *not* notice and offers his own right hand first, the crippled man takes it with his left, rather than leave the other standing awkwardly, hand extended in the air.

⁓ 65 ⁓ For Pets and People

A dog may be man's best friend and a cat by the hearth a very cozy sight, but their owners are responsible for seeing that they behave in such a way as to make them the real friends of everyone with whom they come in contact. Pets other than dogs and cats may be fewer in number, but their good manners are just as important. And if your children's rabbit or hamster cannot be trained not to make a nuisance of himself, *your* good manners take over, and you must insist that he be kept in his pen when visitors are in the house.

DOGS

For years people have complained to me about the unnecessary problems created by neighbors' pets. Is there anything that the Joneses can do to protect themselves from the ill-mannered dogs of neighbors or visitors or even houseguests? I could quote instances by the dozen of pleasant neighborhood friendships that have become strained and even broken by the Smith dog that barks all night or the Pope dog that runs through flower beds and possibly rolls or digs in them. Then there are other dogs brought by their owners into friends' houses and allowed to jump up on the furniture in spite of muddy paws or sharp claws that dig into the sofa cushions. There are some owners who complacently believe that their pet is perfectly trained to stay exactly where ordered. It never occurs to them, engrossed in conversation, to notice that less than a minute after being told to "stay" their pet has quietly slipped away on an exploring expedition. If he is a dog of mature intelligence he may, it is quite true, make an entirely impersonal and dignified survey of the premises. But if he is young and eager to test the taste, texture, and toughness of every new thing he sees, his investigation may all too soon become a foray of destruction. Should his adventuring result in damage of any sort, his owner is *obliged* to pay for it, just as he would if he had broken something himself. *For suggestions about the note of apology to be written after such an unfortunate episode, see Chapter 9.*

The behavior of a dog—like that of the rest of us—is seldom better in company than it is at home. If Kiltie (bright little Sheltie though he is) is allowed to run around the dinner table and beg, he will do the same in every other house.

Then there is that unaccountable lapse from trustworthy behavior that *can* overtake a dog who is allowed to wander at liberty in a strange house—particularly a new house. Dog owners sometimes fail to realize that it is the thoroughly impregnated scent of "human habitation" that tells him he is indoors. To his sense of smell, new upholstery or a newly laid carpet, which has had almost no human handling, is easily mistaken for outdoors. He can't tell the difference between indoor decoration and outdoor view just by sight. It is always safest in a strange house to keep him on a short leash unless his obedience is so perfect that wherever he may be he pays attention to nothing but his position at his master's side. On the street, at the command "Heel!" he takes his place at his master's side and remains there until told "All right, go!" You might test your own dog's training by noticing when you take him out whether he is welcomed by your neighbors' "Hello, Topsie," "Good morning, Blackie!" or by a frown that clearly says, "Oh dear, there's that dreadful dog again!"

Some people, it is true, do not like dogs at all. Unfortunately, if you are invited to stay with friends who do not welcome four-footed visitors, you cannot take your pet, and you must stay home unless you have someone with whom you can leave him or a good kennel at which you can board him. On the other hand, an absolutely obedient dog is almost always welcome, even as a houseguest. But the dog who is told "Come here" and responds by running in the opposite direction, the puppy who nips people on the ankle, the one who chews on everything in sight, the big, loose-lipped dog who on hot days drools like a teething baby over the suits and dresses of visitors—these animals are not social assets even in the opinion of dog-lovers.

Training a dog to such a degree that he obeys every word spoken, or every gesture made to him, requires consistent as well as persistent patience directed by practical common sense. That perfect training is entirely possible has been proved not only by the miracle dogs that are Seeing Eyes for the blind and by the dogs trained as assistants to the police, but by all other breeds of dogs that perform in the theater, industriously herd sheep, and work flawlessly in the hunting field. Surely, then, it is not too much to ask that adequate education be given to the four-footed members of the family. One thing is certainly true: The rewards of good manners are very great. Not only does the behavior of a canine gentleman (or lady) reflect the good sense and good manners of his master, but the dog himself acquires stature as a companion, a guardian, and a friend —in short, a recognized personality.

CATS

In some ways cats present different problems, for they are taken visiting far less often. When your cat has the run of the neighborhood, however, you may have to take steps to see that he does not become a regular visitor to the house of someone who once innocently set out a saucer of milk in the kitchen only to find the cat later perched between the Dresden figurines on the mantel. It is perfectly proper, before an accident has a chance to occur, to ask your neighbor not to feed your pet, as the habit is hard to break and can easily become a neighborhood problem.

In your own house you may be quite accustomed to having your cat jump into your lap without warning, but remember that your guest probably isn't. Not only will there be a suit or dress covered with hairs and possibly snagged; there may be a broken teacup or a burned carpet as a result of the natural and involuntary start of surprise. Until you know your visitor well, it is far safer to put Fluffy securely in another room. This is no way unkind to your pet, for very likely you are saving him from the discipline his overenthusiasm might cause.

Some people, of course, have real aversions to all cats, even the best behaved, and you should no more force Fluffy's presence on them than you would force crabmeat on a guest who is allergic to it.

THE OTHER SIDE

If you are one of those people who have an allergy or an aversion to dogs, cats, hamsters, white mice, or any of the other pets you are likely to encounter, it is only sensible to tell your host or hostess quietly and unobtrusively, just as you would mention a food allergy to avoid embarrassment at the dinner table. No one will wish you to suffer while you are a guest in his house, and a few words can usually prevent much discomfort and possibly an unpleasant misunderstanding.

On the other hand, if you are fond of household animals you should take every care to respect their training and encourage their good habits. Don't, for example, thump the sofa beside you and invite Kiltie to jump up until you have asked whether he is allowed to sit on the furniture. Don't feed an animal without his owner's permission—you would not give a child candy without asking his mother first. If you wish your pet-owning friends and neighbors to respect your rights, do remember that your thoughtless actions may undo months of careful training.

And one final word from the side of the pet. Don't acquire a pet—whether dog, cat, turtle, or canary—unless you are prepared to give it the best physical care you possibly can, as well as your love and respect.

If you have a young child who has been begging for a puppy, a rabbit, a baby crocodile, or whatever it may be, think twice before you give in. It is *you* who will end up cleaning the messes, feeding the crocodile, or attending the accouchement of the mother rabbit. No matter how firmly you start out—"You can have a puppy if you will take care of it entirely by yourself"—it rarely works that way. Little Susie goes to Sally's for the night, Dickie goes off to camp, and Mom takes care of the pet! I know, and from sad experience! When my daughter was very small we gave her a parakeet, thinking that would surely be easy enough to care for. To my horror and shame, one morning I found her parakeet dead in its cage—she had fed it religiously, but had forgotten for days to give it any water. So, a pet is a wonderful thing for a small child, and having one can teach the youngster valuable lessons in tenderness, patience, and responsibility. But parents *must* realize that small children have not yet developed a strong sense of duty, nor an understanding of the needs of dependent animals, and they must be willing to supervise the pet's care and take responsibility for its well-being.

⋅≲66≳⋅ Gifts and Giving

This chapter discusses gifts and giving in general, and in a variety of situations. *You will find detailed information on presents for specific occasions in other chapters—for wedding gifts, see Chapter 51; for shower gifts Chapter 35; and for anniversary gifts, Chapter 45.*

GIFTS OF MONEY

Although giving money is sometimes a lazy way of avoiding the trouble of choosing a gift, there are occasions when a check is the most welcome present of all. There are many elderly couples with a limited income who love the opportunity of shopping for some long-desired object, and there are few teenagers who don't relish the idea of a little extra cash. *For a description of a "money tree," see Chapter 45, pages 498–499.*

For people who dislike the idea of giving cash or a check, a gift certificate is a good compromise. One couple I know took the trouble to send for a gift certificate in the leading department store of the town to which their neighbors were moving, and presented it at their going-away party. Somehow the thoughtfulness of this gesture made the gift seem far warmer and more personal than a check.

In most circumstances it is incorrect to include a request for money on the invitation to any private party such as an anniversary celebration or open house. If, however, the people giving the party have planned a special group present such as tickets for a vacation trip, a new television set, or a fine painting, it would be proper to enclose a short note with the invitation explaining what has been planned and asking the guests if they would like to make a contribution in place of bringing an individual gift. Each guest who contributes should sign the card accompanying the gift.

When a great number of checks or gifts of cash are received, as at a wedding reception or a big anniversary party, the envelopes need not be opened at the time. At smaller parties, or when just a few envelopes are given, the recipient opens them and thanks the giver, but does not mention the amount in front of others.

THANK-YOU LETTERS *(For examples, see Chapter 9.)*

Thank-you letters are not necessary for presents that have been given in person on a birthday, at a house party, a shower, or other similar occasions. Although it is in no way wrong to write a note, sincere verbal thanks at the time you receive the gift are sufficient. Nor do thank-you or "bread-and-butter" letters themselves require any reply: That would be inviting a never-ending exchange of correspondence. A thank-you gift sent with, or in place of, a bread-and-butter letter should, however, be acknowledged if only so that the sender will know it has been received. Sending printed cards of thanks is inexcusable, unless a personal note is added. In cases where a delay in sending handwritten notes is unavoidable, a printed card acknowledging receipt of the gift and stating that a letter will follow is the best way of keeping people from wondering what happened to their present. But the handwritten note must follow as soon as basically possible.

A NEWSPAPER "CARD OF THANKS"

In certain localities, most especially small towns and rural areas, it is not only permissible but expected that recipients of a large number of gifts, or kindnesses, put a public "thanks" in the paper. Here is a typical "card of thanks."

> *CARD OF THANKS*
> *We wish to express our thanks*
> *to all those unselfish people*
> *and organizations from whom we*
> *received cards and gifts on the*
> *occasion of our fiftieth wedding*
> *anniversary*
> *Sincerely,*
> *Mr. and Mrs. Joseph Horne*

When this is done it is not necessary to send written thanks to each and every donor and card-sender. But it would be most unappreciative not to write a personal note to those close to you who have gone out of their way to give something very special or to assist or participate in your celebration in any way.

These "cards of thanks" are published for occasions such as funerals, retirement parties, anniversaries, birthdays, political campaigns, professional advancements, and any other events that result in special kindnesses, assistance, gifts, or contributions.

OPENING PRESENTS AT A PARTY

Half the fun of giving and receiving presents at any party is to see and enjoy what everyone else brought. The nicest way to do this is to have all the presents collected in one place until everyone has arrived, at which time the guest of honor opens them. Whether a gift is a fifty-cent "joke" present or a more expensive article is not important. The recipient reads the cards enclosed, particularly if they are funny ones, and shows enthusiasm for each gift. It is important to include a card even with a gift you deliver personally because many people like to collect and save the cards they receive at these times as mementos of the occasion. If anybody has given money instead of a present, the amount should not be mentioned but the recipient may well say something like, "This is a really welcome contribution toward the china we are saving for," or whatever else may be appropriate.

On occasions when gifts are not necessarily expected, but two or three people bring them regardless, they are opened in the donor's presence but without drawing the attention of other guests. This might happen, for instance, when a couple bring a gift to a dinner hostess. She must show her appreciation, but making a display of the present could embarrass guests who did not bring one.

FLOWERS AS PRESENTS

Flowers may be sent by almost everyone to almost anyone. There are certain times when sending them—if you can possibly afford it—is obligatory. These occasions include funerals, debutante parties, dinners at private homes in Europe, and others where local custom demands it. Flowers may be used in place of, or in addition to, the "gifts for many occasions" listed on pages 795–802.

Some thoughtful people are constantly sending flowers; other people seldom do. Most of us send them much less often than we might because we think those we can afford to buy are not good enough. This reminds me of our daughter, who as a teenager received, at times, corsages and gifts of flowers. I can truthfully say the one she treasured most was a single red rose from a boy whose knowledge of how to please a girl was well in advance of his years.

Flowers make the best gifts for a dinner hostess. Ideally, they should be sent ahead of time, so that the hostess may have them on display when the guests arrive. If you are taking them with you, it is best to have them already "arranged" so that your hostess does not have to leave her guests to put them in a container. Should you want to take a few flowers from your own garden, which are easily arranged, you might even say as you give them to your hostess, "Show me where there is a vase, and I'll put them in water for you" —especially if a number of other guests are arriving at the same time.

In Europe it is customary to take cut flowers to a hostess, and if you do not do so, you should send flowers, with a thank-you card, the next day.

This is also much appreciated in our own country.

When you are the guest of honor at a private party, you should send your hostess a flower arrangement the day of the party.

Now that it is possible to order flowers from a local florist and have them delivered in a distant town or city by an associated florist there, there is no excuse for not remembering birthdays, anniversaries, and other special occasions in this way. Those careless or lazy people who "just don't think" to get a package off in time need only pick up the telephone and make a local call to give pleasure to someone far away.

For many years flowers were not considered an appropriate gift for men. In recent years, however, the attitude has changed, and men are no longer ashamed to show their appreciation of beauty— as represented by a lovely plant or flowers. Both are acceptable as gifts to a man who is ill, who is opening a new office, or as a birthday gift. If you fear that he may think a flower arrangement too "feminine," don't hesitate to give him a plant or terrarium. The latter, especially, requires little care and is ideal for a man's apartment or office.

UNWANTED GIFTS

Many people are far more sensitive than their friends suspect. For this reason it is important never to choose a gift that might be construed as a show of criticism. A present of a cookbook can be most welcome, provided your friend knows that you have enjoyed her cooking and—even more important—you know she likes to cook. This same cookbook might well be resented if given shortly after a disastrous dinner at which the food was all but inedible.

Presents requiring constant care when given to people who are not interested or able to give that care can be a real disaster. Foremost among these are live birds or fish or animals. The well-meaning family friend who gives a young child a puppy or kitten without first clearing the matter with his parents will not long remain a family friend.

Then there are the white elephants that seem to grow in every gift shop. Before buying any present in this category think to yourself, "What will she do with it? Does she have a place for it?" and if you can't find an answer, don't buy it.

Ostentatious gifts are in very poor taste. The gift that has obviously stretched the purse strings of the sender, or is not in keeping with the life-style of the receiver, is a gift that gives no pleasure at all.

Many people get into a pattern of exchanging gifts with friends or relatives and then find it difficult to stop, even though their relationship has changed to the point where the exchange of gifts has become a meaningless nuisance.

I can only say, "Be frank." Well ahead of the occasion (Christmas, birthday, or whenever the gifts habitually arrive), either write or say to the person, "I've loved your gifts, but what with inflation [or the new baby, or redecorating the house, or whatever seems a good reason] let's just send cards this year. Write us your family news—that will be the best present of all."

When someone arrives at your door with an unexpected Christmas present, you are "on the spot." Unless you have a supply of small gifts ready for such an emergency (not a bad idea in some localities!) you can only say, "Thanks so much—but you really shouldn't have done this." This will indicate that you do not expect to start an annual exchange of gifts.

"NO GIFTS, PLEASE"

When an invitation says "No gifts, please," the request should be followed. If you are very close to the sender or the guest of honor, you may take or send a gift to his home before or after the party.

791

But to take it to the celebration is only embarrassing to the hostess and rude to the guests who *have* complied with the request.

GIFT WRAPPINGS

Just as a picture needs a frame, a gift needs an attractive wrapping—as well as a card—to go with it. Most department and gift stores provide special gift wrapping free or at a slight extra charge. For those who have neither the time nor the inclination to wrap their own presents, this is a great boon. On the other hand, devising a

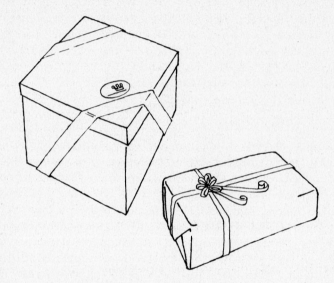

clever or entertaining way to present a gift can add to the fun of giving it. In many cases an unusual or attractive package adds greatly to the present itself. Wine bottles packaged in picnic baskets or golf balls sold in cigarette boxes are examples of this. The original packaging you do yourself, however, can be even more entertaining or useful. A friend of mine camouflaged his Christmas present of ski poles for his teenage daughter as a poinsettia plant. The handles of the poles were stuck into a pot filled with sand, and red-and-green construction paper was used to make the petals and leaves to complete the illusion.

In recent years we have been made to realize the importance of saving our forests and therefore the importance of not using paper extravagantly and needlessly. I have received many letters suggesting ways to conserve paper and I pass a few on to you!

The first and most obvious—reuse wrapping paper. Instead of ripping it off packages, remove it carefully, fold it, and store it where it can be laid flat, or roll it.

Use pretty boxes that do not require an outside wrapping of paper. To decorate plain boxes, you can paste colorful cards or cut-outs of any kind on them.

Inventive packages can be made by using brown paper bags, colorful shopping bags, and even newspaper. Pieces of thick, colorful, leftover yarn serves well as "ties," instead of paper ribbons.

At Christmas one or two large boxes can be wrapped for each member of the family, and the smaller packages placed in them, unwrapped.

MARKING GIFTS

Discussion of a gift's appearance leads to the question of whether to personalize or monogram it. The obvious drawback is that once an article has been initialed it can never be returned. Therefore, before you have anything of value marked, be sure it is something you know is wanted and also that it is the right size, color, and style. If you *are* sure of this, then initials are a handsome addition to many gifts.

It is always possible, also, for the receiver to have the gift marked later. If free engraving is offered with the purchase, it will be honored at any time later. If there is a charge, however, you should have the bill for the marking sent to you, and be sure that the recipient knows this.

When handkerchiefs or other articles that may be marked with a single letter are given as a gift, the initial of a woman's first name is used, whereas the initial of his last name is used for a man.

For details on marking silver, glass, linen, etc., see Chapter 47.

"JOINT" PRESENTS

There are many occasions when it is perfectly permissible to send a "joint" present.

The staff in an office may contribute to a single present for a co-worker.

Friends invited to a birthday or anniversary party may be asked by the hostess to contribute to one big present rather than give individual gifts.

Engaged couples may give "joint" wedding and birthday gifts. However, they usually give individual presents to members of their own families on Christmas.

Two people or two couples may get together to give a weekend hostess something nicer than they could afford individually.

On the other side of the fence, you may sometimes give a "joint" present *to* several people. Godparents who hesitate to give a gift only to a godchild who has brothers or sisters, stepparents, and many other face this problem. Rather than give a present to each of the children in the family, you may give *one* gift—a game, puzzle, etc. —that can be used by all.

"WHAT DO YOU WANT FOR CHRISTMAS?"

When someone asks you what you want for Christmas, or for a wedding present, or for *any* occasion, don't say, "Oh, I don't know," or "I'd rather *you* picked something out." Many people honestly have very little imagination about gifts, and in your own interests they need help. Unless you know it is within their means and easily available, don't mention a specific item. But suggestions such as "You know I love to cook, and *all* kitchen gadgets fascinate me," or "I'm crazy about plants—anything green would be perfect," or "John and I love modern things, and our walls are very bare—any sort of a drawing or print would be great," can be very helpful to the person who is puzzling over a gift for you.

RETURNING AND EXCHANGING GIFTS

If an engagement is broken, the woman must return to her former fiancé the ring and all other gifts of value that he has given. Gifts received from relatives or friends, if they are not monogrammed, should also be returned with a short note of explanation. Shower gifts, too, should be returned if the marriage is called off. Once the wedding has taken place, however, gifts are not returned, no matter how short the marriage. Strictly speaking, the presents belong to the wife, but the usual procedure is for the husband to keep those items that came from his own family and friends, and those particularly meaningful or useful to him, while the wife keeps the others.

If a gift arrives broken, take it, with its wrappings, to the shop where it was purchased. If it comes from another city, return it by mail, accompanied by a letter explaining how it arrived. Any good store will replace the merchandise on reasonable evidence that it was received in a damaged condition. Do not involve the donor in this transaction; do not even let him or her know what happened if you can possibly avoid doing so. Of course, when an *insured* package arrives damaged in the mail, you must inform the sender so that he can collect the insurance and replace the gift.

Although a bride should not exchange presents chosen for her by her own or her bridegroom's family—unless told she may do so—other duplicate wedding gifts may be exchanged. She need not mention the fact that she is exchanging a present in her thank-you letter, especially if the donor lives far away and is not apt to visit her soon. However, it would be wise to explain the exchange to someone who will be in her house and will surely notice the absence of the gift. To avoid embarrassment a donor should never ask, "Where is that lovely bowl we gave you?" The time-honored custom permitting the exchange of duplicate wedding presents is so practical and sensible that no one should be offended by it.

Exchanging gifts received on other occasions, however, may require a little more tact. A present should not be exchanged just because it doesn't happen to be exactly what you want. If it is a duplicate, it would be thoughtful to call the giver and say, "Mary, I happen to have two bottle warmers already. Would you mind terribly if . . . ?" Or "Sue, I adore the sweater you sent but it's a thirty-two and I take a thirty-six. I'm going to try to find one as nearly like it as possible in my size." Then in your thank-you note tell Mary or Sue how much you are enjoying what you got as a replacement.

Gifts given to prospective nuns or priests who decide against a religious life should be returned also. The situation is similar to that of a broken engagement.

GIFTS FOR MANY OCCASIONS

ENGAGEMENTS

Presents are expected only from close relatives and intimate friends and are almost always intended especially for the bride.

Towels for bathroom or guest towels
Luggage for honeymoon
Blanket cover
Jewelry

Lingerie
Plastic table mats
Bar or kitchen towels
Table linen

SHOWERS

Gifts should be chosen to meet the specifications (including color and size) given in the invitation.

Literally any useful or decorative article appropriate to the particular occasion is acceptable, but it should not be elaborate and should not be intended to take the place of a wedding present. Something made personally by the donor is traditional, and no matter how simple, is often the most appreciated gift of all.

WEDDINGS

See Chapter 51, "Wedding Gifts."

BRIDAL ATTENDANTS' GIFTS TO BRIDE OR GROOM, OR BOTH

After-dinner coffee spoons, each engraved with the initials of one attendant
Silver tray, pitcher, or cigarette box engraved with attendants' names
Coffee table with copper plaque engraved with attendants' initials

FROM BRIDE TO HER BRIDESMAIDS

Small silver picture frame with bride's picture
Bracelet with disk engraved with wedding date
Gold charm for bracelet or neck chain
Needlepoint napkin rings, with design of bridesmaids' initials

FROM BRIDEGROOM TO HIS USHERS

Monogrammed key case or key ring
Initialed silver belt buckle
Monogrammed leather jewel case
Pewter beer mugs or "jiggers"

ANNIVERSARY PARTIES

Picture album (to be filled later if possible with pictures taken at the party)
Picture frame with a family portrait
Bottle of wine or champagne

Plant—one that can be planted outside if the couple have a yard

Books—especially those related to the couple's hobbies or interests

It is not necessary to limit gifts to the traditional materials for each anniversary, but for those who wish to do so, a list of the appropriate choices is found in Chapter 45, page 499.

FAREWELL PARTIES

FOR THOSE PERMANENTLY LEAVING A NEIGHBORHOOD

Scrapbook with mementos of the years spent together (if you have the imagination and inclination)

Gift certificate from a department store in their future hometown

Framed picture of their home, or any other place that has special meaning for them

Subscription to your local newspaper

BON VOYAGE PARTIES

Books

Small games

Trip diary

Guidebooks

Champagne or wine (especially welcome if you arrange with the wine steward to have it served as a surprise during the voyage)

Passport folder

Money-exchange guide

Playing cards in a case

Small leather picture frame with a family picture

Travel kit of cleaning and laundry products

Camera film

HOUSEWARMINGS

Cigarette box

Wastebasket

Bookends

Magazine rack

Leather or silver stamp holder (especially nice when filled with postage stamps)

Potted plant

Seeds or bulbs for the garden

Address book including names, addresses, and phone numbers of recommended local services and stores

NEW BABIES

Sweater or other clothing
Blanket or comforter
Crib toys
Baby food
Bath articles
Furnishings for the baby's room (picture, little chair, etc.)
Spoon and fork
Bibs

CHRISTENINGS

Silver porringer
Hairbrush and comb
Savings bond
For a girl, one pearl or charm—to be added to later
Baby's memory book or album

BIRTHDAYS

FOR TEENAGE BOYS
Clothing
Sports equipment
Records or cassettes
Books on favorite sports or hobbies
Wall posters
FOR A "SWEET SIXTEEN"
Enameled or embroidered picture frame
Gold circle pin
Pocketbook or carryall
Books
Crystal or china ornament for her room
Silk scarf, belt, or other accessories
FOR A WIFE OR HUSBAND
Any little present you know he or she wants but has avoided
buying because *you* maintained that it was foolish or extrava-
gant
FOR AN OLDER COUPLE
Travel tickets for a special vacation
Gift certificate
Newspaper subscription
Plant
Books

FOR FRIENDS
>Any foolish "gag" present. Unless a very close friend, to avoid embarrassment, don't give expensive gifts.

FOR EVERYONE
>Anything you have knitted, baked, constructed—in short, MADE—yourself!

FIRST COMMUNION

>Bible
>Prayer book
>Jewelry
>Fine book
>Religious charm or pendant

BAR MITZVAH

A gift of money is most generally given. The amount depends on the closeness of the donor to the youngster. Otherwise, see suggestions for "Teenage Boys."

GRADUATION

>Money, gift certificate, savings bond, or stock
>Initial deposit in a new savings account
>Bedside clock or clock-radio
>Desk pen-and-pencil set or desk lamp
>Books (especially those useful for his or her chosen career, or standard reference works)
>Luggage
>Camera
>Sports equipment
>Stereo or hi-fi equipment
>Jewelry (tie-tack, ring, watch, etc.)
>Leather belt
>If he has a car: emblem for side door or bumper
>Leather case for maps and registration
>Key ring

FOR WEEKEND VISIT

>Gourmet hors d'oeuvres
>A pair of *good* scissors
>Toys for young children
>Liquor or wine
>Plastic place mats

Steak or casserole dish ready for heating (check with the hostess
in advance)
Record album
Flowers or plant
A new game or jigsaw puzzle (especially good if hostess has
children)
Cookies, a cake, or candy

GIRL TO A BOYFRIEND

Key case
Wallet
Imprinted stationery
Picture frame with her picture
Something she has knitted or personalized herself, such as a
sweater, mittens, or golf-club covers
Books
Records

BOY TO A GIRL FRIEND

Pair of tickets to a hit show
Costume jewelry
Inexpensive charm
Clothing accessories (gloves, scarf, belt, etc., but not "personal"
clothing)
Books
Records
Stuffed toy animal

**TO NURSES AND MEDICAL AND OTHER PROFESSIONAL PEOPLE IN
APPRECIATION OF SPECIAL CONSIDERATION**

FOR HOSPITAL NURSES
Cookies, candy, or fruit sent to nurses' desk on patient's floor
FOR DOCTORS, LAWYERS, AND OTHERS
Desk set
Food specialty (e.g., homemade fruitcake)
Liquor or wine
Golf balls
Carving set
Contribution to his favorite charity

FOR SICK PEOPLE AND HOSPITAL PATIENTS

Light reading matter (both in weight and content)
Homemade soup, cookies, or other specialty (clear *all* food gifts
with doctor first)

Flower arrangements or potted plants (not loose, cut flowers)
Autobridge game
Crossword-puzzle book
Bed jacket or dressing gown
Pillow-type backrest, if illness is prolonged
Cologne

FOR A DEBUTANTE

Flowers or corsage
Simple "good" jewelry
Pretty ornament for her room
White leather picture frame for debut picture
Perfume
Good stationery

FOR A TEACHER

Suggest to your classmates that you all give a combined present in place of individual gifts. This might be an atlas or leather-bound dictionary or any other professional book, or something more personal, such as a sweater, or ornamental, such as a desk clock or a picture for the wall. If individual gifts are preferred:

Handkerchiefs
Bud vase
Homemade jelly or Christmas cookies
Inexpensive jewelry
Christmas tree ornament

FOR A NUN

Check or cash
White linen handkerchiefs
Religious picture or statue
Books (including light novels)
Small luxury items (lotion, powder, bath accessories)
Black gloves
Black stockings
Magazine subscription
Cookies and candy
Warm blanket or shawl

FOR A NEWLY ORDAINED PRIEST OR MINISTER

Magazine subscription
Leather diary
Pen-and-pencil set

Gift certificate at a local department store
Pipe and/or pipe rack, or a cigarette lighter
Leather address book
Wristwatch
Briefcase or wallet

✦67✦ Tipping

Although information about how and when to tip is given throughout this book, I believe that a complete list of suggested tips for all situations will be useful to my readers.

Tipping, whether we like it or not, is here to stay. It would, of course, be ideal if everyone who offered a service of any kind were paid so well that he did not need to depend on tips, but this, unfortunately, is not the case. Therefore we must remember that many, many people are dependent on a "reward" for good service, in addition to their regular salaries.

I do believe firmly, however, that the tip should be merited. Where service is bad and the personnel is deliberately rude, inattentive, or careless, the amount should be reduced. If it is bad *enough*, no tip should be left at all. If everyone continues to tip at the same rate, regardless of the effort made to please, there is no incentive to make any extra effort at all. We are all at the mercy of the "system," but by rewarding good service more generously and withholding a gratuity when the service is bad, we can help to make tipping acceptable.

RESTAURANTS

Waiter or waitress—15 percent of the bill. If service is extraordinarily good, slightly higher. In a few very famous, elegant restaurants, 20 percent is expected. Odd pennies should not be left on the plate.

Headwaiter or maitre d'—No tip, if he does no more than show you to a table. If he arranges a special table, cooks a special dish in front of you, or offers other special services, he is given $2 to $5 as you leave, depending on the type of restaurant and the number of people in your party. The headwaiter at a restaurant you patronize regularly should receive $5 to $10 from time to time.

Hostess—No tip, except as described above.

Wine steward—15 percent of wine bill.

Bartender—If you have a drink at the bar before eating, he is given 10 to 15 percent of the bill before you go to your table.

Waiter in smorgasbord restaurant—10 percent of the bill if he does nothing but remove plates. If he assists in other ways, serves coffee, drinks, etc., 15 percent of the bill.

Busboys—No tip. Tips in restaurants large enough to employ busboys are usually pooled, and busboys are given a percentage. If tips are not pooled, the waiter gives a portion of his tip to the busboy for his tables. Busboys in cafeterias are given 25¢ for carrying trays to tables.

Lunch-counter help—15 percent of bill—never less than 15¢. No tip necessary for a cup of coffee or a soft drink without food.

Checkroom—25¢ for each coat. No extra for parcels unless very many, or very large.

Ladies'-room attendant—25¢ if basin is cleaned, towel is offered, etc. No tip necessary if you do nothing but use the toilet.

Cigarette girl—25¢ in addition to the price of the cigarettes. In a nightclub or expensive restaurant, the change from a dollar bill is left for the girl, even though the cigarettes only cost 65¢ to 70¢.

Restaurant musicians—No tip for strolling players unless they play a specific request. Then the tip is usually $1. If several members of a large party make requests, the tip might be up to $5. A pianist or organist also receives $1 or $2 for playing your request.

Parking attendant—25¢ when he brings your car to you.

TIPS ON CREDIT CARDS

When the charge slip is brought to you, it shows the total of your charges for your meal and the amount of the tax on that total. Below that there is a space for the tip, which you must fill in. It is perfectly correct to base your 15 percent on the total of the meal alone, but most people use the total plus tax, making the tip slightly higher than 15 percent.

In some restaurants a bill is presented to you before the credit-company charge slip is prepared. You add the amount you wish to tip and sign the slip. The charge slip is *then* brought in for your signature, with the total amount, including tip, already filled in. This is done to avoid any future complications between restaurant and credit company.

You may also leave the tip in cash, rather than add it to the bill. Many people prefer to do this, feeling that it will get to the right person faster than if he had to wait until the credit company reimbursed the restaurant.

DINNER PARTIES IN RESTAURANTS AND CATERED DINNERS

Some restaurants and caterers add a service charge (usually 15 percent) to the bill for a dinner party. This is divided among the waiters and/or waitresses. The host is not obligated to do any more, unless he wishes to give an additional amount if he has been especially pleased. After a large dinner the host should, in addition, give the person in charge—headwaiter, maitre d', or whoever it may be—a separate tip of $5 to $10, depending on the size and elaborateness of the party. If no service charge is added to the bill, the host gives the person in charge 15 percent of the cost and asks that he divide it among the waiters. When a caterer sends one or two waiters or perhaps a bartender and waitress to serve at a dinner party at home, the host or hostess gives them their tips personally before they leave. For a dinner of ten people, for which the bill might be $100, each would receive about $10, or his share of 20 percent of the bill.

HOTELS

Chambermaid—Transients (businessmen, people "enroute" leave no tip for a one-night stay. This change in custom has been brought about by the popularity of motels, where little or no tipping at all is required. For a stay of several days tip 50¢ a night; for one week, $3 to $5, depending on the class of hotel.

Waiter—15 percent of the check for each meal as a transient. In an American-plan or resort hotel, where the same waiter serves you every day, one-half of 20 percent of the total hotel bill. The remainder is divided among others who have served you.

For more details, see Chapter 23.

Room waiter—15 percent of the bill for each meal, even though there is a service charge for room service.

Headwaiter—*see page 803, information on headwaiter, under*

"restaurants." After a prolonged stay, $5 a week if he has rendered good service.

Bellboy or bellhop—25¢ for opening the room, plus 25¢ for each bag. Generally $1 is the maximum tip, unless the amount of luggage is unusually large. Tip, as well, 25¢ for paging, and 25¢ for the delivery of messages, ice, set-ups, newspapers, packages, etc.

Porter—50¢ a trunk, or $1 for an extraheavy load.

Checkroom attendant—25¢ for a coat and hat.

Doorman—No tip for opening the door for an arriving guest; no tip for merely calling a cab from a stand; 25¢ if he assists with unloading baggage; 25¢ if he must make an effort to call a taxi; for a prolonged stay, $1 or $2 a week rather than individual tips.

Valet—No tip for pressing or cleaning. The charge is added to the hotel bill.

Barbers, manicurists, beauty-parlor operators—Tip on the same basis as in shops outside of hotels. *See page 809, under "beauty parlors."*

Bootblacks—25¢.

Desk clerks—No tip unless, during a prolonged stay, special service is rendered, in which case $5 would be ample.

Parking attendant—25¢ when car is delivered.

MOTELS AND MOTOR LODGES

Transient—No tips except for dining-room waiters. *See page 803, information on waiters, under "restaurants."*

Large chain and "full-service" motels—Exactly the same as tips for hotel personnel.

TRAINS

Dining-car waiters—15 percent of the bill, no less than 25¢.

Bar or club-car stewards—15 percent of bar bill; no less than 25¢ for bringing setups to sleeping cars.

Pullman porter—$1 per person per night; more if he has rendered special services.

Redcaps (luggage porters)—Rates as fixed and posted. The charge is generally 25¢ a bag. A tip of 25¢ to 50¢ is usually added, depending on the amount of luggage.

PLANES

No tip is ever given to "in-flight" personnel—stewardesses, stewards, hostesses, or flight officers. Skycaps (porters) receive 25¢ a bag or $1 or more for a baggage cart full of luggage.

SHIPS *(see also Chapter 24.)*

Transatlantic crossing (five days):

PER PERSON	FIRST CLASS	CABIN CLASS	TOURIST
Cabin steward (or stewardess)	$10	$7	$5
Dining-room steward	10	7	5
Head dining steward	5	3	2
Deck steward	3	2	1

When a "team" of stewards serves you, you tip only one, and they will divide it themselves. In addition, tip as follows:

Cabin boy—25¢ for errands performed.

Bath steward—If no private bath, $1.

Lounge and bar steward—15 percent of the bill at the time of service, no less than 25¢.

Wine steward—15 percent of the total wine bill.

Purser and other ship's officers—No tip.

Stevedores—$2 to $5 for heavy trunks. For large suitcases, 50¢ apiece.

CRUISE SHIPS

Tip 10 to 15 percent of the total fare. Divide one-half the amount between the cabin steward and the dining-room steward. The remainder is divided among those mentioned immediately above, in commensurate proportions. It will be appreciated if you give an appropriate portion of the total tip at the end of *each* week, so that the personnel will have cash to spend during stops in ports.

Some travel agents recommend $1 to $1.50 a day to dining-room and cabin stewards, depending on the "class" you travel and the service you receive. Others are tipped in the neighborhood of $2 or $3 a week.

Certain cruise-ship lines include a charge for "gratuities" in the fare. Check to be sure about this, and if there is such a charge, you need do no more than give $1 or $2 to someone who has been especially helpful.

TAXI DRIVERS

FARE	TIP
Less than 50¢	20¢
50¢ to $1.50	25¢
$1.50 to $2	30¢ to 35¢
$2 to $3	40¢ to 50¢
$4 to $5	75¢ to $1
higher fares	15 percent of fare

Privately hired limousines or taxis—15 percent of fare.
Airport limousines—No tip.

CHARTER BUSES AND BUS TOURS

Charter- and sightseeing-bus drivers—no tip.

Driver-guides—Some chartered buses and sightseeing-bus services provide guides or driver-guides. Passengers generally tip 25¢ to 50¢ per person for this service, but it is not obligatory. On a prolonged tour, driver and guide (if there are both) are tipped $2 to $5, depending on the length of the tour, unless gratuities are included in the fare. The person in charge of a private charter sometimes asks for contributions of $1 a couple as a tip for the driver.

CLUBS

Personnel in most private clubs are not tipped at the time they render service. Members are requested to give to a Christmas fund for employees, and most give additional tips to those who have given them personal attention—the ladies'-room attendant, locker-room attendants, the headwaiter, etc. These personal tips are generally $5 to $10, depending on the type of club and the amount of service. Additional tips are often given for special services throughout the year.

Guests in clubs are not expected to tip personnel unless they are residents for a time. In that case, if no service charge is added to their bill, they tip as they would in a first-class hotel.

Employees in private clubs are usually paid well enough so that they are not dependent on everyday tips for their livelihood.

Caddies receive 15 percent of the regular club charge for eighteen holes. For nine holes, the tip may be closer to 20 percent.

BARBERS

Haircut in a small rural area for a child—25¢ to 35¢.

Haircut in a city barber shop—50¢.

Shampoo, shave, manicure, etc.—$1 to $2, depending on the type of shop and the number of services used.

Regular customer to shopowner—No tip for each haircut, but a gift at Christmas.

BEAUTY PARLORS

When one operator shampoos and sets—15 percent of the bill.

When several operators divide services—20 percent of the bill, divided (the person who sets usually gets 10 percent, and the others divide the remaining 10 percent.)

Proprietor (when he or she sets hair)—In some cases no tip. However, with rising costs, many appreciate a tip and will gladly accept 10 percent of the bill, as would other operators. If you are a new customer, watch to see what other customers do, or ask the receptionist.

Manicurist—50¢ to 75¢ depending on the cost of the manicure.

Regular customers give the proprietor, stylist, and shampooer small gifts at Christmas.

USHERS

Theater (U.S.A.)—No tip.

Movies—No tip.

Concert and opera—No tip.

Sports arenas—25¢ per party if actually shown to your seat, especially in boxes and loges. No tip in upper balconies or bleachers.

GROCERY LOADERS

Tip 25¢ for normal number of bags placed in car; 50¢ for a large week's marketing.

ANSWERING SERVICE

Each girl who takes a shift on your service should receive a minimum of $5 at Christmas.

PARKING ATTENDANTS

Tip 25¢ to the man who delivers your car to you from a hotel garage or in a regular garage.

There is no tip at open-air parking lots unless the car is brought off the ramp, overhead platform, etc.

If the car is kept in a garage with a monthly rental, attendants are not tipped for delivery, but are given gifts at Christmas and occasionally throughout the year for special services. Service will be faster if $5 is offered to each employee at different times, or if it is contributed to a "kitty" (if there is one).

MOVING MEN

No tip for one or two crates or pieces of furniture delivered to your home. If they move furniture, put down carpets, or perform other special services for a big load, $1 to $2 per man.

DELIVERY MEN

Christmas gifts:
Newspapers—daily, $5 to $10.
Mailman—$5 to $10.
Milkman—Daily, $5 to $10.
Garbage collectors—Daily, $10; two to three times a week, $5.
Laundry, butcher, cleaners, etc.—If they come regularly, once or twice a week, $5.

HOUSEHOLD HELP

Live-in help will appreciate an extra $5 to $10 when extra work is required for a large party.

Guests in private homes tip the host's maid and/or cook after a weekend visit—for a single guest, $3; for a couple, $5.

No tip—ever—for servants in a private home at a dinner party.

Christmas gifts for apartment house help depending on the type of building:
Doormen—$5 to $10.
Janitors—$3 to $5 depending on the amount of service.
Elevators—$5.
Superintendent—$25 if full-time, live-in; $10 if part-time.

HOSPITALS

No monetary tips.

A gift of candy, fruit, or cookies to "the staff on the 5th floor, Wing B," will be appreciated.

Private nurses on prolonged duties may be given Christmas gifts or a gift on departing, but not money.

EUROPEAN CUSTOMS

In most European restaurants and hotels, a 15-percent (approximate) service charge is added to your bill. You ARE NOT EXPECTED TO GIVE ADDITIONAL TIPS. You do *not* tip the bellboy, the maid, or the concierge. In a restaurant you may leave the small coins the waiter brings back in change, but you should never—if you wish to help the Europeans preserve their system—add another dollar or two.

When no service charge appears on the bill, or if you think it is too low or "nominal," you tip exactly as you would in the United States.

Theater ushers are tipped in Europe. They are not tipped in England, but there is a charge for the program. It is essential to find out what coin is the closest equivalent to, and serves as, our quarter. That coin, like the quarter, is used for many purposes when there is no bill with a service charge included. A quarter is happily accepted everywhere in Europe as the small tip, because in most countries it is worth more than the closest corresponding coin.

Americans have the reputation of overtipping in Europe, so if you possibly can, observe and talk to the residents of the country you are visiting and follow their example or advice.

Part Eleven

ON HOW TO DRESS

~§68~ Women's Clothes

> *Beau Brummel's remark that when one attracted too much notice, one could be sure of being not well-dressed but over-dressed, has for a hundred years been the comfort of the dowdy. A person may be stared at for any one of many reasons. It depends very much on the stare. A woman may be stared at because she is indiscreet, or because she looks like a left-over member of the circus, or because she is enchanting to look at.*—Emily Post, 1922

Suggested clothing for specific occasions is discussed in the chapters related to those occasions. This chapter is limited to a discussion of appropriateness, becomingness, and your choice of clothes and accessories in general. Fashions change, and I am not a fashion editor, so specific "in" styles, in most cases, are neither recommended nor deplored. I am interested only in helping you decide on the practicality, good taste, and appropriateness of the clothes you select.

Clothes literally "make" our appearance, and the first impression we make on others depends almost entirely on what we wear and how we wear it.

THE CLOTHES THAT SUIT

Skill in presenting oneself is something for which it is difficult to give directions, because it is a talent rather than a formula. Naturally, someone who is young and whose figure is size 10 or 12 can wear almost any dress she likes, and it will be becoming. Yet a woman who lacks the knack of choosing what is suitable will find buying a becoming dress such a trial that she finally buys, not one she likes, but the one she dislikes least.

The sense of what is becoming and the knack of wearing clothes well are the two greatest assets of smartness, but neither is possible if a woman is unwilling to look at herself as she really is.

SHORT WOMEN

There are certain basic principles that all women should consider when they are buying their clothes. Very short women should choose clothes with long vertical lines rather than those broken at the waist by a belt or band of contrasting color. They should not wear horizontal stripes. High heels add height, but it is better to wear a moderate heel if one is unable to walk gracefully on the higher. Hairdos that are teased or have "body" and tall hats add inches to the short woman.

TALL WOMEN

Tall women should choose outfits with a break in the middle—a wide belt, a suit with a jacket, or contrasting colors in skirt and blouse. Pretty shoes are sold especially for the tall woman, with heels of low or moderate height. When a hat is worn, it should not add inches to the head, nor should the hairdo.

FAT WOMEN

The plump woman must avoid large prints, loud plaids, and bulky materials. Black and navy blue are the most slimming colors, but any solid color or small print looks attractive if it is becoming to her complexion. Clothes should not be tight enough to reveal a bulge, but they should not be "baggy" or gathered at the waist, either. A flared skirt is much more flattering than either a "dirndl" or a straight style. Upswept hairdos, if becoming to the face, and long earrings help to lengthen a short neck. Evening dresses should be as simple as possible, and if practical a style that covers the upper arm (having a matching stole, for example) is desirable. A bathing suit with a skirt of reasonable length will help hide chubby thighs; and please, no "stretch" suits "to hold in the tummy"! Bikinis and two-piece suits may be charming on a slender figure, but if you have even a suggestion of a "roll," you MUST stick to the one-piece suit. The fat woman, alas, should give up wearing shorts and slacks in public.

THIN WOMEN

The thin woman has relatively few problems, as most clothes are becoming on a slim figure. If the neck bones are prominent, however, a low neckline should be avoided, and because a long neck often goes with a thin figure, turtlenecks, high collars, and scarves are usually most attractive. The interesting "nubby" materials, which so many women cannot wear, look nice on the thin woman, as do more extreme styles, such as short, straight skirts. She is also fortunate in being able to wear shorts or slacks with style.

THE AVERAGE FIGURE

If you have a more or less average figure, choose clothes in the colors and styles that exaggerate your good points. Minimize your less attractive features—heavy hips, perhaps, or a thick waist—by choosing clothes that disguise those faults. And consider your age. The older sportswoman will carry on her game better in a smartly tailored skirt than in brief shorts. Graying hair should not be worn in a long, loose hairdo; the shorter, fuller, or upswept styles are more becoming to a mature face.

FAD FOLLOWERS

Even the woman of beautiful taste succumbs occasionally to the epidemics of fashion, but she is more immune than most.—Emily Post, 1922

Until recently fashion publications had the power to make any style seem acceptable, even though it had few elements of flattery or beauty. If you doubt it, look at old fashion plates. But lately women have succeeded several times in rejecting a new style that the majority felt was unbecoming, in spite of concerted efforts by stores and fashion publications to promote it. Bravo! We need more independence of that sort! Even a woman with excellent taste succumbs occasionally to the epidemics of fashion, but she is more immune than most. All women who have any clothes sense whatever know more or less the types of things that are their style—unless they have a temporary attack of "fashionitis" that makes them completely irresponsible.

There is one unchanging watchword that must be remembered by everyone who wants to be well dressed—*suitability*. A great number of women do dress with this in mind, but there are many others who, like sheep, follow every new fad without the slightest sense of whether it is a good one or absurd or whether it is at all becoming to them. As each new season's fashion is shown they race to dress themselves as perfect replicas of one another; their own types and personalities have nothing to do with the case. The designers say, "Wear your skirts six inches above the knee," and daughter, mother, and grandmother all wear the same length. Utility, becomingness, suitability, and beauty are forgotten. Fashion is followed to the letter—therefore they believe that they are the last word in smartness.

A WORD ABOUT SLACKS

Slacks as sportswear have been accepted for a number of years. They are certainly the most practical dress for an active woman engaged in sailing, hunting, heavy housework, gardening, and many other activities. Originally worn only by young girls, they are now acceptable for women of all ages—as long as they feel comfortable in pants. However, a woman who has a weight problem or who is particularly heavy through the hips should avoid wearing slacks on all other occasions. They may be comfortable, but unless the wearer is reasonably slim they are anything but flattering.

The same is true of evening slacks and pants suits. They cannot be surpassed for comfort and for smartness when worn by the woman with a good figure, but on anyone else a long "at-home" skirt or a cocktail or dinner dress would be far more appealing.

Slacks used to be limited to country wear, but city dwellers and career women have discovered how comfortable and practical they are. By changing the blouse and accessories, many outfits can be made from one pants suit. I have been doing a personal research project recently, and after keeping a careful count, find that over three-fourths of the women on any city block in midtown Manhattan are wearing slacks. Therefore, although we hear from time to time that they are going out of style—and long skirts have largely replaced evening slacks—I believe that for daytime wear, slacks are here to stay. I, for one, am glad.

While pants suits and outfits are correct for almost all everyday activities, and especially for traveling, they should not be worn on occasions which, by their nature, demand a conservative and ultradignified attitude. Funerals, official functions, weddings, and church services, for example, are "off-limits" for slacks.

VULGAR CLOTHES

The difference between clothes that are smart and clothes that are merely conspicuous is something very elusive. Vulgar clothes are those which are too elaborate for the occasion, are immodest, are too exaggerated in style, or have accessories out of harmony with the dress and the wearer.

Beau Brummell's remark that when someone attracted too much notice he could be sure of being not well dressed but over-dressed has for years been the comfort of the dowdy. It is, of course, very often true, but not invariably so. A woman may be stared at for any one of many reasons, because she is ill-behaved, because she looks like a freak in the circus, or because she is simply "lovely to look at." If you are the object of frequent stares, be sure you don't delude yourself about their cause.

ACCESSORIES

Accessories are as important to the budget-conscious woman as the basic dress. They provide the accents that can vary the costume, giving it versatility as well as adding to its beauty. In planning your wardrobe it is well to stick to a narrow range of colors so that the same accessories may be used with a number of outfits. That is not to say, however, that accessories should limit your wardrobe; instead, they should broaden it. A simple dress may be perfect for lunch at a restaurant or for afternoon shopping when it is worn with a gold pin, single-pearl earrings, and a daytime watch or wide gold bracelet, and accompanied by black kid shoes and a plain leather pocketbook. But change these accessories to a diamond or zircon clip, add a single or double strand of pearls, pendant earrings, a bracelet and ring of glittering stones, suede pumps, and a suede or patent-leather purse, and you may appear at any but the most formal party that night.

GLOVES

The "little white glove" seems to be almost a thing of the past. Gloves are still worn by fastidious older women in large cities when they go to weddings and receptions, to the theater, to dinner parties at friends' homes or in restaurants, and even for shopping. But young women, "liberated" women, women in the suburbs and country, wear gloves during the daytime only when it is necessary to keep their hands warm, and then they are rarely "little" or "white." Gloves *are* worn in all areas, however, for occasions such as weddings, funerals, receptions, teas, formal dinners, and dances, but they are removed on arrival.

Gloves are chosen for practicality as well as appearance, but a handsome pair of leather or suede gloves greatly enhances one's costume. They are generally chosen to match the handbag and shoes, or in some cases, the color of the dress or coat. Long white kid gloves are still worn with elegant evening dresses and as part of the "costume" are kept on all evening except while the wearer is eating. Short white kid gloves are the dressiest glove possible for weddings, receptions, the theater, etc.

There are very few occasions when gloves must be kept on. It used to be required that women going through receiving lines kept their gloves on; today gloves are more apt to be left in a coat pocket when it is checked. The women standing in the line *do* keep their gloves on, however.

Gloves should be worn to church, but there, too, they may be removed for the service.

A woman *never* removes her glove to shake hands with someone she meets. However, she *always* removes them before eating—anything, anywhere.

A bracelet, but not a ring, may be worn outside a long glove.

HATS

If hats are becoming to you, wear them! Don't let the fact that yours is the only hat in the crowd deter you. A well-chosen hat may add dash and distinction to your outfit that a bare head can't possibly achieve. If you are one of the many women who feel that there is no hat in the world becoming to you, settle for a little veil or a band or bow on those occasions when it is necessary to "cover" your head. They are few. It is always correct, but no longer obligatory, to wear a hat in churches of every faith. Certain European cathedrals and churches require that tourists wear some form of head covering, but a scarf or handkerchief will do. At official luncheons and receptions hats are still almost a requirement, and they may be, of course, worn at any time and on any occasion you wish during the day. A hat is appropriate, but not necessary, with a cocktail dress. A hat, even the smallest veil, is never worn with an evening dress. The only exception, and it is not truly an exception, is the practical one of wearing a plastic or net scarf tied over your hair to protect it from wind and rain on the way to a formal party.

FUR CAPES AND STOLES

For many years women adhered to an arbitrary and, to me, inexplicable rule that fur capes, stoles, and jackets should not be worn before five o'clock in the afternoon. I have always enjoyed the story of the Midwestern lady who went to spend a weekend at a fashionable Eastern resort. She appeared at luncheon at the exclusive club with her beautiful mink stole over her shoulders. One of the dowagers, looking down her nose at the visitor, said, "My dear Mrs. Newcomer, don't you know you can't wear a fur before five?" Mrs. Newcomer smiled politely and replied, "That's what I thought, too, Mrs. Goldbrick, until I had one."

Actually, there is no reason for a fur stole's not being worn to any "dressy" affair from noon on if the costume the fur is worn over is of a comparable degree of elegance, whether a cocktail suit or "afternoon" dress. Morning wear is invariably less formal, and therefore a dressy fur would not be in keeping. But for luncheons, receptions, weddings, etc., held at or after noon, it would seem most ridiculous to leave a lovely fur hanging in the closet. Women who have a choice might prefer to wear a cloth coat in the daytime and save their fur for evening, but those who can have only one "dress" coat, and prefer a fur to all others, may feel free to wear it at almost any hour.

Mink, chinchilla, and other luxurious and expensive furs should never be worn with sports clothes such as heavy wool suits or "tweedy" slacks.

Fur stoles may be worn on cool summer evenings with dinner or evening dresses, and also on southern cruises when nights are chilly.

SHOES

The first consideration in buying shoes—and this cannot be stressed too strongly—is the importance of comfort. The most beautiful pair of shoes in the world will destroy the appearance of the wearer if the tightness of the toes causes her to stand painfully—first on one foot and then the other—or worse yet, if she has to sink thankfully onto the nearest chair, saying, "My feet are killing me—do you mind?" and kick off the offenders! When you find a last (the form on which the shoe is made) that really fits your foot you will do well to continue to choose shoes produced by the maker of that last.

When picking out shoes try to find colors and styles that will go with more than one dress. Red, for instance, is an excellent choice for spring and summer, as it goes well with black, navy, white, and most of the light summer shades.

If you are more comfortable in "flats" or low heels, stick to them—there are many attractive styles for daytime, and dressier shoes are available with low, medium, or high heels to fit every requirement. Loafers, sneakers, sandals, and gaily colored flat-soled shoes in every conceivable material and to fit any budget are cool and comfortable in summer. Patent leather, which until recently appeared only in black and was traditionally worn only in the summer, now comes in every conceivable color and is acceptable the year round.

In winter a pair of high boots is invaluable, and both country and city dwellers have found them a wonderful replacement for galoshes or rubber boots, which must go on and off a dozen times a day. They may be worn with pants suits or dresses, and are seen everywhere, day and night, except in very formal situations. They are considered an indispensable part of the "total" look with "midi" skirts and coats.

The working girl who is on her feet much of the day should sacrifice some smartness for comfort and choose a shoe that has a thick, soft sole and gives her foot some support. A good suggestion, if feasible, is to keep an extra pair of shoes at your place of business, as a change in the middle of the day is very restful to the feet.

Shoes to be worn with more formal clothes should match or blend with the costume in color and be appropriate in material and style. You wouldn't, for example, wear kid pumps with satin, even though they might both be brown. Generally speaking, leather shoes such as suede or kid are correct for daytime in the winter. Black shoes go well with almost every winter costume, but beige, red, navy, and other colors are in equally good taste when they complement your outfit. Suede, patent, or peu de soie shoes in black or a color matching your dress are worn for more formal occasions or in the evening. Pumps in gold, silver, or a color matching your dress, or gold or silver sandals, are worn with a formal evening dress. During the summer months shoes of any color of the rainbow are attractive as long as they complement the rest of the outfit. But if you do not wish to buy a variety of colors, a pair of "spectators" (white pumps trimmed with black, brown, or navy) or colored linen pumps for daytime occasions, and white linen or patent-leather pumps or sandals for after dark will go happily with almost any summer ensemble.

High heels and dress shoes used to be unacceptable with slacks, but they are now considered correct with evening pants outfits.

HANDBAGS

Styles in handbags have changed as much as those of any accessory or clothing. The result is that over the years the best features of many types have been retained, and bags can now be found in a literally unlimited variety of colors, styles, and materials. There is little to be said about color—you simply decide on one that will go with a special outfit or will blend with all of your costumes. Your own taste will be your guide in selecting your purse, but there are a few suggestions that may be helpful. A good-quality black leather bag, large enough to contain all the items you may need for a whole day, will last for years and pay for itself many times over in usefulness, durability, and beauty. A straw or white plastic handbag for daytime use in the summer will go with all cottons and sports clothes.

A summer bag with changeable linen covers is very practical. These are not inexpensive, but the cost is more than made up for by the versatility, and one bag may comprise your entire pocketbook wardrobe.

Most young women prefer shoulder-strap bags, and they are surely practical for everyday use. They should not, however, be used with formal clothes. I find them ideal for traveling and shopping, when one wants one's hands free, but I confess that I have difficulty in keeping them on my shoulder if the strap is long!

Evening bags, which come in many materials and colors, can add greatly to your costume. Gold metallic bags, sometimes adorned with artificial (or very occasionally, real) jewels, are popular; and for older people, embroidered black velvet, silk, and satin are good choices. For cocktail time, small suede or satin bags come in a variety of pretty colors and shapes. They should be small and easy to carry, since one is apt to remain standing and a large bag is heavy and difficult to manage. Also, a small bag is less in the way if left on a table during a dance, or in the lap during a dinner party.

CORSAGES

Corsages rise and fall in popularity, and as this is written they are "out," at least among the young. However, they may well return to favor, possibly as clothes become more conservative. There is no rule in existence about where a woman wears a corsage. She pins it wherever and however she thinks most becoming to her dress, to herself, and to the flowers themselves. All things being equal, she wears them on her left shoulder. If the dress is so designed that a corsage does not go well on it, if the material is flimsy, or if the wearer is afraid of crushing the flowers while dancing, she may pin them on a cloth evening bag, or attach them to a ribbon on her wrist.

Corsages should be pinned on the shoulder with the stems *down.*

JEWELRY

> *Don't wear too much jewelry; it is in bad taste in the first place, and in the second, is a temptation to a thief. And don't under any circumstances, distort your figure into a grotesque shape.*—Emily Post, 1922

The wearing of too much jewelry is, at most times, considered ostentatious and in poor taste. However, with the improvement in quality and the consequent rise in popularity of costume jewelry women have increased the amount of jewelry they wear in public as well as at home. Certain gems, such as sapphires, can be manufactured now, and others are beautifully imitated. Cultured pearls rival "real" pearls in beauty, and such semiprecious stones as zircons, garnets, or jade come in a variety of colors. With the lower cost of these substitutes for expensive gems many more women than ever before are able to wear beautiful jewelry.

Jewelry, like clothing, should be chosen and worn with an eye to suitability rather than to fad. A woman with stubby, unattractive hands, for example, should not draw attention to them with a large, flashing ring, no matter how fine a gem it may contain. Furthermore, the type of jewelry worn changes with the time of day and the activity. When engaging in an active sport, jewelry other than a watch and a wedding band and engagement ring is out of place. In the daytime gold and silver, pearls, enamels, wood, costume jewelry of all kinds, and semiprecious stones are more suitable than the brilliant stones that go well with evening clothes. At any hour a gold-link necklace, a pendant, or a string of pearls dresses up a plain blouse and skirt. Bracelets, earrings, rings, and a pin or clip set off a dress or suit at any hour. In short, the choice of jewelry is limited only by the good taste and budget of the wearer. When she has occasion to wear a formal evening gown, a woman may bring out her most brilliant precious stones—as long as she does not overload her wrists and fingers.

Personally, I dislike the current fad of overloading oneself with three or four bracelets on the same wrist, and a ring on almost every finger. Not only does it appear ostentatious (too much of *anything* is in poor taste), but it totally conceals the charm of each individual piece. I suspect that with the current trend toward more conservative styles, the wearing of jewelry, too, will become more reasonable. Celebrities, who frequently set a style such as this and who want to be constantly "in," are the first to adopt a fad but are also the first to drop it when they see the pendulum swinging. Swinging, it surely is, and their followers will be close behind.

RINGS

Of all the various kinds of jewelry, rings give rise to more questions than any other. Information about engagement and wedding rings will be found in Chapters 47 and 53, but there are many other types of rings that are almost as important to the wearer.

"Friendship" or "promise" rings are really preengagement rings. Therefore they may, if you wish, be worn on the fourth finger, left hand, as would a real engagement ring. However, if you wish it to be clear that you do *not* consider yourself engaged, it is best to wear a "promise" ring on your right hand.

"Pinky" rings may be worn at all times on the right hand, but not on the left if you have an engagement or wedding ring on the next finger.

Cameo rings, crest rings, and initialed rings are usually worn with the design facing the wearer. Years ago, when a crest was pressed into sealing wax to close a letter, the fist was clenched and the backs of the fingers pressed down, so the design had to face *away* from the wearer to make the imprint come out right side up. Now that rings are no longer used for this purpose, most people prefer to wear the ring so that they can see and enjoy the design. There is no "rule"—it is a matter of preference.

"Mothers' rings" are very lovely mementos given to a mother by her child or children. The mother's ring contains a tiny birthstone of each child set into a silver or gold band. Some include the father's birthstone set into the middle, and also the birthstone of a deceased child. Stones may be added as additional children are born.

Some school and class rings are traditionally worn on the fourth (or fifth) finger of the left hand, whether they are from the school attended by the girl or are given to her as a preengagement ring. In other cases they are worn on the right hand, according to the school custom.

PIERCED EARS

In many countries—especially Latin countries—it is customary for girls to have their ears pierced when they are tiny babies. It is obviously quite correct for them to do so. However, the same tradition—and the reason behind it—does not exist in the United States. Here, it is not considered in good taste for little girls to wear much jewelry of any sort. The feeling is that they are being made into adults too fast, in any case, and this is just another way of speeding the process up. Therefore, while I would never criticize the act of piercing children's ears for Cubans, Italians, or any others in whose homeland it is common practice, I would not recommend it for American children under thirteen or fourteen years old.

MAKEUP AND HAIRSTYLES

Mrs. Worldly wore a squirrel fur cap in the evening as well as the daytime; she said it was because it was so warm and comfortable. It was really because she could not do her hair!—Emily Post, 1922

Except for special occasions a little powder to dull the shine on your nose, lipstick of a color becoming to your complexion, a little eye makeup if you live in the city, and a neatly combed hairdo are sufficient to make every woman appear well groomed. A good powder base that contains a lubricant for the skin is an excellent idea for older women. The powder should be applied lightly and evenly over the base, and when properly done, the two together will cover the natural blemishes and wrinkles that come inevitably with the years.

Eye makeup should also be applied with discretion. A heavy outline intended to enlarge the eye can, if badly applied, destroy the natural line and appear nothing short of grotesque.

Lipstick, if used at all, should follow the line of the lips. An attempt to enlarge or change the shape of the mouth by running the lipstick over the natural outline of the lips generally gives the impression that your hand has slipped.

Hairdos should be chosen to flatter your face. Of course, if you are young and pretty, many styles will be becoming, and it is fun to attempt different effects and to experiment with current fashions. It is not worth doing, however, if the latest thing could be harmful to the hair—such as cheap coloring or too much spraying with excessively drying lacquers. The well-groomed woman finds a style that is pleasing to her and not difficult to maintain, and while she may vary her coiffure on special occasions, she returns to the simple, becoming style for ordinary dress.

Finally, always remember that a mask can never take the place of a face. The face of a clown is grotesque, for it is meant to be. If cosmetics are to add to beauty, they must be the allies, not the enemies, of nature.

BUDGET BUYING

A very beautiful Chicago woman who is always perfectly dressed for every occasion, worked out the cost of her own clothes this way: On a sheet of paper, thumbtacked on the inside of her closet door, she put a complete typewritten list of her dresses and hats, and the cost of each. Every time she put on a dress she made a pencil mark. By and by when a dress was discarded, she divided the cost of it by the number of times

*it had been worn. In this way she found out accurately which were
her cheapest and which her most expensive clothes.*—Emily Post, 1922

To begin with, sales can be of great help to the budget-conscious
woman, but only if taken advantage of with thought and planning.
End-of-season sales are generally limited to leftover, odd sizes and
the less attractive styles, but if you should happen to find your size
in a rather unusual color that is becoming to you, you may land a
wonderful bargain to wear the following season. Beware, however,
of buying anything "high style" at these sales—it will probably be
"out of style" in a year's time.

In buying at one of the "cut-rate" stores, you may also find
fabulous bargains, but again, take care! These stores get their merchandise from the stocks of more expensive houses for several reasons. The clothes may be defective in workmanship, faulty in cut,
or out of style. Or (and you are in luck if you happen to go in on the
day this shipment arrives) they may be bargains simply because too
many of one design were ordered. If you are knowledgeable about
clothes and able to recognize good design and workmanship, as a
penny-wise shopper you will do well to frequent these stores.

Wherever you decide to do your shopping, you must plan your
needs in advance. If you wish to be able to use the same accessories
with all your clothes, your color scheme must be in harmony. For
example, for fall wear you might choose dresses and suits in olive
greens, golds, browns, and beiges. With all these colors, you can use
the same pair of brown suede or kid pumps, brown or dull-green
leather "flats," a brown purse, and a brown or beige coat.

Outfits that can be changed to fit different occasions are useful.
Skirts are most versatile—with a sweater they are practical for everyday use, and if not too "tweedy" they can be dressed up by a silk
blouse or a decorated sweater for informal evenings at a restaurant
or with friends. A short-sleeved or sleeveless wool or silk dress with
a jacket is a good choice. Without the jacket it is suitable for a dinner
party or an evening of theater and nightclubs. By putting on the
jacket you are ready for a luncheon, tea, or cocktail party.

To make your budget wardrobe truly adequate, you should try
to choose two or three basic dresses—one for afternoon and two for
evening—of good quality. The higher cost of these dresses will be
amply repaid in durability and excellent fit. They should not be

conspicuous in color or style, so that you can wear them time and time again without feeling that your friends are saying, "There comes Janey in her polka-dots again!"

Coats are a problem to the budget-minded. Not only are they the most costly items to buy, but no one coat can cover all your needs. A camel's-hair coat, a tweed, or a lined gabardine is most practical for country wear, and all three go well with daytime clothes from slacks to afternoon dresses. But for winter evenings and for city living it is essential to have a different coat—a well-cut black wool will fit any occasion, but best of all, if your budget allows, or if you have a generous husband or parents, is a fur coat. A full-length fur coat, cut in a simple style, will last for years, and of all coats it provides the greatest warmth and beauty. In choosing a fur coat you will do well to follow the recommendations of a reputable furrier, and you should *never* buy the fur of an animal that is one of a "protected" species.

Imitation furs are so beautifully made today that they are an acceptable substitute. They must be of good quality, however, or they will seem exactly what they are—a cheap copy of the real thing.

Spring and summer coats are less expensive and more versatile. A lightweight wool in white, beige, or red can serve for daytime or evening, although a small fur cape or stole, if one can afford it, is a comfort on a cool summer night. Raincoats come in such attractive fabrics that they can also serve as all-purpose summer coats even when the sun is shining.

YOUR TRAVELING WARDROBE

When you plan a wardrobe for a trip, whether it be by airplane, car, train, or boat, there are two considerations—space and weight. Air travel is not the only means of transportation where weight is a factor. Have you ever tried to carry your own fifty-pound suitcase through the train station when no porter could be found, as is now so often the case? Or have you seen your host take your bag from your car trunk and stagger gasping up his steps because the days of the butler and houseman have passed?

Even more consideration should be given your travel wardrobe than your regular outfits, because of the need for traveling with as few accessories as possible. Nothing takes up more space or weighs more than handbags and shoes. If you can plan your costumes so that one pair of the most comfortable, sturdy shoes available for sightseeing can be exchanged in the evening for a dressier pair of the same color, your packing and overweight problems will be almost solved.

The handbags with changeable covers mentioned earlier in this chapter are ideal for traveling. You can carry the bag itself onto the boat or plane and pack only the lightweight covers. For evening a small flat silk or patent-leather bag will complement any costume and add little to the weight of your suitcase.

Dresses of wrinkleproof material are a "must," and they can now be found in all styles and weights for summer or winter travel. Banlons and knits come in every variety of pattern and color. Take along a cleaning fluid or powder put up specially for travelers—a spot on a dress that forms an important part of your clothing scheme can be a disaster.

Think again of the versatility of your clothes. Sweaters should be chosen because they go well with *all* your slacks, shorts, and dresses. A skirt with a matching coat makes a stunning costume for cruise or country wear and is better than a dress and coat because with a change of blouse you have a different outfit. One rarely needs an evening dress when traveling, but a long skirt or cocktail dress may be worn in any restaurant or theater or at any party to which you are invited.

Until recently slacks were not worn in European cities, but today pants suits are seen on chic women of every nationality. Shorts, however, are rarely worn by European women except at such resorts as the Riviera, and therefore American women should "in Rome, do as the Romans," or they will appear conspicuous and typically "tourist." If you are traveling on the Continent rather than on a cruise ship (where the same clothes as those worn at any resort at home are appropriate), save space by not taking more shorts than you will need for the days you plan to spend in Cannes. Don't forget a bathing suit—even a wayside stream can provide refreshing relief from the heat of southern France, Italy, or Spain in summer, and swimming pools and lakes are found near resort hotels all over the world.

ᴇ𝔰**69**ᶏᴇ Men's Clothes

Recently, radical departures from the conservative men's clothes considered essential for many years have occurred, and men are at last permitted a wider choice of colors and styles than has been true for many years.

Fashions in business suits have not changed drastically. A well-made suit bought ten years ago should still be perfectly wearable today, although its age would be noticeable in some details. Lapels have become narrower, trouser legs slimmer and sometimes flared, and many jackets have double vents in the back rather than a single slit in the center. Neckties go from wide to narrow and back again. Particular styles may come and go, and the well-dressed businessman may choose to follow these fashions if they are not overly flamboyant and if they are becoming to him. Certain colors have a temporary vogue too—in shirts, for instance. One year yellow shirts may appear with gray or brown suits; the next year they will be replaced by blue. Bow ties are popular in some years; in others one sees only the four-in-hands.

Whatever the fashion of the moment, if a man's suit fits him well, is appropriate to whatever he may be doing, and is not overly conspicuous in style or color, he will be labeled "well-dressed" in any community.

Outside the business office a man may now choose from an infinite variety of "new looks." Most of the fads are temporary, but they have had the happy effect of releasing the male population from the rigidity and stuffiness that characterized men's wear for so long. Since there are few rules governing leisure-time clothes other than those of decency and cleanliness, this chapter is devoted mainly to appropriate clothing for the business and social worlds.

THE IMPORTANCE OF FIT AND GOOD CARE

Whether you buy your clothes at a men's store or a department store or have them made by a tailor, the most important consideration is excellent fit. Although you may be on a strict budget and are buying your clothing as inexpensively as possible, be sure to spend he extra time and money required to have any necessary alterations made. Any suit appears more costly than it is if it hangs well and does not sag or stretch.

Another means of adding years to the life of your clothes and adding immeasurably to their appearance is the care that you give them. Suits and sports jackets should be pressed, brushed, and spot-cleaned after two or three wearings. They should be sent for general cleaning only when they are soiled all over or have a stain that cannot be removed at home. Trousers should be pressed as soon as the crease is gone or if they are very wrinkled at the seat or knee. But if you invest in a good "silent valet" (a stand over which you hang the trousers, which are then pressed by another hinged board that is clamped tight against the hanging legs) a suit, because the jacket does not show signs of use to the extent that the trousers do, may be worn many more times before either a pressing or a trip to the cleaner's is necessary.

The immediate replacement of a missing button is a "must." Not only does it ruin the appearance of the clothing, but it can actually cause the material of the suit or jacket to lose shape if it is left unrepaired for a long period of time.

Another worthwhile investment is a pair of shoe trees for each pair of shoes. Nothing increases the life of shoes so much as being properly stretched on trees each time they are removed, and nothing improves the appearance or preserves the leather so much as proper shining.

THE MAN ON A BUDGET

Even though a suit costs more than a dress of equivalent quality, the man on a budget is more fortunate than the woman in the same situation. A man does not need so many complete changes of outfit as a woman, because the same suit with different shirts, ties, and socks may be used for almost every day and for any occasion. But the budget-minded man must consider the same things as his female counterpart. If a limited supply of ties, shirts, socks, and shoes must go with all his suits and jackets, then he must restrict himself to one or two colors. A gray suit for business, a dark-blue suit for evening, and a sports jacket in a gray-blue tweed could be worn, for example, with white, blue, pink, or yellow shirts, blue, maroon, or black socks, and ties with a basically blue background. Since a white shirt is more formal than a colored one, it is always correct with the blue suit in the evening as well as at any other time. Dark-brown shoes could be worn with all three, although some well-dressed men prefer black with a blue suit. A good solution for a two-pair wardrobe would be a black pair to wear with the two suits, and a pair of brown loafers or other casual shoes to wear with the sports jacket.

Because of its versatility, and in spite of the ultraconservative image, a solid-color or faintly patterned suit is an invaluable asset to the man on a limited clothes budget. It may appear anywhere in the daytime and yet go to the theater, a restaurant, or any informal gathering in the evening. In addition, if a neutral color, the trousers may be worn separately with a sports shirt or jacket.

BUSINESS WEAR

Rules for daytime clothes are less rigid than they used to be, but the man who works in an office in the city must dress according to a set pattern if he wishes to impress his clients and his employers or superiors favorably. His clothing is meant to reflect the conservative, responsible, reliable image that his company wishes to impart. Sports jackets, open-necked shirts, and loud plaids are worn in the city only on weekends or in your own home. For weekday wear during office hours, a suit is the proper attire. Only a man who is coming in from the country for a short visit—an author to see his publisher, for example—might wear a sports jacket or blazer. And then only if he does not plan to go to a top-grade restaurant, a reception, or any place where others will be dressed more conventionally.

The business suit is supposed to be an inconspicuous garment, and should be. Today's suit usually consists of trousers and a single-breasted coat. Some men do wear double-breasted suits—they go in and out of style. Vests, like double-breasted suits, come and go. A few rules for men's business clothing follow:

Don't choose striking patterns or materials, although a quiet plaid or muted stripe or herringbone pattern can be very handsome. Suitable woolens come in endless variety, and any that look inconspicuous at a short distance are safe.

Dark gray, dark blue, and brown are first color choices, although olive greens and lighter grays are also correct. But don't get too light a blue, too bright a green, or anything suggesting a horse blanket. If you must be eccentric, let yourself go (within reason) in the pattern of your tie or the color of your shirt, but keep your big investment —your suit—conservative.

Lisle or cotton socks are correct in winter as well as summer for those who are not comfortable in wool. But don't wear white socks with a suit. Don't cover yourself with chains, fobs, lodge emblems, etc. Although they are popular with "mod" dressers, you will be wise to avoid plaid shirts with striped neckties, stripes with polka dots, and other wild combinations. If a salesman offers you anything that has "never been seen before," the safest rule is to shun it unless you are sure your judgment is totally reliable.

White shirts, even though their popularity declined abruptly when men were liberated from the "gray-flannel suit," are always correct with a business suit. Solid-color and pin- or narrow-striped materials are also acceptable, as are broader stripes and stronger patterns when worn with an appropriate necktie.

Summer suits are lighter in color as well as weight, and their accessories are much less conservative. Ties of printed silk or any of the new synthetic fabrics can be gaily colored, and patterns are almost unlimited.

A tan, gray, blue, or olive-green suit in lightweight, crease-resistant summer fabric has the advantage of being correct for the city and not looking out of place in the country.

Some of the new materials are so cool and light that the wearer is comfortable in even the hottest weather, and the necessity of removing the coat, especially in an air-conditioned office, has been almost eliminated. However, most firms do allow their employees to take off their coats—but not their ties—during summer months, unless they are in a position of serving the public.

THE COUNTRY OFFICE

Most men who work in offices in the country prefer to wear a sports jacket rather than a suit. However, some large companies with branch offices require their employees, even in small towns, to wear suits because they feel this is more dignified and makes a better impression on clients or customers. While a suit is always correct for business wear, if your work is such that you do not have to meet outsiders—as does, for instance, a salesman—it is certainly not incorrect to wear a comfortable sports jacket in your office.

WHEN NOT AT WORK

It would not be possible to go into all the types of clothing that may be worn out of working hours. But there are certain general observations that may be made.

Clothing should be appropriate to the occasion. If you have been asked to spend a weekend at a fishing camp, you would be foolish to take light-colored, easily spotted linen slacks rather than dungarees or khakis. Nor would you be wise to appear at an exclusive beach club in clothing appropriate for a weekend on a farm. Don't wear loafers on board a boat. Not only might you slip and fall overboard, but most owners will shudder at the marks that the hard soles may make on their polished decks. In other words, choose your vacation-time clothes with an eye toward what your activities will be, and if you don't know, ask! No one has ever been criticized for wanting to have the appropriate clothes, but many a friendship has been dampened by the need to outfit or lend clothing to someone who didn't take the trouble to find out what might be needed.

In general, men in the city wear the same clothes in their own homes as do their brothers in the country. But when they appear in public, they are more apt to put on jacket and tie, as they do for most social activities.

The country dweller need not be so formal. Open-necked polo shirts and slacks are standard attire in the summer, and in the cooler months flannel shirts and sweaters are seen all over the country. But even the suburbanite or farmer puts on a sports jacket, shirt and tie, or turtleneck when going to any sort of social gathering, from a friendly brunch to a PTA meeting. Men attending weddings, cocktail parties, luncheons, or any other daytime function, sometimes wear a suit, especially in the winter, but more and more often they choose slacks and a blazer or sports jacket.

FORMAL WEAR

When it is necessary to wear formal clothes in the daytime, the cutaway or a dark sack coat with striped trousers is the correct dress. In the evening "white tie" or "tails" is the most formal costume. All three of these outfits are described in detail in Chapter 49. The only difference to be noted is that for a state funeral, or whenever pallbearers or others are dressed in cutaways, a black four-in-hand tie is worn with a fold collar, rather than an ascot or a striped tie. The fourth type of formal dress is the "black tie" or "tuxedo" also described in Chapter 49 but discussed again here because of the many variations possible on occasions other than weddings.

To go out for the evening dressed in black tie means that you are wearing a dinner jacket or tuxedo. The term *tuxedo* appeared in the early 1890s when the dinner jacket was introduced at the Tuxedo Club in Tuxedo, New York, as something less formal to wear than the "swallowtail" or full evening dress. Today black tie is accepted as correct on almost every formal occasion, and few men ever have any need to dress in a more formal manner. Therefore, while it is more practical for most men to rent a "set of tails" when the occasion demands, it is advisable for those who can invest in a good-quality, well-fitted tuxedo, which will last for many years. It consists of:

JACKET

In winter or summer, black or midnight blue is always correct, and the material is usually tropical worsted, or if it is not shiny, one of the new blended materials. The lapels are faced with satin. In hot weather, white linen is worn for very formal affairs, but for less formal parties plaid (madras), paisley, or a solid-color cotton, Dacron, or other blend is appropriate, attractive, and gay. On all jackets the lapels may be rolled or peaked and of whatever width current fashion demands. Dinner jackets are usually single-breasted, but a few men still prefer the double-breasted form, which requires neither waistcoat nor cummerbund.

TROUSERS

When a dark jacket (black or midnight blue) is worn, the trousers are always of the same material. If a colored jacket is worn, the trousers are of a good-quality black material, usually the same pair worn with a black jacket. In either case they do not have cuffs but do have a single stripe of black braid or satin.

WAISTCOAT OR CUMMERBUND

The waistcoat is of white piqué or plain or patterned black silk. A needlepoint vest made by a loving and patient wife makes a very "special" accessory. Today, instead of a waistcoat a cummerbund is usually worn. The most formal are of black or maroon silk, but they may also be plaid or figured, especially in the summertime.

SHIRT

A daytime white shirt with soft fold collar may be worn, but for a formal occasion, a piqué or pleated bosom makes a better appearance.

TIE

A black silk bow tie is worn with a waistcoat or black cummerbund. If a cummerbund other than black is worn, the bow tie should be of a matching color and material.

SOCKS

Black silk or lisle socks are worn.

SHOES

The shoes are black patent leather.

ACCESSORIES

Pearl, mother-of-pearl, or black onyx studs are used if an evening shirt is worn. Cuff links may be gold or mother-of-pearl to match the studs. The handkerchief is white linen, with or without initials, and a white silk scarf is worn when appropriate. A boutonniere—usually a white or red carnation, completes the outfit.

Variations of the above come into vogue from time to time, but few have had more than a brief span of popularity. Typical are the string ties popular recently, and turtlenecks or ruffled shirts worn instead of conventional shirts. Velvet Edwardian jackets are in vogue for young grooms. Those who want to show their up-to-dateness are quick to adopt these fashions, but they are just as quick to drop them when they lose favor. This they invariably do because a majority of men find the traditional costume either most comfortable or most handsome.

COATS AND HATS

Men's topcoats come in an infinite variety of colors and materials. For the man who lives a very active social life and frequently wears evening clothes, a solid black, navy, or dark-gray coat is a necessity. For daytime wear he must also have a less formal coat in the color that goes best with his suits. The dress coat may or may not be double-breasted—the daytime sports coat, never.

For the average man, and especially the young man who is starting his wardrobe, a coat that will be appropriate in any circumstance is preferable to the very dressy or very sporty one. For the city dweller a dark-gray herringbone tweed is most practical. Brown tweed is handsome but should not be worn with formal evening dress. For either city or country wear, a polo coat for the cold months and a straight gabardine (or one of the newer waterproof materials) to double as a topcoat in the summer are ideal solutions.

Some men, in both city and country, prefer not to wear hats unless it is absolutely necessary. For these men, or for anyone whose wardrobe is limited, a soft, gray-felt fedora is the best choice. It may be worn with any color and in any circumstance, except with "white tie."

Men who live in the country may prefer a fedora in a rougher material than the regular felt. They may have special bands of braid or cloth other than black silk, and occasionally they have a feather or other ornament tucked into the band at the side. This type of hat should not be worn with a tuxedo, however.

In the summertime coconut straw hats (fedora-shaped) are handsome and cool. The bands may be of any solid color, or figured or plaid. These are acceptable for all daytime wear, even in the city, but with evening clothes the more conservative Panama hat is correct.

LIFTING OR TIPPING THE HAT

Lifting or tipping the hat is a conventional gesture of politeness shown most often to strangers or mere acquaintances. In lifting his hat a man merely raises it slightly off his forehead—by the brim of a stiff hat or by the crown of a soft one—and replaces it. A man generally tips his hat when he says, "Excuse me," "Thank you," "How do you do?" or when he greets, or is greeted by, a lady in passing.

WHEN TO REMOVE A HAT AND GLOVES

A man takes off his hat and holds it in his hand when a lady enters the elevator in an apartment house or hotel—or any other building that can be classified as a dwelling. He puts it on again in the corridor. A public corridor is like the street, but an elevator in a hotel or apartment house has the character of a room in a house, and in a room a man does not keep his hat on when women are present. However, in public buildings, such as office buildings or stores, the elevator is considered as public a place as a bus or train, and hats stay on. What is more, the elevators in such business structures are often so crowded that the only room for a man's hat is on his head!

A man who stops on the street to speak to a woman must remove his hat and take his right glove off to shake hands. If they walk on together he puts his hat back on, but if they remain standing in the street talking he should stay hatless unless, of course, she says, "Please put your hat on—you'll catch pneumonia in this freezing wind."

As discussed in Chapter 14, out-of-doors every American citizen stands with his hat off at the passing of the flag, and both indoors (in a public place) and outdoors when the national anthem is played. Also, every man should take his hat off in the presence of a casket and in all Christian churches.

A gentleman wearing *outdoor* gloves never shakes hands with a lady without first removing his right-hand glove. But at a formal ball, or when he is an usher at a wedding, he does *not* remove his glove, which is intended to be worn indoors. When outside, if for some reason he cannot get his right glove off, he may say, "Excuse my glove," but he does not ask that an indoor glove be excused.

SHOES AND SOCKS

Dark brown, cordovan, and black are the best color choices for shoes and go well with all business or sports clothes. Loafers are only appropriate with sports clothes. White shoes may be worn in hot weather, but only with a very light suit, such as a seersucker stripe. If you have a tuxedo you should have black patent-leather shoes to go with it, if you can possibly afford them. If not, a plain black-calf tie, well polished, is acceptable.

The better the quality of your shoes, the more wear they will give you. Good leather, properly cared for with wax polish, will last for many years. Expensive shoes are well worth resoling, and you should have it done before they become too worn. Since better-quality shoes will also fit better, the added cost is quite justified, especially if your work requires many hours of standing.

As to style, plain leather, perforated insteps and toes, or "capped" toes are chosen according to your taste. It is best to avoid pointed toes, and in spite of their popularity as this is written, higher-than-average heels. Loafers are fine for country wear but tend to look too casual during business hours in the city. Openwork, suede, and novelty leathers may ruin an otherwise well-chosen outfit.

Socks are selected according to the color of your suit. Black, navy, and maroon are best with blue suits; black, gray, green, or maroon with gray; and brown or green with brown. They may be solid-color, ribbed or plain knit, with or without clock, and they may have a small stripe or a pattern, such as an Argyle plaid.

When you are selecting socks, remember that there is nothing attractive about an expanse of bare masculine leg below the trouser cuff. Unless, like Uriah Heep, you sit primly with both feet on the floor at all times—as is not likely—you will do well to avoid ankle-length socks, especially with a business suit; and you should invest in a good pair of garters unless you prefer a style of sock that has built-in support.

NECKTIES

Neckties should, of course, go well with the color of your suit, and often they match the socks as well, but ties that match shirts—

white on white, for example—are not a good choice. Solid colors, paisleys, stripes, or small patterns go well with business suits. If the shirt has a strong pattern, the tie should be plainer, and vice versa. They may be of foulard (silk), knit, or smooth wool in winter, or cotton or silk in summer.

Choosing a tie to go with a sports jacket can be difficult. With a loud plaid you must avoid stripes or a bold pattern. A solid-color knit or bumpy wool is the safest choice with a wool jacket, and the color should match one of the tones in the plaid. A tie with a very sparse pattern—perhaps two or three flying birds, or a single emblem of some sort—can also be worn with a sports jacket. Cotton or silk ties are worn with madras or patterned lightweight jackets.

The four-in-hand is by far the most popular style, but the bow tie is very becoming to some men and provides a good way of giving your outfits a little variety. When choosing a bow tie, try several lengths and shapes, as certain styles are definitely better suited to one shape of face than others. And practice tying the bow until you are truly adept—if you can't avoid a flying and/or sagging loop, stick to the four-in-hand.

Widths of ties vary from year to year. Follow the current style if you wish to look your best, but within reason. A very tall man with a thin face should not wear the thinnest tie possible, nor a fat man the broadest. On the other hand, an old two-inch-wide tie looks ridiculous when four- or five-inchers are in style.

Bow ties, too, vary in popularity and in style. They are "out" at the moment, except for the "avant-garde" dresser who may wear a "string" bow tie or a wide "butterfly" tie. Undoubtedly, in the near future, bow ties will be "in" once again.

An ascot in gray or silver-gray silk is worn by the bridegroom at a formal wedding—with a cutaway.

A less formal type of ascot is one made of patterned silk in any color. It is worn, tucked inside an open-necked shirt, at sports events in the country and sometimes at informal gatherings such as barbecues or brunches. This type of ascot may be simply a square silk handkerchief folded into a triangle and then into a scarf shape, looped over once, and tucked into the front of the shirt. Or it may be scarf-shaped silk made for the purpose. When wearing an ascot the top button—sometimes two—of the shirt is left undone.

VESTS OR WAISTCOATS

The vest or waistcoat (those worn with evening clothes are always called "waistcoats") rises and falls in popularity. There are always some men, however, who wear them for added warmth and extra pockets, as well as for appearance.

When worn with a business suit, the vest is of the same material as the suit. With a sports jacket, it may be of gaily colored flannel, a checked or plaid wool (often called "tattersall"), or other pattern. Many wives enjoy embroidering vests with the emblems of their husbands' schools or with designs derived from their favorite sports or hobbies. Vests such as these make wonderful "conversation pieces" and add a distinctive note to a man's sports clothes.

One warning, however: If you are wearing a vest remember to remove it if for any reason you take off your jacket. Vests were never meant to be seen uncovered from the rear.

JEWELRY

The two most important requisites for men's jewelry are, first, that it be of good quality, and second, that it be inconspicuous.

Naturally, not everyone is able to buy solid-gold or platinum tie clips or cuff links. So, until you can buy expensive jewelry, take great care in choosing what you can afford. The best rule is to select the simplest design that can be found—it invariably gives the appearance of being more costly than does ornate or gaudy jewelry. There is a great deal of imitation jewelry available that is handsomely designed and well made. The problem is to choose something that not only looks very smart but will not tarnish, lose its finish, or otherwise fall apart.

Cuff links for wear with a business suit should be made of solid metal—usually gold or silver—and should be of moderate size. They may be initialed, have a personal or other crest, or a raised or etched design. Flashing stones in the daytime are not in good taste, but there are some "novelty" links made of wood, stones, synthetics, etc., that are, if not "gaudy," very acceptable.

For evening wear, mother-of-pearl cuff links are usually accompanied by matching studs. They may or may not have a circle of tiny diamonds around the edge. Darker pearl and black onyx are handsome with a tuxedo, and white gold or platinum may be worn. But other colored stones are to be avoided, especially if they are large and conspicuous.

Collar pins are made of gold or are gold-plated, and tie clips may be of almost any metal or combination of metals. The width of the clip depends on the taste of the wearer, and its length, on the width of the tie. Tie pins to hold ascots or scarves in place may be set with pearls, diamonds, or other precious stones. Tie "tacks" are as popular as tie clips, perhaps more so, and are correct with all business and sports clothes. They may also be worn for informal social events.

The most attractive man's ring, in my opinion, is one of gold, with initials or crest, worn on the little finger. Rings may also be set with a single stone. Onyx, opals, moonstones, star sapphires, or rough-cut stones are more masculine than other gems. Seal rings from school, college, or military service are popular and handsome. These are often worn on the fourth finger of either hand rather than on the little finger. Wedding rings are almost always of plain gold, although occasionally they have a pattern or design. They are usually chosen to match the ring of the bride.

Other than the articles mentioned above, accessories for men are of a practical rather than an ornamental nature. Money clips, cigarette lighters, and watches are all utilitarian; although they may not, in the strictest sense of the word, be *jewelry*, they may be *jeweled*. A cigarette case or lighter used in the evening may bear a design or initials done in precious stones, and a watch may be so beautiful and have such a fine gold band that it is as decorative as jewelry. But all these things and many more, like key chains or gold pencils, that have not been discussed, must be carefully chosen to suit the taste of the wearer and the purse of the buyer.

HANDKERCHIEFS

Whether or not a man wears a handkerchief showing above his breast pocket is entirely a matter of taste. Handkerchiefs carried in this way are decorative only—an additional utilitarian one should be carried in a trouser pocket.

The breast-pocket handkerchief worn with a business suit should be white, either initialed or plain. The color of the initial—which is either a two- or three-letter monogram, or the single initial of the last name—should be white or should go with the suit, the shirt, or the tie. Colorful cotton handkerchiefs or silk squares may be worn in the pocket of a sports jacket.

To achieve the correct "casual" look of the pocket handkerchief, open it, pick it up at the center, shake it so that the corners fall together, and turn the part you are holding down into the pocket. The corners should stick up one and a half to two inches above the pocket. If one corner is initialed the handkerchief may be arranged so that that corner is in front.

MONOGRAMS ON MEN'S CLOTHING

The same rule applies for all the rest of a man's clothing as that mentioned for handkerchiefs. All of his initials may be arranged in a monogram—with the last initial larger and in the center if it is a diamond or round decorative pattern, or in a row of three letters of the same size in the order of his name. If he uses a single letter, it must be the initial of his last name.

A three-letter "straight" block monogram on a man's shirt pocket undeniably looks very "special." Shirts may also be monogrammed on the sleeve between elbow and cuff, but I find this rather a waste, since it is rarely noticed. Monograms on pajamas, bathrobes, etc., may be more ornate, since they are only seen in a personal setting.

Monograms on suitcases, briefcases, and other leather articles should also be plain block letters. Since they are meant to be used for identification, they should be as legible as possible.

⊷70⊷ Clothing for Various Sports

Although there are no "dos" and "don'ts" at all about the proper dress for certain sports, others require considerable knowledge of the right clothing if one does not wish to appear a rank amateur. It is hardly necessary to tell people about to go on a trout-fishing trip that they need waterproof waders or hip boots, or to tell hunters that they should wear red hats or shirts in order to avoid being shot by other hunters. Except for this sort of essential clothing, there are no rules as to what one wears—it is simply a matter of what is most practical and most comfortable.

And this is the basis for the choice of clothing that, over a period of time, has come to be considered correct for a number of other sports. Some of these rules for dress have become so much a part of the game that one is required to dress in a prescribed style in order to be allowed to participate.

TENNIS

For some years tennis players have recognized that in the heat of the summer white clothes are the coolest (white does not absorb heat as do darker colors) and the freshest-looking on the court. White became so traditional that many clubs and organizations would not allow players on the court in colored clothes at any time, and others required white on weekends and for tournaments. Gradually, however, this "rule" is changing. First, a little color appeared in the trim—a girl's belt, or a border on a man's shirt. Slowly, more colors appeared on the court, and today the United States Lawn Tennis Association allows yellow and blue (if it is pale enough) to be worn in its tournaments. So, although white is still the basic tennis color, one does see, almost everywhere, pastel shirts or shorts, and dresses with even more colorful decorative designs or trim.

MEN'S CLOTHES

Shorts and polo or T-shirts are standard attire for men. Flannel, the "uniform" of earlier days, is rarely seen, partly because it is too hot for the summer months or in a Southern climate and partly because it cannot be laundered. Shirts may be open-collared or round-necked, and they may have a narrow band of color at the neck, or as mentioned above, be a yellow or light blue. There may be a shield on the pocket, often the colors of the club, school, or team that the player represents. Plain white wool socks and sneakers—or special tennis shoes—and a visor or cap complete the outfit. Wool socks are better than synthetics, because they are more absorbent. For after the game, a heavy ribbed or cabled V-neck sweater with or without a stripe of color at the neck will mark you as a well-dressed tennis player.

WOMEN'S CLOTHES

Women play either in shorts or short skirts, depending on their age and figure. The short (above the knee) tennis dress with full or pleated skirt and matching "short-shorts" underneath is so becoming that most women, even very young girls, are wearing it instead of shorts. There is no rule as to style or material—round neck, shirt-waist, or any other design that is comfortable and attractive—but unless the wearer has lovely slim legs, it must not be too short. If shorts are worn they should be of medium length—not so brief as a bathing suit.

Unless their hair is worn very short, braided, or tied in a ponytail, women should wear a cap or head-band. It is untidy and distracting to have hair flying wildly over the face in the middle of a fast rally. Furthermore, it is safer to wear a hat when playing in the hot sun.

GOLF

SHORTS AND SLACKS

As far as I know there are no golf clubs left that do not allow members of both sexes to play in shorts or permit women to wear slacks in cool weather. Many clubs specify, however, that they be long shorts or "Bermudas." As long as this rule is followed, and if you have reasonably presentable legs and at least a "medium" figure, shorts are acceptable. Many women prefer very short skirts. They are generally more becoming, and in very hot weather, cooler. There is no limit to color combinations for either men or women. Solid-color shorts or skirts with blending, printed shirts or blouses are popular, but the scheme may be reversed. Also, the same color may be used for the whole outfit. Plaid or madras shorts are favored by many men.

The male golfer may prefer slacks to shorts and has his choice of linen, cotton, or any other lightweight material. In cool weather, flannel, whipcord, or corduroy are good choices, and colors range from gray or brown to blue, green, rust, and almost any other shade. Slacks should be reasonably full for ease in bending and walking, and shirts should be generously cut to allow free movement of the arms. In chilly weather men may prefer a flannel or wool shirt or turtle-neck so that they need not wear a sweater or jacket.

SKIRTS AND DRESSES

Women who feel that their figures are not suited to shorts (or whose clubs do not allow them) should choose dresses or skirts of a comfortable, simple design—with pockets. Any color is acceptable, and dresses are sometimes sold with a matching sweater. Skirts should be flared—not pleated or gathered, as billowy material will blow in the wind and may distract the most avid golfer just as she is about to sink a putt. In cool weather, slacks, if becoming, are the warmest and most comfortable clothing, but if they do not look well, or are not allowed, flannel or wool skirts and knee-length socks or wool stockings will ward off the chill.

JACKETS

Golf jackets for both men and women come in all colors and styles. They may be open-down or pullover, long or short, but they must be windproof, waterproof, lightweight, and loose fitting.

SHOES

Shoes should be chosen for comfort, waterproofing, and durability, and therefore they must be of good quality. Men's shoes should be brown, black, or a combination of either of these with white. They should not be yellow or any other light color except for tournament players whose distinctive costumes become their trademarks. They may have a flap over the laces or not, as the wearer chooses.

Women's shoes are much the same as men's, with the addition of navy blue to the list of colors.

It should be remembered that golf shoes must be changed right

843

after playing because spikes are rarely allowed in any part of a club except the locker room, or possibly a golfer's bar.

HATS

The frustrated male who must restrict himself to conservative business clothes may indulge himself and go "all out" in his choice of a golf hat. Be it straw, felt, or cloth, he may pick any style or color that will keep the sun out of his eyes and the rain from his head. He may decorate it with golf insignia, feathers, colored bands, or anything else he likes, and as long as it stays on when it should and suits him well, the wilder it is the more admiration it will arouse in his foursome.

SKIING

The trend in ski clothes in recent years is toward nonski clothes, and the majority of young skiers pursue the sport in their everyday blue jeans, covered by a pair of quilted warm-up pants if it is very cold. Any warm jacket, parka or otherwise, is worn on top, and the only obvious ski clothing is the boot.

However, certain types of clothing have proved to be comfortable, practical, and appropriate, and there are plenty of more conservative skiers, both young and old, who enjoy the "well-dressed" look. It is for them, and for the new skier who wants to *look* like a skier, that this section is written.

TROUSERS AND SHIRTS

"Stretch" pants have proved to be most flattering to almost every sort of figure, as well as most practical, because they do not buckle, flap, or sag out of shape. While they must fit snugly, without fullness or wrinkles, there must be enough "give" so that the seams do not split with the first fall. They come in every color of the rainbow, but the best men skiers stick to the more masculine colors—brown, olive, maroon, dark blue, black, and the like.

Any type of shirt that is comfortable and goes well with your outfit is perfectly correct—cotton, flannel, turtleneck, man-tailored, whatever becomes you best.

For cross-country skiing, knickers with high wool socks are the approved outfit.

PARKAS

Parkas come in an infinite variety of colors and should be chosen to match or complement the pants. The wildly patterned parkas that used to be popular have disappeared, and the more serious lady skiers tend to choose more conservative patterns or solid colors in the same style as those worn by the men.

The lightweight quilted parka (preferably down-filled) is standard for both men and women—it is waterproof, windproof, and warm. Some are reversible, a good idea for those who ski frequently and cannot afford more than one outfit. The tendency is toward longer parkas, a fine idea as they protect the upper legs and seat from bitter winds (especially while you stand in the ever-present line for the lifts) and from the wet or freezing seat of the chair lift. The parka may be belted or not, according to your own taste, but it should have a hood, which usually rolls up under the collar when not in use.

Cross-country skiers who work up more of a "sweat" should choose absorbent wool underwear, a lightweight shirt, and a "shell," or thin parka. The strenuous exercise involved makes the heavy downhill parka unnecessary and undesirable.

SKI BOOTS

The heavy ski boot, with inner boot and adjustable clips for ease in doing up the outside boot, is the most important item of your ski clothing. Before buying leather boots, wear them for several hours with the socks you plan to use when skiing. Many, many pairs of boots have been bought without taking this precaution, only to be exchanged after the first ski trip because blisters have appeared on the skier's heel, ankle, or toe after the first hour's skiing. This is not practical with the high rigid plastic boots, but since the foam lining is molded to fit your feet, it should not be necessary. Boots should *always* be bought from a reputable ski shop, and it is wise to seek the advice of a knowledgeable salesman who can tell you which is the best boot for the price you can pay. As this will be your most expensive clothing investment, choose carefully, remembering that the better-quality boot, though more costly, will be more comfortable and will give you many more years of wear.

Leather ski boots must be well cared for to keep the leather pliant and waterproof. They must be put on racks made for the purpose immediately upon removal, and from time to time they should be treated with a leather conditioner and waterproofer. Rigid plastic boots do not require these precautions, and need only be kept clean and dry.

Cross-country boots, lightweight and comfortable, are no problem. Just be sure that they are large enough to fit over fairly heavy wool socks. Since one exercises violently in cross-country skiing, the wool is most important to absorb perspiration, which could otherwise condense and chill your feet seriously.

HATS

No particular style of hat is correct or incorrect for the skier. Whatever the style, it should be chosen for warmth, comfort, a fit that will not let it fly off, and especially for the girls, appearance. Fur and make-believe-fur hats are very popular with the ladies and are attractive as well as warm. Wool hats in all colors, knits, and shapes can be found to match any parka, and the men are often seen in caps with flaps that come down to cover the ears.

"SNOW BUNNIES"

As I have said all through this chapter on sports clothing, the most important thing of all is appropriateness. And one of the least appropriate sights I know is a "snow bunny"—a girl dressed in lavender stretch pants so tight that they appear to have been painted on, a pink-and-purple fur-trimmed parka, an enormous white fur hat, and a face made up for a nightclub act—struggling miserably down the beginner's slope on Skiball Mountain. Or worse yet, sitting at the bar in the lodge attempting to look as though she has just come in from the expert trail! These women are not there to ski, and their outfits announce the fact by their very conspicuousness. The true enthusiast makes no special attempt to catch the eye of all the members of the opposite sex on the slope.

BOWLING

A full skirt or slacks, worn with a loosely cut cotton or cotton knit blouse, is the standard outfit for women who bowl. If you are blessed with the right figure for slacks, they are the most practical choice, as they combine complete freedom of movement with modesty. A skirt must be flared to allow for a full stride and long enough not to ride up too high in the back when you bend over. A box-pleated skirt is ideal, as it hangs smoothly and yet allows freedom of movement. The short-sleeved blouse worn with either slacks or a skirt may be of any style most comfortable and becoming to the wearer.

A man wears slacks and any open-necked sports shirt or whatever shirt is worn by his team or club.

Most bowlers have their own shoes, but if you don't, you must rent them. Almost all alleys have shoes available because they require them for the protection of their alleys. If there is no such regulation, sneakers will do, but never hard-soled shoes.

Except by young children, shorts are not worn at the bowling alley.

RIDING

A riding habit, no matter what the style happens to be, must be beautifully fitted, smart, and conventional. Don't wear loud plaids, pockets, or eccentric cuffs or lapels. The coat may be of a plain dark color, but small checks, herringbone tweed, or muted plaids can be handsome too. A medium-weight closely woven material holds its shape better than a light, loose weave. The trousers are a solid color, usually fawn or gray.

There are two acceptable types of riding habit for women—the jodhpur and the high boot—but men are more correctly dressed in the high boot.

Jodhpurs are breeches that widen slightly in the lower leg so that they fit *over* a low boot rather than inside a high one. For both men and women the rest of the outfit is the same as that worn with high boots.

High boots should be low heeled and have a straight line from the heel to the top of the back. The tops should be no wider than absolutely necessary to get the boots on and off, and they should not be curved or fancy in shape.

Low boots for wear with jodhpurs should be of plain leather. The ornamental Western boots that are available in some sections of the country are suitable only with Western "Cheyenne" pants or blue jeans.

The hat must fit the head well, and the shape must be conventional. The peaked velvet cap is most often worn, but derbies are correct, especially for show riding. Hats are worn straight—never on the back of the head or tipped over the nose.

Gloves should be leather.

Neckties or stocks should be tied so as to make them as flat and neat as possible, and they should be anchored so securely that nothing can possibly come loose.

If you are asked to ride with a hunt, you wear your most formal riding clothes, with collarless shirt and stock and a derby if you have one.

Members of a hunt, on special occasions, wear the red (but called pink) coats peculiar to the sport, white or fawn breeches, high black boots, and a black derby. The style is rigidly prescribed, although some details may be varied to identify a particular hunt.

The riding habit is proper for riding in city parks, in classes or at clubs, or in horse shows. Riding clothes for the country are completely casual, and shirts, sweaters, or jackets may be chosen according to the weather. Open-necked cotton or flannel shirts, turtleneck or polo shirts, are all comfortable and appropriate, and sweaters may be worn instead of jackets. Jodhpur boots are easier to care for than the highly polished boots, and therefore jodhpurs are often worn by those who ride a great deal.

"WESTERN STYLE"

If you are going to a dude ranch, whether in the West or in the East, or perhaps simply riding in the country "Western" style, you will not need the clothing described above. Blue jeans or any tight-fitting country pants will do, worn with whatever type of shirt is comfortable and right for the weather. The trousers should not be widely flared or they will flap around, ride up, or get caught in the straps of the stirrups. If you prefer a softer material than the denim that jeans are made of, be sure that it is sufficiently tough so that it will not wear through at the "pressure points"—inside the knees and on the seat. If you don't want to look like a real "dude," don't tuck your pants into your boots—no real rancher ever does that.

One of the sometimes unexpected hazards of going to a ranch is the inevitable chafing on the insides of the legs if you have not been riding regularly at home. An excellent preventive is to wear pantyhose under your jeans. Even my six-foot-two husband found he could use women's "extra large" because they stretch up as well as out, and he was eternally grateful to the kind lady who donated a pair.

Wide-brimmed Western hats are not an affectation—they are a protection from both sun and rain. However, *be sure* to select a hat that will stay on, either because of its tight fit or because you can tie it under your chin. I cannot even count the number of times I have seen horses shy because the hat of the rider in front blew off.

Western boots are handsome and comfortable—once you get used to them. But they are expensive and they are not essential. Any sturdy pair of high boots with a real heel can be worn. The heel is necessary to keep the foot from slipping forward through the stirrup if you are thrown off balance or are bouncing along at a rough trot.

Be sure to take a rainproof jacket along, for weather can change fast in the mountains. It can be rolled and tied to the back of the saddle when not in use.

IN GENERAL

There are many other sports that we could discuss in this chapter, but most of them either need no particular costume or require clothing so prescribed that those taking part know what they are to wear without having to read a book. The figure skater, for instance, knows without being told that she wears a short flared skirt and tights to keep her legs warm.

If you are taking up a new sport, make a point of observing those who are old hands—they will know what is correct. Then you can choose the features that will be most becoming to you and most suited to your degree of skill. The rank beginner need not choose the very expensive equipment that the expert requires, but remember, as in choosing all clothes, quality, simplicity, and appropriateness are the most important requisites of dressing well.

Part Twelve

HOME LIFE

◆§71ß~ *Household Help—Old and New*

When I was planning this present edition of *Etiquette* I thought of leaving out of it entirely the sections about the duties of the butler, the footman, the housekeeper, and so on. I thought so few of these people remained that the information would be superfluous. And then I heard this story: A young bride was given a copy of *Etiquette* by her aunt. She raved so much about it, saying she could not run her house without it, that her aunt asked what she meant. "Why," she said, "I carefully read the chapter about the work done by the cook, the chambermaid, and the butler, and I did it."

This seemed such a sensible approach that instead of omitting this chapter, I decided merely to change the emphasis. Also, since it is true that a modern housewife's chores are much the same as those performed by yesterday's staff, it is still interesting to read about how they were carried out in the days of enormous households. When you read the following description of a "great house" of years ago, it is hard to believe that most of today's housewives take care of all the duties described by themselves—with only the aid of a few appliances or possibly with part-time help. But they do, and a well-run, beautifully kept home is something in which a woman should take great pride.

THEN—THE STAFF OF A LARGE ESTABLISH-MENT—FIFTY YEARS AGO

The management of a house of great size was usually divided into several distinct departments, each under its separate head. The housekeeper, if there was one—otherwise, the lady of the house—was in charge of the appearance of the house and of its contents, and the manners and appearance of the maids as well as their work; taking care of linen was also her responsibility.

The butler took charge of the pantry and dining room. He engaged the footmen, apportioned their work, and was responsible for their appearance, manners, and efficiency. He was also responsible for silver and wines.

The cook was in charge of the kitchen and the kitchen maids, if any.

The nurse, the personal maid, and the cook were under the direction of the lady of the house. The butler and the valet as well as the chauffeur and gardener were usually engaged by her husband. When garage or garden required more than one person, the head chauffeur usually engaged his own assistant, and the head gardener always did so.

THE BUTLER

The butler was not only the most important servant in every big establishment, but it was by no means unheard of for him to be both steward and housekeeper.

Where there was no housekeeper the butler engaged not only the menservants but the housemaids, parlor maids, and even on occasion the cook. In a smaller house the butler had charge of the dining room and pantry or possibly the whole ground floor. In all smaller establishments, and in many great ones, he was valet to his employer. In a small house the butler worked a great deal with his hands and not so much with his head. In a large establishment the butler worked very much with his head, and with his hands, very little.

At Golden Hall, when guests used to come in dozens at a time, his stewardship was a job that only a man of real ability could fill. He had perhaps twenty men under him at big dinners, he had the keys to the wine cellar and the combination of the silver safe. He also chose the china and glass and linen as well as the silver to be used each day, and he oversaw the setting of the table and the serving of food.

At all meals he stood behind the chair of the lady of the house so that at the slightest turn of her head he need only take a step to be within reach of her voice. The husband, by the way, was "head of the house," but the wife was "head of his table."

The butler often had considerable knowledge of, and insight into, his employer's family and their affairs. Brendan Gill, in his delightful book *Happy Times,* reports that Jules Bache, "a big man in Wall Street . . . had a butler who was known to be at least as clever about money as his master. Sometimes . . . Bache would recommend a certain stock to his guests, and the butler, standing with suitable deference behind his master's chair, would gravely shake his head in silent veto."

In a smaller house where the butler worked alone, he did all the work—naturally. Even when he had a parlor maid or waitress he cleaned the silver and answered the front door and passed the main courses at the table. The assistant passed the secondary dishes and also washed dishes and cleaned the dining room and pantry. Every other afternoon they took turns in answering the door and serving tea. The butler was also valet not only for the gentleman of the house but for any gentlemen guests as well.

FOOTMEN

In 1922, when the first edition of *Etiquette* was published, the position of "live-in" footman was becoming nonexistent, and when the butler needed extra help for a special occasion, the footmen were hired from a caterer or an agency. They were provided by the agency with regulation "liveries" consisting of trousers and tailcoat to match, buttons of either brass or silver, stiff-starched collar and shirt, white lawn tie, striped waistcoat, and white cotton gloves. Usually there were three buttons on each side of the front of the coat in addition to two linked together on each side of the front edge to hold the coat nearly closed over the waistcoat. There were also twelve buttons on the tails of the coat.

In the rare establishment large enough to require a permanent assistant to the butler, his duties were the following: cleaning the dining room, pantry, lower hall, entrance vestibule and sidewalk, attending to the furnace, carrying wood to any open fireplaces in the house, cleaning the windows, cleaning brasses, cleaning all shoes and boots, carrying everything that was too heavy for the maid or moving furniture so that they could clean behind it, assisting the butler in setting and waiting on table, attending the front door, and cleaning and polishing silver.

The butler himself usually answered the telephone; if not, it was answered by the footman. The footman was deputy butler and took his place whenever the butler was off duty.

THE CHAUFFEUR

The position of chauffeur differed from that of other domestic employees in two respects. The first was that he usually had no regular days off. Second, he usually found and paid for his own board and lodging. Sometimes a single man might eat with the servants in the kitchen, but this was not common. Sometimes, too, there was a room over the garage—or a whole apartment—for him and his family.

His duties were irregular, sometimes extremely so. In a large family, particularly where there were half-grown sons or daughters, a chauffeur's life could be inhumanly strenuous. He was, for example, expected to take the younger children to school, come back and take the lady shopping, go back to school for the children, drive various members of the family during the afternoon, come back and take his employers out to dinner, go back later to fetch them, and perhaps take a debutante daughter to a nightclub or ball. Or if his employers were entertaining that evening, he might perhaps have to stand on the sidewalk to open the car doors of the arriving guests, and be there again when they departed.

On the other hand, there were situations in which the chauffeur was almost a man of leisure; his employer might be an old lady, perhaps, who went to church on Sunday morning from eleven to half-past twelve, who liked to drive from three to five every afternoon, and who went out to dinner not oftener than once a week. The typical schedule was midway between the two. As far in advance as he could, every considerate employer would tell his chauffeur when he was not going to want the car, because only in these circumstances could the chauffeur make any personal engagements.

THE COOK AND KITCHEN MAID

The cook was always in charge of the kitchen. In a small house or in an apartment she did all the cooking and all the cleaning of the kitchen and pantry, answered the back-door bell, set the servants' table, and washed their dishes as well as her kitchen utensils.

In a larger house the kitchen maid prepared vegetables, did all cleaning of the kitchen and pots and pans, answered the bell, set the servants' table, and washed the servants' table dishes. She also carried the housekeeper's meals to her.

In most houses the cook did all the marketing, usually by telephone. She saw the lady of the house every morning and submitted the day's menus for her to approve or change. The butler always went into the kitchen shortly after the cook had had the menus checked and copied the day's menus on a pad of his own. From this he knew what table utensils would be needed.

The cook always wore a white dress and usually a high apron with pockets, stockings (often white), and white shoes. She was expected to furnish her clothes herself, but her aprons and uniforms (and her hair coverings if she wore them) were laundered for her. A few fastidious cooks wore small white kerchief-shaped caps or hair nets when they were preparing food.

THE PARLOR MAID–WAITRESS AND CHAMBERMAID

The parlor maid or waitress kept the drawing room and library in order. In some houses she took up the breakfast trays; in others the butler did this himself and handed them to the lady's maid or the chambermaid to be taken into the bedrooms. She cleaned the windows and the brasses if there was no utility man.

The parlor maid–waitress assisted the butler in waiting table and washing dishes and took turns with him in answering the door and the telephone.

The chambermaid did all the bedrooms, cleaned all silver on dressing tables, polished fixtures in the bathroom—in other words, took care of the bedroom floors. She also took care of the rooms of the other servants.

The waitress or parlor maid and the housemaid were dressed alike. Their work dresses were of plain cotton in whatever color the lady of the house preferred, and had just-above-elbow sleeves edged with a turn-back, attached white cuff. The dresses were finished at the neck with a matching turned-down collar. Large white aprons with high bibs were worn with them.

In a formal house at mealtime, the waitress changed to a long-sleeved dress of taffeta or silk, in black or a dark color, with embroidered white collars, cuffs, and a matching white apron.

A maid's hair had to be smooth and neat. Anything suggesting a faddist hairstyle or curls flying long and loose was in almost as bad taste as a butler's wearing a mustache!

THE LADY'S MAID

A first-class lady's maid, often called a "personal maid," was required to be a hairdresser, a good packer, and an expert needlewoman. Her duty was to keep her employer's clothes in perfect order and to help her dress and undress. She drew the bath, laid out underclothes, dressed the lady's hair, and got out the dress to be worn, as well as the stockings, shoes, hat, gloves, handbag, or whatever accessories went with the dress selected.

As soon as her lady was dressed for the day, everything that had been worn was gone over carefully. Everything mussed was pressed, everything suspected of not being immaculate was washed or cleaned, and when in perfect order, was placed where it belonged. Fine stockings and fragile underwear, as well as washable gloves, were always washed by the maid. This was more reasonable than it perhaps appeared since mending these fragile items was her very special task.

Most ladies' maids were never asked to wait up for their employers beyond a reasonably early hour. Those who sat up late were permitted to sleep comparatively late in the morning.

On duty a lady's maid wore a dark skirt, a white blouse, and either a small white apron, the band of which buttoned in the back, or else a small, round-cornered, black taffeta apron with a narrow self-ruffle. Her aprons were supplied by her employer; otherwise, she always wore her own clothes. These, however, were very quiet in color and of shirtwaist plainness. She never wore a cap.

THE VALET AND HOUSEMAN

The valet (pronounced *VAL-et,* not *val-LAY*) was what Beau Brummell called a gentleman's gentleman. He kept his employer's clothes in perfect order, brushed, cleaned, and pressed everything as soon as it had been worn, laid out the clothes to be put on, and put away everything that was a personal belonging. Some gentlemen, particularly those who were very old, liked their valets to help them dress, run the bath, shave them, and hold each article in readiness as it was to be put on. But most merely required that their clothes be laid out for them in good order.

The valet also unpacked the bags of any gentlemen guests when they arrived, valeted them while there, and packed again when they left. He always packed for his own gentleman, bought tickets, looked after the luggage, and made himself generally useful as a personal attendant, whether at home or when traveling.

THE CHILDREN'S NURSE

Everybody knew fifty years ago that the children's nurse was either the comfort or the torment of the house. Many an excellent cook left an otherwise satisfactory job because the nurse was upsetting the kitchen routine. Not only was it important to have a sweet-tempered, competent, and clean person, but her character was of utmost concern, for she was the constant and inseparable companion of children whose whole lives were influenced by her example, especially if busy parents could give only a small portion of time to their children.

When the mother of the children cared very much about appearances their nurse was always dressed in white in the house. On the street she might wear a simple suit or dress and hat. To dress any nurse in the cloak and cap of the English nurse was suitable only if she actually was British.

OTHER HOUSEHOLD ASSISTANTS

In addition to those regularly employed on the staff of any large establishment there were others whose assistance was required from time to time or on special occasions—the tutor, the registered nurse, and so forth. The companion was sometimes a permanent member of any staff, or she could be employed on a temporary basis in a home with no staff at all. In the same way, one household might require the services of a social secretary at all times, whereas another family might employ her for only a few months, to handle the details of their daughter's elaborate wedding, for example.

—AND NOW

And so, back to the present day.

Gone are the footmen, and most of the butlers and chambermaids, but the chores they performed remain and must be taken care of by the help that is available today. Thanks to the conveniences and appliances found in modern homes, the work that used to be done by many can now be done by one or two. This is not to say that there are no homes with large staffs. There are some, and the duties of those staffs are divided in much the same way as they were in the "great house" of yesterday. Their work, of course, is considerably lighter—thanks to modern appliances and to recognition of the importance of better working hours and working conditions.

But the vast majority of home owners who have live-in servants have no more than one or two, and it is to these people that the rest of this chapter is devoted.

COUPLES

A satisfactory solution to the problem of household help for many families who have large houses but cannot or do not wish to employ many servants is the married couple who are hired together. The work is divided according to the abilities of the man and wife, but the usual arrangement is for the woman to do the cooking and to clean the bedrooms while the man waits on table, cleans the living room, dining room, halls, etc., and also does some driving and takes care of the cars. The couple share the work of cleaning up after meals, and he may also help with their preparation, especially if the employer is entertaining.

The couple must have an apartment of at least two rooms, preferably with a private entrance, perhaps over a garage. Some employers do not object if a child lives with the parents, but it must be understood in advance that he or she will not be disturbing in any way and will not be allowed the run of the house except when playing with the children of the employer.

Their working hours must be carefully scheduled so that they will be able to have at least one day off a week together, even though they alternate being "off" at other times.

THE BABY-SITTER

With smaller family homes and small-apartment living and with the tremendous increase in domestics' salaries the absence of a "live-in" staff has created a special demand—and baby-sitters have achieved both amateur and professional standing. Sitters' ages may range from the early teens, if he or she is a responsible youngster and fond of children, up to elderly ladies. In the intermediate group, many high-school and college boys and girls and young business-women are glad to supplement their allowances or salaries by baby-sitting a few times a week.

In many cities girls who live in residential clubs post their names to indicate their availability for baby-sitting, and mothers in the neighborhood may avail themselves of this service. In many communities there are agencies that provide approved sitters at standard rates.

As the rate of payment varies in different localities no set schedule can be fixed. But the customary rate of the community should be observed, and the sitter should be paid at the end of the evening. It should be clearly understood *ahead of time* what the hourly rate will be. The sitter should be told that after the children are asleep she (or he) may use the television set or play the radio, read, or do homework. In some households a sitter is permitted to ask a girl friend to keep her company, but she may never entertain a boy or her crowd when "sitting," and although it may seem unnecessary you should make that perfectly clear. Otherwise you may run into a situation like this: One evening when our children were young my husband and I returned home an hour or so earlier than we had anticipated. The lights were snapped on as we opened the door, and a very red-faced and rumpled young lady ran out of the bedroom. As she was stuttering and stammering, an even more red-faced young man squeezed out the door—as she muttered, "Er, er, Mrs. Post, this is Mouse!" In other words, it should be clearly understood what she is expected to do and what she may not do. It is thoughtful to leave a snack in the refrigerator or to tell her what she is welcome to as a beverage. Be specific about where you are going —leave the address and telephone number, as well as the name, address, and telephone number of the children's doctor. Always tell the sitter when you expect to be back—and try to be on time.

Adequate transportation must be provided for the sitter's safe return home, and this applies for sitters of any age.

Youngsters of twelve or thirteen are often responsible enough to sit for a toddler or preschooler for a short time. They should never be left alone with an infant, however, or left in a situation where the mother or another adult is not immediately available. It is hard to set age limits because a thirteen-year-old with three or four younger brothers and sisters is far more capable than a seventeen-year-old who has never been around a young child. You must know a young sitter personally before hiring her (or him) or else have excellent personal recommendations from a friend who has used her services.

Young adults—married or single—or experienced older women make the best sitters for very young children, and a married couple is ideal if you are leaving your children for several days or even weeks. A couple is unlikely to get restless and bored as would a single person—especially if your home is at all isolated.

If two mothers wish to share a sitter her pay should be adjusted in recognition of the extra responsibility. It need not be double—a sitter would not charge twice as much for two children in a family as she would for one—but it would not be fair to ask her to sit for two separate families for the price of one. This, too, should be settled ahead of time. It is entirely wrong to hire a sitter to take care of your little Sally and then to say, when she arrives, "Oh, by the way, Mrs. Goodwin is bringing Timmy over for the day."

"Baby-sitter–snatching" is perhaps the eighth deadly sin. If you have a neighbor who has a regular sitter, and she generously "lends" the sitter to you in an emergency, don't try to lure the girl away no matter how much you like her. This is true of all household help of course, but because they are far more prevalent than others, it happens most with sitters. If you wish to discuss it with your neighbor, and perhaps make a sharing arrangement, that is fine, but *never* sitter-snatch behind her back if you wish to have a friend left in town.

When someone comes to pick you up, or arrives to spend the evening, your sitter is introduced just as a friend would be—if she is present. You need not call her away from the children, or from whatever she is doing, however, unless it is someone to whom you especially want to introduce her.

PART-TIME HELP

The maid or "cleaning woman" who comes by the hour or day should be treated with the same courtesy that is expected by the permanent servant. She should be paid promptly, daily, weekly, or in any other way agreed upon.

If your house is far from public transportation, you must see that she is transported to bus or train, or if she is not, that her pay is augmented to cover taxi fare.

If you wish her to wear uniforms, you naturally provide them for her. The part-time cleaning woman often prefers to wear her own clothes covered by a large apron, but if she wishes to wear a uniform in order to save her clothes, she may ask you to buy one or two.

The maid's duties should be carefully outlined in advance. Will there be cooking to do? Are washing and ironing expected, and what about heavy cleaning like waxing floors and washing windows? All these points should be clearly understood on both sides, and if you ask her to do any unusual work or stay on late—to help with a dinner party, for example—her hourly rate for this extra service should be agreed upon beforehand.

Unlike the case of other household employees, it is best to hire part-time cleaning women through friends rather than agencies. The turnover is much higher than it is for live-in help, and many agencies that handle temporary help do not have the opportunity to know very much about them. A good recommendation from a friend who has employed your prospective help for a reasonable length of time is by far the most reliable recommendation you can have.

Since your cleaning woman does not have a room of her own in your house, there must be some space allotted to her to hang her coat, change her clothes, use the bathroom, etc. If your kitchen is too small to hold a table and chairs, she must feel free to sit in your living room or dining area for her noontime break and meal. If she stays all day, you must be prepared to provide a lunch for her. Discuss what sort of a noontime meal she is accustomed to when you hire her, and either be sure to buy something for her or tell her what she is—or is not—free to help herself to from your refrigerator, freezer, or cupboard shelves.

THE REGISTERED NURSE

The social position of a registered hospital nurse is, of course, that of a deputy physician, and on a long case she is sometimes the closest of the family's friends. She always eats her meals with the family or has them served to her on a tray in a sitting room. She never eats in the kitchen unless that is where the family also eats, or unless she wants to.

When on duty in her patient's room or anywhere in a private house, she wears her uniform. But when going into the street, going downstairs in a hotel, or traveling with her patient, she dresses as does any other lady.

Other servants in the household—especially longtime family retainers—often resent her position. When you are forced to have a nurse—or perhaps three shifts of nurses—in attendance, you will be wise to talk to the cook and maid—or whoever else is there—beforehand, explaining how important it is to you and to the sick person that everyone make an extra effort to get along, even though there will be inconveniences. If there are extra meals to be prepared, trays to be served, and so on, a small raise in wages may help to smooth over what can be a very difficult situation.

While the nurse is dependent on the cook for meals and trays, she should take care of her own room, her laundry, and so forth.

THE COMPANION

One of the most upsetting things about getting old is the consequent loss of independence. This makes the job of being a companion to an older person one of the hardest—in some ways—there is. The elderly man or woman resents having to be taken care of, resents his or her loss of privacy, and resents having someone around who is generally hired by another member of the family or perhaps a doctor. Added to all this is the fact that there is sometimes mental failure as well as physical, and the old person may be senile, crotchety, repetitive, and vindictive. To handle all this, certain considerations must be given to a companion, who, to hold the job at all, must often be something of a saint. Of course there are companions who have been known to neglect their charges shamelessly, to physically abuse them, and to rob them blind. This is a real danger if no other member of the family lives in the home or nearby. To guard against this, it is best to hire a companion through a reputable agency and even then to check the references carefully. In cases where a companion is hired through a personal ad in the paper, you must be extra careful, talking to previous employers in person, if possible, and if not, by correspondence.

Because of the confining nature of the work, it is essential that companions have more than the ordinary day and a half a week off. Two days, either consecutively, or if she prefers, one midweek and one during the weekend, allow her enough time away from the monotony and irritations of the job. She should also have two or three hours during the day—perhaps when her charge is resting—to go to her room, read, watch television, write letters, or to do whatever else she chooses. Although she often must accompany her charge when he or she goes out socially, she need not stay in attendance when friends come to visit at the home. She should, however, remain within call in case she is needed.

As in choosing a children's nurse, a companion must be sympathetic, patient, and understanding. It is far more important that she have these qualities, and that the older person be reasonably content with her, than that she be a superb cook and housekeeper. Often she must do those chores too, as well as order food and keep accounts of household expenses. If possible, it is ideal to have the person who takes her place on her days off agree to do some of the cleaning chores, to relieve the companion of all that responsibility.

When you hire a companion you must, as you would with any servant, make very clear what she will and will not be expected to do. In a servantless home she may have to do almost everything, and should be paid accordingly. In a house where there are other servants she may have nothing to do except entertain her charge and take care of his or her physical needs.

The companion generally eats with her patient—from trays or in the dining room. If they live with the older person's children, both she and her charge may eat with the family, but the companion, unless she chooses to do so, does not eat with the servants in the kitchen.

She ordinarily wears a white uniform if her duties include any "nursing." Many women prefer to do this to save their own clothes. When she and her charge go out or travel together, however, she generally wears her own appropriate clothing. Companions to more active people, who need no nursing, are often very refined older women who need a little extra money or who want company themselves. In this case they dress as, and are treated as, good friends.

The same considerations (involving the rest of the household help) are necessary as described above under "the registered nurse."

THE MOTHER'S HELPER

Many young couples with small children need an all-around helper more than they need a specialist such as a cook or a nurse.

The duties of a mother's helper are generally related to the care of the children—their meals, their rooms, and their clothes. If there are only one or two children her chores may also include some light housework, some laundry, some cooking, and some washing up. It is essential, because of the loosely defined nature of the job, that the areas and amount of work to be done are discussed and settled upon before the position is accepted. Too often a woman is hired to "take care of the children," and because no guidelines were laid down in the beginning, eventually finds herself taking care of the whole house as well.

The relationship of a mother's helper and her family is usually quite different from that of other servants and employers. She often, over a period of time, becomes almost a member of the family. In some cases she may eat her meals with them, but this can become somewhat of a strain, because every couple is entitled to privacy and the privilege of being alone. When there are young children in the family the ideal solution is for the mother's helper to eat dinner with them at an earlier hour, except, perhaps, on Sundays and special occasions. Some perceptive mother's helpers, in order to avoid imposing, simply say that they prefer to eat earlier or to watch television at that hour, or they make some other excuse. But the mother's helper, with the children, may join the family for a while before dinner if she wishes, and once the children are in bed her time should be her own.

A great many young girls—called au pair girls—come from abroad to fill this position, and they have their special problems. They generally contract to come for a ridiculously low salary, for a period of one year. But the housewife who does not realize that the wage, even though agreed upon in advance, is often completely inadequate in our economy, will find herself with a very unhappy employee. She will also find, if she does not voluntarily offer to pay a reasonable amount, that her mother's helper may suddenly be wooed away by an offer of higher wages from one of the neighbors. These girls are often highly educated and take the job as a means of getting to the United States. Their backgrounds are frequently the same as or better than those of the people they are working for. When this is so, it is even more necessary, if the year is to be a success and the job is possibly to extend beyond the one year, that the employers make every effort to make their helper feel at home. Although she need not be included when they are entertaining, when they are alone as a family she should be a welcome member of the group.

THE COOK-HOUSEKEEPER

The cook-housekeeper is truly the remaining embodiment of the staff of the "great house" of years ago. And even she is found today only in the homes of the relatively wealthy, or more frequently, in the home of a career or professional woman.

The great difficulty in keeping a cook-housekeeper (or general houseworker, as she may be called) comes when you expect too much of her. If you do not work and are home to do your share of the housework most of the time, this is not such a danger, but if you work all day, every day, it is very easy to turn more and more of the household chores over to your housekeeper, who will finally collapse under the load or give up and leave.

Her duties must be clearly defined when you hire her—written down if necessary—and strictly observed on both sides. She should be responsible for all the kitchen work—cooking, cleaning up, and ordering the food if that is part of your agreement. She also takes care of the downstairs or "living" area—living room, hall, and dining room. She cleans the silver, brass, etc. How much work she does in the bedroom area depends on your arrangement. If there are no children to cook for or pick up after, she may dust and vacuum upstairs, too, as well as clean the bathrooms. Or she may not go into the bedrooms at all. The size of the house, your needs, and her inclinations must be considered in establishing her routine.

In addition to a day and a half off each week—and that includes an "overnight" off—she should have definite hours in the afternoon to herself. If she wishes to remain at home, she should answer the phone or door for you during those hours, but unless there is some specific reason that she remain in the house (if, for instance, young children are expected home from school) she should be free to take a walk, do errands, or whatever. The more time she has to pursue her own life, the less she will feel "put upon," and the longer she will stay with you.

The cook-housekeeper eats by herself, either before or after you, as she pleases—she serves herself the same food she prepares for you and has free access to the refrigerator and the freezer. If there are things you are saving for a special occasion, it is up to you to let her know about them.

The cook-housekeeper wears a uniform—either a simple white or colored dress with an apron. If she serves you at dinner, or when you have guests, she changes to a slightly dressier, colored dress with white collar and apron. She should of course be neat and clean, and if she has long hair it should be put up or tied back before serving a meal.

When you entertain more than one or two other people you should hire an extra person to help your cook-housekeeper, unless you intend to do a great deal of the preparation yourself and plan to serve a buffet meal.

If your cook-housekeeper happens to be a man, the basic regulations and requirements are exactly the same. He may also—in addition to, or in place of, some of the chores mentioned above—act as handyman, gardener, or chauffeur. Oriental housemen may or may not choose to wear dark trousers with white mandarin-style jackets during the day, and often in the evening too. American housemen wear khakis or slacks and open-neck shirts when they are doing housework. To serve meals they dress in black trousers and jackets with soft white shirts and (usually) bow ties.

CHAUFFEURS

A goodly number of older people who cannot or do not wish to drive themselves, have chauffeurs. So do businessmen and officials who use the time they are driven to and from their offices to work on papers, dictate, study, etc.

The chauffeur—especially if his employer has a suburban or country home—often doubles as handyman and/or gardener. He is also in charge of keeping the car, or cars, in top condition.

Although a chauffeur's duties today can be almost as confining as those described on page 854, he is now given specific days off so that he can count on certain hours for his own use. The considerate employer "now" as "then" will tell him as far in advance as possible when he will or will not be needed, and since he generally does not live at his employer's home, he may go to his own whenever he is off duty.

Chauffeurs no longer wear "livery." Even those driving diplomatic cars are most often seen in plain black or dark-gray suits with soft hats. If his employer wishes, a chauffeur may be required to wear the traditional peaked cap instead of a fedora, but that is almost the only remaining sign of the old-fashioned uniform.

As with all servants, the chauffeur's duties, his hours, and his salary must be fully agreed upon in advance.

~§72§~ The Employer-Servant Relationship

In these days of "do-it-yourself" housekeeping, a large household staff is rare indeed. A moderate number of households have one maid living in, but the most that a great majority of the women of today expect is to have help with the housecleaning chores once or twice a week. Beyond that, they may hire a combination cook-waitress to assist on special occasions.

Everyone who employs a servant is at some point faced with the problem of doing so for the first time. Even the young woman who has grown up in a household with a large staff is confronted by a new situation when she begins to look for her own maid for her own home. Too many people give too little thought to what is involved in the employer-servant relationship, not only when they interview applicants but throughout the months and years that follow.

If you have never kept house before and do not know what a maid should be able to do, you can go to a reliable employment office where the personnel will tell you about hours and wages and an average working plan. On the other hand, if you advertise in the paper, you should ask a friend whose household is similar to your own to give you advice on making a fair and practical schedule and establishing a wage.

INTERVIEWING AN APPLICANT

If the applicant has a written reference from her last employer, read it carefully but do not put too much stock in it. Most housewives hesitate to write down derogatory comments and then give them to their ex-employees. A written reference is worthwhile only if it gives the name and telephone number of the writer. Before hiring anyone the houswife should take advantage of that information because she will get a far more complete and honest appraisal over the phone than the note of reference can possibly give.

Let us say that the references of an applicant are good and that the wages you can pay meet her expectations. Let us say, too, that you find her personality pleasing. (Perhaps this feeling is not always reliable, but it is an important point to consider.)

The next move is to give her briefly but accurately the schedule of both working and time-off hours. Accuracy is emphasized because misrepresentation of facts or intentions is unfair. It is unfair, for example, to assure the maid that she is to have no care of the baby and then gradually ask that she do just about everything that would be expected of a nurse—as well as her other work.

Another important point is to try to visualize what you offer her as well as what you expect of her. Don't say that you are always prompt, when you are not; don't say that your meals will be very simple and then expect her to be an expert chef. Don't say that you don't entertain much, when you regularly give Saturday-night dinner parties. Don't say that her work will take a certain number of hours a day without having the vaguest notion of how much work can be reasonably expected in this length of time. At the other extreme, it isn't necessary to exaggerate whatever inconveniences there may perhaps be, particularly when there will be much compensating pleasantness that could make her quite happy with you.

Even though you make your contact with a prospective employee through an agency, and they arrange the first interview at their office, it is wise, if possible, to have another follow-up interview in your home. Your aim is to show her, and make her feel at ease in, what may be her new surroundings. In the familiar atmosphere of your own house you will be much better able to see how she will fit in, and she, too, will understand much more about you and about the way you live. If you have children they should meet her at this interview also, because their reaction to her—and hers to them—is of the utmost importance.

While most of the questions should come from you, it is only to be expected that she will have questions, too, and you must answer them *honestly,* to the best of your ability. You have every right to inquire about her state of health, her age, her interests, her family responsibilities, and of course her past working experience. You also should find out whether she smokes and/or drinks. She in turn is quite within bounds in asking how much entertaining you will do, how often older children are home, how much time she will have to herself, how you feel about her friends coming in, etc. You should, in turn, offer as much information about you and your family, and your habits, as seems pertinent. If you have had previous employees who stayed with you for a long time, don't hesitate to mention that—it makes it clear that you are a considerate employer.

HOW MUCH WORK?

The details of just how much, and just what, one maid should do, constitute a subject that is almost impossible to treat in a general statement, because her work must be adjusted not only to the needs of the particular family by whom she is employed but also to her own capabilities.

Out of every twenty-four hours, every normal human being should have at least nine hours for sleeping, dressing, and undressing, in addition to plenty of time for eating three meals. During the rest of the day she must be able to find the time for rest and recreation as well as for work. It is impossible to establish a fixed schedule for working hours and time off, because these are in many cases subject to personal requirements and agreements.

If in your household it is possible to employ someone with the promise that she will work a normal eight-hour day, from nine to five or ten to six, for example, you will find it far easier to fill the position. There have been, and are, union moves in this direction, and if more hours are put in, overtime should be paid. However, such a schedule is simply not practical in most households, especially if the maid's job involves the care of children or the mother works and needs someone to prepare the evening meal. In short, domestic service is almost impossible to organize like business work. It must be fitted to the individual household and to all the people involved.

Your employee's days off must be clearly stated—and respected. If for a very important reason you wish to change her day off on occasion, you must ask her if she would be willing to do so well in advance so that she may change her own plans.

MAY SERVANTS ENTERTAIN FRIENDS?

Of course they may! Domestic help enjoy entertaining friends just as their employers do, and whenever their duties are finished and it does not interfere with the plans of the people they work for, they should be allowed to do so.

In a house where no sitting room for a maid is possible, one end of the kitchen can sometimes be attractively fixed up for her leisure hours. Or the maid's room, especially one on the ground floor, may be furnished as a sitting room.

In homes with one servant the relationship is sometimes on such a friendly basis that the use of the living room is offered the maid when the family is not at home. Naturally, she and her friends should not abuse this privilege by helping themselves to cigarettes or liquor. If he wishes, the man of the house may suggest that her callers will find beer or soft drinks in the refrigerator. The maid, of course, makes the room immaculate when her friends leave.

AN ATTRACTIVE ROOM

When fixing up a room for a new maid, try to imagine yourself in her place and take pains to make it as attractive as possible. Surely nothing could be more discouraging to any normal woman than to arrive in a strange place, which is to be her "home," and be taken to a drab and comfortless room all too plainly furnished with the family discards.

After all, a comfortable bed, attractively painted furniture, and a little gay chintz are not very difficult to supply, especially in this day of spray paints that can be applied by the merest amateur. In other words, dingy brown and "landlord cream" are inexcusable. The same attention to attractiveness and convenience should be evident in the kitchen—where most maids work and take their meals, and where they may also spend much of their leisure time.

If you have a downstairs room that can be furnished as a bed-sitting room, that is ideal. It provides more comfortable surroundings for her leisure hours and a more attractive place to entertain her friends. If this is not possible, and her room must be on the third floor or "in back," at least take the measures described above to give it some charm. Make sure the bed is comfortable, with a good, firm mattress. An aching back will not help the quality of your maid's service.

Every maid's room should have a radio, and if you can possibly provide it, a television set.

UNIFORMS

All maids' uniforms as well as aprons and collars and cuffs are furnished by the employer, with the exception, possibly, of those worn by a cook, for whom the employer furnishes only the aprons.

THE COMMON COURTESIES

Years ago the butler was "Hastings" and the chauffeur, "Campbell." Today they are called "John" or "Jim." Young maids are called by their first names, but an older woman—mother's helper or houseworker—is often called "Mrs. Sykes." In a large, formal household, however, chambermaids and waitresses are called by their first names, although the cook's title is sometimes used. When hiring someone for a one-servant household, or as a part-time helper, it is thoughtful do ask her what she would like to be called. Older employees who are called "Mrs. Sykes" or "Miss Stanley" automatically seem to be accorded more respect—especially by children—than if the familiar first name is used.

Household employees, whether young or old, in a large house or a small apartment, call their employers "Mrs. Grant" and "Mr. Grant." The only exception might be an old family nurse who stayed on to help out in her charge's household after the latter married. Children in the family are called by their first names or nicknames by all employees older than themselves. A maid in a very formal household would, however, call adolescent—or older—sons or daughters "Mr. Bob" or "Miss Jill."

Every courteous employer says "Please" in asking that something be brought to her or him: "Would you turn on the lights, please," or "Some more bread, please." One is equally careful to say "Thank you" for any service rendered. No lady or gentleman barks, "Turn on the lights!" or "Give me the bread!" In refusing a dish at the table one says, "No, thank you," or "No, thanks." Children *must* be taught these courtesies with relation to servants as well as friends at the earliest possible age.

A new servant in any capacity is always introduced *to* the members of the household: "Bobby, this is Mary McCormack—she is going to be our new cook."

When guests come to your house for dinner or a party of any sort, it is not necessary to introduce your servant(s) to them. However, when someone comes to stay overnight, or longer, and they will have occasion to talk to each other, introductions are in order. Again, the employee is introduced *to* the guest, and only the name by which the maid is known to the household is used. For example, when your friend Marion comes in, and your maid-of-all-work, Sally, is in the hall to take her bag, you say, "Marion, this is Sally, our housekeeper. Sally, will you take Mrs. Harmon's bag to the guest room, please?" If Sally is normally called Mrs. Loveman, that is the name you use in introducing her.

When it is necessary to write a note to your maid, the rules are slightly different from those for your other correspondence. Although you may start it "Dear Barbara," just "Barbara" is sufficient. The signature, rather than the usual "Sarah Carnes," may be either "S. L. C." or "Mrs. Carnes." Notes left to deliverymen are also signed "Mrs. Carnes."

PRIVACY

Your employee's private life is her own business—not yours. As long as her problems do not interfere with her work, there is no reason for you to be "in" on them. Her mail, her telephone calls, and what she does with her spare time are just as inviolate as your children's or your friends'.

Naturally, if she *comes* to you with her problems, you must do your best to help her. It may be advice she needs, or it may be financial help, and you may want to assist with either one. If it is money that is the problem, you are free to advance her a sum or not, as you see fit, but if you do, be sure that it is clearly understood that you will take a certain amount out of future salaries to pay it back—or whatever arrangement you care to make.

Her room is her own domain, and you should not "snoop" when she is on her day off, but you *do* have a right to knock on her door occasionally when she is in, to be sure that she is keeping it in at least reasonably good order.

DISMISSAL

There are several reasons for instant dismissal, with no accompanying reference nor special consideration. They are robbery, dishonesty of other kinds, cruelty to children, drunkenness, or use of drugs. When a servant is caught in any of these acts, the sooner she is out of the house, the better.

In almost all other circumstances a degree of tolerance and understanding pays off. Even a "second chance" if the misbehavior is not too severe is often better than the necessity of finding and training a new employee. I have, over the years, put up with plates being broken carelessly, with oversleeping, with mops or dust rags being left in the living room, cobwebs on the lampshades, and a variety of other situations, because the mistakes were unintentional, the perpetrator was truly sorry, or simply because I liked her, and she liked me. Having someone who is pleasant and *simpática* in the household, and especially someone who is trustworthy with your children and your possessions, more than makes up for all the little slips that are relatively so unimportant.

When it is necessary to dismiss a domestic it is best to do it promptly, immediately after the episode causing the dismissal takes place, and firmly. You must have a good reason—it is very difficult to tell someone you just don't like her, or her looks, or the way she walks. If these are the reasons, try, in order to leave her her self-respect, to find a more specific reason, even by putting the blame on your financial situation, your future plans, or whatever. Of course, if your reason is more legitimate and definite, you must tell her that too.

With the difficulty in finding servants today, however, you will be wise to try to correct the faults or change the conditions that bring on the faults—overwork, overlong hours, etc.—before you decide on dismissal. Of course if you feel there is no rapport between you, no hope for training, nor any possibility of changing the routine, then you must face up to it and "fire" your employee as tactfully and kindly as you can. If circumstances warrant it, you should give her as good a letter of reference as you can, and you might also help her to find another job to which she would be better fitted.

LETTERS OF REFERENCE

As stated above, there are some situations in which no letter of reference need be written, but ordinarily it would be most unkind to withhold one. The girl you find lazy or sloppy might suit someone else to a "T."

The most considerate letter will point out all the good points of the employee and will not mention the bad. The omission will, of course, speak for itself, but the good points will at least prompt a prospective employer to call you, and you can then give a full and honest explanation.

An excellent recommendation—written by hand—might read:

Julia Corbin has been my general housekeeper for four years. She is completely reliable, honest, and responsible. She is also neat, efficient, and pleasant. Her duties included keeping the downstairs clean, preparing and serving breakfast and dinner. She is an excellent cook and enjoys cooking. My children are devoted to her, and the whole family will miss her terribly. She is only leaving because we are moving to California and she does not wish to go so far from her family, who live in New York.

I will be happy to answer any questions about Julia personally, at 914–286–6343.

An adequate but less enthusiastic reference could be worded:

Sandra Parkins has been in my employ for two years as a mother's helper. I found her at all times honest and good with the children. She cooked simple meals for them and kept their rooms in order. Sandra is leaving because the children have now reached school age, and I no longer need help with them. For further reference, you may call me at 203–966–7274.

When someone does call to check on a written reference, you must be honest, but again, try not to emphasize the drawbacks unless they are serious ones.

SOCIAL SECURITY AND WORKMEN'S COMPENSATION

Every person who employs domestic help is responsible for filing a return and paying at least one-half of the employee's Social Security tax. Even though your cleaning woman is a part-time worker, she must, if you pay her wages of over fifty dollars in any quarter (three-month period) of the year, pay a Social Security tax. The employer is supposed to deduct half of the amount to be paid from the employee's wages, and pay it, plus the other half from his own pocket, to the government. This must be clearly understood by the employee at the time of hiring, so that there will be no question of why the salary is lower than had been promised. Be sure that she *has* a Social Security number and gives it to you when you hire her, as you are *both* legally liable if you do not comply with the regulations. Many employers, instead of paying a higher weekly sum, pay the full amount of the Social Security tax themselves. This is both legal—since the government does not care so long as it receives its (current) 11½ percent of the wages—and simpler, if the arrangement is clearly understood by the employee, who may *not* get the same "break" from her next employer. You will be sent a tax return automatically each quarter, and you will be fined if it is not returned within the specified time. You must of course furnish the employee with a yearly record of how much you have withheld for her, so that she may file a correct income tax return.

The sensible employer carries sufficient liability insurance to cover any accident that might occur to anyone in his employ. This should be discussed with your insurance company before anyone comes to live in your home.

SUCCESS IN HOUSEHOLD MANAGEMENT

Those who have servant trouble might do well to remember a basic rule that is often overlooked: Justice must be the foundation upon which every tranquil household is constructed. Work and privileges must be as evenly divided as possible; one servant should not be allowed liberties not accorded to all.

Neglect of this rule, perhaps, explains why some people are always having trouble—finding servants difficult to get and more difficult to keep. Perhaps a servant problem is more often an employer problem. I'm sure it is! Because, if you notice, families that have woes and complaints invariably have them continually, just as others never have any trouble at all. Problems do not depend on the size of the house—the Lovejoys never have any trouble, and yet their one maid-of-all-work has a far from easy job.

It is not fair to be too lenient, any more than it is just to be unreasonably demanding. To allow impertinence or sloppy work is a mistake, but it is also inexcusable to show unwarranted irritability or to be overbearing or rude. And there is no greater example of injustice than to reprimand people about you because you happen to be in a bad humor, and at another time to overlook offenses that are greater because you are in an amiable mood. Nor is there ever any excuse for correcting an employee in front of anyone else.

In analyzing the spirit of a happy house, I believe it consists of the understanding and fairness that are shown by both sides. Proper pride on the part of an employee demands that he or she give fair value for wages received. On the other side, the obligation of the lady of the house and the other members of the family is to show understanding and fairness in what they require. If their point of view is just, and if they themselves are kind and trustworthy, then they naturally believe that people serving them have the same traits and they are very unlikely ever to have any housekeeping difficulties.

875

Part Thirteen

YOU AND
YOUR FAMILY

✺73✺ The Young
Child

Training a child is exactly like training a puppy; a little heedless inattention and it is out if hand immediately.—Emily Post, 1922

Several years ago I wrote a book called *Please, Say Please—A Common Sense Guide to Bringing Up Your Child.* The book is based on the principle that to be a well-rounded, happy individual, to *give* the most as well as to *get* the most out of life, a child should be taught from the earliest age that he must fit into the society that is already there—the world is not going to revolve around him. This, I believe, is the great flaw in the permissive method of child-rearing. The child does what *he* wants regardless of how it affects others, and while his family may be able to understand and live with his "independence," society at large, when he is ready to become a part of it, will not be. To enjoy other people and in turn to be liked by them, a child must learn to think of them—to consider them. Good manners, which are no more than the most attractive, most practical, or least offensive ways of doing anything, help the child to learn and to exhibit that attitude. When people ask me, "Are manners really important anymore?" I can honestly reply, "Of course they are." Without the instruction and example set by one generation for the next, the experience of civilization over hundreds of years would be lost. This would be a tragedy, because out of all the thousands of "manners"— the contradictory, the changing, and the useless—there are hundreds of others of value. It is your job to sort out and pass on the best. By teaching your child what you consider worthwhile manners you will give him a start toward being an attractive, acceptable, considerate member of society, and he will then have the prerogative, as he grows older, to discard, add to, or change the ones he has learned from you—for others more appropriate to his time. The most important thing of all is that each generation *does* create a set of standards of its own, based on those it learned in its childhood and adapted to its own life-style. Without its parents' instruction it would have no-place to start. And the greatest tragedy of all would be an absence of standards and manners—a kind of "anarchy" that would result in totally chaotic behavior.

This book, unlike *Please, Say Please*, is not designed to tell you how to bring up your children. But it *is* concerned with teaching them manners, and this chapter will discuss the "why," the "when," and the "how."

I am often asked what is the best way to teach rules of etiquette to young people and whether there are special rules that they should be taught. Of course etiquette applies to everyone, old or young, and the best way to teach etiquette to children is the best way to teach anything—by patient instruction, consistency, firmness, and example. Indeed, children are people—and parents and teachers will do well to remember it.

Children who are spoken to in baby talk and treated like adorable idiots are inclined to act like babies or idiots. But children who are treated as interesting individuals with minds of their own will react by trying to prove that they *are* intelligent and that they *are* individuals.

Children can scarcely be too young to be taught the rudiments of good manners, nor can the teaching be too patiently or too conscientiously carried out. Any child can be taught to be well behaved with patience and perseverance, whereas to break bad habits once they are acquired is a herculean task.

FAIR PLAY

Quite young children are able to understand the principles of justice, and they should be taught, even before they go to school, to "play fair," to respect another's property and rights, to give credit to others, and not to take too much credit to themselves. They must be taught to share playthings and to take care of their own toys as well as those that belong to other children. A bright, observant child should never be allowed to brag about his own achievements or to tell his or her mother how inferior other children are. If he wins a medal at school or is praised, the family naturally rejoices, and it is proper that they should; but a wise mother teaches her child that selfishness and conceit will get him nowhere.

"BECAUSE EVERYONE ELSE DOES"

All young people feel a need to conform to the mores of others of their own age. They express this need in their speech, their play, their choice of clothing, and their relationships to each other. This conformity is quite normal and is to be respected as part of the development of individual personality as well as of social responsibility. Adults, after all, conform to their world too. Young people in time learn that through conformity with most of the social customs of the adult world they will be able to take their place in that world.

Children should be permitted to follow the cutoms of their community, so as not to differ too radically from the other children in the neighborhood. However, there are necessary and obvious qualifications to this advice. It is possible for children to be well brought up even though the community where the family lives may seem to have accepted lower standards of behavior than the family's own. The phrase one hears so often from children—"Everyone else does thus-and-so"—is not sufficient excuse for lowering standards. Surely, to take an extreme example, no one could condone cheating at games or on examinations just "because everyone else does."

Of course parents sometimes must make a decision at the risk of having their children a little different in some particular from their friends. There are times when children should be required to set an example, rather than follow others. There is a certain element of risk involved in this position, but there is also an element of discipline that is far more important.

Parents and teachers must never underestimate the problems that a child has in adapting himself to a world full of contradictions that can only be reconciled by experience.

THE PARENT'S ATTITUDE

First and foremost, every parent must realize that each child is an individual and as such must be treated with respect.

The first outward sign of respect you can show your toddler is, never talk *down* to him. Of course you must use simple words and sentences or he will not understand you at all, but baby talk is an insult to the intelligence of a normal child and does nothing to encourage him to increase his vocabulary or to speak as fluently as possible. Nor should you talk about a child in front of him. Why some people talk about their child's shortcomings, or tell "funny" stories about him, as though he were deaf, is more than I can understand.

This same attitude of treating a child as an individual carries through to your judgment of what he can or cannot do. I have found that most children are far more capable than their elders believe. If you expect good behavior or assume that your child will react to a situation in a reasonable way, you will generally find that he will live up to your expectations. If, however, you start out by saying to Johnny, "I'll cut your meat for you, dear—you're too little," he will certainly not be encouraged to make the effort to learn to do it himself. One word of warning, however: This can be overdone, and nothing will frustrate Johnny more than being required to do things that he simply is not capable of handling. To scold him for not being able to do up his snaps or buttons will quickly cause him to rebel against all attempts to teach him to dress himself.

Study your child as an interesting person, increase his responsibilities as he seems able to cope with them, reprove him when he falls short, and praise him when he takes a step forward. Include him in your conversation, correcting his mistakes and teaching him new words, and share as many family activities with him as you can. Don't laugh at his mistakes or ridicule him, but at the same time try to appreciate his developing sense of humor and laugh *with* him. Encouragement, appreciation, and lots of love are the most essential elements in a baby's happy environment.

OBEYING THE RULES

Little children must be taught from their earliest years that there are certain rules that have to be obeyed. You may be one of the many parents who believe in self-regulating schedules for small children (I happen to believe that a certain amount of regulation is better for both children and their parents), but this does not mean that they cannot be taught the rules that govern the relationships between themselves and other people. I firmly believe that too much permissiveness can contribute to delinquency. Young people, no matter what they may say aloud, want and need direction and correction, and the more honest ones will even admit it. I have actually heard a young girl say, "I wish my mother would say 'No'—then I wouldn't have to make up my mind."

THE VALIDITY OF "NO"

Obedience to "No" is perhaps the earliest lesson a youngster must learn. "No's" fall into various categories—from very important, which requires instant response, to "probably not," which may be discussed. The most important "No" is the one that will prevent your child from getting hurt or hurting someone else. This "No" requires instant, unquestioning obedience. If he goes too far out on thin ice, or goes right on touching a match to little Joannie's dress while he decides whether or not to obey, it will be too late. The tone of your voice, reserved for this real emergency "No," is usually enough to enforce it.

The next "No," in importance, is that which prevents destruction of property. This "No" is used continually with small children— "No, Johnny, don't touch," "No, Susie, don't step on the flowers," and so on and on. It is a vital part of teaching respect for possessions, and as the child gets older, will become less necessary.

From there on "No" is used for an infinite number of reasons— some good, some bad. It is important that you recognize your motive for saying "No." Is it for your child's good or for your own satisfaction? Are you simply feeling too lazy to get him dressed to take him to meet Daddy, or should he *really* be in bed and asleep before Daddy's plane comes in? The "good" reasons for a firm "No" are:

Protection of your child's safety or health

Protection of your own—or someone else's—property

The child's education—to help him differentiate between right and wrong

Any legitimate reason—for example, he wants you to buy a toy that he doesn't need and/or you cannot afford. Or he wants to go out and play when he is tired and it is time for his nap.

The "bad" reasons for a "No" are:

Vindictiveness—because you are "mad"

Laziness and/or selfishness. It is simply less trouble for you to say "No" at the time.

Having learned to respond to "No" the child must then learn that "No" is inviolable. Temper tantrums, refusal to eat, begging, or feigning sickness will not change "No" to "Yes."

There are only two exceptions to the rule. "No" *should* be changed to "Yes" when:

The reason for the original "No" is gone.

You realize that the "No" was wrong or unfair.

DISCIPLINE

The single most important thing about disciplining a child is to make your point and stick to it. If you say "No" to an extra half hour at bedtime, and then say "Yes" when Susie says, "But Mommy, this is my favorite TV program," how will Susie ever know whether or not you mean what you say? And how much respect will she have for your decisions?

The severity of the punishment should be directly related to the seriousness of the misdeed. If it is a minor infraction it should not result in a major penalty, or you will have nowhere to go when a more serious misdeed is committed, and the child will have no way of differentiating between an important and an unimportant offense. If possible the punishment should be related to the error. If Judy, who loves cherries, insists on throwing her cherry pits on the floor, she might be deprived of her favorite fruit for several meals. Or if Johnny refuses to remove his muddy rubbers time after time, he might be forbidden to go out to play in the mud puddles the next time his best friend calls him.

Unless you know that you will be able to hold to them, don't make threats. When you have retracted a threat once, your child will pay little attention when you make another. A simple one, such as, "Bobby, if you don't stop throwing the wrappers on the floor, I will have to take away the rest of your chewing gum," is all right, because it is simple and easily carried out, but to say, "Karen, if you don't go to bed at once, I won't let you go to kindergarten for a week," when you know perfectly well (and so does Karen) that she will be there the next morning, carries no weight at all and only makes you appear ridiculous in her eyes.

When a child has committed a serious misdeed, especially if he has repeated it after being corrected, take the time and trouble to explain the reason for the rule. The most obvious example of this, and unfortunately one of the commonest, is lighting matches and setting fires. I am not of the school that believes you should burn the child to prove your point, but for an offense as dangerous as this, punishment should be quick and severe. First show him, with paper or kerosene or however you can make it the most impressive, how quickly a fire can spread, and explain the consequences from his point of view—his favorite toy would be burned up, his dog might be killed, etc. And then decide on the punishment that you think will make the deepest impression. It might be deprivation of certain privileges like watching television, or the cancellation of a longed-for treat, or something equally important.

In some situations where in spite of all your efforts your child continues to be destructive, disorderly, or whatever it may be, an effective punishment is sometimes the "tit-for-tat" method. One little girl's mother was driven to distraction because her four-year-old would not stop writing all over the walls with her crayons. Finally, in desperation, she took easily washed-off chalk and scribbled all over her daughter's walls, furniture, and favorite books. When Julie came in from playing with a friend, she started to cry. Her mother sat down and explained that if Julie didn't care about her things, she certainly didn't care about Julie's, and the problem was solved. This is not always practical, of course, but it *can* work very well, if properly done.

In extreme cases of misbehavior, where repeated admonitions and punishments have brought no results, I believe there is no substitute for a good, hard—not brutal—spanking, with the palm of Daddy's hand! No one but a parent should ever be allowed to spank a child—in other words, sitters, nurses, or parents of your child's friends have no right to discipline in this way. They may—and should—"correct," of course, but not physically.

Finally, spankings should be administered in private, and only after the child is made to understand the seriousness of the offense. They should never be carried out in anger, and never in front of strangers. Not only does the child feel degraded and mortified by the indignity, but it is embarrassing for the witness too.

RESPECT

In relationships between children and their parents today, the quality that is most lacking is respect. In large part, this is the result of the atmosphere that psychologists advocated when they went overboard in recommending that parents be their children's "pals" rather than continue the relationship between the generations that has existed for centuries. If children are taught that their parents should have no authority over them and are their equals regardless of age, education, and experience, how will respect arise? This trend, which fortunately has been somewhat modified and even reversed, showed itself in families whose children called their parents by their first names, where they were never required to rise when older people entered the room nor adhere to any other social conventions. This resulted in a directionless youth, and instead of becoming mature, independent adults, these children grew up as lazy, confused individuals, lacking respect not only for their parents but for all society. If you, as parents, lead your youngsters to believe that your experience, your education, and your attitudes are worth emulating, respect will follow of its own accord. This, in turn, will be expanded, as your children grow up, to include relatives, friends, and finally, more mature people in all walks of life.

ORDERLINESS

GOOD GROOMING

Unfortunately, children are not born with an innate desire to be neat and clean. It must be instilled by patient urging, correcting, and directing. As soon as a child is old enough to feed himself he should learn that he must wash his hands before meals. As he learns to dress himself he must be taught that doing up buttons, tying laces, buckling belts, are all essential parts of being "dressed." Combing his hair, brushing his teeth, taking a bath, must become habits that need no reminding.

Constant encouragement is necessary. You may discover your daughter trying at an early age to comb her doll's hair. Help her and let her know that you think it's great that she cares about Suzanna's appearance, just as you care about hers.

Fathers can help little boys to take an interest in their appearance by inviting their sons to keep them company while they shave, to share their showers, to discuss their shirt-and-trouser combinations—and by outspoken praise when their hair is combed and their hands are clean.

The evening meal—the one time when the whole family is apt to get together "socially"—is the time to insist that everyone be neat and clean, and to point out that one dirty, messy individual can spoil the dinner for everyone else.

As soon as a child shows any interest in what he is wearing, he should be allowed a voice in choosing his clothes. Naturally, his mother must make the final decision, as a little child will not consider cost, practicality, or suitability, but within the limits of these requirements the child can be given a choice of garments. He will thus absorb some principles of dressing well, and he will also be happy to wear the clothes that are bought for him.

There are several offenses committed by doting mothers that should be avoided:

Don't overdress your child. If he or she is invited to a party, ask the mother of the host or hostess what type of clothing will be appropriate. Nothing could make a little girl more miserable than to wear a frilly organdy dress to a party that turns out to be an outdoor barbecue. Even school clothes should conform to those of the other children. If wearing a jacket is not required of the small boys, let your son go in a sweater, and if the girls all wear brown loafers, don't insist on tie shoes.

Never dress your child in clothes that are too old for him. Your three-year-old son, dressed in long gray flannels and a sports jacket, may look, to you, too "cute" for words, but this is as inappropriate as his father going to business in shorts and an Eton jacket.

Don't let little girls wear makeup or dress their hair elaborately. Of course they want to imitate Mommy, but let them play at being grown-up in the privacy of their home or at a costume party, never in public. This is not to say that their hair should not be arranged in an attractive, simple style and neatly combed. They have many years ahead when they will need makeup to enhance their looks, but for the present their natural look is the most attractive sight in the world.

A NEAT ROOM

There *are* people who are naturally neat, but they are few and far between. Most children must be *taught* to be neat with their possessions, as well as in their personal grooming. The small child's first responsibility in this line is to take care of his own clothes and his own room. You will get much further with your efforts if you make it easy for him. Clothes hooks and rods in his closet should be at *his* level, so that he can hang up his own clothes. A laundry hamper in his *own* room—not the bathroom—will encourage him to put his dirty clothes where they belong. Plenty of big boxes to throw non-breakable toys into, and shelves for more delicate things, will make it easier for him to keep his room picked up. A chest of small drawers for crayons, marbles, jacks, etc., is indispensable.

Having provided him with the facilities for keeping his room neat, all you can do is to keep reminding him, encouraging him, and praising him when he does well. An occasional reward—a surprise or something promised—will help too. If he isn't making progress, and it is more than you can stand, shut the door so you won't have to look at the mess. But *don't* break down and pick it up for him—that is probably just what he hopes you will do. And don't lose your temper—he will enjoy the excitement he is creating. Of course you must be willing to help if things get beyond his ability to "catch up," but be sure that it is a "joint" effort and you are not doing more than your share.

The next step, after he has the idea that he must keep his *own* things neat, is to teach him his responsibilities toward the rest of the house. By the time he is between three and four, he can begin to understand that the house belongs to everyone in it, including himself, and that everyone must share in the care of it. Here is the way one mother convinced her child that neatness "pays off."

Mrs. Dunbar was having a very difficult time convincing little Jeremy that he could not leave his toys all over the living room. She finally told him that if he would not pick them up, she would have to. But since he was not shouldering his responsibilities, she felt none toward him and would not necessarily take good care of his things or even tell him where they were. After several days of losing one toy after another, Jeremy decided it was better to take his things to his own room.

MANNERS IN CONVERSATION

BABY TALK

Learning to talk is the most demanding challenge a child faces. It is one part of his education that he learns almost entirely by imitation, and although you will, of course, teach him certain words and phrases and correct him frequently, his choice of words and his inflections will, at least in the beginning, be patterned after yours.

When your baby is tiny you will naturally talk to him in some form of baby talk. He will respond to a certain pitch and rhythm long before he responds to words. But as he grows older, baby talk can become a danger. If you continue to talk to him in a squeak, his first words will be a squeak too. If you say "num-num" for "food," "itsy" for "little," he will say it too. It may sound cute at first but it is a hard habit to break, and he will be unmercifully teased if he continues to talk baby talk when he begins to play with other children. Baby talk indicates that the mother subconsciously thinks the child is not intelligent—is inferior to adults. Children sense this and resent it. Listen to yourself to see how you sound when you talk to any small child.

I hope that you use the same tones you would in talking to a contemporary, instead of sounding falsely enthusiastic, condescending, or impatient.

"BAD" LANGUAGE

Your child, no matter how careful you may be at home, is going to pick up "bad" or "dirty" language sooner or later. He will go through a stage, probably around four, when he thinks "toilet" words or words relating to the body are funny. "Popo" or "fanny" or "weewee" may reduce him to hysterics. Ignore it. There is nothing really objectionable in these words—they are universally used and understood—and as he grows older he will develop a natural modesty about bodily functions. He will soon learn to say, "I want to go to the bathroom," rather than, "Peepee, Mommy!" Later, at school, he will inevitably pick up "four-letter" words. Many of them, for years unmentionable, are now heard all over, and are used by educated people and the media. So you can hardly tell your child that it is "wrong" to use those words. What you *can* tell him is when, and with whom, he may use them. You should be sure that he knows the meaning of the words he uses, and then explain to him that since you don't want him to be offensive or disliked, he should not use them in certain places and in front of certain people. In the schoolyard, no matter what you say, he is going to use the same language as his schoolmates, but he can, and should, be taught that he does not use that language in church, or at Grandmother's.

RESPECTFUL LANGUAGE

As mentioned briefly above, one of the problems with some youngsters today is lack of respect—for anything. And if a child is going to grow up with respect for authority and respect for his elders, it must start at home with his parents.

The parent-child relationship is a natural one and should be maintained. You can be very good friends with your child but you cannot be his contemporary. You *are* older, you *do have* more experience and more education. Therefore, unless you do something to lose the right to it, you do merit some respect. One way of preserving the correct parent-child relationship is by having your child call you "Mom" and "Dad," or any derivative he chooses of "Mother" and "Father." [The use of these names also contributes to his feeling of security.] This same attitude should prevail with your contemporaries. They are not his "pals," and he should address them as "Mr." and "Mrs." There is nothing old-fashioned or stuffy about these titles, but there are some adults—especially young ones—who prefer to be called by their first names. This is their prerogative, and if they ask your child to call them "Betsy" and "Bill," he should do so. But *you* should make it clear that this is a special case, and that normally "Mr." and "Mrs." are used for your other friends.

The old custom of using "Aunt" or "Uncle" for close family friends has gone out of style, but again, if your best friend would rather be called "Aunt Sue" than "Mrs. Jones," she certainly may ask that your child do so.

INTERRUPTING

Children should not be allowed to get into the habit of interrupting. This is part of learning to respect other people's rights. It is up to you to teach your child to wait for a break in the conversation before butting in. The mother who invariably stops and says, "What is it, dear?" when her child interrupts, is helping him to establish a habit that will do him a disservice all his life.

The first "lesson" is to say to him, every time he breaks into your conversation, "Johnny, Mrs. Smith is talking. Wait until she is finished." Some children react to this well; others seem to be deaf to it. It may help to discuss it before your visitor comes. Explain that you expect him to stay outside, or to play in his room for half an hour, so that you can talk to your friend. You can also make a bargain—if he will give you one hour uninterrupted, you will devote one hour to him later in the day.

But most important, when he does "barge in," don't answer him—just keep insisting, "Johnny, I'll talk to you when Mrs. Smith and I are through." If he is very small you must help him out by saying to your friend after a few minutes, "Excuse me, Sue, Johnny is waiting to tell me something . . . etc." It is not fair or reasonable to keep a two- or three-year-old waiting while you and Sue catch up on an hour's worth of neighborhood news.

"PLEASE" AND "THANK YOU"

"Please" and "Thank you" are still the "magic" words, and you will be doing your child a favor if you insist that he use them until they become a habit. Everyone likes to be appreciated, and "Thank you" is the accepted way of showing appreciation. "Please" turns a demand into a request and indicates an option—it turns an unpopular request into a more palatable one.

The essential requirement in teaching your child to use the "magic" words is—use them yourself. Too many parents say, "Hand me that hammer," "Go get my knitting," "Put on your jacket," without even a "Would you?" let alone a "Please." Then they consistently respond to their youngsters' demands by saying, "What do you say?" or "If you say 'please.'" You must do this constantly with both "Please" and "Thank you" when he is small, as a reminder, but he will get the point much faster if you use them when speaking to him.

GREETINGS

If you want your child to be considered attractive and intelligent by your friends (and who doesn't?) he must learn to greet people pleasantly. No one thinks much of the two- or three-year-old who responds to "Hello, Timmy," by running away, saying, "I don't like you," or hanging his head and squirming with embarrassment.

The best preventive is to prepare your toddler in advance. Make up some games with him to make it seem like fun. Show him how to shake hands, and give him and yourself silly names. Say to his Teddy bear, in a gruff voice, "Why, hello, Teddy," and then, shaking Teddy's hand, say in a high, squeaking voice, "Oh, hello, Mrs. Looneybird." Then get Timmy to take your part and say "Hello" and shake hands with Teddy.

When visitors are expected, practice beforehand, using their names. If he is familiar with the situation he will be far less embarrassed, and most of his faults are the result of shyness. If he does fall apart and refuses to shake hands, don't make an issue of it—simply give him more patient instruction before you thrust the situation on him again.

Every child should, in due course, learn to shake hands willingly and with a firm grip. The youngster should smile and look the person he is greeting in the eye. As soon as he can, he should learn to add the person's name to a simple "Hello." Curtsies and bows are no longer considered necessary, but they can be very cute when practiced by a small child. They also give the child something definite to do, which can be easier than doing nothing. But curtsies should not be continued past three or four—they look ridiculous today for an older child. A boy, however, may continue to nod his head in a modified bow indefinitely.

TABLE MANNERS

THE YOUNG BABY

The real "teaching" of table manners starts when the baby indicates a desire to feed himself—to hold his own spoon or mug. This may be well before he is a year old, or it may not be until he is eighteen months or more. Don't force him before he is ready—you may think it will save you time but actually your troubles will just begin! You cannot leave a little one to feed himself untended, and it will take longer than if you fed him yourself.

In the beginning, it doesn't matter *how* your child holds his spoon. Instead of showing him which side is up, let him use the spoon to get the food from plate to mouth any way he wants. As he gets more adept, but possibly not until he is three or four, when his hands are under better control, you can begin to urge him to hold his implements in the adult manner.

All babies love to spit and blow their food. If you make too big an issue of it, he will persist because he will enjoy the excitement he is causing as much as the blowing. Try to keep your temper but let him know that that is not the way big people do it. He will also, undoubtedly, throw things on the floor. If you pick them up every time, or if you get mad, he will go on doing it. Pick them up once or twice, in case it is a mistake, and then tell him fondly, "No more." If he goes on, take his dinner away and put him to bed, or whatever comes next in his schedule. It won't hurt him to miss most of his meal, and he will soon learn that that particular naughtiness is not worthwhile.

Don't give in to the temptation to laugh at your baby when he smears chocolate pudding all over his face, or splashes his milk, or makes bubbles in it. If it is an honest mistake, you will hurt his feelings and discourage him, and if he is doing it to get attention, you will be playing right into his hands. Clean him up, give him another chance, and then, if he repeats the act, take his dinner away.

As soon as the child has learned to eat well enough so that his presence at the table is not offensive, he should be allowed to eat with the family, occasionally at first, and more often as his manners improve. When be becomes a regular member of the family group at meals, there are more advanced lessons to be learned:

He must be clean and neat when he comes to the table.

He must chew quietly, with his mouth closed.

He must not overload his spoon or fork.

He must not interrupt the adults, but at the same time, he should be included in the conversation. If it is beyond his understanding, his mother or father should from time to time introduce a subject that is within his range of interests.

He must ask for something he wants, rather than reach across his neighbor for it.

He must not fidget or play with his food or the implements at his place.

He must use his fork and spoon properly and never leave the spoon in his cup or mug.

If he finishes before the others, he must ask, "May I please be excused?" and wait for permission before leaving the table. Very young children should be given this privilege, because if they are forced to remain at the table when their food is gone, they are sure to resort to wriggling, fiddling, and noisemaking to pass the time.

If he refuses to be good, the best course is to say nothing but lead him as quietly as possible from the table. The child will learn much more quickly to be well behaved if he understands that good behavior is the price of admission to grown-up society.

There are many ways in which the child's mother can help to pave the way for him. His plate should be brought to the table ready for him to eat. The portions should be of small or moderate size—never a heaping plateful. Meat should be cut in small, bite-size pieces, as should vegetables such as asparagus and string beans. To avoid accidents his glass or cup should have a broad base and be of plastic or silver. If he is very small his fork and spoon should be of appropriate size. He should wear a bib large enough so that an accidental spill will not ruin his clothes. And he should either sit in his high chair or have cushions on a regular chair that will raise him to the proper height. If you think this is unimportant, try sometime to eat neatly while kneeling at a table that comes approximately to the level of your chin.

All these small aids put together help to make the child look forward to his meal with pleasure, rather than as a time of strain. Mealtime should, above all, be pleasant. The child who sees his family enjoying their food and enjoying each other's company cannot help but follow their example. Constant nagging and correction are as detrimental as a total lack of instruction. If older children are allowed to complain about the food, if Father refuses to eat anything but steak and potatoes, and if there are continuous arguments at the table, the young child will come to dread the dinner hour, and the unhappy associations will result in antagonisms to food and to good manners in eating.

THE LEFT-HANDED CHILD

Many, perhaps most, very young children are ambidextrous. The baby in his crib will reach for his rattle with either hand for some time. Unless your child shows a very strong tendency to left-handed-ness, you will be doing him a favor if you teach him to eat with his right hand as he gets a little older. Simply because the whole table setup is organized with right-handed people in mind, he will find it simpler to be one of them. I have consulted with several eminent pediatricians, and as long as the one-year-old child still shows a tendency to use either hand, it will do him no harm to urge him to eat with his right.

Never reverse the place setting to accommodate him if he *is* strongly left-handed. After all, much of the normal pattern *favors* the left-hander. The butter plate is on the left, and so is the fork—the most-used implement. It should be no harder for him to reach over to pick up his glass on the right than it is for the right-hander to butter his bread or eat his salad on the left! Therefore, set the left-handed child's place normally, so that he will be accustomed to using the setting that he will invariably encounter outside his home.

MONEY MATTERS

From the time a child is old enough to buy a candy bar or an ice-cream cone for himself he should be given a small, regular allowance. In return he should be expected to perform certain everyday chores, such as helping with the dishes or keeping his room neat. But extra duties—washing the dog or running an errand—deserve special consideration and are paid for separately if the parents feel that they merit a reward. Only by having money of their own can children begin to appreciate its value, and they should be permitted to use an allowance as they wish. The amount must be decided upon by considering what uses the money will be put to and the approximate amount small friends are given. It is as bad for a child to have twice as much as the neighborhood children (even though his parents can well afford it) as it is to have him always saying, "I can't go to the movies with you—I don't have enough money." Some parents give the child a larger allowance but insist that a part be set aside for the weekly church contribution or that a certain sum be put in a piggy bank or otherwise saved for birthday presents or a special hobby or treat. This seems to me to be a wise system, as the child acquires a sense of the value of money that he cannot learn if his parents simply put his quarter in the plate each Sunday or pay for birthday presents as the dates arrive.

As the child grows, so must his allowance, and so must the expenses he is expected to pay himself. If he is working toward something worthwhile that he really cares about, his parents will be wise to encourage him by giving him extra chores that they may pay for at an hourly rate and by adding to his fund with a small check for Christmas or his birthday.

CHILDREN'S PARTIES

A child's party that has been well planned can be a joy for everyone. Parties for very young children, under six, let us say, should be quite short, preferably not more than two hours long. The span of attention of tiny children is very limited, and they also tire quickly, which leads to crankiness and naughtiness. Refreshments should be simple enough to allow the mother and her assistants more time for supervision and less time in the kitchen. Also, a large amount of rich food can upset little stomachs that are already in a turmoil with excitement. Finally, to avoid confusion and permit better organization, the guest list should be short. Five or six guests would be ample for a second-birthday party, and ten or twelve should be the limit for a six- to eight-year-old. The formula for a successful party for the very young is as follows:

Guests arrive at four. A half hour is allowed for opening presents and letting off steam. One hour of organized games or entertainment follows. A magician is always popular, and comedy movies, if you have a projector or can borrow one, are invariably a great success. Treasure hunts, "pin-the-tail-on-the-donkey," and musical chairs for tiny children, and guessing games, a "three-legged" race, or other contests for older ones—all help to make the hour fly. At five thirty refreshments are served. A sandwich (peanut butter and jelly cannot be surpassed for popularity), ice cream, and the birthday cake are all that are necessary. If the weather is warm, a fruit punch, soda, or ice-cold milk may be served, and in the winter hot chocolate is always welcome.

Parties for older children can be extended to two and a half or three hours if enough entertainment is planned. Games can be more complicated, thus taking more time, and a short feature movie could be shown rather than "shorts." A scavenger hunt is always popular outside the city, or if you have the use of a swimming pool, that may be all that is necessary to have a successful summer party. As children reach the age of ten or eleven or even older, hay rides, sleigh rides, trips to baseball or football games, or circuses or rodeos become more fun than the "game party" at home. When a group is taken to this sort of entertainment, the invitation should make it clear whether or not lunch or supper will be provided and whether the guests should take money of their own for snacks or souvenirs. Remember, when planning a trip to the ball park or anywhere, a small group will be easier to chaperon, it will be less expensive, and your child will enjoy it every bit as much as a large, rambunctious crowd.

If the birthday child is old enough he may help in deciding on the guest list, sending out invitations, and setting the table. A girl may even help prepare the refreshments—mixing the cake batter or making sandwiches.

Whether they are three or ten, the essential manners for party guests are identical. They must say "Hello" to their host and the host's mother when they arrive, and they must shake hands and say, "Goodbye, and thank you," when they leave. The young host or hostess must, in turn, greet them when they come, thank them for their presents, and in answer to their farewell, say, "Good-bye. Thank you for coming."

THE ADOPTED CHILD

There is a tremendous interest among the concerned young people of today in adopting children. Many feel that it is one way in which they can help control the population explosion, and each adoption alleviates the problem of unwanted children. Young couples are not necessarily against large families, but they may plan to adopt after having one or two babies of their own, instead of further adding to the census figures.

Adoption, when carried out through reliable channels, is completely satisfactory and thoroughly rewarding, but it does entail some problems. One is the question of when, how, or even whether to tell the child he is adopted. The answer is that he should be told as soon as he can begin to understand, probably when he is about four years old. And the information should be repeated from time to time so that he cannot possibly misunderstand or be confused by questions or remarks from outsiders. It would be hard to find a better way to break such news than this:

Julie, aged four, ran into the house with tears streaming down her face. Her playmate's chant followed her through the door—"You haven't any mommy, you haven't any daddy. You're just adopted, you're just adopted!"

Julie's mommy took her on her lap and started out, "Of course you have a mommy and daddy." She explained that some little boys and girls are born to their parents, and those parents have to keep whatever baby they get. But other children, like Julie, are adopted, and they are chosen by their parents. "Daddy and I looked and looked for a baby until we found you. When we saw you, we knew you were exactly the one for us. So don't let anyone tell you you don't have a mommy and daddy. We chose you and we love you more than anything!"

Inevitably the adopted youngster will begin to wonder who his real parents were. Most adoption agencies never divulge this information, and you must help your youngster to accept the fact that he will never know. If he has been brought up with the same combination of love, respect, and good sense that a natural child would receive, the urge to delve into his own past and upset his life and that of his parents will subside quickly.

When a child is a relative, or the orphan of friends who died, he should be told as much as possible about his real parents so that he will not be upset by curious or thoughtless remarks from acquaintances who may have known his real parents.

The problem may be more serious in the case of children who are old enough to remember their natural parents and their life with them. In these children there may be a well of uncertainty, possibly of bitterness, and surely, for a while at least, loneliness. Whether the crisis will come and be gone quickly without serious aftereffects, or whether the child will be deeply scarred, depends on two things: first, his adopted parents' support, without their adding more turmoil by expecting his undivided affection; second, his unquestioning belief that his adopted parents truly want him and love him.

There are specific things the parents can do to help. They can keep the "Who am I?" question in proportion by bringing it into the open at such an early age that the child accepts it without even thinking about it. They can build up his sense of security by convincing him that the tie of ideal adoption is love, just as the tie of an ideal marriage is love. It should be made clear that a mother and father are never related by blood, yet their relationship is the foundation of every home. This tie of love, therefore, is of the same quality between the parents and the adopted child.

~§74§~ School and College Years

Even though your particular interest may be in the "manners" of your teenager or college student, I would suggest that you read the preceding chapter, "The Young Child," as well as this one. The teaching of manners must begin very early—long before the child becomes a teenager—and Chapter 73 deals with the essential beginnings. This chapter is concerned more with the *new* problems that arise as the youngster approaches adulthood. His basic attitudes—consideration for others, response to those around him, respect for his elders, and so on—*must* be established before he reaches his teens. If they are, you will be able to teach him the adult "refinements" without too much difficulty, as long as you are willing to be tolerant, be patient, stand firm—and love. I would also suggest that you get a copy of my *Emily Post's Etiquette for Young People*, which deals with these problems in far more detail than can be done in these pages.

Boys and girls who have reached their teens have a whole new set of problems to face. This is the time when they really begin to emerge from the constant supervision of their parents and to develop independence and a social life of their own choosing. Because they are well on their way to becoming adults they are expected to act in an adult manner. They must make the adjustment from childhood with its complete dependence on parental care to adulthood, which brings not only the joys of independence but the trials as well.

Parents of teenagers must try to recognize this transition. The wise mother and father will, from the very early teen years when the child is still "in between" and under a good deal of supervision, encourage him to make his own decisions and offer him guidance and help rather than dictate to him.

THE EARLY TEENS

If parents have had a good, intelligent relationship with their sons and daughters during childhood, with confidence and respect growing on both sides, the problems will be greatly modified. Even though the emotional makeup of a teenager is vastly more complicated and often more high-strung than that of younger children, the same characteristics of patience, give-and-take, and restraint will tide the family over what can be difficult years.

However, this is not a book designed to discuss the psychological aspects of the young, but rather to discuss their manners and what they should or should not do. Just remember, when making a rule or saying "No" to a teenager, to consider the importance of the decision to him (does it really *matter* if Bob stays out a half hour longer?), the customs of his friends and classmates, and whether it will actually help him, either from his own point of view or in the eyes of others. The last reason in the world for making a regulation is, "Well, *I* always had to wash the dishes when I was your age!"

A family is a unit, but it is made up of individuals. Each of these individuals has his own likes and dislikes, his own talents, his own personality, which may clash violently with the characteristics of other members of his family. Parents must recognize these differences—there may even be actual antipathy between certain of their children—and in order to make the home a livable place, must work out a mode of conduct.

Every member of the family has a right to his own separate life and his privacy. Don't insist on involving yourself in every problem. For instance, if you see Sally and Anne having a serious discussion, don't ask, "What are you two talking about?" Leave them alone—if either one wants to tell you about it or ask for advice, that is her choice, not yours.

It is most important that your teenagers share willingly in the chores. It is up to you as parents to decide in what areas you need their assistance, and together you should settle on a reasonable schedule. In the interest of fairness chores should be rotated, so that the monotony of doing the same old thing day after day will be avoided.

Enthusiasm for family projects is important, and up to a certain point you should insist that your youngsters participate. However, we all have moods and times when we just don't feel like taking part in a group activity. When this happens to one of your children, respect his feelings and don't force him. On the other hand, don't let him be a "wet blanket." Suggest that he go to his room and read, play records, or snooze until the mood passes.

In every way the parents must set the example. If they don't act in a reasonable and considerate way, their children certainly won't. There's nothing wrong in admitting a mistake, so when you are at fault, say so. If an apology is in order, make it. This will not lower your image in your children's eyes—it will only heighten their respect for your honesty and "human-ness."

The place for your children to learn plain, everyday good manners is at home. If they practice their manners with the family and your guests, they'll never have any problems in other homes or among strangers. Of course you are going to relax some of the formalities at home, and life wouldn't be much fun if you didn't, but you must insist on unselfishness and consideration and the manners that preserve those qualities.

When your friends come to your home your children have a wonderful chance to practice their manners. Remind them that a prompt, firm handshake is the proper response to an introduction. Urge them to come in and chat for a few minutes so that they will learn to be at ease with adults and to talk to them without self-consciousness. When they bring a stranger of their own age to the house, insist that they introduce him to you in the proper way, and by your own example show them how much an enthusiastic and proper response to an introduction means.

Mealtime provides another opportunity for teaching good manners. Because it may well be the only hour of the day when your family is together, you should try to make it as pleasant as possible. Don't use that time to scold Jimmy for the mess in his room, or Sue for borrowing your sweater without asking. Try to keep the conversation on subjects of interest to everyone. A good, honest difference of opinion can be stimulating and educational for the youngsters. Let them hear your side, and pay them the courtesy of listening to theirs.

It is important for their own sakes—for the good impression they will make on others—as well as for the enjoyment of people who eat with them, that young people learn good table manners. Slouching, tipping the chair back, and fiddling all seem to be indigenous to the teenager, but not even the gangliest sixteen-year-old should be incapable of sitting still and upright in his chair. It is up to the parents to instill in him the importance of good posture. Since teenage boys' appetites are generally tremendous they must be constantly reminded not to bolt their food and to wait for the others at the table. Their faults are more likely to be errors committed than good habits omitted, and because they can hardly be sent to eat in another room like small children, their mothers and fathers must improve their manners with firm, patient, repeated corrections. In many cases the problem is not their willful disregard of directions—they simply do not absorb them. Their minds are on a thousand other more interesting matters—girls, boys, parties, school, sports, ad infinitum—and the only hope of penetrating the screen is repetition, in the hope that eventually your words will "sink in." By the tone of your voice and the way you give them, repeated corrections can avoid the undesirable effect of "nagging."

APPEARANCE

Most teenagers from thirteen to nineteen have one trait in common: They apparently *like* to be sloppy. This applies not only to themselves but to their rooms and possessions. It doesn't seem to do much good to remind them that they will be more popular with the opposite sex if they keep their hair combed and their clothes clean, nor are they interested in keeping warm in cold weather if no one else is wearing a coat. Shoes seem to be a forgotten item of clothing in the summer everywhere except in the largest cities. My feeling about this general attitude is that they should be allowed to dress as casually as they please during vacations, in their own homes, on the beach, or at picnics. But at school (fortunately most schools set certain standards, which the pupils must adhere to), at meals, on any excursion with adults, on all public conveyances, and at all social functions, they should be properly and neatly dressed. This does not mean that they should not go to an informal gathering without a tie and jacket. Of course they may wear a sports shirt, jeans, and a sweater, or whatever the favorite local costume is, but the jeans and shirt should be clean, the hair combed, and the shoes ON.

Young boys must constantly be reminded to wash and to shave. Nothing looks dirtier or messier than a stubble of whiskers on a young face, but many boys who are not accustomed to regular shaving habits simply do not realize that their beards are becoming heavier each year. The only thing to do is keep calling this to their attention day in and day out until shaving becomes a habit.

Teenage girls need less urging to fix their hair—in fact most of them spend interminable hours under a hair dryer. What they do need is guidance as to style, length, becomingness, and good hygiene. Extreme styles should be avoided in the younger teen years—the simplest hairdo currently popular is generally the most becoming.

As they get older they will want to experiment with more complicated arrangements, and the only restriction should be that they refrain from becoming too extreme, for such styles invariably make a young girl look "cheap."

The same suggestion applies to makeup. A thirteen- or fourteen-year-old may start to wear a little eye shadow, or lipstick, or whatever the current fad in cosmetics happens to be, as long as she does it in moderation. As she matures she may use darker shades or vary the application as she learns what brings out her best features. During the early teens mothers should teach their daughters as much as they can about proper skin care. It is hard to impress on a young girl with lovely skin that some effort is necessary to keep it that way, but your daughter will bless you later if you implant a habit of good care to prolong that youthful glow.

At some point in her early teens your daughter may want to have her ears pierced. Let her, but be sure that she has it done by a physician who has had experience in piercing ears or a reputable jeweler, and not by a contemporary self-proclaimed "expert." It is no longer considered in bad taste for young girls to wear earrings so long as they are not dangling or ornate. During the day she should wear only the tiny gold studs necessary to keep the holes open, and even when she dresses up, the thirteen- to fifteen-year-old should wear no more than a small gold earring or perhaps one of enamel or with a tiny colored stone.

Among some ethnic groups it is customary to pierce little girls' ears when they are babies. This is, of course, acceptable if you are a member of one of those groups, but I would not recommend that other youngsters have their ears pierced before they reach their teens.

ALLOWANCES

As children advance into their teens allowances may become a question of what the parents can afford and how much responsibility the youngster himself wants to assume. Some parents with a limited income feel that by fourteen or fifteen their child should work for any money he receives, but others, who can do so, continue to help out their children through high school and even through college.

The question of a "clothes allowance" usually arises in the middle teens. Some youngsters can't wait to be given enough money to dress themselves and pay all their own expenses, while others cling to the security of letting their parents pay for their clothes and receiving a small weekly or monthly allowance for "expenses." As a general rule, the year a boy or girl enters college, or reaches college age, is the time to give him or her financial independence.

But there is no set rule—the time might come a year or two earlier for a teenager who is responsible and understands the value of money and the danger of wasting it, while the youngster who has had little experience in shopping or managing a checking account should perhaps wait longer.

A system that seems to me to be excellent is practiced by one of my neighbors. Her daughter of fourteen, a sensible, intelligent girl, was most anxious to be given a clothing allowance. Instead of telling her that she was just too young or putting her on a large allowance all at once, the parents started her out with a monthly sum that was to cover school clothes—blouses, slacks, skirts, shoes, socks, underwear, etc.—but no expensive ones such as party dresses or overcoats. In this way she is learning to shop carefully and to understand the handling of money, but she does not have a large sum at her disposal, which might prove to be a temptation to spend irresponsibly. They plan to increase the sum and the variety of clothing she is expected to buy each year, so that by the time she finishes high school she will be completely responsible for her clothes and incidental expenses.

Most parents pay as much of their children's tuition at school and college as they can, but if it is too severe a strain on the family budget, teenagers should certainly help as much as possible by applying for scholarships, working part-time at one of the jobs (in the cafeteria, dormitories, or library) that most colleges provide, or taking an evening job, preferably one like baby-sitting that will allow the student to study during working hours. Parents should never be ashamed to discuss the need for financial assistance of this sort with their children. Young men and women, if they really care about a good education, are more than willing to do what they can to attain it. If they have been brought up with love and respect for their families, they will never criticize parents who may not have amassed great wealth, but rather will take pride in what they have achieved.

As to the actual amounts for suitable allowances, it is impossible to say, because the requirements vary so in different areas. A city child needs more—every time he takes a bus or subway it costs him something, while his country cousin can ride the same distance on a bicycle. Prices are higher, too, in the city. Movies, food, and entertainment are much bigger budget items than the equivalent ones in the country. The country boy might take his date to a square dance at the local grange for a dollar or so, while the city boy, if he wishes to dance, must go to a nightclub or hotel where the admission or cover charge may be as high as three or four.

Insofar as is possible, your child's allowance should fall in the same range of those of his friends. It is not good for him, simply because you can afford it, always to be the one with more money than the others. Nor is it right to keep him from being able to pay his share and to do the things his friends can do, if you are able to give him enough to make that possible.

LEARNING TO ENTERTAIN

Youngsters who learn how to entertain their friends nicely during their adolescence will have a good background for more formal and ambitious entertaining later on. Parents who encourage a child to invite his or her friends in reasonably often and who help him to plan and prepare parties will be more than rewarded by the young person's gratitude and enthusiasm. Because girls are more inclined to give parties than boys—just as it is the wife who plans a couple's social activities—my suggestions may be of special interest to young girls and their mothers. However, a boy who is planning a party may profit from them too.

Although the following subjects should be discussed and decided on by mother and daughter (or son) together, the word *hostess* will refer to your daughter, since the party will, of course, be hers.

First of all, I want to make it clear that parents should be at home when teenagers entertain. They need not be in evidence except perhaps to make their presence known by saying "Hello" to arriving guests, but they should be in the house, possibly with friends of their own if they think they may need support. This is not so much a matter of "chaperoning" as of being available to help the young hostess if any problems—liquor, crashers, or whatever—arise.

The most attractive written invitations for young people are the colorful cards available at all stationery stores. Your daughter may choose any appropriate design and fill in the blanks with the necessary information. She adds "RSVP" with your telephone number below it, or she may, if she wishes, write "Regrets only" with the number.

If she prefers to issue her invitations by telephone in order to get definite answers immediately, she may do so, but she runs the risk of her guests forgetting the date, the hour, or the location of the party.

THE GUEST LIST

Like adults, young people must choose congenial guests who will enjoy each other's company. A group of friends who all know each other well is easy and fun but not particularly interesting or stimulating. On the other hand, a group of strangers who have little in common, or don't know that they do, can be a nightmare for the young hostess trying to get the party off the ground. A combination of a few friends and two or three "outsiders" from a different school or another neighborhood works best, as long as the hostess sees that the strangers are included in the conversation and activities.

The number of guests invited depends, first, on the size of your home, and second, on the amount you can afford to spend. Discuss these questions frankly with your teenager. Overcrowded rooms and lack of space can ruin an otherwise good party, and grandiose ideas, forgetting the family exchequer, must be restrained before she goes too far.

If it is to be a "singles" party, with invitations issued to both boys and girls, the hostess must see that there are even numbers, or extra boys. If only the girls are sent invitations, with "Bring a date" written on them, those receiving them should let the hostess know whether they are successful in finding a date, and if so, who he is. If a girl cannot find a boy to go with her, she should enlist the help of her friends to get her a blind date. If she has no luck at all, she must refuse the invitation.

When a boy or girl is going steady, or has a previous date for the night of a "singles" party, it is perfectly proper to call and ask whether the date may be included. At the same time, if this will make too many people, or upset the boy-girl ratio, the hostess has every right to refuse—politely, and with an explanation, of course.

Even teenagers like to get dressed up once in a while, so don't let your daughter be afraid to suggest a "jacket-and-tie" or "semiformal" party. Then dress up the party to suit the outfit—fancier food, prettier decorations, and perhaps live music. The whole affair will take on the glamour that a less formal party never has.

There are a few things that you should insist on, no matter how informal the party. Guests should wear shoes and socks. At VERY informal parties they may sometimes kick them off later, but at a real dance girls should not be allowed on the floor without shoes. It lowers the tone of the party, and the tone is what makes a more or less formal party rather special. The same is true of jackets and ties—at a formal party they should be kept on.

When an invitation says "black tie" or "formal" a boy should not try to go unless he is wearing a tuxedo, or in some communities, a dark suit. The hostess has set the tone of the party, and he should respect her wishes.

MAKING A PARTY "GO"

There is no question about it—young people love to dance, so be sure there are plenty of good records available, and enough cleared floor space. The most popular parties are those which combine the opportunity to dance with the chance to sit around and talk and eat. Boys especially, but most girls too, like to take time out between dances to relax and enjoy a little conversation.

A piano is a tremendous asset if one of the group can play, and so is a guest with a guitar. Active games such as Ping-Pong, pool, carpet bowls, or Twister are not to be scorned. If one or two people start playing, the rest of the group is often quick to join.

FOOD AND DRINK

The most important consideration in thinking about food and drink is quantity. It doesn't matter too much *what* is served, as long as your daughter knows the preferences of her guests. But it is a calamity to run short before the end of the evening. For an after-dinner party she should count on the guests drinking at least two soft drinks apiece, and add half again as many for emergencies.

Food is generally very simple. It may be that snacks such as pretzels, popcorn, corn chips, etc., are all that is necessary. If your daughter likes to bake or has a special cake or cookie recipe, those foods will disappear as fast as she serves them. You and your husband might offer to help cook up a batch of hot dogs and hamburgers around midnight, and if you help serve, you will have an excellent opportunity to check on how things are going without seeming to "chaperon." Other popular late-evening foods are pancakes, pizzas, or cheese fondue. If a fondue is served, be sure to cover the table with a plastic cloth, for it is almost impossible to eat without dripping.

As long as there are teenage parties there will be boys who try to smuggle in liquor. You and your daughter must decide in advance on how you will cope with this if it occurs. She, because she will be there all the time, must keep her eyes open for signs of hidden flasks or bottles. If she does not think she can handle the situation herself by asking the offenders to stop drinking, to remove the liquor, or to leave, you should be available to help her out. You may ask the boy or boys to hand their liquor over to you for the duration of the party, and when it is over, if the boys are of legal age to drink, return it to them before they go home. If they are not of legal age, their parents should be notified. As for serving liquor in states where it is prohibited—don't do it. Not only is it illegal, but you are indicating to the youngsters that it is all right to flaunt the law, and therefore indirectly encouraging them to do so.

In areas where the minimum drinking age is eighteen, there is more of a problem at graduation parties and other events involving high-school seniors. Because of the guests who are under eighteen, and also because of the possible dangers involved in serving alcohol to youngsters, most parents sensibly prefer not to do so. If your daughter is at that "in-between" age, you will want her guests to enjoy themselves, of course, but you should not give in to that old threat of "But no one will come if we don't." If there is a prospect of plenty of good music, good food, and good company, they *will* come, and they *will* have a good time, even though you serve only soft drinks or punch.

If it is legal, you may also compromise by serving beer. If you buy a keg and have your husband or another adult "man" it, he can keep an eye on the number of beers the boys are drinking and refuse to serve more to anyone who seems to be getting a little "high."

"CRASHERS"

To be forewarned is to be forearmed, and every young person planning to give a large party must decide what she is going to do about "crashers."

When the doorbell rings and two or three uninvited classmates are standing there, what *does* she do?

The answer, I feel, does depend a little on the circumstances. If they are friends who couldn't be included because the guest list had to be limited, if they are sober and polite and dressed in appropriate clothes, they *might* be invited in. The "Oh, we didn't know you were having a party!" line may not fool her, but if she will be seeing the boys frequently, it may make for pleasanter relationships in the future. However, if she does not know the boys, if they claim to be friends of friends, if they have been drinking, or if they are not properly dressed, she should not let them in. She may need your help to keep them out, and if it is a large party, you and your husband should have another couple or perhaps some relatives there to help if need be. In some areas the problems of "crashing" and of boys sneaking liquor in have become so acute that parents hire a police-man to be in evidence and keep an eye out for any offenders.

ENDING A PARTY

When your daughter sends out her invitations she should give an "until" time as well as an "at" time, by stating "eight to twelve" or whatever the hours may be. If she does this, parents of nondrivers will know what time to come for their youngsters, and their arrival will start breaking up the party.

It is also a good idea to cut off the supply of food and drink a half hour or so before the party should end. If all else fails, and nobody seems to have the slightest intention of leaving, your daughter should ask you to put in an appearance, and that will be a sufficient hint!

After all parties are over, the teenage hostess (or host) should empty ashtrays, dispose of empty bottles, wash glasses, dispose of paper plates and other trash, and generally "pick up." If this is faithfully done, parents will rarely object to another party in their home.

SWEET-SIXTEEN PARTIES

All of the suggestions above apply to sweet-sixteen parties. Some girls prefer to celebrate their sixteenth birthday with a family party or a "slumber" party with their best girl friends, but the majority choose the boy-girl party. It may be a buffet dinner, an after-dinner party, or during the summer, a picnic or barbecue.

The gifts are essentially the only things that differentiate the sweet-sixteen party from any other. If boys and girls receive individual invitations, each one takes a gift. If the girls receive "bring-a-date" invitations, the girl and the boy she invites give a gift together. Whether she pays for it herself or he pays a share, depends on their relationship. If they are going steady or know each other very well, he would undoubtedly want to pay his half, but if she invites a relative stranger, she might feel that she was imposing on him if she asked him to contribute.

When a girl asks a boy to go with her to a sweet-sixteen party she is responsible for the transportation unless he is old enough to drive. Her parents should take them and pick them up or arrange with other parents for a car pool. If this is impossible, and the boy and girl live some distance apart, they should make plans to meet at the party.

When a girl and her father go to pick up her date she should go to the door to tell the boy they are there. This may seem odd but is far better than sitting in the car and honking!

PROMS AND GIRL-ASK-BOY PARTIES

Proms are back in style! There was a time when they were so unpopular and poorly attended that many schools gave them up entirely. But now they are coming back into favor, and in some areas the boys are wearing tuxedos and the girls, long skirts or dresses. If a girl is invited to a prom and the invitation does not say "formal" or "informal," she should be sure to ask the person who has invited her what sort of clothes are worn to parties in that particular school. It can still vary from slacks to evening clothes, but her date will be able to tell her what is right for the prom. If it says "semiformal" it probably means ties and sports jackets for the boys and dresses or long skirts for the girls. "Informal" means school clothes—but neat, clean, and the nicest ones she owns. Again, it is best to check with the person who invites her.

A prom at a public or coeducational school poses few problems, since all the members of the class are invited and will pair off as they usually do. Some mixed proms permit the members of the class to bring outside dates—others do not. Proms at girls' schools or boys' schools, or those given by the girls only or the boys only in a particular class, give rise to more questions. Since most of those questions come from girls I will concentrate on their proms, but most of the information will answer the boys' questions too.

If a girl and boy are going steady, she may invite him to her prom as soon as the date is announced. But if she is inviting someone she does not date regularly, she should not make it difficult for him to refuse by asking him too far in advance. Three or four weeks ahead of time is ample. On the other hand, if she waits until a week or ten days ahead, it looks as though the boy were her second choice, so she must not wait too long. When a girl *receives* an invitation that close to the day of the prom she must decide whether she wants to go enough to swallow her pride at playing "second fiddle."

Boys and girls who come as out-of-town guests pay for their own transportation. They are usually "put up" at the home of their host or hostess unless the parents will not be at home or there is not enough room. In that case the boy or girl who issued the invitation should pay for the guest's lodging in a nearby hotel or motel. At boarding schools, facilities are always prepared for the guests—in dormitories, masters' homes, etc.

When a girl knows that transportation costs are stretching the boy's pocketbook as far as it can go, she should plan meals at home, or picnics, or anything that will cost him nothing. If she knows him well enough, she may also tell him the whole weekend is "on her," or that if they go out on the town, they will "go Dutch."

When a prom is given by a coed class each member simply pays his own share—and an extra share for a date if he brings one. When boys ask girls or girls ask boys to their prom, the host or hostess pays for the tickets. In both cases the boy usually pays all other expenses— late-night snacks, flowers for his date, etc. When a girl asks a boy she may have him for dinner beforehand, or perhaps she gets together with her friends and arranges a dinner party. But her expenses end when they leave the prom itself.

Girls do not give boys boutonnieres unless it is a school custom. If it is a custom the girl buys it, just as he buys her corsage. Occasionally a prom committee buys boutonnieres to be given to the male guests, and each girl contributes toward them.

When a boy gives a girl a corsage she *must* wear it. Even if it looks ghastly with her dress, it would be most ungrateful not to pin it to a pocketbook or to a ribbon tied around her wrist. The pocketbook is best—you can leave it on a table while you are dancing, and the "clash" with your dress won't be noticed.

These rules for proms apply, in general, to all girl-ask-boy (sometimes called Tolo) parties. The girl pays for both tickets to whatever the event may be as well as dinner beforehand if a meal is not served at the party. The boy pays all extra expenses. The girl arranges for transportation unless the boy can drive. In that case they would go in his car, or perhaps in her family's car if they have no objections. If they must go by bus or subway the boy pays their fares.

If a girl happens to get tickets to the theater, a concert, a baseball game, or any special event, she may ask a boy to go with her. Again, he is responsible for all expenses other than the tickets, unless she specifically says *"dinner* and the theater." She should make it quite clear when she invites him just what the afternoon or evening will involve, because he may not be able to afford the extras, and he would be put in a very embarrassing spot.

DATING

A young girl may not, even with her fiancé, lunch in a road house without a chaperon, or go on a journey that can by any possibility last over night. To go out with him in a small sail-boat sounds harmless enough, but might result in a questionable situation if they are becalmed, or if they are left helpless in a sudden fog. The Maine coast, for example, is particularly subject to fogs that often shut down without warning and no one going out on the water can tell whether he will be able to get back within a reasonable time or not. A man and a girl went out from Bar Harbor and did not get back until next day. Everyone knew the fog had come in as thick as pea-soup and that it was impossible to get home; but to the end of time her reputation will suffer for the experience.—Emily Post, 1922

Chaperons, like high-button shoes, are a thing of the past.

From an ethical standpoint, the only chaperon worth having today is a young girl's own efficiency in chaperoning herself. The girl who has been taught to appraise every person and situation she meets needs no one to sit beside her and tell her what to do. She must be able to handle any situation herself, because today's girl is on her own. She must learn to gauge the reactions of various types of people, particularly men, in varying circumstances.

Many parents, unfortunately, become overprotective of their teenage children and restrict their activities and friendships unreasonably. Perhaps they are afraid that more lenient guidance would give the impression that they are indifferent to their daughter's well-being. They should realize that overzealous guarding will hamper their child's development of responsibility and judgment and that unnecessary restriction may separate her from her friends. It is admittedly difficult to achieve the middle road of reasonable supervision, but it is important to the child's social development to receive freedom as well as guidance during these years of adolescence.

The age at which a girl may go out alone with a boy in the evening and how late she may stay out will vary according to the responsibility of the girl herself and the custom of the community. Only a parent can make the exact decision. A girl of thirteen or fourteen might go out with a boy as part of a group of four or more to an early movie, dinner, sports match, or some other special event. Most of her dates will, however, be those at the homes of friends or at parties organized by her school. Her parents should at all times know where and with whom she is and at what time she will be home.

At fifteen, assuming that she has proved herself responsible, she should start having an occasional "real" date. As long as she is open with her parents, introduces her dates to them, asks permission to go out, abides by their mutual decisions as to when she should be home and where she may go, she is ready to start going out on her own. Her parents must realize that she is rapidly becoming an adult, and if she is too restricted now, she will have no experience to lean on when she is finally set free. This is as dangerous for a young girl as being allowed too much freedom before she is ready for it. As she grows in age and experience, her dates will naturally include many more activities, she will go out more frequently alone with a boy, and the time she is to return home will be extended.

HOMECOMING HOURS

The hour at which a teenager must be home is one of the most difficult problems to be settled between children and their parents. The customs of the community, the hours kept by friends, the amount of sleep the individual child needs, and the confidence of the parents in their daughter—and her escort—are all important factors. During the early teen years, when children do not have the wisdom to recognize their own needs, the parents must set time limits on dates and see that they are kept, even though this may mean waiting up to greet the returning son or daughter. This is a simple matter of good health, as well as setting a high standard of behavior. It is wise to discuss homecoming hours with other parents and try to arrive at an hour to which everyone, including the children, agrees. If this is impossible, try to choose a time you think sensible—not the earliest, for this will only cause resentment and disobedience, or the latest, which may cause criticism, as well as be detrimental to the child's health.

Friends of mine evolved what seemed to me to be a very sensible solution to the problem of enforcing a curfew and avoiding the agonizing necessity of waiting up for their daughter. At the door of their room they placed an alarm clock, set for fifteen minutes or so after the hour their child was supposed to be home. When she came in, she turned off the alarm without waking them. They could go to sleep unworried, knowing that they would not be awakened if all went well, but that if there were cause for worry, the alarm would wake them up and they could take whatever steps they felt necessary to locate their daughter.

As a general rule, ten thirty or eleven is a reasonable time for a thirteen- or fourteen-year-old to be home. On occasion he or she may attend a school club dance or other special party until twelve. The hours should be made a little later each year, so that sixteen- or seventeen-year-olds might stay at parties until twelve thirty or one. If they plan to go to a friend's house or a snack bar afterward, their parents should know in advance or be called on the telephone so that they may know the whereabouts of the child and readjust the hour when he or she is supposed to be home. When a youngster reaches his late teens, his hours should be regulated only by his or her own need for sleep or the rules of his school or university. Parents of a child living at home should realize that were he away at college, he would be making his own rules as to hours, and allow him the same privilege. They may, of course, point out that he is not getting enough sleep, or suggest that he needs a "health night," as my teen-agers called an early-to-bed evening. But many eighteen-year-olds live away from home—they work, they are in the armed forces, and they are even married—so it seems a little ridiculous for parents, simply because they are fortunate enough to have their youngster at home, to attempt to treat him as a child rather than an intelligent, if young, adult.

Dates should be absolutely restricted to weekends and vacations. Even high-school students who are "going steady" should not be permitted to date during the week, even to study together. The only exceptions might be very special occasions, such as if a boy were given theater tickets to an excellent and difficult-to-see show or to a championship game or some other extraordinary event.

If a young girl's family is not at home, she should not, on return-ing from a party, invite or allow her date to "come in for a while." However, if her parents are home and have no objections, it is per-fectly all right to invite him in. He should not stay overly long, and if he shows no inclination to leave, the girl should tell him that her parents have set a definite "curfew" hour.

A boy taking a girl home to an apartment house with a doorman and/or an elevator operator, says goodnight to her in the lobby. If it is an unattended building and a self-service elevator, he should accompany her to her own door.

Some families insist on a practice that is quite sensible—merely that their daughter telephone home just before leaving a dance if she plans to go on to someone's house or bring friends to her own.

BREAKING THE ICE

Women's Lib, feminists, and the changed relationship between men and women in general are challenging the established order of "boy asks girl" for a date. The girls say, "Why should we sit at home and wait to be invited out? Why, if we are equal to men, shouldn't we be free to ask them out?"

911

There is a certain amount of justice in this attitude, but I believe it is self-defeating. Men *like* to think of themselves as the aggressors. They may be flattered by a woman who pursues them, but they may also feel that their masculinity is being threatened. If a girl wants a man to like her—and presumably she does if she wants to ask him out—she will be much wiser to let him *think* that it is his idea than to be too obvious. Of course she *can* do all the asking she wants, and she probably won't even be criticized with the current approval of women's independence, but she may find that she is alienating the very person she wants to impress. A girl who knows how to use her femininity and her charm to get the man she wants, instead of displaying her independence and "strength" to bowl him over, has a far better chance of success. The same general rule applies to telephone calls and to writing letters. The girl who wants to make a boy aware of her, without seeming to be pushy, can:

Persuade a mutual friend to invite them both to a small party.

Go to all school events in which he takes part.

Join clubs and organizations to which he belongs.

Ask a girl who knows him to arrange a blind double date.

Be as attractive and vivacious as she can with her other friends whenever she is near him.

If she is successful, and they do get to know each other, he may ask her for a date when they happen to meet or he may telephone her. In either case he should mention the following details:

What time he will call for the girl.

Their means of transportation.

What kind of date it will be—movies, a party at a friend's, a picnic, etc.

Who else, if anyone, will be with them.

If he forgets to offer any of this information, the girl may, and should, ask for it.

Unless a boy and girl are going steady he should ask for a date:

Two to four days ahead for any ordinary date.

At least two weeks ahead for a formal dance or party.

A month or more ahead for a big college weekend.

There are exceptions, such as when a party is planned on the spur of the moment, but these are good general rules.

ACCEPTING OR REFUSING A DATE

Ordinarily, accepting a date presents no problem. If she wants to go, the girl need only say, "I'd love to!" promptly and enthusiastically. The worst mistake she can make is to be evasive. If she has promised to baby-sit and doesn't know whether she can get a substitute, or if she is not sure whether the family is going to the country for the weekend, she must say so. But it must be true, and she must be sincere, or he will surely know it. No one should ever say, "Can I let you know tomorrow?" without saying why.

Once a girl has accepted, she must keep the date unless a real emergency arises. One should *never* break one date to accept another.

To refuse a date politely a girl need only say, "I'm so sorry, but I have a date for Saturday night." As long as she doesn't make the mistake of saying, "I'm sorry, I can't go out that night," she is free to accept someone else who calls. If, however, she would really like the boy to ask her again, she should give him a more detailed excuse that sounds, and is, true.

OTHER DATING DATA

A girl should introduce a new friend to her parents on her first date with him. She should brief her parents a little before he arrives so that they can carry on a conversation easily. Five minutes or so is enough for the visit, and the girl should be ready to say, "We'd better go now or we'll be late for the movie."

Men—and boys—should call for their dates at their homes. Only if the boy knows the girl well and has a good reason (a late class or hockey practice, for example) might he meet her at the movie house or the snack bar.

Unless a couple have been going steady and have agreed to share at times, the boy pays all expenses on a date. The girl may help considerably by suggesting inexpensive entertainment—or choosing the lower-priced items on a menu. If after a few dates she wishes to pay for their next dinner or to share the costs, she should bring it up in advance and not surprise him with the offer in front of strangers. Although most boys are happy to go along with this new approach, some are still hesitant about accepting a girl's money publicly. But in general, "going Dutch" is becoming the rule rather than the exception.

On a first date, or when a couple date infrequently, the boy plans the entertainment in advance and asks the girl to go to a movie, to bowl, or whatever. When they go out together often they generally discuss what they would like to do and plan it together.

The boy should arrive for his date on time, and the girl should be ready. There is no truth in the old idea that she makes herself more desirable by keeping him waiting. Quite the opposite!

The girl should be dressed suitably, assuming that her date has told her what they are going to do. If he has been vague, a simple rather than a "dressy" costume is a safer choice, and if she is totally at sea, she should, as mentioned above, call and ask him what they are going to do.

THE BLIND DATE

The "blind date" is sometimes arranged by a third person—such as Mrs. Towne, who thinks that Gloria Gorgeous and Harry Handsome would enjoy each other's company. She first makes sure that Harry would be interested in getting to know Gloria; then she asks Gloria if she would like to meet an attractive boy. Only after both parties have indicated that they would like to be introduced should Mrs. Towne proceed. She may invite both of them to her house, with or without other friends, or if she is sure they will "hit it off," she may give Gloria's number to Harry and let him arrange a date with Gloria directly.

The date may be proposed by a boy who has a date with a girl and asks her to get a date for a friend of his who would like to go with them.

The most frequent type of blind date, however, occurs when a boy or girl arranges a date for his or her overnight guest. A girl may call a good friend and say, "Tom, Sally, my roommate at college, is spending the weekend with me, and I think you'd like her, so how about taking her to a movie with Jim and me on Saturday night?" Or she might ask Jim to find a date for Sally.

Dates arranged in any of these ways should not be expected to result in anything more than a pleasant evening. Even close friends do not always agree on whom they like or dislike, and while Cindy may think Charley is divine, her friend Jane may well be bored to death in his company. So make the best of a blind date, and no matter what you may think to yourself, act as though you are enjoying every minute. After all, it is probably better than sitting at home by yourself, and whether he or she is enchanting or not, you may meet more attractive people through your new acquaintance.

The dangerous blind date is the one arranged through a chain of people, or people you do not know. For example, a boy calls and asks your roommate, Jane, to get a date for a friend of his. Jane barely recognizes the name of the caller, but she asks if you would like to go. Don't! You don't know the caller yourself, let alone his friend, so hold off unless Jane arranges to meet the friend first.

"GOING STEADY" AND "PINNING"

To the chagrin of many parents and teachers, "going steady" has become a fact of American teenage life. Gone for the most part is the traditional stag line at the high-school dance; today a girl usually dances only with her escort. When a boy and girl date each other consistently, and they have an agreement that neither is to date anyone else, they are "going steady"; this may be formalized by an exchange of friendship rings or identification bracelets.

For several reasons, this is an unfortunate practice. A wise young person wants to widen rather than narrow his circle of friends. Unfortunately, many girls fear not having a date for Saturday night, and some boys are afraid to be told "No" when they call a girl for a date. But these young people are restricting the development of their own personalities when they limit their dating friendships. Only by meeting many other young people of varied backgrounds and interests can a boy or girl gain enough insight to be capable of making a good choice of a wife or husband when the time comes.

The constant "togetherness" of going steady also poses a sexual problem. Boys and girls are put in a position where it is difficult, if not impossible, to resist their urges, even though they may want to.

Finally, it is usually extremely difficult to "break up," especially for the girl. Other boys have gotten out of the habit of calling, and she is bound to be dateless for a time, at least. The boy has fewer problems in that way, but they both may find it a traumatic experience, to be alone with no one to lean on, especially if they had been "steadies" for a long period of time.

If he has given her a ring, it should be returned when the couple break up.

The presentation of a fraternity badge by a college man to his girl, known as "pinning," may be merely another type of "going steady," or it may mean that the couple are "engaged to be engaged," depending on the customs of that particular college. Generally the couple intend to marry, but in the somewhat distant future, and this relationship allows them to examine their compatibility without committing themselves formally to an engagement. It is not right for a girl to collect fraternity pins as trophies of her dates. If the pinned couple break up, the girl is expected to return the pin to the young man. In many cases pinning does lead to a formal engagement and then to marriage.

After leaving college, of course, unmarried young men and

915

women do not follow these customs. Although a couple in their twenties or thirties may be dating each other exclusively, there will usually be no formalizing of their relationship until they decide to become engaged.

SMOKING, DRINKING, AND DRUGS

The best possible deterrent for all three of these pitfalls is education. If you can show your youngster the results, you may succeed in convincing him that all three are monsters—sometimes in sheep's clothing.

If you can persuade your child to do volunteer work (when he or she is old enough) in a drug-rehabilitation center, he will soon understand the disastrous effect of taking drugs. If he works on a hospital floor where there are victims of lung cancer or emphysema, he will rapidly be convinced that he doesn't want to smoke. A visit to a meeting of Alcoholics Anonymous, or a trip to the Bowery, where the "winos" lie passed out on the streets, is visible evidence of the dangers of alcohol.

The best way, perhaps, to keep your child from smoking is not to smoke yourself. He will try it, with his friends, no matter how dire a picture you paint of the results, but if he is conspicuous as the only smoker at home, he will be less inclined to smoke habitually. Be sure that he reads as many of the reports put out by the Surgeon General's office as possible, and do not give him "permission" to smoke. Your best approach may be to *ask* him to refrain from smoking until a certain age—perhaps until he graduates from college. If he holds out that long, and reads the facts and figures about the dangers of smoking, there is a good chance that he will never start.

Many parents prefer to introduce their teenager to alcohol at home, instead of letting them have their first experience at a bar or in a place where loss of control could be a disaster. The French give very young children wine mixed with water—it does them no harm. Offering your midteenager an occasional glass of wine is a good way of letting him learn how a mild drink makes you feel. A little later he may try a beer—but always with you, and under your supervision. When he approaches college age it is wise to let him try a cocktail or a little whiskey—always in your home. He *will* try it when he goes away to college, and he will be much better equipped to cope with it, and to know how much he can take, if he has become accustomed to it with your assistance.

Again, your example is important. If you do not drink too much, or at all, your children are bound to be influenced by your behavior and may drink no more than an occasional beer. If your habits prove to him that limited "social" drinking does no harm, he is apt to limit himself, as you do. You can and should, however, be sure that he is aware of the dangers and horrors that are inevitable for the alcoholic.

Drugs, as this is being written, are the greatest of the three pitfalls. Most parents are convinced that "it can't happen here," but it can. Drug addiction hits rich and poor, good and bad, old and young—and especially the last. Children who are not even out of elementary school are getting "hooked" by despicable pushers. Here again education is the most important weapon. Aside from providing your children with reading material, take them to as many films, discussions, and lectures on the subject as you can. And equally important, don't let a "communications gap" develop. If your child will discuss the drug problem openly with you, the pressures on him will be dissipated and with your support he will be better able to resist the urgings of his peers that "everyone does it." The National Institute of Mental Health will provide you with a wealth of material on drugs at very little expense. The address is Chevy Chase, Maryland 20015.

Don't panic if you find that your child has smoked marijuana. Whether it is injurious or not is still being debated, but it seems fairly well established that the drug is not in itself addictive. Naturally, you should emphasize that it is illegal and point out the fringe dangers of going on to harder drugs, getting "in" with a bad crowd, etc. But it seems to be almost universally tried by teenagers, and if your child is well educated and self-controlled, he will probably suffer no ill effects from his experiment.

THE TELEPHONE

Teenagers are absolutely *compulsive* about using the telephone! Jane leaves Sue at her gate, walks across the street into her house, and picks up the telephone to call—Sue. It is a phenomenon that adults cannot understand, but it's there, and "if you can't fight 'em, join 'em!"

To avoid knock-down, drag-out fights with your youngsters, you must, with their agreement, establish some rules. There should be hours when they can make and receive calls and hours when they cannot. Dinnertime and after a certain hour at night should be taboo. So should any hours at which you are apt to receive important calls

917

—if, for instance, Grandmother regularly calls from California at about eight oclock on Wednesday nights.

If you can afford to have a separate telephone for your teenagers, you are in luck. But if you cannot, you must all make some concessions. You might ask your friends to call during the afternoon, or early in the evening when your youngsters are doing their homework. After eight or eight thirty, perhaps, they might be allowed free use of the phone.

Finally, the length of calls should be limited. Nothing is more frustrating than trying to get an important call through, only to get a busy signal hour after hour. You might settle on a reasonable time with your children—shorter than they want and longer than you want. Something in the neighborhood of fifteen minutes will give them time to say and resay everything they can think of, and will leave your callers short of apoplexy.

I am frequently asked whether it is all right for girls to call boys on the phone. It is hardly a "sin," but it is not a good idea to do it too frequently, for the reasons discussed on pages 911–912, under "breaking the ice."

There are many perfectly good reasons for a girl to call a boy, and the five most common ones are:

To return a call by request.

To apologize.

To issue or answer an invitation.

To give important or long-awaited news.

To tell him about a change in plans.

TEENAGE VISITORS

When a teenager—whether a boy or a girl—goes to spend a weekend with friends, the same basic rules apply as do for adults. The visitor should take a gift, preferably a "house" present rather than a "hostess" present. A game, a plant, a record, or anything that can be enjoyed by the whole family is the best choice.

While visiting, the guest should be especially careful to pick up after himself, to make his bed, and to leave the bathroom clean. He should *not* leave socks, shoes, sweaters, etc., lying around the house, and he should be reminded, before going, to be polite and helpful— not only to his own host or hostess, but to his or her mother. Even though the menus do not offer the foods to which he is accustomed, he should try everything and keep his feelings to himself if he is disappointed. He must, of course, obey any household rules laid down by his host's or hostess' parents.

Finally, he—or she—must write a thank-you letter to the host's or hostess' mother. He need not write his friend if he is going to see him soon, but the bread-and-butter letter to the mother is a must. This is not necessary at all, of course, for the casual "sleep-over" at a neighbor's. Then verbal thanks in the morning is all that is necessary.

AT COLLEGE

DORMITORIES

Consideration is the key to successful dormitory living, whether it be for a roommate, your hall mates, the dormitory personnel, or the maintenance staff. The facilities of the dormitory are yours, but they're also your roommate's. This means sharing the mirror, the shower, the desk, the lounge; it means preserving the life of all dormitory property; it means keeping "your side" in order. It also means being considerate of your roommate's sleeping and studying habits and observing the quiet hours (if any) that the dormitory imposes.

An unfortunate custom, but one that is not likely to disappear, is that of borrowing among dormitory mates. Avoid borrowing if you can, but you must, of course, respond pleasantly when asked to lend an article of yours, whether you accept or refuse the request. If you must borrow, never do so without asking permission, and always take better care of borrowed property than of your own. Whether you borrow a book or a sweater, its prompt return to the owner as soon as you have finished with it is essential if you want to keep your friends.

There is little to be said in this book about "open" dorms—where men and women students live together, in some cases on separate floors, in others, sharing rooms. Parents have the very deep obligation of preparing their youngsters for the decisions they will be forced to make, and if their daughters—or sons—are not mature enough to form and adhere to an acceptable standard of behavior, they should not be sent to a college where these conditions exist. Many educators feel that it is far more normal and healthy to allow the sexes to mix and to grow up in close proximity than to enforce segregation as colleges used to do. I agree, as long as there is a refuge for the youngster who is not ready for total "togetherness." The young people who seem to be self-assured and able to handle themselves should be taught to be tolerant of other youngsters who may not be so well adjusted.

In any case, whether mixed or segregated, the main requirement for getting along in a dormitory is consideration. Obey whatever rules there may be, be pleasant and helpful, be tolerant, and
be aware of how your actions are affecting your fellow students.

COLLEGE WEEKENDS

The visitor on a college weekend, whether boy or girl, pays for
his own transportation to and from the campus. The host should help
out by providing information about planes, buses, or highway routes.
He should always be on hand to meet his guest, or if that is absolutely
impossible, have someone there in his place. The guest should be
forewarned: "I'll have to be at band practice just when your plane
lands, but my roommate, Gordon Coxe, will be there to meet
you."

Men and women visitors stay in fraternity or sorority houses,
dormitories emptied for the guests, reputable hotels and motels, or
masters' houses. A man ordinarily pays for his date's lodgings, unless
their relationship is such that she shares expenses when they are
together. When a man invites a girl he does not know very well for
the weekend, he should let her know exactly what they will be doing
and where she will be staying. If he doesn't, she should ask. Otherwise she may find herself in the same spot as did a friend of my
daughter's. After spending all day going to a football game, parties,
etc., she asked her host to take her to her room so she could get
dressed for the evening. "Why," he said casually, "this is where you
are staying." "This" was his apartment, and since she had no interest
in sharing his quarters with him, she spent most of the night in her
car—driving home.

In general, the man pays for all the weekend expenses other
than his date's transportation. However, if they are very close
friends, engaged, or going steady, and she knows it would stretch his
budget painfully, she may offer to pay for her hotel accommodations,
or to "go Dutch" on some of their meals.

A LIST OF "DON'TS"

The courtesy "dos" at a college weekend need not be listed,
since they are the same "dos" as are listed throughout this book.
There are, however, certain specific "don'ts," which, if observed, will
make the weekend more fun for everyone, and will help ensure a
repeat invitation.

DON'T arrive with a shabby, down-at-heel suitcase with straps
carelessly hanging out. Neat, compact luggage will please a man
much more than you might suspect.

DON'T forget to dress mentally as you pack. Panty hose, shoes?

Dress? What goes with it? Belt, scarf, or other accessories, bag? No one is less pleasing than the girl who begins to borrow from the other girls the moment she arrives. And yet: DON'T make your luggage one inch bigger or one ounce heavier than necessary. Any girl who brings more than one moderate-sized bag will not add to her popularity either with the others who are going in the same car or with her host who perhaps has to carry her luggage up a steep hill to the house where she is to stay.

DON'T show an alive and interested manner toward the boys and total indifference toward the girls. When you are shown to the room you are to share with another girl, DON'T claim the bed you like best by throwing your bag on it. At least make the gesture of asking the other girl if she cares which you take.

DON'T take up more than exactly your share of the closet space and drawer space. If you have brought too many things for the space that is yours, you must leave some of them packed in your bag and leave the bag neatly closed.

DON'T monopolize the bathroom; remember that others are waiting. DON'T leave your personal belongings around on all the bedroom furniture. Later, when you pack to leave, DON'T leave used tissues and bobby pins in the bureau drawer. Also, open dresser drawers wide to be sure you have not left panties or other personal items behind. DON'T leave rubbish behind you, either. Remember that the regular occupant of the room may have to move back in before there is time to have the room cleaned.

Throughout your stay, DON'T think only of what you like to do; that is, DON'T insist on playing Ping-Pong if your host would rather play pool, unless your Ping-Pong is expert and your pool so bad it would ruin the game for everyone else. In general, do what the majority wants to do—unless you think it is wrong. For example, you are under no obligation to drink or to smoke "pot" anywhere, at any time, if you don't want to.

DON'T be jealous of every attention your date pays to another girl. The more you show your dislike for this interest, the more jealous he is likely to try to make you. DON'T show that you hate to be teased, or you'll be a target for every practical joker around.

DON'T show chagrin or disappointment. The fundamental secret is to show delight in everything pleasing, and to be blind, deaf, and insensible to annoyance or disappointment. Above all, DON'T do anything to seem unappreciative of the efforts made for your pleasure by the man who is your host. It should not be necessary to try to impress him with your powers by attracting one of his classmates. In other words, DON'T try to be the house-party coquette!

❧75❧ Family Relationships

HUSBANDS AND WIVES

Nor does a gentleman ever criticise the behavior of a wife whose conduct is scandalous. What he says to her in the privacy of their own apartments is no one's affair but his own, but he must never treat her with disrespect before their children, or a servant, or any one.—Emily Post, 1922

There are no two people in the world, no matter how much in love they are when they get married, who do not have to make adjustments to each other. There is simply no way of getting to know each other completely when still living apart, and the first months, and even years, of married life are an exciting, stimulating time of discovery and deepening affection—if, that is, each partner is willing to make concessions to the habits of his mate that annoy him and to look for and enjoy the traits that please. The wife who starts nagging soon after marriage because her husband does not hang up his suit every night or the husband who can't stand her stockings drying in the bathroom will have a difficult period of adjustment. Of course he should try to improve his bachelor habits in order to make his wife's housecleaning easier, and she should try to do her wash early enough so that her stockings can be put away before he gets home, but this type of irritation should never be allowed to become so important that the happy times are forgotten in a constant stream of recriminations.

I don't know why people should feel that because they are married they may give up all pretense of good manners and treat their partners like "old shoes." During courtship, both men and women put their best foot forward, and instead of being a trap to catch their mate, this attitude should set the pattern for the marriage. But it does not always work that way, and many a marriage has failed because one (or both) of the partners allowed his attitude toward the other to become careless, ill-mannered, or just plain bored. It takes an effort to keep a good marriage going, and the close proximity of home life makes the constant presence of good manners more important than in any relationship outside the family.

So many people save up all their troubles to pour on the one they love most. Why, when her husband's prize rosebush has just burst into bloom, does his wife tell him first about the hole the neighbor's dog dug in the strawberry bed? Why, instead of noticing his wife's new hairdo, or the slipcover she has just finished, does her husband come in complaining about the milk carton the children left on the lawn? If something is really wrong, or one or the other is truly ill, that is another matter. But beware of dwelling on petty things in order to get sympathy. There is a big deposit of sympathy in the bank of love, but don't draw out little sums every hour or two. By and by, perhaps when you need it most, it will all be withdrawn, and you won't know how or on what it was spent.

Constant nagging or complaining can also produce another reaction—closing one's ears. If a wife knows that the first thing she hears every time she and her husband meet is criticism, she will soon plan to be next door or busy with the children or working late when he is due to get home. A husband coming home to the same kind of complaints will bury himself in the paper and not talk at all, or he'll go out to join the "boys" for a beer.

The couple who greet each other with enthusiasm, who keep the unpleasantnesses until after they've had a chance to relax, and who then listen to each other's problems or triumphs with equal interest, are off to a wonderful start. Nothing is better for a marriage than a partner who is the one person in the world with whom you can discuss anything—and vice versa.

Neither a husband nor a wife should make social engagements without consulting the other—unless he or she is absolutely sure that there is no other commitment and that it is something his spouse would like to do. On the husband's side, this usually involves bringing people home from work without warning. If a man suddenly finds that he *must* entertain a client or someone important to his business, he should call his wife and tell her either that they are taking Mr. X *out* to dinner or that Mr. X is coming to dinner but he (the husband) will pick up a steak and cook it himself on the grill.

In general, wives make most of the social plans for the couple.

If her husband works hard during the week, she would be very thoughtless to plan a dinner party for Friday night, accept an invitation to a dance Saturday night, and organize an all-day picnic on Sunday. Of course, if she has been taking care of the baby all week, she wants to get out of the house on weekends, but there must be some compromise so that her husband can get the rest *he* needs while she gets the diversion *she* needs.

Not many men can endure for long the sight of a wife in a dirty housecoat, with her hair in curlers and her face smeared with cold cream. Nor is a wife charmed by an unshaven husband slouching around in his undershirt. The wife who combs her hair, puts on fresh makeup, and if she has been working around the yard or house, changes her clothes before her husband comes home, is the wife he'll be glad to come home to. The husband who straightens his tie, tucks in his shirt, washes up as soon as he comes home, and perhaps changes into fresh clothes, is the husband who will receive an enthusiastic welcome.

A man who lived in a bachelor apartment or whose mother picked up after him before he married, may need a bit of tactful educating. This should be done by discussion—not by carping and nagging. If he has never had to do it, he will not think about hanging up his clothes, putting the cap on the toothpaste, putting the toilet seat down, or cleaning the sink after shaving. These are common masculine failings, and a smart bride won't follow in her mother-in-law's footsteps. Today, partners share the household chores as they never did before, and each is responsible for his own department. Even the cooking, vacuuming, and "community" chores are often done by turns in a modern marriage where both members work and contribute to the exchequer. This, it seems to me, is a very healthy trend, and will surely remove many of the resentments that women used to feel when they were irrevocably tied down to babies and housework.

Educating a spouse—either husband or wife—is one thing; trying to reform him is another. Education implies growth; reform implies change. The former is a good and natural progression that you achieve together; the latter is selfish—indicating that your partner must do it *your* way. If your husband (or your wife) has the *important* virtues that make a good mate, don't worry too much about his small faults. If he is considerate, tolerant, gentle, and he loves you, don't go to pieces because he won't wipe his feet on the mat or hold the car door for you. If you can't educate him by telling him how you feel, or by tactful hints or discussion, learn to live with the little "lapses" and concentrate on what he *does* do right. Above all, don't let little resentments fester—bring them out at once and solve them by discussion, not by an attempt to "reform." No one should ever, ever enter into marriage thinking that he is going to reform his mate.

This does not mean that good manners are not important to a successful marriage. Nothing could be farther from the truth. Lack of manners may not actually put a good marriage on the rocks, but it can surely rock the boat. A husband helping with the dishes, a wife shining her husband's shoes may be small things, but they are thoughtful things. A woman who lights her husband's cigarette or a man who holds his wife's coat for her are not making earthshaking gestures, but they are showing courtesy and respect for each other. When this sort of consideration is lacking in a marriage, it is indicative of far greater trouble, and the importance of manners cannot be minimized.

AIRING THE PROBLEMS

There are endless other suggestions that might well be considered by newlyweds. Minor, but frequently repeated irritations—interrupting each other, making fun of idiosyncrasies, not laughing at his or her jokes, never being on time, the wife's using the husband's razor, and a thousand others—can build up a huge wall of resentment. And there are greater ones—basic differences of opinion on bringing up children, on spending vacations, on where each member wants to live, and so on—that can undermine an otherwise sound marriage. But great or small, the only way to handle these problems is by bringing them into the open and keeping the lines of communication free between husband and wife. The moment that one or the other feels he cannot discuss a problem and it is left to fester and grow inside, is the moment the marriage begins to dissolve. The couple who agree not only to listen to each other's problems but to make an effort to see the other side and to DO something to correct the situation, is certain to stay out of the divorce courts.

THE IMPORTANCE OF *OUR*

Of all the advice one could give a young bride or groom, perhaps the best would be to use the words *we* and *our*. How many times have you heard a wife say, "Yes, *I* have three children," instead of "Bill and I . . ." or "We have. . . ." Or a husband introducing his son: "I'd like you to meet *my* son, Billy."

When a man and woman marry they become a unit made up

of two parts. Their major possessions, whether their children or their worldly goods, become *theirs*, not *his* and *hers*. To refuse to recognize this by using *I* and *my*, instead of *we* and *our*, is not only discourteous but indicates a dangerous attitude toward the marriage itself.

INVASION OF PRIVACY

While, as discussed above, possessions are "pooled" in a good marriage, some things are not. Each member of the couple has a right to his own opinions, to his own interests, and to his privacy. *No one* has a right to pry into the personal correspondence of another person or to listen in on his phone calls or private conversations. Neither a husband nor a wife should *ever* open a letter addressed to the other unless it is obviously an advertisement or unsolicited "nuisance" mail.

SOCIAL RELATIONSHIPS BETWEEN RELATIVES

Just as no chain is stronger than its weakest link, no manners can be expected to stand a strain beyond their daily test at home.—Emily Post, 1922

Relations between relatives are usually more informal than those between friends, but not necessarily. Good friends *can* be far closer than brothers or sisters. Merely being related is no excuse for invasion of privacy, for imposing, or for expecting too much of people. It is the latter—too much expectation—that causes more problems between relatives than anything else. Aunts *expect* their nieces to invite them to see the new baby; parents *expect* their married children to have them for visits; fathers *expect* their sons to want to go into business with them; and on and on.

"DROP-IN" RELATIVES AND OTHER VISITORS

Many people feel that they are free to drop in on their relatives at any time, and they are resentful if they are not welcomed with open arms. They are totally wrong. Of course there are some sisters who visit back and forth without a word of warning, or children who drop in on their parents, etc., but aunts and uncles, cousins, and in-laws should follow the same rule they would with an unrelated friend and *call first* to arrange a time to visit. If you have relatives who "surprise" you frequently, you must be frank. Tell them you love seeing them, but if they would call before they arrive to give you a chance to pull yourself together or to make sure that you had made no other plans, you would enjoy their visits much more.

When relatives who live far away come to visit, a good deal of rivalry and jealousy may develop. Judy wants them to stay with her and her family, John wants them to visit him so they can see the new baby, and their parents assume that of course they will stay with them in the old homestead. Instead of trying to divide up their time and stay a day or two with each, the best solution is for the visitors to insist firmly that they prefer to stay in a motel. There may be some hurt feelings, but they will not last. In this way the visiting couple can divide their time more or less evenly among their relatives, and besides, they will be able to see old friends and do some of the things they would like to—on their own.

When you are the visiting relative, don't sit in your motel room and wait for your sisters and brothers to call you. They cannot know just when you will arrive unless they are actually meeting you. After you have recovered from your trip, call them and say, "We're here— when can we come out to see you?"

Relatives who move to a new house are sometimes hurt because members of the family do not rush over to see it. Chances are, their brothers or sisters or aunts or cousins are saying, "I'd love to see Joanie's house, but I don't know whether she's ready for visitors." If you have moved, or if you have a new baby to show off, or any other reason for wanting people to come to see you, don't sit and wait for the doorbell to ring. Call your relatives and invite them—that's the way to let them know they are welcome.

ELDERLY PARENTS

Elderly people frequently complain that their grown children or their grandchildren or their nieces or nephews don't come to see them often enough. This can be very sad, especially if the elderly person is alone. It is particularly hard at holiday seasons, and I can only urge children of elderly parents to remember their loneliness and to have them visit at those times, no matter how busy the household may be.

On the other hand, elderly parents should do their best to understand how busy their children are—and *everyone* seems to be "busy" today—and not be selfishly demanding. The older person who stays "young" by keeping busy himself, by keeping up his interest in what is going on in the world, by participating in as many activities as he can and as he enjoys, will not be sitting around feeling sorry for himself.

When a mother or father must live with a married child the situation demands the wisdom of a Solomon, the tact of a Récamier, and the self-control of a Stoic. Moreover, she or he must conscientiously practice the art of "invisibility" at frequent and lengthy intervals. This does not mean that the mother, for example, must scuttle out of sight like a frightened mouse, but that she should have or find occupations of her own that will keep her from being idly, plaintively, or forcefully present—particularly when friends of her daughter-in-law or her son are present. Perhaps she can find some friends who play bridge or canasta one or·two evenings every week. Her room should be equipped with radio and television so that she can always be free to enjoy her own favorite programs. She should assist with household chores or caring for the children as much as she easily can, but she should not be imposed upon or made to feel like a built-in baby-sitter.

On the other hand, there is no excuse for the ruthless unkindness that some wives show when they are obliged to have a parent-in-law living with them. This attitude not only is distressing to the helpless victim, but is certainly resented by all who see it.

If it is physically possible, it is far better for parents to live apart from their married children. The young people should, if necessary, help to support the older ones, especially a widow, but the parents should be allowed to feel that they are handling their own affairs and managing their own lives until they are no longer capable or do not wish to do so. Love and affection will flourish in an atmosphere of independence, supplemented by close family ties. But people of different generations living together are bound to find some friction even though they may feel great affection for each other.

IN-LAW SITUATIONS

One is likely to overlook the fact that when John Jones marries Mary Smith, a number of Smiths and Joneses are suddenly forced into the closeness of a family relationship. Even when a man or woman has no family, he or she becomes son or daughter, sister or brother, to those who hitherto may have been total strangers.

The two most difficult situations to meet happily and successfully are that between the husband and his father-in-law and that between the wife and her mother-in-law. The other positions are easier, and there is little reason for failure. In any case the very first rule that every father-in-law—and especially every mother-in-law—must learn is DON'T INTERFERE. Never mind what small blunders your daughter or daughter-in-law or your son or son-in-law may make; remember that it is the individual's right to live and do and think as he or she pleases. If you are asked what you think, answer truthfully, of course; but don't, upon being given one opening, cram in every item of good advice you've been storing up for just this chance —or you will risk never being asked again.

In spite of all the mother-in-law jokes one hears, a great many couples—perhaps a majority—establish very happy relationships with their in-laws—not only the parents, but also the brothers and sisters. The ties may be as strong or stronger than those with their own families, and often continue long after the death of the husband or wife.

Unfortunately, however, there are people who feel that the blood relationship is the only important one, and when the blood relative dies they feel no responsibility toward the widowed in-law or his or her children. It is very sad when this happens, as it seems to indicate that the fondness shown before either was very shallow or existed only for the benefit of the one who has died. This is so wrong! People should be loved—or disliked—for themselves, not because they married someone's relative. And the affection should not die because the spouse has passed away, unless of course the bereaved in-law kills it herself (or himself) by becoming demanding, omnipresent, or self-pitying. Sisters—or brothers—in-law should remember that *their* in-laws need just as much support in their loneliness as would any member of their "own" family.

A brother-in-law, according to the dictionary, is "a brother of a husband or wife, a sister's husband, or loosely, a *wife's sister's husband.*" Someone in this "looser" relationship merits the same affection and consideration as his wife. He is called "Uncle" and continues to be called by that name even after his spouse dies.

A WORD ABOUT COUSINS

The children of sisters and brothers are first cousins. The grandchildren of sisters and brothers are second cousins. A sister's child and another sister's grandchild are first cousins once removed.

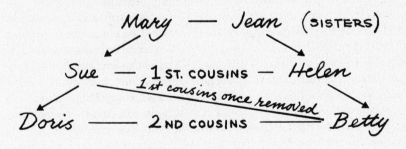

929

SEPARATION

Unfortunately, there has been an epidemic of divorce raging in this country for the past fifty years, and it has accelerated even more in the last ten. There are cases, of course, where divorce is the best—sometimes the only—solution for everyone concerned. If two persons are truly mismated, they certainly, and perhaps their children too, are better off if they part. One of the most unfortunate circumstances is when couples part because of a love-for-another attack that frequently proves to be transient.

Sometimes a period of separation can head off a too-hasty divorce, for separation and divorce are different not only in terms of the law but to some extent in terms of the behavior expected of the people involved.

A separation may be legal or it may simply be arranged by the unwritten consent of both parties. It may be a "trial" separation or it may be viewed from the beginning as permanent. The latter is more often true if the faith of the couple forbids divorce, as does Catholicism.

A trial separation is exactly what it sounds like. Two people have found it increasingly difficult to live together and wish to find out if they can readjust, and be happier, living alone. But for one reason or another—because of children, finances, or any number of other considerations—they want time to think before taking the final steps toward divorce. If they find they are better off apart, and if they are not interested in remarriage or are forbidden by their church to remarry, they may make the separation legal, and papers making property settlements, arrangements for children, financial support, and so on, will be drawn up by their lawyers.

When a couple separate, it is never publicly announced, although the news generally spreads quickly. Because they are still legally married, the woman continues to use her husband's name and wear her wedding ring. He quietly moves out of their home, or she may take the children for a visit to her family. They refuse invitations that come to "Mr. and Mrs.," although if they accidentally meet, they should act as friendly and normal as possible. They may even attend certain family functions or holiday gatherings together. Friends, of course, should respect the situation and never invite them both to the same party without their knowledge and consent.

Whether or how much they see each other while they are separated depends on their feelings and the situation. A couple with no children might feel it would do them the most good to sever all ties

for a certain period. A wife with small children might, on the contrary, need her husband's presence at times to enable her to fulfill
appointments or obligations. There are no rules—each couple must
work out their own separation agreement to their mutual satisfaction.

Men and women who are separated are free to go out with
members of the opposite sex, but if they are sincerely trying to save
their marriage, they will scrupulously avoid any serious entangle-
ments.

If they decide that life together was better than life apart is, they
simply move back together and make as little of the separation as
they can. For this reason, it is wise for the wife or husband—
whichever has remained there—to keep the home and other property intact, rather than sell or rent it in a moment of bitterness.

DIVORCE

*A man of honor never seeks publicly to divorce his wife, no matter
what he believes her conduct to have been; but for the protection of
his own name, and that of the children, he allows her to get her
freedom on other than criminal grounds. No matter who he may be,
whether rich or poor, in high life or low, the man who publicly
besmirches his wife's name, besmirches still more his own, and proves
that he is not, was not, and never will be, a gentleman.*—Emily Post,
1922

When a divorce is finally and irrevocably decided upon, both
parties must accept the fact that their marriage no longer exists. The
husband who insists on "dropping in" to see the children, or the wife
who keeps calling his office to ask his advice on this or that, is only
prolonging the agony and achieving nothing but more unhappiness.
People who have made the decision to part should have done so with
enough serious thought so that once it is accomplished all ties are
severed and they can start to make new lives for themselves and
leave their ex-partners to do the same.

LETTING PEOPLE KNOW

A divorce is almost always a tragic experience for at least one
of the couple. Therefore it should not be announced publicly, and
under no circumstances should printed announcements be sent out.
Certain people have done it and are doing it, and doubtless others
think it is very "with it" or very chic or amusing, but it is in the worst

of taste. In the first place, a divorce *is* a failure, even though both people may agree that it is best, and there is little reason to be proud of a failure. Second, as mentioned above, there is almost invariably one injured party, and it is surely rubbing salt in his wound for the other to shout publicly, "Hooray! I'm free!"

The situation will become public knowledge very quickly, as soon as the divorcée starts calling herself "Mrs. Helen Broderick." If she moves, she may have change-of-name-and-address cards printed, and of course her Christmas cards will serve as announcements. She may add a note to them—"As you can see, Bob and I were, unfortunately, divorced last August. Hope to hear from you at my new address." To those who might not recognize "Susan Smith," she may add in parentheses, "Formerly Mrs. James Smith." Naturally, either the man or the woman may send as many personal notes telling of the divorce as he or she wishes.

DIVORCÉES AND IN-LAWS

Divorcées who have been on friendly terms with their ex-in-laws often remain so, especially if there are children. They may and should continue to exchange Christmas cards, notes of condolence, birthday cards, etc., and in the case of the children's grandparents, gifts. The children, too, should be encouraged to maintain contact with their father's family, and they may need the support of those aunts, uncles, and cousins if their mother has no family of her own.

If the divorce was a very bitter one, however, it is perhaps better if the person who was at fault waits to see whether the ex-mate's family wishes to have anything to do with him (or her) or not.

The parents-in-law of a girl who has been divorced from their son are often terrified that they will "lose" their grandchildren, and yet they hesitate to contact their ex-daughter-in-law, fearing this will seem disloyal to their son. If you should find yourself in this position, do not hesitate. You need not "take sides" or even discuss the divorce if you do not want to, but the grandparent-grandchild relationship is one that should not be abandoned. Actually this attitude, far from being disloyal, is unprejudiced and commendable, and is often a tremendous help to a newly divorced girl who may be very unhappy.

Your friendship with your son's ex-wife need not end because the girl remarries. Her new husband may be a fine addition to the family and a wonderful father to your grandchildren. If your affection for your former daughter-in-law has remained steadfast, any children she may have with her new husband, although in no way related to you, may make happy additions to your circle of grandchildren.

THE DIVORCÉE'S BEHAVIOR

If a lady has been so unfortunate as to have married a man not a gentleman, to draw attention to his behavior would put herself on his level.—Emily Post, 1922

Whether you are separated or divorced, you must hold up your head and face the situation openly. There is no stigma attached to divorce anymore, and even though you may feel that you have failed, or been betrayed, that is no one's business but your own. Don't dwell on your problems with everyone you see, but don't be ashamed to mention your state. When you run into someone who says, "Where's Joe?" or "How is Joe doing these days?" just say, "I honestly don't know—we were divorced in April." The first few times it will be hard, but you will find that you will soon think nothing of it.

As discussed in Chapter 2, most divorcées today prefer to use "Mrs. Sandra Jacobs" to "Mrs. Rothschild [maiden name] Jacobs," and I feel that this is sensible and acceptable. If for whatever reason she prefers to use her maiden name and her husband's last name, that is still perfectly correct. For example, "Mrs. Mary Smith" might feel that that name was so very common that she would be better identified by "Mrs. Hooper Smith." Today, she is free to choose whichever name she wishes or to take back her maiden name if she prefers. A woman whose marriage has been annulled almost invariably uses her maiden name, since an annulment rejects the fact that a marriage ever existed.

A divorcée, unlike a widow, does not necessarily continue to wear her wedding ring. If she has children, she may do so for their sake, or she may transfer it to her right hand to indicate that she is no longer married. Her engagement ring may be kept for their use later, or she may have the stones reset into something that she can use herself.

A divorcée does not give back any wedding gifts, although a bride whose marriage was annulled, and who never lived with her husband, should do so.

The divorced couple's friends, and if possible their families, should extend their sympathetic support—never criticism or censure—but at the same time respect their privacy and avoid prying or questioning the reasons for or the mechanics of the divorce, unless their advice is asked for.

When a divorce is agreed upon by mutual consent, perhaps because of nothing more than "incompatibility," the couple generally remain friendly—often quite close, in fact. When a third person is involved, or when there are grounds such as cruelty, desertion, nonsupport, etc., there can be, of course, tremendous bitterness. But whatever the reasons for the divorce, in the thousands of cases where children are involved, it is far, far better that the divorced parents make every effort to remain on friendly terms. Nothing in all the world is so devastating as living in an atmosphere infused with hatred. Anything is better for children than that!

At present the breaking up of homes is so widespread it may be that young people who grow up without ever having known the completeness of home will find it unessential. Or will it be the other way around? Perhaps the children of today's divided houses will be twice as earnest in their efforts to provide their own children with the priceless security of a father and mother together in one place called HOME!

Before her divorce becomes final, a divorcée must conduct herself with considerable restraint. She may, of course, go out with as many men as she wishes, but her behavior must be examplary—not only because she is laying herself open to criticism, and to the inevitable dangers of a "rebound" if she allows herself to become too intimate with one man, but also because she must consider the legal results if she is found in a compromising situation. This is equally true, of course, of the male divorcé.

Once the final papers are signed, the divorced couple behave like any single people. The divorcée who is a mother, however, *must* consider her children. Naturally, she will want to ward off loneliness and depression with all sorts of social activities and dates, but she must remember—assuming that she has custody of the children— that her first responsibility is to them. In the absence of their father they need her company and the security of knowing that she is there when they need her, more than ever before. A steady stream of dates and other people coming in and out of their house and their lives can be upsetting and confusing to little children. Their mother has the obligation of trying to organize her social activities so that the tremendous change in the family's life is minimized as much as possible. Assuming that she is aware of this responsibility, her own inclinations and her own moral values should then determine her behavior.

WIDOWS

A widow is written to, referred to, introduced, and announced using her late husband's name. She also continues to wear her wedding and engagement rings on the same finger, even though she may be looking for a new husband. (It is never very difficult to make one's marital status clear in the first few moments of a conversation by using such phrases as "When my husband was alive . . ." or "Before my husband died. . . .") The rings are removed, of course, as soon as she becomes engaged, or if she has children, when she remarries. She and her new husband should decide between them what is to be done with them. She should not continue to wear them at all—even on her right hand. This indicates no lack of love for her first husband—only consideration for the second.

Once a widow has remarried, she should no longer be referred to as "the widow of the late Mr. X," no matter how prominent Mr. X was. John F. Kennedy's widow was a case in point. For some time after Mrs. Kennedy married Aristotle Onassis, she was referred to in the press as "the late President's widow." Once a widow remarries, she is a *wife* and she *must* be known as "Mrs. Newhusband." It is most disrespectful to *him* not to do so, and furthermore, she is no longer "a widow" at all.

Widows and divorcées, too—especially those with children—need not discard all the personal mementos of their first marriage when they remarry. Photograph albums, for example, should certainly be kept so that the youngsters will know more about their parents' life together. Other things such as portraits, personal gifts, etc., may be saved. They should, however, be put away carefully and not left in evidence where they might cause the new mate unhappiness.

SINGLE WOMEN IN SOCIAL SITUATIONS

When an invitation to a party is extended to a single woman, it seems obvious that she should not be treated as an "odd" person, but this is just what frequently happens. Games are planned in which sides must be "even," or in which four or six make a "table." The lone woman in a group of several couples inevitably feels like a "fifth wheel." It is not asking too much of a hostess to plan to play poker or blackjack or any of the many games in which five or seven players are as appropriate as six or eight.

The considerate hostess will also suggest that a friend who lives nearby pick up and take home a lone woman, unless she insists that she prefers to be on her own. Many women refuse invitations time after time because they are afraid to drive alone or travel by bus or taxi at night.

A problem frequently faced by widows and divorcées is that of thoughtless friends and relatives who tend to "lump" them all together. One widow wrote me recently saying that she had been delighted to receive three wedding invitations in the past few months. But she had been very disappointed at each reception to find herself seated with three or four other widows, and at one, the table included two old men who were total strangers. Why married people feel that widows and divorcées are a separate clan who do not enjoy the company of married couples or males is more than I can understand. Widows, widowers, and divorced people should be seated with contemporaries and their own friends, female *and* male, on the infrequent occasions when they have the opportunity to enjoy mixed company.

Widows no longer need wait for a long mourning period to pass before taking up a normal social life. They would seem very callous, of course, if they threw themselves into a round of gaiety before the dirt settled on the grave, but as soon as they feel that they *want* company and diversion, they should have it. At first the widow may want to be only with relatives or close friends, but after a few weeks she will feel like expanding her activities, and she should do so. At this time, a vacation, a new job, or a change of scene of any kind is therapeutic and helps the recently widowed *or* the newly divorced woman to renew her interest in life.

~§76§~ You and Your Neighbors

Getting along with your neighbors is mainly a matter of applying the Golden Rule. If you make every effort to treat them as you would like them to treat you, you can be fairly certain you will be good friends—as well as good neighbors.

The fact that two families live close to each other does not mean that each should be included in all the other's activities. It is important to recognize that your neighbors have other friends, other commitments, and other things that they like to do, and you should not expect to be included in all their entertainments and activities—nor should you try to involve them in all of yours.

Privacy is essential too. Good neighbors do not pry, do not push, in no way invade the other's privacy.

To be able to live in close proximity with others, you must have tolerance. Perhaps your neighbors are members of another religion, a different nationality, or come from different surroundings. They will do things differently, and you must accept, and teach your children to accept, their ways. You can learn a great deal from people with different backgrounds if you have an open mind and are willing to study rather than criticize.

There will inevitably be irritations—the neighbor who constantly borrows a cup of sugar, or drops in every morning when you are busiest, or runs the power mower at seven o'clock on Sunday mornings when you are trying to sleep. Don't let these annoyances blow up out of all proportion. Tell your friends how you feel about them. Nine times out of ten, they won't have realized that they were bothering you and will be happy to call before dropping in, or to mow the lawn in the evening. It is all a matter of give-and-take, and remember, the neighbor who upsets you by a trivial act today may be the one who takes care of the kids when you are sick in bed tomorrow.

This chapter has been inspired—at least partially—by the great number of very varied questions that come in every week regarding neighborhood relations. They are so individual and so diverse that I believe the most informative and interesting way to present them is just as they are—in question-and-answer form. Perhaps you will recognize some of your own problems among them and will benefit by the answers.

GETTING ALONG WITH THE CHILDREN

Q. Our property lies in the direct line between the local school and the neighborhood where many children live. Naturally they walk across our yard rather than going around by the street. I have no objections except for one thing. They litter. I have asked them repeatedly to stop but with no success. What can I do now?

A. First, put an unobtrusive wire receptacle at either end of your yard. Put a silly sign or drawing on it, asking them to discard litter there. This will serve as a constant reminder. Then, talk to them and explain how much you care about your yard. Try to get them to discuss ecology and the environment with you. Ask the youngsters' parents to talk about it at home, too.

If all else fails, you may have to threaten to put up a fence, and you might even have to do it. I doubt it, though. Most young people are very environment-conscious, and if you make it easy for them to be neat, I believe they will.

Q. The other day a seven-year-old boy accidentally broke our dining-room window. He nervously came to the door to admit his guilt and to offer to pay for the damage. I admire him for the honesty and hesitate to present him or his parents with the thirty-dollar bill. How should I take care of this?

A. Although the youngster deserves great credit for his courage and honesty, you should not feel obligated to pay for *his* error. Therefore I would suggest that you call his parents, compliment them on their son's behavior, and ask them over for a cup of coffee to discuss the replacement of the window.

Q. My mother had a very clever way of handling children who cut through the property, making a muddy path across the lawn. What do you think of her solution?

A. I think it's great. Here it is:

She made a point of being in the yard every day when the gang came through. She was very friendly, asked how their families were, etc. By implying that she knew their mothers, she scared them off without any threats or unpleasantness.

She used the same tactic with a group of boys who were ambling down the middle of the road and refused to move over for her car. She leaned out and called, "Hi, how's your Mom?" It cleared the road in a hurry, with no one hurt or angry.

A little subtlety and tact can often solve quite easily what might otherwise be an unpleasant situation.

GIVE-AND-TAKE

Q. I am a housewife—not a career wife—and therefore am called on frequently to "canvass" my neighborhood—to collect for the Red Cross, Heart Fund, cerebral palsy, etc. I would enjoy this except for the offensive manner in which I am received at some homes. For example, the wife who says, "We don't choose to give," and slams the door in your face. Or the six-figure-income family who fill out a pledge for one dollar. If only these people realized I am doing this *for* them, and often *in place of* them, they might give me the polite attention that would make the job worthwhile!

A. For neighbors to be short, or actually rude, to anyone who is giving time and effort for the benefit of others, is inexcusable. On the other hand, a volunteer really has no right to criticize the amounts given—she has no way of knowing what the extenuating circumstances might be. But whatever the householders' decision, it is entirely out of line for them to inflict their resentment or their feelings about the "cause" on the volunteer.

Q. After a delicious meal at a friend's house, I asked her to give me the recipe for the dessert. To my surprise, she flatly refused. I would welcome your opinion as to whether she—or I—was at fault.

A. Asking for a recipe is a sincere form of flattery and should certainly not be resented. Nor should the request be refused, except in two cases:

1. If it is an old family recipe, handed down with the understanding that it be kept as a family secret.
2. If it was given to the hostess by someone who exacted her promise that she would not reveal the secret.

Q. What is the polite way to refuse to lend neighbors articles such as vacuum cleaners and electric appliances? I have loaned things often and had them returned damaged, soiled, or with parts missing.

A. "Neither a borrower nor a lender be" is a safe rule for neighbors. Unless you *want* to lend an appliance to a friend you know will take good care of it, you need not do so. If you refuse firmly, pleasantly, and consistently, neighbors will soon give up asking. To keep things amicable, try to soften your refusal with a logical excuse: "I'll be needing it myself tonight," or "I promised to let my daughter use it this weekend," etc.

Q. Several times over the years we have asked for special help from our local police department. We have written a note to the chief, expressing our appreciation, but I wonder whether more tangible thanks are expected.

A. Although the police give assistance in any way they can without thought of payment, it would be a fitting gesture to send a contribution to their Benevolent Association, Athletic League, or whatever organization your particular police force supports.

The following letter is not a question and needs no answer.

In reference to the woman who had been in this hospital, and didn't know how she could repay her neighbors for their kindness in taking care of her family, I always give the answer my landlady gave me when I was young and couldn't afford a sitter. She listened and checked on my baby for nothing. When I said I didn't know how I could ever repay her she said, "Oh, it doesn't work that way—you pass it on to someone else."

COMING AND GOING

Q. Our next-door neighbors have sold their house to people we have not met. I would like to help them out on moving day, but hesitate to intrude on strangers. Is there any rule about greeting newcomers?

A. Yes there is—DO IT. When you see that they have arrived, or perhaps when the moving van leaves, go over with a casserole prepared for their dinner. They will be tired, dirty, and will not only be unprepared to cook a meal, but will probably not feel like getting dressed up to go out. I know of nothing that can get you off to a better start with new neighbors than to greet them with dinner—and a drink if you wish—in hand.

Q. A lovely family lived next to us for four years, and we got along very well. One morning I awoke to see a moving van outside their house and was shocked to see them moving away. They never let us know or said "Good-bye." Later I heard that *they* were hurt that we hadn't bid them farewell! Am I wrong in thinking they should have let us know they were leaving?

A. I do not believe you can have been very close to them and not known they were moving away. However, if you wish to maintain your friendship, write to them at once and tell them their move was a surprise to you. I'm sure they assumed you knew about it.

SUPERMARKET SHOPPING

Q. I wish you would comment on the rudeness of people with loaded shopping baskets who refuse to let someone behind them, who has only two or three articles, go through the check-out line ahead of them.

A. I'll comment gladly. The shopper with a loaded basket should definitely let someone with only a couple of items go ahead of her. However, she need *not* let more than one person in ahead of her or she could spend hours waiting for the small-order trade to pass her by.

Q. Do you approve of a customer packing her own bags as the checker rings up the rest of her order?

A. I certainly do. I cannot understand women who stand by and watch the checker ring up the order, pack it, and make change while they do not lift a finger. I am surprised that they have so much time to spare themselves to begin with, and also sorry that they do not consider the time they would save for the people behind them—who might be in more of a hurry.

Q. It is extremely annoying to drive into the supermarket lot and find all the parking places filled by abandoned shopping carts. Is there something we, the customers, can do to remedy this situation?

A. Indeed there is. Talk to your store manager and urge him to:
1. Provide shopping-cart stations—designated by signs and lines on the pavement—at intervals throughout the parking lot.
2. Send out employees to collect the carts more frequently.
3. Put signs up requesting customers to bring their carts to the entrance or leave them out of the way of the cars.

You can also push two or three carts to the proper area yourself, thereby setting an example for other shoppers in the lot.

IMPOSITIONS

Q. How do we put a stop to neighbors who park their car across the street from our driveway or so close to the end of the driveway that it is very difficult to get in and out? Can we ask the police to mark off a "no-parking" zone?

A. You *could* do that, although I don't know whether the police would consider your request justified or not. However, the crux of the situation is really not who parks where, but your relationship with your neighbors. If tempers are kept under control, there should be no need for drastic action. Ask your neighbors over for a cup of coffee or a drink and discuss it rationally. Something can be worked out—they may be able to park a few feet one way or the other, and you might widen the end of your driveway to make the turn easier.

Q. A group of us get together almost every morning for coffee, and it makes a pleasant break in the routine of housework and baby-tending. But these gatherings are getting longer and longer, and the girls are vying with each other to produce the most elaborate snacks. I simply don't have the time or the money to keep up with them, yet I don't want to lose my friends. What can I do?

A. Tell the girls that if the coffee breaks go on getting longer and fancier, you'll have to drop out. Make it clear that you would love to have them to your house in your usual turn, but that the snacks will be fresh donuts or a coffee cake—from the bakery. I am sure that some of the others will heave a "sigh of relief" too.

Q. My husband is an accountant, and our neighbors don't forget it when income tax time rolls around. He is a kind man and winds up giving these people his evenings and weekends until April 15 is past. He would not mind if they didn't all expect help right at the deadline. Could you remind them that they are demanding more of a friend than they have any right to expect?

A. Respect for another's privacy is a cardinal principle of etiquette. Before you look for a little "free advice," remember that the professional man, like any other, needs to escape from his business. This applies to men in all fields—doctors, teachers, clergymen, and so on. They need relaxation as much as anyone else, and common courtesy demands that they be allowed to enjoy their leisure hours without constant requests for professional advice or performance.

AROUND THE NEIGHBORHOOD

Q. We have just bought a house in the suburbs, and after moving in, found that the previous owner and our next-door neighbor have a horseshoe pit in the corner of our yard, and a spotlight in our tree to light it. Apparently all the neighborhood men have been enjoying the horseshoe games during the summer. We do not pitch horseshoes, we would like our yard to ourselves, and we don't like the glare of the light. And yet we do not want to alienate our new neighbors. What can we do?

A. You have every right to use your yard as you wish, but if you want to establish friendly relations with your neighbors, you will have to be very tactful. Think of something *specific* you would like to do with that corner of your yard. Then say to Mr. Neighbor, "We had really been planning to put a rock garden [or a pool, or a barbecue fireplace, or whatever] in the corner of the yard, so would you mind very much moving your horseshoe pit over to your yard?" They will undoubtedly move the light without your mentioning it, to light their new location. Then, of course, you must do whatever you said you would with that corner of your yard.

Q. After moving into our new home, we found that our next-door neighbor is a real "pack rat." His yard is filled with every sort of trash imaginable. I don't want to start off on the wrong foot with him, but is there any way we can get him to clean up his place?

A. Let this be a warning to home buyers. Look around at the neighbors and the neighborhood *before* you buy your house!

You are not your brother's keeper, and there is not much you can do by yourself. You could, however, ask other neighbors if they would be interested in joining you in a clean-up campaign to improve the neighborhood, and of course, ask the man next door to join, too.

If the situation could be construed as a fire hazard or dangerous in any way, you should go to your town sanitary officers. It is their job to inspect and correct conditions that are hazardous to health or to other property.

Q. My children and I walk our dog every evening. Recently an unleashed dog attacked our dog. We managed to pull Tinker away and take him home. The next day the same dog started after us again. I now carry a stick, but it bothers me to think of having to hit an animal. Would it be wrong under the circumstances?

A. If an unleashed dog attacks your dog or your children, you surely have every right to chase him away by any means short of actual injury. You can give him a good rap—enough to chase him off without injuring him—if you do not hit him about the face or head. If your town has an ordinance against dogs running loose, you should also report him to the SPCA or the police.

If you believe he belongs to one of your neighbors, however, you will avoid an unpleasant situation by telling him that the dog has attacked you and asking him to keep the animal penned. You might also find another route to walk your dog, if possible, until the owner or the SPCA has taken care of the situation.

Q. Whenever my next-door neighbor cuts his grass he cleans up his side of the adjoining lawns and leaves the cuttings that have fallen on my side. It is most annoying, and I would like to know how I can tactfully put a stop to it.

A. If you don't care about being friends with your neighbor, go out and rake his cuttings over onto his lawn. But if you want to maintain a pleasant relationship, don't do that! The next time he cuts his lawn, go out and watch and chat with him. If, even while you are there, he leaves the same mess, ask him to please clean it up. If you do it in a nice way, he will not resent it, and he probably doesn't even realize what he has been doing.

SWIMMING POOLS

Q. My twelve-year-old daughter has been told she can have occasional pool parties this summer, and of course, wants no supervision by her father or me. I feel this could be dangerous, and we might be severely criticized, but we would like your opinion.

A. Much as I hate to sound stuffy, you're right! You would quite justly be criticized because no matter how competent your daughter's friends are in the water, accidents do happen. Twelve-year-olds just aren't old enough to cope with emergencies, so you and your husband or another competent adult must be present at all times.

Q. Is it necessary to provide towels for all the guests who come to swim in our pool? I love to have people over, but it's quite an expense to provide so many (and they do have a way of disappearing), and it's a lot of work to keep them washed.

A. It's perfectly OK to ask your friends to bring their own towels when you invite them to swim. But you should also keep six or more available for those who forget, or for when the swimming idea comes up unexpectedly. The same goes for extra bathing suits. Incidentally, I find that although a lot of my towels disappear, an equal number are left behind and can't be traced, so that I come out about even, although with rather an odd assortment.

Q. We have just built a swimming pool, and it will soon be ready for the summer. There are many children in our neighborhood, and we are afraid we will be overwhelmed by constant requests for permission to go for a swim. Can you tell us how to handle this, if it happens?

A. It probably *will* happen, especially if yours is the only pool in the neighborhood. But I *can* tell you an excellent way of handling it.

Install a small flagpole at the gate to the pool and tell all the neighborhood children that they are invited to swim whenever the flag is raised. This means that you or a grown son or daughter or another qualified adult will stay at the pool to supervise the youngsters. When you have guests, or simply want the pool to yourselves, keep the flag down, and the children will know that the pool is "closed" to them.

Q. We love to have our neighbors join us at our pool whenever they can, but it gets very expensive offering them food and drinks. Is it necessary to do this, and if not, how can I break the habit?

A. If they are such good friends that they are at the pool frequently, it should be no problem. Tell them quite frankly that you can't go on providing snacks and drinks. You might suggest that if they will make afternoons at the pool 'BYOB" parties, you will have chips or simple snacks. Close neighbors, in return for your hospitality, should, from time to time, bring sandwiches for the gang and help you out by offering beer, soft drinks, or iced tea. Pools are great fun to have, but you must stand firm in some ways, or thoughtless neighbors will inevitably impose on you.

Index

947

clothes (cont.):
  for businesswoman, 518
  for widow, 518
  for movies, 189
  for opera, 188
  for prom, 907
  for public speaking, 52
  for radio and television appearances,
    196–197
  for resorts, 262
  for restaurant, 164, 825, 827
  for ship travel, 235, 237
  for sports activities, 841–849
    bowling, 846–847
    golf, 842–844
    riding, 847–849
    skiing, 844–846
    tennis, 769, 841–842
  for sports events, attending of, 193
  for sweet-sixteen party, 346
  for tea party, 316, 825
  for teenager, 899, 903–905, 907
  for theater, 185, 825, 827
  for wedding guests, 582–583, 681,
    701–702
  for White House dinner, 145
  women's, 813–827
    accessories for, 817–823, 825, 826
    for afternoon wear, 582, 583, 819,
      820, 825, 826
    age differences in, 153–154, 815,
      817, 821, 824
    appropriateness in, 817–818, 819,
      820, 822
    "at-home" skirts, 816
    for average figure, 815
    basic dresses, 825–826
    bathing suits, 814–815, 827
    boots, 820
    for bride, see brides, costume for
    budget buying of, 817, 824–826
    for business, 751, 820
    coats, 819, 820, 826, 827
    for cocktail parties, 582, 583, 816,
      818, 819, 825, 827
    color use in, 582, 583, 814, 817,
      819, 820, 821, 825, 826
    at concerts, 189
    corsages with, 821
    for country, 817, 820, 826
    earrings with, 814, 817, 823
    evening dresses, 582, 814, 818,
      819, 820, 821, 822, 825, 827
    fads in, 815–816, 822
    in fashion publications, 815
    formal, 461–462, 582, 583, 819,
      820, 821, 823, 825, 826
    fur capes and stoles with, 819, 826
    gloves with, 582, 583, 585, 817–818
    for golf, 842–844
    hair ornaments with, 582, 583
    hair styles and, 814, 815, 824
    handbags with, 817, 818, 820–821,
      826–827
    hats with, 582, 583, 814, 818
    jewelry with, 585, 817, 818,
      822–823

  makeup and, 585, 824
  matching of, 817, 818, 819, 820, 821
  materials for, 814, 815, 820
  for morning wear, 819
  pants suits, 327–328, 816, 820, 827
  for plump figure, 814–815, 816
  rings with, 817, 818, 822, 823
  scarves, 815, 818
  shoes with, 585, 814, 817, 818,
    819–820, 826
  for short figure, 814
  shorts, 815, 827
  for skiing, 846
  skirts, 814, 815, 816, 825, 827
  slacks, 462, 815, 816–817, 820, 827
  suitability of, 813–815, 816, 817,
    819, 822
  sweaters, 825, 827
  for tall figure, 814
  for tennis, 842
  for thin figure, 815
  for traveling, 228–229, 235, 237,
    245, 250, 261–262, 816, 819,
    821, 826–827
  vulgarity in, 817, 822
clubs, 736–746
  country, 338–339, 739–740
  guests and privileges in, 740–742
  listings of, 71
  men's, 742–743
  municipal, 739
  new member in, 739
  private, joining of
    by application, 736–738
    by invitation, 88, 736–738
  resigning from, 745–746
  stag dinner at, 364
  tipping in, 744–745, 808
  women's, 743–744
  yacht, 739
coasters, 301, 320
coats:
  men's, 834–835
  women's, 819, 820, 826, 827
cocktail buffets, 324–325
  housewarming as, 359
  menu for, 324, 325
  table for, 324–325
cocktail dresses, 582, 583, 816, 818,
  819, 825, 827
cocktail parties, 318–325
  for anniversary, 343
  bartenders and waiters at, 321–322
  buffet and, 324–325
  cocktails only at, 319–320
  before college or school games, 193
  before dance, 323–324
  vs. dinner party, 318
  drinks served at, 320–321
  engagement parties as, 531
  guests at, 320–321
  without help, 322
  housewarming as, 359
  invitations to, 319, 323–324
  merits of, 318–319
  nonalcoholic drinks at, 320
  overstaying welcome at, 323

952

drinking *(cont.):*
    deterring children from, 916–917
    driving and, 243
    in foreign travel, 263–264
    on planes, 230–231
    as problem for host, 472–473
    at teenager party, 904–905
driving courtesy (*see also* automobile
    travel), 239–249
drugs, deterring children from, 916, 917
duck, serving of, 290
"Dutch-Treat Dinner," 348
Dutch treats, 160
    in dating, 908, 913
    at dinner and theater, 183–184
    and neighbors, 945
    picnic as, 349
    and prom, 908
    in restaurant, 173–174

earrings, 814, 817
    piercing for, 823, 900
    for young girls, 900
egg dishes, serving of, 309
elderly, *see* older people
elevator etiquette, 157
elopements, 629, 684–685
*Emily Post's Etiquette for Young
    People,* 896
employers, entertaining of, 755
employer-servant relations, 867–875
employment agencies, household help
    from, 279, 280, 858, 860,
    862, 867
enamelware, for barbecues, 356
engagement parties, 531–532
    form of, 531–532
    toasts at, 54, 532
engagement rings, 526–528, 822
    birthstones for, 526–527
    and death of fiancé, 534
    wearing of, 527–528
    widow's or divorcée's, 528
engagements, 523–544
    announcement of, 528–531
        formal, 528
        in newspaper, 529–531
        at party, 532
        personal, 528
        in unusual situations, 529–531
    broken, 534
    couple's behavior during, 534–535
    courtship and, 523–524
    fidelity during, 535
    gifts for, 532, 534, 535, 795–796
    gifts to fiancé in, 528
    hope chest and, 535–536
    length of, 533–534
    parents' approval and, 524–525
    parents becoming acquainted in,
        525–526
    trousseau and, 536–544
    wedding rings and, 533
engraving:
    of gifts, 543, 793
    of invitations, 305, 306, 336, 341, 437,

442, 489, 547, 594, 595
    vs. printing, in writing paper, 64
    of silver, 543
    of thank-you card, 105–106, 632
    of visiting card, 127
    of wedding ring, 533
entertainers:
    courtesy towards, 774–777
    friends as, 775–776
entertainment:
    at barbecues, 358
    at cotillion, 336
    at dinner party, 465–466
    at showers, 374
    at sweet-sixteen party, 346
    at teenager party, 904
entrées, serving of, 290
envelopes:
    addressing of, 72–74
    dinner, 8, 274
    instructions on, 73–74
    for invitation reply, 438, 446
    for visiting cards, 126
    for wedding invitations, 597–599
Episcopal church, baptism in, 481
escargots, eating of, 414
escorts, at cotillions, 335–336
"Esquire," in correspondence, 64, 72
ethnic insults, 46
Etiquette, first edition of, 853
etiquette, thoughtfulness and, 153
Europe:
    flowers and gifts in, 265–266, 789, 790
    gracious manners in, 265
    handshaking in, 13, 265
    hotels in, 223–224
    restaurants in, 254
    tipping in, 254, 265, 811
    traveler's attitude in, 260–264
evening dresses, 582, 814, 818, 819, 820,
    821, 822, 825, 827
executives:
    business card for, 134–135
    as "gentlemen," 748–749

family:
    child-rearing in, 877–895
    introducing members of, 3–5
    meals of, 366–367, 399, 430–434
    and teenager, 896–902
family relationships, 922–936
    and divorce, 931–934
    elderly parents in, 927–928
    between husbands and wives, 922–926
    in-laws in, 928–929
    during marital separation, 930–931
    between relatives, 926–929
    widows in, 934–935
farewell parties, 347
    gifts for, 797
farewells (*see also* leave-taking):
    informal, 15–16
    at large party, 17
    to strangers, 17
fathers (*see also* parents):
    of brides

luncheons *(cont.)*:
    invitations to, 305–306
    vs. "lunch," 305
    menu for, 309–311
    number of guests at, and room size, 305
    of sewing circle, 366
    table settings for, 306–308, 429–430
    before wedding, 641–642

"Ma'am," local usage of, 26
"Madam(s)," in salutation, 67
maids:
    at buffet dinner, 297
    at luncheon, 308
    of past, 852, 854, 855, 856
    and seated dinner, 279, 281, 285–286,
        291, 295
maids (and/or matrons) of honor, 560,
        648, 656, 658, 660, 663, 664–665,
        667, 688
    at double wedding, 685, 686, 687
main courses, serving of, 290, 302
maitre d', tipping of, 803–804, 805
makeup, 196
    for bride, 585
    child's use of, 885
    teenager's use of, 900
    for television appearance, 196
marijuana, teenager and, 917
marriage, 922–926
    education vs. reform in, 924–925
    grooming in, 924
    nagging in, 922, 923
    newlyweds and, 925
    privacy and, 926
    sharing in, 924, 925–926
    social plans in, 923–924
married couples:
    at dance, 338–339
    as household help, 858
    names for, 22–23
    remarriage after divorce of, 496–497
    at seated dinners, 272, 466
    social cards of, 131–134
masculine role, dating and, 912
"Master," boys addressed as, 73
master of ceremonies, at wedding
        reception, 673
mayors:
    forms of address for (chart), 78–79
    social card of, 131
meat carving, 286, 288, 291, 308
meetings, 198–201
    board, 198–199
    chairman's duties at, 198–199, 200
    of charitable organizations, 198–199,
        200–201
    dressing for, 198, 200–201
    in home, 200–201
    of large organizations, 198–199
    maintaining order at, 199, 200
    officers at, 200
    preparation for chairing of, 198–199,
        200
    refreshments at, 200

melons, serving of, 290, 309
memorials, 522
memorial services, 514–515
men:
    appetites of, 301
    clothes for, *see* clothes, men's
    as cooks, 291, 353, 356
    at dances, informal, 338, 339
    at formal dinners, seating of, 272,
        275, 277
    as gentlemen
      in business, 748–749
      definitions of, 34–35
      in elevator, 157
      giving up seat by, 157
      and ladies, before or after, 155–156,
        242–243, 251–252
      with ladies, on street, 154–155
      removing hat and gloves by, 835–836
      rising of, in greeting women, 14–15,
        748–749
    as hosts, *see* hosts
    as luncheon guests, 305, 306
    in passing and serving food, 399
    at restaurants
      ordering meal by, 168–169
      in seating, 164–166
      as woman's guest, 174
    at single woman's dinner party, 288
    social cards of, 130–131
    at stag dinner, 364
    stationery of, 59
men's clubs, 742–743
menu cards, 91
menus:
    for barbecue, 356–358
    for buffet dinner, 301–303
    for cocktail buffet, 324, 325
    for luncheon, 309–311
    for picnic, 351–353
    for seated dinner, 268, 290–291
    for wedding reception, 567–568, 682
    for wedding rehearsal dinner, 646
"Mesdames," avoiding of, 67
"Messrs.," correct use of, 73
military officers, forms of address for,
        83–84, 141
Minister Plenipotentiary of the United
        States, forms of address for
        (chart), 78–79
ministers of foreign countries, forms of
        address for (chart), 78–79
"Miss":
    in business use, 753
    divorcée's use of, 26, 27
    in envelope address, 61
    vs. first name, 23
    graduate's use of, 491
    on invitations, 73, 439
    for professional woman, 28
    in salutation, 67
    in signature, 70, 220
    on social cards, 129
    unmarried mother's use of, 27
    for young girl, 73
money (*see also* paying):
    card games for, 763–764